The Government and Politics of
the Middle East and North Africa

The Government and Politics of the

MIDDLE EAST AND NORTH AFRICA

Seventh Edition

Edited by

Mark Gasiorowski

Formerly coedited with

David E. Long
Bernard Reich

WESTVIEW PRESS

A Member of the Perseus Books Group

A Member of the Perseus Books Group

WESTVIEW PRESS was founded in 1975 in Boulder, Colorado, by notable publisher and intellectual Fred Praeger. Westview Press continues to publish scholarly titles and high-quality undergraduate-and graduate-level textbooks in core social science disciplines. With books developed, written, and edited with the needs of serious nonfiction readers, professors, and students in mind, Westview Press honors its long history of publishing books that matter.

Published by Westview Press,
A Member of the Perseus Books Group

Find us on the World Wide Web at www.westviewpress.com.

Every effort has been made to secure required permissions for all text, images, maps, and other art reprinted in this volume.

Westview Press books are available at special discounts for bulk purchases in the United States by corporations, institutions, and other organizations. For more information, please contact the Special Markets Department at the Perseus Books Group, 2300 Chestnut Street, Suite 200, Philadelphia, PA 19103, or call (800) 810-4145, ext. 5000, or e-mail special.markets@perseusbooks.com.

Designed by Jeff Williams
Set in Times New Roman and Arno Pro Display by the Perseus Books Group.

Library of Congress Cataloging-in-Publication Data
    The government and politics of the Middle East and North Africa / Edited by Mark Gasiorowski; formerly edited by David E. Long, Bernard Reich.—Seventh Edition.
        pages cm
    Includes bibliographical references and index.
    ISBN 978-0-8133-4865-0 (pbk.)—ISBN 978-0-8133-4866-7 (e-book)   1. Middle East—Politics and government—1945–   2. Africa, North—Politics and government.
I. Gasiorowski, Mark J., 1954–
DS62.8.G68 2013
956—dc23
                                    2013012742

10 9 8 7 6 5 4 3 2

CONTENTS

PREFACE

This seventh edition of *The Government and Politics of the Middle East and North Africa* updates the previous edition and introduces the reader to the growing challenges now facing the region. Substantial change has occurred in the Middle East and North Africa since the last edition went to press in late 2009. Most notably, the popular uprisings dubbed the "Arab Spring" have roiled the region, affecting every country there in one way or another. The region also has been affected in recent years by the continuing challenges posed by radical Islamist movements, severe geopolitical tensions, high oil prices, the global recession, and the steady advance of globalization. The contributors to this volume address the effects of these and other factors on the contemporary politics of each country in the region.

Several changes have occurred since the previous edition. Most importantly, David Long and Bernard Reich, who published the first edition in 1980 and have inspired and overseen each edition since then, have moved on to other things, leaving Mark Gasiorowski as the sole editor. Mark thanks them for doing an excellent job on the previous editions and giving him the opportunity to follow in their footsteps. In addition, several new authors have joined the list of contributors for this edition. Joshua Stacher and Christopher Alexander have taken over authorship of the Egypt and Tunisia chapters, respectively. And Raymond Hinnebusch has joined David Lesch as coauthor of the Syria chapter.

The introductory chapter of this volume gives a broad overview of the region, sketching its geography, history, social and economic conditions, and prevalent types of political regimes. The subsequent chapters cover the domestic politics and foreign policy of every country in the region, as well as the Palestinian Authority. Each of these chapters follows a common format, examining a country's historical background, the factors that shape its domestic politics, and its foreign policy. These chapters also contain maps showing the geography of each country, fact boxes giving key details, and annotated bibliographies with references for further reading. Each chapter is written by a leading scholar and updated through late 2012, providing comprehensive, up-to-date coverage of the region's politics.

The editor would like to thank Karen Hopkins and Timothy Joyner, who created the maps used in this volume. He would also like to thank his wife and daughter, Mary and Elena, for their patience, support, and love.

Note from the
Original Editors

David E. Long and Bernard Reich

In the 1970s, Frederick A. Praeger, the well-known publisher of numerous works concerning international relations, politics, and history, approached us to produce (write and edit) an introductory work on the politics of the states of the region known as the Middle East. It was to be suitable for students, analysts, journalists, government officials, and general readers with an interest in the region. From the beginning, we made the decision to ensure its comprehensiveness by including the states of Arab North Africa.

In addition, we not only sought the assistance of a diverse group of Middle East specialists who had academic and policy-oriented experience in the two regions but also chose specific specialists in each country in the region to produce a current and comprehensive chapter focusing on the political dynamics of that particular country.

We presented a common outline for each author to follow, but we were always aware that there were differences and peculiarities in each country's political system and in the style of each author. A common format added continuity to the book, but we never imposed our perspectives or points of view on the authors. They were the experts on their subject matter, and as scholars with the country specialty, they could best provide unparalleled expertise and analysis and permit the reader to compare and contrast the politics/political dynamics of each state.

Thus, all in all, we felt that by having the editors and authors working together toward presenting the region to our readers, students, and others interested in the region, we were able through the years to provide scholarly analysis while at the same time allowing comparisons of the countries throughout the region.

That said, in looking back over the years we have been involved in editing *The Government and Politics of the Middle East and North Africa,* it seems incredible it has been three decades since the first edition came out in 1980 and that we have produced six editions in that time. It is also incredible to think back on how much the Middle East, and indeed the entire world, has changed during that time. For example, in 1980, the Cold War was still considered very much a regional issue as well as an international problem, terrorism was for the most part centered on the regional Arab-Israeli problem and just beginning to become an international problem, and the information revolution had not yet expanded to include ordinary people.

Over the six editions that have been published, we have updated each of the chapters for each edition and have recruited new authors as older authors have retired. As times have changed, they have brought the latest expertise and reflected the altering nature of the academic fields they represent. And now we believe it is time for us to pass the torch on to a younger generation.

This seventh edition of *The Government and Politics of the Middle East and North Africa* is the first edited entirely by Mark Gasiorowski, who joined us beginning with the fifth edition, published in 2007. It marks another transition from the original concepts to a revised approach, reflecting Mark Gasiorowski's approach to the region. As times change, we wish him luck, and to him and to all our readers, farewell.

ABOUT THE CONTRIBUTORS

Christopher Alexander is associate dean for international programs and the John and Ruth McGee Director of the Dean Rusk International Studies Program at Davidson College. He holds a PhD in political science from Duke University. He is author of *Tunisia: Stability and Reform in the Modern Maghreb* and several articles and chapters on Tunisia and the Maghreb.

Henri J. Barkey is the Bernard and Bertha Cohen Professor of International Relations at Lehigh University. He served on the US State Department's policy planning staff (1998–2000), working on issues related to the eastern Mediterranean and the Middle East. His works include *Turkey's Kurdish Question* (with Graham Fuller), *Preventing Conflict over Kurdistan*, and "Turkey's Transformers," in *Foreign Affairs* (with Morton Abramowitz).

Robert D. Burrowes holds a PhD from Princeton University. He recently retired from the Political Science Department and Henry M. Jackson School of International Studies of the University of Washington. He has authored *The Yemen Arab Republic: The Politics of Development* and *The Historical Dictionary of Yemen,* 2nd ed. His recent articles include "Yemen: Political Economy and the Effort Against Terrorism," in *Battling Terror in the Horn of Africa*, edited by Robert I. Rotberg.

Jill Crystal is professor of political science at Auburn University. She received a PhD from Harvard University and has authored *Oil and Politics in the Gulf: Rulers and Merchants in Kuwait* and *Qatar and Kuwait: The Transformation of an Oil State*, as well as several articles and book chapters.

Mary-Jane Deeb is chief of the African and Middle Eastern Division at the Library of Congress. She was editor of *The Middle East Journal* from 1995 to 1998 and taught at American University for a decade. Deeb is author of *Libya's Foreign Policy in North Africa* and coauthor with Marius K. Deeb of *Libya Since the Revolution: Aspects of Social and Political Development*.

Mark Gasiorowski is professor of political science at Tulane University. He was a visiting professor at Tehran University in 1994, 1996, and 1998 and a visiting fellow at the Middle East Centre of St. Antony's College, Oxford University, in 2001–2002. He is author of *U.S. Foreign Policy and the Shah* and coeditor (with Nikki Keddie) of *Neither East nor West* and (with Malcolm Byrne) of *Mohammad Mosaddeq and the 1953 Coup in Iran*.

David H. Goldberg is a Toronto-based policy analyst specializing in Israel. He holds a PhD in political science from McGill University. He has taught at York University and was the publisher of *Middle East Focus*. He has authored or edited seven books, including (with Bernard Reich) *Historical Dictionary of Israel,* 2nd ed.

William Harris holds a PhD from the University of Durham and is a professor in the Department of Politics, University of Otago, New Zealand. He is author of *Lebanon: A History, 600–2011* and *The Levant: A Fractured Mosaic*, which won a Choice Magazine Outstanding Academic Title Award.

Raymond Hinnebusch is professor of international relations and Middle East politics and director of the Centre for Syrian Studies at the University of St Andrews, Scotland. He is author of *Syria: Revolution from Above; Authoritarian Power and State Formation in Ba'thist Syria;* and *Peasant and Bureaucracy in Ba'thist Syria* and coauthor of *Syria and the Middle East Peace Process* and *The Syrian-Iranian Alliance*.

Azzedine Layachi is professor of politics and former associate director of the Center for Global Studies at St. John's University. He received a PhD and MA in politics from New York University and a BA from the Institut des Études Politiques of the University of Algiers. He is author of numerous books, chapters, and articles on North Africa, including *Economic Crisis and Political Change in North Africa; State, Society and Liberalization in Morocco; The United States and North Africa: A Cognitive Approach to Foreign Policy;* and *Global Studies: The Middle East.*

David W. Lesch is professor of Middle Eastern history at Trinity University, Texas. He has a PhD in history and Middle Eastern studies from Harvard University. Among his authored books are *Syria: The Fall of the House of Assad; The Arab-Israeli Conflict: A History; The New Lion of Damascus: Bashar al-Asad and Modern Syria;* and *1979: The Year That Shaped the Modern Middle East*. He is coeditor (with Mark Haas) of two books published by Westview Press: *The Middle East and the United States: History, Politics and Ideologies,* 5th ed., and *The Arab Spring: Change and Resistance in the Middle East.*

Sebastian Maisel is assistant professor of Arabic language and Middle Eastern studies at Grand Valley State University. He holds a PhD in Arabic and Islamic studies and anthropology from the University of Leipzig. Among his publications are *The Customary Law of the Bedouins in Arabia; Saudi Arabia and the Gulf States Today: An Encyclopedia of Life in the Arab States* (with J. Shoup); and *The Kingdom of Saudi Arabia* (with David Long). He was the program researcher for the Saudi Arabian National Arts Foundation and has taught at King Saud University.

Glenn E. Robinson holds a PhD from the University of California, Berkeley, and is associate professor of defense analysis at the Naval Postgraduate School. He has written extensively on the Palestinian issue. His publications include *Building a Palestinian*

State: The Incomplete Revolution; The Arc: A Formal Structure for a Palestinian State; and *Building a Successful Palestinian State.*

Curtis R. Ryan is associate professor of political science at Appalachian State University in North Carolina. He holds a PhD from the University of North Carolina, Chapel Hill. He served as a Fulbright scholar at the Center for Strategic Studies in Jordan (1992–1993) and was twice named a peace scholar by the United States Institute of Peace. He has authored *Inter-Arab Alliances: Regime Security and Jordanian Foreign Policy* and *Jordan in Transition: From Hussein to Abdullah,* as well as articles in *The Middle East Journal, Middle East Insight, Arab Studies Quarterly, Israel Affairs, Southeastern Political Review, Journal of Third World Studies, Middle East Policy,* and *Middle East Report.*

Joshua Stacher is assistant professor of political science at Kent State University and was a fellow at the Woodrow Wilson International Center for Scholars in 2012–2013. He is author of *Adaptable Autocrats: Regime Power in Egypt and Syria.* He is also a frequent contributor to, and member of the editorial committee of, the Middle East Research and Information Project.

Omer Taspinar is director of the Turkey Program at the Brookings Institution's Center on the United States and Europe and an adjunct professor at the Johns Hopkins University, School of Advanced International Studies (SAIS). Prior to joining Brookings, he was assistant professor in the European Studies Department of SAIS and a consultant at the Robert F. Kennedy Center for Justice and Human Rights.

Gregory W. White is professor of government at Smith College, Northampton, Massachusetts, where he directs the Global Studies Center. He is a former Fulbright scholar to Morocco and Tunisia and author most recently of *Climate Change and Migration: Borders and Security in a Warming World.* He is an editor of the *Journal of North African Studies.*

Judith S. Yaphe is a Distinguished Research Fellow for the Middle East in the Institute for National Strategic Studies at National Defense University and a professorial lecturer at George Washington University. She has authored many articles on Iraqi history and politics and US policy.

1

INTRODUCTION

Middle Eastern and North African States in Comparative Perspective

Mark Gasiorowski

Recent years have seen extensive political change in the Middle East and North Africa. Touched off by a Tunisian fruit vendor's self-immolation, popular protests spread throughout the region in 2011, in what became known as the "Arab Spring." These protests soon brought down entrenched authoritarian regimes in Tunisia, Egypt, Libya, and Yemen. Rulers in several other countries scrambled to avoid a similar fate by implementing limited political reforms, co-opting opponents, or increasing repression. By late 2012, Tunisia and Morocco had undergone considerable political liberalization, Syria and Yemen were gripped by civil war, and the future remained unclear in Egypt, Libya, and several other countries. Moderate Islamists were the biggest beneficiaries, winning elections in Morocco, Tunisia, and Egypt.

These events highlight the importance of studying the politics of the Middle East and North Africa. This book contributes to our understanding of the region by presenting concise overviews of the history and politics of each of its countries and of the stateless Palestinians. It is intended to serve as a textbook for university-level classes and a general reference work for people interested in the region.

The book contains a chapter on each of the fourteen larger countries in the region, as well as a single chapter covering the five small eastern Arabian states (Kuwait, Bahrain, Qatar, United Arab Emirates, and Oman) and one on the Palestinians. Each chapter begins with a historical overview, focusing especially on recent trends. The chapters then examine the general environment within which politics unfolds in each country, including geographic, social, cultural, economic, and geopolitical factors. Next they discuss each country's political structure and dynamics, examining its political institutions and the main factors animating its politics. Each chapter also includes a section on the country's foreign policy as well as a country map, table of facts and figures (based on the CIA

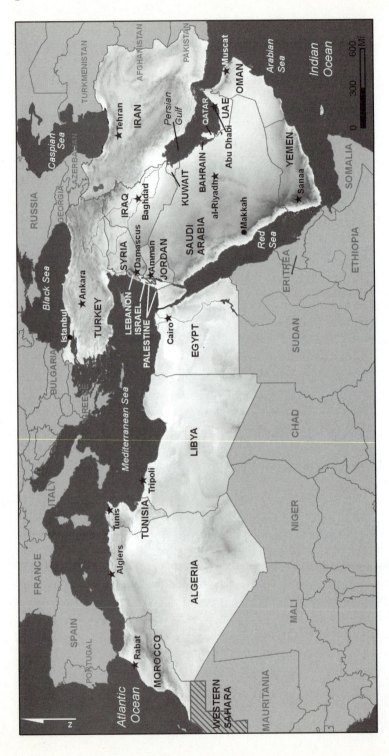

The Middle East and North Africa

World Factbook and Wikipedia), and annotated bibliography. The remainder of this chapter provides an overview of the region.

Physical and Social Geography

The terms *Middle East* and *Near East* refer to the area stretching from Egypt in the west to Iran in the east and from Turkey in the north to Yemen in the south. (See Map 1.1.) In common parlance these terms sometimes include the North African countries Morocco, Algeria, Tunisia, and Libya, a region also known as the Maghreb ("West" in Arabic). Palestine is a common name for the area today comprising Israel and the occupied Palestinian territories. The Levant comprises this area and Lebanon, Syria, and Jordan. The main land area of Turkey is known as Anatolia or Asia Minor. Arabia refers to the large peninsula that includes Saudi Arabia, Yemen, and the smaller Persian Gulf Arab countries.

Most of the region is hot and arid, consisting of deserts or grassy steppes. The biggest desert is the Sahara, comprising large portions of the four North African countries, Egypt, and their southern neighbors. The Sinai and Negev Deserts straddle the border between Egypt and Israel. The Syrian Desert includes large portions of Syria, Iraq, Jordan, and northern Saudi Arabia. The Arabian Desert includes southeastern Saudi Arabia and parts of the neighboring countries. The Dasht-e Kavir and Dasht-e Lut Deserts are in north-central and eastern Iran. These deserts vary considerably in soil composition, elevation, and other features. They are marked by occasional oases, where geological conditions provide enough water to support plants and animals. Some oases are inhabited; others are visited by nomads, who usually raise sheep and other livestock.

The steppes are transition zones between deserts and well-watered areas, with enough moisture to support grasses, bushes, and small trees. Many are located in or near mountain ranges, where rain and springs provide some water. These include the Atlas Mountains of northern Morocco, Algeria, and Tunisia; the Western and Eastern Mountains of Lebanon; the Taurus and Pontic Mountains of Turkey; the Zagros and Alborz Mountains of Iran; and the Hejaz, Asir, Yemeni, and Al Hajar Mountains of Arabia. Temperatures are moderate in some mountain areas, even permitting winter snow. Other steppes are located in the hinterlands of rivers, seas, and oceans. These steppes support scattered sedentary populations that raise livestock and cultivate grain and other crops, as well as small nomadic pastoral groups.

Most of the region's population is concentrated in cities and towns located along coasts and rivers. The most populated area historically has been the Fertile Crescent, stretching from the Nile River delta northeast along the Mediterranean coast, east across northern Syria and southern Turkey, and southeast along the Tigris and Euphrates Rivers. Many Middle Eastern cities, including Alexandria, Baghdad, Beirut, Cairo, Damascus, Fez, Istanbul, Jerusalem, Mecca, and Tunis, date back over 1,000 years and have great historical and cultural importance.

HISTORY

The Middle East was home to the earliest human civilizations: the Sumerians, who emerged in present-day Iraq around 3,500 BCE, and the Egyptians, who emerged around 3,200 BCE. Other major early civilizations included the Babylonians, Assyrians, and Phoenicians. Ancient Israel emerged around 1,000 BCE, establishing Judaism as the first great monotheistic faith. Carthage emerged in present-day Tunisia around 800 BCE and controlled most of the western Mediterranean. The first Persian empire emerged around 550 BCE in present-day Iran. Alexander the Great conquered much of the Middle East before dying in 323 BCE, leaving a lasting Greek imprint on the region.

The Romans conquered most of the Middle East and North Africa during the second and first centuries BCE. Jesus Christ lived in the Roman province of Iudaea, located in and around modern Israel. His teachings gave rise to Christianity, the second great monotheistic faith, which gradually spread throughout the Roman Empire. A series of Jewish rebellions against Roman rule occurred between 66 and 135 CE, leading the Romans to expel most Jews from the area, in what became known as the Jewish diaspora. Roman emperor Constantine I (r. 306 to 337 CE) legalized Christianity, became a Christian, and moved the empire's capital to Byzantium, known later as Constantinople and now as Istanbul. This produced the Byzantine Empire, a Hellenized Christian empire that controlled much of the region. Its main rival was Persia, which ruled most of modern-day Iraq and Iran.

Beginning around 610 CE, a merchant named Muhammad living in the Arabian city of Mecca received divine revelations. Muhammad claimed to be the last prophet sent by God to spread his word. His teachings became the basis for Islam, the third great monotheistic faith. Muhammad and his followers conquered most of Arabia before he died in 632 CE. His successors defeated the Persians and drove the Byzantines back into Anatolia, bringing most of the Middle East under Islamic rule. The new Arab-Islamic empire expanded further in the following decades, conquering North Africa, Spain, and parts of Pakistan, Afghanistan, and central Asia. Most of the conquered people gradually adopted Islam and the Arabic language. Their new rulers, in turn, absorbed many cultural and administrative practices from the peoples they conquered.

The new empire was deeply factionalized. The first factional dispute focused on which of Muhammad's companions should lead the faithful after he died. Some favored Ali, his cousin and son-in-law, but another companion was chosen instead. Ali later became the fourth leader, or caliph, but was assassinated by a member of the Umayyad clan, which then established a dynasty based in Damascus. The Umayyads were unpopular, resulting in a series of uprisings. One was led by Ali's son, Hussein, who was killed in battle in 680. Hussein's followers refused to recognize the Umayyads, instead supporting a line of Hussein's descendants. This rift developed into the division between the majority Sunni branch of Islam, which supported the caliphs, and the minority Shi'a branch, which supported Hussein's descendants. The Umayyads were overthrown in 750 by the (Sunni) Abbasid clan, which moved the capital to Baghdad.

The Abbasids remained in power for more than five centuries, overseeing extensive economic, administrative, and cultural development. However, this period also saw growing fragmentation of the empire, with local rulers sometimes exercising considerable autonomy. In addition, European Christian Crusaders invaded the empire repeatedly starting in 1096, establishing Christian states in coastal areas of the Levant. The Abbasids were finally overthrown in 1258, when Mongol armies sacked Baghdad. Mongols and local leaders ruled in different parts of the region during the next two centuries.

In addition to the Mongols, Turkic people migrated from central Asia into the northeastern Middle East during this period. One such group was the Ottoman Turks, who established themselves in Anatolia in the thirteenth century and began to conquer the surrounding area. They seized Constantinople, the last remnant of the Byzantine Empire, in 1453 and then conquered southeastern Europe and most of the Arab lands. In 1517 the Ottoman sultan proclaimed himself caliph, appropriating the religious authority of the earlier Islamic empire. At about the same time, the Safavid dynasty established a new Persian empire and proclaimed Shi'ism the state religion, becoming bitter rivals of the Ottomans.

The Ottomans were the most powerful force in the Mediterranean region for several centuries. However, their frequent wars with the Habsburg and Safavid empires and growing European might weakened them in the eighteenth and nineteenth centuries. European powers drove the Ottomans out of southeastern Europe and North Africa in the nineteenth and early twentieth centuries. Nationalist movements emerged in the Levant, further threatening Ottoman control over this region. By World War I, the Ottoman Empire was on the brink of collapse.

The Ottomans sided with Germany and Austria-Hungary during World War I. Britain fomented anti-Ottoman rebellions in northern Arabia and the Levant during the war, promising to create an independent Arab state there. The resulting Arab Revolt helped drive Ottoman forces out of the region. However, Britain and France also secretly agreed to divide the region between themselves. They implemented this agreement after the war, with Britain taking what became Palestine, Jordan, and Iraq and France taking what became Lebanon and Syria, ruling these territories as mandates under the League of Nations. Iraq became independent in 1932. Lebanon, Syria, and Jordan became independent in the mid-1940s.

In the late nineteenth century, a Jewish nationalist movement known as Zionism emerged in Europe. Its main focus was to encourage European Jews to emigrate to Palestine and establish a Jewish state there to escape the persecution they had long suffered in Europe. Small numbers of Zionists moved to Palestine before World War I. During the war, British foreign secretary Arthur Balfour declared that Britain would help the Zionists achieve their goal. Britain then allowed much more extensive Jewish immigration into Palestine after the war, producing a substantial Jewish population there for the first time since the Roman-era diaspora. Clashes grew between the Zionists and Palestinian Arabs, who wanted their own independent state. Full-scale civil war occurred between 1936 and 1939.

World War II briefly defused the conflict in Palestine, but tensions reemerged after the war. Britain now was weak and unable to resolve the crisis, so the United Nations took over. With strong encouragement from the United States, the United Nations decided to partition Palestine into Jewish and Arab states in May 1948. When the new State of Israel declared independence, Egypt, Jordan, Syria, and Iraq invaded it, beginning the first Arab-Israeli war. Israel managed to conquer not only the land awarded it by the United Nations but also much of the land designated for an Arab state. Most Arabs fled or were driven out of Palestine, becoming refugees in the neighboring Arab countries.

The creation of Israel and the Palestinian refugee crisis produced great anger throughout the Arab world. This anger, together with continuing European colonial or neocolonial domination in many areas, fueled a wave of instability and the emergence of radical nationalist movements in many Arab countries. In Egypt, radical Arab nationalists led by Colonel Gamal Abdel Nasser seized power in 1952. Nasser then nationalized the British-owned Suez Canal, leading Israel, Britain, and France to invade Egypt in an unsuccessful effort to depose him. The radical nationalist governments of Egypt and Syria merged in 1958, creating the short-lived United Arab Republic, and radical nationalists overthrew Iraq's monarchy in 1958. Radical nationalists in Algeria began a bloody uprising against French colonial rule in 1954, leading France to grant independence to Morocco and Tunisia in 1956 and finally to Algeria in 1962. Radical nationalists also seized power in southern Yemen and Libya in the late 1960s.

In June 1967, provocative actions by Nasser led Israel to invade its neighbors and conquer the remaining parts of Palestine, Egypt's Sinai Peninsula, and Syria's Golan Heights. This fueled further radicalism in the Arab world, including a sharp increase in Palestinian terrorist attacks against Israel. In 1973, Egypt and Syria jointly attacked Israeli forces in the Sinai and Golan, trying unsuccessfully to retake these territories. Palestinians staged numerous terrorist attacks against Israel from southern Lebanon, producing harsh Israeli retaliation and tensions that triggered a civil war in Lebanon in 1975. Egyptian president Anwar Sadat signed the Camp David peace agreement with Israel in 1978, establishing a precedent for Arab-Israeli peace negotiations and leading radical Islamists to assassinate him in 1981.

In 1978–1979, Islamists in Iran led a popular revolution that overthrew the US-backed monarchy there and installed an Islamic regime. The Iranian revolution inspired Islamists throughout the region, beginning an era in which Islamists replaced nationalists as the main advocates of change in the region. Iran's new leaders became increasingly radical during the next few years, carrying out a thorough domestic Islamization program and supporting radical Islamists in neighboring countries. The resulting turmoil led Iraqi president Saddam Hussein to invade Iran in 1980, producing a devastating war. Israel invaded Lebanon in 1982, leading Iran to create the radical Islamist militia Hizballah, which carried out numerous terrorist attacks against Israeli and US targets. Powerful Islamist movements also emerged in Afghanistan, Egypt, Algeria, and the Israeli-occupied Palestinian territories in the 1980s.

The Iran-Iraq War ended in 1988. Iraq then invaded Kuwait in 1990, leading the United States to organize a coalition of forces that drove Iraq out in early 1991 and then imposed harsh UN sanctions on Iraq. US officials also tried to forge an Israeli-Palestinian peace agreement in the 1990s. This effort finally collapsed in 2000, triggering a Palestinian uprising against Israeli occupation that lasted several years and took thousands of lives. These events created great anxiety in the Arab world, fueling anti-Americanism and radical Islamism. The most important manifestation of this was the emergence of the Islamist terrorist group al-Qaida, which established bases in Afghanistan in the late 1990s and carried out a series of terrorist attacks against US and pro-Western targets.

Al-Qaida's most dramatic effort was the September 11, 2001, attacks in New York and Washington. In the following months, the United States and its allies launched a global effort to destroy al-Qaida and its affiliates, beginning with the radical Islamist Taliban government in Afghanistan. The United States then invaded Iraq in 2003, though the country posed little threat to US interests. US forces became bogged down in a bloody war there, which continued until 2011. This war diverted US resources from Afghanistan, enabling the Taliban to reemerge and challenge the governments of Afghanistan and Pakistan. A border clash with Hizballah led Israel to invade Lebanon again in 2006. In the Palestinian territories, the Islamist movement Hamas won parliamentary elections in 2006 and pushed the moderate Fatah party out of Gaza in 2007. Israel then began a harsh blockade of Gaza and invaded it in late 2008, hoping to undermine popular support for Hamas.

The past few years have been a watershed period in the region. The Arab Spring transformed the Arab world, producing democratic or semidemocratic regimes in several countries, spurring civil war elsewhere, and giving moderate Islamists an unprecedented role in politics. The Arab Spring also has had important regional effects, aggravating Arab-Israeli and Arab-Iranian relations, raising the regional profiles of Qatar and Turkey, and fueling rebellion in the Sahara region. In 2011 US forces finally killed al-Qaida's leader, Osama bin Laden, eliminating a radical Islamist icon and raising doubts about the future of the movement. And Iran's nuclear program became a major concern, leading Western powers to impose crippling economic sanctions on Iran and raising the possibility that Israel or the United States might use military force to prevent Iran from developing nuclear weapons.

ETHNIC AND RELIGIOUS DIVISIONS

Numerous ethnic and religious groups live in the Middle East and North Africa. Some 62 percent of the region's residents speak Arabic as their primary language and thus can be considered Arabs. Arabic speakers live throughout the region but comprise only small minorities in Israel, Turkey, and Iran. The next largest ethnolinguistic group is the Turks, who constitute 16 percent of the region's population and 70 to 75 percent of Turkey's population. Smaller Turkic minorities include the Azeris of northwestern Iran, the

Qashqais of south-central Iran, and the Turkmen of Turkey, Iraq, and Iran. The next largest group is the Persians, who comprise 10 percent of the region's population and 61 percent of Iran's population. Related to Persians are the Kurds, who constitute 6 percent of the region's population and live in adjoining areas of Turkey, Iraq, Iran, and Syria, and the Baluch people of southeastern Iran, Pakistan, and Afghanistan. Another 4 percent are Berbers, who live mainly in Morocco and Algeria. Hebrew-speaking Jews make up about 1 percent of the region's population and 76 percent of Israel's population, with Palestinian Arabs comprising most of the remainder. Small numbers of Armenians live in Syria, Lebanon, and Iran.

Some 92 percent of the region's population is Muslim, with roughly two-thirds following the Sunni branch of Islam. Most of the remainder are Ja'fari Shi'a, who venerate a line of twelve male descendants of Muhammad, including Ali and Hussein. Ja'fari Shi'a comprise roughly 90 percent of Iranians, 65 percent of Iraqis and Bahrainis, 35 percent of Lebanese, and smaller proportions in Saudi Arabia and elsewhere. Other Shi'a populations include the Alevis and Alawis of Turkey and Syria and the Zaydis of Yemen. Most Omanis follow the ancient Ibadhi branch of Islam, while small minorities in Lebanon, Syria, and Israel follow the Druze offshoot of Islam. Most of the region's remaining population is Christian, including Copts, who comprise about 10 percent of Egypt's population, Maronites, who comprise about 25 percent of Lebanon's population, Armenians, and Greek Orthodox. About 1 percent of the region's population is Jewish, including most Israelis and small communities in Iran and elsewhere.

ECONOMIC CONDITIONS

The region's economies vary considerably, as shown in Table 1.1. The most striking pattern is that gross domestic product per capita, which represents the average income of a country's population, varies tremendously across the region, with the richest country (Qatar) being forty-one times wealthier than the poorest (Yemen). While these two countries are atypical, incomes nevertheless vary substantially, with seven countries in the region lying above $20,000 per year and six (including the Palestinian territories) below $6,000. The comparable figure for the United States is $48,100.

The main factor driving these income disparities is the huge variation in oil and gas revenue across the region. The second column in Table 1.1 shows each country's net fuel export revenue per capita (i.e., oil and gas exports minus imports, divided by population size). Six of the seven countries with gross domestic product (GDP) per capita above $20,000 are major fuel exporters, while all but one below $6,000 (Iraq) have small or negative net fuel exports. The region's major fuel exporters fall into three categories: three with net fuel exports per capita above $20,000 (Kuwait, Qatar, and the United Arab Emirates), three between $4,000 and $11,000 (Bahrain, Oman, and Saudi Arabia), and three others above $900 (Algeria, Iran, and Iraq). These levels correlate closely with GDP per capita.

The oil and gas that produces this income is government owned, so most of this revenue goes into government coffers. In countries with large fuel exports, governments receive large revenue inflows from abroad and therefore have little need to tax their citizens, reducing an important potential source of unrest. These governments can reduce unrest further by using this revenue to provide free or low-cost education, health care, utilities, transportation, and even housing and by giving citizens lucrative employment and business opportunities. Moreover, with low taxes and extensive public services and other opportunities, these governments generally face less pressure for political representation and accountability. Countries of this sort are often called "rentier states" because much of their income consists of "rent" based on government-owned resources. Countries with high net fuel exports per capita, like Kuwait, Qatar, and the United Arab Emirates, are quintessential rentier states and face little unrest or pressure for political representation. The other oil and gas producers in the region experience these effects roughly in proportion to the size of their net fuel exports per capita, with lower-income countries like Iran and Algeria feeling only weak effects, especially when fuel prices are low.

Most countries in the region with small or negative net fuel exports are quite poor. As shown in Table 1.1, many of these countries have relatively large agricultural sectors, providing extensive low-income employment—even though some have little arable land. These countries also have relatively large, inefficient service sectors that provide additional low-income employment. Some have large manufacturing industries, though most are inefficient and cannot compete in world markets. Most of these poorer countries rely heavily on remittances from expatriate workers, and the Palestinians, Egypt, and Jordan receive considerable foreign aid. The Palestinian territories are under Israeli occupation, and some countries have experienced persistent political instability, discouraging investment and therefore undermining economic growth.

Three countries in the region depart from the general pattern in which oil and gas revenues largely determine income per capita. Most notably, Israel has a dynamic, modern economy, due mainly to its high education levels, extensive foreign aid and donations, and careful economic management. Its economy features a technology-intensive agricultural sector, a large tourism sector, and advanced defense, electronics, and software industries. Lebanon has important banking and tourism industries, considerable expatriate remittances, and close ties to Europe. Turkey has liberalized its economy in recent decades and established a customs union with the European Union, giving it a strong agricultural sector and various globally competitive manufacturing industries.

DEMOGRAPHIC AND SOCIAL CONDITIONS

Demographic and social conditions also vary substantially. Table 1.2 shows that the countries of the region differ widely in population size, with three having populations of more than 60 million and six, populations below 5 million. Moreover, the second column in the

Table 1.1   Selected Economic Indicators

Country	GDP per Capita (US $)	Net Fuel Exports per Capita (US $)	Arable Land (%)	Agriculture (% of GDP)	Services (% of GDP)	Industry (% of GDP)
Algeria	7,200	1,542	3	8	29	63
Bahrain	27,300	4,096	3	0	36	64
Egypt	6,500	10	3	14	48	38
Iran	12,200	938	10	10	52	38
Iraq	3,900	1,330	13	10	30	60
Israel	31,000	−1,353	15	3	65	31
Jordan	5,900	−551	3	4	65	31
Kuwait	40,700	33,056	1	0	52	47
Lebanon	15,600	−934	16	6	76	20
Libya	14,100		1	3	47	50
Morocco	5,100	−249	19	17	51	32
Oman	26,200	10,201	0	1	49	50
Palestinian Territories	2,900		18	4	83	14
Qatar	102,700	37,883	2	0	27	73
Saudi Arabia	24,000	7,947	2	2	29	69
Syria	5,100	13	25	17	56	27
Tunisia	9,500	−45	17	11	55	35
Turkey	14,600	−312	30	9	63	28
United Arab Emirates	48,500	24,685	1	1	45	54
Yemen	2,500	165	3	8	50	42

Sources: Net fuel exports data from World Bank, *World Development Indicators Online*. All other data from *CIA World Factbook*. All data are for 2011 or most recent year available.

table shows that the Persian Gulf oil-producing countries host large numbers of immigrant workers, leaving Bahrain, Kuwait, and Qatar each with fewer than a million citizens. The third column shows that most of these countries have fertility rates well above the population-replacement rate of just over two babies per woman, producing high population growth rates. Moreover, as shown in the fourth column, countries with high fertility rates and few immigrant workers (who are mainly adult males) have very youthful populations, often creating youth-unemployment problems and potentially volatile unrest. A few countries (Iran, Tunisia, and Turkey) have brought fertility rates down substantially with family-planning programs, reducing these problems.

Table 1.2   Selected Demographic Indicators

Country	Population (Thousands)	Percent of Population Immigrants	Fertility Rate (Live Births per Woman)	Percent of Population Under 15	Percent of Population Urban
Algeria	35,468	1	2.3	27	67
Bahrain	1,262	25	2.5	20	89
Egypt	81,121	0	2.7	32	43
Iran	73,973	3	1.7	23	70
Iraq	32,031	0	4.7	43	66
Israel	7,624	39	3.0	27	92
Jordan	6,047	49	3.8	38	79
Kuwait	2,736	77	2.3	27	98
Lebanon	4,227	18	1.8	25	87
Libya	6,355	11	2.6	30	78
Morocco	31,951	0	2.3	28	57
Oman	2,783	30	2.3	27	72
Palestinian Territories	4,152	46	4.5	42	72
Qatar	1,759	74	2.3	13	96
Saudi Arabia	27,448	27	2.8	30	84
Syria	20,447	11	2.9	37	55
Tunisia	10,549	0	2.0	23	67
Turkey	72,752	2	2.1	26	70
United Arab Emirates	7,512	44	1.7	17	78
Yemen	24,053	2	5.2	44	32

Source: World Bank, *World Development Indicators Online*. All data are for 2010 or most recent year available.

The last column of Table 1.2 shows that all countries in the region except Egypt and Yemen are very urbanized, with at least half of their populations living in cities. While cities like Dubai and Tel Aviv in the wealthier countries boast glittering skyscrapers and broad boulevards, those in poorer countries are often dysfunctional, with inadequate infrastructure, serious environmental problems, and vast, impoverished shantytowns. The urban poor in these cities have difficult lives and are susceptible to populist appeals, providing the main base of support for the region's Islamist movements.

Table 1.3 shows several indicators of poverty in the region. Israel and the wealthy Persian Gulf countries have infant-mortality and life-expectancy rates rivaling those in

Table 1.3   Selected Social Indicators

Country	Infant Mortality (per 1,000 births)	Life Expectancy (at birth)	Adult Literacy (%)	Adult Female Literacy (%)	Telephone (per 100 people)	Internet Users (per 100 people)
Algeria	31	73	73	64	101	13
Bahrain	9	75	91	90	142	55
Egypt	19	73	66	58	99	27
Iran	22	73	85	81	128	13
Iraq	31	68	78	70	80	2
Israel	4	82			172	65
Jordan	18	73	92	89	118	39
Kuwait	10	75	94	92	182	38
Lebanon	19	72	90	86	89	31
Libya	13	75	89	82	191	14
Morocco	30	72	56	44	112	49
Oman	8	73	87	81	176	62
Palestinian Territories	20	73	95	92	54	36
Qatar	7	78	95	93	149	82
Saudi Arabia	15	74	86	81	203	41
Syria	14	76	84	78	78	21
Tunisia	14	75	78	71	118	37
Turkey	14	74	91	85	107	40
United Arab Emirates	6	77	90	91	165	78
Yemen	57	65	62	45	50	12

Source: World Bank, World Development Indicators Online. All data are for 2010 or most recent year available.

Europe, reflecting their modern health and sanitation systems. Infant mortality and life expectancy are far worse in Yemen and, to a lesser extent, in Morocco and Iraq (following decades of war and economic sanctions), reflecting the severe poverty and poor infrastructure in these countries. Adult literacy is very high in Israel and fairly high in the wealthy Persian Gulf countries, where oil income has fueled a big expansion of educational infrastructure. Moreover, Table 1.3 shows that women have benefited substantially from this expansion, despite the conservative character of these countries. By contrast, male and especially female literacy are much lower in Yemen and Morocco, where poverty sharply limits educational opportunities.

The last two columns in the table show that the availability of telephones (including mobile phones) and the Internet also varies widely, being highest in Israel and the wealthy Persian Gulf countries and lowest in Iraq, the Palestinian territories, Syria, and Yemen, where poverty and repressive regimes limit them. These figures give a good indication of how isolated or connected people in these countries are, both nationally and globally.

POLITICAL REGIMES

The countries of the region have very diverse political regimes. Their regimes can be grouped into three categories: authoritarian or semidemocratic monarchies, authoritarian republics, and democratic or semidemocratic republics.

As shown in Table 1.4, Jordan, Morocco, Saudi Arabia, and the eastern Arabian states (Bahrain, Kuwait, Oman, Qatar, and the United Arab Emirates) all have monarchical regimes. Egypt, Iraq, Yemen, Libya, and Iran also had monarchies that were overthrown in the 1950s, 1960s, or 1970s. Most of these monarchies were established upon independence, based on a precolonial ruling family (Egypt, Morocco, the eastern Arabian states, and Yemen), a powerful family from a neighboring region (Jordan and Iraq), or a prominent religious family (Libya). The Saudi monarchy was established after the Saud tribe conquered much of Arabia in the 1920s. Iran's monarchy dated from ancient Persian times.

The monarchies of today are similar in some ways but different in others. In each case, substantial power is concentrated in the hands of the monarch, known formally as the king, emir, or sultan. As Table 1.4 shows, some are absolute monarchs who rule directly as heads of government, while others are constitutional monarchs ruling indirectly through prime ministers. The United Arab Emirates is ruled by a council consisting of the absolute monarchs of its seven federated emirates. Most of the monarchies now have popularly elected parliaments or consultative councils, though only those in Kuwait and Morocco wield much power. Most also now have constitutions that codify the structure of government, including the monarch's powers. Relatives of the monarch often occupy powerful positions, and considerable rivalry sometimes exists within a royal family. The monarchs claim legitimacy on the basis of their historical, tribal, and/or religious backgrounds. They all maintain close ties with traditional and modern elites, giving these elites some influence but also cementing their loyalty. All of these monarchs also maintain close ties with the United States and other Western countries, further strengthening them. Finally, as discussed above, the Persian Gulf monarchies all receive extensive oil revenue, reducing domestic unrest and pressure for representation.

With traditional claims to legitimacy and close ties to domestic elites and Western powers, these monarchs are all inherently conservative, upholding rather than challenging the status quo. Nevertheless, after decades of autocratic rule, most have allowed at least limited political liberalization in recent years, enacting or revising constitutions or basic laws, establishing parliaments or consultative bodies, expanding the electorate, holding elections, allowing parties to operate, and/or easing censorship. These reforms have been most extensive in Kuwait and Morocco, which are now semidemocratic ("partly free" in Table 1.4). Little or no political liberalization has occurred in Saudi Arabia and the United Arab Emirates.

Of the authoritarian republics, Algeria, Egypt, Iraq, Libya, Syria, Tunisia, and southern Yemen each established radical Arab nationalist regimes in the 1950s or 1960s. These regimes were similar in many ways, though important differences also existed among them. Their leaders all espoused Arab nationalist ideology, though some added doses of Marxist-Leninism (southern Yemen) or Islam (Libya). To implement their agendas, they all built strong state apparatuses featuring powerful executive branches, vanguard political parties, extensive state control over the economy, and powerful security apparatuses. All were authoritarian, excluding their opponents, rigging elections, and controlling the media. Some were highly repressive (Iraq and Syria), while others were more liberal (Tunisia). Some leaders were popular and charismatic (Nasser in Egypt, Habib Bourguiba in Tunisia), and most initially sought to mobilize popular support with rousing speeches, mass parties, and populist economic and social policies. But most were more feared than loved. These regimes generally claimed to be allied against Israel, the West, and the conservative Arab monarchies, but deep rivalries existed among them.

The leaders of these regimes largely abandoned Arab nationalism in the 1970s and 1980s, though they continued to pay lip service to it. However, their political institutions remained stubbornly resistant to change. All remained authoritarian, with strong state apparatuses, powerful executive branches, dominant parties or ruling cliques, and fearsome security apparatuses. Some allowed limited opposition activity but kept it carefully controlled. Most carried out some economic liberalization, but their economies remained state dominated. Charismatic leadership and mass mobilization ended, replaced by colorless or fearsome leaders, stultifying bureaucracy, and ossified parties that served mainly to dispense patronage in exchange for loyalty. The powerful state apparatuses established to implement Arab nationalist agendas now served mainly to keep their leaders in power.

As these regimes became increasingly sclerotic, popular unrest grew. Starting in the late 1970s, riots or other forms of mass protest emerged in each of these countries. Many of these protests were led by Islamists, whose popularity grew rapidly. Popular unrest sparked major rebellions in Syria in the early 1980s, Iraq in 1991, and Algeria beginning in 1992; lesser challenges emerged elsewhere. Iraq's Ba'thist regime collapsed after the 2003 US invasion, triggering extensive fighting between its supporters and opponents. And when the Arab Spring emerged in 2011, these radical Arab nationalist successor regimes were the most severely affected: those in Tunisia, Egypt, and Libya soon collapsed, and Syria's Ba'thists unleashed a bloodbath that continued in late 2012. It remains unclear what will replace these regimes.

Iran and the Palestinian territories both have authoritarian republics, though meaningful political competition has occurred at certain times under these regimes. Iran established an Islamic republic after its 1979 revolution. Under its constitution key positions of

Table 1.4 Selected Political Indicators

Country	Year of Independence	Executive System	Constitution Year Adopted (*=temporary)	Suffrage, Minimum Voting Age	Political Freedom, 2011
Algeria	1962	presidential republic	1963	universal, 18	not free
Bahrain	1971	constitutional monarchy	2002	universal, 20	not free
Egypt	1922	presidential republic	2011*	universal, 18	not free
Iran	1501	presidential theocracy	1979	universal, 18	not free
Iraq	1932	parliamentary republic	2005	universal, 18	not free
Israel	1948	parliamentary republic	none	universal, 18	free
Jordan	1946	constitutional monarchy	1952	universal, 18	not free
Kuwait	1961	constitutional monarchy	1962	universal, 21	partly free
Lebanon	1943	semi–presidential republic	1926	universal, 21	partly free
Libya	1951	transitional	2011*	universal, 18	not free
Morocco	1956	constitutional monarchy	1972	universal, 18	partly free
Oman	1650	absolute monarchy	none	universal, 21	not free
Palestinian Territories	not independent	semi–presidential under Israeli occupation	none	noneuniversal, 18	not free
Qatar	1971	constitutional monarchy	2005	universal, 18	not free
Saudi Arabia	1932	absolute monarchy	none	men, 21	not free
Syria	1946	dominant–party dictatorship	1973	universal, 18	not free
Tunisia	1956	presidential republic	1959	universal, 18	partly free
Turkey	1923	parliamentary republic	1982	universal, 18	partly free
United Arab Emirates	1971	constitutional federation of monarchies	1971	none	not free
Yemen	1918/1967	presidential republic	1991	universal, 18	not free

Notes: Political freedom classifications from *freedomhouse.org*. All other data from *CIA World Factbook* and *Wikipedia.org*.

government are reserved for unelected Shi'a clerics, who are empowered to screen candidates in presidential and parliamentary elections, dismiss the president, and veto legislation passed by parliament. Elections were fairly competitive in the late 1990s, enabling reform-oriented Islamists to win the presidency in 1997 and gain control over parliament in 2000. However, hard-liners then began a crackdown, marginalizing these reformists. When allegations of vote rigging sparked large protests after the 2009 presidential election, hard-liners carried out an extensive crackdown that destroyed the reformist movement and ended political competition.

Under the 1993 Oslo peace agreement, Palestinians in the Israeli-occupied West Bank and Gaza established a self-governing body featuring an elected president and parliament. The secular nationalist Fatah party won the first elections for these institutions in 1996, while the Islamist Hamas party boycotted. Turmoil in the Palestinian territories delayed the next presidential election until 2005, when Hamas again boycotted. Hamas then won a plurality in the 2006 parliamentary election. Tensions quickly grew between Hamas and Fatah, leading to armed clashes in 2007 that left Fatah in control of the West Bank and Hamas in control of Gaza. Continuing tension between these parties has delayed the next set of elections indefinitely.

Israel, Lebanon, and Turkey each have democratic or semidemocratic regimes dating from the 1940s. Upon independence in 1948, Israel established a Western-style democracy that continues to thrive. However, while its citizens enjoy extensive opportunities for political participation, Israel continues to impose severe restrictions on political activity by the large Palestinian population living under Israeli occupation. Since independence in 1943, Lebanon has had a semidemocratic regime that apportions representation among its various confessional groups, though disproportionately favoring Christians. This system broke down in the mid-1970s, producing a devastating civil war. When the war ended in 1989, the system was restructured to benefit the Muslim majority, though inequities remain. Turkey's leaders established a Western-style democracy after World War II. However, the country's armed forces have repeatedly intervened in politics, producing a persistent legacy of "guided democracy," and its Kurdish minority continues to suffer human rights abuses.

Bibliography

For histories of the Middle East, see James L. Gelvin, *The Modern Middle East* (New York: Oxford University Press, 2011), and Arthur Goldschmidt and Lawrence Davidson, *A Concise History of the Middle East,* 9th ed. (Boulder, CO: Westview Press, 2009). For general overviews of the region, see Ellen Lust, ed., *The Middle East,* 12th ed. (Washington, DC: CQ Press, 2011), and Jillian Schwedler and Deborah J. Gerner, eds., *Understanding the Contemporary Middle East,* 3rd ed. (Boulder, CO: Lynne Rienner, 2008).

On the region's international politics, see Louise Fawcett, ed., *International Relations of the Middle East,* 2nd ed. (New York: Oxford University Press, 2009); Fred Halliday,

The Middle East in International Relations (Cambridge: Cambridge University Press, 2005); and L. Carl Brown, *Diplomacy in the Middle East* (London: I. B. Tauris, 2004). On the Arab Spring, see Marc Lynch, *The Arab Uprising* (New York: PublicAffairs, 2012).

For introductory works on Islam and political Islam, see Ira M. Lapidus, *A History of Islamic Societies,* 2nd ed. (Cambridge: Cambridge University Press, 2002), and Peter Mandaville, *Global Political Islam,* 2nd ed. (New York: Routledge, 2013). On Middle Eastern culture, see Lawrence Rosen, *The Culture of Islam* (Chicago: University of Chicago Press, 2002), and Halim Barakat, *The Arab World* (Berkeley: University of California Press, 1993). See also classic works of modern Middle Eastern literature such as Abdel Rahman Munif, *Cities of Salt* (London: Cape, 1988), and Naquib Mahfouz, *The Cairo Trilogy* (New York: Everyman's Library, 2001).

On regional geography, see Colbert C. Held and John Thomas Cummings, *Middle East Patterns,* 5th ed. (Boulder, CO: Westview Press, 2010), and Ewan W. Anderson and Liam D. Anderson, *An Atlas of Middle Eastern Affairs* (New York: Routledge, 2009). On the region's economics, see Clement M. Henry and Robert Springborg, *Globalization and the Politics of Development in the Middle East,* 2nd ed. (New York: Cambridge University Press, 2010), and Alan Richards and John Waterbury, *A Political Economy of the Middle East,* 3rd ed. (Boulder, CO: Westview Press, 2007). On social conditions, see United Nations Development Programme, *Arab Human Development Report 2012* (New York: United Nations Publications, 2012).

For useful websites, see Middle East Institute (www.mei.edu), Middle East Policy Council (http://mepc.org), the Gulf 2000 Project (http://gulf2000.columbia.edu), Human Rights Watch, Middle East/North Africa (www.hrw.org/middle-east/n-africa), New York Times—Middle East (http://nytimes.com/pages/world/middleeast), BBC News—Middle East (http://bbc.co.uk/news/world/middle_east), Middle East Newspapers (www.world-newspapers.com/east.html), Perry-Castañeda Library Map Collection—Middle East Maps (http://lib.utexas.edu/maps/middle_east.html), and MidEast Web Gateway (http://mideastweb.org).

2

REPUBLIC OF TURKEY

Henri J. Barkey and Omer Taspinar

HISTORICAL BACKGROUND

The history of the Turkish people goes back to pre-Islamic central Asia, where shamanism defined the religious context. Their conversion to Islam came in the ninth and tenth centuries as a result of westward territorial expansion. The new religion played a crucial role in consolidating central state power, mainly by legitimizing sultanic rule in the name of protecting and expanding the Islamic realm.

Among the new Muslim-Turkic states, the Seljuks rapidly stood out with their territorial expansion into Persia and further west. In 1071, the Seljuks defeated the Byzantine armies in the eastern Anatolian province of Manzikert. This historic victory opened the gates of Anatolia to the Turks. With their new capital in Konya, the Seljuks conquered a large swath of Anatolia, where they established a great civilization. The Ottomans emerged from the Seljuks after their demise.

The Ottomans continued the Turkish tradition of westward territorial expansion. Their spectacular rise from a small principality to a legendary empire took less than two centuries. After taking Constantinople in 1453, they conquered the Balkans and most of eastern Europe, and by the mid-sixteenth century, Ottoman armies had reached the gates of Vienna. During these centuries the image of the "terrible Turk" symbolized a sort of religious "other," consolidating Europe's own Christian identity. Yet a long and agonizing Ottoman decline had already started by the late seventeenth century. During the empire's last century, the Ottoman ruling elite sought salvation in one of the earliest projects of westernization. During the nineteenth century the Young Ottoman and Young Turk movements emerged in an attempt to arrest the empire's decline by introducing reforms modeled after European military, political, and legal systems.

A flair for bureaucratic organization distinguished the later Ottomans from their earliest days. Initially the armed forces dominated the government apparatus, but once the era of conquest ended, the problems of administering the huge Ottoman territories demanded increased attention. In response, the civilian hierarchy expanded in prestige, size, and

Republic of Turkey

complexity. Thus, though the army always played an important role, the Ottoman Empire was far more than a praetorian state run by a dominant military caste. It was a bureaucratic empire in which the state enjoyed political legitimacy in the eyes of its subjects.

This deeply rooted state tradition also meant that reforms were state-led and promulgated from above. This tradition duly continued under the Young Turks and Mustafa Kemal Ataturk, the founder of modern Turkey, with greater secularist zeal.

At the same time, the effort to keep the Ottoman state competitive triggered severe intraelite conflict. On the one hand, secular modernizers, who emerged in the nineteenth century, saw the adoption of European technology as the way to cope with Western intrusions. On the other hand, traditionalists advocated a return to religious purity and a rejection of Western materialism as the recipe for staving off Europe.

By the time the empire collapsed after World War I, however, the religious class was in full retreat. The need to embrace European technology was generally accepted, but dispute centered on whether wholesale cultural Westernization was essential to complement Western technology. This debate continued into the republican era.

Organization by religious community proved a cost-effective method of rule in the centuries before national consciousness was awakened among the subject peoples. But the persistence of communal identity provided fertile ground for separatist movements once nationalism's seeds had been planted. These ethnic separatists threatened to dismember the empire from within while the European powers were pressing from without.

Turkish nationalism did not emerge full-blown until the Ottoman Empire disintegrated. But as early as the Young Turk period, proponents of Turkism were in evidence. After the 1908 Young Turk revolution, forces of economic nationalism emerged, mainly in reaction to the financial controls imposed by European creditors. Yet, although Enver

Pasha, one of Turkey's triumvirs in World War I, urged that the world's Turks be assembled in a single state, neither he nor his fellow Young Turks ever abandoned their hope of maintaining the empire, especially its Arab and Islamic elements.

Modern Turkey was built on the political structures erected by the Young Turks. The Ottoman parliament that had been restored in 1908 continued on as the Grand National Assembly in Ankara, and the Committee of Union and Progress served as the model for Ataturk's own political vehicle, the Republican People's Party.

The First Republic

Ataturk is rightly credited with having established Turkey out of the ruins of the Ottoman state. Yet he built on local "defense of rights" organizations in Anatolia and Thrace that the Committee of Union and Progress had set up to resist the European effort to carve up the Turkish heartland after World War I. Ataturk served as a critical rallying point against the invading Greeks, who landed in Izmir in May 1919. Under his charismatic leadership, Turkey regained its independence, expelled the Greeks, and convinced the Western powers to end their occupation.

Ataturk then began extensive modernization of Turkish society. One of his major contributions was to recognize the folly of trying to retain Arab dominions. But he insisted on keeping a Kurdish-inhabited segment of the Anatolian core area, which he considered essential to modern Turkey. To boost Turkish pride, he tried to translate religious attachment into patriotic fervor for the new state. Ataturk sought to transform Turkey quickly and radically. His reforms ran the gamut, from establishing modern dress codes to replacing the Arabic alphabet with the Latin one. Turkey, he declared, had to join "contemporary civilization."

The new Turkish state was a parliamentary republic in form, though an autocracy in practice. The basic slogan of the republic was "Sovereignty belongs to the people"—a sovereignty formally exercised by a unicameral parliament. Ataturk used his Republican People's Party to dominate politics. Backed by a handpicked parliamentary majority, he shut down rival political groups, starting with supporters of the caliph in the 1923 elections, the Progressive Republican Party in 1925, and even his own tame "opposition" Free Party in 1930. Thereafter he attempted to fuse his single party with the government. This effort at a corporate state, however, led the party to atrophy and government organs to become dominant.

Following Ataturk's death in 1938, the regime became even more authoritarian, lashing out at domestic minorities. Ataturk's successor, Ismet Inonu, though a respectable former comrade in arms, lacked his charisma and natural authority. In their search for legitimacy, his successors transformed Ataturk into a cultlike figure. Following the Allied victory in World War II, the Inonu regime sought to align itself with the victors and secure their support against the Soviet Union. Inonu decided to liberalize the regime to gain favor with the West.

REPUBLIC OF TURKEY

Capital city	Ankara
Chief of state, 2012	President Abdullah Gul
Head of government, 2012	Prime Minister Recep Tayyip Erdogan
Political parties (share of vote in most recent election, 2011)	Justice and Development Party (49.8%), Republican People's Party (25.9%), Nationalist Movement Party (13%), Motherland Party, Democratic Party, Democratic Left Party, Democratic Society Party, Felicity Party, Freedom and Solidarity Party, Grand Unity Party, People's Rise Party, Social Democratic People's Party, Young Party
Ethnic groups	Turkish (70%–75%), Kurdish (18%), other minorities (7%–12%)
Religious groups	Muslim, mostly Sunni (99.8%), other (0.2%)
Export partners, 2009	Germany (10.3%), Iraq (6.2%), United Kingdom (6%), Italy (5.8%), France (5%), Russia (4.4%)
Import partners, 2009	Russia (9.9%), Germany (9.5%), China (9%), United States (6.7%), Italy (5.6%), Iran (5.2%)

Inonu allowed four prominent defectors from the Republican People's Party to form the Democrat Party in 1946. Although the Republicans prevented a free and fair contest in the July 1946 elections, the Democrats won handily in 1950, capitalizing on widespread discontent generated by years of Republican People's Party rule.

The Democrats had the support of rural areas as well as the private sector they had championed. By contrast, the old state elite remained ensconced in the civilian and military bureaucracy, suspicious of the Democrats' willingness to relax Ataturk's reforms, especially regarding religion. Military officers perceived themselves as losers in the new economy, and some began secretly to agitate for a coup as early as the mid-1950s. The absence of a tradition of tolerance engendered a climate of oppression. The Democrats, while winning the 1953 and 1957 elections, feared Inonu and the Republicans and sought to muzzle the opposition.

The Second Republic

Upset with the Democrats, mid-level officers executed a coup in 1960. The officers' reign was short. They banned the Democrat Party, executed three of its leaders after a sham trial, and introduced a new constitution that was surprisingly liberal and progressive. They created a new upper chamber and Constitutional Court and organized new elections. By the end of 1961, they had transferred power to a new parliament that chose Inonu as prime minister. Inonu formed a series of weak and unstable coalitions that nonetheless served to reassure the officers that there would be no retaliation for their coup.

The new rising star of Turkish politics was Suleyman Demirel and his Justice Party. Ironically, the party was nothing but an extension, or reincarnation, of the Democrat Party. It successfully challenged Inonu and the Republicans by winning an overwhelming electoral victory in 1965. Economically, it benefited from the beginning of import-substituting industrialization and workers' remittances from Europe. The Justice Party scored a second electoral victory in 1969.

Demirel was challenged, however, by growing extremism. Government indecisiveness toward mounting student and labor disorder led senior military commanders in March 1971 to issue an extraordinary public demand for more effective rule. Otherwise, they warned, the armed forces would seize power.

Demirel was forced to resign, and parliament voted into power a series of technocratic cabinets under nonpartisan prime ministers. Under the military's tutelage these governments imposed martial law, narrowed some of the more liberal facets of the 1961 constitution, banned Turkey's only legal Marxist party, and made widespread arrests to suppress terrorism. Intellectuals, journalists, and labor leaders filled the jails.

Satisfied with these changes, the military allowed new elections in 1973. These were indecisive, as the Justice Party's right-of-center constituency fragmented and the Republicans, under a new leader, Bulent Ecevit, won a plurality of seats. Noteworthy was the emergence of Necmettin Erbakan and his National Salvation Party, which appealed to Islamic activists.

The next seven years were marked by a series of coalition governments, with Ecevit and Demirel alternating as prime minister. Each in turn relied on support from the National Salvation Party. Ecevit's first coalition sent Turkish troops into Cyprus in July 1974, following a Greek-inspired coup against President Makarios. But when Ecevit resigned, hoping to force early elections to cash in on the popularity of sending in troops, he was outmaneuvered and blocked by Demirel.

Elections in 1977 failed to resolve the political impasse. Bitter personal rivalry between Ecevit and Demirel exacerbated political paralysis. Turkey was buffeted by one economic crisis after another, producing shortages of foreign currency that left it unable to import basic necessities. Violence among left- and right-wing student groups increased dramatically. Although a Justice Party minority government in early 1980 was able to take bold economic departures to satisfy the International Monetary Fund (IMF) and shore up Turkey's external credit worthiness, parliament remained deadlocked. It failed to elect a president. The opposition ignored repeated warnings from top generals to cooperate with the government in granting additional authority to the military to impose order. Instead, the National Salvation Party demonstrated open disrespect for the constitutional provisions against exploiting religion, Kurdish unrest began to grow in the east, and no-confidence motions against cabinet ministers challenged the government's existence.

The Third Republic

Once again the military acted to resolve the political paralysis, ousting the civilian government in September 1980, shutting down parliament, and arresting thousands of people. On the economic front the generals initially co-opted Demirel's financial team, led by Turgut Ozal, who had been the architect of a wide-ranging economic-stabilization program. Coup leader General Kenan Evren and the ruling generals promised a return to civilian rule but made it clear they intended to transform Turkey's political system.

It would be three years before a new constitution, election law, and political parties' act could be put in place and elections held. During the first two years of this period, party propaganda was prohibited, the old parties were abolished, and institutions such as universities and unions were fundamentally restructured. The generals then banned all officials of the previously existing parties from political participation for ten years before permitting new parties to be established. The 1982 constitution was approved in a referendum—no one was allowed to campaign against it—that also ratified General Evren's seven-year term as president. The military also decided to create a two-party system and fashioned the new parties to serve its interests. Much to their surprise, Ozal formed his own party, the Motherland Party, and decided to challenge the generals.

In a clear rebuff of the generals, the Motherland Party won a solid majority in parliament in the November 1983 elections. Ozal used his parliamentary majority to enhance economic liberalization and continued to challenge military prerogatives. Within a few years, the two military-created parties had disappeared, and the old parties reemerged under different names and guises. All the banned politicians—Ecevit, Erbakan, and Demirel—would also resurrect themselves.

One change introduced by the generals had a lasting impact: a 10 percent electoral threshold prevented smaller parties from entering parliament and strengthened larger ones. In 1987, for instance, Ozal's Motherland Party won 36 percent of the vote and commanded an absolute majority in parliament. This has also served to prevent pro-Kurdish parties from making it into parliament, except as individual independent deputies.

The late 1980s saw the emergence of Kurdish unrest in the southeast, renewed religious agitation, and difficult inflationary pressures. Ozal's reforms, while improving Turkey's economy, fed corruption and a general dissatisfaction with the new class of rich entrepreneurs who made their fortunes thanks to the liberalized foreign exchange system.

Recognizing the downward spiral in his party's popularity, Prime Minister Ozal used his parliamentary majority to secure election as president in 1989. Although he resigned from the Motherland Party, as required under the constitution, he remained a power behind the scenes in both the party and the government. In April 1991, at Ozal's initiative, restrictions were eased on use of the Kurdish language, and prohibitions on the right to espouse class or religious ideologies were dropped from the penal code.

Ozal could not stem his party's slow decline. The Motherland Party came in second to Demirel's True Path Party in the October 1991 elections. Turkey again faced coalition politics in which personal rivalries played a major role. Not surprisingly, Demirel reached across the philosophical divide to bring the Social Democrat Populist Party into the cabinet rather than seeking Ozal's support, despite their similar views on many issues.

The unexpected death of President Ozal in April 1993 brought about significant change: Demirel was elected president; he then named a newcomer, Tansu Ciller, as Turkey's first woman prime minister. Ciller would disappoint all those who had hoped she would usher in a new era in Turkish politics. Inexperienced, she alienated key constituencies and allowed rampant corruption in her immediate entourage. By the time of the December 1995 elections, Ciller had become just another Turkish politician, and her True Path Party ran slightly behind Necmettin Erbakan's Welfare Party—the successor to the National Salvation Party of the 1970s. Welfare's appeal as untainted by corruption apparently overcame voters' reluctance to support a religiously oriented party.

The Welfare Party's success sent shock waves through the secular civilian and military elite. Thus, as an expedient, Motherland Party leader Mesut Yilmaz overcame his strong personal animus toward Tansu Ciller and formed a coalition government in early 1996. This artificial alliance collapsed after only a few months, and Ciller did the unthinkable: she formed a coalition government with the Welfare Party that rewarded Erbakan, the bête noire of Turkish politics, with the prime ministry. Ciller assumed the roles of foreign minister and deputy prime minister.

Tension between the government and the military quickly materialized. In February 1997, the generals issued an eighteen-point set of demands to the government to preserve secularist institutions, directly contradicting the policies espoused by the Welfare Party. So began what some Turkish political observers called Turkey's postmodern coup: the military, working in tandem with and directing civil society groups, engineered the government's downfall in June 1997. It was replaced by a Yilmaz-led left-of-center/right-of-center coalition. This led to a period in which the military appeared to play a much more active role in politics.

Under the military's influence, the Constitutional Court banned the Welfare Party and Erbakan from politics. Welfare, however, reconstituted itself as the Virtue Party, a common occurrence in Turkey where, in anticipation of party banning, shell parties are created to absorb members of parliament and activists. The Yilmaz government did not last long and was replaced by a minority one led by Ecevit. Ecevit's fortunes received an unexpected boost in February 1999 when US officials handed Abdullah Ocalan, Kurdistan Workers' Party (PKK) leader and Turkey's archnemesis, to Turkish authorities. Ocalan, who had lived in Damascus since 1980, was forced to go on the run when the Turkish military threatened the Syrian regime. He had found refuge in Kenya when the Americans located him.

Ecevit's personal probity and the capture of Ocalan catapulted his Democratic Left Party from fourth to first place in the 1999 elections, winning a plurality of the popular vote. Close behind was the Nationalist Action Party, whose leader, Devlet Bahceli, maneuvered the party into a coalition with Yilmaz's Motherland Party. The new government's policies seemed largely set by Ecevit who, over the objections of the Nationalist Action Party, blocked the execution of Ocalan. This coalition also appeared more serious than its predecessors about budgetary discipline and trying to meet the criteria for inclusion in the European Union (EU).

These promising developments were set back when Ecevit and the president, Ahmet Necdet Sezer, engaged in a public and undiplomatic row over corruption. The February 2001 dispute occurred at a time when the banking sector was reeling from poor management and fictitious loans. Overnight the currency depreciated by half, inflation rose, and credit dried up. To deal with the most serious economic crisis Turkey had ever faced, Ecevit called in World Bank vice president Kemal Dervis to introduce an IMF-approved stabilization program. The Dervis reforms continue to this day; he first helped arrest the decline and then pushed for a series of rapid structural reforms that produced economic recovery.

The Ecevit government eventually fell victim to its internal feuds, some the result of having strange bedfellows under one roof, others of the uncertainties associated with Ecevit's frail physical condition. As his party splintered, new elections were called for November 2002. For the first time since Ozal's electoral victories, one party, the Justice and Development Party (AKP), captured almost two-thirds of the seats in parliament, although it garnered only 34 percent of the vote.

The AKP was an offshoot of the Islamist Virtue Party, which had been banned by constitutional authorities, initiating a major division among Erbakan's followers. Some, such as former mayor of Istanbul Recep Tayyip Erdogan and Abdullah Gul, decided to seek a more conciliatory approach to the secular state. They distanced themselves from—and even repudiated—Erbakan and his hard-core followers, who had elected to form the Felicity Party. Earlier, the authorities had banned Erdogan from politics when he had recited in public a poem by a well-known nationalist poet. Many perceived his removal from the Istanbul mayoralty following his conviction to be a miscarriage of justice, augmenting his popularity. In 2002, with the ban on Erdogan still in place, the AKP entered the elections under Gul's leadership. The party's success was electrifying. This time an Islamist party, though a much more moderate one, had come to power on its own and would not need to rely on coalition partners to form a government. Gul became prime minister, and the party worked successfully to reverse the ban on Erdogan, who, by March 2003, had assumed the reins of power.

The Erdogan government's first priority was to deepen the reforms needed to advance Turkey's EU candidacy. The AKP quickly introduced a series of reforms that began to curtail some of the powerful military's constitutional prerogatives. It continued the Dervis economic reforms and introduced a series of wide-ranging political changes designed to improve political conditions, especially those of minorities. Erdogan also engineered an about-face in Turkey's Cyprus policy. As a result, the EU in December 2004 announced that Turkey had become a candidate for membership and in October 2005 officially initiated accession negotiations. While there is still a long way to go, the Erdogan government has made far more progress in this area than its predecessors.

The 2003 Iraq War overshadowed many developments in Turkey. It has made Turks of all stripes and ideologies uncomfortable with the United States, especially because it led to an autonomous Kurdish entity in northern Iraq. The war has strained relations between the two countries, and dealings between the military and the governing party also have been tense at times. Secular elites have no confidence in the AKP government and believe it has a hidden agenda to undermine secularism and further an Islamist agenda that will enable women to cover their heads in public spaces, a practice hitherto proscribed by the courts.

The AKP is still the dominant party. Its only opposition in parliament, the Republican People's Party, has been woefully ineffective, failing to address the shortcomings of the ruling party—corruption and cronyism—or offer a coherent alternative vision. Until 2007, the military operated as the sole de facto opposition to the government, conspiring at times to overthrow the government. Finally, Turkey's Kurdish problem has reemerged, as Kurds have started to openly challenge the state.

POLITICAL ENVIRONMENT

Turkey is a land of pronounced physical contrasts and sharp economic disparities. Extending 780,576 square kilometers (301,380 square miles)—40 percent larger than France—it ranges from sea level to the 5,165-meter (16,945-foot) peak of Mount Ararat, which is higher than any European mountain. The western part of the country, bordering the Aegean and the Sea of Marmara, is a region of developed communication and easy access to the inland plateau. Well-watered farming areas produce cash crops such as cotton, tobacco, and raisins. Eastern Turkey, abutting the Caucasian republics, Iran, and Iraq, is mountainous, cut by rivers into more or less isolated valleys. Income disparity between relatively wealthy western Anatolia and underdeveloped eastern Anatolia is highly visible.

The population of Turkey is about 70 million and increasing at a rate of somewhat under 1.5 percent a year—significantly lower than in recent decades. Demographers project that by 2050 Turkey's population might stabilize at about 90 to 95 million. The AKP government has taken symbolic and policy initiatives to increase the birthrate.

Istanbul, the former Ottoman capital, remains Turkey's largest city, with a rapidly growing population of approximately 14 million. Ankara, the capital, is a magnet second only to Istanbul, with 5 million inhabitants. Izmir, on the Aegean coast, Adana, on the Mediterranean (with some 3 million each), and newly industrializing Anatolian cities such as Denizli, Mersin, Kayseri, and Gaziantep complete the roster of major urban foci.

With a 99 percent Muslim population, modern Turkey is far more homogeneous than the multiethnic and multireligious Ottoman Empire. Sunni Islam predominates, while the heterodox Alevi-Shi'a branch of Islam constitutes a sizable minority. Although census data does not distinguish between Sunni and Alevi Islam, the Alevis are estimated to represent about 10 to 15 percent of the total population.

The Alevi-Sunni cleavage remains one of the most important divisions in Turkish society, and there are some signs that the rebellion in Syria against the Alawite regime of Bashar al-Asad is exacerbating Turkey's own polarization. Under the Sunni supremacy of the Ottoman Empire, Alevis were a persecuted minority. Their Shi'a proclivity and heterodox practice of Islam turned Alevis into a perennial fifth column in the eyes of imperial Istanbul. The Ottomans' historic rivalry with the Shi'a Safavid Empire further complicated the status of Alevis and put in question their loyalty to the Sunni-led Ottoman government.

It was therefore with great enthusiasm that the Alevis supported the secularist reforms of Ataturk that led to the abolition of the Sunni religious establishment in Turkey. Yet the peculiar nature of Turkish secularism, where the state recognizes, controls, and administers the Sunni branch as the only legitimate practice of Islam, is an ongoing source of disappointment for Turkey's Alevi minority. Perhaps more problematic is the anti-Alevi societal and political bias in Turkey, based mainly on the grounds that Alevis do not attend mosques and have their own community centers and religious rituals. To this day intermarriage between Alevis and Sunnis remains quite exceptional.

Kurds constitute the most significant ethnic minority in Turkey. Inspired by France, Turkey's official understanding of citizenship does not recognize ethnic minorities. This is why precise data once again is missing. Yet it is commonly estimated that about 20 percent of Turkey's population is of Kurdish origin. Kurds represent a clear majority in Turkey's southeast provinces and speak a distinct Indo-European language with several different dialects. Due to conflict-induced migration, over half of Turkey's Kurdish population inhabits the western and southern regions of the country. Istanbul, for instance, is today home to the largest urban concentration of Kurds in the world.

Most Kurds in Turkey used to have tribal connections, but the influence of traditional leaders has been waning rapidly. These chiefs frequently also head branches of dervish orders (Nakshibandi and Kadiri) or belong to religious sects, such as the Nurcular, to which Kurds seem particularly drawn. Especially in eastern Turkey, this social organization historically both perpetuated an identity separate from that of the rest of the Turkish population and divided the various tribes and clans into rival units. This fragmentation caused the Kurdish ethnic uprisings in the 1920s and 1930s to remain limited in scope.

Without endorsing Kurdish separatism, Turkey's political parties have often tacitly exploited Kurdish ethnicity in the past to expand their bases of support in the southeast. A popular tactic has been to offer tribal leaders prominent places on the ticket to capitalize on the propensity of their followers to vote for their chiefs. Such policies are part of populist electoral politics in Turkey, where patronage networks matter greatly.

By Middle Eastern standards, Turkey is a vibrant democracy and model of capitalist economic development. The country has a complex political environment characterized by peculiar historical and socioeconomic circumstances. Perhaps the most important underpinnings of the Turkish political environment are the following:

- A deeply rooted imperial state tradition
- Until recently, a politically intrusive, highly secular military
- A heartfelt personality cult built around Ataturk
- Democratic elections since 1950 that confirm conservative political tendencies
- Severe income and regional disparities
- An increasingly robust private sector driving economic growth
- A strong, though diminishing, European vocation, due to Turkey's own economic success and Europe's lack of interest

Such complexity makes for a rapidly changing society in an increasingly urban context. By 2010 the urbanization rate of Turkey had reached 70 percent. Over the last thirty years, the rapid influx of traditionally oriented, religiously observant peasants has given urban areas a bifurcated appearance, where the modern and traditional chaotically coexist. On the gender front, the picture is also quite mixed. Turkey has brought urban women into the mainstream of political, professional, and cultural life. The educational level of women has risen steadily, and the literacy rate of school-age girls is approaching that of boys. Male literacy is around 95 percent, while female literacy is at 80 percent. Although social barriers still exist, females have not faced legal obstacles hindering employment opportunities since the 1930s. In the villages, however, the traditional male-dominated pattern of life persists, as it does to some extent in the urban ghettos where new migrants from the countryside have settled.

Economic development has been a major engine of political transformation in Turkey. Until the early 1980s, the public sector and import-substitution industrialization dominated the Turkish economy. Market dynamics and the private sector remained secondary forces. A state-led industrialization drive characterized most of the 1960s and early 1970s. Starting in the 1950s, Turkey also witnessed significant improvements in agricultural productivity, thanks to improved mechanization and large-scale irrigation. Yet, more than agricultural productivity, industrialization behind protective walls fueled Turkish economic growth, particularly throughout the 1960s. Public investment in heavy industry and the creation of state-owned enterprises created a manufacturing base targeting the local market.

Yet, there were also clear limits to economic growth during the 1960s and 1970s. Turkey, unlike South Korea and other East Asian models, never managed to switch from import-substitution to export-led growth. The vagaries of electoral democracy, major labor disputes, populist economic policies, and systemic fiscal deficits negatively affected economic performance. By the late 1970s, the surge in oil prices, growing trade deficits, an overvalued currency, and high inflation paralyzed the economy. To cope with this challenge, Turkey had to adopt IMF-led liberalization packages in the early 1980s. Under Prime Minister Ozal, the Turkish economy dismantled its subsidies for energy and other basic commodities, devalued its partially privatized public enterprises, and stimulated exports.

Despite considerable structural reform between 1983 and 1987, by the end of the decade Turkey was still unable to control its fiscal deficit and public debt. In the absence of strict fiscal and monetary restraint and because of populist economic policies during electoral cycles, Turkey failed to deal efficiently with rampant inflation.

In addition to serious economic problems, by the 1990s serious identity issues with ethnic and religious dimensions also plagued Turkey. In fact, since the end of the Cold War, two major issues have sharply polarized Turkish politics: Kurdish dissent and political Islam. Neither Kurdish nationalism nor political Islam was totally new in Turkish politics. Both issues have their roots in the country's difficult transition from a cosmopolitan Muslim empire to a secular nation-state.

During the first two decades of the republic, nationalism and secularism emerged as the twin principles of Ataturk's republic. These two fundamental principles of Kemalism rapidly generated twin threats, namely, Kurdish rebellions and Islamic reaction during the 1920s and 1930s. It took the military suppression of a long series of Kurdish and Islamic rebellions for a sense of Kemalist stability to be established after the foundation of the republic.

With Turkey's transition to multiparty democracy during the Cold War and its 1952 accession to NATO, Left-Right political divisions came to dominate Turkish politics. Yet under this new ideological divide, the Kurdish question and political Islam never totally disappeared from Turkey's agenda. Political Islam was part of the anti-Communist Right, while Kurdish dissent was part of the socialist Left. Kurdish dissent was therefore expressed in terms of class conflict rather than ethnic grievances. Such dynamics enabled Kurdish political assimilation within Turkey's leftist movements.

Ideological polarization and the democratic process were punctured by short-term military interventions in 1960, 1971, and 1980. Each intervention had different causes. The 1960 coup was instigated by young officers unhappy with their economic lot and diminished importance in society. They, in the process, opened the door for future interventions, as groups in society often turned to the military to resolve difficult and stalemated situations. It also gave the military an expectation that, as the self-declared guardian of the republic, it would have strong influence in the management of the Turkish polity. In fact, in

1971 a group of senior generals decided to overthrow the government for failing to deal with growing political violence and immobility. Unwilling to see a repeat of the 1960 coup, when the military hierarchy was ignored, the service chiefs and chief of staff outmaneuvered the generals. The 1980 coup was triggered by political paralysis stemming from the Left-Right divide, increasing unrest in Kurdish provinces, and Islamist flouting of Kemalist principles.

However, the real threat of Kurdish nationalism or Islamic activism would not materialize fully until after the end of the Cold War and the reemergence of identity problems. Ironically, many of the Kurds who escaped the post-1980 military dragnet found an opening in the repressive years of military rule to launch an insurgency in the southeast. The PKK-led insurgency, which had gained considerable regional support by the end of the 1980s, proved a substantial challenge to the Turkish military. Between 1984 and 1999, the Kurdish conflict caused some 35,000 deaths among insurgents, the local population, and security forces and cost the Turkish economy an estimated $120 billion. Perhaps more importantly, the Kurdish conflict completely derailed Turkey's European agenda. To the dismay of Ankara, the EU—to which Turkey had officially applied for membership in 1987—saw in the Kurdish conflict the rebellion of an ethnic group whose cultural and political rights were denied by an authoritarian regime.

By the mid-1990s, things had gone from bad to worse. In addition to the Kurdish conflict, political Islam came to haunt the Kemalist republic. The Islamist Welfare Party triumphed in local elections (1994), controlled important municipalities such as Istanbul and Ankara, and won a plurality in national elections (1995). By 1996, the secular republic had its first Islamist-led coalition government, triggering a soft, or indirect, coup in 1997. With Kurdish separatism and political Islam on the rise, the political environment was ripe for a military backlash. The counteroffensive by the secular establishment came first with the ousting of the Welfare Party coalition government in June 1997. In February 1999, Kurdish separatism received a severe blow with the capture of PKK leader Ocalan.

The EU also emerged as an important factor in Turkish politics, especially after the 1999 Helsinki summit, which opened the door for negotiations on Turkey's candidacy. The EU's importance grew further with the November 2002 elections, when the newly established moderate Islamist AKP, which had embraced the EU, won in a landslide. The fact that a major financial crisis in 2001 had completely discredited Turkey's corrupt and bankrupt political establishment greatly contributed to the AKP victory. In short, the political environment of Turkey in 2003 was radically different from that of the 1990s.

So was the global environment. In the wake of the September 11 terrorist attacks, the "clash of civilizations" scenario turned into a self-fulfilling prophecy. In such a polarized global context, the symbolism of a Muslim country governed by a moderate Islamist government seeking membership in an exclusive European club gained unprecedented civilizational relevance.

The AKP's embrace of Europe initially helped it win time and perhaps some much-needed legitimacy from the traditional establishment. The military was much more willing to give the benefit of the doubt to a political party with a European vocation rather than to one with anti-Western proclivities, like the banned Welfare Party. The Kemalist backlash against the Welfare Party in 1997 created a genuine sense of appreciation among moderately Islamic politicians for the benefits of liberal democracy. This, in itself, explains why the leadership of the AKP supported pro-EU democratization. Its pro-EU stance made the AKP much more appealing to the business community, the middle class, and liberal intellectuals.

During its first term, the AKP remained strongly committed to its reformist agenda. It undertook radical reforms in the judicial system, civil-military relations, and human rights practices. The party also attacked corruption and continued to implement an IMF-led structural-reform package. By 2005, the Turkish economy had stabilized, and inflation had fallen to levels that allowed a lopping of six zeros off the currency. Such political and economic reforms, combined with the AKP's constructive approach in Cyprus, convinced the EU that Turkey had fulfilled the criteria necessary to begin accession talks.

The AKP, however, also lost steam after the EU's decision to start accession negotiations in 2004, becoming distracted by other issues discussed below. Commensurate with the AKP's ascent, one particular moderate Islamist movement, that of Fethullah Gulen, though unaffiliated with the AKP, began to gather momentum. Gulen is a charismatic preacher who, fearing prosecution, sought refuge in the United States in 1999. Gulen and his associates made great efforts to build up their support base primarily by guiding their followers to engage and invest in civil causes, such as building schools in Turkey and abroad. They also created an informal but successful economic network, as well as a formidable media operation designed as much to expand their influence as to protect them from the secular establishment that came to loathe and fear them as a mortal threat, despite Gulen's moderate message.

POLITICAL STRUCTURE

Turkey is a unitary republic and a parliamentary democracy. Cabinet ministers are jointly responsible for the execution of the government's general policy and personally liable for their ministries' acts. The prime minister, as the top executive, heads the Council of Ministers and can dismiss ministers at will.

The 1982 constitution, as amended, centers on a 550-seat unicameral legislature. The senate of the Second Republic was abolished in an effort to strengthen and improve the efficiency of the executive at the expense of the legislative branch. The president of the republic is elected by the Grand National Assembly for a seven-year term. As a result of constitutional amendments in 2007, the people will elect future presidents for five-year terms, and assembly members will serve for four years instead of five. Elections, however, can be held earlier by consent of parliament.

One of the most important objectives of the 1982 constitution was to strongly reassert the authority of the state, partly as a reaction to the 1961 constitution, which was perceived as too liberal. Drafted by the 1980 military junta, the 1982 constitution prioritized law and order and set up state security courts, where military judges served with civilian judges. These courts were abolished in 2004 under the AKP's pro-EU democratization program.

Although superior administrative and military courts have final jurisdiction over cases within their competencies, the Turkish judicial system provides for the Constitutional Court to rule on the constitutionality of laws and decrees. The Constitutional Court functions as the Supreme Court and therefore decides all cases relating to political parties.

Understanding Turkey's political structure requires a basic grasp of the republic's foundational principle. Unlike most other Western democracies, Turkey has an official state ideology. This ideology, Kemalism, is named after Mustafa Kemal Ataturk, the founding father of modern Turkey. In the context of the 1930s, Kemalism represented a secularist, nationalist, and progressive political agenda based on establishing a Turkish nation-state. Modernization and Westernization were the main traits of Kemalism.

More problematic, however, is determining what exactly Kemalism represents as a contemporary political project. There is, in fact, no consensus among Kemalists themselves on what Kemalism stands for in the twenty-first century. This difficulty is understandable because Kemalism is in many ways already a success story. Modern Turkey is a secular nation-state and a democratic republic. There is certainly room for improvement in terms of establishing a truly liberal democracy in Turkey; however, as liberalism was never on the Kemalist political agenda, it would be unfair to blame Kemalism for this. After all, liberalism was not on the global agenda of the 1930s. It is therefore possible to argue that Kemalism, as a secularist-nationalist political project aimed at nation building, modernization, and Westernization, achieved its mission.

In today's Turkey, this success transforms Kemalism into a conservative ideology. Turkey's official state ideology, in other words, displays an understandable urge to conserve and protect the republic's historic achievements and structure. Especially for Turkey's politically powerful military, Kemalism represented a defensive political reaction against the enemies of the secular republic. More than a coherent ideology, Kemalism became a secularist and nationalist reflex against Kurdish nationalism and political Islam.

The military is the main institution serving as the ultimate guardian of the republic's Kemalist legacy. Unlike in other Western democracies, the armed forces had a special position in Turkey. Their political weight entered into a broad range of government calculations. At the end of the Ottoman Empire, the armed forces, with their secular schools, were the main window on the West. As a result, officers were the reformists par excellence. Ataturk himself and his chief lieutenants were career officers who represented the Young Turk tradition of positivism, nationalism, and secularism with great reformist zeal.

After the foundation of the republic, Ataturk wanted to separate military and political tracks, mainly to protect the military's professionalism and keep the armed forces out of day-to-day politics. Abiding by this civilian-military divide, he and his loyal associates gave up their own active-duty status. Yet, Ataturk and Inonu maintained close ties with the armed forces, and Ataturk continually cited the army as the ultimate guardian of the republic, making clear that its role was to defend the cultural and political revolution in addition to protecting the country against foreign foes.

In that sense the Turkish military effectively functioned as the guardian of the Kemalist system. No matter what happened in the "realm of politics," the armed forces defended the "realm of the Kemalist state." This is why the Turkish military was associated with the state rather than with politics in the eyes of the Turkish public. The Turkish army served as a sort of deus ex machina. Whenever it intervened in the realm of politics, it did so on behalf of the republic. Unlike Latin American militaries, the Turkish army did not stay in power for long. To preserve its professionalism and nonpolitical image, it went back to its barracks. This is why none of the three major military interventions in Turkish politics (1960, 1971, and 1980) lasted more than three years.

In the post–Cold War era, the pattern of military interventions changed. Instead of directly overthrowing governments, the military used a variety of means to dislodge or pressure elected governments, sometimes through pronouncements, as in February 1997 and April 2007. Civil-military relations, however, began to change following the 2007 attempted military interference with the selection of a new president. The ruling AKP stood its ground and called for early elections, which it won decisively. As a result, for the first time in the history of the republic, the balance has radically changed in favor of civilians and against the armed forces.

While the 1960 military coup had strong Kemalist undertones, the second and third interventions had unmistakable anti-Left tendencies. In a NATO member bordering the Soviet Union, it was not particularly surprising that the military had serious concerns about the appeal of socialism. In the early twenty-first century, however, the real threat to the Kemalist republic changed from communism to Kurdish nationalism and political Islam.

As far as these threats were concerned, there was no room for ambiguity in the Kemalist position of the military. The Kurdish problem, whether in the form of political violence or political activity calling for minority rights, is viewed as an existential threat. Hence any assertion of Kurdish ethnic identity, no matter how minor, is perceived as a major security problem endangering Turkey's territorial and national integrity. A similarly alarmist attitude characterizes the military's approach to Islam. Display of Islamic sociopolitical and cultural symbols in the public sphere—such as head scarves in public schools—is seen as the harbinger of a fundamentalist revolution.

The Turkish republic's political structure, especially Kemalism's understanding of secularism and nationalism, was influenced by the French model. Turkish secularism was modeled after anticlerical French *laïcité* rather than the less confrontational Anglo-Saxon secularism. According to Kemalist secularism, Islam had to become part of private life. As in France after the 1789 revolution, the state came to control and administer the religious establishment in order to prevent political threats of a conservative and religious nature. The Kemalist state banned religious sects and brotherhoods. Religious activities not controlled by the state had to operate underground.

France proved to be the model for nationalism as well. The Turkish republic refused to recognize ethnic minorities and multiculturalism. All citizens were to be assimilated into Turkish citizenship. The only officially recognized minorities were non-Muslims. In short, all Muslims were to become Turks. With the benefit of hindsight, one can argue that, behind the facade of a successful nationalist-secularist revolution, the repression of Kurdish and Islamic identities remained the Achilles' heel of the Kemalist project.

POLITICAL DYNAMICS

Political patterns in Turkey show remarkable continuity, despite frequent military interventions. On the one hand, that continuity reflects the longevity of political figures in Turkey, where tenures of thirty or even forty years for major political leaders are not uncommon. On the other hand, voting blocs themselves have changed little in proportion over the years, which would give the right-of-center a marked edge were it not torn by such intense personal rivalries. Another major aspect of continuity has been the tenacious commitment to elective parliamentary rule, which all political elements, including the military, see as the principal legitimizing process. Turkey's political parties operate with relative efficiency in mobilizing voters. Participation in elections has generally been high, involving between 64 and 94 percent of eligible voters.

The predominance of right-of-center votes in the Third Republic convincingly shows that Turks do not cast ballots on a class basis. Rather, the ups and downs in party performance appear to confirm that Turkish voters seek successful leaders who keep their promises and avoid the appearance of corruption—an image that has proven difficult to maintain. This pattern was visible in the multiparty era of the First Republic; it continued in the Second Republic and has repeated itself in the Third.

The AKP government, which won elections in 2002, 2007, and 2011, appears to challenge these dynamics. The AKP has proven exceptionally successful so far in maintaining its grasp on power. The origins of political Islam in Turkey date back to the 1970s, when an anti-Western, antisecular, antiliberal political movement first emerged. Despite their orientation, Turkish Islamist parties have always played by electoral rules. Thus, compared to its Middle Eastern counterparts, Turkish political Islam was much more moderate and inclined toward gaining electoral legitimacy. Yet the political ambitions of Turkish Islamists clearly surpassed their competence. In 1996, when political Islam came to power under its third incarnation as the Welfare Party, it failed to rise to the challenge of running a complex, diversified country. The military's forced resignation of the Welfare Party–led coalition government in 1997 created a generational and ideological rift in the ranks of the movement. As the patrimonial structure of the old guard broke up,

Turkish Islamists split into two parties, the AKP and the Felicity Party, with the latter representing the small, traditional, hard-line wing of the movement.

The AKP followed its 2002 win with unprecedented victories in 2007 and 2011, increasing its share of the vote from 34 to 47 and then 50 percent—the first time an incumbent government had increased its vote share since 1954—and won two successive elections after coming to power. All these victories amounted to political earthquakes in Turkish politics, with the AKP winning comfortable majorities in parliament, thus enabling the moderate Islamist party to govern alone.

From very early on, the AKP continued a pro-EU reform process initiated in the summer of 2002 by the previous government. While more progress still must be made, the initial reforms passed by parliament have achieved some progress toward improving human rights and democracy, paving the way for accession negotiations with the EU. Key areas of reform included the following:

Civil-Military Relations. New laws have substantially reduced the military's role in politics. As of August 2004, a general no longer heads the National Security Council (NSC)—a platform through which the military traditionally has exerted influence over the government. NSC meetings are not as frequent and are more transparent. The removal of military representatives from the boards that oversee broadcasting and higher education has also enhanced civilian control. New limits on the jurisdiction of military courts over civilians have been enacted. In the ten years of AKP rule, the military's influence has eroded. Military pronouncements used to be given extensive coverage by all media outlets, as both the public and the political class perceived the military to be the ultimate source of authority on issues relating to secularism, ethnicity, and national security. However, starting with an April 2007 pronouncement on the military's website aimed at thwarting the AKP's choice for president, the pendulum has swung away from the armed forces. Gul, whose wife wears a headscarf, was bitterly opposed by the Turkish secular establishment, which went to great lengths to block his nomination.

The AKP rose to the military's challenge in 2007 and forced a showdown that resulted in the 2007 electoral victory. The Erdogan government capitalized on the military's missteps and was aided in its concerted effort to narrow the military's influence in politics by the onset in 2008 of the Ergenekon investigation. The military's reputation was dealt a severe setback as scores of officers were implicated in attempted coups. When in 2011 the chief of staff and the service chiefs resigned en masse to protest the treatment of their comrades, the government calmly accepted their resignations and appointed new generals to replace them. Within weeks, the public and media had forgotten the whole episode. The military's musings about politics had become a nonevent.

Human Rights. Provisions on the rights of detainees and prisoners have been improved. Pretrial detention periods have been shortened, and detainees are guaranteed immediate access to an attorney. Legislation also has broadened freedom of expression, the press, association, assembly, and demonstration. The repeal of Article 8 of the Anti-Terror Law, which prohibited the dissemination of separatist propaganda, has led to a significant reduction in the number of political prisoners. However, there remain important shortcomings in the Turkish penal code, such as Article 301, which punishes free thought. The AKP has been reluctant to repeal this provision. As a result, many authors, journalists, and others, including Nobel laureate Orhan Pamuk, have been prosecuted for "denigrating Turkishness." Some of the progress has been reversed as the judiciary has been used to silence critics and persecute Kurdish activists who have been jailed without trial.

Cultural Rights. Under the leadership of the AKP, the Turkish republic reluctantly has acknowledged the existence of minorities based on "racial, religious, sectarian, cultural, or linguistic differences" and repealed laws curtailing their rights. Recent reforms introduced the right to broadcast, publish, and receive instruction in languages other than Turkish, in effect officially allowing the use of the Kurdish language. In practice, however, the use of Kurdish in the broadcast media remains strictly controlled. In fact, the only nationwide Kurdish TV station is run by the state.

Judicial Reform. The Turkish judicial system has been significantly reformed, and criminal and antiterrorism laws have been amended, in line with EU requirements. The death penalty was abolished in August 2002. Reforms also allow for the retrial of legal cases invalidated by the European Court of Human Rights, although this policy has been implemented sporadically. A constitutional referendum in 2010 enabled the government to introduce a number of judicial reforms, especially when it came to the composition of the Constitutional Court and other supervisory bodies. However, these did not fundamentally alter the functioning of the judicial branch, as evidenced by the multitudes of trials and detentions targeted at regime opponents. Typically, suspects are jailed for many years before their cases are ever heard by judges.

Cyprus Policy. Turkish efforts to find a solution to the division of Cyprus were never explicitly made a precondition for EU accession, but the political reality has always been that Turkey's opposition to a Cyprus settlement would undermine its chances of joining the EU. Reversing the course of the hard-line Ecevit government, the Erdogan government made a Cyprus settlement a high priority, largely in the name of removing the issue as an obstacle to EU accession. Erdogan invested significant political capital and defied Turkish nationalists in urging Turkish Cypriots to approve a UN plan for political settlement. In the April 2004 referendum on the plan, 65 percent of Turkish Cypriots supported it, whereas 75 percent of Greek Cypriots rejected it. The Turkish government's strong support for the plan (in contrast to the Greek Cypriot leadership's opposition) earned it much political credit with the EU and has helped Turkey's case for membership. However, Greek Cypriot opposition to the plan did not prevent the Greek part of Cyprus from becoming an EU member in 2005. As a result, a solution to the Cyprus problem remains elusive, and Turkey's own prospects for EU accession have been negatively affected.

Economic Reform. Turkey experienced its most severe economic crisis since World War II in 2001, forcing it to adopt painful, wide-ranging structural reforms. The most important of these reforms included a restructuring of the banking sector. These reforms paid off and helped the Turkish economy post significant growth rates from 2002 to 2008. Thanks to its fiscal discipline, mostly dictated by the IMF, Turkey has succeeded in containing its high inflation rate and attracting significant foreign investment. When the 2008 global financial crisis came about, Turkey's economy was not immune, although its banking sector weathered the crisis better than most. The sharp fall in Turkey's exports following the global crisis has proven temporary. More importantly, Turkey has experienced an economic restructuring with the emergence of the Anatolian Tigers—medium-size businesses that flourished in Anatolia, led by a new class of pious, conservative businessmen. Their emergence was due to the structural reforms undertaken by Ozal in 1980, which provided opportunities to new enterprises that were willing to export, especially to non-traditional markets. This new class of entrepreneurs has come to embody the political-economic base of the AKP, which has wholeheartedly embraced laissez-faire policies. Turkish exports have risen dramatically, helping make it the seventeenth largest economy in the world and a member of the G-20.

FOREIGN POLICY

Ataturk was determined to transform and modernize Turkey and make it an integral member of what he termed "contemporary civilization." His most famous adage about foreign relations, "peace at home, peace abroad," also implied a degree of introversion and autarky. To the Kemalists, Ataturk's legacy would be a mixture of Westernization with isolation. Effectively, this meant that Ataturk and his followers would turn their backs on the Middle East and the emerging Arab world.

World War II was a particularly trying time for the new republic. Bereft of its strong leader, who had passed away in 1938, Ankara was caught between the entreaties of the Allied and Axis powers. Its military weakness prevented it from entering the conflict, save for during the last months of the war. With the Allied victory in 1945, Turkey hitched its future to an alliance with the United States and Europe. It joined NATO and later applied for membership in the EU. Even after the demise of the Soviet Union, Turkey's Western alliance has a solid foundation in the modern Turkish state. Ankara had little choice after the war but to align itself with the West. The Soviet Union was decidedly interested in enlarging its zone of influence, as Stalin tried to make the most of Turkey's wartime neutrality to extract concessions ranging from territory in Turkey's east to privileged access to the Turkish Straits. In some respects this was a continuation of nineteenth-century Russo-Ottoman rivalry and therefore conjured up unpleasant memories in Turkey.

The Truman Doctrine—enunciated on March 12, 1947, to support Turkey and Greece in the face of continuing Soviet pressure—heralded the beginning of both countries' active participation in the Cold War.

The Truman Doctrine notwithstanding, Washington had reservations about the utility of Turkey and Greece as alliance members and therefore initially resisted their inclusion in NATO. By contrast, Ankara did its utmost to convince the United States to accept it as a member, since it viewed NATO as the ultimate shield against an aggressive Soviet Union. The ruling Democrat Party even sent a contingent of troops to fight in Korea as a means of proving its bona fides. Finally, in 1952, three years after the inception of NATO, Turkey and Greece joined the alliance. Turkey under the Democrat Party became a close US ally; it helped set up the Baghdad Pact, a defense alliance among Great Britain, Iraq, Iran, Pakistan, and Turkey. Military cooperation between the United States and Turkey enabled Ankara to revamp its creaky armed forces. Turkey, as the sole NATO member bordering the Soviet Union, became an important asset in the US policy of containment.

The military leaders who overthrew the Democrat Party in 1960 were too preoccupied with domestic problems to devise major foreign initiatives. In any case, because they came out of Turkey's military tradition, they were, for the most part, satisfied with US-Turkish relations. Yet, the broader political debate permitted in the Second Republic, especially with the rise of the socialist movement in the early 1960s, set the stage for problems in Turkey's Western orientation. Like Europe, Turkey experienced an upsurge in student activism that contributed to increased pressure on the US-Turkish relationship.

Cyprus was the main foreign policy issue to confront Turkey in the mid-1960s. In December 1963, violence between the small Turkish and much larger Greek Cypriot communities led Ankara to send planes over the island to demonstrate its commitment to the Turkish minority. Continuing communal troubles caused Turkish Cypriots to group themselves in enclaves and the Turkish government to consider landing troops to protect Turkish Cypriots' rights, a remedy provided in the Treaty of Guarantee that had established the Cypriot state in 1960. In June 1964, Turkey threatened to dispatch forces to the island. This elicited a harsh warning from US President Lyndon Johnson. The Johnson letter, as it came to be known, warned Prime Minister Inonu that NATO might not protect Turkey from Soviet intervention if it took military action on Cyprus, and it categorically forbade the use of American-made weapons in Cyprus. Ironically, it is unclear whether Turkey could have followed up on its threat in view of the fact that it lacked the wherewithal to mount an invasion, not having even a single landing craft. Yet, the appearance of Turkish capitulation in the face of US pressure provoked intense public resentment toward the United States. The Johnson letter henceforth would come to represent an act of perfidy in the annals of US-Turkish relations and marked the beginning of an era of unquestioning Turkish cooperation with Washington.

The 1974 Cyprus crisis was a real turning point in US-Turkish relations. Turkey felt obliged to respond to a coup against the legitimate government of Archbishop Makarios in Cyprus by Greek Cypriot nationalist elements supported by the military junta in

Athens. Although the coup was not directed against the Turkish community per se, the man who seized power, Nicos Sampson, was known as a longtime advocate of unification with Greece and a dedicated foe of Turkish Cypriots. On July 20, Turkey landed troops on Cyprus, claiming that it was exercising its treaty rights to repair a clear violation of the Cypriot constitution. Under strong international pressure, however, the Turks halted their military action after two days, having secured merely a foothold in the Kyrenia region, north of Nicosia. During the ensuing peace talks, when the Turks thought the new regime in Athens was stalling, Turkey resumed military operations and speedily secured control over slightly more than the northern third of the island.

Despite its insistence that these actions were sanctioned by the Treaty of Guarantee, Turkey found itself largely isolated in the international community. The US Congress in February 1975 imposed a complete embargo on all arms deliveries to Turkey, which lasted until September 1978. In retaliation, Turkey closed all US installations (leaving the NATO air base in Incirlik open, however) and abrogated the 1969 Defense Cooperation Agreement. The embargo, whose origins had more to do with infighting between the executive and legislative branches in the United States, nonetheless left a deep imprint on the Turkish psyche regarding the reliability of the United States.

In this context, Turkey's relations with Greece took a decided turn for the worse. Tensions generated by Cyprus were further enflamed by an emerging dispute over the continental shelf and air rights in the Aegean Sea. The geography of the Aegean, with numerous Greek islands hugging the Turkish coast, presented complex problems in apportioning the seabed. Behind its difficulties in dealing with Greece and Cyprus in the 1970s lay a new and painful fact for Turkey: the US Congress, not the executive branch, had become the articulator of Turkish-US problems. Whereas American presidents understood the compulsions that led Turkey to act in Cyprus, Congress was far less willing to credit Turkish arguments. This contest of wills in Washington slowed renegotiation of defense cooperation arrangements. But after the Jimmy Carter administration finally convinced Congress to lift the arms embargo in September 1978, US facilities were reopened, and a new Cooperation on Defense and Economy Agreement was signed in March 1980.

This was followed by a new challenge: the 1980 military coup. Most Europeans, who were critical of military rule as well as of the treatment of former Turkish politicians, received the advent of the generals in Turkey badly. By contrast, the United States was alarmed by the increasing domestic violence and instability in Turkey just after the shah of Iran lost his throne to anti-American clerics and the Soviets invaded Afghanistan. Turkey's strategic importance once again became crystal clear to Washington, which decided to support the regime.

Economically, Turkey was on the mend. Ozal's reforms had made the economy more competitive, especially in the Middle East. In fact, the Iran-Iraq War turned out to be a boon for Turkey, the only country to border both belligerents. Short on foreign exchange and in need of various finished goods, Iran and Iraq became large consumers of Turkish exports, facilitating Turkey's economic transformation in the early 1980s. To cement these favorable trends, Turkey deepened its involvement in the politics of the Islamic world and for a while reduced its diplomatic ties with Israel.

In the 1980s, Cyprus once again became a problem in Ankara's relations with its allies. Turkey's encouragement of Turkish Cypriot independence dismayed the United States and Europe. Faced with concerted European and American pressure, no one, save for Turkey, would recognize the Turkish Cypriot Republic of Northern Cyprus. In the United States, congressional critics of Turkey, especially those with close ties to diaspora Greek and Armenian communities, were able to propose or push through punitive resolutions, including one commemorating the 1915 Armenian genocide.

By 1991, Turkey's strategic environment had been radically transformed by the Soviet Union's disintegration. Unlike that of its long-term rival Greece, Turkey's strategic importance to the West did not vanish together with the Soviet border. Turkey assumed a new and quite different role in the post–Cold War era. For Washington, whose relations with Tehran were highly acrimonious, Ankara represented a perfect foil for Iran's ambitions in central Asia—an area freed from direct Soviet control. Turkey's linguistic and cultural affinity with Azerbaijan, Turkmenistan, Kazakhstan, and Uzbekistan, several of which had extensive energy reserves, was an asset. The US supported Ankara's fledgling ambitions to become an agent of Western, secular influence and a conduit for hydrocarbon riches, which otherwise would be transported through either Russian or Iranian pipelines. US support for non-Russian transportation routes led to construction of the Baku-Tbilisi-Ceyhan pipeline, which has been transporting Caspian Sea oil to Turkey's Mediterranean coast since 2006.

Ataturk wanted to distance Turkey from the Middle East; in fact, in 1926, after putting down the first of many Kurdish insurrections, he agreed to cede the mostly Kurdish-inhabited region of Mosul to Iraq, which was under a British mandate. Some sixty years later, Turkey found itself again mired in the affairs of its southern neighbors. A new Kurdish rebellion in Turkey meant that Ankara could no longer be immune to developments in neighboring countries with Kurdish populations. This was especially true of Iraq, where Iraqi Kurdish groups, long active in a struggle to free themselves from Baghdad's rule, took advantage of every opportunity to rebel against the central government. The 1980–1988 Iran-Iraq War was no exception. During this war the PKK benefited from the absence of Iraqi government authority in the north to establish bases there. In response, Turkey conducted hot-pursuit operations with the Baghdad government's consent. At the end of that war, when Saddam Hussein took revenge on his rebellious Kurdish population by massacring tens of thousands, many Iraqi Kurds fled to Turkey.

Iraq's 1990 invasion of Kuwait and the resulting war further complicated Turkey's relations both with its neighbors and with its main ally, the United States. Initially President Ozal backed the UN sanctions against Iraq and closed the oil pipeline running from northern Iraq to the Mediterranean. Although Ozal wanted to support, and perhaps even participate in, the war against Iraq, he found that not only the public but also his military chiefs opposed this. For the first time in Turkish history, the armed forces chief of staff resigned rather than execute his orders. More than half a million Kurdish refugees streamed toward the Turkish border during the turmoil following Iraq's 1991 expulsion from Kuwait.

Faced with a humanitarian crisis and a world riveted by the plight of these refugees (1 million others fled to the Iranian border), Turkey, the United States, and Britain helped establish a no-fly zone over northern Iraq and pushed Iraqi troops back from the Kurdish regions. This enabled the refugees to return home and restart their lives. However, Iraqi Kurds, protected by a US-UK air umbrella and no longer under the tutelage of Saddam Hussein, began to manage their own affairs. Because the air assets enforcing the no-fly zone were based at Incirlik airbase, Turkey paradoxically became the midwife to an autonomous Kurdish entity in northern Iraq at a time when it confronted its own Kurdish insurrection. Operation Provide Comfort (OPC), as this endeavor was called, caused tensions between Turkey and the United States because of the uncertainty that surrounded its periodic renewal by the Turkish parliament. The conundrum for Ankara was that Iraqi Kurds—divided among themselves—were incapable of exercising complete authority over their territory and controlling PKK activities. Ankara, sometimes with the cooperation of Iraqi Kurdish guerrillas and sometimes on its own, conducted cross-border operations against PKK camps near the border in its efforts to end the Kurdish insurgency at home. Ankara made no secret of its preference for a return of Saddam Hussein's regime to the north and an end to the sanctions regime, putting it at odds with Washington's containment of Baghdad. Thanks to OPC, Turkey became an indispensable element of US policy toward Iraq, enabling Washington both to protect the Kurds and to ensure that Hussein's regime was kept on a tight leash. OPC was a double-edged sword, binding the United States to Turkey, heightening the latter's importance, and enabling Ankara to extract concessions from Washington. Washington rewarded Ankara by unconditionally supporting its bid for EU membership, providing help against the PKK (including the delivery of PKK leader Ocalan to Turkish authorities), and assisting it economically whenever necessary. On the other hand, Ankara, despite its misgivings, felt compelled to maintain OPC for fear of a backlash in Washington.

Perhaps the greatest success for US diplomacy came after the EU's 1999 decision to reverse its earlier rejection of Turkey's candidacy for EU membership. The United States, despite its own criticism of Turkey's human rights shortcomings, aggressively lobbied the Europeans to give Turkey a chance at membership.

Iraq would come back once again to haunt US-Turkish relations. In the run-up to the 2003 war against Iraq, the United States wooed the new AKP-led Turkish government and secured its agreement for the United States to open up a second front against Iraq from Turkish territory. Turkish troops were supposed to follow the Americans and establish a cordon sanitaire, ostensibly to prevent a repeat of the 1988 and 1991 refugee outflows. Washington also promised to put together an economic aid package to protect Turkey from the turbulence the war was expected to cause. The AKP government, then led by Gul, with the support of Erdogan as party leader, decided to endorse the second front. With almost 90 percent of the Turkish public adamantly opposed to this venture, the AKP sought to share the political burden with the military. But the Turkish general staff, which had reluctantly decided to allow the operation in the face of American pressure, was unwilling to offer the AKP political cover. As a result, the army's apparently noncommittal approach confused both the public and politicians. Still, on March 1, 2003, with the Turkish parliament set to debate and vote on the matter, the AKP estimated it commanded a comfortable margin to pass it. To everyone's surprise, however, the proposal to approve the deployment of US troops failed narrowly.

The invasion of Iraq went ahead without the northern front. The March 1 vote was hailed as an example of democracy in action, but it had long-term repercussions for US-Turkish relations. The next crisis was not long in coming. On July 4, 2003, US troops raided the offices of the Turkish-affiliated Iraq Turkmen Front (ITC), where they arrested a number of party officials and Turkish special forces personnel on suspicion of plotting the assassination of the governor of Kirkuk. The Turkish personnel, who were in northern Iraq with US permission, were handcuffed and hooded and sent to Baghdad for interrogation. The Turkish press, public, and political class erupted with indignation. This was seen as the worst kind of insult by a trusted ally. No one paid much attention to the underlying reason. Within a year, and very quietly, the Turkish military high command sidelined three generals who were in charge of the special forces personnel, signaling that this was probably a rogue operation.

The reaction to this incident had much to do with the unease Turks felt with US intentions in Iraq. Having dealt themselves out of the Iraq War, they watched the rapprochement between Iraqi Kurds and Americans with increasing anxiety. The Kurdish north turned out to be immune from the Iraqi insurrection and the slow descent into chaos. This enabled the Kurds to consolidate their power and enhance their role in Iraq as Jalal Talabani, the leader of the Patriotic Union of Kurdistan, was elected president of Iraq, and his longtime rival, Massoud Barzani of the Kurdish Democratic Party, became president of the federal autonomous region of Iraqi Kurdistan. Turks feared that an Iraqi civil war might lead to the division of the country and an independent Kurdish state. Turkey also found out that its ability to influence events in Iraq was limited. Initially it opposed an Iraqi federal state, preferring a unitary one. When Turkey agreed to a US request to deploy peacekeeping forces in central Iraq, Iraqi Kurds and Shi'a vetoed their deployment. Similarly, the Turks' main client in Iraq, the ITC, which they hoped would represent the 900,000 Iraqi Turkmen, did poorly in Iraqi elections. Turkey's desire to keep the oil-rich city of Kirkuk out of Kurdish hands also is proving difficult. Ankara has stated on many occasions that Kurdish control of Kirkuk is unacceptable. However, many displaced Kurds have managed to return to the city with the help of Kurdish political parties, as Turkey has watched helplessly.

All these developments have strained US-Turkish relations. Anti-Americanism in Turkey has increased considerably, and in response Turkey has lost much support in Washington. Following a number of spectacular PKK raids on Turkish military outposts, the Bush administration, under pressure from Ankara and facing the prospect of Turkish military intervention into northern Iraq, decided to increase US military and intelligence cooperation with Turkey significantly. This helped avert a potentially crippling crisis and improved US-Turkish relations.

Although the Iraq War was the main source of deteriorating US-Turkish relations, the AKP's attempt to develop a more self-confident and activist foreign policy also has helped increase tensions. The AKP government strongly believes, with significant justification, that Turkey has traditionally punched well below its weight. Its presence in international organizations has been limited, and it has not made enough of its geostrategic location and material strengths to exert influence in the immediate region and beyond. Since the AKP came to power in late 2002, its foreign policy has been based on what Prime Minister Recep Tayyip Erdogan's top foreign policy adviser and now foreign minister, Ahmet Davutoğlu, calls "strategic depth" and "zero-problems with neighbors." Davutoğlu's main argument is that Turkey is a great power that has neglected—partly because of its obsession with the West—its historic and cultural ties as well as its diplomatic, economic, and political relations with its immediate strategic hinterland in the Middle East, North Africa, and Eurasia. Instead of a security-first approach that often resulted in confrontational relations with neighbors such as Greece, Iraq, Syria, and Iran, the zero-problems policy favored a more self-confident strategy of diplomatic engagement with all the countries surrounding Turkey.

In what represents a remarkable departure from the Kemalist tradition, Ankara under the AKP has become a very active and important player in the Middle East during the past decade: Turkey established closer ties with Syria, Iran, and Iraq; it assumed a leadership position in the Organization of the Islamic Conference; it attended Arab League conferences; and it contributed to UN forces in Lebanon and NATO forces in Afghanistan. It also actively mediated in the Syrian-Israeli conflict and the nuclear standoff with Iran. Ankara's diplomatic engagements with Iran and Hamas led to differences with the United States and Israel and left many wondering whether Turkey was turning decidedly away from its Western orientation or whether this turn was just a long overdue completion of Turkey's full circle of relations.

Another interesting factor in Turkey's foreign relations has been its rapprochement with Russia. Russia has become Turkey's main trade partner, thanks mainly to Turkey's dependence on Russian natural gas. Beyond growing economic relations, Ankara and Moscow have also improved their military and intelligence cooperation on issues related to terrorism. There seems to be more-active collaboration between the two countries in the Black Sea region and on the Kurdish and Chechen questions. Despite such enhanced partnership, however, it is too early to speak of a strategic convergence between Russian and Turkish national interests. In fact, a major factor behind Ankara's rapprochement with Moscow was its frustration with the policies of the George W. Bush administration, especially in Iraq and the greater Middle East.

The atmospherics of Turkish-American relations improved somewhat with the coming of the Barack Obama administration to power. Willing to put strategic relations back on track after the tumultuous 2003–2007 period, President Obama selected the country for one of his first overseas visits and described the relationship as a "model partnership" during his visit to Turkey in April 2009. Yet what began as a promising fresh start in Turkish-American relations quickly turned into mutual frustration. From the point of view of the Obama administration, the most disappointing part no doubt was Ankara's Iran policy, culminating with the no vote at the UN Security Council on the question of tighter financial sanctions against Tehran in the summer of 2010. For its part, Ankara was frustrated with Washington's reluctance to give the Tehran agreement—a deal brokered by Turkey and Brazil with the Iranian regime prior to the UN vote on sanctions—a chance. According to the agreement, signed jointly by the Iranian, Turkish, and Brazilian leaders, Tehran was to ship 2,640 pounds of low-enriched uranium to Turkey and in exchange would have the right to receive about 265 pounds of uranium enriched to 20 percent for civilian use.

Shortly after the Iran crisis, in June 2010, relations between Ankara and Washington went from bad to worse because of the Gaza flotilla incident and the Obama administration's refusal to condemn Israel's actions. Turkish-Israeli relations had hit their lowest point when the Israeli military attacked an aid flotilla in international waters and killed nine Turks (one a dual national with American citizenship) after it encountered resistance by activists on the flagship *Mavi Marmara*.

In addition to Iran and Israel, a third factor contributed to the negative mood in Washington: Turkey's failure to normalize relations with Armenia. Turkey and Armenia signed an accord in October 2009 calling for the reopening of the Turkish-Armenian border, which has been closed since 1993, and the establishment of diplomatic relations. These protocols needed to be ratified by the Turkish parliament to become effective. As the AKP government dragged its feet on the matter, many in Washington blamed Ankara for not showing enough vision and courage. In the meantime, the looming threat of an Armenian genocide resolution in the US Congress continued sporadically to dominate the bilateral agenda.

In many ways, one can argue that the Arab Spring, which shook the core of the Arab world and led to the emergence of new regimes in Tunisia, Egypt, and Libya, dramatically changed the Western discourse about Turkey. Instead of asking "who lost Turkey" or complaining about the Islamization of Turkish foreign policy, analysts began discussing whether the new regimes in the Arab world would follow the "Turkish model." As the most democratic and secular Muslim country in the region, Turkey did not hesitate to call for democratic change in Egypt and—after initial reluctance—gave its blessing to the NATO military effort in Libya. Even in Syria, where Turkey had invested significant strategic and diplomatic capital in rebuilding its tattered relations with the Asad regime, Ankara ultimately aligned with the West and became one of the strongest supporters of the anti-Asad rebellion.

FUTURE PROSPECTS

The 2007 and 2011 elections confirmed that the AKP is the dominant political force in Turkish politics. If in 2002 it achieved the impossible, removing from power a whole generation of politicians, some of whom had been there since the 1950s, in 2007 it reaffirmed its hold on the political center. The combination of a majority government, better economic performance, and a determined effort to join the EU has provided Turkey with the kind of stability unseen since the mid-1980s. The AKP has no challengers: the military has been subdued, with many retired and serving officers, including many generals and admirals, behind bars, and the main opposition party is inept and incapable of appealing to the broader public. The hard-line nationalists have limited appeal because the AKP has largely managed to appropriate the nationalist discourse. The only opposition, which is limited to only one or possibly two regions of the country, comes from the pro-Kurdish Peace and Democracy Party. Ironically, the Gulen movement, though generally sympathetic to the AKP, also occasionally has challenged its writ.

Moreover, Erdogan has emerged as Turkey's uncontested leader. He dominates everyday politics, taking an active interest in miniscule details, and the AKP has been reduced to a reflection of his will. Whereas the AKP and Erdogan were on the defensive until after the 2007 elections, when the republic's prosecutor charged them with fostering an Islamic agenda because they sought to open universities to women who wear Islamic head scarves, today the tables have been reversed. The media, in particular, have felt his heavy hand, as numerous journalists have been sacked for daring to criticize him. Erdogan, who had promised to replace the 1982 military constitution with a more democratic document that also would help resolve the Kurdish question, has instead focused on transforming Turkey's parliamentary system into a French-style semi-presidential system. Without his ever articulating his preferences, Turkish politics has already factored in Erdogan's desire to become Turkey's next president in 2014.

Despite these changes, the country remains polarized over identity issues, especially the secular-religious and Turkish-Kurdish divides. The AKP—partially because it garnered a significant segment of the Kurdish vote and partially because Erdogan calculated that without a resolution to the Kurdish issue, Turkey's future ambitions would suffer—took some bold steps. Freed from the military's watchful eye, it even engaged in secret negotiations with the PKK, which it has always termed a terrorist organization. Neither the government nor the PKK proved willing to move to the next stage. As a result, the AKP's much-heralded opening to the Kurds faltered. In 2012, fighting between the PKK and Turks had reached a crescendo of sorts.

Turkey's perceived difficulties with the EU, including the EU's insistence that it open its ports to Greek Cypriot shipping, as called for by its customs union agreement with the EU, have reduced the EU's influence as the main driver of Turkish reforms. This has enabled the AKP to pursue a more multidimensional foreign policy. Europe has become one factor among many that determines Turkish foreign policy. The opposition of French president Nicolas Sarkozy and his German counterpart, Chancellor Angela Merkel, to full Turkish EU membership has jeopardized both the future of reforms in Turkey and Turkish confidence in Europe.

Some in the EU, especially Germany's Christian Democrats, France, and Austria, would prefer to have Turkey seek a privileged partnership instead of full membership. If the EU were to renege on its commitment to a fair accession process, Turkey's diminishing enthusiasm could turn into a backlash against Europe and the West. Nonetheless, the backlash itself would be contained by the very fact that the bulk of Turkish trade is with Europe.

Moreover, Turkey's strategic importance for Europe is likely to increase in parallel with the EU's quest for energy diversification and a supplier more reliable than Russia. In that sense, the Nabucco pipeline, which would transport natural gas from the Caspian Sea to central Europe via Turkey, would radically alter Turkey's strategic relationship with the EU.

Hence, Turkey's economic relationship with the EU will likely remain intact. All things considered, Turkey has come a long way; it has managed to overcome difficult situations, albeit sometimes quite slowly. The dynamism and flexibility of Turkish society and its workforce point to a potential yet to be realized.

BIBLIOGRAPHY

Bernard Lewis's *The Emergence of Modern Turkey* (New York: Oxford University Press, 1961) remains the classic volume on Turkey. Feroz Ahmad's *The Making of Modern Turkey* (London: Routledge, 1993) covers Turkish politics up to the 1990s. Erik J. Zurcher, *Turkey: A Modern History* (New York: Tauris, 1994), gives a good overview. Stanford J. Shaw's two-volume *History of the Ottoman Empire and Modern Turkey* (London: Cambridge University Press, 1976–1977) contains a mine of data on the events it chronicles. Andrew Mango, *Ataturk: The Biography of the Founder of Modern Turkey* (Woodstock, NY: Overlook Press, 2000), gives a somewhat more reliable account of Turkey's great leader than Lord Kinross (Patrick Balfour) did in *Ataturk: A Biography of Mustafa Kemal, Father of Modern Turkey* (New York: William Morrow, 1965).

The political system of the Third Republic is analyzed in Ergun Ozbudun, *Contemporary Turkish Politics: Challenges to Democratic Consolidation* (Boulder, CO: Lynne Rienner Publishers, 2000). For an earlier view, see George S. Harris, *Turkey: Coping with Crisis* (Boulder, CO: Westview Press, 1985). Hugh Poulton's *Top Hat, Grey Wolf and Crescent: Turkish Nationalism and the Turkish Republic* (London: Hurst & Company, 1997) is a detailed study of the nationalist roots of modern Turkey. For the evolution of political parties up to 1989, consult Metin Heper and Jacob M. Landau, eds., *Political Parties and Democracy in Turkey* (London: I. B. Tauris, 1991). Andrew Finkel and Nukhet Sirman, eds., *Turkish State, Turkish Society* (London: Routledge, 1990), offers a broad analysis of political trends and ethnicity in the Third Republic.

Peter A. Andrews, ed., *Ethnic Groups in the Republic of Turkey* (Wiesbaden: Dr. Ludwig Teichert Verlag, 1989), gives a magisterial treatment of Turkey's cultural geography.

Z. Y. Herslag's *The Contemporary Turkish Economy* (New York: Routledge, 1988) examines the Turkish economy through the post-1980 period of export orientation. Anne O. Krueger and Okan A. Aktan provide an analysis of Turgut Ozal's reforms in the 1980s in *Swimming Against the Tide: Turkish Trade Reform in the 1980s* (San Francisco: Institute for Contemporary Studies Press, 1992).

For an excellent series of articles on Kemalist modernization, see Resat Kasaba and Sibel Bozdogan's *Rethinking Modernity and National Identity in Turkey* (Seattle: University of Washington Press, 1997).

The role of the military in politics is well depicted by William M. Hale, *Turkish Politics and the Military* (London: Routledge, 1995). For an anthropological approach to civil society relations in Turkey, see Ayse Gul Altinay, *The Myth of the Military Nation: Militarism, Gender, and Education in Turkey* (New York: Palgrave, 2004).

Morton Abramowitz, ed., *Friends in Need: Turkey and the United States After September 11* (New York: The Century Foundation, 2003), is a comprehensive approach to US-Turkish relations. Philip Robins's *Suits and Uniforms: Turkish Foreign Policy Since the Cold War* (Seattle: University of Washington Press, 2003) is a novel approach to Turkish foreign policy. Alvin Z. Rubinstein and Oles M. Smolansky, eds., *Regional Power Rivalries in the New Eurasia: Russia, Turkey, and Iran* (Armonk, NY: M. E. Sharpe, 1995), covers the early stages of Turkey's relationship with the newly independent states of the former Soviet Union. Heinz Kramer performs a tour de force on Turkey's role in Europe and its neighborhood in *A Changing Turkey: The Challenge to Europe and the United States* (Washington, DC: Brookings Institution Press, 2000). On the Cyprus issue, see Michael Emerson and Nathalie Tocci, *Cyprus as Lighthouse of the East Mediterranean: Shaping Re-unification and EU Accession Together* (Brussels: Center for European Research, 2002); Tozun Bahcheli, *Greek-Turkish Relations Since 1955* (Boulder, CO: Westview Press, 1990); and Meliha Altunışık and Lenore G. Martin, eds., "Turkey and the Middle East," special issue, *Turkish Studies* (December 2011).

Richard Tapper, ed., *Islam in Modern Turkey: Religion, Politics, and Literature in a Secular State* (London: I. B. Tauris, 1991), gives the background to recent religious developments. A more specialized treatment is in Jenny White, *Islamist Mobilization in Turkey: A Study in Vernacular Politics* (Seattle: University of Washington Press, 2002). Serif Mardin's *Religion and Social Change in Modern Turkey: The Case of Bediuzzaman Said Nursi* (Albany: State University of New York Press, 1989) is a sophisticated sociological study of the role of religion in Turkey viewed through an analysis of one of the most influential Turkish religious leaders of the twentieth century. On the Gulen movement, see Berna Turam, *Between Islam and the State: The Politics of Engagement* (Palo Alto, CA: Stanford University Press, 2007). Women's issues are treated in Sirin Tekeli, ed., *Women in Modern Turkish Society: A Reader* (London: Zed, 1995). The Kurdish challenge is covered in David McDowall, *A Modern History of the Kurds* (New York: I. B.

Tauris, 1996). See also Henri J. Barkey and Graham E. Fuller, *Turkey's Kurdish Question: An Example of a Trans-State Conflict* (Lanham, MD: Rowman & Littlefield, 1998), and Kemal Kirişçi and Gareth Winrow, *The Kurdish Question and Turkey* (London: Frank Cass, 1997). See also Omer Taspinar, *Kurdish Nationalism and Political Islam in Turkey: Kemalist Identity in Transition* (New York: Routledge, 2005).

Useful websites on Turkey include those of the German Marshall Fund (www .scribd.com/collections/2588599/On-Turkey), the independent Turkish think tank TESEV (www.tesev.org.tr/en/homepage), the pro-Justice and Development Party think tank SETA (www.setadc.org), and the newspapers *Today's Zaman* (www.todayszaman.com) and *Hurriyet Daily News* (www.hurriyetdailynews.com).

3

Islamic Republic of Iran

Mark Gasiorowski

Iran has preserved its unique identity since the dawn of history, despite the Arab, Turkic, and Mongol invasions that once swept through the region. Known as Persia until 1935, it boasted major empires that rivaled the ancient Greeks, Byzantines, and Ottomans. It was one of the few countries in the Middle East that was not colonized in the modern era, though European powers exerted considerable influence there in the early twentieth century. Iran is heir to a very rich culture, renowned for its poetry, visual arts, music, and cuisine. It is also the birthplace of the Zoroastrian and Baha'i faiths and the main bastion of the Shi'a branch of Islam.

Iran was convulsed by a popular revolution in 1978–1979, replacing 2,500 years of monarchical rule with an Islamic republic. Its new Islamist leaders were very radical during their first decade in power, transforming political and cultural life inside the country and engaging in bitter confrontations with the West and with most neighboring countries. Iran then became increasingly moderate in the 1990s, easing cultural restrictions, undertaking political reform, and improving relations with its neighbors and with Europe, though not with the United States. However, the momentum behind this moderation faded, and hard-liners swept the parliamentary and presidential elections of 2004 and 2005, establishing a new era of radicalism that continues today.

Historical Background

The Great Persian Empires

The ancestors of modern Iranians migrated into what is now Iran in the eleventh and tenth centuries BCE. The region was occupied at the time by other ethnic groups, mainly Assyrians, Elamites, and Urartians. In the sixth century BCE, Cyrus the Great united two Iranian tribes to form the first great Persian empire, known as the Achaemenian Empire. Cyrus and his descendants conquered vast areas, including much of what is now Egypt, Syria, Iraq, Turkey, and central Asia. Their efforts to conquer Greece were stopped at the

Islamic Replublic of Iran

battle of Marathon in 490 BCE. The Achaemenian Empire was finally defeated by Alexander the Great in 330 BCE.

The next great Persian empire was established in 224 CE, when Ardeshir Babakan, a local ruler in what is now southern Iran, conquered the neighboring areas and established the Sassanian dynasty, which ruled Iran until the seventh century. Ardeshir's son Shahpour attacked the Roman Empire's Middle Eastern provinces, seizing Antioch and even capturing the Roman emperor Valerian. During the next few centuries the Sassanians fought frequently with Rome and its successor, the Byzantine Empire, eventually capturing Jerusalem and Egypt and even laying siege to Constantinople, the Byzantine capital. The Byzantines then achieved a series of victories in the early seventh century, weakening the Sassanian Empire.

Following the death of Muhammad, the great prophet of Islam, in 632 CE, Muslim armies attacked the Sassanian Empire and achieved major victories at Qadisiya in modern-day Iraq in 637 and at Nahavand in central Iran in 641, seizing the Iranian heartland. Many Arabs settled in Iran in the following decades, introducing Islam and the Arabic alphabet and vocabulary. Iran's new Arab rulers adopted the Sassanians' advanced administrative techniques and many aspects of Iranian culture, strengthening and enriching the vast empire they created during this period.

From the seventh to the eleventh centuries, Iran was ruled either as part of the Arab Empire or by local dynasties. During the next two centuries, a series of Turkic military commanders ruled Iran at the behest of local elites and caliphs. This was a rich period in Iran's cultural life, with a flourishing of poetry, the visual arts, and urban development. This period ended in 1251, when Mongol invaders swept into Iran from central Asia, looting and pillaging and leaving Iran in a state of near anarchy for many decades.

Iran's last great empire, ruled by the Safavid dynasty, was established in 1501 by Shah (King) Ismail, who made the Shi'a branch of Islam the state religion and united territory roughly comprising the boundaries of today's Iran. The Safavid dynasty was at its height during the reign of Shah Abbas I (r. 1587–1628), who conquered much of central Asia and parts of the Ottoman Empire. Shah Abbas established his capital in Isfahan, building superb palaces, mosques, bridges, and gardens that make this city one of the most beautiful in the world. The Safavids gradually fell into decline and were conquered by Afghans in 1722, initiating decades of instability.

In the late eighteenth century, the Turkic-speaking Qajar tribe defeated the other tribes and warlords of Iran and re-created much of the Safavid Empire. They also moved the capital to Tehran, which was then merely a village. The Qajars ruled until 1925. This was an era of decline for Iran, with the Qajars losing substantial territory in the Caucasus and central Asia to imperial Russia and becoming increasingly indebted to European bankers and entrepreneurs. Internally, Qajar Iran was shaken by the Babi and Baha'i movements in the 1840s and 1850s, the tobacco boycott of 1891–1892, and the constitutional revolution of 1906, which brought Iran the first constitution in the non-Western world. Iran's decline under the Qajars culminated during World War I, when foreign armies occupied parts of the country and famine was widespread. In 1919, Ahmad Shah Qajar signed a treaty with Britain that made Iran essentially a British protectorate.

The Pahlavi Era

In 1921, Reza Khan Pahlavi, the commander of one of Iran's few effective military units, led a coup against the current government. During the next four years, he gradually consolidated power by eliminating his rivals, defeating various tribal forces, and packing the *majles* (parliament) with his supporters. He then had the *majles* vote to depose the last Qajar shah and name him the new shah. He was crowned in April 1926, establishing the Pahlavi dynasty.

Reza Shah Pahlavi was a modernizing despot, establishing the foundations of a modern economy and society but also severely repressing political activity. Like his Turkish contemporary Mustafa Kemal Ataturk, he did much to develop Iran's economic and social infrastructure, building roads, a large rail network, a modern banking system, a professional civil service, modern educational institutions, and the country's first modern

ISLAMIC REPUBLIC OF IRAN

Capital city	Tehran
Chief of state, 2012	Supreme Leader Ali Khamenei
Head of government, 2012	President Mahmoud Ahmadinejad
Political parties, 2012	Islamic Society of Engineers, Combatant Clergy Association, Islamic Coalition Party, Executives of Construction Party, Association of Combatant Clerics, Islamic Labor Party
Ethnic groups	Persian (61%), Azeri (16%), Kurd (10%), Lur (6%), Baloch (2%), Arab (2%), Turkmen (2%), other (1%)
Religious groups	Shi'a Muslim (89%), Sunni Muslim (9%), other (2%)
Export partners, 2011	China (21%), India (9.3%), Japan (8.9%), Turkey (8.7%), South Korea (7.9%), Italy (5.2%)
Import partners, 2011	United Arab Emirates (30.6%), China (17.2%), Germany (4.8%), Turkey (4.2%)

factories. Much of this activity was financed by proceeds from Iran's rapidly growing oil industry, which had been established in 1901 and was controlled by the British-owned Anglo-Iranian Oil Company. Reza Shah also took steps to increase Iran's independence, rescinding the treaty with Britain and reorganizing and strengthening its armed forces. But he was very repressive, brutally suppressing his opponents, forbidding political parties and other civil society institutions, and undermining the Shi'a clergy and religious practice.

Britain and the Soviet Union jointly occupied Iran during World War II to establish a supply route for Soviet forces, which were fighting desperately against German invaders in areas to the northwest of Iran. Reza Shah opposed this and was promptly deposed and sent into exile. The occupying powers then installed Reza Shah's twenty-one-year-old son, Mohammad Reza Pahlavi, in his place. The young shah was at this time a weak and timid figure with no political experience. His installation on the throne therefore produced a flourishing of political activity, with various traditionalist, Islamist, nationalist, tribal, and leftist tendencies emerging. During the last years of World War II, the Soviet Union and its close allies in Iran's Communist Tudeh (Mass) Party began to encourage Azeri and Kurdish separatist movements in northwestern Iran, producing an incipient crisis. These movements collapsed in 1946, however, as a result of the skillful diplomacy of Prime Minister Ahmad Qavam and support from the United States.

Political activity continued to flourish in Iran in the late 1940s. Nationalist, leftist, and Islamist forces agitated against British influence in Iran, especially against British control over the oil industry. In 1949, several moderate nationalist parties and assorted individuals created an umbrella organization called the National Front to promote nationalization of the oil industry. Many National Front leaders also wanted to establish democracy in Iran, which would entail wresting power from the pro-British traditional upper class and weakening the monarchy. The National Front was led by Mohammad Mosaddeq, a venerable politician who had long campaigned for oil nationalization and opposed the Pahlavi monarchy.

As the oil nationalization movement grew, the shah felt compelled to appoint Mosaddeq prime minister in April 1951. Mosaddeq then nationalized the oil industry, triggering a confrontation with the British government. The British organized a worldwide embargo of Iranian oil exports and began covert efforts to undermine Mosaddeq's government. They also began preparations to invade Iran, which ended in September 1951 when US President Harry Truman expressed opposition. The United States made extensive efforts to negotiate a solution to the oil dispute, but Britain and Iran could not reach agreement. As the crisis dragged on during 1952, Mosaddeq's coalition began to weaken, with key Islamist and nationalist allies joining the opposition. US officials increasingly feared that Mosaddeq would become dependent on the Tudeh Party, giving the Soviet Union growing influence in Iran. Soon after US President Dwight Eisenhower was inaugurated in January 1953, the United States agreed to a British proposal to stage a joint coup d'état against Mosaddeq. The US Central Intelligence Agency (CIA) then organized and carried out the coup, overthrowing Mosaddeq in August 1953.

The 1953 coup began a dramatic shift in Iran's political evolution, ending the flourishing of political activity that had occurred since 1941 and beginning a long period of authoritarian rule. Mosaddeq's successor, Fazlollah Zahedi—who had been handpicked by the United States and Britain—declared martial law, arrested thousands, and closed down all opposition parties and newspapers. Mosaddeq was put on trial, imprisoned for three years, and then kept under house arrest until he died in 1967. Most of Mosaddeq's key associates were imprisoned as well, and his foreign minister was executed. A large Tudeh Party network in the armed forces was discovered and dismantled in September 1954, crippling the party. The United States made extensive efforts to prop up the Zahedi government, giving it considerable economic and security assistance and working tirelessly to negotiate an end to the oil dispute. An oil agreement was finally signed in October 1954 under which a consortium of foreign oil companies purchased Iranian oil produced by the state-owned National Iranian Oil Company.

The shah dismissed Zahedi in April 1955 and appointed a loyalist in his place, beginning a long period in which the shah gradually consolidated power in his own hands. Political unrest continued to simmer, especially among the rapidly growing urban middle class. The shah finally lifted martial law in April 1957. He also authorized the creation of two political parties, the Nationalists (Melliyun) Party and the People's (Mardom) Party, but he put loyalists in charge of both. During this period, the CIA established a new Iranian intelligence service, Sazeman-e Ettela'at va Amniyat-e Keshvar (SAVAK), which soon became a key pillar of the shah's authoritarian regime.

By 1960, political unrest had grown considerably. In January, high school students in Tehran staged the first public demonstrations since 1953. Soon after, the shah announced that the upcoming *majles* elections would be completely free, prompting various politicians to announce their candidacy, including several members of the National Front. The elections were held in August and featured widespread irregularities and violence, forcing the shah to cancel them. New elections were held in January 1961 and again were rigged. The National Front, students, and teachers organized large protest demonstrations. US officials began discreetly pressuring the shah to initiate liberalization measures. As a result, the shah fired several unpopular officials and appointed the US-backed moderate reformer Ali Amini as prime minister.

Amini quickly took steps to appease the shah's critics, announcing a series of reforms, including a much-needed land-reform program and measures aimed at stimulating the sluggish economy. The shah also called for new elections. The National Front rejected these measures and organized large demonstrations after Amini's appointment. Amini responded by arresting all of the National Front's leaders and many supporters, and he did not schedule new elections. More demonstrations occurred in January 1962. The security forces attacked the demonstrators, leaving hundreds injured and arresting hundreds more. Under severe pressure, the National Front began to split into moderate and radical factions.

With his opponents growing weaker, the shah dismissed Amini in July 1962. He then announced his own package of reforms in January 1963, dubbed the "White Revolution," which included a large land-reform program, the enfranchisement of women, and efforts to improve literacy and public health. These measures mollified many of the shah's urban middle-class critics, and the land-reform program weakened the traditional upper class. However, many members of the traditional middle and lower classes were angered by the modernizing thrust of the White Revolution. Ayatollah Ruhollah Khomeini and other Islamists organized a series of strikes and demonstrations to protest the White Revolution. Khomeini was arrested in June 1963, triggering huge demonstrations by his traditional middle- and lower-class supporters. The security forces viciously attacked the demonstrators, leaving hundreds dead and thousands injured. Khomeini was soon released but was arrested again and sent into exile in October 1964, after denouncing a new law giving US military personnel immunity from prosecution.

After these events, the shah allowed no genuine opposition activity. His security forces effectively suppressed all overt political activity. He replaced the Nationalists Party with the New Iran (Iran Novin) Party in late 1963 and later replaced both official parties with a single party, the Resurgence (Rastakhiz) Party. These parties gained little popular support, serving merely as mechanisms of co-optation. Iran's oil revenue grew rapidly in the 1960s and skyrocketed after the large price increases of the early 1970s, producing a long period of rapid economic growth that helped defuse unrest. The United States stopped pressuring the shah for reform after the early 1960s, and its strong support for him led many Iranians to believe he was invincible. Viewed from afar, Iran appeared to be an "island of stability," as US President Jimmy Carter famously remarked on New Year's Eve of 1977.

Nevertheless, despite the appearance of calm, several opposition currents existed in Iran in the 1970s. The National Front, with its aging leadership and moderate rhetoric, became increasingly irrelevant. The Liberation Movement of Iran (Nezhat-e Azadi-ye Iran), an Islamic modernist faction led by Mehdi Bazargan, had broken off from the National Front in 1961 and secretly remained active during this period, though its base of support was limited. Both the National Front and the Liberation Movement spawned important student organizations among the many Iranians studying in the United States and Europe in the 1960s and 1970s, creating powerful opposition networks among the educated elite.

In addition, several leftist guerrilla organizations were established in the late 1960s and early 1970s by young Iranians who had become disillusioned with the moderate positions of the National Front and Liberation Movement and the weakness of the Tudeh Party. The most important of these were the People's Warriors (Mojahedin-e Khalq), which had a radical Islamic-leftist ideology, and the People's Guerrilla Warriors (Cherikha-ye Fedayan-e Khalq), which had a Third World–oriented Marxist-Leninist ideology. These organizations sent some of their members to Lebanon and elsewhere for guerrilla training and maintained contact with the Iranian student movements in the United States and Europe. They launched an armed uprising in 1971, attacking police stations and other targets and assassinating government officials and six American military and civilian advisers. The security forces responded with severe repression, torturing and executing many suspected guerrillas. By 1975, these organizations had been severely weakened.

Finally, a variety of Islamist movements emerged in the 1960s and 1970s. The most important was a network of Shi'a clerics, most of whom had studied under Ayatollah Khomeini. Khomeini lived in the Shi'a holy city of Najaf, Iraq, from 1965 until 1978 and communicated with this network through a series of emissaries who relayed messages back and forth and brought tapes of his fiery sermons to be played in Iran's mosques. He also wrote his seminal book *Islamic Government* during this period, providing a blueprint for the Islamic regime he hoped to establish in Iran. Closely affiliated with this clerical network was a small cell of Islamist laymen called the Coalition of Islamic Societies (Jamiat-e Motalafeh-ye Islami), which assassinated Prime Minister Hassan Ali Mansur in January 1965. The Islamic modernist intellectual Ali Shariati developed a large following before he died mysteriously in 1977, drawing many students and middle-class Iranians toward political Islam. Inspired by the Mojahedin-e Khalq and Fedayan-e Khalq, many small Islamist guerrilla cells emerged in the late 1970s and staged attacks on the shah's regime. These various Islamist movements were loosely connected with one another, with the Liberation Movement, and with Islamist movements in Lebanon and elsewhere.

The 1978–1979 Revolution

Several factors exacerbated popular unrest in Iran in the 1960s and 1970s. The absence of political freedom and growing repression alienated many Iranians, especially among students and the urban middle class. Inequality remained high, despite the huge influx of oil revenue in the 1970s, creating unrest among the lower classes. The shah drew even closer to the United States in the early 1970s, buying large quantities of US arms, signing lucrative contracts with US corporations, and bringing tens of thousands of Americans to Iran to administer these projects. He promoted rapid Westernization in Iran by fostering the growth of Western culture, creating a new Westernized elite, and deemphasizing traditional Persian and Islamic values. He also maintained close relations with Israel. These various trends angered not only traditionalist Iranians but also many modernists, who believed the shah was compromising Iran's rich cultural identity and creating a growing chasm between the traditional and modern segments of society.

In 1976 and 1977, several new conditions emerged that further increased this unrest and facilitated opposition activity. The mid-1970s oil boom produced higher inflation, shortages of goods and services, unprecedented corruption, and extensive rural-urban migration, which severely strained public services. The oil boom also forced the shah to take steps that further angered certain segments of society, such as implementing price controls, higher interest rates, an antiprofiteering campaign, and spending cuts. During the 1976 US presidential campaign, candidate Jimmy Carter stated that he would promote human rights if elected president and specifically mentioned Iran as a likely focus. Although in practice Carter made little effort to promote human rights in Iran, the shah anticipated that he would and eased up on his opponents. Finally, the shah was secretly diagnosed with lymphatic cancer in 1974 and began to take powerful medication, forcing him to consider his legacy and probably impairing his cognitive ability.

Under these conditions, opposition leaders began to test the limits on political activity during 1977. Secular activists circulated open letters calling for political reform. Several new civil society organizations were established and began to hold public meetings. The National Front and Liberation Movement began to agitate. These organizations became increasingly active in the fall of 1977, holding rallies and issuing public statements. After Ayatollah Khomeini's son Mostafa died suddenly in October, Khomeini's Islamist allies organized a series of memorial services around the country, which were widely attended. Responding to these pressures, the shah replaced his docile prime minister, Amir Abbas Hoveida, with a respected technocrat and permitted the Resurgence Party and other official bodies to discuss matters more openly. The security forces did not crack down on opposition activity until November 1977, leading many Iranians to believe that a new era of openness had begun.

Encouraged by these events, Khomeini's allies organized large demonstrations in the city of Qom in January 1978 to protest a slanderous newspaper article about Khomeini. The security forces attacked the demonstrators, killing seven and arresting over a hundred. Following traditional Shi'a mourning practices, the Islamists then organized more demonstrations throughout the country forty days later to commemorate those killed in January. Mobs attacked government buildings, theaters, and stores selling liquor and again clashed with the security forces, leaving nine more dead and hundreds arrested. More violent demonstrations then occurred at forty-day intervals in the following months, leaving more dead and filling the country's prisons. By the summer of 1978, Iran had become dangerously unstable.

The shah responded erratically to this challenge, trying to suppress these demonstrations but also making important concessions. This ambiguous approach merely encouraged the opposition, which was increasingly dominated by Khomeini's allies. Islamist guerrillas began to provoke the security forces by shooting at them from crowds and carrying out arson and bombing attacks. Khomeinist clerics called on security personnel to defect, and many did.

A key turning point came in mid-August 1978, when unknown arsonists set fire to a crowded theater in Abadan, killing hundreds. Huge demonstrations then spread throughout the country, fanned by rumors that SAVAK had burned the theater. The shah tried to end the chaos by again replacing his prime minister, releasing hundreds of political prisoners, calling for free elections, and making other conciliatory gestures. Moderate opposition leaders appealed for calm. These measures failed to stop the crisis. The shah then declared martial law. On September 8, army units opened fire on a crowd demonstrating at Zhaleh Square in eastern Tehran, killing scores and injuring hundreds.

Martial law kept demonstrators in check during the following weeks. However, labor unrest began to spread throughout the country, crippling the oil industry and public services. Islamist and leftist guerrillas increasingly attacked the shah's regime. Khomeini moved from Iraq to Paris in October, enabling him to exercise better leadership over events. Islamist and secularist leaders traveled to Paris to meet with Khomeini, further strengthening his leadership. The shah tried unsuccessfully to persuade moderate opposition figures to form a government that would carry out reforms but preserve the monarchy. He also continued to release political prisoners and make other conciliatory gestures.

A new wave of violent demonstrations swept through Tehran in early November, leading the shah again to replace his prime minister, this time with a military government. Massive demonstrations, guerrilla activity, and strikes continued in the following weeks, leaving hundreds dead and paralyzing the economy. During Shi'a holy days in early December, millions of demonstrators appeared in the streets of Tehran and other cities. The armed forces began to disintegrate. The shah continued to meet with moderate opposition leaders about forming a new government. He finally persuaded National Front leader

Shahpour Bakhtiar to head a new government, but only on the condition that the shah leave the country, release all political prisoners, and meet other demands. Bakhtiar became prime minister on December 30. The shah left Iran on January 16, 1979, never to return.

Bakhtiar quickly took a number of conciliatory steps, lifting press restrictions, freeing all remaining political prisoners, promising to dissolve SAVAK, and canceling foreign arms purchases. The United States backed Bakhtiar and sent General Robert Huyser to Iran to bolster support for him among military officers. These actions did little to calm the situation. Khomeini declared Bakhtiar's government illegal and appointed a Revolutionary Council to oversee the transition to a new regime. The National Front expelled Bakhtiar. Huge demonstrations and strikes continued. Khomeini returned to Tehran on February 1 and was greeted by millions of jubilant supporters. He then appointed Liberation Movement leader Mehdi Bazargan to head a new provisional government. Revolutionary committees sprang up in many neighborhoods and towns, taking over public services and administering "revolutionary justice." Air force technicians mutinied in Tehran on February 9, distributing large stocks of weapons and clashing with loyalist army units. Islamist and leftist guerrillas attacked military and police bases, seizing more weapons and leaving hundreds dead. On February 11 military commanders declared that the armed forces would remain neutral in the fighting, ending their support for Bakhtiar's government. Bakhtiar went into hiding the next day.

The Radical Phase of the Islamic Regime

From February through early November 1979, the moderates in and around Bazargan's provisional government were harshly attacked by radical Islamists and radical leftists. Radical Islamists also dominated the Revolutionary Council and several other revolutionary institutions that emerged during this period; these institutions served as a parallel government that increasingly marginalized the Bazargan government. Ayatollah Khomeini acted as an arbitrator in the tense struggle among these factions, but he generally backed the radical Islamists. As a result, Iran moved steadily in a radical Islamist direction.

The first major dispute between these factions emerged when members of the revolutionary committees began to arrest top officials from the shah's regime, bring them before hastily created revolutionary courts, and execute them. Bazargan and other moderates protested but were unable to stop the executions, which numbered over six hundred by November. Another dispute emerged in March over the wording of a referendum on Iran's new regime. Bazargan pushed for a "democratic republic" or "democratic Islamic republic," but Khomeini and his allies demanded that the referendum offer a simple choice for or against an "Islamic republic." The referendum was held in late March and produced a resounding victory for the radical Islamists. Additional disputes occurred over freedom of the press and women's rights. During the spring of 1979, Iranian Kurds, Arabs, and other ethnic minorities began to rebel, Islamist extremists assassinated several prominent moderates, and the radical leftist guerrilla organizations became increasingly powerful. Radical Islamists therefore created the paramilitary Islamic Revolutionary Guard Corps to protect the new Islamic regime against these various threats. Iran's relations with the United States and neighboring Iraq deteriorated sharply during this period.

Tension also emerged over efforts to write a new constitution. Bazargan appointed a commission that produced a draft constitution providing full democratic rights and giving the Shi'a clergy only a limited role in government. Khomeini supported this draft constitution, but radical Islamists, leftists, and ethnic leaders attacked it. Radical Islamists then manipulated the August 1979 election for the constitutional assembly that was to finalize the constitution, achieving a decisive victory. They continued to attack their opponents in the following weeks, closing newspapers, banning demonstrations, and outlawing two major secularist parties. Heavy fighting also occurred in Iran's Kurdish and Arab regions. The radical Islamists used their control over the constitutional assembly to enact major revisions of the draft constitution, creating the institutional foundations for a clergy-dominated Islamic regime. (See "Political Structure" below.) Bazargan and other moderates despaired about their inability to stop the radical Islamists; many fled into exile.

On November 4, hundreds of radical Islamist students stormed the US embassy compound in Tehran and took sixty-one Americans hostage. After Bazargan and Foreign Minister Ibrahim Yazdi tried unsuccessfully to persuade Khomeini to order the hostages released, Bazargan and his cabinet resigned. Some of the hostages were soon released, but fifty-two were held until January 1981. The students wanted to humiliate the United States and push Iran in a more radical direction. They succeeded on both counts.

The Revolutionary Council temporarily succeeded Bazargan's government. The council oversaw a December 1979 referendum that overwhelmingly approved the new constitution. It then held presidential elections in January that were won by Abol Hassan Bani-Sadr, a relatively moderate Islamist intellectual who had lived in Paris for many years and become a key aide to Khomeini in 1978. The students holding the US embassy considered Bani-Sadr too moderate and soon began to attack him. Radical Islamists associated with the recently created Islamic Republican Party (IRP) swept the March 1980 parliamentary elections and soon began to attack Bani-Sadr as well, demanding that he accept their nominees for cabinet positions. Led by IRP head Ayatollah Mohammad Beheshti and Speaker of Parliament Akbar Hashemi Rafsanjani, they eventually forced Bani-Sadr to accept their nominee for prime minister, Mohammad Ali Raja'i. During this period Bani-Sadr became increasingly dependent on support from the Mojahedin-e Khalq, whose large cadre of urban guerrillas posed a serious threat to the radical Islamists.

Following more than a year of clashes along their common border, Iraq invaded Iran in September 1980. Iraqi forces seized some 4,000 square miles of Iranian territory, including much of the oil-producing region in southwestern Iran. The Iranian government began a massive effort to mobilize resistance to the invasion, producing a huge outpouring of volunteers and a groundswell of support for the Islamic regime. Both Bani-Sadr and his radical opponents tried to take advantage of the situation by identifying themselves with the war effort and using the war as a pretext to attack one another.

Clashes between Bani-Sadr and the radical Islamists became increasingly tense in early 1981. Bani-Sadr's moderate backers and the Mojahedin organized a series of rallies that were attacked by radical vigilantes. The radicals held rallies of their own, which generally were much larger than the pro–Bani-Sadr rallies. By April, violent clashes were occurring almost daily. Parliament and other institutions controlled by the radicals began to strip Bani-Sadr of his powers and close down moderate newspapers, leading Bani-Sadr to demand a popular referendum to resolve the confrontation. Frustrated by the factional infighting, Khomeini in late May began to criticize Bani-Sadr publicly. With Khomeini apparently on their side, the radicals moved to eliminate Bani-Sadr, filing frivolous legal charges against him, arresting many of his associates, attacking his supporters, and finally calling for his execution. Khomeini dismissed Bani-Sadr on June 22, forcing him to flee underground with help from the Mojahedin.

With the radical Islamists now poised to consolidate control, the Mojahedin tried to spark a counterrevolutionary uprising. They organized a huge rally on June 20 that was brutally attacked by the radicals, leaving dozens dead and over 1,000 arrested. Large numbers of Mojahedin and secular leftist guerrillas were executed in the following days. The Mojahedin then carried out a series of bombings and assassinations aimed at decapitating the radical Islamist leadership and overthrowing the Islamic regime. The most dramatic was a June 28 bombing that killed seventy-four IRP leaders, including Beheshti, four cabinet ministers, and twenty-seven members of parliament. The radicals reacted with fury, arresting thousands and executing hundreds. Additional bombings and assassinations occurred in the following months. Raja'i was elected president in late July, but he and the new prime minister were soon killed in another bombing. The arrests and executions continued for many months, leaving many thousands dead and decisively weakening the Mojahedin. Most of its surviving members fled to Iraq, where they were armed by the Iraqi government and launched frequent attacks into Iran.

In October 1981, Ali Khamenei, a radical cleric, was elected president, and Mir Hossein Musavi, a radical lay Islamist, was appointed prime minister. These men, together with Speaker of Parliament Rafsanjani, worked under the general guidance of Ayatollah Khomeini to consolidate the radical Islamists' control and bring order and stability to Iran. After defeating the Mojahedin, their most urgent priority was to drive Iraqi forces out of Iran. They accomplished this in May 1982. Iran then carried the war into Iraqi territory, hoping to bring down the government of Saddam Hussein and establish an Islamic state in Iraq. Iran's forces soon became bogged down, producing a brutal war of attrition that lasted until 1988. Khamenei was reelected in August 1985, and Musavi was reappointed in October 1985.

Having defeated their various opponents, the radical Islamists began to feud among themselves in the mid-1980s. The most important dispute was between the Islamic leftists associated with Prime Minister Musavi, who favored a radical redistribution of wealth and statist economic policies, and Islamic conservatives associated with the traditional clerical and business elite, who favored laissez-faire economic policies. This dispute persisted throughout the mid- and late 1980s, preventing the government from carrying out effective economic policies.

Another dispute surfaced in November 1986, when it emerged that the United States had been selling arms to Iran in exchange for the release of US hostages held in Lebanon by guerrillas backed by Iran. US officials then used the profits from these arms sales to assist Nicaraguan guerrillas, in what became known as the Iran-Contra Affair. Information about these arms sales was made public in October 1986 by the son-in-law of Ayatollah Hossein Ali Montazari, Khomeini's designated successor. Most of Iran's leaders had backed the arms-for-hostages deal and were deeply embarrassed by the revelation. Yet another dispute emerged in the late 1980s, when Montazari and others began to call for greater liberalization. Khomeini tried to slow this trend in early 1989 by dismissing Montazari and issuing a death sentence for British author Salman Rushdie, whose book *The Satanic Verses* had offended many Muslims.

The Moderate Phase

Several key changes in 1988 and 1989 initiated a trend toward moderation in Iran. In July 1988, after its ground forces had been severely weakened and driven out of Iraq, Iran finally agreed to a UN proposal to end the Iran-Iraq War. Ayatollah Khomeini died in June 1989, after a long illness. In July, Rafsanjani, who had emerged as a leading advocate of moderation, was elected president. At the same time, Iran's voters approved a package of constitutional reforms designed to reduce the gridlock that had largely paralyzed the political system since the mid-1980s. The most important of these reforms was a measure to eliminate the position of prime minister and concentrate executive power in the hands of the president.

President Rafsanjani assembled a government dominated by centrist technocrats. His highest priority was to reform the economy, which had deteriorated sharply as a result of the war and years of ideologically driven policy making. Rafsanjani's economic reforms met with strong opposition in parliament, which was dominated by Islamic leftists. He therefore drew closer to the conservatives, who vetoed many leftist candidates for the 1992 parliamentary elections. Most of the remaining leftists were defeated at the polls, giving the conservatives a large majority in parliament, which they retained in the 1996 elections. The conservative-controlled parliament soon turned against Rafsanjani and the centrists, however, blocking most of the reforms they sought to implement.

The leftists' defeat in the 1992 elections demonstrated that they had lost most of their popular support, leading many to become more moderate. In the run-up to the May 1997 presidential election, the leftists established a pro-reform coalition with the centrists, who were disillusioned with the conservatives' opposition to their economic reforms. This reformist coalition backed Hojjat ol-Islam Mohammad Khatami, a moderate leftist cleric, in the presidential election. Khatami won a landslide victory, demonstrating that the reformists' program was much more popular than that of the conservatives.

Khatami's election temporarily threw the conservatives off balance and gave the reformists a chance to carry out reforms. The reformists' highest priority was to promote democracy, since free elections would likely give them control over parliament. They therefore began to pursue political reform, liberalizing the press, loosening restrictions on political activity, and challenging the conservatives' control over state institutions. The conservatives soon responded, assaulting and arresting reformist leaders, closing their newspapers, and attacking them with demagogic rhetoric. Ayatollah Khamenei largely backed the conservatives, using the broad powers of his office to block many reformist initiatives. By the summer of 1998, the two factions were locked in a bitter power struggle, bringing the reform process largely to an end.

The reformists won another landslide victory in the 1999 municipal council elections. The conservatives continued their attacks, however, focusing especially on the reformist press. In July 1999 they closed a popular reformist newspaper, triggering six days of severe rioting that shook the regime's foundations. The reformists then won yet another landslide victory in the February 2000 parliamentary elections, gaining control over this crucial body. The conservatives reacted bitterly, arresting reformist leaders, shooting a key reformist strategist, and closing down most remaining reformist newspapers. Rumors circulated that hard-liners in the security forces might carry out a coup. Once the new parliament was convened, the conservative-dominated Guardian Council vetoed much of its legislation. The reformists pursued a strategy of "active calm," pressing for reform but avoiding confrontational actions that might give the conservatives a pretext for cracking down even further.

As the June 2001 presidential election approached, tensions began to emerge in the reformist camp, with radical reformists calling for a more confrontational approach and some even breaking with their colleagues. President Khatami publicly admitted that he was powerless and refused for many months to say whether he would run for reelection. In the end, Khatami entered the race and won another landslide victory, indicating that the reformists remained very popular, despite growing unease.

The conservatives continued to attack the reformists and block their reform initiatives during Khatami's second term. In addition, the terrorist attacks of September 11, 2001, the subsequent US declaration that Iran was part of an "axis of evil," and the US invasion of Iraq in March 2003 created growing fear that the United States might attack Iran, strengthening the conservatives' determination to stop the reformists. Fissures continued to grow in the reformist camp during this period, and Khatami openly threatened to resign.

Municipal council elections were held again in February 2003. Conservative candidates in Tehran and other major cities won a sweeping victory. Voter turnout fell dramatically from its 1999 level, undermining support for reformist candidates and demonstrating that the Iranian public had become disillusioned with the reformists.

In the run-up to the February 2004 parliamentary elections, many reformists talked openly about staging a boycott, though most finally chose to participate. The conservatives were determined to control these elections. Accordingly, they vetoed almost all prominent reformist candidates, including eighty incumbent members of parliament. Reformist members of parliament staged a sit-in strike and threatened to resign if the vetoes were upheld, and protests occurred in many cities. Although some minor reformist candidates were reinstated, the conservatives remained firm. Most reformist leaders eventually backed down, giving up their strike and their threats to resign. They were then punished by the voters, winning only 17 percent of the seats filled in the first round, compared with 68 percent for conservative candidates. Turnout was higher than expected, indicating again that many Iranians had become disillusioned with the reformists and backed conservatives instead.

As the June 2005 presidential election approached, the conservatives continued to attack the reformists and block their initiatives. With Khatami ineligible for a third term and most popular reformists likely to be vetoed, the reformists did not have a strong candidate for the election. In the end, Speaker of Parliament Mehdi Karrubi and Mostafa Moin, a little-known former cabinet minister, were the main reformist candidates. Several prominent conservatives entered the race, along with former president Rafsanjani, a centrist. Rafsanjani led the first round of voting, followed by Tehran mayor Mahmoud Ahmadinejad, a little-known hard-liner whose populist campaign and humble demeanor attracted many voters. Ahmadinejad then won the second round, shocking most observers and ending the moderate era that had prevailed since 1989.

Radical Resurgence

Ahmadinejad's election marked the beginning of a shift back toward the radicalism of the 1980s. During Ahmadinejad's first term, this resurgent radicalism was manifested mainly in Iran's foreign policy, as discussed below. Domestically Ahmadinejad pursued populist economic policies and governed in a very cronyistic manner, alienating not only his reformist and centrist opponents but also many conservatives. Opposition to Ahmadinejad had become widespread by the end of his first term, though Supreme Leader Khamenei continued to support him.

After his inauguration, Ahmadinejad nominated a cabinet dominated by hard-liners, including several of his close associates. The conservative-led parliament voted down four of his nominees on the grounds of incompetence, beginning a series of clashes over presidential appointments that continued throughout Ahmadinejad's tenure. As they settled into office, Ahmadinejad's cabinet members began to purge reformists and centrists from their ministries and appoint hard-liners. Ahmadinejad also began to implement the populist economic policies he had campaigned on, increasing public spending and driving down interest rates. These actions produced sharp criticism from economists and additional clashes with parliament.

Ahmadinejad's cronyism, partisanship, and controversial policies sparked growing criticism from all political factions. Even Khamenei seemed concerned, creating two new mechanisms to oversee Ahmadinejad's performance. As the December 2006 elections for municipal councils and the Assembly of Experts approached, most centrists gravitated to the reformist camp, and Rafsanjani and Khatami made a series of joint campaign appearances. The new reformist-centrist coalition did fairly well in the election, while conservatives backed by Ahmadinejad did poorly. Rafsanjani was the big winner, taking the largest number of votes in the Assembly of Experts election and later becoming chairman of this powerful body. Students, women, and labor leaders staged frequent demonstrations during this period. Another important trend was the sudden emergence of new, ethnically based terrorist movements in Iran's Arab, Kurdish, and Baluch regions, which carried out numerous violent attacks. Iran blamed these movements on the United States, Britain, and Israel.

In the months leading up to the 2008 parliamentary election, the conservative camp split into pro- and anti-Ahmadinejad factions. The anti-Ahmadinejad faction was led by Ali Larijani, a Khamenei protégé who had emerged as a major critic of Ahmadinejad. This faction produced a list of candidates, though many also were backed by the pro-Ahmadinejad faction. Two reformist factions also produced lists of candidates, though many were vetoed by the Guardian Council. The reformists did poorly in the election, partly as a result of these vetoes and other restrictions. The new parliament overwhelmingly elected Larijani as speaker, indicating that the anti-Ahmadinejad conservatives had done quite well and setting up a new round of confrontations between this body and President Ahmadinejad.

Factional tension continued to grow, fueled by rising inflation, scandals involving Ahmadinejad's cronies, and a harsh crackdown on violations of Islamic cultural restrictions. As the June 12, 2009, presidential election approached, speculation grew about which reformists would run and whether a prominent conservative would challenge Ahmadinejad. Reformist leaders Mehdi Karrubi and Mir Hossein Musavi entered the race, energizing the reformist camp and alarming conservatives. Despite widespread opposition to Ahmadinejad, no strong conservative candidate emerged to challenge him.

In the weeks leading up to the election, hard-liners repeatedly harassed Karrubi and Musavi and undermined their efforts to campaign, and Khamenei implicitly encouraged Iranians to vote for Ahmadinejad. Nevertheless, popular support for the two reformist candidates visibly surged. When the election results were announced, however, Ahmadinejad took 62 percent of the vote, Musavi took 34 percent, the pragmatic conservative Mohsen Rezaie took only 2 percent, and Karrubi took only 1 percent.

Reformists erupted in fury. Reformist leaders charged that the election had been flagrantly rigged. Thousands of protesters poured into the streets on June 13, chanting anti-Ahmadinejad slogans. Much larger demonstrations occurred in the following days, with many hundreds of thousands protesting and clashing with the security forces on June 15 and 18. People also began chanting "God is great" and other slogans from rooftops to support the protests. On June 19, Khamenei made a speech lauding the election as a "divine assessment" and warning that further protests would not be tolerated. The security forces brutally attacked protesters the following day, killing at least ten, injuring dozens, and arresting hundreds. Additional protests and violent clashes occurred during the following week but then gradually died down. Dozens were killed during these events, and some 4,000 were arrested, including many reformist leaders, journalists, and intellectuals. Hard-liners began to blame the unrest on foreign powers.

Although protests over the election gradually died down, a series of broader protests occurred in the following months, mainly at regime-sponsored events, when the security forces could not easily ban marches or disperse crowds. The first occurred on July 17 at a Friday prayer sermon led by Rafsanjani, who subsequently was dropped from the roster of Friday prayer leaders. Similar protests occurred on Ahmadinejad's inauguration day, Jerusalem Day, and the anniversary of the US embassy seizure, as well as at the funeral of Ayatollah Montazari, who had become a reformist icon. The protesters clashed with security forces and increasingly chanted slogans denouncing Supreme Leader Khamenei and the Islamic regime itself. These protests, which became known as the Green Movement, were largely spontaneous, with little involvement by reformist leaders. Several Iranian diplomats defected in this period to support the protesters.

The regime's leaders reacted harshly to the Green Movement, brutally attacking protesters, arresting thousands, and suppressing new-media outlets that were being used to organize protests. They also used the protests as an opportunity to destroy the reformist movement, placing Karrubi and Musavi under house arrest, arresting most remaining reformist leaders, subjecting some to humiliating show trials, and outlawing the two main reformist parties. Several Rafsanjani relatives were even arrested. As a result, the Green Movement gradually dissipated in 2010, and the reformist faction was severely weakened, with almost all of its leaders in prison or in exile. The climate of repression that descended over Iran in this period remained firmly in place in late 2012.

After the suppression of the Green Movement and the reformist faction, politics in Iran consisted mainly of disputes between the pro- and anti-Ahmadinejad conservative factions. Ahmadinejad and his opponents in parliament clashed over the budget, plans to phase out consumer goods subsidies, funding for the Tehran metro system, and other matters. Some members of parliament talked openly about impeaching Ahmadinejad. In December 2010, Ahmadinejad abruptly fired his foreign minister, triggering weeks of recrimination. In March 2011, Ahmadinejad fired his intelligence minister but then was forced to retain him by Khamenei, triggering more recriminations and leading many observers to conclude that Khamenei had turned against the president. In November, Khamenei floated the idea of replacing the presidential system with a parliamentary one, reinforcing these conclusions. Hard-liners also managed to remove Rafsanjani from his position as chairman of the Assembly of Experts and arrested his daughter, further undermining this key centrist leader.

In the fall of 2011, Iran's various political factions began to prepare for the March 2012 parliamentary elections. Musavi, Karrubi, and most other reformist leaders called for a boycott, though Khatami and some others opposed this. Election authorities banned the three main reformist parties from participating. Over 5,000 candidates registered for the election, though many were vetoed by the Guardian Council. Ahmadinejad chose not to back a slate of candidates, apparently fearing this might backfire, but three other conservative slates emerged. Predictably, conservatives took some 57 percent of the seats, while reformists took only 7 percent and independents and minority candidates took 36 percent. In late May, Ali Larijani was reelected speaker, ensuring that the new parliament would continue to oppose Ahmadinejad and support Khamenei.

While conservatives loyal to Khamenei remained firmly in control, several urgent problems continued to threaten the Islamic regime in late 2012. Most importantly, the harsh economic sanctions enacted by the United States and its allies (discussed below) were now having dire consequences, producing shortages and sharp price increases and threatening to push the economy into recession. Scattered strikes and rioting occurred as a result, despite the repressive climate. The United States and Israel apparently began carrying out a series of deadly covert operations against Iran. Kurdish and Baluch rebels remained active, though the security forces had substantially weakened them. And sharp tensions remained between reformists and conservatives and between pro- and anti-Ahmadinejad conservatives. Iran seems likely to face considerable turbulence in the coming years.

POLITICAL ENVIRONMENT

Geography

Iran is located in Southwest Asia, bounded to the north by the Caucasus region, the Caspian Sea, and the steppes of central Asia; to the south by the Persian Gulf and the Gulf of Oman; to the west by Turkey and Iraq; and to the east by Afghanistan and Pakistan. It is divided by two high mountain ranges: the Zagros, running from the northwestern part of the country to the southeast; and the Alborz, running from the northwest to the northeast, looping below the Caspian Sea. The Zagros range creates natural borders in western and southern Iran, marking the boundary between Iran's predominantly Persian population and their Arab neighbors. The Alborz range and the Caspian Sea create natural borders in northern Iran, separating it from the various ethnic groups that inhabit the Caucasus and central Asia. These natural borders have helped preserve Iran's unique identity through the ages, despite its vulnerable location at the crossroads of central Asia, south Asia, and the Middle East. Today they offer ample protection to the large majority of Iran's population located in the northern and central parts of the country from the various hostile powers located to the west and south.

The central region of Iran, bordered by the Zagros and Alborz ranges, is a high, arid plateau. The eastern part of this plateau features two large, barren deserts. The remainder supports limited agricultural activity and includes Tehran, Isfahan, and Mashad—Iran's three largest cities. North of the Alborz lies the lush Caspian coastal region, where plentiful rains support extensive rice cultivation and other crops. Across the Zagros to the southwest lies Iran's Khuzestan Province, a hot coastal plain that features Iran's only large river (the Karun), marshes, and most of the country's oil reserves. The Caspian and Persian Gulf coastal regions support fishing, shipping, and tourism. Most of Iran's border areas are lightly populated and have rough terrain, so smuggling is common in these areas.

Ethnicity and Religion

Iranian society is ethnically diverse. Persians are the largest ethnic group, comprising 61 percent of the population and dominating the central and eastern parts of the country. Persians are an Indo-European people whose language is based on Sanskrit, making it distantly related to most European languages. Most Iranians speak Persian, or Farsi, the largest of the Iranian (or Persianate) subfamily of languages. Persian contains many Arabic and Turkish loanwords but nevertheless is related to Kurdish, Tajik, Pashto, and other Iranian languages. Kurds comprise 10 percent of the population and live in the mountainous northwestern part of the country, bordering on the Kurdish regions of Turkey and Iraq. Iran's Lur and Baluch minorities also speak Iranian languages. Lurs comprise 6 percent of the population and live in western Iran. Baluchis comprise 2 percent and live in southeastern Iran, adjacent to the Baluch regions of Afghanistan and Pakistan.

Iran's second-largest ethnic group is Azeri Turks, who comprise 16 percent of the population, live mainly in the northwest, and speak the same Azeri Turkic language as the residents of Azerbaijan, just to the north. In recent decades, many Iranian Azeris have moved to Tehran and other cities elsewhere in the country, and there has been considerable intermarriage between Azeris and Persians. Another 2 percent of the population consists of the Turkic-speaking Turkmen, who live in northeastern Iran near the border with Turkmenistan, and Qashqais, who live in southern Iran near Shiraz. Around 2 percent of Iranians are ethnic Arabs, living mainly in Khuzestan and along the Persian Gulf coast. There are also small numbers of Armenians and Assyrians, living mainly in Tehran and other major cities.

Some 89 percent of Iranians are Shi'a Muslims—adherents of the largest minority branch of Islam, who believe that leadership of the Islamic community should have passed from Mohammad to his son-in-law, Ali, and his descendants. Shi'a Islam differs from the majority Sunni branch in having an elaborate clerical hierarchy, following a different school of Islamic law, and observing rather different rituals and practices. Iran's Safavid dynasty made Shi'a Islam the country's official religion in the 1500s, establishing a close connection between the country and this sect that persists today. Iraq, Bahrain, and Azerbaijan also have Shi'a majorities, and the most important Shi'a holy sites are located in Iraq. Lebanon, Saudi Arabia, Pakistan, and several other countries have significant Shi'a minorities, which maintain religious and political ties with their coreligionists in

Iran. Thus, Iran's Shi'a identity sets it apart from most other countries in the region and creates suspicions—sometimes justified—that it is meddling in their internal affairs.

Almost all of Iran's Persian and Turkic population are Shi'a. Some 9 percent of Iranians are Sunni Muslims, including the Baluchis and most Kurds. Iran's Armenian and Assyrian populations are Christian, mainly following the Armenian, Nestorian, or Chaldean rites. Iran has had a small Jewish population for over 2,500 years, though most have emigrated to Israel or the United States in recent decades. Iran also has a small population of Zoroastrians, whose faith dominated the country before the introduction of Islam. Finally, a small number of Iranians follow the Baha'i sect, which emerged in Iran in the mid-1800s. Baha'is are considered apostates by most Shi'a, producing frequent persecution and leading many to emigrate. By contrast, Iran's Christians, Jews, and Zoroastrians are free to practice their faiths and follow their own customs in matters of family law, and the constitution reserves several seats in parliament for them. Almost all Iranian Jews, Zoroastrians, and Baha'is are ethnic Persians.

Social Change

Driven mainly by economic development, Iran's social structure has changed tremendously since the mid-nineteenth century.

Roughly half of Iran's population consisted of tribal nomads in the early nineteenth century, typically living in tents, tending flocks of sheep and goats, migrating between summer and winter pastures, and maintaining distinctive tribal customs, dress, and folklore. Most nomads lived in extended family groups organized into loose federations headed by *khans* (chiefs), which protected and exercised authority over their members and maintained considerable independence from the central government. Almost all of Iran's nomads became sedentary during the late nineteenth and twentieth centuries, as economic development provided better opportunities for them in agriculture or in towns and cities and as the Pahlavi shahs forcibly disarmed and settled them. Only about 2 percent of Iranians now are fully nomadic, though considerably more maintain tribal cultural affiliations of some sort.

Most other Iranians were landless peasants in the early nineteenth century, usually working on agricultural estates and living near the subsistence level. As Iran's economy developed and provided new employment opportunities, many of these peasants moved to towns and cities, seeking better living standards. This rural-urban migration was especially rapid in the 1960s and 1970s, when oil revenue transformed the economy and the last shah's land-reform program pushed many peasants off the land. Iran's urban population grew from about 20 percent of the total in 1900 to 34 percent in 1960, 50 percent in 1980, and 71 percent today. About 10 percent of the country's population—7 to 8 million people—live in Tehran, the capital; another 10 percent live in the Tehran metropolitan area; and the cities of Mashad, Tabriz, Isfahan, and Shiraz each have more than 2 million residents.

Economic development also has transformed urban society in Iran. Modern industrial plants began to emerge in Iran's major cities and in the oil-producing areas of Khuzestan in the first few decades of the twentieth century, creating an industrial working class. In the same era, the expansion of the state bureaucracy, the creation of a modern educational system, and the growth of services such as journalism and banking began to create a modern middle class, which differed from the traditional middle class of shopkeepers and artisans in that its members had Western-style education and a more cosmopolitan outlook. In the post–World War II era, a modern upper class of businessmen, investors, and cronies of the royal court emerged, distinguished from the traditional upper class of wealthy landowners also by its Western education and relatively cosmopolitan outlook.

These changes in the structure of Iranian society shaped the main contours of Iranian politics during the twentieth century. The gradual emergence of a modern middle class propelled the constitutional movement of 1906, Reza Shah's modernization efforts, and the various secular nationalist and leftist movements that emerged from the 1940s through the 1960s. The industrial working class also helped propel nationalist and leftist movements. The modern upper class became the shah's main base of support in the 1960s and 1970s, though it was not strong or loyal enough to keep him in power. The emergence of these modern classes and their prominent role in both the shah's regime and the secular opposition increasingly aggravated Iran's traditional classes, creating tensions that led to the 1978–1979 revolution and gave the revolution its Islamist character. The extensive rural-urban migration of the 1960s and 1970s brought large numbers of poorly educated, deeply religious people into Iran's cities, providing a large mass of foot soldiers for the revolution and further strengthening its Islamist character. Many members of the modern upper and middle classes emigrated to Western countries after the revolution, creating a large, prosperous Iranian diaspora community.

Two other social trends have had a big impact on Iranian politics in recent decades. First, a sharp drop in Iran's infant-mortality rate and a persistently high birthrate created a large baby boom generation born in the 1970s and 1980s, before Iran's leaders had embraced family planning in the 1990s and 2000s. These young Iranians generally are better educated than older Iranians and better connected to the outside world through the Internet and contacts with Iranians living abroad. They are also too young to have been caught up in the idealism of the 1978–1979 revolution and the early years of the Islamic regime, experiencing instead the economic stagnation and cultural restrictions that followed; so they are generally less loyal to the Islamic regime and more interested in reforming or abolishing it than older Iranians. This large cohort of young Iranians provided the main social base for the reformist movement that emerged in the late 1990s and the 2009 Green Movement. Second, rapid increases in educational opportunities for women both before and after the revolution have led women to become increasingly involved in politics in recent years. Many Iranian women resent the restrictions imposed on them under the Islamic regime, so women also strongly supported the reformist movement in the late 1990s and the Green Movement.

Political Culture

Iran's history and social structure have shaped its political culture in numerous ways.

Iran's long, rich history and frequent foreign intervention during the past two centuries have made most Iranians deeply nationalistic and wary of foreign interference. These sentiments produced strong support for nationalist movements in Iran from the late 1940s through the early 1960s and led many Iranians to consider the last shah a puppet of foreign powers. The Islamist movements that emerged in the 1970s emphasized similar themes, expressing their opposition to foreign influence and the shah's foreign connections in language that ranged from the anti-imperialism of the Mojahedin-e Khalq to the culturally oriented, often xenophobic views of many traditionalists. These themes have remained central to Iran's foreign policy discourse ever since the establishment of the Islamic republic.

Shi'a Islam's strong emphasis on martyrdom has been a recurring theme in Iran's modern history. Even before the upsurge of Islamist movements in the 1970s, figures like Mohammad Mosaddeq were widely revered by secularists and Islamists alike for their willingness to make sacrifices for a just cause. Martyrdom and morality then became central motifs in the discourse of the 1978–1979 revolution and the Islamic regime it spawned, leading many Iranians to sacrifice their lives willingly during the revolution and the Iran-Iraq War.

Another recurring theme in Iran's modern history has been an emphasis on political pluralism, reflecting not only the growing importance of the modern middle class but also the country's Shi'a traditions, which include a tendency to support multiple religious leaders and norms of legalism, inclusiveness, and consensus building among the clergy. This emphasis on pluralism has led all major popular movements in modern Iran to claim to speak in the name of the Iranian people and advocate political freedom, constitutionalism, and representative institutions. These pluralistic themes have been stressed not only by avowedly democratic, secularist movements like the National Front but also by Islamist movements like the Liberation Movement, Khatami's reformist movement, and even the revolutionary Islamist followers of Ayatollah Khomeini. As a result, before the election crisis of 2009, Iran's Islamic regime featured an unusual mixture of authoritarian and democratic features, including a powerful repressive apparatus and institutions that ensure clerical control but also relatively free elections, a fairly open political climate, and often intense contestation among the diverse factions of the Islamist elite.

Despite the many pressures on Iranian society since the early nineteenth century, family bonds remain very strong and have a substantial impact on patterns of social and political organization. As Iran's economy has developed and its citizens have become more mobile, these family bonds have been replaced in part by connections based on childhood friendships or relationships established in universities, seminaries, or public service. These family bonds and other close connections have a considerable impact on Iranian politics. Politicians often rely heavily on their children, siblings, and old friends for assistance, and the latter benefit considerably from these connections. Political organizations also rely heavily on connections of this sort, giving them a personalistic character. Iranians judge politicians very much on the basis of family background and other personal connections and rely on their own relatives and close friends for connections and advice. As a result, Iranian politics has strong patrimonial and clannish tendencies, and the country's civil society institutions are fairly weak.

Finally, political culture often differs considerably from one segment of Iranian society to another, making it difficult to speak of a single Iranian political culture. Most importantly, the political culture of the modern segment of Iranian society differs substantially from that of traditionalists, who are generally more religious, less educated, less cosmopolitan, more reliant on personal connections, and often deeply concerned about the decline of Islam and the spread of Western culture and values in Iran. The sharply different outlooks of the modern and traditional segments of society were a fundamental cause of the 1978–1979 revolution and have remained the most important theme in Iranian politics ever since, underlying the clashes between Islamic leftists and conservatives in the 1980s, centrists and conservatives in the early 1990s, and reformists and conservatives since the late 1990s. The large Iranian diaspora community that emerged after the revolution is especially modernist in its outlook and very antagonistic toward the conservatives.

Another important political cultural division exists between younger and older Iranians. As discussed above, Iranians born during the 1970s and 1980s are better educated, more cosmopolitan, less committed to the Islamic regime, and more deeply affected by the economic stagnation and cultural restrictions of recent decades. These young Iranians strongly favor increased political and cultural freedom and greater economic opportunity. While most are quite religious, many oppose extensive clerical involvement in government. They also have little interest in socialism and other secular ideologies. Many young Iranians are strongly attracted to Western culture, which they follow avidly on the Internet and satellite television. A large majority at first enthusiastically supported President Khatami but then grew disillusioned with the reformists' failures. Consequently, while most young people strongly favor reform, many are apathetic and cynical about politics. Indeed, in one of the great ironies of the Islamic regime, many young Iranians today dream of emigrating to the West.

Economic Conditions

Iran's economy was based mainly on agriculture before the 1920s, though trade and production of textiles, carpets, and other handicrafts were important activities as well. Iran's large nomadic population produced most of the country's meat and dairy products, using land unsuitable for farming. Oil was first discovered in Iran in 1901 and began to play an important role in the economy in the 1920s and 1930s, when it helped finance Reza Shah's development efforts. Reza Shah's key economic achievements during this period included building a nationwide network of roads and railroads; establishing factories to produce textiles, cement, and other products; creating a modern banking system; and establishing a modern educational system that produced a new class of modern businessmen, managers, and public officials.

Iran's oil revenue began to grow rapidly in the late 1950s as a result of production increases and the higher profits resulting from the 1954 oil agreement. Oil prices then increased eightfold from 1970 to 1974, creating another huge increase in oil revenue. Iran's oil revenue went into the state treasury, where it helped finance the state's operating budget and a series of five-year development plans. Through these mechanisms, oil revenue generated a huge expansion of Iran's economy, with real gross domestic product (GDP) growing by an average of 9.8 percent annually in the 1960s and 12.1 percent from 1970 to 1976, after which it stagnated for several years and then declined sharply as the revolution unfolded. Although much of this growth was in the oil and gas sector, the manufacturing sector grew by an average of 11.5 percent annually in the 1960s and 16.4 percent from 1970 to 1976, when large steel mills, automobile plants, and other factories were built. The service sector grew by an annual average of 8.1 percent in the 1960s and 18.3 percent from 1970 to 1976, while the agricultural sector stagnated. The oil boom also had several adverse consequences that helped fuel the 1978–1979 revolution, including higher inflation, shortages, corruption, and rural-urban migration.

The revolution and the Iran-Iraq War together had a devastating impact on Iran's economy. Oil production fell sharply, and domestic consumption of oil products grew substantially. As a result, by 1981 Iran's oil revenue had fallen to 16 percent of its prerevolution high, despite much higher oil prices, and it remained below 43 percent of this high throughout the 1980s and below 61 percent of it in the 1990s. This sharp decline in oil revenue and higher wartime military spending substantially reduced public investment. The revolution and the war also sharply reduced private investment, damaged production facilities and infrastructure, disrupted foreign borrowing and imports of critical goods, and led many entrepreneurs and skilled workers to emigrate. These factors produced a 21 percent decline in real GDP from its peak in 1976 to its 1988 level. With the high birthrates of the 1980s, real GDP per capita fell by 48 percent between 1976 and 1988. In 2009 it finally returned to its 1976 level.

Since the late 1980s, Iran's leaders have carried out a series of development plans whose main goal has been to stimulate economic growth and employment by liberalizing the economy and expanding non-oil industries. None of these plans have been very successful.

The first plan covered the period from 1989 to 1993 and was drawn up in consultation with the International Monetary Fund (IMF). It faced strong opposition from Islamic leftists in parliament, who feared that privatization, subsidy cuts, exchange rate liberalization, and tight monetary policy would hurt the poor. Most of its key goals were never achieved. In addition, the Rafsanjani government undertook massive foreign borrowing and a sharp expansion of imports in conjunction with the first plan, putting severe pressure on Iran's exchange rate and foreign reserves and driving inflation higher.

The Islamic leftists lost control of parliament in 1992, raising hopes that economic reform might move forward. The second development plan (1994–1999) had very ambitious objectives, including exchange rate liberalization, banking reform, fiscal and monetary restraint, subsidy cuts, and privatization. However, opposition from the conservative-controlled parliament and lower world oil prices prevented implementation of many of the second plan's objectives. As a result, Iran's economy stagnated during the second-plan period, barely growing in per capita terms.

Most Islamic leftists became much more moderate during the mid-1990s, embracing not only political liberalization but also economic reform. Consequently, after his election in 1997, President Khatami continued to implement the reforms embodied in the second plan. His main economic achievement was to adopt a unified, floating exchange rate system. The Khatami government also drew up a third development plan (2000–2004), which called for further privatization, subsidy cuts, increased foreign investment, an expansion of non-oil exports, and efforts to increase tax collection and reduce bureaucracy. However, conservatives blocked key elements of the third plan before the reformists gained control over parliament in 2000 and worked to undermine the plan as it was being implemented. Moreover, many of the plan's goals were unrealistic. As a result, the third plan also failed to achieve most of its objectives. Nevertheless, due partly to higher oil revenue, Iran's economic performance was substantially better during the third-plan period than in previous years, with real per capita growth averaging 3.8 percent and inflation averaging 16 percent. Unemployment, however, remained close to 12 percent.

President Ahmadinejad campaigned for the 2005 election on an economic populist platform. Once in office he implemented this platform, sharply increasing public spending, pushing interest rates below the inflation rate, allowing consumer-goods subsidies to grow even further, and financing these efforts from Iran's rapidly growing oil windfall. He fired several top officials who warned that his policies were inflationary and dismantled the Management and Planning Organization, which for decades had overseen Iran's macroeconomic and development policy. As predicted, these actions increased inflation, which reached 29 percent in late 2008. Monetary tightening then brought inflation back to single-digit levels in 2009 and 2010.

As the election-related turmoil of 2009 began to subside, Ahmadinejad and his opponents in parliament began an effort to trim the vast array of subsidies on energy, food, and other products, worth an estimated $100 billion per year. They agreed on a plan to replace most subsidies with cash payments to families, beginning in late 2010. Critics warned that this plan would sharply increase inflation and hurt the poor.

Beginning in 2010, the United States and its allies sharply increased economic sanctions on Iran, hoping to stop its nuclear program. Together with the subsidy-reduction plan and Ahmadinejad's populist economic measures, these actions had a devastating impact on Iran's economy in 2012: oil exports fell by more than 60 percent, the exchange rate fell by 70 percent, shortages of imported parts crippled the manufacturing sector, unemployment grew, and inflation again rose above 20 percent. The IMF predicted that Iran would slip into recession in 2013, unemployment would top 15 percent, and inflation would remain above 20 percent. These conditions could have a substantial impact on Iranian politics.

POLITICAL STRUCTURE

The 1978–1979 revolution swept away Iran's monarchy and most other political institutions. Ayatollah Khomeini then appointed Mehdi Bazargan to head a transitional government, whose main responsibilities were to oversee the process of writing a new constitution and govern Iran until this constitution could be implemented. However, radical Islamists created a series of additional institutions during this period that overshadowed the transitional government, leading many observers to describe them as a "parallel government." These included the Revolutionary Council, revolutionary courts, revolutionary committees, and the Islamic Revolutionary Guard Corps. Bazargan resigned mainly because these parallel institutions made it impossible for him to govern effectively.

Radical Islamists gained control over the constitutional assembly and used it to write a constitution embodying the principle of *velayat-e faqih* (guardianship of the jurist), which Khomeini had developed in his seminal book *Islamic Government*. Under this principle, high-ranking Shi'a clerics would oversee the state apparatus to ensure that public policy conformed with Islamic law, though they would not necessarily serve in executive positions. The new constitution was approved in a December 1979 popular referendum. The Revolutionary Council was soon dissolved, and the revolutionary courts and committees were integrated into the new judicial and security apparatuses. The Revolutionary Guard Corps was greatly expanded, eventually including its own navy and air force and a large paramilitary force, the Basij (Mobilization).

The new constitution created two key institutions that enabled Shi'a clerics to oversee the state, as envisioned by Khomeini. First, it created the office of *faqih* (jurist), commonly known as the (supreme) leader (*rahbar*), which would be occupied by a *marja-e taqlid* (source of emulation), the highest rank of the Shi'a clergy. The leader would be chosen and overseen by the Assembly of Experts (Majles-e Khobregan), a popularly elected council of Shi'a clerics. The leader was empowered to set general policy guidelines, supervise policy implementation, appoint the head of the judiciary, dismiss the president, and oversee the armed forces. This position was created for Khomeini, who was succeeded by Ayatollah Ali Khamenei in June 1989. Khomeini and Khamenei gradually built up a large staff, including policy advisers, representatives in all major government and religious bodies, an office to oversee Friday prayer sermons, and the heads of various parastatal foundations and organizations. Second, the constitution created the Council of Guardians (Shura-ye Negahban), consisting of six Shi'a clerics and six laypeople empowered to interpret the constitution, judge whether legislation was compatible with Islamic law, and supervise elections. The six lay members are selected by parliament from nominees proposed by the head of the judiciary, while the six clerical members are appointed by the leader.

The constitution also created a directly elected president and unicameral parliament, whose seats are allocated to Iran's provinces in proportion to population size. In addition, five seats are reserved for Iran's Christian, Jewish, and Zoroastrian minorities. The Council of Guardians oversees presidential and parliamentary elections, which are held every four years. The council inevitably vetoes many minor candidates and all candidates who do not fully support the Islamic regime, but generally it approves enough candidates for each position to ensure some competition among the main factions supporting the regime. It also generally does not interfere in the voting process itself, though the 2009 election apparently was manipulated extensively. The council also frequently vetoes parliamentary legislation, limiting the influence of parliament and often creating severe tensions. Finally, the 1979 constitution also created the position of prime minister but failed to delineate clearly how power would be divided between this office and the presidency.

During the 1980s, it became increasingly apparent that the many checks and balances embodied in the constitution were paralyzing the government. Ayatollah Khomeini tried to eliminate one source of paralysis in February 1988 by creating the Council for the Discernment of Expediency (Majma-e Tashkhis-e Maslehat-e Nezam), which was empowered to resolve disputes over legislation between parliament and the Guardian Council. Although the Expediency Council was fairly effective, disputes continued to emerge between these two bodies, and several other sources of paralysis remained. Another problem that emerged as Khomeini's health deteriorated in the late 1980s was that no cleric with the rank of *marja-e taqlid* strongly supported the Islamic regime and therefore was a suitable replacement for Khomeini as leader.

To resolve these problems, Khomeini created a panel in April 1989 to study and revise the constitution. This panel made several major changes. It eliminated the position of prime minister, concentrating executive authority in the hands of the president. It spelled out the responsibilities of the Expediency Council. It eliminated the leader's ability to dismiss the president and the requirement that the leader be a *marja*. It also created a Supreme National Security Council to oversee foreign policy. These changes were approved in an August 1989 referendum.

The head of the judiciary, who is appointed by the leader, has far-reaching powers, including the power to appoint the prosecutor-general, all judges, and all Supreme Court justices; the power to draft legislation affecting the legal system; and oversight over all aspects of the judicial system. The minister of justice is responsible mainly for administrative matters. The constitution bans torture; it guarantees freedom of the press and assembly, except when this violates "the principles of Islam"; and it allows Sunni Muslims and the Christian, Jewish, and Zoroastrian communities (though not Baha'is) to practice their own faiths freely and to be governed by their faiths in personal-status matters. There are special courts for cases involving the security forces, government officials, the clergy, the press, and national security matters.

Iran's security forces include the regular armed forces, the Revolutionary Guard Corps, the Basij, the Ministry of Intelligence and Security (MOIS), and the Law Enforcement Forces (LEF), which consist of the national police, prison guards, border guards, and rural paramilitary forces. The MOIS is responsible to the president; the other branches are responsible to the leader. Revolutionary Guard and Basij personnel are specially selected and indoctrinated to ensure their loyalty to the Islamic regime, and these forces have specialized units for crowd control. The Revolutionary Guard, Basij, and LEF sometimes work with informal gangs of thugs to attack reformists or opponents of the Islamic regime.

The 1979 constitution created five levels of regional and local government: provinces, subprovinces, districts, cities, and villages. It also called for popularly elected councils to govern these bodies. This latter provision was not implemented until 1999, when Khatami and the reformists promoted it in the hope that these councils would nurture politicians oriented toward democracy. Since that time, elections have been held every four years for municipal councils in cities and villages. These councils appoint mayors for their jurisdictions and representatives to provincial, subprovincial, and district councils. Provincial governors-general are appointed by the interior ministry and, in turn, appoint the heads of subprovinces and districts.

The constitution also allowed for the establishment of political parties, provided they support the principles of the Islamic regime. This provision also was not implemented until the late 1990s, though several party-like organizations existed before then. Legislation authorizing the creation of parties was adopted in 1998, and many parties emerged in the following years. The main reformist parties were the Executives of Construction Party (Hezb-e Kargozaran-e Sazendegi), which had close ties to former president Rafsanjani, and the Islamic Iran Participation Party (Hezb-e Mosharakat-e Iran-e Islami), which was banned in early 2010. The main conservative parties were the Militant Clerics Association (Jameh-ye Ruhaniyat-e Mobarez) and Islamic Coalition Party (Hezb-e Motalafeh-ye Islami), which continue to operate. The Liberation Movement and several other Islamic modernist and secular nationalist parties were officially outlawed but allowed to operate on a limited basis before the 2009 election. None of these parties were particularly popular or effective.

Several other civil society organizations emerged in the 1990s. The Office for Consolidating Unity (Daftar-e Takhim-e Vahdat) was a prominent reformist student organization. The Labor House (Khaneh-ye Kargar) was a pro-reformist, government-sponsored labor federation. Both were heavily suppressed and have become inactive. The Supporters of the Party of God (Ansar-e Hizballah) is a vigilante group that specializes in attacking reformists, often in cooperation with the security forces. Various other professional, student, women's, and religious organizations emerged in the 1990s, with some supporting one or another political faction and others remaining apolitical.

In addition, a wide range of parties and civil society organizations exist among the large Iranian exile communities in North America, Europe, and elsewhere. The most important is the Mojahedin-e Khalq, which had a large guerrilla force based in Iraq after the early 1980s, secret networks inside Iran, and a large network of supporters in other countries. The Iraqi government had largely dismantled its guerrilla force by 2012. Various exile monarchist, nationalist, and leftist organizations exist as well, though none are very important.

Another aspect of civil society in Iran is the news and entertainment media. From mid-1979 through the 1980s, Iran's newspapers were heavily restricted, providing one-sided news coverage and a narrow range of opinion. This changed in the early 1990s, when the Rafsanjani government allowed several critical newspapers and magazines to appear. The print media flourished during the first few years of Khatami's presidency, with some newspapers going so far as to accuse top officials of complicity in murder. However, hard-liners in the judiciary began to crack down on the press, closing the most critical newspapers and imprisoning or assaulting editors and journalists. This crackdown increased sharply after the February 2000 parliamentary elections, when dozens of newspapers were closed, and has increased further since then. In 2011–2012, Reporters Without Borders ranked Iran 175 out of 179 countries on its Press Freedom Index.

The domestic radio and television media are controlled by Islamic Republic of Iran Broadcasting, a state agency based in the leader's office. Its programming is narrow and dull and generally reflects the views of the leader. However, many Iranians listen to Persian-language radio broadcasts beamed to Iran by Britain, the United States, and other countries or watch the many Persian-language satellite television stations broadcast to Iran from abroad. These broadcasts provide a wide range of programming, giving most Iranians access to diverse sources of news, commentary, and entertainment. The government makes some effort to block these foreign broadcasts by jamming them and outlawing satellite antennas, but these measures have little effect. Iranians also increasingly use the Internet through Internet cafes or computers at home or in offices. This gives them access to the many Persian-language websites featuring news, commentary, and entertainment and enables e-mail contact with friends and relatives living abroad. The government has increasingly blocked access to various Internet sites and claims to be developing an "Islamic Internet" that would likely prevent most Iranians from accessing foreign Internet sites altogether.

Before the 2009 election crisis, Iran's Islamic regime contained some democratic elements and was more representative than many other regimes in the region. The Council of Guardians sharply restricted elections for the presidency, parliament, and other bodies, but these elections offered voters considerable opportunity to express their preferences, both by voting and by abstaining. The formal powers of these elected bodies were constrained by the Guardian Council and other institutions and their authority was overshadowed by that of the leader, but they nevertheless exercised substantial influence, both formally and informally. The judiciary and much of the security apparatus were not responsible to popularly elected bodies, but repression was not severe. Political parties, the media, and other civil society institutions could not express opposition to the Islamic regime and were restricted in other ways, but they were more open and more numerous than in many neighboring countries. Indeed, Iranians could express their views quite openly, and the country's leaders clearly were concerned about, and responsive to, trends in public opinion.

These democratic features were suspended and perhaps eliminated permanently during the crisis that began with the 2009 presidential election. That election was apparently manipulated extensively, raising strong doubts about the prospects for future elections. Repression increased substantially after the 2009 election, with many thousands arrested, torture widespread, all reformist and centrist leaders still in prison or facing severe restrictions, and civil society organizations rendered largely impotent. Many Iranians live in a climate of fear. The country's conservative leaders seem intent on imposing their vision of an Islamic regime on the populace. Supreme Leader Khamenei has orchestrated this process, relying heavily on the security forces, the judiciary, and his bickering allies in the executive and legislative branches of government. It is unclear how long this era of repression will last or what sort of political structure will emerge from it.

POLITICAL DYNAMICS

Iran has changed substantially since the Islamic regime was established in 1979.

The early 1980s were a time of revolutionary social transformation. The radical Islamist leadership undertook a comprehensive effort to "Islamicize" Iranian society in this period, restructuring the country's laws and political institutions; turning schools, religious institutions, and the media into instruments of indoctrination; and forcing all Iranians to observe strict Islamic standards of dress and behavior. To accomplish this transformation, the radicals sought to mobilize their supporters with inflammatory rhetoric and dramatic actions like the US embassy hostage crisis and the war with Iraq. They also had to neutralize not only their political opponents but also many secularized Iranians, who strongly opposed these measures. As a result, repression was fairly high during this period, though it did not approach the levels reached in the Soviet Union and China after their revolutions. Although many Iranians opposed the Islamic regime, many others supported it, giving it a populist character.

Much of the revolutionary fervor that animated this period dissipated in the mid-1980s, and popular unrest grew considerably as a result of the war with Iraq, continuing repression, and economic deterioration. When Rafsanjani became president in 1989, he responded to these changes by initiating a period of moderation. His strategy was to reduce unrest by revitalizing the economy and loosening cultural restrictions while keeping the political system largely intact. As discussed above, opposition first from Islamic leftists and then from conservatives blocked many of Rafsanjani's economic reforms, producing anemic economic growth in the early and mid-1990s.

Rafsanjani's failure to revitalize the economy led many Iranians to conclude that more extensive change was necessary, though most apparently did not want to eliminate the Islamic regime altogether. In 1997, this discontent led many Iranians to support the candidacy of Mohammad Khatami. Two important societal changes helped pave the way for Khatami's victory. First, the baby boom generation mentioned above was coming of age in the mid-1990s, producing a large cohort of young people who were more sophisticated than their elders and had not developed strong attachments to the Islamic regime by participating in the revolutionary upheaval or the war with Iraq. Second, Iranian women, who had made greater sacrifices than men under the Islamic regime and whose education levels had increased sharply, had become more politicized. These trends produced a large constituency for Khatami's reforms in 1997.

Khatami's landslide victory, the reformists' overwhelming success in the 2000 parliamentary elections, and Khatami's strong reelection in 2001 demonstrated that a large majority of Iranians wanted fundamental change. However, the conservatives still controlled key political institutions and used them to block most of Khatami's reforms. As a result, many Iranians became disillusioned with Khatami and the reformists, regarding them as ineffective or even insincere in their promises of reform. The ramifications of this discontent first emerged in the 2003 municipal council elections, when sharply lower turnout by pro-reformist voters led to the defeat of most reformist candidates. Much the same happened in the 2004 elections.

The final blow came in 2005, when Ahmadinejad defeated his reformist and centrist opponents. In the first round of voting, the three reformist candidates together took 35 percent of the vote, the centrist (Rafsanjani) took 21 percent, and the three conservatives together took only 39 percent, indicating that Ahmadinejad's victory did not reflect a sharp increase in support for the conservatives. Rather, his victory was due to continuing popular disillusionment with the reformists, widespread opposition to Ahmadinejad's second-round opponent (Rafsanjani), and Ahmadinejad's populist appeal. The elections of 2006 and 2008 demonstrated that disillusionment with the reformists remained high and that Ahmadinejad's hard-line views and style were not very popular.

The likely manipulation of election results in 2009, the reformists' boycott in 2012, and the absence of reliable polls in Iran make it difficult to assess the implications of these elections. However, Iran clearly has been deeply polarized since the crisis of 2009, with a large bloc of Iranians strongly opposed to the views of Ahmadinejad and Khamenei—and many opposed to the Islamic regime itself—while another large bloc continues to support the Islamic regime and Khamenei, if not Ahmadinejad. It is impossible to judge the size of these two blocs with any certainty. The latter bloc clearly has the upper hand for now, but the former could well reassert itself in the coming years, perhaps bringing fundamental change to Iran.

FOREIGN POLICY

Before the 1978–1979 revolution, Iran was closely allied with the United States and becoming increasingly Westernized. The various factions that seized power in 1979 generally opposed these trends but nevertheless held very different views on how Iran's foreign policy should be conducted. Consequently, disputes over foreign policy were a major focus of the power struggles that emerged after the revolution, and the character of Iran's foreign policy has closely paralleled its domestic political dynamics.

Iran's foreign policy was highly confrontational during the first decade of the Islamic regime. Although Prime Minister Bazargan wanted to change Iran's pro-Western orientation, he wanted to do so in ways that would avoid confrontation. Most of Bazargan's radical Islamist opponents were intensely anti-Western and wanted to break off relations with the United States, and many wanted violent confrontation with the West. Moreover, the radical Islamists were encouraged by their radical leftist rivals, whose anti-Western views were equally intense. As a result, the radical Islamists and radical leftists opposed Bazargan's nonconfrontational foreign policy and undercut him at every opportunity. This struggle culminated in the November 1979 seizure of the US embassy by radical Islamist students. The radical Islamists used the resulting hostage crisis to drive Bazargan from power and push Iran's foreign policy in a more confrontational direction, hoping to humiliate the United States, position Iran as the leader of a region-wide radical Islamist movement, and mobilize additional support for their efforts to carry out revolutionary change at home.

The central focus of Iran's confrontational foreign policy during this period was hostility toward the United States. This was manifested not only in the hostage crisis, which lasted more than a year and drove President Jimmy Carter from office, but also in harsh anti-American rhetoric and indirect attacks on US targets. Iran's leaders routinely called the United States the "great Satan" and chanted "Death to America" at meetings and rallies. Aware that Iran was too weak to attack the United States directly, they undertook a variety of indirect assaults. Most importantly, they encouraged and assisted radical Islamist terrorists in Lebanon who bombed a US marine base and the US embassy (twice) in Beirut, killing some three hundred US and Lebanese citizens and taking thirteen Americans hostage, two of whom died in captivity. They also assisted terrorists who hijacked US airliners and a cruise ship, killing several Americans, and laid mines targeting US warships and US-flagged commercial vessels in the Persian Gulf. The United States responded by backing Iraq in the Iran-Iraq War, attacking Iranian naval vessels in the Gulf, and undertaking covert operations against the Islamic regime.

Iran also carried out or facilitated attacks against various US allies in the region and in Europe during this period. Its leaders made extensive efforts to export their Islamic revolution, especially in Lebanon, where they created and assisted the radical Islamist group Hizballah, and in Bahrain, Kuwait, and Saudi Arabia. Although Iran's allies in these countries did not manage to foment revolutions, they caused severe problems for their

US-backed governments and carried out frequent attacks against Iran's enemies. In particular, Hizballah and other radical Shi'a forces attacked not only US targets in Lebanon but also Israeli occupation forces and British and French peacekeeping forces, killing hundreds, and they seized many hostages. Iranian officials repeatedly fomented unrest during the annual Hajj pilgrimage to Mecca in the mid-1980s, leaving hundreds dead and severely embarrassing the Saudi government.

Iran's biggest efforts to export revolution and foment unrest were directed at Iraq. Iranian officials made extensive efforts to trigger a Shi'a uprising in Iraq, both before and after the September 1980 Iraqi invasion, and their July 1982 invasion of Iraq was aimed at toppling its secularist government and establishing an Islamic republic. Although Iraq certainly was not a US ally, Iran claimed it was and portrayed its invasion of Iraq partly as an effort to drive the United States and Israel out of the region.

Iran's confrontational, anti-Western posture during the 1980s left it very isolated and desperately in need of allies to sell it arms and provide other forms of assistance. This led Iran's radical Islamist leaders to establish close relationships with several very unlikely countries. During the first few years of the Islamic regime, Iran purchased large quantities of weapons from Israel, which was the only country willing to flaunt US efforts to block the flow of US-made arms to Iran at this time. These Israeli arms sales eventually led to the 1985–1986 Iran-Contra Affair, in which Iran bought arms directly from the United States. Iran also established close relations in the early 1980s with Syria, gaining an important ally in the Arab world. This left Iran's leaders in the uncomfortable position of being closely allied with a country ruled by the same secularist Ba'th Party they were trying to overthrow in Iraq and remaining silent while Syria's leaders carried out a brutal crackdown on their Muslim Brotherhood opponents in 1982. Iran also bought large quantities of arms during this period from China and North Korea, whose Communist regimes were avowedly atheistic.

As the radical phase of the Islamic regime ended, Iran's foreign policy became increasingly contradictory, with radicals seeking to maintain a confrontational, anti-Western posture and moderates hoping to ease the country's isolation in order to concentrate on reconstruction. Iran's July 1988 agreement to stop the war with Iraq ended its most ambitious effort to export revolution and produced considerable optimism that its foreign policy would become more moderate. However, in February 1989, Ayatollah Khomeini denounced Salman Rushdie and called for Muslims to kill him, creating severe tension with Europe. Iran also began a more concerted effort to assassinate Iranian exile opposition activists, which ultimately claimed scores of victims in Europe and elsewhere. Nevertheless, despite these hostile actions, President Rafsanjani began to make overtures to the West, apparently hoping this would facilitate his economic reform program. Most importantly, he indicated that Iran would help gain the release of US and other hostages still being held in Lebanon in exchange for better relations with the West. The last of these hostages was released in 1992. Iran also stayed out of the 1990–1991 Gulf War and reestablished diplomatic relations with Morocco and Saudi Arabia during this period.

Iran's foreign policy remained contradictory during the mid-1990s. It maintained its close connections with Hizballah. Iran and Hizballah apparently cooperated in bombing the Israeli embassy and a Jewish cultural center in Argentina in 1992 and 1994 and the Khobar Towers US military complex in Saudi Arabia in 1996, killing many innocent Argentines and US military personnel. Iran also helped foment Shi'a unrest in Bahrain and cooperated closely with radical Islamist Palestinian organizations and the radical Islamist government in Sudan during this period. Iran's program of assassinating exile activists continued, and it worked to develop nuclear weapons and medium-range missiles in the mid-1990s. Nevertheless, Rafsanjani at the same time continued to make overtures toward the United States, most notably by reaching an agreement with the US oil company Conoco to develop a large Iranian natural gas field. The Bill Clinton administration rejected Rafsanjani's overtures, blocking this agreement and expanding US economic sanctions on Iran.

An important turning point in Iran's foreign policy came in late 1996 and early 1997. After the Khobar Towers bombing, US and Saudi officials confronted Iran with evidence of its involvement and exposed a large number of Iranian intelligence officers operating abroad, making clear that they would take harsher action if Iran undertook additional attacks of this sort. In early 1997, a German court ruled that top Iranian officials had been involved in the 1989 assassination of four Iranian Kurdish dissidents in Germany, greatly embarrassing Iran and leading most European Union (EU) countries to withdraw their ambassadors from Iran. These two events seem to have enabled the moderates to wrest control over foreign policy from the radicals: Iran's direct involvement in terrorist attacks against Western targets and its assassinations of Iranian exiles abruptly ended in early 1997.

By the time President Khatami was elected in May 1997, many reformists had concluded that Iran should normalize its relations with the United States and most other countries, though not with Israel. Accordingly, during his first few months in office, Khatami repeatedly called for better relations with the United States. Most conservatives still opposed the United States and were alarmed by Khatami's actions. In January 1998, Supreme Leader Khamenei declared his opposition to rapid rapprochement with the United States, which he described as Iran's enemy. US officials at first reacted cautiously to Khatami's overtures, waiting until June 1998 to reciprocate. By this time opposition from Khamenei and his allies made it impossible for Khatami to move forward. Nevertheless, until the end of the Clinton administration, US officials made concerted efforts to improve relations with Iran.

Although Khatami did not manage to forge rapprochement with the United States, he did establish better relations with many other countries, continuing trends begun under Rafsanjani. Khatami soon negotiated an agreement under which all EU members returned their ambassadors to Iran. In September 1998, his government promised Britain it would not enforce the death threat against Salman Rushdie, eliminating a major source of tension with Europe. Iran's economic ties with Europe grew rapidly thereafter.

Iran's relations with most of its neighbors improved as well. In December 1997, Crown Prince Abdullah of Saudi Arabia visited Iran to attend the Organization of the Islamic Conference summit. Khatami then sent Rafsanjani to visit Saudi Arabia a few months later, and the two countries agreed to normalize relations. Iran forged better ties with most of the other Persian Gulf Arab countries as well, though its relationship with the United Arab Emirates remained strained over their conflicting claims to three strategically important islands in the Gulf. Iran also held talks with archfoe Iraq, and the two countries exchanged their last remaining prisoners of war. Iran continued to enjoy good relations with Pakistan, Turkey, and most of the countries to its north, though its relations with Azerbaijan remained strained over the latter's claims to Iran's Azeri region. The only neighbor that Iran had hostile relations with during this period was Afghanistan, which was ruled by the hard-line, anti-Shi'a Taliban faction. The Taliban were fighting bitterly at this time against factions in northern and western Afghanistan that had close ethnic and political ties to Iran. In August 1998, the Taliban killed several Iranians working with these factions, bringing the two countries to the brink of war.

Elsewhere in the region, Iran maintained its close relationships with Syria, Hizballah, and the radical Islamist Palestinian organizations Hamas and Islamic Jihad. However, it also worked diligently to improve its relations with Egypt, which had been severely strained since the early days of the Islamic regime, and with other moderate Arab countries. Iran's relations with Sudan became much more distant after the radical Islamist leaders of that country were deposed in 1999. Iran's relations with Israel even thawed slightly, with Khatami making several conciliatory statements and secret meetings occurring between the two sides.

Iran continued to develop close relations with Russia and various East Asian countries under Khatami. Russia agreed to finish building a nuclear power plant in Bushehr and sold Iran large amounts of military equipment. The two countries also worked closely to support anti-Taliban guerrillas in Afghanistan. Iran expanded its commercial relations with China, Japan, and other East Asian countries as well during this period.

As the reformists grew weaker in 2000 and 2001, Ayatollah Khamenei seems to have decided that Iran could begin to improve its relations with the United States, since the reformists would no longer benefit. Iran made several significant gestures toward the United States in this period. Iranian officials expressed sympathy for the victims of the September 11, 2001, terrorist attacks in New York and Washington. When the United States then attacked Afghanistan in an effort to destroy al-Qaida and its Taliban allies, Iran provided assistance to US forces. Iran also played a key role in helping the United States establish a friendly new government in Afghanistan.

As these events were unfolding, Israel intercepted a freighter carrying weapons from Iran to the Palestinian Authority, producing harsh criticism of Iran in the United States. Soon after, US President George W. Bush bitterly denounced Iran, describing it as part of an "axis of evil." Deeply angered by this statement after the conciliatory gestures they had made, Iran's leaders ended most cooperation with the United States. The Bush administration kept up its harsh criticism of Iran.

Another crisis began to unfold in 2002, when evidence emerged that Iran's nuclear program was more advanced than previously known and included activities aimed at building nuclear weapons. Britain, France, and Germany then began talks with Iran over the matter, and the EU suspended negotiations with Iran over trade and investment. In 2003, Iran agreed to suspend its efforts to enrich uranium and accepted other demands made by the International Atomic Energy Agency. However, additional concerns soon emerged, and Iran announced it would resume work on enrichment. In 2004, the Europeans negotiated a second agreement with Iran to suspend enrichment.

Ahmadinejad's election in 2005 produced yet another turning point in Iran's foreign policy. In August 2005, Iran rejected a major European proposal on the nuclear dispute and resumed enrichment work. In April 2006, Iran announced it had mastered the enrichment process, and by 2009 it had produced enough low-enriched uranium to make, if enriched further, a single nuclear weapon. Evidence also emerged in 2009 that Iran had built a second enrichment plant deep beneath layers of rock near the village of Fordo, where it was almost invulnerable to missile attack. Iran deployed dozens of missiles capable of hitting Israel and southeastern Europe in this period, though it could not yet produce nuclear warheads for these missiles. In 2006, the UN Security Council voted to impose a package of economic sanctions on Iran, aimed at stopping its nuclear program. It then approved additional sanctions in 2007, 2008, and 2010.

Iran's foreign policy became more aggressive in other ways as well. Ahmadinejad and other officials regularly denounced the United States and other Western countries. Ahmadinejad made a series of statements calling for the destruction of Israel and expressing doubt about the Holocaust. Iran continued to give extensive financial assistance and weapons to Hizballah and radical Palestinian factions. More ominously, beginning in early 2007, US officials charged that Iran had been supplying roadside bombs and other assistance to insurgents in Iraq, contributing to the deaths of hundreds of US soldiers. US forces arrested several Iranian operatives inside Iraq. Iranian officials repeatedly charged that Britain, Israel, and the United States were supporting terrorist attacks inside Iran by Arab, Baluch, Kurdish, and Mojahedin-e Khalq guerrillas, so Iran's actions in Iraq may have been a response to these attacks. Numerous unconfirmed reports about US support for these guerrillas appeared in the Western press as well. US and Israeli officials repeatedly hinted that they might use military force against Iran's nuclear facilities during this period. Iran indicated it would respond harshly to such an attack with missiles and other means, and Hizballah declared it would use its large missile stockpile and other means to retaliate for an attack on Iran.

Tensions between the United States and Iran eased somewhat in 2008 and 2009, with diplomats from the two countries holding bilateral talks for the first time in almost thirty years and US President Barack Obama making a series of conciliatory statements. No real progress was made in resolving the various outstanding disputes, however, and sharp tensions soon reemerged.

Beginning in June 2010, the United States imposed a series of additional unilateral economic sanctions aimed at stopping Iran's nuclear program, ending almost all bilateral trade and harming Iran in other ways. In January 2012, the EU voted to end all oil imports from Iran. Together with the UN sanctions of 2006 to 2010 and unilateral sanctions by other countries, these actions severely disrupted Iran's economy. In addition, the United States and/or Israel apparently carried out a series of deadly covert operations against Iran in this period, assassinating several Iranian nuclear scientists, launching cyberattacks that crippled Iran's nuclear-enrichment facilities, and possibly carrying out sabotage attacks against Iranian oil facilities. Iran apparently retaliated with a series of unsuccessful terrorist attacks against Israelis, a plot to assassinate the Saudi ambassador to the United States, and cyberattacks on Saudi oil facilities. Reports emerged that Iran was helping Taliban guerrillas in Afghanistan and rebels in Yemen and Senegal. Iran also began to help the Syrian government in its brutal effort to suppress a popular uprising in 2011–2012. Although another round of negotiations over Iran's nuclear program was scheduled to begin in late 2012, the prospects for better relations between Iran and the West seemed very remote.

BIBLIOGRAPHY

Standard reference works on Iran include the seven-volume *Cambridge History of Iran* (Cambridge: Cambridge University Press, 1968–1991) and *Encyclopedia Iranica* (Costa Mesa, CA: Mazda Publications, 1992–present), also available at www.iranica.com. See also Ali Ansari, ed., *Politics of Modern Iran* (London: Routledge, 2010). A good general survey is Homa Katouzian, *The Persians: Ancient, Mediaeval, and Modern Iran* (New Haven, CT: Yale University Press, 2009). On Iranian culture, see William O. Beeman, *Language, Status, and Power in Iran* (Bloomington: Indiana University Press, 1986). On modern Iranian politics, see Ali Gheissari and Vali Nasr, *Democracy in Iran* (New York: Oxford University Press, 2006); Fakhreddin Azimi, *The Quest for Democracy in Iran: A Century of Struggle Against Authoritarian Rule* (Cambridge, MA: Harvard University Press, 2008); and Ervand Abrahamian, *A History of Modern Iran* (Cambridge: Cambridge University Press, 2008). A useful travel guide is Anthony Burke et al., *Iran,* 6th ed. (London: Lonely Planet, 2012).

On Iran before the Islamic revolution, see Rouhollah K. Ramazani, *Iran's Foreign Policy, 1941–1973* (Charlottesville: University Press of Virginia, 1975); Richard Cottam, *Nationalism in Iran* (Pittsburgh, PA: University of Pittsburgh Press, 1979); Shahrough Akhavi, *Religion and Politics in Contemporary Iran* (Albany: State University of New York Press, 1980); Ervand Abrahamian, *Iran Between Two Revolutions* (Princeton, NJ: Princeton University Press, 1982); Asadollah Alam, *The Shah and I* (London: I. B. Tauris, 1991); Mark J. Gasiorowski, *U.S. Foreign Policy and the Shah* (Ithaca, NY: Cornell

University Press, 1991); Janet Afary, *The Iranian Constitutional Revolution, 1906–1911* (New York: Columbia University Press, 1996); Sirus Ghani, *Iran and the Rise of Reza Shah* (London: I. B. Tauris, 1998); Stephanie Cronin, ed., *The Making of Modern Iran* (London: Routledge-Curzon, 2003); Mark Gasiorowski and Malcolm Byrne, eds., *Mohammad Mosaddeq and the 1953 Coup in Iran* (Syracuse, NY: Syracuse University Press, 2004); and Abbas Milani, *The Shah* (New York: Palgrave Macmillan, 2011).

On the revolution and its aftermath, see Shaul Bakhash, *The Reign of the Ayatollahs* (New York: Basic Books, 1984); Said Amir Arjomand, *The Turban for the Crown* (New York: Oxford University Press, 1988); Misagh Parsa, *Social Origins of the Iranian Revolution* (New Brunswick, NJ: Rutgers University Press, 1989); H. E. Chehabi, *Iranian Politics and Religious Modernism* (Ithaca, NY: Cornell University Press, 1990); Mansoor Moaddel, *Class, Politics, and Ideology in the Iranian Revolution* (New York: Columbia University Press, 1993); Ervand Abrahamian, *Khomeinism* (Berkeley: University of California Press, 1993); Hamid Dabashi, *Theology of Discontent* (New York: New York University Press, 1993); Mehrzad Boroujerdi, *Iranian Intellectuals and the West* (Syracuse, NY: Syracuse University Press, 1996); Baqer Moin, *Khomeini: Life of the Ayatollah* (New York: St. Martin's Press, 1999); Vanessa Martin, *Creating an Islamic State* (London: I. B. Tauris, 2000); Nikki Keddie, *Modern Iran: Roots and Results of Revolution* (New Haven, CT: Yale University Press, 2003); Charles Kurzman, *The Unthinkable Revolution in Iran* (Cambridge, MA: Harvard University Press, 2004); Mark Bowden, *Guests of the Ayatollah* (New York: Atlantic Monthly Press, 2006); and Abbas Amanat, *Apocalyptic Islam and Iranian Shi'ism* (London: I. B. Tauris, 2009).

On Iran since the revolution, see Samih K. Farsoun and Mehrdad Mashayekhi, *Iran: Political Culture in the Islamic Republic* (London: Routledge, 1992); Anoushiravan Ehteshami, *After Khomeini* (London: Routledge, 1995); Bahman Baktiari, *Parliamentary Politics in Revolutionary Iran* (Gainesville: University Press of Florida, 1996); Asghar Schirazi, *The Constitution of Iran* (London: I. B. Tauris, 1997); Jahangir Amuzegar, *Iran's Economy Under the Islamic Republic* (London: I. B. Tauris, 1997); Haleh Afshar, *Islam and Feminisms: An Iranian Case-Study* (New York: St. Martin's Press, 1998); Maziar Bahrooz, *Rebels with a Cause* (London: I. B. Tauris, 1999); Fariba Adelkhah, *Being Modern in Iran* (New York: Columbia University Press, 2000); Eliz Sanasarian, *Religious Minorities in Iran* (Cambridge: Cambridge University Press, 2000); Wilfried Buchta, *Who Rules Iran?* (Washington, DC: Washington Institute for Near East Policy, 2000); Daniel Brumberg, *Reinventing Khomeini* (Chicago: University of Chicago Press, 2001); Mehdi Moslem, *Factional Politics in Post-Khomeini Iran* (Syracuse, NY: Syracuse University Press, 2002); Eric Hooglund, ed., *Twenty Years of Islamic Revolution* (Syracuse, NY: Syracuse University Press, 2002); Anthony H. Cordesman, *Iran's Developing Military Capabilities* (Washington, DC: Center for Strategic and International Studies Press, 2005); Mehran Kamrava, *Iran's Intellectual Revolution* (Cambridge: Cambridge University Press, 2008); Steven R. Ward, *Immortal: A Military History of Iran and Its Armed Forces* (Washington, DC: Georgetown University Press, 2009); Said Amir Arjomand,

After Khomeini: Iran Under His Successors (New York: Oxford University Press, 2009); Ray Takeyh, *Guardians of the Revolution: Iran and the World in the Age of the Ayatollahs* (New York: Oxford University Press, 2009); Hamid Dabashi, *Iran, the Green Movement, and the USA* (London: Zed Books, 2010); and David Crist, *The Twilight War: The Secret History of America's Thirty-Year Conflict with Iran* (New York: Penguin Press, 2012).

Useful Internet sites on Iran include Payvand (http://payvand.com), Gooya (http://gooya.com), Iranian Newspapers (www.world-newspapers.com/iran.html), Perry-Castañeda Library Map Collection—Iran Maps (http://lib.utexas.edu/maps/iran.html), Iran Review (www.iranreview.org), (www.iranreview.org/iranSpectrum/index.aspx), Radio Free Europe/Radio Liberty—Iran (www.rferl.org/section/iran/156.html), and The Iran Primer (http://iranprimer.usip.org).

4

KINGDOM OF SAUDI ARABIA

Sebastian Maisel

Early History

In 1932, King Abd al-Aziz ibn Abd al-Rahman Al Saud formally united the Hijaz and Najd to form the Kingdom of Saudi Arabia. The Saud regime, however, dates back over 250 years to when its founder ruled a small desert principality in Najd, as central Arabia is called. The story of Saudi Arabia, therefore, is the story of the evolution of a small oasis principality into the mighty oil kingdom of today.

The founder of the Al Saud dynasty, Muhammad ibn Saud (c. 1703/1704–1765), was emir of Dar'iyyah. Dar'iyyah is a small oasis town located on the Wadi Hanifah, a usually dry streambed in central Najd. In 1744–1745, he became the patron of Muhammad ibn Abd al-Wahhab (1703–1793), a zealous religious revivalist who had been driven from his home, the neighboring town of Uyainah, because of his strict, puritan religious beliefs. The religious leader and the political leader formed a bond that has provided ideological cohesion for the Saudi state to this day.

Muhammad ibn Abd al-Wahhab's revival movement was based on the Hanbali school of Islamic jurisprudence, the most conservative of the four recognized schools of Sunni Islam. Many of the revival's teachings were drawn from the writings of an early Hanbali jurist, Taqi al-Din Ahmad ibn Taymiyyah (c. 1262–1328). The revival stressed a return to the fundamentals of Islam based on the strict monotheistic doctrine of *Tawhid* (monotheism) and condemned many of the religious practices that had cropped up since the time of the Prophet as heretical and those who followed them as idolaters and polytheists.

Outside detractors called followers of the revival "Wahhabis," after Abd al-Wahhab. The followers themselves, however, rejected the term as implying worship of a human being rather than God. They preferred to be called *Muwahhidin* (unitarians or monotheists), expressing adherence to the central monotheistic doctrine of *Tawhid*. Muhammad ibn Abd al-Wahhab was known as the teacher, or "the Shaykh." His descendants, called Al

Kingdom of Saudi Arabia

al-Shaykh (House of the Shaykh), are second in prestige to the Al Saud and still provide religious leadership for the country.

By the end of the eighteenth century, the Al Saud ruled over nearly all of Najd and were preparing to expand even farther. Saudi control of Najd was accomplished with little notice by the outside world, but when in 1801 the Saudis sacked the Shi'a holy city of Karbala, in what is now southern Iraq, they came to the attention of the world, particularly the Islamic world. Convinced that pilgrimages to tombs of holy men constituted idolatry, the Al Saud destroyed the tombs of a number of revered Shi'a "saints," including that of Hussein, the grandson of the Prophet Muhammad. Hussein's tomb is venerated by Shi'as as a site for pilgrimage second in importance only to Mecca and Medina. In 1806, *Muwahhidin* forces defeated the Ottoman garrisons in the Hijaz and seized Mecca and Medina. In the east they pushed into Oman, forcing the Sultan of Muscat to pay annual tribute. Persian Gulf mariners, newly converted to the religious revival movement, sent privateers against British and local merchant vessels, deeming the former to be nonbelievers and the latter to be heretics. Thus, in a few short years, Saudi domains had expanded from a small oasis principality to much of the Arabian Peninsula, and Saudi influence extended to the Gulf and the Arabian Sea.

One can speculate about how far the forces of the Al Saud might have gone had they not encountered the Ottomans' vastly superior military technology. The capture of the holy places of Mecca and Medina roused the sultan in Constantinople to action. He bade his viceroy in Egypt, Muhammad Ali, to send an army against the invaders. In 1811 Muhammad Ali sent his son Tusun to retake the holy places and invade Najd. Tusun was able to recapture most of the Hijaz but could not defeat the *Muwahhidin*. In 1816, Tusun's brother Ibrahim Pasha arrived with a well-equipped army and finally captured the Saudi capital at Dar'iyyah in 1818. Ibrahim's forces laid waste to the city, whose ruins can still be seen, and exiled the Saudi emir, Abdallah ibn Saud Al Saud, fourth in the line, to Cairo along with other members of the Al Saud and Al al-Shaykh. Abdallah was later sent to Constantinople, where he was eventually beheaded.

During the next four years, the Ottoman-Egyptian occupiers set out to destroy the Al Saud base of power so that it could no longer threaten the holy cities of the Hijaz. They installed Abdallah's brother, Mishari, as a puppet emir and finally withdrew from Najd in 1822 after concluding that the *Muwahhidin* were no longer a threat to Mecca and Medina.

In 1823–1824, Turki ibn Abdallah, a second cousin, reestablished Saudi rule and moved the capital twenty kilometers down the Wadi Hanifah to Riyadh, where it has remained to this day. He was assassinated in 1834 and succeeded by his son Faisal. In 1837, Egyptians ousted Faisal and installed his cousin, Khalid, but he in turn was overthrown by another cousin, Abdallah ibn Thunayan. Finally, in 1843, Faisal escaped from exile in Cairo, ousted Abdallah ibn Thunayan, and again became undisputed ruler of Najd. During Faisal's second reign (1843–1865), Saudi leadership reached the apex of its power and influence in the nineteenth century. Faisal restored peace, extended his rule to Jabal Shammar in the north, and laid claim to Buraymi Oasis on the Omani frontier.

Faisal's death in 1865 signaled another eclipse in the fortunes of the Al Saud. He was succeeded by his son Abdallah, but Abdallah's leadership was almost immediately challenged by a second son, Saud, who became emir in 1871. After Saud's death in 1875, Abdallah again became emir, but by this time, the Al Saud's grip on Najd was slipping; the Ottomans had recaptured Eastern Province (al-Hasa) in the east; the Jabal Shammar area was lost to the Al Rashid and the Shammar tribe; and Buraymi Oasis was lost in the south. In 1887, the Saudi state again collapsed. This time, Muhammad ibn Rashid, emir of the Shammar, seized Najd and ruled it from the Shammari capital at Hail. Abd al-Rahman bin Faysal, a younger brother of Abdallah and Saud, served briefly as the Rashidi governor in Riyadh, but in 1891, after failing in an abortive revolt, he and his family were forced to flee. He settled for months with the al-Murrah tribes at the edge of the Rub' al-Khali (Empty Quarter), where his son Abd al-Aziz, the future king of Saudi Arabia, learned the Bedouin lifestyle and customs. Later, Abd al-Rahman and his family moved to Kuwait, where they lived off the hospitality of the ruler, Mubarak the Great.

KINGDOM OF SAUDI ARABIA

Capital city	Riyadh
Chief of state, 2012	King and Prime Minister Abdallah bin Abd al-Aziz Al Saud
Head of government, 2012	King and Prime Minister Abdallah bin Abd al-Aziz Al Saud
Political parties, 2012	None
Ethnic groups	Arab (90%), Afro-Asian (10%)
Religious groups	Muslim (100%)
Export partners, 2011	Japan (13.9%), China (13.7%), United States (13.4%), South Korea (10.2%), India (7.2%), Singapore (4.9%)
Import partners, 2011	China (12.8%), United States (11.9%), Germany (7.1%), South Korea (6%), Japan (5.6%), India (5.3%), Italy (4.1%)

From Desert Principality to Modern Oil Kingdom

The rise of the Al Saud from exile to rulers of the world's foremost oil state was due primarily to Abd al-Rahman's son Abd al-Aziz, known in the West as Ibn Saud. He was an imposing figure. The true measure of his greatness, however, was in his breadth of vision. Even though he did not fully comprehend the revolutionary changes that his acts would ultimately produce, he brought his country from centuries of desert isolation to a seat on regional and world political and economic councils.

The first step was the legendary recapture of Riyadh in 1902. It took another two decades from that January morning for Abd al-Aziz to complete the conquest of the Ibn Rashids. His success was greatly facilitated by the fratricidal rivalries that split the Al Rashid, much as the Al Saud had been split just a generation before. Saudi control continued to expand; in 1912, Abd al-Aziz raised his Najdi state from an emirate to a sultanate, as befitted his growing status. By the time he captured the Rashidi capital of Hail in 1922, he had also recaptured in eastern Arabia the large oasis of al-Hasa from the Ottomans.

In his military campaigns, Abd al-Aziz relied on tribal warriors called the Ikhwan (liter-ally "the Brethren" in Arabic), whom he indoctrinated in the teachings of Abd al-Wahhab, provided with subsidies and a share of the booty from raids against enemies of the Al Saud, and settled in agricultural communities. The Ikhwan, fighting under the banner of *Tawhid*, might have defeated the Ibn Rashids sooner had not World War I intervened. The war tem-porarily brought the Arabian Peninsula into the arena of great-power politics, with the British and the Turks in competition for the support of the peninsula's three major rulers, Abd al-Aziz of Najd, Saud ibn Rashid of Jabal Shammar, and Sharif Hussein of Mecca. Ibn Rashid sided with the Turks (and the Germans); the other two chose the British.

During the war period, three Britons came to fame in Arabia: Captain W. H. I. Shake-speare, Colonel T. E. Lawrence (Lawrence of Arabia), and H. St. John B. Philby. Shake-speare, as British political agent in Kuwait, had informally contacted Abd al-Aziz in 1910 and, while on a trek through Arabia in 1913, had visited him in Riyadh. On the eve of the war, Shakespeare was sent back to Riyadh in 1914 as the British political representative to Abd al-Aziz.

In 1916, the British sent Lawrence to the Hijaz to encourage Sharif Hussein to revolt against the Ottomans. Lawrence subsequently won a place in history by leading Arab raiding parties against Turkish supply routes along the Hijaz Railway. The following year, the British sent another mission to Abd al-Aziz to persuade him to side with Sharif Hus-sein and the Allies and attack the Ibn Rashids. The mission included Philby, who re-mained in Arabia as an explorer and later became one of the closest confidants of Abd al-Aziz.

With the war's end, Abd al-Aziz finally conquered the capital of Ibn Rashid, but in the meantime, the Al Saud's relations with King (formerly Sharif) Hussein of the Hijaz had begun to deteriorate. Hussein proclaimed himself "King of the Arabs" and claimed prece-dence over the Al Saud, whom he regarded as mere desert chieftains.

The tide was turning, however. The same year, Abdallah, another of Hussein's sons, set out east of Ta'if to claim the Khurmah Oasis for the Hijaz. While encamped at nearby Turabah, his army was wiped out by the Ikhwan. Only men with horses (including Abdal-lah) escaped.

Because of British support for the Hijaz, Abd al-Aziz did not press his advantage until 1924, when King Hussein proclaimed himself the caliph after the Ottoman caliphate had been dissolved. This was more than the devout Abd al-Aziz could accept, and he set out to invade the Hijaz. Ta'if surrendered without resistance, but for a still unexplained reason, a shot rang out and the zealous Ikhwan sacked the city. When the rest of the Hijaz learned of the fate of Ta'if, they panicked and forced King Hussein to abdicate in favor of his son, Ali. Ali fared no better, however, and in January 1926, he also set sail from Jiddah into exile.

In a quarter century, Abd al-Aziz, who had started with forty men, had regained the Saudi patrimony. In 1934, he acquired the Wadi Najran after a brief war with Yemen, completing the present frontiers, pending settlement of remaining boundary disputes. After Abd al-Aziz conquered the Hijaz, he ruled the two countries as the Kingdom of the Hijaz and Sultanate of Najd, then the Kingdom of the Hijaz and Najd. In 1932, the two countries were consolidated as the Kingdom of Saudi Arabia.

With the restoration and consolidation of the kingdom, peace came to Saudi Arabia for one of the few times in recorded history. With no more wars to fight, the Ikhwan became restless, and the king had to put down a tribal uprising at Sibilah in 1929, perhaps the last great Bedouin battle in history. The Ikhwan were subsequently disbanded (except for the brief Yemen campaign), and on the eve of World War II, Saudi Arabia was one of the few countries in the world with no standing army. It did declare war on Germany, however, and became a charter member of the United Nations.

The Postwar Era

The postwar history of Saudi Arabia has been one of unprecedented economic and social development. The enabling factor has been oil, first found in commercial quantities in 1938 but not exported in quantity until after the war. King Abd al-Aziz, by the time of his death in 1953, had constructed a firm foundation on which his successors could build a modern oil state.

He was succeeded by his eldest surviving son, Saud. More at home with tribal politics, Saud lacked the breadth of vision to propel Saudi Arabia from a desert kingdom to a major oil power. Intrigue and lavish spending characterized his reign. Despite growing oil revenues, the treasury was often virtually empty. In 1962, Saud was obliged to turn government operations over to his half brother Faisal, and in 1964, the royal family withdrew its support entirely, forcing him to abdicate. Saud left Saudi Arabia, choosing to remain in exile until his death in Athens in 1969.

King Faisal began his reign with nearly a half-century's experience in public affairs. In 1919, at the age of fourteen, he represented his father on an official visit to England. After his father conquered the Hijaz, Faisal was made its viceroy in 1926, and when the Ministry of Foreign Affairs was created in 1930, he became foreign minister, a position he held for the rest of his life, with the exception of a short period during the reign of his half brother, Saud, when Faisal retired to private life.

King Faisal, whose mother was an Al al-Shaykh, was dedicated to the preservation of a conservative Islamic way of life both in Saudi Arabia and throughout the Muslim world, while he at the same time encouraged material and technological modernization. These goals, initiated by his father, were articulated in a ten-point reform program, which Faisal announced in 1962 while he was still heir apparent and prime minister. The measure of his success can be explained by his capacity to introduce modern economic- and social-development programs while never being so far out in front that the conservative Saudi public would not follow. By balancing tradition and modernization, he was able to win over even the most conservative segments of the population to such innovations as public radio and television and education for women. To dispel religious opposition to radio and television, for example, Faisal ordered large portions of programming time to be devoted to religious instruction and readings from the Qur'an.

Faisal's greatest interest, however, was foreign affairs. As foreign minister, he became one of the most widely traveled Saudi officials of his time. For example, he attended the 1945 San Francisco conference that established the United Nations. Faisal's primary focus was on the Muslim world and the preservation of its values.

His reign coincided with the Cold War, and his strident antipathy toward the Soviet Union was based in large part on his Islamic bipolar worldview that atheistic communism was a threat to the entire Muslim world. Likewise, his strong support of the Palestinian cause was based not only on his belief in the injustice of partitioning Arab lands to create a Jewish state but also on the Israeli capture during the 1967 war of the al-Aqsa Mosque in Jerusalem, the third holiest site in Sunni Islam after Mecca and Medina.

King Faisal was assassinated by a deranged nephew on March 25, 1975, and succeeded by his half brother, Khalid. Quiet, retiring, and pious, King Khalid was a very popular ruler. During his reign, in 1979, fanatical followers of Juhayman al-Utaybi and the self-proclaimed Mahdi (Redeemer) Muhammad al-Qahtani seized the Haram Mosque in Mecca, demanding political, religious, and economic reform. With foreign technical support they were killed or captured. King Khalid died of a heart attack in June 1982 and was succeeded by Fahd.

Fahd's half brother Abdallah became heir apparent and first deputy prime minister, also retaining command of the Saudi National Guard, to which he had been appointed by Faisal in 1962. Fahd's full brother Prince Sultan, the minister of defense, became second deputy prime minister.

King Fahd carried on the evolutionary political and economic policies of his predecessors while continuing to maintain the Islamic nature of the state. In 1992, he promulgated a Basic Law of Government designed to modernize the political process and also promulgated a Consultative Assembly (Majlis al-Shura) designed to institutionalize more public participation in the political process commensurate with the Islamic constitutional system. (See "Political Structure," below.)

In foreign policy, Fahd followed the lead of King Faisal in seeking cooperation with Western as well as moderate regional states to address Middle East regional problems. Radical Arab nationalism had lost its credence after the Arab defeat in the 1967 war, and as heir apparent and ultimately king, Fahd could be more active in regional affairs.

Fahd felt vindicated by the failure of the Camp David Accords of 1979 to lead to an Arab-Israeli agreement that addressed any Palestinian core issues, and in 1981 he offered the Fahd Plan for an Arab-Israeli peace. It was, however, summarily rejected by Israel and the United States. Succeeding peace negotiations came to naught, and in 2002, Crown Prince Abdullah offered yet another peace proposal that got some support from Israelis but no results. However, he succeeded in reconciling the main Palestinian political parties, Hamas and Fatah, which signed the Mecca Accord in 2007.

Coping with Modernization in a Hostile World

By the end of the 1980s, the collapse of the Soviet Union heralded the end of the Cold War, which, for almost a half century, Saudi Arabia had considered to be the greatest security threat to the Islamic way of life, not only in the kingdom but throughout the Muslim world. It remained concerned about regional threats, however, and its fears were justified in 1990 when Iraq's President Saddam Hussein invaded Kuwait, threatening the rest of the Arabian Peninsula as well. After initial reluctance, King Fahd welcomed a coalition of Arab states and others led by the United States to counter the Iraqi invasion, and in 1991 Operation Desert Storm was launched to drive Hussein out of Kuwait.

Iraq's invasion of Kuwait in 1990 and expulsion by coalition forces the following year was the greatest crisis for Saudi Arabia of that period. The Saudi military acquitted itself well during the war, particularly the Royal Saudi Air Force.

In the 1980s, many young Saudis volunteered to fight the Soviets in Afghanistan. Returning home after the war, many felt more marginalized than ever and turned to militant Islamism to give meaning to their lives, spreading this solution to their pain to younger marginalized youths. In this way they were drawn to terrorist groups, the most effective of which was Osama bin Laden's al-Qaida. Thus, modern terrorism, which had never before been a major problem, gradually became the greatest national security problem facing the country.

King Fahd was incapacitated by a series of strokes in 1995 and passed the reins of government in 1996 to his half brother, Abdallah, the heir apparent. The next decade was a difficult period for the kingdom in terms of meeting the challenges of social change, measuring up to economic and political expectations, and maintaining national security.

These pressures have been expanding for years, but at such a slow pace that they can best be described as a "creeping crisis." They were mostly unfocused until the 1990s, when the stationing of US troops in the kingdom became a rallying cry for the politically disaffected. But they did not reach a flash point until September 11, 2001, when the country faced fierce hostility, particularly in the United States, for alleged collusion with the terrorists, fifteen out of nineteen of whom were Saudis. (See "Foreign Policy" below.)

But national security really struck home in the kingdom in May 2003 when terrorists attacked residential compounds, killing not only Western expatriates but Muslims as well. Since then, the government has initiated a successful counterterrorism program, attacking and rounding up terrorists as well as rehabilitating young recruits for reentry into society. It is not possible to eradicate all terrorist threats, but the Saudis certainly have reduced them to more manageable proportions.

When Abdallah became king in 2005, upon the death of Fahd, one of his major concerns was growing public support for more participation in the political process. Adjusting to the challenges and changes of the era of global economy and security, he initiated a reform of the political process and the judicial system as well as the educational sector. The arguably slow process aims at a renewal and revitalization of the origin of Saudi rule:

a balance of politics and religion for the sake of not only the survival but the strong, lasting impact of the "country of the two holy places." He has set about establishing his own personal style of government, though one based on precedent; Saudi domestic and foreign policies will likely continue to follow the lead of Kings Abd al-Aziz, Faisal, and Fahd, emphasizing economic development and social welfare within the framework of Islam and moderation.

POLITICAL ENVIRONMENT

The Land

Saudi Arabia occupies about 2 million square kilometers (772,000 square miles), but political borders have traditionally been relatively meaningless to Saudi rulers, who have looked on sovereignty more in terms of tribal allegiance. Recognized tribal territories were huge and carefully defined, as Bedouin tribes followed the rains from water hole to water hole and wandered over broad areas. Later, when oil became so important in the region, fixed regional and international borders acquired much more importance. A deviation of a few centimeters from a common point could translate into hundreds of square kilometers when projected for long distances over the desert.

It has taken many years for Saudi Arabia to demarcate its borders. In 1922, the Saudi-Kuwaiti Neutral Zone and the Saudi-Iraqi Neutral Zone were created to avoid tribal border hostilities. The first was abolished in 1966 and the second in 1975, and their territories were divided among the parties. The decades-old Buraymi Oasis territorial dispute among Saudi Arabia, Oman, and Abu Dhabi was settled in 1974 when Saudi Arabia agreed to give up its claim to the oasis and adjacent territory in return for an outlet to the Gulf through Abu Dhabi. Since then, the kingdom has agreed in principle to demarcate the rest of its long border with Oman. In 2000, Saudi Arabia and Yemen signed a treaty on their international land and sea borders, ending a dispute that went back to the 1934 Saudi invasion of Yemen.

The same can be said for offshore territorial limits. Saudi Arabia claims a twelve-nautical-mile limit offshore, as well as a number of islands in the Gulf and the Red Sea. With extensive offshore oil discoveries in the Gulf, establishing a median line dividing underwater oil and gas fields among the Gulf states became imperative. Nevertheless, not until the 1970s could such a line finally be negotiated.

Because of Saudi Arabia's predominantly desert terrain, a shortage of water is a major concern. In the interior, nonrenewable aquifers are being tapped at an unprecedented rate, particularly as urbanization and population growth expand and as irrigated agricultural-development projects have been created in the interior. To augment water supplies, the kingdom has created a massive desalination system.

Despite the arid climate, sporadic rains do fall in Saudi Arabia, and there is occasional snow in the mountains. This water has to run off somewhere, and as a result, there is a drainage system of numerous intersecting wadis, which are usually dry riverbeds and valleys. After local, and occasionally heavy, rains, the wadis can become rushing torrents.

Although nearly all of Saudi Arabia is arid, only a part of it consists of real sand desert. There are three such deserts in the kingdom: the Great Nafud, located in the north (*nafud* is one of several Arabic words meaning "desert"); the Rub' al-Khali (Empty Quarter), stretching along the entire southern frontier; and the Dahna, a narrow strip that forms a great arc from the Great Nafud westward and then south to the Rub' al-Khali. The sand in all three bears iron oxide, giving it a pink color that can turn to deep red in the setting sun.

Excluding the Empty Quarter, the kingdom is divided into four geographical regions: central, western, eastern, and northern. Central Arabia, or Najd (highlands), is predominantly an arid plateau interspersed with oases and is both the geographical and the political heartland of the country.

Many cities and towns are scattered throughout Najd. The largest is the national capital, Riyadh, which means "gardens," referring to the numerous vegetable gardens and date groves that were located there. Riyadh has grown from a small oasis town—about 7,500 in 1900—to a major metropolis with a population of over 3.5 million a century later; by 2010 it was estimated to be approaching 5 million.

Riyadh remained generally closed to Westerners until the 1970s, when the Saudis opened it up to Western development. Between 1969 and 1975 the number of Western expatriates living in the capital rose from fewer than three hundred to hundreds of thousands. Just a few kilometers north, the ruins of Dar'iyyah, ancestral home of the Al Saud, have become a virtual suburb of the capital. Northeast of Riyadh is the district of al-Qasim, with its neighboring and rival cities of Unayzah and Buraydah. The inhabitants of al-Qasim are among the most conservative in the kingdom. Further north is Jabal Shammar and the former Rashidi capital of Hail on the edge of the Great Nafud.

Western Saudi Arabia is divided into two areas, the Hijaz in the north and Asir in the south. The Hijaz extends from the Jordanian border to just south of Jiddah, the kingdom's second-largest city.

The economic and social life of the Hijaz has traditionally revolved around the annual Hajj, or great pilgrimage to Mecca. With so much attention given to Saudi oil and Middle East politics, few Westerners are aware that to the Muslim world—comprising around 1.4 billion people, or one-fifth of the world's population—the kingdom is even more important as the location of the two holiest cities in Islam, Mecca and Medina. Performing the Hajj once in their lifetime is an obligation for all Muslims who are physically and financially able. In addition, many Muslims perform the lesser pilgrimage, or Umrah, to Mecca. Observed each year by 2.5 to 3 million of the faithful, the Hajj is not only one of the world's greatest religious celebrations but also one of the greatest exercises in public administration. The number of those going on Umrah reaches 8 million.

The Saudi government seeks to ensure that all those who make pilgrimages do so without incurring serious injury and with a minimum of discomfort. This requires the concerted effort of health, housing, transportation, security, diplomatic, customs, and finance officials, working with large private-sector guilds, to meet, guide, and look after the Hajjis throughout their stay. Over the centuries, an extensive service industry has grown up to cater to Hajjis. With the discovery of oil, the Hajj has lost the economic importance it once had, but with millions of visitors to Mecca and Medina throughout each year, many staying three to five weeks, it is still a major commercial season, somewhat analogous to the Christmas season in Western countries. Physical infrastructure to accommodate the Hajj is extensive, including one of the largest commercial airports in the world at Jiddah, a modern commercial hub of over 3 million on the Red Sea and the traditional port of entry for the Hajj. The Saudi government has also spent billions of riyals upgrading the Haram Mosque in Mecca and the Prophet's Mosque in Medina, the two holiest sites in Islam.

Asir and southern Tihama (the Red Sea coastal plain) were quasi-independent until the Saudi conquest in the 1920s and 1930s, and they remained relatively isolated until modern roads were built in the 1970s. Its main cities are Jizan, a modest city on the coast; Abha, the provincial capital atop the escarpment; and Najran, located inland on the Saudi-Yemeni border. Not far from Abha is Khamis Mushayt, site of a major Saudi military cantonment area.

Eastern Saudi Arabia is a mixture of old and new. Called the Eastern Province, it includes al-Hasa, the largest oasis in the world, and Qatif Oasis on the coast. The primary significance of the region is that it sits above the bulk of Saudi Arabia's huge oil reserves, one-fourth of the planet's total. The Ghawar field, which stretches over two hundred kilometers from north to south, is the largest single oil field in the world.

The capital and principal city of the province is Dammam, just south of Qatif. Once a small pearling and privateering port, it is now a bustling metropolis. South of Dammam is Dhahran, whose name is far more familiar in the West. It is actually not a city but the location of the Saudi Aramco headquarters and King Faisal University. Nearby, on the coast, is al-Khobar, which grew from virtually nothing into a major service town.

North of Dammam to the Kuwaiti border are located a number of oil towns and facilities, including Ras Tanura, the principal Saudi Aramco oil terminal, and farther north, Khafji, in what was formerly part of the Saudi-Kuwaiti Neutral Zone. Just north of Ras Tanura is Jubayl, only a tiny village when the first American oil men landed there in 1933 and now a major industrial city and the site of much of Saudi Arabia's petrochemical industry. The largest town in al-Hasa Oasis is the ancient town of Hufuf, now home to many Saudi Aramco workers and the kingdom's Shi'a minority.

The area extending along the kingdom's northern frontiers with Jordan and Iraq is physically isolated from the rest of the country by the Great Nafud. It is geographically a part of the Syrian Desert, and tribesmen in the area claim kinship with fellow tribesmen in neighboring Jordan, Iraq, and Syria, as well as Saudi Arabia, occasionally possessing passports from all four countries. This area was the traditional caravan route for traders from the Fertile Crescent traveling to central and eastern Arabia.

There are no cities in the region. The two principal towns, Dumat al-Jandal (al-Jawf) and Sakaka, the provincial capital, are located in oases just north of the Nafud. Prior to the 1967 Arab-Israeli War, the most important installation in the region economically was the Trans-Arabian Pipeline (TAPLINE), which carried crude oil from the Eastern Province to the Lebanese port of Sidon. With access to Lebanon now closed, TAPLINE has lost much of its economic importance, although oil is still sent through the pipeline to Jordan.

Saudi Arabia has the harsh, hot climate typical of a desert area. There are variations, however. In the interior, the lack of humidity causes daytime temperatures to rise sharply. In the summer, daytime readings can register over 54°C (130°F), then drop precipitously after the sun goes down, sometimes by as much as 20°C (70°F) in less than three hours. In the winter, subfreezing temperatures are not uncommon, and the ever-present winds create a windchill that can be very uncomfortable.

The coastal areas combine heat and high humidity. The humidity usually keeps the temperature from exceeding 40°C (around 105°F) in the summer but likewise prevents it from dropping more than a few degrees at night. Winter temperatures, in contrast, are balmier and warmer at night than those in the interior, particularly the farther south one goes. Both along the coasts and in the interior, rainfall is very sporadic. Torrential rains can flood one area and entirely miss areas a few kilometers away. At other times, the same area can go without rain for five to ten years. The sporadic nature of the rains is the main reason desert pastoralists must cover wide areas in search of pasturage for their livestock.

The mountain areas are cooler, particularly in the Asir, where it can get quite cold at night. The Asir also gets the moisture-laden monsoon winds from the south in the winter, when it gets most of its annual rainfall of around five hundred millimeters (twenty inches).

The People

In 2012 Saudi Arabia had an estimated population of 28.7 million, of which roughly 5.6 million were expatriates. Though the country's population is relatively small in comparison to its great wealth, it has experienced a population explosion in the past quarter century that has radically changed its demography. There are some indications that the population growth rate is stabilizing, declining from over 3.5 percent per year to around 3.2 percent. However, with a median age of about eighteen and a rapidly expanding life expectancy due to vastly improved health care, the kingdom still faces major socioeconomic problems far into the twenty-first century. Every year there are more young Saudis for a finite number of jobs, and more and more of the aged must be supported by their children, with both groups increasingly living off their families' income.

The indigenous Saudi population is among the most homogeneous in the entire Middle East. Virtually all Saudis are Arab and Muslim. Bloodlines, not geography, determine nationality, and being born in Saudi Arabia does not automatically entitle a person to citizenship. The extended family is the most important social institution in Saudi Arabia. If put to the test, loyalty to one's family would probably exceed loyalty to the state. The state has been in existence for a few decades, but most Saudis trace their families back for centuries.

With genealogy so important, there is relatively little social mobility in Saudi Arabia. Not only is Najd the center of Saudi political power, but its tribal affiliations are among the most aristocratic on the Arabian Peninsula. Members of the leading tribal families of Najd are at the top of the social order, and nontribal families are near the bottom.

The Hijazi population is far more cosmopolitan than that of Najd because of centuries of immigration connected with the Hajj. The leading families historically constituted a merchant class that grew up in the Hijaz to serve the Hajj. The Eastern Province, with its concentration of the oil industry, also has a polyglot population, and many families there have close ties in other Gulf states.

The Eastern Province is the home of the only significant minority in the kingdom, the Shi'a community, estimated at around 2 million, or 12 percent of the total population. They live mainly in al-Qatif and al-Hasa oases. Unlike much of the rest of the population, the Shi'a are willing to work with their hands and over the years have become the backbone of the skilled and semiskilled workforce in the oil sector. They are members of the predominant Twelver Shi'a sect. Another group of Shi'a is concentrated in the Najran area near Yemen. They are followers of the Isma'ili, or Sevener, sect.

A few families of non-Arabian origin have also become Saudi nationals. Most of them are found in the Hijaz and are descended from Hajjis who never returned to their homelands after the pilgrimage. Some of these families have lived in Jiddah and Mecca for centuries and have attained stature in society and senior government rank. These families came from Java, China, and other, mostly Far Eastern Asian regions. Another group, the Hadhramis, originally came from the Wadi Hadhramaut in what is now western Yemen, particularly in the nineteenth century, and number among the leading merchant families of Jiddah. Also, after the abolition of slavery in 1960, many former slaves stayed in the kingdom and became citizens, often remaining closely allied with their former masters.

The distinction between foreigners and natives breaks down somewhat when one looks at neighboring states. Many of the old Sunni families of Kuwait and Bahrain migrated from Najd some three hundred years ago. Northern Saudis have close tribal ties in Iraq, Jordan, and Syria. Gulf ties are reflected during the Hajj, when members of the Gulf Cooperation Council (GCC) states are not required to obtain Saudi visas. No matter how long a person's family has resided in the country, however, he is still identified by his family's place of origin.

The foreign community constitutes about one-fifth of the total population. European diplomats, bankers, and merchants have long resided in the Hijaz to service the Hajj trade, but few lived in other parts of the country until recently. The original function of foreign diplomats and consuls, located in Jiddah, was to look after Hajjis from their home countries, and many countries continue to maintain consulates in Jiddah for that purpose, although all foreign embassies moved to Riyadh in the 1970s.

As the oil-based economy grew, the foreign workforce rapidly expanded. By the 1950s, Aramco employed thousands of foreign workers, from senior American executives to manual laborers from the Persian Gulf states and South Asia. In the 1970s, the oil boom spurred unprecedented economic development throughout the kingdom, and Najd was opened up to Westerners for the first time in a major way. A new diplomatic enclave, separate from the rest of the city, was created in Riyadh by the Saudi government, and many foreign and local businesses moved their headquarters to Riyadh as well. Thus, the capital not only is now the largest city in the kingdom but probably contains most of the kingdom's foreigners. Skilled laborers, clerks, and teachers have come from nearby Arab states, and manual laborers have come from many Arab and South Asian countries. Yemeni workers, for instance, numbered as many as 1 million until many of them were expelled after Desert Storm for security reasons.

Contrary to fears often expressed in the West, the social and political influence of foreign workers on the society has been relatively slight. Not only does the kingdom have a basically closed society, but most foreign workers are there primarily to make as much money as possible before returning home, not to spread some radical political ideology.

In all, with the breathtaking pace of modernization in the past few decades, the miracle of Saudi society is not how it has changed but how resilient it has been in the face of change. The extended family system is still intact and, indeed, is probably the most stabilizing force in the country. Whatever Saudi Arabia's political or economic future, it is difficult to visualize it without the paramount importance of family ties.

Finally, it is within the context of the extended family that one must view the role of women in government and politics. Although they have constitutional rights under Islamic law, which are actually quite detailed, they have no formal participatory political rights in a Western sense. But within the extended family, which is the basic unit of the society, they have tremendous power because women run the family and thus can exercise significant influence over public affairs informally through their spouses and male siblings. King Abd al-Aziz's closest political adviser was his blood sister Nura, and King Faisal's closest political adviser, particularly on women's affairs, was his wife Iffat, called "the Queen" by the people out of respect, although no such title formally existed. In recent years, women have been appointed ministers and have been elected to professional boards and business associations.

Economic Conditions

The backbone of the Saudi economy is oil, accounting for 75 percent of revenues and 90 percent of export earnings. The kingdom holds roughly one-fourth of the world's proved oil reserves, the largest reserves in the world.

When one looks at Saudi Arabia's huge oil wealth, it is difficult to imagine that, prior to World War II, the country was one of the poorest on earth. Following the incorporation of the Hijaz into the Saudi realm in the 1920s, revenues generated from the Hajj became the major source of foreign exchange. When the global economic depression and political disorders leading to World War II greatly reduced the number of Hajjis in the 1930s, the Saudi economy was badly hit, and although oil had been discovered, revenues were insufficient to fill the gap.

In the pre-oil era, economic activity outside the Hijaz consisted largely of subsistence agriculture in oases and the western mountains, fishing along the Red Sea and Gulf coasts, and pearl diving in the Gulf. Even before oil wealth, Saudi Arabia had one of the most freewheeling market economies in the world. The predominant Hanbali school of Islamic jurisprudence, while ultraconservative on social and political issues, is one of the most liberal schools on economic and commercial matters, and caveat emptor (buyer beware) is still the order of the day.

The transition of the Saudi economy from subsistence to oil wealth did not occur overnight. The first Saudi oil concession was sold in the 1920s but allowed to lapse. Despite his chronic shortage of funds, King Abd al-Aziz feared that granting a concession to European oil companies would lead to imperialist penetration. In 1933, he granted a new concession to an American company, Standard Oil of California (SoCal). This came about in part through the good offices of Philby and Karl Twitchell, an American geologist who had explored for water in the kingdom, and in part because Abd al-Aziz believed the United States had no imperialist designs on Arabia. The company, originally named the California Arabian Standard Oil Company, was later renamed the Arabian American Oil Company (Aramco).

Oil was first discovered in commercial quantities in 1938, but the advent of World War II prevented its export in significant quantities to international markets. Thus, Saudi Arabia did not begin the process of becoming a leading oil state until the late 1940s.

In the 1960s, the kingdom joined the Organization of Petroleum Exporting Countries (OPEC) and quickly became the dominant member, with roughly one-quarter of the world's reserves and most of its production available for export. The original intent of OPEC was to pressure the foreign-owned oil companies to keep prices from collapsing in a buyers' market, but by the late 1960s, the United States, once the world's leading exporter, became a net importer, creating a sellers' market. This resulted in a major oil shortage, exacerbated by the 1970s Arab oil embargo. The oil-producing countries, including Saudi Arabia, were able to gain control of production rates from the companies and ultimately gained ownership of the oil itself.

Many OPEC countries simply nationalized the producing companies, but Saudi Arabia acquired ownership of Aramco in a gradual buyout called "participation," a concept developed by Zaki Yamani, then Saudi oil minister. Yamani feared that without extended oil company participation, the oil-producing countries would engage in cutthroat competition that could collapse the entire oil market. By 1980, Saudi Arabia had acquired full ownership of Aramco and renamed the company Saudi Aramco.

The high revenues of the 1970s enabled the Saudis to accelerate their economic and social welfare programs greatly. Ultimately, however, high oil prices also led to increased worldwide energy efficiency and a drop in per capita demand, and in 1980 the market entered a glut from which it did not fully recover for two decades.

Saudi Arabia's evolution from a traditional mercantile state to a major oil-producing state has wrought rapid changes throughout the economy, structurally, institutionally, and operationally. A vivid example is in the area of financial and fiscal transactions. Prior to the oil age, there were no commercial banks except foreign banks in the Hijaz established to handle the Hajj trade. There was no paper currency, which the local population distrusted, and Aramco had to fly in planeloads of silver coins to meet its payroll and royalty payments.

The government turned to Britain, France, and the United States for technical assistance in creating a modern monetary and banking system, and in 1952 it created a central bank, the Saudi Arabian Monetary Agency (SAMA). One of its first tasks was to introduce local paper money. SAMA issued promissory paper notes called "Hajj receipts," ostensibly for use by Hajjis in changing money and payable to the bearer on demand in silver coins. Once the public became accustomed to paper money, the notes were simply identified by denomination.

The evolution of Islamic banking is another creative endeavor, for Islam proscribes charging interest, considered usury. To avoid interest charges and payments, a banking system based on fees has been developed, and there are now a number of Islamic banks in the kingdom.

With advice from Western consultants and following his development philosophy of "modernization without secularization," King Faisal instituted a formal planning process, beginning with the first five-year plan adopted in 1970. The process bears no resemblance to Communist central planning, however, and could better be described as a combination of wish lists and statements of intent. The five-year plans are not intended as detailed instructions for budgetary expenditures and should be viewed impressionistically rather than literally. They are nevertheless fairly accurate indicators of Saudi priorities and the direction in which Saudis believe they should be heading, as well as the lessons they believe they have learned from the previous five years.

Early plans concentrated on building economic and social infrastructure and on economic diversification. Because of the huge increase in oil revenues in the 1970s, these early plans were very ambitious. With the oil glut of the 1980s and 1990s, revenues dropped drastically, creating deficit financing. Development plans were sharply reduced. The sixth plan (1995–2000) further reflected the need to restructure the economy, stressing human resource development, economic diversification, privatization, and liberalization of trade and investment. The current (ninth) plan (2010–2014) focuses on social projects and human resources to eradicate poverty.

Oil prices have always been cyclical, and the early years of the twenty-first century have witnessed a return of high oil prices. With the global recession beginning in November 2008, prices again declined but recovered to about $70 to $75 per barrel by the summer of 2009, in part due to speculators investing in future production.

In sum, although economic conditions do affect political stability in Saudi Arabia, the kingdom's tight-knit, family-based society continues to be insurance against the kind of political unrest found in many developing countries. But with the demographic problems the kingdom faces and inherent cyclical fluctuations in world oil prices, the end of the latest oil glut is no cause for complacency.

Political Culture

Saudi culture is overwhelmingly Islamic. More than a religion, Islam is a totally self-contained, cosmic system. In assessing the influence of Islam on Saudi political culture, one must emphasize cultural values rather than religious piety. Several characteristics of Saudi culture are basic to Saudi politics. Among the most salient are a heightened sense of inevitability, a compartmentalization of behavior, a high degree of personalization of behavior, and a strong sense of personal honor.

The sense of inevitability derives from the Islamic emphasis on God's will, often expressed in the Arabic phrase *Inshallah*, or "God willing." Nothing can happen unless God wills it. Thus, Saudis (and other Muslims) tend to accept situations as inevitable far more quickly than people from Western cultures. Conversely, if convinced that a situation is not God's will, they will persevere against it long after others would give up.

Compartmentalization of behavior, common in non-Western societies, is a tendency to view events within a single context rather than to explore all the ramifications of how it might appear in another context. As a result, a single issue can elicit different, and occasionally incompatible, policy responses, depending on the context in which it is viewed. Because these overlap and cannot be neatly separated, tolerance of major policy inconsistencies is inherent in the Saudi decision-making process.

A third cultural characteristic is the personalization of behavior. In contrast to problem-oriented Western cultures, Saudis are mainly people oriented. Good interpersonal relations are the sine qua non of good political relations, and losing face is to be avoided at all costs.

Two other characteristics of Saudi culture, derived in large part from its tribal origins, geographic isolation, and historic insularity, are a strong sense of personal and collective honor (*sharaf*) and a high degree of ethnocentricity. The ancient code of honor is still a guiding principle in interpersonal relations, often more compelling, for example, than contractual obligations, and the desire to avoid the personal and family shame associated with dishonor is very powerful.

Ethnocentricity is also very powerful, particularly in Najd, and Saudis tend to see themselves as the center of their universe. Personal status is conferred more by bloodlines than by money or achievement, and nearly all Saudis claim a proud Arabian ancestry. Having never been under European colonial rule, Saudis have not developed a national inferiority complex, as have many colonized peoples. They do not merely see themselves as equals of the West but in fact believe their culture is vastly superior to secular Western culture. Close personal relationships aside, they tend to look on outsiders as people to be tolerated as long as they have something to contribute.

POLITICAL STRUCTURE

Saudi Arabia is one of the few countries without a constitution in the Western political understanding. The country's political system is based on the interpretation and application of divine guidelines from the Qur'an and other primary Islamic sources.

The creation of modern Saudi political institutions over the past decades was bred of necessity as the kingdom evolved from a traditional desert principality into a modern oil power. It has made government operations a great deal more orderly, but it has not fundamentally changed the traditional, interpersonal system of government.

The Judicial Branch

Islamic law has always formed the basis of the Saudi constitutional system and is supreme, even over the king. The most recent reaffirmation is Article 1 of the Basic Law of Government, issued by King Fahd on March 1, 1992:

> The Saudi Arabian Kingdom is a sovereign Arab Islamic state with Islam as its religion; God's book and the Sunna [which together form the sources of Islamic law] are its constitution; Arabic is its language; and Riyadh is its capital.

Islam is basically a system of divine law. Islamic theology is quite simple, consisting of five basic tenets, or "pillars," of the faith: profession of faith ("There is no god but God, and Muhammad is the messenger of God"), prayer (five times a day, facing Mecca), alms, fasting (during Ramadan), and performing the Hajj once during one's lifetime if one is physically and financially able to do so. Another tenet, sometimes called the sixth pillar, is jihad. Often translated as "holy war," it is in fact a much broader concept, referring to both the private and the corporate obligation to encourage virtue and resist evil, by force if necessary.

Islamic law, or sharia, on the other hand, is quite complex. It is the primary area of specialization of Islamic scholars. Despite theological differences among the various branches of Islam (for example, between Sunni and Shi'a), Islamic law is universally respected by all Muslims. The primary sources of the law are the Qur'an and Sunna, or "traditions," of the Prophet Muhammad, comprised of Hadiths, his divinely inspired sayings and deeds.

The Saudi legal system is based on Sunni interpretations of Islamic law, principally but not exclusively according to the Hanbali school of Islamic jurisprudence. The most conservative of the schools in social and family law, it reinforces conservative social mores practiced by societies of Arabia for millennia, such as the veiling of women as an expression of modesty.

Saudi courts are presided over by an Islamic judge, or *qadi*. Because Islamic law is considered to be divinely inspired, however, there is no legal precedent based on previous court decisions. Islamic law does provide, however, for binding legal opinions (fatwas), issued without a court case by a mufti. Historically, the principal Saudi judicial official was called the chief *qadi* and grand mufti. In 1970, the title was changed to minister of justice, but the functions of the ministry have remained basically the same.

Because the sharia is considered divine, legislative or statutory law is proscribed. There is, however, a means for regulating and adjudicating issues that did not exist during the time of Muhammad. Royal decrees (nizams) issued by the king are used to provide regulatory and administrative rules, and special administrative tribunals have been created to adjudicate labor and commercial disputes. In addition, a Board of Grievances (Diwan al-Mazalim) adjudicates grievances between citizens and the government.

The Executive Branch

Saudi Arabia is an Islamic monarchy, ruled by the Al Saud. Royal succession is technically legitimized through an ancient Islamic institution, Ahl al-Hall wa'l-Aqd (The People Who Bind and Loose), made up of the elders of the royal family and religious leaders, technocrats, businessmen, and heads of important families not otherwise included in those categories. In reality, however, no king can remain in power without the consensual support of the Al Saud.

The king is both the chief of state and head of government, but he is not above the law. Thus, despite there being no democratically elected representatives of the people, Saudi Arabia is not an absolute monarchy in the historic European sense; the doctrine of divine right of kings would be considered heresy. Moreover, despite all the powers residing in the ruler, he cannot act in the face of a contravening consensus. Thus, the king must be more than a chief of state and head of government. In order to legitimize government policies, he must also act as the chief consensus maker through consultation with all those considered part of the national decision-making process.

Prior to the capture of the Hijaz in 1925, the Al Saud regime had few, if any, formal political institutions, other than the Islamic judicial system, and they ruled by interpersonal consultation with leading members of the royal family and tribal and religious leaders. The Hijaz, in contrast, had a much more formal system of government, including cabinet ministers. When Abd al-Aziz annexed the Hijaz in 1926, he left its political institutions intact. The evolution of Saudi political institutions had no master plan. It can be seen as the expansion of institutions initially found only in the Hijaz to the rest of the country, augmented by the creation of new institutions and a bureaucracy to run them as the need arose. Interpersonal relations within the government, as throughout the society as a whole, are still highly personalized, but they are increasingly carried out within the parameters of formal political institutions and more standardized procedures. Moreover, it is still a work in progress.

The first nationwide ministry, the Ministry of Foreign Affairs, was created in 1930, followed by the Ministry of Finance in 1932. Both ministries initially overlapped with separate Hijazi ministries, which continued to exist for a number of years. The Ministry of Finance was initially responsible not only for financial affairs but also for most of the administrative machinery of the entire kingdom, as its predecessor, the Hijazi Ministry of the Interior (abolished in 1934), had been.

Many of the subsequent national ministries thus began as departments under the Ministry of Finance, some becoming independent agencies before being elevated to the ministry level. One of Abd al-Aziz's final acts was to create a Council of Ministers, which he decreed in October 1953, just a month before his death. Nevertheless, because many of the ministries and independent agencies existed before the Council of Ministers, interministerial and interagency cooperation have evolved at a slower pace.

The evolution of local government institutions has faced another set of problems. The country is divided into thirteen provincial regions, all of which have representatives from national ministries who report directly to Riyadh but must also work closely with the regional governors. Each regional governor is responsible for subregional governorates, districts, and local government centers. The Regions Statute, issued by royal decree on March 1, 1992, did not greatly clarify the situation. For example, although the national interior ministry is directly in charge of regional and local government, the decree confers equal ministerial rank on the regional governors. The decree also stipulates a ten-man advisory council for each region.

Consultative Participation

The term *legislative branch of government* is obviously inappropriate for a country that proscribes statuary law. Thus, when King Fahd decreed the creation of an appointed Consultative Assembly (Majlis al-Shura) on March 1, 1992, his intent was not to create an embryonic legislature modeled after a Western parliamentary concept. Rather, it was to employ a formal Islamic institution for *shura* (consultation) with "people of knowledge and expertise and specialists" in order to create a consensus legitimizing public policy. With rapid modernization acquired with oil revenues, it was increasingly obvious that an informal personalized system was no longer adequate to create a true consensus and that public participation in the political process must be expanded.

A Majlis al-Shura existed in the Hijaz when it was annexed by the Saudis. King Abd al-Aziz wished to extend it into a national institution then but met with opposition from Najdi religious authorities, who objected that by in effect dealing with statutory law, the assembly was incompatible with the sharia, a wholly self-contained, revealed system of divine law. Thus, in some respects, the 1992 decree completed the process of expanding Hijazi political institutions to the entire country, which had begun in the early years of Abd al-Aziz's reign.

The Majlis al-Shura was inaugurated by the king in December 1993 with 60 members; it was expanded to 90 in 1997 and 150 in 2005. Members are appointed for four-year terms and meet in closed sessions at least every two weeks. They are charged with suggesting new regulatory decrees and reviewing and evaluating foreign and domestic policies.

Members include businessmen, technocrats, journalists, Islamic scholars, and professional soldiers and represent all regions of the country. In a break with tradition, most members are in their forties and fifties, young by Saudi leadership standards. Thus, although the majority come from well-known families, they tend not to be the family patriarchs that speculation had suggested would be appointed. Many have doctorates from the United States, Europe, Australia, or the Middle East. Similarly, an ever-increasing number of Saudi religious community members are younger men with outside exposure, in contrast with the older generation of Islamic leaders, many of whom have never been outside the Muslim world or even outside Saudi Arabia. The real test for the Majlis will be the degree to which its members actually participate in the consultative process. But whatever its future, it reflects a remarkable vision as an adaptation of a classical Islamic concept to modern government.

In 2005, King Abdallah succeeded his half brother King Fahd, ending a ten-year hiatus during which Fahd was incapacitated due to medical problems and Abdallah headed a caretaker government. As king, Abdallah has reenergized the process of political evolution and increased public participation in the political process. Even before his succession, however, he was seeking new opportunities for more political participation by all Saudi citizens. In response to petitions signed by over 350 intellectuals in 2003, the government, under Abdallah's auspices, initiated the National Dialogue (al-Hiwar al-Watani), a forum headquartered in Riyadh to bring together interest groups to discuss topics of public concern such as the role of women, religious tolerance, and future prospects for youth.

Another political concession by Abdallah was for half the members of the 179 municipal councils to be chosen by popular elections held in 2005. Among the main issues discussed by the candidates were political reform, corruption, environmental issues, and better public service. The second round of elections was postponed until September 2011, when 1,056 seats in 285 councils were elected. However, despite initial announcements to the contrary, women were not allowed to participate.

The Decision-Making Process

Islamic cultural traits have often made the Saudi decision-making process appear arbitrary and capricious to the untrained eye. There is a systemic logic to the process, however. At the heart of the system are two fundamental concepts: *ijma'* (consensus), which is derived through *shura* (consultation). Consensus has been used to legitimize collective decisions in the Arab world for millennia, whether in government, business, or family, and has been incorporated into Islam.

With the coming of the oil age, government operations have become far too large and too complicated for the traditional, personalized decision-making process that had existed virtually unchanged until the mid-twentieth century. In addition, the advent of the information-technology revolution has increased exponentially the need to expand the number of citizens participating directly in the decision-making process. Evolutionary reform is vital, but to maintain legitimacy, it is more likely to reflect the teachings of Islam than those of Thomas Jefferson.

THE POLITICAL PROCESS

The Saudi political process basically works on three separate but highly interrelated levels: royal family politics, national politics, and bureaucratic politics.

Royal Family Politics

Few outside the Al Saud know how the royal family actually operates or even its size (estimated to be in the thousands). It has historically been rife with rivalries and contention, yet assiduously shuns publicity and always seeks an outward appearance of unanimity. Consensus is key, but ties based on family, branch, generation, seniority, and siblinghood (particularly among siblings of the same mother) are very important. The ruling branch is composed of the surviving sons of King Abd al-Aziz. Some grandsons have been appointed to senior positions—for instance, Prince Saud al-Faisal serves as foreign minister—but they are generally less influential than members of their fathers' generation.

There are also collateral branches of the family, descended from brothers of former rulers. The two leading collateral branches are the Saud al-Kabir, who descend from an older brother of Abd al-Rahman (Abd al-Aziz's father), and the Ibn Jaluwi, who descend from an uncle of Abd al-Rahman, Jaluwi. Technically, the head of the Saud al-Kabir branch outranks all but the king, since the founder was an older brother of Abd al-Rahman; however, the ruling branch has a monopoly on influence.

Among the sons of Abd al-Aziz, seniority of birth is important but not absolute in determining political influence. Older princes not deemed capable of maintaining high government positions are excluded from the decision-making process except with regard to purely royal-family business.

Succession is also determined by seniority among the sons of Abd al-Aziz with the oldest son being nominated as king and the next in age as crown prince. However, crown princes Sultan and Nayef died unexpectedly in 2011 and 2012. The king and other senior members of the Al Saud then formed a council to determine the next crown prince. This Allegiance Council did not specifically adhere to the seniority concept, theoretically allowing consideration of younger brothers and grandchildren of Abd al-Aziz. Their first selection, however, Prince Salman, was the next in line.

National and Bureaucratic Politics

National politics is played out not in the royal family per se but in the national ministries. The royal family has ensured that family members fill most senior national security related cabinet posts. However, the regime has consistently named technocrats to ministerial positions not connected with national security. These posts deal mainly with economics and social welfare, and in those areas it may be said that a technocracy has developed.

As the government expanded rapidly over the years, the sheer size and complexity of its operations made it impossible for the king to be personally involved in all but the most pressing national issues. Thus, senior technocrats have considerable powers as principal advisers to the king in their areas of responsibility and as operational decision makers.

In recent years, an increasing number of the younger generation of Western-educated royal-family members, including those from collateral branches, have entered government, creating a new category of "royal technocrats." However, because the more senior positions are occupied, the younger princes join the government in junior positions. It is too soon to know how they will ultimately affect the political equation, but so far the most successful have won respect on merit as much as rank.

On balance, the evolution of public administration in Saudi Arabia has consisted of a gradual shift from the traditional rule of King Abd al-Aziz to a more institutionalized, bureaucratized government. However, the creation of a government bureaucracy has not diminished the personalization of the policy process so much as rechanneled it, and it is within the present structure that bureaucratic politics has grown and flourished.

POLITICAL DYNAMICS

Saudi political culture is inseparable from Islam. The country is the cradle of Islam and Arabic, the language of the Qur'an, which is indigenous to northern Arabia. Moreover, from the time of the founder of the ruling family 250 years ago, the teachings of Muhammad ibn Abd al-Wahhab have constituted the political ideology of Saudi Arabia. Those teachings have provided the Saudi regime with an egalitarian, universal, and moral base that has bound rulers and ruled together through many crises and troubles and served as a major factor in the survival of the Saudi state throughout its often turbulent history. One must use care, however, in looking at Saudi political ideology as analogous to secular political ideologies in the West. Considering that there is no separation of church and state in Saudi Arabia, there is no political culture independent of Islam.

The government and mainstream establishment in Saudi Arabia are challenged by two internal forms of religious opposition: from Sunnis, who contest the elite's legitimacy and ability to protect the country from Westernization, and from Shi'as, who generally feel rejected by and discriminated against in a Wahhabi-dominated kingdom. After tensions with the Shi'as during the late 1970s and early 1980s had ebbed significantly, a new round of clashes between active Shi'as and government forces broke out in 2003 and continue to flare up, especially during the Hajj or Ashura. King Abdallah, through the National Dialogue and his reform agenda, uses both force and concessions to prevent the conflict from having any impact on the oil industry, which is largely housed in the Eastern Province.

On the other end of the religious spectrum are Sunni scholars, preachers, and activists, who were influenced by the Muslim Brotherhood and started to agitate against the ruling elites. Radical preachers in local mosques called for young Saudis to do something more meaningful with their lives and join the jihad in Afghanistan and Iraq. Some went even further by including corrupt Arab regimes as targets for jihad actions. Al-Qaida is a product of this inflammatory speech, and the government is working hard to crack down on those radicals, arresting and reeducating them. Support is provided by the highest religious authorities in the country, who also recognize that more needs to be done on the ideological front to cut the relationship between militants, disillusioned youth, and religious extremists.

FOREIGN POLICY

Saudi foreign and national security policies revolve around four major goals: preserving an Islamic way of life at home and abroad, protecting against external threats to national and regional security, providing for the national economic welfare and extending economic assistance to those in need throughout the Arab and Muslim world, and survival of the regime. How these are translated into relations with other states is largely a product of a uniquely Saudi view of the world.

The Saudi worldview conforms closely to the classical, bipolar Islamic theory of international relations that contrasts believers (monotheists) with unbelievers (atheists and polytheists). The believers—who include Christians, Jews, and Zoroastrians, as "People of the Book"—inhabit *Dar al-Islam,* the Abode of Islam (i.e., the land of those who live by God's law), while the unbelievers inhabit *Dar al-Harb,* the Abode of War (i.e., the land of those who live outside God's law). This worldview is a product of three strong, though seemingly contradictory, themes: a strong sense of Arabian self-identity, a deep and abiding allegiance to Islam, and millennia of physical isolation from the non-Islamic outside world until well into the twentieth century, particularly in Najd.

Most Arabs equate their self-identity with pan-Arabism, a relatively recent political movement based on the rebirth of secular Arab nationalism. Secular Arab nationalism reached its apogee in the 1950s and 1960s as the idiom for expressing political hostility toward the West after centuries of political domination. The Saudis, while sharing an Arab self-identity, reject secular Arab nationalism as a political ideology, considering it incompatible with Islamic political theory. They base their self-identity on bloodlines, equating it with their Arabian tribal genealogy, which they trace back to the beginning of history.

Saudi Arabia takes special pride in being the birthplace of Islam and in the fact that Arabic, the language of Islam's holy book, the Qur'an, is indigenous to northern Arabia. Moreover, the Saudi sense of responsibility for the preservation of the Islamic way of life was substantially strengthened in the 1920s when Abd al-Aziz occupied the Hijaz and the holy cities of Mecca and Medina. As guardians of these two holy sites, the Saudis assumed responsibility for defending the Islamic way of life throughout the Muslim world. It is in this context that one must view the title adopted by King Fahd in 1986, Khadim al-Haramayn al-Sharifayn (Custodian of the Two Holy Places). Centuries of isolation from the Western world have further reinforced Saudis' sense of Arabian self-identity and their role as custodians of Islamic values. Although the oil age has transformed the kingdom into a global oil state, the traditional Saudi worldview has remained largely intact.

Saudi foreign and national security policy making is imbued with two strong, though seemingly contradictory, themes: extraordinary cultural self-assurance based on a sense of Islamic heritage and Arabian, tribe-based self-identity and a heightened sense of insecurity based on the historical experience of an insular people eternally surrounded by enemies. A basic tenet of foreign policy, therefore, has always been to avoid confrontations whenever possible and to seek alliances and cooperation in the face of external threats to political, economic, and national security interests.

In accordance with its worldview, Saudi Arabia has developed close ties with fellow Arab and Muslim states. It is a member of the Arab League and the GCC, as well as a charter member of, and prime mover in the 1969 creation of, the Organization of the Islamic Conference (OIC), the premier international organization serving the Muslim world. The OIC Secretariat is located in Jiddah.

Alliance politics with powerful partners sharing mutual interests has traditionally been the major focus of Saudi foreign security and economic policies. In the years leading up to World War I, King Abd al-Aziz relied on the British, the paramount Western power in Arabia, for both protection and economic assistance. Gradually, however, he turned to the United States, in part because he was convinced that they had no imperial designs on the region and also because his earliest experience with Americans was largely positive. American Protestant medical missionaries located in Bahrain began bringing modern medicine to the kingdom in 1913, and in 1933 American oil men began searching for oil in the Eastern Province, establishing what would become important and lasting mutual Saudi-US commercial, and later strategic, oil interests.

Yet, not until World War II did the United States establish a resident diplomatic mission in the kingdom and extend lend-lease economic assistance. Perhaps the cementing of close political relations between the two countries during the reign of King Abd al-Aziz resulted from his meeting with President Franklin D. Roosevelt aboard the USS *Quincy* in the Great Bitter Lake of the Suez Canal on February 14, 1945.

Since then, a special relationship between the two countries has evolved, due not only to mutual interest in reliable supplies of oil flowing to the West but also to their close cooperation in Middle East regional security. During the Cold War, Saudi Arabia considered atheistic Soviet Communist ideology to be the greatest threat to Muslim hearts and minds. Thus, the kingdom also opposed radical Arab leaders such as President Gamal Abdel Nasser of Egypt, who had established cordial relations with the Soviet Union. Even after the end of the Cold War, Saudi Arabia looked to the United States for military training and for a great proportion of its arms purchases.

US-Saudi relations have not always been smooth, however. The greatest source of stress has been what the Saudis see as the disproportionate US support for Israel. US rejection of Saudi efforts to help in the quest for an Arab-Israeli peace has added to the stress. In general, the most stressful Saudi-US relations have coincided with periods of polarization of the Arab-Israeli conflict, beginning in 1948 with the initial partition of Palestine to create a Jewish state. From the Saudi perspective, not only did the lead US role in the partition of Palestine and the creation of Israel constitute grave injustice, but for President Harry Truman to ignore President Roosevelt's oral and written word to King Abd al-Aziz in 1945 that the United States would not act on partition without first consulting him and other Arab leaders was considered the height of dishonor. Against the advice of the State Department, Truman bowed to US domestic political pressure in engineering the partition and creation of Israel in 1948.

The three periods of greatest polarization since 1948 have resulted from Israel's annexation of Arab East Jerusalem in the wake of the 1967 Arab-Israeli War, the Arab oil embargo led by King Faisal during the 1973 Arab-Israeli War, and a wave of American anti-Arab and anti-Muslim sentiment following the terrorist attacks on the World Trade Center in New York City and Washington, DC, on September 11, 2001, in which fifteen of the nineteen terrorists were Saudis.

Following the Israeli occupation of the Palestinian West Bank, Gaza, and East Jerusalem in the 1967 war, the UN Security Council passed Resolution 242, which called for a return of Palestinian territory in exchange for an end of hostilities—land for peace. Israel ignored the resolution, but particularly egregious from the Saudi perspective was Israel's unilateral "annexation" of Jerusalem. Not only did this violate international law, but it granted Israel sovereignty over the Muslim shrines of al-Aqsa, located in East Jerusalem. Al-Aqsa is the third holiest site in Sunni Islam after Mecca and Medina. The United States did not recognize the annexation but did nothing to prevent it. Nor did it have the domestic political capital to push for an Arab-Israeli peace settlement based on Resolution 242.

The 1973–1974 Arab oil embargo ironically ran counter to the Saudis' estimate of their own economic and security interests. Saudi Arabia has always been moderate on oil prices due to the reality that expansion of alternative sources of energy due to high prices could do irreparable damage to the Saudi oil economy. The embargo also strained Saudi reliance on the United States to deter external military threats against the kingdom that were in neither country's interest.

Apparently the embargo was the result of King Faisal's anger over what he considered President Richard Nixon's going back on his word. Two days after Nixon had sent a secret message to Faisal assuring him that the United States would be evenhanded during the war, the president announced $2 billion in military aid to Israel, presumably to assuage domestic fears over the heavy equipment losses Israel was sustaining in the war. Faisal had never forgotten President Truman's breaking of Roosevelt's promise on partition in 1948. As Saudi foreign minister at the time, Faisal had urged his father to break diplomatic relations.

The embargo quickly strained Saudi relations with the United States. Not only did it bring economic hardship to the United States, but politically it resulted in a strong anti-Saudi campaign in the US media, exploiting domestic anger at high oil prices and fears that the "Arab oil weapon" could threaten US interests in the region, including Israel's national security. Saudi Arabia originally benefited from high oil prices, but fearing strained relations would undermine its national security interests, which depended heavily on US support, it sought to negotiate a rapid end to the embargo. In the longer run, however, relations returned to normal. The embargo forced the United States and other Western oil consumers to reduce demand by increasing energy efficiency. By the 1980s, the oil shortage was replaced by a glut, keeping oil prices low for a whole generation, and US-Saudi relations based on mutual security as well as petroleum interests normalized.

The September 11, 2001, terrorist attacks traumatized most Americans, who had for years believed themselves impervious to such assaults. The fear and anger aroused by the attacks brought broad support for the government's hard-line response of all-out global war against terrorism—with the perpetrators identified as chiefly Arabs and Muslims—and Israel was praised as a partner in the war. Saudi businessmen, students, and those seeking medical care were singled out at ports of entry as potential terrorists. The heightened xenophobia was further fueled by another anti-Saudi campaign in the US media, which denounced the kingdom not only as a supporter of terrorism but as thoroughly evil. In Saudi Arabia, American policies and attitudes were in turn met with anger, fear, and a sense of betrayal by a longtime friendly ally, leading to a sharp decline in travel to the United States and a significant flight of Saudi investment capital.

As time has passed, mutual fears and feelings of grievance appear again to be receding, and relations have once again begun to normalize. Nevertheless, it is likely that the Saudis will increase the diversification of their foreign policy, as well as commercial and security relations, to safeguard against a repeat of their post–September 11 experience. Following the military occupation of Iraq by the United States and Britain in 2003, Saudi Arabia rejected the US proposal to use its airfields for attacks on Iraq. US headquarters was thus relocated to Qatar, but the tensions kept growing. The Saudis were against the war due to concerns over growing inter-Arab conflicts. At one point, Abdallah even called it an "illegal foreign occupation," showing his frustration with the dangerous and hazardous directions of the conflict. However, there was also a deep mistrust that a Shi'a-dominated government in Baghdad would become an agent of Iran. The Saudi government had long warned about the growing influence of Iran and started to support Sunni tribal militias long before the coalition troops discovered their value.

To challenge the growing security needs of the country, a multilevel and well-equipped security force, headed by the very diverse (for Saudi Arabia) National Security Council, protects the traditional and current form of leadership and government. This gives Saudi Arabia the necessary prowess, strength, and credibility to continue acting like a power broker in broader Gulf and Middle East affairs, and it is utilizing its position to call for a Middle East free of weapons of mass destruction.

Although Iran has for many years been considered a major threat to the national and regional security of the Gulf, Saudi Arabia continues to work with the Iranians to solve bilateral issues. While the existence of nuclear weapons in Iran would obviously be seen as a security threat, Saudi Arabia has always accepted the right of other states, including Iran, to develop peaceful uses of nuclear power and retains the right to do so itself sometime in the future.

As a leading Arab-Islamic state and regional power broker, Saudi Arabia is also committed to mediating in regional conflicts. Following political examples and strategies that have evolved over centuries, the Saudis consider moderation, negotiation, reconciliation, and alliance building the necessary tools to bring together rival factions in Lebanon, Palestine, and other Arab countries. When in neighboring Bahrain the ruling Sunni family of the Al Khalifah was threatened by a politically motivated uprising of the country's Shi'a majority, Saudi Arabia sent troops to restore calm. Other Arab Spring–related events have had little impact on the kingdom. A balanced foreign policy based on mediation, collaboration, and the building of alliances serves as a tool to lower domestic and international threats to the national security of the kingdom. Thus, Saudi Arabia supported Hosni Mubarak of Egypt until it was obvious that he could no longer stay in power. The Saudis did not participate in the military operation against Muammar Qaddafi of Libya, and that is why Saudi Arabia is only covertly helping the Syrian opposition in its struggle against Bashar al-Asad. However, when stability in neighboring Yemen was in jeopardy, the GCC led by the Saudis worked hard to find a compromise solution allowing President Ali Abdullah Saleh to step down and to go into exile.

BIBLIOGRAPHY

Definitive works on Saudi Arabia are comparatively few. R. Bayly Winder's *Saudi Arabia in the Nineteenth Century* (New York: St. Martin's Press, 1985) is still the standard work in English on earlier history. Any of the several works by H. St. John B. Philby, though not scholarly, capture the feel of Saudi Arabia in the interwar and immediate post–World War II period. Two of his books, *Arabian Jubilee* (London: Robert Hale, 1952) and *Saudi Arabia* (London: Ernest Benn, 1955), written to commemorate the fiftieth year of King Abd al-Aziz's reign, would be good places to begin. Another classic is T. E. Lawrence's *The Seven Pillars of Wisdom* (Garden City, NY: Doubleday, 1935), about his exploits in the Hijaz during World War I. For a good study of the earlier history of the Hijaz, see William Ochsenwald's *Religion, Society and the State in Arabia: The Hijaz Under*

Ottoman Control, 1849–1908 (Columbus: Ohio State University Press, 1984). For a general historical overview, both Alexander Vassiliev's *The History of Saudi Arabia* (London: Saqi, 1998) and Madawi al-Rasheed's *A History of Saudi Arabia* (Cambridge: Cambridge University Press, 2002) are recommended.

For readers interested in the modern Hajj, see David E. Long's *The Hajj Today: A Survey of the Contemporary Makkah Pilgrimage* (Albany: State University of New York Press, 1979). An interesting account of Mecca and the Hajj in the nineteenth century is C. Snouck-Hurgronje's *Mekka in the Latter Part of the Nineteenth Century*, trans. J. H. Monahan (Leiden: E. J. Brill, and London: Luzac and Co., 1931). Natana DeLong-Bas's extensive study on Wahhabism, *Wahhabi Islam* (Oxford: Oxford University Press, 2004), is the standard in this field. On modern extremist expression of Islamism, see Thomas Hegghammer's *Jihad in Saudi Arabia: Violence and Pan-Islamism Since 1979* (Cambridge: Cambridge University Press, 2010). The impact of the generation gap and new evolving identities are discussed in Mai Yamani's *Changed Identities: The Challenge of the New Generation in Saudi Arabia* (London: The Royal Institute of International Affairs, 2000).

There are a number of good studies on the development of the Saudi oil industry. Daniel Yergin's exhaustively researched best seller, *The Prize: The Epic Quest for Oil, Money and Power* (New York: Simon and Schuster, 1990), is a must-read. Toby Jones's *Desert Kingdom* (Cambridge, MA: Harvard University Press, 2010) describes how oil and water forged modern Saudi Arabia, while Steffen Hertog's study sheds light on the deep connections between the government and the oil sector in *Princes, Brokers and Bureaucrats: Oil and the State in Saudi Arabia* (Ithaca, NY: Cornell University Press, 2011). A fascinating book on the Saudi Arabian Monetary Agency, the Saudi central bank, is *Saudi Arabia: The Making of a Financial Giant* (New York: New York University Press, 1983) by Arthur N. Young, who played a major role in the agency's creation.

Works on political, military, and strategic issues are highly uneven. David E. Long's *The United States and Saudi Arabia: Ambivalent Allies* (Boulder, CO: Westview Press, 1985) is a short but authoritative overview of US-Saudi political, economic, oil, and military relations up to 1985. Anthony Cordesman emerged as the leading authority regarding Saudi Arabia's national security and strategic issues with his *Saudi Arabia: National Security in a Troubled Region* (Santa Barbara, CA: ABC-CLIO, 2009). A recent study of US relations with Saudi Arabia, Rachel Bronson's *Thicker Than Oil: America's Uneasy Partnership with Saudi Arabia* (New York: Oxford University Press, 2005), documents post–September 11 events.

Two nonscholarly books are worth looking into for their wealth of narrative, if not their interpretative analysis: Robert Lacey's *The Kingdom* (London: Hutcheson, 1981) and David Howarth and Richard Johns's *The House of Saud* (London: Sidgwick and Jackson, 1981). The most recent survey of Saudi Arabia is David E. Long and Sebastian Maisel's *The Kingdom of Saudi Arabia* (Gainesville: University Press of Florida, 2010). Those interested in the Rub' al-Khali should read Wilfred Thesiger's *Arabian Sands* (New York: Dutton, 1959). Finally, David E. Long also provides the most concise study on Saudi Arabian culture in transition: *Culture and Customs of Saudi Arabia* (Westport, CT: Greenwood, 2005), which in combination with Sebastian Maisel and John Shoup's *Encyclopedia of Life in Saudi Arabia and the Arab Gulf States* (Westport, CT: Greenwood, 2009) gives the reader a rare insight into the evolution and functioning of Saudi lifestyles.

5

REPUBLIC OF IRAQ

Judith S. Yaphe

Since the first modern government of Iraq was created by and under British mandate in 1920, observers inside and outside the country have argued over its imperial and colonial legacies, identity, and viability. Some saw Iraq as an artificial creation of secret agreements between greedy British and French diplomats eager for booty following the Great War. Iraqis were Arabs or Kurds, Sunnis or Shi'as, Christians or Jews. What they were not, according to this perspective, was Iraqi. For Iraqis, however, Iraqi nationalism was born in the ashes of the Ottoman Empire and was the force that shaped modern Iraq, despite British efforts to impose foreign values, government institutions, and rulers on the new country. Iraq has survived three occupations: the Turks in the sixteenth century, the British twice in the twentieth century, and the Americans in the twenty-first century. Ten years after liberation, and after two national parliamentary elections and a constitutional referendum, Iraq has had an opportunity to showcase its successful transition from dictatorship to democracy. The inability of political factions to agree on national versus provincial power, disputed territories, ownership of Iraq's singular resource—oil—and an end to de-Ba'thification laws indicates that national reconciliation is still more dream than reality.

HISTORICAL BACKGROUND

Iraq is a land rich in resources and history. Known until the twentieth century as Mesopotamia ("the land between the rivers," the Tigris and Euphrates), Iraq has been a battleground of strategic importance due to geography and the availability of oil and water. As a result, it has experienced foreign invasions and occupations, tribal wars, ethnic and sectarian factionalism, violence, and decay. Bordered by deserts in the south and high mountains to the north, Iraq is virtually without natural defenses against invasion. Its occupiers—the Greeks, Romans, Persians, Arabs, Turks, and, in modern times, the British and Americans—have all left their mark on the country's diverse people and cultures, fashioning a society in search of identity.

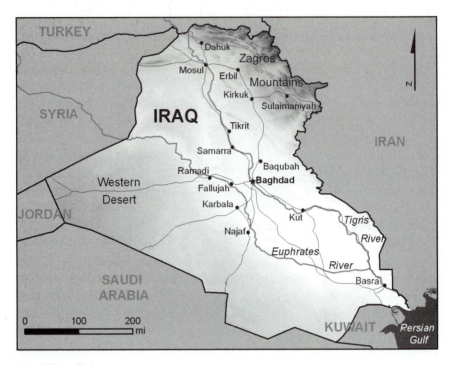

Republic of Iraq

Arab Conquests, 633–1258

The Arab-Islamic conquest of Iraq began in 633 CE, one year after the death of the Prophet Muhammad. It was one of the most decisive events in Iraqi history. Arabic became the predominant language, and Islam became the religion of virtually all inhabitants. For over a century after the conquest, Iraq was governed as a province from capitals of the Islamic empire, first in Medina and later Damascus. Iraqis came to resent the power of Damascus—a theme that persists even in modern times—and often revolted against it. In the process, Iraq acquired a reputation, which it retains, as a territory difficult to govern.

Moving the Islamic capital to Damascus produced a religious schism that still divides the Islamic community. In 680, Hussein, grandson of the Prophet Muhammad and son of Ali, the fourth caliph, challenged the Umayyads and, along with a small band of followers, was killed near Karbala in Iraq. Ali's followers, known as Shi'a (short for *Shi'at Ali*, the "partisans of Ali"), went underground as opponents of the established order. Followers of the Umayyads came to be known as Sunnis, those who adhere to the Prophet's traditions (Sunna). Gradually, the Shi'a became a distinctive sect within Islam, with different leaders (called imams rather than caliphs) and different doctrines, considered heresy by the Sunni victors. As a persecuted minority, the Shi'a acquired a sense of social alienation, oppression, and injustice, characteristics still evident in the twenty-first century.

In 747, Abd al-Abbas, a descendant of Muhammad's uncle, revolted against the Umayyads, and in 750 he established the Abbasid caliphate. In 762, the Abbasids moved the capital to the new city of Baghdad. The Abbasid period (750–1258) was a great era in Iraqi, Arab, and Islamic history. Iraq became the center of a prosperous empire that stretched from southern France to the borders of China and a brilliant civilization in which science, architecture, and literature flourished.

The decline of the Abbasid caliphate was gradual. Prosperity was concentrated in the urban upper classes; little filtered down to the rural and urban poor, who often revolted. Turkish captives were used as warriors and administrators, and factionalism within the ruling elite led to economic decline and neglect of the irrigation system. Weakness within encouraged incursion from without, including the intrusion of the Seljuk Turks in 1055.

It was the Mongols, however, who caused the ultimate demise of the Abbasid caliphate. In 1258, Hulagu, the grandson of Genghis Khan, destroyed much of Baghdad and the irrigation system on which its prosperity depended. Even more devastating to Iraq was the invasion of Timur the Lame in 1401. He so ravished the country that it did not recover until the mid-twentieth century. Iraq's strategic location astride the major East-West trade routes was also greatly undermined by the Portuguese discovery of the sea route around the Cape of Good Hope. Although Iraqis recall their glorious Abbasid past, their political and social environment—and much of their psychology—has been shaped mainly by the centuries of stagnation that followed.

Ottoman Rule, 1258–1918

From 1258 until 1534, Iraq was divided into provinces ruled by Turkish tribal dynasties from capitals in Persian territory. Because of the lack of a central government, neither the irrigation systems nor the urban culture could be revived. The Ottoman conquest began in 1514 as an outgrowth of a religious and dynastic war between the Sunni Ottoman sultan and the Shi'a Safavid shah of Persia. Most of Iraq was incorporated into the Ottoman domain, and the country was divided into three provinces: Mosul, Baghdad, and Basra.

The Ottomans were unable to bring stability or prosperity to Iraq, primarily for two reasons. The first was a succession of Ottoman-Persian wars that continued until 1818, ravaged the Iraqi countryside, and renewed Shi'a-Sunni distrust. The second was the weakness of Ottoman power. As Ottoman society declined in the seventeenth and eighteenth centuries, direct administration ceased in Iraq, and local tribal chiefs held sway in Arab and Kurdish areas. In the late eighteenth century, Ottoman efforts to gain control over Iraq's fractious Arab tribes and restrict the growing influence of Persian Shi'a clerics in southern Iraq hastened the conversion of many Arab tribes from Sunni to Shi'a Islam. By the nineteenth century, the fragmentation was complete. What little Ottoman control

REPUBLIC OF IRAQ

Capital city	Baghdad
Chief of state, 2012	President Jalal Talabani
Head of government, 2012	Prime Minister Nuri al-Maliki
Political parties, 2012	Badr Organization, Da'wa Party, Da'wa Tanzim, Fadilah Party, Goran List, Hadba Gathering, Iraqi Covenant Gathering, Iraqi Constitutional Party, Iraqi Front for National Dialogue, Iraqi Islamic Party, Iraqi Justice and Reform Movement, Iraqi National Accord, Iraqi National Congress, Islamic Supreme Council of Iraq, Kurdistan Democratic Party, Future National Gathering, National Iraqiyun Gathering, National Movement for Reform and Development, National Reform Trend, Patriotic Union of Kurdistan, Renewal List, Sadrist Trend, Sahawa al-Iraq
Ethnic groups	Arab (75%–80%), Kurdish (15%–20%), Turkoman, Assyrian, or other (5%)
Religious groups	Shi'a Muslim (60%–65%), Sunni Muslim (32%–37%), Christian or other (3%)
Export partners, 2011	United States (23.3%), India (19.2%), China (14%), South Korea (12.2%), Japan (5%), Netherlands (4.5%)
Import partners, 2011	Turkey (25%), Syria (18.1%), China (11.5%), United States (7.3%), South Korea (4.6%)

remained was inefficient and corrupt. Most of the local population despised the Ottoman Turks as occupiers.

During the nineteenth century, Iraq was drawn into international politics and economics. The opening of the Suez Canal in 1869 increased Iraq's trade, and in the south some landlords shifted from subsistence agriculture to cash crops. Because of its strategic location astride overland routes to India, Iraq attracted increasing British attention, while international commerce produced a small class of urban merchants and farmers tied to the new market economy. These benefits, however, could not overcome centuries of indifferent and often corrupt Ottoman rule. Iraq entered the twentieth century a profoundly underdeveloped country, only marginally touched by the economic, scientific, and political developments that had transformed Europe in the nineteenth century.

British Occupation, 1920–1932

The impact of the British in shaping modern Iraq was second only to that of the Arab-Islamic conquest of the seventh century and the Mongol invaders of the thirteenth century. The British created the modern state of Iraq, established its present boundaries, and introduced a non-Iraqi monarch with impeccable Arab and Islamic credentials. They also incorporated a diverse ethnic and sectarian population that would prove to be a source of both strength and instability for the new state.

Britain occupied Iraq during World War I, starting with Basra in 1914, Baghdad in 1917, and finally Mosul in 1918. British control over Iraq was formalized at the San Remo Conference in April 1920, which granted Britain a mandate over the country, subject to supervision by the League of Nations. Several factors constrained British control over the territory and its government. First, the mandate itself was designed to prepare the country for independence, but the British could not agree among themselves on who should rule Iraq, how it should be ruled, or when Iraqis would meet European standards of political responsibility. Second, Great Britain faced a growing demand to cut back on financial commitments and military deployments in Iraq. This sentiment was underscored by an anti-British revolt in 1920, the suppression of which cost nearly £40 million and hundreds of British lives. The final constraint was the emergence in Iraq of a vigorous nationalist movement, which began agitating for an end to British occupation even before the war ended. Arabism and nationalism had held the imaginations of Iraq's Arabs since 1916, when Sunni Arabs who had served in the Ottoman army joined the Arab Revolt against the Turks. In 1920, Sunni and Shi'a Arabs joined together to oppose British occupation, creating a rite of passage that resonates still.

As a result, the British sought a less expensive means of governing Iraq. They found it in three instruments of indirect rule. First, they established a monarchy in Iraq in the person of Amir Faysal, third son of the Hashimite ruler of Mecca, who had cooperated with the British during the war. In 1921, after a carefully controlled plebiscite, Faysal became the first of three Hashimite kings to rule Iraq. Under the British-written constitution, the king was given considerable powers, including the right to appoint the prime minister and dismiss parliament. Britain exercised its influence through the monarchy and a network of British advisers in key ministries. Second, the British outlined their mandatory relationship through a series of treaties signed between 1922 and 1932. These provided the British with bases and other facilities in return for help, advice, and protection for the new state. Third, they expanded their use of air power to monitor tribal movements and quell threats to security.

Although the British created Western-style democratic institutions in Iraq, including a parliament, constitution, and indirect elections, responsibility for governance was unclear. King Faysal obeyed British directives but also helped his Iraqi supporters—many of whom had fought with him in the Arab Revolt—to create an Iraqi and Arab identity in a secular state. The result was an army dominated by Sunni Arabs and an educational system focused on promoting Arab identity and Iraqi national unity. The British also relied on this small group of nationalists and on a parliament increasingly filled with tribal leaders and wealthy urban elites willing to trade political acquiescence for self-interest and economic privileges. They became the backbone of the new state.

Not everyone was satisfied with the British distribution of power. The Kurds rebelled against Arab rule and eventually were given special consideration, particularly in the use of their language in schools. Shi'a religious leaders led a rebellion against the mandate, and its leaders ended up in exile in Iran. For much of the mandate period, Faysal was able to maintain the balance between British and nationalist interests. In 1929, the British negotiated a treaty that met British security interests and nationalist demands. The mandate ended formally in 1932, Iraq was admitted to the League of Nations, and a new Anglo-Iraq treaty gave Britain air bases and Iraq military protection.

Constitutional Monarchy, 1932–1958

The end of the mandate and the reduction of British control ushered in a period of instability that revealed the weakness of the constitutional structure and the fragility of Iraq's sense of nationhood. Several religious and ethnic groups asserted claims to a greater share of power, and the Iraqi army entered the political arena and committed its first act of ethnic cleansing.

In 1933 the Assyrian (Nestorian Christian) community demanded the right to self-government and was put down by the Iraqi army. In the process, a massacre of Assyrians occurred in northern Iraq that besmirched the reputation of the new government. In the mid-1930s rebellions broke out among the Shi'a tribes of southern Iraq. Shi'a religious leaders used this occasion to demand more Shi'a representation in government and more recognition of their religion and culture in the emerging state system. Little heed was given to these requests, and both Shi'as and Kurds continued to be underrepresented in cabinets dominated by Arab Sunnis. In 1936 the army staged the first of a series of coups aimed at replacing the cabinet but not the king.

By 1939 the Iraqi political leadership was in disarray. Two factions had emerged: a pro-British group led by Nuri al-Sa'id, an Ottoman-trained officer who had joined Faysal in the 1916 revolt, and an Arab nationalist anti-British faction supported by the army and led by Rashid Ali al-Gaylani, a civilian politician. The latter group looked to Germany for support and in 1941 led a coup that ousted regent Abd al-Ilah, Nuri al-Sa'id, and other pro-British politicians. Fearful that this outcome would alter the balance of power in the Middle East in favor of the Axis, Britain reoccupied Iraq from 1941 to 1945, restored Abd al-Ilah and Nuri to power, and encouraged removal of the anti-British elements in the army and bureaucracy. This move restored stability to Iraq and placed the country firmly in the Western orbit, but it also created resentment inside Iraq toward the ruling group and its association with a foreign power. The 1941 coup was a forerunner of the 1958 revolution. It also helped shape the worldview of Saddam Hussein, whose uncle was among those arrested by the British.

From 1945 to 1958 the power structure of Iraq remained relatively stable. Nuri al-Sa'id was prime minister thirteen times during that period. Stability was enhanced by the development of Iraq's oil resources and the expenditure of oil revenue on dams, roads, health, and education. As education spread to rural areas, more Shi'a and Kurds entered the political establishment, quieting ethnic and sectarian tensions. In 1955, Iraq joined the Baghdad Pact, a Western-oriented, anti-Soviet defense alliance, together with Turkey, Pakistan, Iran, and Great Britain, and with the United States as an observer.

However, the relative stability of the postwar period could not conceal the flaws of the political and social structure that eventually resulted in the regime's overthrow in a violent revolt. Behind a parliamentary facade, Nuri ruled with a heavy hand. Although elections were held periodically, Nuri manipulated them to assure favorable results. Political parties were controlled, and opposition leaders, especially Communists, were jailed; some were executed. Riots and demonstrations erupted in 1948 (against a proposed new Anglo-Iraq treaty), in 1952 (against the establishment of foreign bases, including an attack against a US facility), and in 1956 (against the British, French, and Israeli invasion of Egypt). Nationalist sentiments were fanned by Egyptian president Gamal Abdel Nasser, who attacked the Baghdad Pact and urged the people of Iraq to overthrow the regime. These antiforeign sentiments took root in the army, where younger officers formed a Free Officers group to plan the overthrow of the regime. On July 14, troops under the command of General Abd al-Karim Qasim and Colonel Abd al-Salam Arif, both Free Officers, moved on Baghdad and in a violent and bloody coup ended the monarchy, killing the royal family and Nuri al-Sa'id and imprisoning many "old regime" leaders.

Republican Iraq, 1958–1968

The overthrow of the monarchy ushered in a decade of political instability. Between 1958 and 1968 there were four changes of regime, several involving considerable bloodshed. Although a facade of civilian government was maintained, the revolution placed the army in power, with officers assuming the most important political positions.

The republican period began with a military regime headed by Abd al-Karim Qasim (1958–1963). Qasim, now prime minister, instituted social and agrarian reforms, including laws limiting the size of landholdings and placing a ceiling on rent, and revised the personal-status law, giving women more rights and security. Finally, in 1961, Qasim expropriated 99.5 percent of the foreign-owned Iraq Petroleum Company (IPC) concession area. These acts may have brought a measure of social justice, but they were poorly managed, and a period of economic decline began.

In foreign policy the new regime abrogated the Baghdad Pact and recognized the Soviet Union and the People's Republic of China. In 1959, Iraq signed economic and arms-supply agreements with Moscow. This orientation toward the Communist bloc and the break in treaty relations with the West began a period of increasingly tense relations with the West, which persisted long after the end of the Cold War. A power struggle pitted Qasim against his deputy prime minister and chief rival, Abd al-Salam Arif. Their personal differences soon crystallized around a key policy issue: whether Iraq should move toward union with Egypt or remain independent and concentrate on reform at home. Arif, backed by Nasserites and the Ba'th Party, favored union. Qasim, supported by the Communist Party and the Kurds, opposed it. Qasim also faced growing opposition from Arab nationalists, who precipitated a rebellion in Mosul in 1959. The final blow came in 1961 with Qasim's inept claim to Kuwait. Qasim refused to recognize Kuwait's newly acquired independence, claiming that it had been part of Iraq under the Ottoman Empire. On February 8, 1963, Qasim was overthrown in a coup led by the Iraqi Ba'th Party, sympathetic army officers, and Arab nationalist groups. He and his followers were executed.

The regime that succeeded Qasim lasted only nine months. The Ba'thists were young, inexperienced, and not ready to govern. Moreover, they were split between moderates, who wanted to consolidate power in Iraq and move slowly on union with the United Arab Republic (UAR), and radicals, who favored closer unity with the new Ba'thist government in Syria and radical domestic reform. Attempts to unite with the UAR failed, and the first Ba'thist government was overthrown in November 1963. Army officers gained control of the government, but in 1967 the military in Iraq, like its counterparts elsewhere in the Arab world, was humiliated by its defeat in the Six-Day War with Israel. On July 17, 1968, a bloodless coup brought General Ahmad Hasan al-Bakr and a group of Ba'thists and non-Ba'thist officers to power. This time the Ba'thists were determined not to let power slip from their grasp, as they had in 1963. Two weeks after the coup, they removed all non-Ba'thists from power. Then they inaugurated their rule with a series of secret trials and brutal executions designed to stamp out dissidents, terrorize the populace, and stabilize the country by force. This modus operandi kept them in power for the next thirty-five years.

Ba'th Party Rule, 1968–2003

The government established by the new Ba'th regime was based on a Revolutionary Command Council (RCC), buttressed by the regional (Iraqi) command of the Ba'th Party and a cabinet. The two leading figures were Iraqi president and RCC chairman Ahmad Hasan al-Bakr and RCC vice-chairman Saddam Hussein, who was Bakr's kinsman. In July 1970, an interim constitution indicating that Iraq would follow a socialist economic path was promulgated. This constitution, with some modifications, remained in effect until the collapse of the Ba'th regime in 2003. The RCC was given authority to promulgate laws, deal with defense and security, declare war, and approve the budget. The president was given authority to appoint, promote, and dismiss judiciary, civil, and military personnel and members of the party's regional command, thereby ensuring party control of government. Cabinet ministers were reduced to executing RCC decisions. The constitution provided for the election of a national assembly, but it was not created until 1980.

The first decade of Ba'th rule was notable for increased oil revenue, expanded economic and social development, and sustained stability. Nationalization of oil resources in 1970 and the oil price increase of 1973 greatly increased the government's revenue. As a consequence, the regime embarked on an ambitious economic and social program, mainly in the public sector. Programs to distribute land to the peasants were expanded, as were education and health services, especially in rural areas. Heavy industries—iron, steel, and petrochemicals—were established, mainly in the south. The regime also embarked on a military-industrial program that included chemical and nuclear weapons.

The greatest challenge to the regime in the early 1970s came from the Kurds, whose festering war with Baghdad was encouraged by the shah of Iran. In 1970, after two years of intermittent warfare, the Ba'thist regime negotiated a settlement more comprehensive than any previous agreement. The Kurds were offered autonomy and an elected regional executive and legislative authority, a Kurdish vice president in Baghdad, and a larger share of oil revenues. However, there was to be a four-year delay so that a census could determine the boundaries of the new autonomous zone. When it became clear to the Kurds that they would not receive the degree of autonomy or the extent of territory they desired, Kurdish leader Mustafa Barzani led a revolt, this time with military aid from Iran and financial help from the United States and Israel. The revolt collapsed in March 1975 when Saddam Hussein, by now vice president of the republic, negotiated the Algiers Accord with the shah. Iran agreed to withdraw its support for Iraq's Kurds in return for Iraqi recognition of Iranian sovereignty over half the Shatt al-Arab River. Barzani was forced into exile and later died in the United States. That same year, the Kurdish movement split into two factions, the Kurdish Democratic Party (KDP), eventually led by Barzani's son, Massoud, and the Patriotic Union of Kurdistan (PUK), led by Jalal Talabani.

After the Algiers Accord, Baghdad unilaterally established an autonomous region in the heavily Kurdish north with its own legislative and executive council and budget, named a Kurdish vice president, and appointed at least one Kurd, Jalal Talabani, to the cabinet in Baghdad. Real control over the region, however, remained in the hands of the central government. Baghdad instituted some land reform and economic development in the north. To prevent renewed guerrilla activities, the government razed Kurdish villages along its borders with Turkey and Iran, forcibly resettled Kurds in southern Iraq, and encouraged Arabs to settle in the north, especially in Kirkuk. These activities stirred renewed hostility among the Kurds, and by 1979 the Kurdish opposition had once again begun guerrilla activities.

The Saddam Years, 1979–2003

The stability established and enforced by Saddam Hussein and the Ba'thist government would not survive the decade of the 1970s. Saddam had been patient in sheltering his ambition behind the image of Bakr, but his desire to take charge finally won out. In July 1979, Saddam announced Bakr's resignation, claiming that the president was suffering from ill health, and declared himself president of the republic and head of the party. He also purged many party faithful whom he accused of plotting with Syria to eliminate him. This act marked a final transition from party rule to personal dictatorship. Saddam's tenure would be marked by the ruthless suppression of all real and suspected opponents and any form of organized activity not under his control, total concentration of power in his person, elimination of party and military leaders unconvinced of his superiority, and increased reliance on a coterie of family members and cronies from his home village near Tikrit (a small city north of Baghdad) to maintain his power. Saddam's belief in his leadership capabilities plus the absence of any checks on his power soon led to miscalculations in foreign affairs that plunged the country into two devastating wars in little more than a decade.

The Iran-Iraq War began on September 23, 1980, when Iraqi forces invaded Iran. Saddam had mixed motives for going to war. One was defensive. For over a year, the Islamic government in Iran had incited opposition elements in Iraq (Shi'a and Kurd) to overthrow the regime. He feared that if he did not move against the new regime, Iraq would soon face a greater threat. Saddam also had more opportunistic motives. The collapse of the shah's regime provided Saddam with the opportunity to reverse the 1975 Algiers Accord and possibly "liberate" Iran's oil-rich Khuzestan Province, inhabited largely by Arabs. Iran was also vulnerable; revolutionary judges were busy purging the American-trained armed forces of the politically unreliable, leaving the image of a weak state ripe for the plucking.

The war proved a profound strategic miscalculation. Saddam expected a quick victory; instead, the war lasted eight years. After an initial thrust into Iranian territory, Iraq adopted a defensive strategy and soon lost the initiative. With the aid of waves of suicide troops, Iranian forces counterattacked and had driven Iraq out of Iran by June 1982. Iran then made the mistake of carrying the war into Iraq, hoping to unseat the regime in Baghdad. Iran was unable to marshal sufficient forces to win, and Iraqis, now defending their homeland, fought hard. The conflict settled into a long war of attrition. Both sides used long-range missiles to attack major cities. In addition, Iraq used chemical weapons on the battlefield and on the Kurdish population, which Saddam suspected of harboring Iranian military forces. Iraq received approximately $80 billion in loans from the oil-rich Arab Gulf states, as well as support from Europe, the United States, and the Soviet Union in the form of weapons, loans, credits, and intelligence. It was also helped by a growing US military presence in the Gulf to protect oil shipping. The war ended in July 1988 after intensive Iraqi missile strikes on Iranian cities, attacks into Iran using chemical weapons, and the accidental downing by the United States of an Iranian civilian airliner carrying nearly three hundred people.

The costs of the war were high for Iraq. Iraq's offshore oil-export facilities were destroyed, and the Shatt al-Arab waterway was closed to traffic and filled with sunken ships, chemical weapons, and other ordnance, making Iraq almost a landlocked country. As a result, Iraq had to turn to the port of Umm Qasr, bordering Kuwait, as its main shipping terminal. Estimates place Iraq's war casualties at nearly 500,000, with about 150,000 killed. Iraq was also deeply in debt to Saudi Arabia, Kuwait, Qatar, and the United Arab Emirates, as well as to Europe and the United States. But Iraq emerged from the war with its territory and its military intact and with a sense of nationalist pride at its defense of the country.

Most observers assumed Saddam would settle down after the war, rebuild Iraq's economy, and repay its debt. He did not. Eager to continue work on expensive military programs, including acquisition of biological, chemical, and nuclear weapons, while providing expensive subsidies to his support base, Saddam looked for a new source of money. He challenged the US military presence in the Gulf, threatened to burn half of Israel with chemical weapons, and accused Kuwait of stealing oil from fields that spanned their mutual, contested borders, leaving Iraq unable to meet its debt payments. Baghdad demanded large sums of money from Kuwait and the other oil-rich Gulf states as the price of rescuing them from Iranian efforts to export its revolution. When Kuwait refused to accede to Saddam's extortion, he invaded his small and vulnerable neighbor. The invasion was over in one day. One week later, Saddam announced that Kuwait had become Iraq's nineteenth province.

Once again, Saddam had miscalculated. The UN Security Council imposed an oil embargo on Iraq and sanctions on imports of goods except for food and medical supplies, while the United States, operating through the United Nations, organized a thirty-nation coalition to force Iraq out of Kuwait. On January 16, 1991, US-led coalition forces began Operation Desert Storm with an air bombardment of Iraq's economic and military infrastructure and its military forces in Kuwait. The ground war began on February 23. It lasted one hundred hours and resulted in Iraq's retreat from Kuwait in complete disarray.

The devastating defeat very nearly unseated Saddam Hussein and his regime. On March 1, retreating soldiers started a popular rebellion in Basra. Within days, most of the Shi'a-inhabited territory from the outskirts of Baghdad to Basra was under rebel control. In the predominantly Kurdish area of the north, the two Kurdish factions tried to incite a similar rebellion, but their reluctance to coordinate with rebels in the south or cooperate with each other doomed their efforts. Both the Kurds and the Shi'a had hoped the US-led coalition would help them. Saddam controlled only three of Iraq's eighteen provinces, but within three months he had brutally suppressed the revolt in the south and was moving north against the Kurds. Nearly 2 million refugees fled across the borders into Turkey, Iran, and Saudi Arabia. Saddam sent his Republican Guard force, which had been left untouched by the war, to suppress the Shi'a rebels. Approximately 60,000 Shi'a were killed and a 1,000-year-old Marsh Arab culture destroyed when the marshes were drained. The

Turks refused to give the Kurds asylum, seeking instead help from the coalition. Under UN auspices, the coalition created a safe haven in northern Iraq, prohibiting Iraqi aircraft and ground forces from flying or driving north of the thirty-sixth parallel. Free of control from Baghdad for the first time in their history, the Kurds established a virtually autonomous government. To prevent Iraqi forces from threatening Saudi Arabia and Kuwait, the coalition instituted a no-fly zone south of the thirty-second parallel, later extended to the thirty-third parallel, but Saddam's troops kept control on the ground.

The rebellions scarcely touched Baghdad and the Sunni-dominated center of the country. By the following year, much of the infrastructure in Baghdad and its environs had been repaired, although sanctions made maintenance difficult. Saddam's reluctance to adhere to the cease-fire provisions instituted through UN resolutions, particularly those requiring elimination of his weapons of mass destruction (WMD), kept sanctions and the oil embargo in place for the next twelve years.

Saddam Hussein's strategy at the end of the Kuwait war was to survive with Iraq's political and territorial integrity intact. He shunned cooperation with the United Nations and the special commission established under UN Resolution 687 to identify and dismantle Iraq's WMD programs. He taunted the coalition, harassed UN inspectors looking for his nuclear, biological, and chemical weapons, and in general refused to comply with the demands placed on Iraq by the United Nations and the international community. He flirted with the Kurdish factions, who spent much of the 1990s at odds with each other, tried to assassinate former President George H. W. Bush during his visit to Kuwait, and constantly challenged the no-fly zone in southern Iraq. He reinstated tribal law and authority in many areas of the country and rewarded tribal leaders who helped Baghdad maintain a semblance of order in the countryside. He took revenge on those he believed had betrayed him, from Ba'th Party and RCC cronies to his sons-in-law, who defected in 1995 and revealed details of his WMD efforts. And he believed he had won because he had survived.

The second Gulf War proved even more devastating for Iraq than the first. The loss of life from war and rebellion was substantial, though undocumented. Unable to sell its oil or trade except with UN approval, Iraq's economy declined drastically. Saddam's family benefited from oil smuggling and monopolies on goods made scarce by sanctions, but Iraq's once burgeoning middle class was virtually wiped out by high inflation, low salaries, and a dysfunctional political and economic system that rewarded only those loyal to an authoritarian leader out of touch with reality. Iraq's isolation was intense: its sovereignty was curtailed by intrusive international inspections of its weapons facilities, no-fly zones that denied the regime unchallenged access to its northern and southern provinces, and the emergence of a secure zone in the north where regime opponents could operate under coalition protection. From August 1990, when sanctions were first imposed, until April 2003, when Saddam's regime fell, sanctions prevented full rehabilitation of the economy and greatly impacted Iraq's economic well-being and social structure. International support for Iraq's isolation and sanctions began to erode by 2001, but the long-term damage to the country and its people had been done.

Politics in Saddam's Iraq

Ba'thism, meaning "renaissance" or "awakening," was a secular movement founded in the late 1940s in Syria by two Syrians—one Christian and the other a Sunni Arab—and an Iraqi Shi'a Arab. It provided a secular nationalist identity and an ideology based on principles of Arab unity and vague theories of economic and social justice. More importantly, it provided the opportunity to compete on a more equal basis without the advantage or stigma of ethnic, tribal, or sectarian ties. At least that was the theory. Under Saddam, party membership became the key credential for education, jobs, higher salaries, and a modicum of political and personal security. Membership expanded from a few thousand in the 1950s to more than a million in the early 1970s. As Saddam tightened his hold on power, the party lost its principles and its intellectual leaders. In their stead, Saddam fashioned a party of adherents loyal to him and the state. Ba'thist ideology—or what was left of it— became more identified with Iraqi hegemony and Saddam's cult of personality.

Most of those who came to power under Saddam shared his background. They were Arabs from the smaller towns and villages of central Iraq, mostly but not exclusively Sunni, party members and clan loyalists from rural and tribal roots. To many Iraqis the party represented capability, influence, and a sense of exceptionalism. They were administrators, civil servants, and educators with high expectations of power and status. Their intellectual self-view remained strongly secular and nationalist. Other Iraqis joined the party as part of their military service or to protect family or tribal interests. They came from the Arab Sunni tribes of the so-called center, an area bounded by Mosul, Fallujah, Tikrit, Baqubah, and Baghdad, and provided most of the recruits and personnel for the officer corps of the military, Republican Guard, Special Republican Guard, and other security and intelligence units. They filled the upper ranks of the Ba'th Party and the elite group of advisers around Saddam. Shi'a, Kurds, and Christians joined the party, but few broke through the glass ceiling of Sunni Arab loyalism. Saddam used the military to police society and the tribes to help maintain control of the countryside.

Saddam's Ba'thists exhibited a strong sense of elitism and exceptionalism, sentiments that in many Iraqis run deeper than modern political loyalties. In the politics of cultural identity, to be an Iraqi, an Arab, and a Ba'thist was to be the best of all Arabs, with a sense of entitlement and exclusivity—Iraq was meant to lead the Arab world, and the party was the channel for upward mobility, egalitarianism, modernity, and secularism.

Iraq Under American Occupation, 2003–2011

The American presidential election in 2000 brought to office George W. Bush, son of former president George H. W. Bush, and an administration that seemed determined to reverse policy on Iraq. Their opportunity came after the al-Qaida terrorist attacks on New York and Washington on September 11, 2001. Administration officials sought to blame Iraq for the actions of al-Qaida and, after the fall of the Taliban government in

Afghanistan (which had harbored al-Qaida and its leader, Osama bin Laden), began to plan for regime change in Iraq. They claimed to have information confirming Iraqi support for al-Qaida and plans to produce nuclear weapons. They warned that Saddam would share his new weapons with terrorist groups and raised the specter of a nuclear holocaust, even though the United Nations had declared that Iraq had been stripped of virtually all its nuclear components and matériel.

When British general F. S. Maude entered Baghdad in 1917, he said the British came "as Liberators, and not as Conquerors" and the war "was not about Religion." Unconsciously echoing these sentiments, the American administration predicted that the US-led coalition would be welcomed as liberators, rather than seen as occupiers, and showered with rice and rose petals. Iraq, it was claimed, would quickly transition to democratic government and become the model to emulate for the region. A new age of political and economic reform would sweep the entire Middle East, they breathlessly concluded. As for the costs of removing Saddam, Iraq's oil would cover all. Saddam's government fell in early April 2003. He did not survive in power; Saddam was pulled out of an underground bunker eight months later, his sons dead and his country in total disarray.

The Bush administration had several goals for Iraq, including identifying and removing all WMD sites and programs, purging all Ba'thist influence, creating democratic political institutions, and restoring civil society and domestic security. With the collapse of Saddam's regime in April 2003, the United States sent to Iraq a retired general, Jay Garner, to oversee aid to Iraqis displaced by the war and establish mechanisms to restore order, run the government, and begin reconstruction. Garner confronted looting and sabotage, ministries ablaze, a disappeared bureaucracy, and a rising insurgency. He was replaced within a month by Ambassador L. Paul Bremer, who, under the direction of the Department of Defense, established the Coalition Provisional Authority (CPA).

Bremer issued two controversial orders shortly after arriving in Baghdad. He disbanded the Iraqi armed forces and security forces and banned members of the now-outlawed Ba'th Party from serving in any public or official position. The first announcement put 450,000 military and security personnel out of work with no pay—in a country with 75 percent unemployment. The second affected approximately 50,000 party members, many of whom had joined the party to obtain education and employment benefits and were members in name only. Both measures ended up targeting the Sunni Arab community and its tribes and prominent individuals, who had held most party and government posts and virtually all senior military positions. Few felt great loyalty to Saddam, but they had always been well provisioned and secure, even in times of scarcity and risk. With Bremer's decrees, Iraq's Sunni Arabs began to feel they were victims of, not participants in, the new order. On the other hand, the demilitarization and de-Ba'thification decrees were popular with the Shi'a Arab and Kurdish communities, which now demanded justice for their suffering.

De-Ba'thification as a process was both necessary and risky. Some Iraqis believed a deep purge of party members was necessary if Iraq was to free itself from its dark past under Saddam. But de-Ba'thification had other, unintended consequences. It put at risk rehabilitation and reconstruction programs by cutting too deeply into government bureaucracies, education, and the officer corps. Many of Iraq's most competent and experienced managers disappeared, afraid of retribution from people who had suffered under Saddam's rule and from insurgents threatening to kill anyone believed to be collaborating with the occupier. Teachers, journalists, and even medical personnel had to join the party to work, so de-Ba'thification led to the collapse of vital education, aid, security, and health-care systems. Finally, de-Ba'thification and demilitarization increased the risk of civil war between those displaced and their victims. In this light, the willingness of disgruntled military officers to join with Saddam loyalists, former Ba'thists, the criminals who comprised Saddam's fedayeen militia, and Sunni religious extremists becomes more explicable. Elements opposed to the American occupation began terrorist operations against the US military and civilian presence as well as the United Nations, the International Red Cross, governments assisting the occupation (Jordan, Turkey, Italy, and Spain), and Iraqis suspected of collaborating with the United States.

Bremer appointed a governing council of twenty-five exiles to be the public face of Iraq. It was a proportionally correct group—thirteen Shi'a Arabs, five Sunni Arabs, five Kurds, a Turkman, and a Christian—and the presidency rotated monthly among nine of the most prominent members. It was replaced by two interim governments, the first under Iyad Allawi, a secular Shi'a politician, and the second elected in 2005, in the first transparent election in Iraq's eighty-five-year history. The prime minister was chosen by the Shi'a coalition, which had won the largest number of seats in the new parliament. The mission of this coalition was to write a constitution and prepare for the election of a permanent government.

Bremer's most significant contribution to the new Iraq may have been the interim constitution, referred to as the Transitional Administrative Law (TAL). Written by Iraqis with guidance from American advisers, it resonated with the protections for individual rights and civil liberties usually contained in Western constitutions. It described Iraq as republican, federal, democratic, and pluralistic. Its key sections dealt with issues of federal versus state's rights, the role of Islam in the state, and the structure and nature of governance. Most of its provisions were written into the constitution that was approved in a nationwide referendum in October 2005.

Under the protection of UN forces in 1991, the Kurds had established a Kurdish Regional Government (KRG) independent of Baghdad in the three predominantly Kurdish provinces: Dohuk, Irbil, and Sulaymaniyyah. Elections had been held in 1992 for a regional assembly, and a cabinet was chosen mainly from the two Kurdish parties, the KDP and PUK. However, the two parties could not maintain the facade of unity for long. A power struggle erupted with frequent military clashes over the next five years. At one point Massoud Barzani invited Saddam's forces to cross the no-fly, no-drive zone and help him defeat his rival, Jalal Talabani.

Today there is a Kurdish parliament, but Kurdistan remains divided, with the KDP controlling Irbil and the PUK controlling Sulaymaniyyah. In regional elections in July 2009, a third party—the Goran (Change) Party—captured a quarter of the votes and seats in the KRG. Despite this apparent opening in the political fabric, however, there are few signs of transparency or real democracy in the KRG and no tolerance for the civil rights of non-Kurds or critics of the leadership.

POLITICAL ENVIRONMENT

Although Iraq is a state, it is not yet a nation. Every Iraqi government since 1920 has attempted to create a single political community from a diverse population, but none have succeeded in overriding residual ethnic, sectarian, and tribal loyalties or undermining the Arab nationalism fostered by Iraq's Sunni Arab leaders. These factors make Iraq difficult to govern.

Iraq's People

Iraq's population is approximately 31 million, growing at 2.3 percent annually. Its capital, Baghdad, is the largest city, with 5.7 million people, nearly one-fifth of the population. Other urban concentrations include Mosul, Iraq's second-largest city; Basra, its port; Kirkuk, an oil center in the north; Irbil, a Kurdish city now under Kurdish control; and Najaf, a Shi'a religious center in the south.

Iraq has two major demographic fault lines. The first and most serious is its ethnic divisions. The overwhelming majority of the population is Arab (75 to 80 percent); they dominate the western steppe and the Tigris and Euphrates valley, from Basra to the Mosul plain. Kurds are the largest ethnic minority, estimated at 15 to 20 percent; their stronghold is in the mountains of northern and eastern Iraq. Saddam killed many Kurds or forced them to migrate to the plains of southern Iraq, replacing them with Arabs from the south. Since 2003, Kurds have been moving into Kirkuk, Mosul, and villages belonging to Christian, Turkmen, and Yazidi tribes. About one-quarter of Baghdad's population was and may still be Kurds. Iraq's Kurds are a portion of the larger Kurdish population inhabiting adjoining regions in Turkey, Iran, and Syria.

The second demographic fault line is sectarian. Iraqis are divided mainly between the two major divisions in Islam: the Sunni and the Shi'a. Sunni Arabs constitute approximately 20 percent of the population. For more than four hundred years of Ottoman, British, and Arab rule, they dominated the military and political life of the country. Under Saddam, they constituted a majority in the officer corps and the upper echelons of the Ba'th Party. As an elite, they benefited disproportionately from modernization and education. In occupation and lifestyle they tended to be more secular than Shi'a Arabs. Since 2003, extremist Sunni Arab religious groups—called salafists or jihadists, they include

KEY PROVISIONS OF THE IRAQI CONSTITUTION OF OCTOBER 15, 2005

- *Iraq* is a country of many nationalities, and the Arab people of Iraq are an inseparable part of the Arab nation. An Iraqi citizen is anyone who carries Iraqi nationality.

- *Islam* is the official religion of the country as well as *a* source, but not *the* source, of legislation.

- *Arabic and Kurdish* are the recognized languages, and Iraqis can educate their children in their own language in state and private schools.

- *All Iraqis* have full equality without regard to gender, sect, opinion, belief, nationality, religion, or origin. All are equal before the law and have the right to a fair, speedy, and public trial.

- *The Iraqi government* shall include a national assembly, a president, a council of ministers, a prime minister, and a judiciary. The assembly elects the president and two deputy presidents from its ranks and approves selection of the prime minister, who shall be chosen by the party winning the most votes in the general election. One-quarter of the assembly's 275 representatives shall be women, and all communities are to be fairly represented. There is separation of powers: legislative, executive, and judicial.

- *Federalism* is defined as a system of separation of powers based on geographic and historical realities and not race, ethnicity, nationality, or religious sect. Formulation of national security policy, as well as foreign, diplomatic, economic, trade, and debt policies, lies with the federal government. The management of the country's natural resources and distribution of its revenues fall under federal authority, but a distinction is made between "old" resources (already discovered and exploited), which come under federal authority, and "new" oil and gas resources, which are to come under provincial authority. This is contested by Sunni Arabs in the Shi'a camp. It is, however, a demand of the Kurds, who are signing contracts and selling rights to explore, repair, and exploit fields they do not yet control.

- *The armed forces and the intelligence services* come under civilian control, and all military personnel are banned from political office and activity.

elements of the once-banned Muslim Brotherhood—have surfaced to demand that Iraq be governed as an Islamic state under sharia (Islamic law).

Shi'a Arabs comprise the majority of the population—55 to 60 percent. Most inhabit the area from Baghdad south to the Shatt al-Arab, the most densely populated section of the country. As a result of sectarian violence after the collapse of the Ba'thist regime, Baghdad has a larger Shi'a population than it had before the occupation. The heartland of Shi'a Islam has always been the shrine cities of Najaf and Karbala in southern Iraq, where Imams Ali and Hussein are buried. Along with Samarra and Kazimiyyah, a suburb of Baghdad, these shrine cities have long been central to pilgrimage rites, religious education, especially in Islamic law, and burial for religious scholars. Shi'a have rarely held senior political or military positions. This increased their resentment of any centralized, Sunni-dominated power structure in Baghdad. In the Shi'a south, where much of the population is rural and agricultural, lower standards of living and literacy historically prevailed. This too fed Shi'a resentment and spawned an organized, clandestine Shi'a opposition to the increasingly popular Arab secular parties, especially the Ba'th and Communist parties.

The original Shi'a opposition movement was the Dawa (Call) Party, founded in Najaf in the 1960s by an Iraqi Arab cleric, Ayatollah Muhammad Baqr al-Sadr. Since the 2005 elections, it has been one of Iraq's leading political parties. Another major Shi'a faction is the Islamic Supreme Council in Iraq (ISCI), formerly known as the Supreme Council for the Islamic Revolution in Iraq. It was created by the Iranian Islamic government in 1982 as an umbrella group of anti-Saddam elements and led by another prominent Iraqi cleric, Ayatollah Muhammad Baqr al-Hakim. Saddam may have mistrusted Iraq's Shi'a and Ayatollah Ruhollah Khomeini may have assumed they would help Iran defeat Saddam, but most Shi'a remained loyal to the Iraqi state and fought Iran in the eight-year war. They have never desired self-determination, as do Iraq's Kurds, but seek representation in a democratically elected government commensurate with their numbers. Not all Shi'a clerics are militants. One of the most revered Shi'a clerics, Iranian-born Grand Ayatollah Ali Sistani, upholds Shi'a political and Iraqi national interests but opposes a role for clerics in government.

The Kurds have long resisted assimilation into Arab Iraq. Traditionally, Kurds lived under the control of the *aghas* (tribal chiefs and landholders), but war, modernization, and land reform eroded their position. In the twentieth century, a sense of Kurdish identity, based on language, close tribal ties, a common history, and a shared sense of victimization by the government, inspired demands for self-rule. Many Kurds are still engaged in agriculture, but a growing number form an urban, educated elite class. Much of the economy and society of the Kurdish north was drastically disrupted by the razing of over 4,000 villages by Saddam's regime, the death and disappearance of many thousands of Kurds during a concerted campaign against them at the end of the Iran-Iraq War, and the displacement of large numbers of Kurds as a result of the 1991 rebellion. Protected from Saddam's depredations after 1991, the Kurds made considerable progress in resettling those who had been displaced and in reviving agriculture and industry. Although the major Kurdish parties formed a regional government and have held three elections, real political authority remains in the hands of patriarchal tribal warlords. There is relatively little democratic transparency in the three predominantly Kurdish provinces, which would like to become an autonomous federated state within Iraq, or if Iraq fails, outside it.

Most Kurds are Sunni, but there are also Shi'a (*fayli*), Christian, and a small number of Jewish Kurds. As a result of sectarian violence and ethnic cleansing after the collapse of the Ba'thist regime, Baghdad now has a significantly larger Shi'a majority than it had before the occupation. Although some Iraqis and non-Iraqis believe ethnic and sectarian differences pose a stumbling block to Iraqi identity, Iraqis have a high rate of intermarriage between Sunni and Shi'a and Arab and Kurd. Until 2003, it also had a large number of integrated communities. The three communities seen as dividing the country—Sunni Arabs, Shi'a Arabs, and Kurds—are not as distinct as some assume.

Iraq has a number of smaller minority groups, many with bonds to similar peoples across Iraq's borders. In northern cities and towns along the old trade routes from Turkey to Baghdad are Turkish speakers, known as Turkmen. Making up 2 to 3 percent of the population, they are mainly Sunni, middle-class, and urban. Turkmen have strong ties to Turkey. Until the onset of the Iran-Iraq War, Iraq had a substantial group of Persian speakers, comprising 1 to 2 percent of the population, inhabiting parts of Baghdad and some southern cities, especially Najaf and Karbala. Saddam forcibly expelled this group from Iraq during the Iran-Iraq War, but many are returning now that Saddam is gone and the borders with Iran are open. In the south, several hundred thousand Shi'a Arabs, known as Marsh Arabs, inhabited the marshes between the Tigris and Euphrates Rivers. For more than 1,000 years, they dwelled in reed huts, raised water buffalo, and fished. As punishment for their alleged role in the 1991 rebellion and to eliminate a refuge for dissidents, Saddam's army drained most of the marsh territory, dramatically degrading the environment and ending, possibly forever, their traditional way of life. Efforts since 2003 to restore the marshes and return the Marsh Arabs to their traditional homes are failing now because of a sharp drop in water levels due to several years of drought and diversion of water by Iraq's upstream neighbors, Syria, Turkey, and Iran.

Finally, about 5 percent of the population is non-Muslim. Iraq has a variety of indigenous Christian sects, including Chaldeans (Nestorian Christians who reunited with Rome), Assyrians (Nestorians who remained independent), Armenians, Jacobites, and Greek Orthodox. Yazidis, a Kurdish-speaking group with an eclectic religion drawn in part from Zoroastrianism, live in areas around Mosul, and Sabaeans, a pre-Christian group, live in the south. Under the Ottoman Empire and the British mandate, Iraq had a large and flourishing Jewish community, but by the early 1950s, most Jews had migrated to Israel.

Iraq's Social Structure

Traditionally, Iraqi society was characterized by a pronounced dichotomy between rural society, organized for the most part by tribes, and urban life. Since 1950, the rural-urban gap has been greatly narrowed by massive rural-urban migration, the spread of education and health services to rural areas, and the emergence of a sizable middle class. At the end of the monarchy, about 70 percent of the population lived in rural communities. In 2012, nearly 70 percent lived in cities, although many of these were recent migrants who had not been thoroughly urbanized, a factor that has sharpened class distinctions.

Rural agricultural areas remain much poorer than most cities, but conditions have improved since mandate times, when a few landlords and tribal leaders controlled large portions of the farmland and peasants were virtual serfs. Successive land-reform measures eliminated most of this landlord class and gradually extended landownership to a class of small and middle-level farmers. Saddam's skewed modernization programs, which favored industrial development and investment in Sunni Arab areas, and long years under economic sanctions and oil-for-food programs mismanaged by the Ba'thist government had a devastating impact on life in both rural and urban Iraq.

The expansion of education significantly affected Iraq's social structure. Until the Iran-Iraq War, elementary education was available to virtually all Iraqi children. High schools graduated students in the hundreds of thousands, colleges and universities in the tens of thousands. Over time, Iraq produced one of the Arab world's largest professional classes, including scientific and technocratic elites. Along with a middle class came an urban working class, particularly in the oil and industrial sectors located in Baghdad and Basra. Under the Ba'th, most of Iraq's urban middle and lower classes worked for the government as industrial employees, teachers, bureaucrats, and army officers. They still do.

One element of Iraq's social structure saw its status improved under Ba'thist rule: women. Encouraged by government legislation, women enjoyed a wider range of freedom and opportunities than did their Arab and Iranian counterparts. They could vote, hold office, receive an education, hold senior positions in the government and the party, and choose whether to follow Western or Islamic dress codes, depending on how tribal and traditional their family culture was. In 1978, a law restricting polygamy and granting women more freedom in the choice of a marriage partner was passed. By the mid-1980s, 50 percent of the students in elementary schools, 35 percent in high school, and 30 percent in universities were women. Women taught in universities, worked in government ministries, and could enter any profession.

Women are probably the biggest losers under the 2005 constitution, which mandates that 25 percent of all seats in parliament be held by women; quotas are also applied for minority groups. Personal-status law follows sharia law, which does not recognize women's rights to child custody in a divorce and restricts the amount of inheritance a woman can receive. Women politicians have a hard time establishing a voice in politics and are not represented in senior government or party positions. Some have been warned that they will eventually lose whatever political status the constitution guarantees them when, not if, more restrictive religious proscriptions are adopted.

Secularism remains strong in the personal lives of Iraq's middle class, but religion plays a much more significant role in society as a whole, especially in shaping governance, civil society, and education. In post-Saddam Iraq, clerics from both sects wield inordinate influence and fuel political debate as well as insurgency. Religious influence is growing among urbanized Sunni Arabs as well as recent migrants to Baghdad, Mosul, and Basra. In many of Iraq's cities, religious and tribal leaders are assuming more significant political roles and eroding the influence secular elites once wielded.

Family, clan, and tribal ties have always been strong in Iraq. Saddam prized traditional tribal values, such as manliness, courage, honor, and loyalty, and these remain strong. As bureaucratic structures and civil society eroded under the impact of wars and sanctions, Iraqis' reliance on tribal and family ties grew stronger. Despite regime change and the introduction of democratic institutions and processes, political life and social security remain essentially tribal and family centered. Only time will tell if Iraq will move beyond the facade of party politics, but even Western democracies function on occasion through traditional patronage and kinship links.

Iraq's Economic Environment

Iraq is one of the few Middle Eastern countries with the potential for a balanced economy, but its economic infrastructure has been so mismanaged that it has rarely achieved its potential. Since the 1950s, two features have dominated the Iraqi economy: the preeminence of oil and increased government economic control. These features, plus a sense of entitlement, are complicating recovery from years of a Soviet-style command economy and the devastation of years of war, sanctions, occupation, and civil violence.

Government planning actually originated during the monarchy, when long-range development plans were created to utilize oil revenues. After the 1958 revolution, development plans followed Soviet models, emphasizing heavy industry, collective farming, and state management of the economy. According to official statistics, the public-sector share in domestic production rose from 31 percent in 1968, when the Ba'th came to power, to 80 percent a decade later. Under Saddam, the state initially dominated economic decision making, investment policy, and industrial modernization. In the name of wartime efficiency, Saddam's regime abolished collective farms, loosened government controls, and encouraged the private sector in agriculture, services, commerce, and light industry. The conversion to a market economy was only partial, however. Saddam's government refused to allow foreign private investment, preferring to hire foreign firms to undertake projects that were turned over to the government upon completion. Since the collapse of Saddam's regime, political factions vie with each other to control resources and distribute revenues, mostly for their own benefit and that of their supporters. Corruption is pervasive in many ministries, which some politicians in the new Iraq view as their private domains.

Iraq's Oil Sector

Oil revenues have long dominated Iraq's economy. Second only to Saudi Arabia in supply, Iraq has at least 115 billion barrels of proven reserves and possibly as much or more in unexplored areas of the north, south, and west. The Iraq Petroleum Company began commercial export of oil from the Kirkuk field in 1934, but Iraq did not earn substantial oil revenues until the 1950s, when the rich Rumailah field was discovered near the Kuwaiti border. In the early 1960s, Qasim's acrimonious dispute with the IPC and his expropriation of its concession initiated a protracted struggle with the oil companies. As a result, the oil companies shifted their operations elsewhere in the Gulf. In 1972, the Ba'thist government nationalized the oil industry and, helped by the 1973 oil embargo, saw a fourfold increase in prices and revenues. By 1980, Iraq was exporting 3.2 million barrels a day and earning revenues of $26 billion, more than 60 percent of its gross domestic product (GDP). Iraq used much of this revenue to expand its oil facilities, building new "strategic" pipelines from Kirkuk to the Persian Gulf, through Turkey to the Mediterranean, and through Saudi Arabia to the Red Sea. It also built two offshore oil terminals in the Persian Gulf, refineries, and a sophisticated petrochemical industry. Years of war, neglect, underinvestment, embargoes, and terrorism under Saddam resulted in declining oil-production capacity. Under sanctions, Iraq's exports fell to three-quarters of pre-1990 levels.

Iraq's long-term oil-exporting potential is good. By 2012, Iraq's export levels had risen to 3 million barrels per day, nearly the 1980 level, and production could double by 2016, as facilities are repaired and production expanded. Realization of this potential, however, will require foreign investment, an end to insurgent attacks on pipelines and facilities, and a stable political climate. Iraq's government will also have to resolve the question of who owns Iraq's oil. The 2005 constitution left control of "old" oil—already discovered and exploited resources—to the federal government, while the provincial governments "own" all new and unexploited oil. The Kurds favor this and, expecting to gain control over the Kirkuk fields, have signed contracts with foreign oil companies to repair and explore fields, including some in disputed territories. The oil ministry in Baghdad has rejected the Kurdish contracts, saying it alone has the right to negotiate contracts. Under sanctions and Saddam's government, the Kurds had been allocated 13 percent of oil revenues. Since 2003, they have argued that because of their suffering under Saddam and the neglect of successive governments in Baghdad, they are due more. Baghdad compromised and raised Kurdish revenues to 17 percent, which is dispensed directly to the KRG. The Kurds are ignoring the constitution, however, and continue to move into "old" oil fields and sign contracts with international oil companies.

Iraq's Non-oil Sectors

Non-oil industries have not played a major role in Iraq's economy. Under the monarchy, indigenous industries consisted almost wholly of food processing, textiles, and cement production. After the oil price rise in the 1970s, more rapid progress was made in economic and social modernization, including expansion in heavy industry—petrochemicals, iron, steel, and aluminum plants—as well as intermediate industries like metalworking, machine tools, and car and truck assembly. One area in which the Ba'th invested heavily was military industry, especially chemical and nuclear weapons and medium- and long-range missile-delivery systems. Like oil, these are not labor-intensive industries and did little to provide employment to native Iraqis. Iraq depended on foreign labor for skilled and unskilled work. In the late 1980s, the industrial sector produced only 10 percent of GDP and employed 8 percent of the labor force.

Under the monarchy, agriculture received the lion's share of the regime's attention. Development programs expanded dams and barrages, and private entrepreneurs introduced pumps to expand production. The amount of land under cultivation in irrigated areas of the south and rain-fed territory in the north increased. Through the 1950s, Iraq was able not only to feed itself but also to export wheat and barley. Unfortunately, most of the surplus profits went to wealthy landlords rather than to cultivators. After the 1958 revolution, land-reform efforts took much of the land away from large landholders but failed to redistribute it in a timely fashion. Under the Ba'thists, agriculture continued to suffer from official neglect.

Farming in the riverain tracts of the south requires intensive investment in drainage, small-scale irrigation systems, and agricultural-extension programs. These were never forthcoming. Saddam preferred to invest in flashy military-industrial projects rather than agricultural reform. The agricultural share of GDP dropped from 17 percent in 1960 to 8 percent in the 1980s, even though agriculture still employed about 30 percent of the population. Food imports increased until they constituted nearly one-quarter of all imports. Agriculture in the Kurdish area, one of the most fertile in Iraq, was disrupted by war, chemical attacks, ethnic cleansing, and the destruction of villages. In the 1990s, sanctions and a Kurdish population haunted by the specter of planes spraying chemicals on villages prohibited Iraq from using chemicals to spray crops.

It will take years for Iraq's non-oil sector, especially agriculture, to return to pre-Ba'th productivity levels. But Iraq's greatest economic difficulty lies not in the agrarian or oil sectors of the economy. Rather, it is water. All of Iraq's water sources lie outside its boundaries. The Tigris and Euphrates Rivers rise in Turkey, and Tigris tributaries flow from Iran. The Euphrates passes through Syria before reaching Iraq. In the past several years, severe drought and the completion of a series of dams in Turkey, Syria, and Iran have drastically reduced the waters of the Tigris and Euphrates. Poor political relations with Syria under Saddam and his successors resulted in that country's cutting Iraq's water flow, an act that has dried up Iraqi irrigation and caused severe crop damage.

Iraq's greatest resource is its people. Wars, the oil embargo, and thirteen years of sanctions have taken their toll here too. Massive inflation fueled by scarcity of goods and corruption reduced the Iraqi dinar to a worthless currency after the Kuwait war, depleting the savings and reserves of both the government and the population. GDP was at one-third of what it had been in 1989, and per capita income and living standards were drastically reduced. Since 2003, goods have become more plentiful, but unemployment remains at 15 percent officially, down from its 2003 high of nearly 75 percent. Erosion of the infrastructure in health, education, electricity, and water supplies, which produced a serious decline in health standards under Saddam, continues. Reconstruction efforts have been slow, with corruption, grandiose planning schemes, and violence undercutting efforts to rebuild. Insurgent attacks on economic infrastructure and on Iraqis alleged to be collaborating with the occupiers—meaning the United States, any other foreign country or company in Iraq, and officials in the new post-Saddam governments—made Iraq's cities unsafe places to work under American occupation. Added to this is the high crime rate, with kidnapping, murder, and extortion keeping many in Iraq afraid to leave home and, in some cases, fleeing the country.

Meanwhile, a new class of urban rich and well-to-do has emerged from the wreckage of war and occupation. Exiles and those in a position to seize wealth or carry it over into the new Iraq are thriving, while appointees to the several governments since 2003 have used their ministries to enrich themselves, their families, and their friends. Although the hardships of the post-Saddam period are easing, and food and imported consumer goods are available for those who can afford them, the effects of more than a decade of sanctions are still evident and still devastating. Too many Iraqis still lack reliable and available sources of electricity, clean water, and health care. The consequences of Saddam Hussein's miscalculations on Iraq's economy will take years to repair.

POLITICAL STRUCTURE AND DYNAMICS

Saddam and his Ba'th Party dominated Iraq for more than three decades. He ruled through a finely tuned cult of personality and with the aid of a multilayered network of intelligence and secret police services. Iraq was a *mukhabarat* (police) state. It had a constitution, parliament, political party, and elections, and everyone voted, even if Saddam was the only candidate. Nearly 70 percent of Iraqis alive today were born after Saddam assumed the presidency in 1979. They have known only wars, sanctions, isolation, terror, and Saddam's overwhelming presence.

Iraq is now a structured democracy. It has a popularly elected government dominated by a majority-Shi'a coalition, a parliament, a constitution, and elections, with much power residing with provincial governors who control their own budgets and security forces. Iraq's politics reflects its diverse population and the need to balance deeply entrenched ethnic, sectarian, and tribal interests. The Shi'a prime minister has two deputies, one Sunni and one Kurd; the Kurdish president has two vice presidents, one Sunni and one Shi'a; and the Sunni speaker of parliament has two subordinates, one Shi'a and one Kurd. Except for the ministries of defense and interior, which since 2010 have been under the prime minister, cabinet posts have been negotiated with the various factions. ISCI has been especially interested in the interior ministry, since its Iranian-trained Badr militia was legitimized by becoming the police force. The Sunni Arab community feels entitled by history and custom to the defense ministry. Each ministry has deputies from the other communities.

The constitution does not guarantee that a Shi'a will always be prime minister, a Kurd will always be president, or the speaker will always be a Sunni Arab. In 2010, a new electoral law increased the number of seats in parliament from 275 to 325, allocated on the basis of the estimated number of voters in each province and abroad. The constitution requires that a census be conducted to determine the actual population, but the political factions cannot agree on when or how this should be done.

Iraq held three national elections in 2005: elections in January for an interim national assembly, which wrote a constitution and prepared for the election of a permanent government; a referendum in October to approve the constitution; and elections in December for a permanent parliament. The new parliament, dominated by the winning Shi'a coalition, chose Ibrahim al-Jaafari from the Dawa Party as prime minister. He was forced to resign in April 2006 and replaced by Nuri al-Maliki, also a Dawa leader.

The constitution establishes a weak central authority, with most power residing in regional or provincial governments. Federalism is defined as a separation of powers based on geographic and historical realities, not on race, ethnicity, nationality, or religious sect. Should a provincial government oppose a law, or should an issue be contested by both the federal and a provincial government, the provincial government's authority is paramount. The federal government has control over defense, security, economic, trade, debt, and foreign policies. It does not have the power to tax. Islam is the official religion of the country as well as a source—not the source—of legislation. Management of the country's natural resources and distribution of revenues fall under federal authority, but a distinction is made between old resources (already discovered and exploited), which come under federal authority, and so-called new oil and gas resources, which are supposed to come under provincial authority. There is separation of powers into legislative, executive, and judicial. The government includes a national assembly (the Council of Representatives), a president, a Council of Ministers, a prime minister, and a separate, independent judiciary. The assembly elects the president and two deputy presidents from its ranks and approves selection of the prime minister, who is supposed to be chosen by the party winning the most votes in the general election. The armed forces and the intelligence services come under civilian control, and all military personnel are banned from political office and activity.

Iraq's constitution leaves many issues unresolved. The reluctance of Iraqis to support a strong central government is understandable, given the long years of living in a highly centralized state where all decisions were made in Baghdad. Shi'a leaders oppose the provision allowing a majority of voters in three governorates the power to veto a new constitution or legislation passed by the majority. Kurds are dissatisfied with the geographic rather than ethnic basis of federalism and probably mistrust the willingness of any Arab-dominated government to share revenues or political offices fairly with them. Sunni Arabs oppose federalism and any other move that could lead to the partition of Iraq. In this, they have Shi'a Arab support. Kurds, Christians, and secular Arabs object to the provision recognizing Iraq as Arab and Muslim. Islamists prefer an avowedly Islamic government with sharia as the foundation of all law. Iraq's Shi'a do not favor rule by clerics, as practiced in Iran.

FOREIGN POLICY

Iraq's leaders have long sought to play a dominant role in regional affairs. Iraq was a founding member of the Arab League in 1945, and in 1955 it joined the Baghdad Pact, a security arrangement linking Iraq with Great Britain, Turkey, Iran, and Pakistan. Until 1958, Iraq's foreign and security policy and its economy were tied to the West; diplomatic relations with the Soviet Union were shunned.

This foreign relations orientation changed with the revolution of 1958. Iraq gradually became isolated and anti-Western. As nationalist ideologies, whether Iraqi or pan-Arab, took hold, Iraqis became unwilling to entertain any foreign influence in their country. Iraq turned to the Soviet Union for arms and technical assistance. Moscow sold Baghdad its first nuclear reactor in 1958 and, after Iraq nationalized its oil industry in 1972, provided help in developing Iraq's southern oil fields. In 1972, the two countries signed a friendship treaty. However, Baghdad never allowed Moscow to establish bases on its soil, and when oil prices rose in the 1970s, Iraq shifted its purchases to higher-quality Western technology. During the Iran-Iraq War, Iraq purchased weapons and other war matériel from the United States, the United Kingdom, France, Germany, and Italy, as well as from the Soviet Bloc.

Iraq and the Neighbors Before Saddam's Fall

Pan-Arabism notwithstanding, Saddam Hussein's regime had uneasy relations with its Arab neighbors, who feared Iraqi attempts to dominate the region and unseat rival regimes. Saddam, in particular, was involved in a personal and party feud with Syrian Ba'thist leader Hafiz al-Asad. Their rivalry reached its peak when Syria supported Iran in the Iran-Iraq War and joined the coalition that fought Iraq in Kuwait. Saddam turned Iraq into a state sponsor of international terrorism, primarily to wreak havoc on Asad. Saddam probably envied Asad's ability to make Syria the focus of all Middle Eastern issues, especially those involving Israel, as well as his negotiation and leadership skills. Iraq has been one of Israel's most strident enemies in its rhetoric, and Iraqi forces contributed to Arab military action against Israel in the wars of 1948, 1967, and 1973.

Saddam may not have been able to rival Hafiz al-Asad's leadership role in the Arab-Israel environment, but he did contain the ambitions of Iran's leaders. In 1975, Saddam negotiated the Algiers Accord with the shah of Iran in order to end Iranian and American assistance to Iraq's Kurds. Iraq was in a weak economic and strategic position, and the shah was strong. In exchange for the shah's promise to cut off all support to the Kurds, Saddam recognized Iranian control of the Shatt al-Arab and made some territorial concessions.

Five years later, Iraq was strong and Iran weak. Saddam had declared himself president of Iraq and hosted a successful pan-Arab summit to isolate Egyptian president Anwar Sadat after he made peace with Israel. Iran's Islamic revolution was in disarray, as the clerics purged the shah's unreliable, American-trained armed forces and threatened to export its revolution to Iraq and across the Gulf. Saddam invaded Iran in September 1980. The war was long, costly, and brutal, with combined casualties estimated at nearly 1 million. Pressure on Iraq's oil-rich Gulf neighbors, combined with pleas that he was fighting their war, resulted in approximately $80 billion in loans and weapons. Iraq also received intelligence assistance from the United States. Saddam was able to fight Iran and at the same time feed Iraq and build his WMD.

In the end, the eight-year war with Iran left Saddam with little to show for his efforts and deeply in debt. Iraq's relations with the Gulf Cooperation Council (GCC) states had always been uncertain, ranging from mere unease to outright hostility, regardless of the government in power in Baghdad. Iraq first invaded Kuwait in 1961, but it was the August 1990 invasion and occupation of Kuwait and the 1991 Gulf War that left a legacy of fear and distrust in most Gulf states.

Baghdad and Washington: Rocky Road to War and Liberation

Iraq's invasion of Iran shifted its foreign policy, of necessity, from a somewhat isolated, pro-Moscow orientation to a more pragmatic, pro-Western direction. Relations with the United States, which had been cut after the 1967 Arab-Israeli War, were renewed in 1984. To offset a possible Iranian victory, and at the behest of Iraq's Arab Gulf neighbors, Washington offered military and financial aid to Baghdad in the form of arms sales, loans, and intelligence on Iranian military dispositions. Saddam was always wary of US intentions in helping Iraq during the war. His suspicions were seemingly confirmed when Washington began a brief tilt toward Iran in 1985, hoping to gain the release of US hostages held in Lebanon and leverage over Tehran by providing it with arms and intelligence on Iraq. The tilt failed, and cooperation between the United States and Iraq in the war against Iran continued, primarily out of necessity, until the Islamic republic accepted defeat in 1988.

This seemingly pragmatic trend did not survive the end of the Iran-Iraq War. Misreading the international climate of détente in the aftermath of the Cold War, Saddam saw a political vacuum developing in the Arab world and sought to fill it. He resumed hostile rhetoric toward the United States, the Gulf Arab states, and Israel, which cooled relations with America and Europe. His defeat in the Kuwait war and the sanctions imposed by the United Nations and enforced by the US-led coalition after the war left the Iraqi regime too weak to play a significant regional or international role. Saddam remained in control of much of Iraq and turned trade in restricted goods to his and his family's advantage.

Iraq and Its Neighbors Since Saddam's Fall

The collapse of the Ba'thist government and disappearance of Saddam Hussein were greeted with joy inside Iraq and caution outside the beleaguered country. As the US-led coalition sought to reconstruct Iraq's political institutions and introduce democratic processes, Iraq's neighbors urged the installation of a strong—and Sunni Arab—leader in Baghdad who could keep the country united and secure. Democracy, said many Gulf Arabs, could wait until a more propitious time. They watched with unease as political disarray, insurgent violence, and terrorism took hold in Iraq, fearing spillover from religious extremists or nationalist-minded insurgents determined to overthrow un-Islamic, corrupt, pro-American rulers and spread crime, drugs, arms smuggling, and human trafficking. On a deeper level, they feared, and continue to fear, the side effects of democracy—the idea of a weak central authority with independent provinces and sources of authority was as worrisome as having to adopt democratic institutions and processes.

Turkey warns about the dangers from the Kurdistan Workers' Party (PKK), an anti-Turkish Kurdish group based in northern Iraq, and the risk to the small Turkmen community in Iraq from Kurds and Arab nationalists. Syria and Iran, which share long and virtually open borders with Iraq, have encouraged and supplied insurgent factions to challenge American occupation. Saudi Arabia supports Iraqi Sunni Arab elements, particularly the reemergent Muslim Brotherhood, which Saddam had long banned. Sunni rulers, such as Jordan's King Abdullah II and Saudi Arabia's King Abdullah, deplore a Shi'a-dominated Iraq linked to an Iran that they see building a Shi'a crescent from Lebanon through Syria, Iraq, and Saudi Arabia.

While all the neighbors fear a failed state, none have really offered Iraq the kind of assistance it needs to stabilize itself, secure its borders, or become an accepted member of the regional community. Some Gulf Arabs say that Iraq should not look to them for help but should solve its own problems. They certainly see no place for Iraq in the GCC and are wary of competing Iranian and Iraqi ambitions for regional hegemony in the future. They long for a return to the pre-Saddam status quo, when British, American, and Western interests balanced power in the region and shielded them from their neighbors and themselves.

Future Prospects

Iraq's Experiment in Democracy: Is It Failing?

Elections in Iraq are an imperfect instrument. They provide a clear sign of both the country's limited political progress and its weakness. Voting is done by a closed list with parties clearly identified. A candidate's place on the party's list reflects personal status and deals between party leaders rather than local support or positions on issues. In the 2005 elections, Iraqis voted according to sectarian and ethnic interests, reflecting deep-seated fears about their status and future. Sunni Arabs boycotted the election and lost their ability to play a role in the new government. Shi'a factions, encouraged by Iran, formed a coalition that gave it the majority of seats in parliament and the right to select the prime minister. That alliance had broken down by 2009, and leaders of Sunni and Shi'a political factions looked to form new coalitions that crossed ethnic and religious loyalties.

For many scholars of revolution, it is the second election, not the first, that confirms a new state's future as an institutionalized democracy operating under the rule of law or as a lapsed democracy where popular participation and public accountability are given lip service and the style of rule has reverted to dictatorship. The current crisis in governance began in 2006 and involves the current prime minister, Nuri al-Maliki. Maliki had survived more than twenty years of exile in Tehran and Damascus as a functionary in the banned Dawa Party. He was a discreet and seemingly unthreatening presence in the short-lived government of Ibrahim al-Jaafari. From his base in the Dawa Party, he first marginalized his opponents within the party and then moved against Jaafari, also a Dawa Party member, replacing him as prime minister in 2006.

At first, Maliki seemed to be the right ruler for the times. He moved against the Sadrist militia in Baghdad and contained feuds among rival Shi'a factions in Basra. He arrested ex-Ba'thists and al-Qaida insurgents. His government moved to bring oil contracts and distribution of oil revenue under control. But other actions had a much darker side.

In 2008, Maliki began targeting the military, the courts, and the ministries. He refused to honor promises to incorporate the Sunni Arab militias that had fought al-Qaida into the government and military services. As the US military transferred responsibility to its Iraqi counterparts, Maliki created several special brigades within the army as counterterrorism units and moved them out of the defense ministry to report directly to him. The office of commander in chief was moved to the prime minister's office and staffed with loyalists. Maliki then consolidated the police and army into one office under one general in order to control all security functions. At the same time, the United States began to implement agreements signed with Baghdad in November 2008 calling for the gradual withdrawal of American combat forces from Iraq by the end of 2011.

In January 2010, Iraq held its second national parliamentary election. Nine months later it finally seated a new government led by Maliki and his new State of Law coalition. The battle for power had been a bitter one. Maliki's rival, Iyad Allawi, and his secular Iraqiyyah coalition had won the popular election by a slim majority of two seats, but Maliki moved closer to the Sadrists and engineered a court decision that allowed his coalition, formed after the election, to emerge the victor. With his hold on power apparently secure, Maliki resumed efforts to strengthen the authority of the central government at the expense of parliament, provincial governments, and other independent checks and balances of post-Saddam governance.

Maliki began consolidating power in April 2010. To paper over the bitterness of the election, he went to Irbil to negotiate with the Kurds and prominent Sunni Arab politicians, including Allawi. He promised a new degree of power sharing among Iraq's Sunni and Shi'a Arabs and Kurds by creating a National Council of Strategic Policies to oversee, approve, or veto any major legislation after the prime minister signed it. Leadership of the council was promised to Allawi. Maliki also promised to appoint a Sunni Arab and a Shi'a Arab to head the defense and interior ministries. Maliki, however, reneged on his commitments.

In January 2011 the judiciary, now under Maliki's control, ended the independence of several agencies established during the US occupation to oversee elections, protect human rights, and fight corruption and placed them under direct control of the prime minister's office. The courts found the Independent Higher Education Commission's link to the legislative branch of government in violation of the separation of powers. Several months later, its chairman, who had worked to preserve the integrity of elections from Maliki's manipulation, was arrested and charged with corruption. The Higher Judicial Council then ruled that new legislation could only be proposed by the cabinet, giving the prime minister and not parliament the ability to propose legislation. It also ended the right of parliament to question ministers. These actions are major setbacks for the institutional checks and balances the United States hoped to ensure in post-Saddam Iraq. On the day of the US withdrawal ceremony in Baghdad in December 2011, Iraqi security forces surrounded the residences of several prominent Sunni Arab politicians and threatened to arrest the deputy vice president, a Sunni Arab, on charges of coup plotting. He has since been tried in absentia and sentenced to death.

Maliki talks about ending the quota system that ensures women and minorities representation in government. Instead, he would like to establish "true democratic rule," meaning that to the winner belongs all the spoils of victory, all appointments, posts, and assignments. For Iraqis who have only known the extremes of dictatorship or weak federal government, Maliki is now seen either as struggling to restore security, national power, and Iraqi patriotism or as aspiring to be the new Saddam. In Iraq today, there is no middle ground.

The constitution created a central government with few powers while assigning greater authority to provincial governments. The structure is somewhat akin to the Articles of Confederation that formed the first Constitution of the United States, but it is the Kurds who insist that the Iraqi constitution create a confederal form of government. Embedded in this assumption is a second Kurdish aspiration—that the government and the allocation of power be shared according to Iraq's primary sectarian and ethnic divisions of Sunni Arab, Shi'a Arab, and Kurd, similar to the Lebanese model of government. Under this plan, Iraq's Kurds would control the presidency and foreign ministry and have a guaranteed presence in cabinet, parliamentary, and military posts. It is a vision not shared by the non-Kurds of Iraq and strongly opposed by the prime minister.

The Arab Spring that swept through the Middle East in 2011 had little effect in Iraq. Many Iraqis watched the demands for political liberalization and economic reform and felt they had inspired the movements with the removal of Saddam Hussein. Popular demonstrations occurred in Baghdad and other cities in Kurdistan, but the demands focused on economic reform, not political regime change. Maliki at first announced he would not seek reelection in 2014, but the demonstrators were quickly dispersed and their demands forgotten.

By retaining the title and role of defense and interior minister, moving special security units out of the defense ministry, streamlining the military hierarchy, and controlling high-ranking appointments, Maliki has circumvented the military chain of command and, in effect, coup-proofed the military. He has also moved to tighten control over the intelligence and security services. At the same time, Shi'a security forces masquerading as militias maintain secret prisons and conduct kidnappings and targeted killings with apparent impunity.

Maliki is seen by many Iraqis, including some Sunni Arabs, as a brave nationalist willing to move against sectarian extremists. A National Democratic Institute poll released in April 2012 shows that Maliki's approval rating jumped from 34 percent in September 2011 to 53 percent the following spring. Others view Maliki as the new Saddam. This view is held primarily by Iraq's Kurdish leaders (especially KRG president Massoud Barzani), by Sunni Arab politicians whose tribes were favored by Saddam's regime and sided with US forces in support of the 2006–2007 surge, and by Americans and British who worked closely with the Sunni Arabs during the US occupation. Maliki has become increasingly skilled at using nationalist rhetoric when it suits him and sectarian manipulation when he perceives it as more useful. He is artful in fashioning political compromises, such as the Irbil Agreement, to co-opt his rivals and in using constitutional arguments to defend his refusal to implement previous concessions while moving to isolate, intimidate, and arrest opponents. He has been helped by the split last year in the Iraqiyyah movement and the reluctance of Sunni Arab parliamentary leaders to break with him openly.

Maliki has made clear his view that power sharing or the creation of more autonomous provincial regions will not solve Iraq's current problems. He argues that in a democratic state the winner has the right to form the government with ministers and officials of his choosing. In a state with a history of free and fair elections, acceptance of the rule of the law, and a system of checks and balances among government institutions, this would apply. But Iraq is not that state, Maliki is not that leader, and Iraqis are too scarred by past decades of oppression and dictatorship to accept Maliki as a "muscular democrat" or protest his actions openly.

Is Maliki's Iraq a fractured, angry, alienated state or a democracy in transition? If the ability to provide goods and services to the people is a measure, then his government has only marginally improved people's lives. Unemployment and underemployment remain high, job security uncertain, and electricity an unreliable commodity in a country where summer temperatures average 125°F. Few, however, see an uprising coming. Iraqis are weary of the long years of war and sanctions under Saddam, followed by more years of violence, deprivation, and political wrangling. Maliki is not solely responsible for Iraq's political stagnation. State institutions are profoundly weak due to rampant corruption; interest groups that purchase ministries using money, violence, or *wasta* (influence); reliance on patronage networks; and politicians playing on blatant sectarian fears. Transparency International's Corruption Perceptions Index ranks Iraq as the eighth most corrupt country in the world.

Would Iraq be better under a national unity government? Probably not. So long as governments reward loyalty with ministry positions, the military is politicized, and there is no independent civil service or other means of imposing accountability on government and its exercise of power, there can be little hope of change.

EXTERNAL STRESSES

Iraqi politics also is influenced by external developments. All Iraqis are watching Syria with great concern. Syria no longer is a safe haven for Iraqi exiles, and Syrian refugees are reportedly seeking protection in tribal areas of northwestern Iraq, which once saw an influx of Syrian-backed terrorists and arms smugglers. Some Sunni Arabs worry that Iran's position and that of Maliki will be strengthened should Asad survive. Other Iraqis—both Sunni and Shi'a—worry that should the Asad regime fail, Saudi-backed religious extremist factions (Muslim Brotherhood and Salafi extremists) will be strengthened and threaten Iraq's tenuous stability. In either scenario, Iraq will be more vulnerable to outside manipulation, either from a Sunni-dominated Syria or as Iran's new line of defense against its enemies to the west. Either scenario could place Iraq at greater risk of civil war.

The crisis in Syria has had some unintended consequences. As Syrian Kurds defy Damascus and the KRG heats up its anti-Arab, pro-Turkish rhetoric and tries to expand its control over disputed territories and oil fields, Sunni Arab opponents of Maliki are expressing their frustration with Kurdish demands and returning to Iraq. The Iraqi army is probably strong and coherent enough to stabilize an uprising, at least in central Iraq, but it is probably not strong enough to fight the Kurds in the north. Many predict that a decision to move against Barzani would lead to a long and protracted conflict. This may be correct in the short term, but in the longer term and with new arms and resources, Baghdad will be stronger and better able to deal with security problems in the disputed territories and on its borders. It would behoove the Kurds to work out their relations with Baghdad to protect their interests, but Barzani's rhetoric and intransigence on cooperation with Baghdad alarm many in Iraq and abroad. Can the KRG survive for long when more than $10 billion annually flows from Baghdad's oil-sharing revenues into its coffers? Only with great difficulty and with foreign support it is unlikely to receive.

The United States withdrew its combat forces from Iraq in December 2011 but still has influence in military affairs because of equipment sales and exchange and training programs. Iraqi leaders, fearing public reproof, refused in 2011 to authorize a new Status of Forces Agreement, which would have permitted US forces to stay in Iraq. Instead, Baghdad looks to implementation of the Strategic Framework, which will govern relations between the two governments, with the Department of State as the senior US agency. Washington, however, is unhappy with the Maliki government's support for the embargoed Asad regime, mostly under pressure from Iran. At stake for Iraq is its purchase of thirty-six F-16 aircraft, now scheduled for delivery beginning in 2014. In October 2012, Baghdad signed a $4.2 billion arms deal with Moscow. The deal includes attack helicopters and surface-to-air missiles but could be expanded to MiG-29 fighters and other heavy weapons. Baghdad probably sees these arms deals as a way of counterbalancing Iran rather than encouraging competition between Washington and Moscow, but the overall goal is independence from outside powers.

Iraq's Future Is Uncertain

Life goes on in Iraq. People go to work and to market; children go to school. Violence was endemic from 2004 through 2007 but has declined, partly as a result of the 2006–2007 US-Iraqi surge and partly because of the decision by Iraq's Sunni community that al-Qaida had become a threat to its interests and well-being. Violence returned in 2011, even before the withdrawal of US combat forces and with the breakdown in law and order in Syria. Progress has been made in reconstruction, although many areas of Iraq still lack sufficient power, fuel, or water.

Iraq almost certainly will remain an Islamic state and a tribal society where democratic-sounding institutions and practices are mingled with traditional tribal politics and competing interests. One thing is clear. Iraq's politicians have learned to act as politicians. They talk about national identity and secular politics. They argue, make nonnegotiable demands, compromise, cut deals, and try to avoid public scrutiny of their actions—the best and worst behaviors of politicians everywhere. Several times since 2005, Iraqis have pulled back from the precipice of civil war. Rather than confront issues that could lead to military confrontation or civil war, such as Kurdish demands and Arab resistance to resolving Kirkuk's status, both sides have backed down and sought more circuitous ways to get what they want.

Iraq has made little progress on several key issues—the nature of federalism (defining the power of the state versus the power of the provinces), a hydrocarbon law (who controls contracts and revenue distribution of Iraq's oil and gas resources), the fate of disputed territories, and a meaningful de-Ba'thification law that would permit the repatriation of thousands of exiles. Iraq also needs laws against corrupt practices in government, an end to armed militias, and ministries run by a professional civil service and ministers loyal to the state rather than personal or private interests. And, finally, Iraq needs a new election law that will define how parties and lists are formed, how Iraqis vote, and who finances elections. Those currently holding power prefer the system as it is—voting by closed lists with candidates chosen by influence and not by ability, issues, or local representation. Currently serving parliamentarians and women and minority groups guaranteed a number of seats under the current system favor voting by closed lists since it protects their participation. Those who are outside the system or cannot gain a place on party lists and those with broader interests in accountability favor open lists, where voters can select candidates they know rather than anonymous party representatives.

One final question remains. Was Saddam an anomaly or a product of his time and political culture? If he was an anomaly, the chances of another era of repression under a patriarchal autocrat are slim. But if he was a product of his political culture and history, then Maliki could represent the next Saddam. Let us hope this is not the case.

Bibliography

The most comprehensive studies of Iraq's modern history are Phebe Marr, *The Modern History of Iraq,* 3rd ed. (Boulder, CO: Westview Press, 2012), and Charles Tripp, *A History of Iraq* (Cambridge: Cambridge University Press, 2000). For the period between the world wars, see Reeva S. Simon, *The Creation of Iraq, 1914–1921* (New York: Columbia University Press, 2004), and Reeva S. Simon and Eleanor H. Tejirian, *Iraq Between the Two World Wars: The Militarist Origins of Tyranny* (New York: Columbia University Press, 2004). Toby Dodge's study *Inventing Iraq: The Failure of Nation Building and a History Denied* (New York: Columbia University Press, 2003) is a brilliant study of the mind-set of Britain's imperial overseers in the making of modern Iraq. A sharply critical study of Iraq under the Ba'th is found in Marion Farouk-Sluglett and Peter Sluglett, *Iraq Since 1958: From Revolution to Dictatorship* (London: I. B. Tauris, 2001). Amatzia Baram, *Culture, History and Ideology in the Formation of Ba'thist Iraq, 1968–1989* (Oxford: Macmillan, 1991), deals with Ba'thist ideology. Baram has also written an authoritative study of Iraq's political elite: "The Ruling Political Elite in Ba'thi Iraq, 1968–1986," *International Journal of Middle East Studies* 21, no. 4 (1989), 447–493. Kanan Makiya, writing under the pseudonym Samir al-Khalil, wrote two brilliant but polemical depictions of Iraqi society under the Ba'th: *Republic of Fear* (Berkeley: University of California Press, 1989) and *Cruelty and Silence* (New York: Norton, 1993). Among the best of recent publications on Saddam's mind-set is Kevin Woods, David E. Palkki, and Mark Stout, eds., *The Saddam Tapes: The Inner Workings of a Tyrant's Regime, 1978–2001* (Boston: Cambridge University Press, 2011). Adequate biographies of Saddam Hussein are Sa'id K. Aburish, *Saddam Hussein: The Politics of Revenge* (New York: Bloomsbury, 2000), and Efraim Karsh and Inari Rautsi, *Saddam Hussein: A Political Biography* (New York: Free Press, 1991).

On Iraq's social and political structure, no work compares to Hanna Batatu's monumental study, *The Old Social Classes and the Revolutionary Movements of Iraq* (Princeton, NJ: Princeton University Press, 1978). Elizabeth Fernea draws a compelling picture of life in a poor southern village in the 1950s in *Guests of the Sheikh* (London: Hale, 1968), as does Joyce Wiley in *The Islamic Movement of Iraqi Shi'a* (Boulder, CO: Lynne Rienner, 1992). Two decent histories of Iraq's Kurds are Edmond Ghareeb's *The Kurdish Question in Iraq* (Syracuse, NY: Syracuse University Press, 1981), and David McDowall's *The Modern History of the Kurds* (London: I. B. Tauris, 1997). The Shi'a are best dealt with in Yitzhak Nakash, *The Shi'is of Iraq* (Princeton, NJ: Princeton University Press, 1994), and Faleh A. Jabar, *The Shi'ite Movement in Iraq,* (London: Saqi, 2003).

The Gulf Wars have spawned a huge number of books on Iraq, many of uneven quality. On the Iran-Iraq War the best are Shahram Chubin and Charles Tripp, *Iran and Iraq at War* (Boulder, CO: Westview Press, 1988); Jasim Abdulghani's *Iran and Iraq* (Baltimore: Johns Hopkins University Press, 1984); and Dilip Hiro, *The Longest War: The Iran-Iraq Military Conflict* (New York: Routledge, 1991). Among the best of the many studies on the Kuwait war are Elaine Sciolino, *The Outlaw State: Saddam Hussein's Quest for Power and the Gulf Crisis* (New York: John Wiley, 1991), and Ibrahim Ibrahim, ed., *The Gulf Crisis: Background and Consequences* (Washington, DC: Georgetown University Center for Contemporary Arab Studies, 1992).

Several books have appeared on the impact of sanctions on Iraq after the Kuwait war. The best are by Sarah Graham Brown, *Sanctioning Saddam: The Politics of Intervention in Iraq* (London: I. B. Tauris, 1999), and Anthony Cordesman and Ahmed Hashim, *Sanctions and Beyond* (Boulder, CO: Westview Press, 1997). Amatzia Baram, *Building Toward Crisis: Saddam Husayn's Strategy for Survival* (Washington, DC: Washington Institute for Near East Policy, 1998), looks at the relations of family, clan, and power after the 1991 war.

The 2003 war for regime change in Iraq has produced a veritable flood of studies. Those worth reading include Anthony Shadid, *Night Draws Near* (New York: Henry Holt, 2005); Anne Garrels, *Naked in Baghdad* (New York: Farrar, Straus and Giroux, 2003); and George Packer, *The Assassins' Gate: America in Iraq* (New York: Farrar Strauss and Giroux, 2005). Michael R. Gordon and Bernard Trainer have written two excellent studies of the United States in Iraq: *Cobra II: The Inside Story of the Invasion and Occupation of Iraq* (New York: Pantheon, 2006), and *The Endgame: The Inside Story of the Struggle for Iraq, from George W. Bush to Barack Obama* (New York: Pantheon, 2012). The first account by an Iraqi written in English is Ali Allawi, *The Occupation of Iraq: Winning the War, Losing the Peace* (New Haven, CT: Yale University Press, 2007). It is preferable to accounts such as that by Coalition Provisional Authority head Paul Bremer, *My Year in Iraq: The Struggle to Build a Future of Hope* (New York: Simon & Schuster, 2006).

A good website on political developments in Iraq is Niquash (www.niqash.org). On Iraqi Kurds, see Washington Kurdish Institute (www.kurd.org).

6

Eastern Arabian States

Kuwait, Bahrain, Qatar, United Arab Emirates, and Oman

Jill Crystal

Historical Background

Archaeological discoveries over the past four decades have revealed much about eastern Arabia's past. An early Gulf trading culture, dating back to the fourth millennium BCE, was linked with the ancient civilizations of Mesopotamia to the north and the Indus valley to the southeast. Centered in the Bahrain archipelago, it came to be known as Dilmun, after its principal urban settlement, the remains of which were discovered in 1953 outside modern Manama. Dilmun extended from Kuwait to Qatar, with a related culture dominating what are now the United Arab Emirates (UAE) and Oman. The fabled kingdom of Magan (or Makan), located in Oman, was a somewhat later culture whose wealth derived from its control of copper sources.

In about 4000 BCE, oasis date cultivation began providing a vital food source. Highly nutritious and easily transported, dates became a major staple in nomadic life. Beginning in about 3000 BCE, increasing climatic desiccation greatly reduced the population in the interior of eastern Arabia. By 1500 BCE, the domesticated camel became indispensable to Bedouin life in the desert interior.

Peoples on the coast generally turned to the sea for their livelihood. Fishing, pearling, and maritime trade reached their apogee in the eighth and ninth centuries CE, and Arab seafarers sailing in ships much like the present-day dhows created maritime trade networks that reached from East Africa to the coast of China. Arab maritime trade was finally superseded by Spanish and Portuguese merchant shipping in the fifteenth and sixteenth centuries.

In the early seventeenth century, the Portuguese yielded maritime primacy to the Dutch and English, whose commercial ambitions were reflected in the establishment of

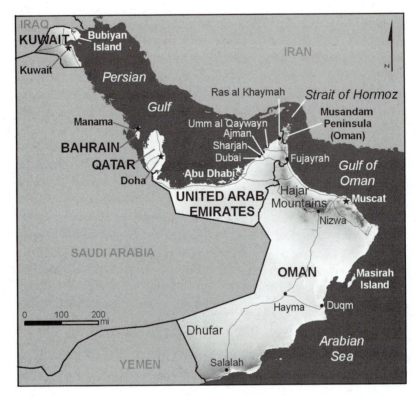

**Eastern Arabian States: Kuwait, Bahrain, Qatar,
United Arab Emirates, and Oman**

the English and Dutch East India Companies in 1600 and 1602, respectively. The Dutch initially gained the upper hand over the British, but by 1765 the British had become the dominant external power in the region and remained so up to the modern era. To protect their commercial interests, the British, like the Portuguese and the Dutch, adopted a policy of indirect rule with minimal interference in local affairs. By the end of the eighteenth century, Napoleonic France had imperial designs on the Middle East. In response, Britain entered into a treaty with Oman in 1788, designed to deny the Gulf to the French and to improve the protection of Britain's lines of communication with its increasingly important Indian possessions.

As the Napoleonic challenge evaporated, another threat presented itself in the form of Arab privateers. Sailing from the shaykhdoms of Sharjah and Ras al-Khaymah, the privateers would strike at commercial maritime shipping, threatening British maritime trade routes to India and beyond. After heavy fighting, Anglo-Indian naval forces decisively defeated the Arab privateer fleet based in Ras al-Khaymah in 1819 and signed a treaty with the local shaykhs that became the cornerstone of Britain's presence in the Gulf area for the next 150 years.

Although the threat of Arab privateering came to an end, tribal warfare continued to threaten stability throughout the shaykhdoms. In 1835, the British prevailed upon all the ruling shaykhs to sign a second treaty prohibiting tribes under the rulers' jurisdiction from raiding each other during the fishing and pearling seasons. In 1838 the ban was extended throughout the year, and in 1853 it was made permanent in the Treaty of Maritime Peace in Perpetuity.

These treaties formed the basis for British colonial rule in the Gulf. Subsequently, treaties of 1861 and 1880 committed the British to protecting the Al Khalifah rulers of Bahrain, and by the early twentieth century, a British political agent resided in that shaykhdom. In 1892 Britain concluded "exclusive agreements" with the Trucial States, assuming responsibility for their defense and foreign affairs. In 1899 a similar relationship, though not then made public, was established with Kuwait, and in 1916 another followed with Qatar. Oman remained outside this treaty system, but the British retained a close relationship with the Al Bu Sa'id sultans of Muscat, who in the nineteenth century had lost effective control over Oman's interior.

In addition to taking direct control of these states' external relations, Britain assumed a degree of oversight over their domestic affairs. This control was minimal in some principalities that rarely crossed British interests, such as Kuwait. In others, advice was freely proffered. Most rulers followed the advice; those who refused risked exile, ouster, or British naval bombardment. In this manner Britain brought a degree of stability to the region.

The British left a lasting impact on the Gulf. Their treaty system stabilized political power relationships and led to the establishment of European-style boundaries that largely exist today. In addition, Britain introduced and developed administrative and legal practices, as reflected in the establishment of municipal councils and the application of Western-style legal codes alongside Islamic law (sharia). It also launched modest economic- and social-development schemes that pointed the way to much more ambitious postindependence projects. An important consequence of the British imperium in the Gulf was the establishment of English as the area's language of international trade, defense, and diplomacy.

After World War II, British strategic interests in protecting maritime trade routes ceased with the independence of India and Pakistan in 1947. Nevertheless, following the trend of granting full independence throughout the British Empire, Britain granted full independence to Kuwait in 1961, and in 1968 it announced its intention to withdraw completely from the Gulf. In 1971 Britain terminated its special treaty relationships with Bahrain, Qatar, and the Trucial States. It failed to create a federation of the Trucial States, Bahrain, and Qatar when Bahrain and Qatar became separate independent states, but the seven Trucial States federated to form the United Arab Emirates. (Ras al-Khaymah finally joined in 1972.)

The 1970s brought both fears and fortunes. The fortunes were the rapid rise in oil revenues due to the Arab oil embargo in the wake of the 1973 Arab-Israeli War. The fears arose as a result of the 1979 Islamic revolution in Shi'a Iran followed by the Iran-Iraq War (1980–1988). The revolution threatened the domestic security of all the Persian Gulf Arab states, but particularly Bahrain, where a Sunni minority rules a Shi'a majority.

In 1981, Kuwait, Bahrain, Qatar, the UAE, and Saudi Arabia founded the GCC. There had been discussions about creating such an organization to enhance regional security since the British departure, but the idea was never realized, largely because of pressure from Iran and Iraq to be included. The Iran-Iraq War provided both a new incentive and the opportunity to exclude both warring states.

During the Iran-Iraq War, the leaders of the GCC states, fearing Iran more than Iraq, threw their support behind Saddam Hussein. In 1987 Iran initiated regular attacks on Kuwaiti oil tankers in retaliation for Iraqi assaults on Iran's tankers and loading facilities. This led Kuwait to request US naval escorts and the reflagging of some of its tankers. This was a dramatic departure from Kuwait's and the eastern Arabian states' policy of maintaining security through nonmilitary means, backed by an over-the-horizon US military presence in the Indian Ocean. When Britain left the Gulf, the United States became the only major Western country with a major military presence in the Gulf.

Oil prices collapsed in the 1980s, forcing the Gulf oil-producing states to cut development expenditures and seek new revenue sources. This was a factor leading to the Iraqi invasion of Kuwait in August 1990. The Kuwaiti royal family escaped into exile, but the Kuwaitis suffered through a brutal Iraqi occupation until February 1991, when an allied coalition of military forces led by the United States drove the Iraqis out of Kuwait in Operation Desert Storm. Desert Storm drew the eastern Arabian states closer to the United States in security cooperation. By the mid-1990s, GCC states had contracted for $36 billion in arms purchases from the United States, a third of US sales worldwide.

The Gulf War had domestic reverberations as well, accelerating a nascent political-liberalization process across the Gulf. Following the Gulf War, these states created or expanded elected or partially elected councils that advise the ruler. In Kuwait, the emir agreed to reopen the parliament he had suspended in 1986, holding elections in 1992. In Qatar, Crown Prince Hamad overthrew his father, Khalifah Al Thani, in a bloodless coup in 1995, and in the following years he wrote a new constitution and held limited elections. In Bahrain, a government crackdown on Shi'as in the mid-1990s ended with another generational leadership change, as Hamad bin Isa Al Khalifah became emir after his father's death in 1999. He took modest steps to liberalize Bahrain's political system, reinstating an assembly that had been dissolved since 1975. In Oman, Sultan Qabus presided over a gradual liberalization.

The al-Qaida attacks of September 11, 2001, on US targets deepened the US military presence in the Gulf by leading to two wars, first in Afghanistan and, more importantly from a GCC perspective, in Iraq from 2003 to 2011. The war in Iraq heightened sectarian tension there, resonating with the growing tension between the Sunni GCC leaders and the leaders of Shi'a Iran. Domestically, the liberalization of the 1990s began to stall. In Bahrain, growing tension over the limited liberalization led the al-Wifaq party to boycott the 2002 elections. In Kuwait, the confrontations between the government and its parliamentary opposition resulted in frequent gridlock. Only in Oman did political liberalization continue.

All five states were shaken by the Arab Spring that swept through the region in 2010–2011. In general, the Gulf monarchies proved more resilient than the region's single-party regimes, largely because of their greater wealth, their well-established succession mechanisms, and their greater political openness owing to the previous period of political liberalization. As a result the opposition that arose challenged rulers' policies and practices but not the system of dynastic monarchism itself. Rulers, in turn, responded more often with economic and political concessions than with force. The notable exception was Bahrain, where the government responded to protests with force.

Today all five countries have economic and political commonalities. All are largely dependent on oil revenues. All have diversified and liberalized their economies in the past decade in an attempt to mitigate that dependence; yet each Gulf economy remains largely government owned and operated, with a small private sector (more vibrant in Dubai and Kuwait than elsewhere) closely tied to the state.

All five are ruled by monarchs, and all but Oman by ruling families who govern through a political form Michael Herb has called "dynastic monarchism," which was adopted first by Kuwait to retain power in a period of rapid economic growth following the arrival of oil revenues, then copied by the other GCC states. All five, and most notably Bahrain, continue to confront the challenges of the Arab Spring.

KUWAIT

Political Environment

Kuwait is a city-state bordering Iraq and Saudi Arabia, with a history shaped by the desert and sea. It was settled in the late seventeenth and early eighteenth centuries when tribes from the central Arabian Unayzah confederation migrated toward the coast. The Bani 'Utub, as they came to call themselves, settled first in Bahrain and then Kuwait. Kuwait's hot, dry climate could sustain little agriculture, so the settlers turned to the sea, developing an economy based on pearling, fishing, and long-distance trade. The tribal structures from their desert past remained largely intact, and Kuwait's ruling elite mainly consisted of descendants of the original Sunni settlers from the Arabian Desert. According to Kuwait's founding myth, these leading families chose one family from among them to rule, the Al Sabah. With time, other groups settled in Kuwait, forming a social hierarchy atop which remained the now urban descendants of these original Sunni families. As the economy shifted from the desert to the sea, the Bani 'Utub became a merchant elite. When oil was discovered and oil revenues overwhelmed other sources of

STATE OF KUWAIT

Capital city	Kuwait
Chief of state, 2012	Amir Sabah al-Ahmed al-Jabir Al Sabah
Head of government, 2012	Prime Minister Jabir al-Mubarak al-Hamad al-Sabah
Political parties, 2012	None
Ethnic groups	Kuwaiti (45%), other Arab (35%), South Asian (9%), Iranian (4%), other (7%)
Religious groups	Sunni Muslim (60%), Shi'a Muslim (25%), other (15%)
Export partners, 2011	South Korea (18.3%), Japan (14.2%), India (13.4%), China (9.9%), United States (8.7%)
Import partners, 2011	United States (11.9%), India (10%), China (9.3%), Saudi Arabia (8%), South Korea (6.3%), Japan (5.9%), Germany (4.8%), United Arab Emirates (4.1%)

income, the original economic basis of their wealth vanished, but the entrenched hierarchies remained.

In the early twentieth century, Persian Shi'as migrated to Kuwait, joining the smaller group of Arab Shi'as originally from Bahrain, Iraq, or Saudi Arabia's Eastern Province. These Shi'as formed the next rung in Kuwait's social hierarchy and constitute about one-fourth of Kuwait's population. In the late twentieth century, Arab Bedouins from the surrounding areas settled in Kuwait, typically on the outskirts of the capital. Those who received citizenship formed the next rung down and now constitute just under half of Kuwait's citizens. In parliamentary elections, their tribal candidates typically win about half the seats, primarily in the outer districts.

With the discovery of oil in commercial quantities in 1938, Kuwait's social structure again changed. As in other GCC states, oil revenues changed the political dynamics of Kuwait by freeing rulers of their financial dependence on the merchants. Oil wealth also brought an influx of expatriate workers who now constitute over half of Kuwait's population. Originally many were Palestinians who fled their country after the partition of Palestine, and many attained high positions in both the government and the private sector. After Desert Storm, however, most Palestinians were expelled from Kuwait due to their perceived support of Iraq.

Since then, most expatriate workers have come from the Indian subcontinent. As a group, expatriate workers form an underclass beneath the Kuwaitis. A hierarchical division also exists within the expatriate community, with Western expatriates at the apex, followed by Arab expatriates, and Asians at the bottom.

A separate group of stateless residents called *bidun* (from *bidun jinsiyyah*, meaning literally "without nationality") constitutes a final element of Kuwaiti society. The *bidun* comprise an umbrella category of stateless people, many long-term residents in Kuwait. Many are from the Shammar and Anayzah tribes, which extend into Iraq (as well as Saudi Arabia and Syria). Some have lived in Kuwait for generations, but their ancestors never registered for citizenship when the Nationality Law was introduced in 1959. Others came to Kuwait in the late twentieth century, with the ruler's encouragement, typically to join the police or military, whose ranks before the Iraqi invasion were largely filled by *bidun*. In the decades before the Iraqi invasion, some received nationality; the rest were slowly stripped of many rights. After the Iraqi invasion, the government considered the *bidun* a suspect group because some had collaborated with the Iraqi authorities. The government began an all-out crackdown, firing en masse *bidun* who worked for the government. Those who had fled Kuwait during the occupation were not allowed to return, and those still in Kuwait remain in *bidun* limbo.

The sharpest social divisions in Kuwait remain those between citizens and expatriates, Sunnis and Shi'as, and *hadar* (the settled, Sunni, urban elite) and *badu* (the much more recently settled Bedouin tribes). Other social identities crosscut these divisions, but none are as salient politically. These affective divisions also reflect differences in wealth; class and communal identities overlap substantially.

Demography is also an important element of Kuwaiti society. Modern health care financed by oil wealth created a population explosion. Almost two-thirds of the population is under twenty, putting pressure on the government to create jobs. Rapid social change has also affected gender relations. The debate over the role of women in society has typically pitted Kuwait's Islamists against its modernists. For years it focused on the issue of women's suffrage. In 2005, however, the emir granted women the right to vote and run for office. In 2009 four women were elected to parliament.

Kuwait's economy is dominated by oil. The Kuwait Oil Company (KOC), originally jointly owned by British Petroleum and (the US-based) Gulf Oil Company, received a concession to search for oil and in 1938 found it in commercial quantities. After World War II, the oil sector expanded dramatically. In 1970 the Kuwaiti government nationalized the KOC, becoming the first Arab Gulf state to achieve total ownership of its oil industry. Most of Kuwait's oil comes from the Burgan oil field, the world's second largest. Burgan, however, has been in production for over fifty years, and some controversy exists over the actual level of remaining reserves.

The Kuwaiti government spent much of its new oil wealth on the public, first in direct handouts of cash and housing (and for the elite, inexpensive land). In time a large welfare state emerged, providing free education, health care, heavily subsidized utilities, and a guaranteed state job to all who wanted one (the constitution guarantees a right to work). Substantial oil revenues were also invested in the Reserve Fund for Future Generations beginning in 1976. By the early 1980s Kuwait was earning more from its overseas investments than from its oil exports. The oil glut of the mid-1980s placed some economic stress on the country, prompting it to pump oil beyond the quota mandated by the Organization of Petroleum Exporting Countries (OPEC). In this period, a political storm also arose over the collapse of the Suq al-Manakh, an unofficial stock market, whose bubble burst after many Kuwaitis, including ruling-family members, engaged in massive speculative stock purchases using postdated checks. When the market crashed, the government bailout was so politically charged that it was not finally resolved by Kuwait's National Assembly until 1998.

The Iraqi occupation of Kuwait in 1990 was a financial as well as a political and psychological burden on the country. Financial support for the Desert Storm operation that ended the occupation emptied Kuwait's Reserve Fund. The postwar cost of rebuilding Kuwait was high, although the pace of physical recovery of infrastructure was quite swift. These expenses, combined with controversy over the mismanagement of investment funds and lingering issues related to the Suq al-Manakh crisis, provoked public calls for greater government financial accountability. In 1993 Kuwait's National Assembly passed legislation enabling it to examine the financial records of all state-owned companies and investment organizations.

In the 1990s the government embarked on a major economic-liberalization initiative to encourage growth, cut government costs, and, it was hoped, create more jobs for younger Kuwaitis, nearly all of whom work for the government. Many restrictions on foreign ownership were lifted in an effort to attract foreign direct investment. Major stakes in state-owned companies were privatized. In the energy sector, the government embarked on Project Kuwait, an ambitious and controversial $8.5 billion plan to invite foreign oil companies to participate in the development of Kuwait's northern oil fields. The Kuwaiti business community, however, was ambivalent about this foreign participation. Much of the tension between the executive and the legislature leading up to the 2009 elections turned on the National Assembly's opposition to Project Kuwait, as well as its success in forcing the cancellation of a $27.4 billion joint-venture project with Dow Chemical and delaying a government stimulus package.

When oil prices rose in 2005, the government budget went from a deficit to a $9-billion surplus. Much of this was again spent on various direct grants to citizens, rebuilding of infrastructure, and investment in the Reserve Fund (by law, 10 percent of Kuwait's revenues are placed in the fund). Virtually depleted by the 1991 Gulf War, by 2006 the fund had grown back to about $100 billion, generating $5 billion in income a year.

Kuwait's economy remains dominated by the state-run energy sector. The majority of the national population works for the state. Of Kuwait's national budget, 40 percent goes to payroll; another 30 percent goes to public subsidies for basic services (such as utilities) and handouts of various sorts. Kuwait benefited from the high oil prices of 2005 and has also suffered from the 2009 recession (it was the only Gulf state in which the government was forced to rescue a bank).

Political Structure and Dynamics

Kuwait has been ruled since the eighteenth century by members of the Al Sabah family. The modern history of Kuwait began in 1899, when Mubarak the Great (r. 1896–1915) took power. Fearing pressure from the Ottomans, who exercised nominal suzerainty over the shaykhdom, Mubarak entered into a protected-state relationship with Britain, establishing ties that would last beyond independence.

Britain concerned itself primarily with foreign policy: first with regional security and later with oil. Internal affairs were left largely to the Kuwaitis. On Mubarak's death, a pattern was established of alternation in power between the lines of two of his sons: Jabir (r. 1915–1917) and Salim (r. 1917–1921). This alternation held through the twentieth century with one exception: in 1965 Abdallah Al Salim (r. 1950–1965) was succeeded by his brother, Sabah Al Salim (r. 1965–1977). Oil revenues began to appear in significant quantities during the reigns of Abdallah and Sabah and with it the establishment of a welfare state and the rapid expansion of infrastructure and industry.

Like the other Gulf monarchies, Kuwait is ruled by both a public set of officials (ministers and department heads) and a ruling-family council. The two institutions overlap. The most important ministries, called the sovereign ministries (interior, defense, foreign affairs, and energy), are nearly always headed by ruling-family members. These ministers are also part of a larger family council that decides broad policy matters and handles succession. Its deliberations are secret and normally invisible. From time to time, however, differences appear, as they did in 2006 following the death of Shaykh Jabir (discussed below). Kuwait's ruling family continues to exercise predominant political power in Kuwait. The Kuwaiti citizenry seems generally supportive of the ruling family. No opposition groups call for its removal, although many have called for a reduction in the emir's powers and an expansion of the assembly's powers.

Kuwait has the longest experience of all the GCC states with a written constitution and elected bodies. Kuwait's constitution was adopted in 1962, making it one of the oldest in the region and the oldest in the Gulf. In accordance with this constitution, Kuwait has had an elected unicameral National Assembly (Majlis al-Umma) since 1963. It comprises fifty members elected for four-year terms. The country's twenty-five districts were gerrymandered in 1981 when the parliament was reconvened after a five-year suspension. These districts were oddly shaped and ranged in population from under 10,000 to under 3,000, making vote buying feasible. Reformist members of parliament (MPs) had long called for limiting the number of constituencies, and in 2006 a new election law reduced their number from twenty-five to five. Each voter may vote for up to four candidates.

Elections (with the exception of the 1967 election) have been largely free and open. Cabinet ministers, one of whom must be elected, also vote. The ruler has intervened unconstitutionally twice to suspend the assembly: in 1976 and in 1986. The 2009 elections were notable for the election of four female MPs, all of whom held PhDs from US universities. The 2012 elections produced a strong Islamist opposition and led to a constitutional crisis over the summer of 2012 (see below).

Suffrage is granted to most adult citizens (police and military may not vote) age twenty-one and over whose official ancestry in Kuwait can be traced back to 1921. Naturalized citizens (a very small segment of the population) must have twenty years of Kuwaiti residency before they may vote. Women's suffrage was introduced in 2005, largely through the efforts of the prime minister and over the objections of Sunni Islamists in the assembly.

The assembly's formal powers are limited. However, it does play an important and vocal role in shaping and challenging government policy. The assembly must approve all legislation. It can (and does) interpellate ministers and entertain votes of confidence for individual ministers.

In January 2006 the assembly played an unprecedented role in the succession crisis that occurred upon the death of Kuwaiti ruler Shaykh Jabir. Unusually open discussion followed about the physical and mental fitness of his named successor, Crown Prince Shaykh Sa'd Abdallah. As the ruling family continued to discuss the issue, the country grew impatient. In keeping with a constitutional provision, the assembly voted unanimously to force Shaykh Sa'd's abdication, prompting the ruling family finally to name an appropriate successor, Shaykh Sabah al-Ahmad Al Sabah, who had been prime minister since 2003 (when the posts of crown prince and prime minister were separated). Sabah's accession was also a departure from the pattern of alternation between the Jabir and Salim lines, moving essentially from one Jabir (Shaykh Jabir) to another (Shaykh Sabah). While not entirely unprecedented, the new emir's selection of his half brother Shaykh Nawaf al-Ahmad al-Jabir Al Sabah (another Jabir) as crown prince suggests that the practice of alternation may have come to an end, reflecting a demographic shift toward the Jabir line. The appointment of Shaykh Nasir Muhammad as prime minister continued the separation of the crown prince and prime minister posts that many MPs had demanded. The assembly's active involvement in a succession that might have played out as a bloodless palace coup in other GCC states has emboldened it as an institution. Some MPs even called for the emir to appoint a prime minister from outside the ruling family.

Kuwait has a civil (rather than common) law legal system, administered since 1996 by the Supreme Judicial Council. On personal-status matters, Kuwaitis are governed by accepted schools of Islamic jurisprudence (Sunni and Shi'a). Kuwait has a mixed human rights record. As with the other GCC states, its primary weakness concerns maltreatment of foreign laborers. Shi'a Kuwaitis are also subject to discrimination. In addition to a private human rights group operating in the country, the National Assembly has a Human Rights Committee.

Kuwait's small size precludes significant local government. Administratively, it is divided into six governorates. Elected local neighborhood cooperatives are an important element of the Kuwaiti political system and often the springboard to political careers. Kuwait's elected Municipal Council, which predates independence, has the power to approve building, construction, and road projects. In 2006 women voted for the first time in municipal elections, and two ran as candidates.

Political parties are banned in Kuwait. However, party-like blocs (tribal, religious, and ideological) compete in elections and function openly in the assembly. Bedouins in Kuwait organize politically around tribes, often holding illegal tribal primaries. One group in the assembly consists of pro-government delegates, mostly tribal, with many campaigning as service deputies. Some of them vote with the Islamist bloc at times.

The largest opposition group consists of Islamists. These include Salafis, the Muslim Brotherhood, and independent Islamists. In 2005 the Salafis tried to press for the legalization of parties by founding Kuwait's first openly political party, the Umma Party (Hizb al-Umma). The government encouraged the growth of Islamists in the 1960s and 1970s as a counterweight to the Arab nationalists. In 1976 and 1986 the Islamists supported the government when it suspended the assembly. But by the 1981 assembly, the Islamists had clearly eclipsed the Liberals, and as they found their own voice, the government turned increasingly to the tribal deputies for support. In the 2003 election, Islamists were very successful, more in the tribal than in the *hadar* districts. In 2009 their numbers dropped, but they surged again in the 2012 elections. The Islamist base is Kuwait's poor and the upwardly mobile urban middle class shut out of money and power by the old economic elite. The Islamists have exhibited political flexibility. For example, Islamists opposed women's suffrage, but once it became law, they moved very quickly to campaign for women's votes. As elsewhere, their strength lies in a class base, an ideological agenda, and an ability to organize: to raise funds, take over associations, and form alliances (for example, at times with Shi'a Islamists).

The Liberals, who have been losing ground, have their base in the old, urban, Sunni, *hadar* merchant families. The Liberals began as Arab nationalists in the 1960s, but in the 1970s and 1980s, they redefined themselves as a secularist pro-democracy grouping.

With little interest in the predominantly Sunni Arab nationalism supported by the liberal Arab nationalists, the Shi'as aligned themselves with the ruling family in the 1960s and 1970s and were reliable supporters of government legislation. However, the Iranian revolution prompted the government to view Kuwaiti Shi'as as a potential threat, and the alliance weakened.

Kuwait's civil society is vibrant. Kuwaitis feel free to criticize the government and the ruling family. Many civic associations exist, including trade unions, cooperative societies, professional groups, and a human rights group. (The nongovernmental Kuwait Human Rights Society was granted a license in 2004, after ten years of operating without one.) Broadcast media are largely state owned; however, print media are privately owned and have, since independence, offered an opportunity for public debate and a lively forum for assembly candidates. As in the other GCC states, Kuwait's Internet penetration is high. Kuwait also has an older institution that plays an important role in shaping debate: the *diwaniyya*, a weekly meeting among men to discuss political and economic issues. At times—for example, during the 1986 suspension—these meetings have become extremely politicized.

Kuwait's opposition has largely been a loyal one. The Arab Spring initially had little impact in Kuwait, in part because Kuwait's political system already allowed substantial room for dissent and in part because the government was quick to offer financial handouts to the population. One exception was the *bidun,* who took the opportunity presented by the Arab Spring to launch new protests. However, by late 2011, long-standing opposition to the prime minister, Shaikh Nasser al-Muhammad Al Sabah, turning largely on the issue of corruption (notably allegations that sixteen MPs had received some $350 million in bribes), prompted growing public dissent, bringing 50,000 protesters to the streets and culminating in protesters storming the parliament in November 2011. By the end of the month the prime minister had offered his resignation, the seventh time this had happened in six years. In December the emir dissolved the government and set new elections for February. While Kuwaitis did not echo the call of revolutionaries elsewhere in the region for the overthrow of the regime, many did call for a reduction of the emir's powers.

In February 2012 National Assembly elections led to a landslide victory for the opposition and a loose alliance between Sunni Islamist and tribal MPs, with the Islamists winning fourteen seats and tribal candidates (about half of whom were also Islamist) taking twenty-one seats. Liberals fared poorly, as did the twenty-three female candidates, none of whom were elected. Shi'a MPs fell from nine to seven seats. A predictably fiery clash between the assembly and the government emerged in the following months. In May the finance minister resigned under pressure from the assembly. In June the minister of labor resigned following efforts by parliament to question him over work permits.

With the new assembly, Islamist issues moved to the forefront of politics. In March a court suspended publication of the newspaper *al-Dar* for three months for allegedly stirring sectarian strife. That month authorities arrested a Shi'a, Hamad al-Naqi, for allegedly insulting the Prophet and his wife in tweets (which he claimed were hacked). In June he was convicted and sentenced to ten years in prison. In May the assembly passed legislation imposing the death penalty for blasphemy. That same month the emir blocked a proposal by thirty-one MPs requiring all legislation to conform to Islamic law.

In June 2012 the political disagreements reached a crisis when the day before the interior minister was to appear before parliament for questioning, the government invoked Article 106 of the constitution, suspending the assembly for a month (into Ramadan, a period when the assembly is typically closed). Although emirs had previously dissolved the assembly seven times (twice unconstitutionally), this was the first suspension in Kuwait's history. Two days after the suspension announcement, the Constitutional Court, ruling on a challenge to the December 2011 decree suspending parliament, took an unprecedented and still more dramatic step, ruling the February 2012 election void and ordering the reinstatement of the previous 2009 assembly (leading presumably to a constitutional dissolution and new elections). This led to protest and the resignation of twenty-four MPs, including several elected in 2009.

The Arab Spring also reshaped Kuwait's foreign policy. In March 2011, during the protests and government crackdown in Bahrain, Kuwait offered to mediate between the pro-democracy protesters and the Bahraini government. Although Bahrain's leading opposition group, al-Wifaq, accepted the offer, the Bahraini government publicly denied that any such offer had been made, while privately rebuking Kuwait for meddling in its affairs. Kuwait then sent a small coast guard reinforcement to Bahrain in May to join the predominantly Saudi GCC Peninsula Shield Force that had entered the kingdom in March to put down the protests. (Kuwait had initially declined to participate, owing to opposition from liberal and Shi'a Kuwaitis.) In March Kuwait also agreed to send medical and logistical support to the rebel forces in Libya.

Both the Arab Spring and tension with Iran prompted the United States to reassess its Middle East policies. The 1990 Iraqi invasion had demonstrated the weakness of Kuwait's army. As a result, in the 1990s the military was restructured with US assistance and rebuilt to about 15,000—nearly the prewar strength. In addition to regular military forces, Kuwait's forces include the paramilitary National Guard. Crown Prince Shaykh Nawaf was a founder of the modern police force and, until his appointment, deputy chief of Kuwait's National Guard. Kuwait's military (and its police) also underwent significant personnel changes in an effort to reduce dependence on *bidun*, who once constituted the overwhelming majority of military and police recruits.

The government also consolidated its close relationship with the United States. In 2001 Kuwait and the United States renewed a 1991 pact permitting US forces to use Kuwaiti facilities and station troops and equipment there. Kuwait was the base for most US troops rotating in and out of Iraq and Afghanistan. In June 2012 the United States decided to maintain a significant continuing US military presence in Kuwait on the order of 13,500 US troops, down only slightly from the existing level of 15,000.

Bahrain

Political Environment

Bahrain is a small archipelago located between Saudi Arabia and Qatar. The largest island contains the capital, Manama. The second-largest island, Muharraq, is accessible by a four-mile causeway from Manama. It contains the state's second-largest city, also called Muharraq. The four main islands are joined by causeways. The population of Bahrain is

Kingdom of Bahrain

Capital city	Manama
Chief of state, 2012	King Hamad bin Isa al-Khalifah
Head of government, 2012	Prime Minister Khalifah bin Salman Al Khalifa
Political societies (share of seats in most recent election, 2010)	al Wifaq (18), Asala (3), Minbar (2), independents (17)
Ethnic groups	Bahraini (46%), non-Bahraini (54%)
Religious groups	Muslim (81.2%), Christian (9%), other (9.8%)
Export partners, 2011	Saudi Arabia (3.3%), United Arab Emirates (2.2%), Japan (2%), India (1.9%)
Import partners, 2011	Saudi Arabia (27.5%), United States (10.2%), India (7.9%), China (7.4%), Brazil (5.8%), Germany (4.7%)

the smallest of the GCC states, about 1.2 million. This population is primarily Arab. Native Bahrainis account for about two-thirds of the total population.

Bahrain's ruling family, the Al Khalifah, is a branch of the Bani 'Utub tribe that rules Kuwait. The Al Khalifah migrated from Kuwait to Zubarah, a settlement at the northwest tip of the Qatar Peninsula, and from there to Bahrain in 1782. There they drove out the Persian-backed rulers, ending Persia's influence along the Arab side of the Gulf.

The Al Khalifah are Sunni; however, a majority of Bahrainis are Shi'a. Opposition leaders contend that the government has granted many Sunni Arabs (perhaps as many as 50,000 or more) citizenship under a 2002 revision of Bahrain's citizenship law in order to help shift the country's demographic balance. Sunnis are divided between those of Arabian tribal origin and, somewhat lower in social status, the Sunni *hawwalah*, descendants of Arabs who migrated to Iran and later returned to Bahrain. The Shi'as are either *baharna*, indigenous to Bahrain, or *ajam*, a smaller group of Iranian origin and somewhat lower in social status. Bahrain's Shi'as, although mostly Twelvers, look to many different clerical leaders, including those in Iran, Iraq, and Lebanon. The Shi'as have faced significant discrimination from the Sunni elite in housing, education, and especially employment: political discrimination has likewise left Shi'as largely out of positions of power.

Less than 20 percent of senior government positions are held by Shi'as, and Shi'as are effectively barred from the security forces. From time to time, Shi'a protests have been severely repressed by government forces. Three periods stand out. The first was in the 1980s, during the years after the 1979 Islamic revolution in Shi'a Iran, when Bahrain's rulers, fearing the revolution would spread to their realm, cracked down harshly on all Shi'a dissent. Many Shi'a dissidents took refuge in Iran during this period. The second period was in the mid-1990s when the government responded, again with great harshness and some brutality, to Shi'a demonstrations. The third was in 2011 when the government responded with substantial force to antigovernment protests.

Before oil, Bahrain's economy was largely dependent on pearling. Oil was discovered in commercial quantities in the 1930s, but the scope of Bahrain's reserves has always been modest, the lowest in the GCC. Bahrain was both the first Gulf state to develop an oil industry and the first oil producer in the region to begin running out of oil. Production peaked at 76,000 barrels per day in 1970 and has been declining since. New recovery methods and the revenues shared with Saudi Arabia from a common offshore field ensure at least modest continuing revenues. Offshore exploration also holds promise for future natural gas production. Bahrain's large oil refinery has, since 1945, processed Saudi oil as well as its own; Saudi oil accounts for 80 percent of the throughput. In 1980 the government acquired 100 percent of the Bahrain Petroleum Company, a subsidiary of Caltex. Despite its depleting reserves, oil production and refining still account for more than half of Bahrain's export and government revenues.

The modest scope of Bahrain's oil made it the first country to make serious efforts to diversify its economy. In the late 1960s Bahrain undertook several industrial projects. The largest was Aluminum Bahrain, which produces over 500,000 tons of aluminum annually and constitutes Bahrain's second major source of exports. Other projects included the Arab Shipbuilding and Repair Yard and the Arab Iron and Steel Company, an ore-pelletizing plant. Another diversification effort was the establishment of offshore banking units, designed originally to capture some of the financial business that had fled Beirut with the outbreak of Lebanon's civil war in 1975. Bahrain's tourism industry, weakened by the government response to the Arab Spring, was until 2011 a growing source of revenues.

Political Structure and Dynamics

Bahrain's ruling family, the Al Khalifah, has reigned since 1783. Unlike in Kuwait, where the ruling family is generally accepted, in Bahrain it has been opposed by the majority of the Shi'a population. As a result, Bahrain's movements in the direction of political liberalization have been much more cautious.

Bahrain's first attempt at political liberalization was short-lived. From 1961 to 1999, power was shared between the emir, Shaykh Isa bin Salman, and his brother and prime minister, Shaykh Khalifah bin Salman. In an effort to create a degree of legitimacy, Shaykh Khalifah, on independence, drew up a constitution promulgated in mid-1973 and held elections in late 1973 for Bahrain's first National Assembly, a unicameral body. However, continuing protests against the government, led by labor organizations, prompted the ruler to issue the State Security Law in 1975, granting the government wide powers to detain and hold dissidents. The young assembly united in opposition to this law, which was never submitted for assembly approval. In August 1975 the government suspended the assembly and the constitution.

The early 1990s witnessed some efforts to introduce a degree of consultation as demands for political participation grew across the Gulf. In 1992 Bahrain's ruler announced plans for a consultative assembly whose members would be drawn from business, professional, religious, and academic backgrounds. This did little to assuage popular demands, however, and a 1994 petition calling for restoration of the National Assembly, signed by 20,000 Sunni and Shi'a professionals, prompted Shaykh Isa to increase the size and power of the consultative assembly. Shi'a protests over high unemployment and lack of political representation continued, however. Throughout the mid-1990s, large Shi'a demonstrations brought a harsh government response, including the arrest and detention of several hundred opposition activists. The violence ebbed and flowed until 1999.

In 1999 Shaykh Isa died and was succeeded by his son, Shaykh Hamad bin Isa Al Khalifah. The new ruler released political prisoners, welcomed back pro-democracy activists exiled in the 1990s, and promised a new era of reform. He called on Bahrain to vote on a new national charter that would reinstate an elected legislature, one with real legislative authority. The bicameral National Assembly would consist of an elected lower house and an appointed upper house. He extended suffrage to women and promised to guarantee freedom of the press and religious belief. He won the tentative support of the Shi'a opposition by agreeing to amnesty four hundred political prisoners and repatriate over one hundred exiles. In February 2001 a popular referendum endorsed the new national charter. The State Security Law was abolished, and the state security police, which many blamed for the severity of the crackdowns of the 1990s, was replaced with the National Security Agency.

Then reform stalled. Some signs of the limits to liberalization were visible early on. Despite the new government, the old prime minister (the king's uncle), Shaykh Khalifah bin Salman Al Khalifah, retained his portfolio. Khalifah, a major power center since independence, was a key architect of the crackdown of the 1990s.

In 1999 Shaykh Hamad ibn Isa issued a new Press and Publications Law that expanded the information ministry's censorship powers and mandated fines, publication closures, and even prison terms for journalists. He issued a blanket immunity for officials suspected of human rights violations. In place of the national charter, he promulgated a new amended constitution, which deprived the National Assembly of the right to introduce legislation directly, gave preponderant power to an unelected upper house, and gave Hamad nearly limitless powers. In February 2002, he promoted himself to King Hamad.

People protested. Nonetheless, elections went ahead. The first elections, held in May 2002, were for municipal councils. The opposition, with some reluctance, participated. A debate then emerged over the merits of participating in upcoming elections for the

Chamber of Deputies in October 2002. In the end, four groups, headed by Bahrain's largest predominantly Shi'a opposition group, al-Wifaq National Islamic Society, boycotted, arguing that more constitutional reforms were needed and that the gerrymandering of districts deprived them of any chance of winning a majority in the lower house. With slightly more than half the eligible voters participating, the outcome of the elections was a body dominated by Sunni Muslims, divided between Islamists and secularists but leaning toward the former. Six women ran, although none were elected. The king then appointed a new *majlis* and cabinet, retaining his uncle as prime minister.

Despite the limitations on the assembly, the impending collapse of two government-managed pension funds, holding the savings of nearly all Bahrainis, brought out a streak of independence in the body in 2004. The legislature formed a commission, over government objection, to investigate the fund's management. In January 2004 the commission submitted a report to the Council of Deputies detailing the extensive mismanagement and malfeasance of the fund managers and recommended the interpellation of the ministers of finance, labor, and state. To deter more radical steps, the government offered to rescue the pension funds at a cost of nearly $40 million.

In 2006, elections were again held, and this time the al-Wifaq society and the three other groups that had boycotted the 2002 elections participated. This decision led to a break in al-Wifaq's ranks, with the minority, which advocated continuing the boycott, leaving to form al-Haq. The forty-member elected lower house included seventeen al-Wifaq MPs, eight Sunni Salafist al-Asala bloc members, seven Muslim Brothers, four Sunni members of the al-Mustaqbal bloc, and twenty-two pro-government MPs. One woman was among those elected. During the election the naturalization issue emerged as a result of publication of the Bandar Report by a government adviser, alleging a host of government improprieties. After entering parliament in 2006, al-Wifaq's main goal was amending the 2002 constitution. In 2008 al-Wifaq paralyzed parliament in an effort to question the government's naturalization of non-Bahraini Sunnis. Political divisions at the top of the ruling family also appeared in January 2008 when the king's cancer diagnosis and absence from the country resulted in tension between the more reform-minded crown prince and the prime minister.

The Arab Spring brought renewed conflict to Bahrain. In October 2010 flawed parliamentary elections and the arrest of opposition activists had already raised tensions. New protests began in February 2011 at Manama's Pearl Roundabout, framed largely in terms of economic and social justice and political and human rights. Although most of the protesters were Shi'a, the calls for reform were initially cross sectarian. Peaceful protests were met with a violent government response with dozens killed. A division emerged between the crown prince, who appeared to back efforts at dialogue, and the long-serving prime minister, whose hard-line views eventually prevailed. In March a predominantly Saudi GCC force moved into Bahrain, crushing the uprising. The king then declared martial law. In the following months many state employees, especially medical personnel and journalists, were fired. Hundreds were arrested; many were tortured and sentenced to prison. Sunnis largely rallied behind the king, and the conflict took on an increasingly sectarian tone. The uprising had been suppressed, but tension continued to resurface in cycles of unrest and repression. In November the Bahrain Independent Commission of Inquiry published a report accusing the government's security forces of using torture and excessive force against the protesters.

Civil society in Bahrain has always functioned within limits set by the government. Political parties are banned, but political societies, professional associations, women's groups, and other associations are permitted. Al-Wifaq is the largest society with some 65,000 members, nearly all Shi'a. It includes Shi'as of many different political slants. Al-Wifaq was a major supporter of the 2011 opposition movement in Bahrain. In July 2011 it walked out of what it felt were meaningless talks with the government. The Islamic Action Society, another Shi'a group, is the next largest. It is Islamist in orientation and successor to the Islamic Front for the Liberation of Bahrain, a militant group that advocated the overthrow of the Al Khalifah during the 1990s. The National Democratic Action Society, Wa'ad, the largest grouping on the left, was suspended by the government in April 2011 for its role in the uprising and its leader sentenced to five years in prison.

The Bahrain Shi'a clergy, as elsewhere, has long maintained independent institutions (mosques and *matams*) and a degree of autonomy unknown to Sunni clergy. However, in 2006 the government began implementing new legislation permitting it to pay salaries to imams, putting some three hundred on salary. This prompted considerable debate in Bahrain about the legitimacy and independence of state-salaried imams.

Bahrain's military, with about 11,000 members, comprises the smallest force in the Gulf. The Bahraini military (and police) forces are filled largely with Sunni expatriates from Jordan, Pakistan, Syria, and Yemen. Bahrain also has a police force of 2,000 and a national guard of 1,000 that handles internal security. The security forces consist largely of Pakistani Baluchis under Jordanian and other Arab officers. Bahrainis working for the military, police, and security services are largely Sunni.

Bahrain's judiciary is divided into two branches: the civil law courts and the sharia law courts. The civil law courts handle commercial, civil, criminal, and personal-status cases involving non-Muslims. Sharia courts have jurisdiction over personal-status matters for all Muslims (Bahraini and expatriate), with separate Sunni and Shi'a courts. Women's groups have frequently criticized sharia court rulings. The Supreme Court, established in 1989, serves as the final court of appeal for the civil law courts and for personal-status case appeals for non-Muslims. The 2002 constitution gives the Higher Judicial Council (created in 2000) oversight over the courts. It also establishes an appointed constitutional court to rule on constitutional issues. Although nominally independent, the courts have experienced frequent interference from the king.

Bahrain has moved in the direction of economic liberalization in recent years. It is a member of the World Trade Organization. In 2005 it signed a free-trade agreement with the United States and created a committee, headed by the chair of the Bahrain Chamber of Commerce and Industry, to oversee its implementation and build public-private partnerships. To diversify, the government has expanded Bahrain's financial sector to include over one hundred offshore banks and twenty-eight Islamic banking institutions. The financial sector accounts for about one-quarter of Bahrain's gross domestic product (GDP). However, Bahrain faces extremely strong competition in this sector from Dubai. Lacking the oil resources its neighbors possess, Bahrain felt the impact of the global financial crisis and recession more keenly than the other GCC states.

QATAR

Political Environment

Qatar occupies a mitten-shaped peninsula that extends for about one hundred miles northward into the Gulf and measures fifty miles across at its point of greatest width. The land is mostly low-lying and consists largely of sandy or stony desert, with limestone outcroppings and salt flats.

STATE OF QATAR

Capital city	Doha
Chief of state, 2012	Amir Hamad bin Khalifa Al Thani
Head of government, 2012	Prime Minister Hamad bin Jasim bin Jabir Al Thani
Political parties, 2012	None
Ethnic groups	Arab (40%), Indian (18%), Pakistani (18%), Iranian (10%), other (14%)
Religious groups	Muslim (77.5%), Christian (8.5%), other (14%)
Export partners, 2011	Japan (26.6%), South Korea (18.3%), India (8.1%), Singapore (6.6%), United Kingdom (6.5%), China (4.1%)
Import partners, 2011	United States (12.9%), United Arab Emirates (12.5%), Saudi Arabia (9.4%), United Kingdom 96.2%), China (5.5%), Germany (5.2%), Japan (4.7%), France (4.6%), Italy (4.5%)

Two-thirds of the population lives in the capital of Doha, on the east coast of the peninsula. Before the production of oil in 1949, Qatar's population was one of the poorest in the
region. Most of its inhabitants lived at subsistence levels, with most of their income derived
from fishing and pearling. Today Qatar's per capita income is among the highest in the
world, owing largely to the development of its substantial gas reserves. Qatar also has a very
small national population: less than 20 percent of Qatar's population of almost 2 million are
Qataris; the rest are expatriate workers, mostly South Asians and Arabs. Most of the indigenous population is Arab, some originally from the peninsula; others are *hawwalah*. Qataris
are about 80 percent Sunni Muslim and generally subscribe to a less conservative version of
the Hanbali school of Islamic jurisprudence than is practiced in Saudi Arabia.

Qatar has developed an extensive educational system open to all Qataris. In the nineteenth and early twentieth centuries, those girls whose parents could afford it typically received a basic education in reading, writing, and religion from a tutor. In 1955 the
government opened the first public school for girls; by the early twenty-first century, girls
graduated from high school at a higher rate than boys. At Qatar University, the disparity is
even more pronounced: over 70 percent of the students are women. In 2004 a woman,
Shaykha bint Ahmad al-Mahmud, was named education minister, and another woman, Dr.
Shaykha Abdallah al-Misnad, was appointed president of Qatar University.

Oil and especially natural gas exports are responsible for much of the dramatic transformation that has taken place in the country's social and economic life. In 1975 the government nationalized the two major oil-producing companies, Qatar Petroleum Company
and Shell. Although Qatar's oil reserves are modest by Gulf standards, its North Dome
field, shared with Iran, is the world's largest deposit of unassociated natural gas. Its gas
reserves are the world's third largest, after Russia and Iran. Exploitation of this large gas
field began in 1991, and in 1997 the second phase of its development, construction of facilities for production and export of liquefied natural gas, was completed. The government has invested these revenues in a large welfare state that provides Qataris with free
education, health care, and guaranteed employment. It has also made continuing investments in infrastructure and taken some steps toward economic diversification, beginning
with the manufacture of fertilizer in the 1970s and moving on to cement and steel plants
as well as flour mills and an expanded shrimping industry.

Political Structure and Dynamics

Qatar has been ruled since the nineteenth century by emirs from the Al Thani family. In its
basic structure, Qatar's political system is similar to those of the other GCC states. At the
top is a ruling family, members of whom hold the sovereign ministries (and, in Qatar's
case, usually several other ministries as well). They rule with advice from appointed and
elected bodies. In 2000 the emir formally established the Council of the Ruling Family,
consisting of thirteen family members. The constitution stipulates that rule be hereditary
within the Al Thani family through the line of the current emir's male offspring.

Qatar's political system differs from those of the other GCC states in two important ways. The first is the largely unconsolidated nature of the country's government. While the emir is the country's leader, other powerful family members run governmental fiefdoms with some independence and often different political agendas. The Al Thani is the largest ruling family in the region, numbering, by some accounts, as many as 20,000. The family has many factions, and some members—among them the very wealthy and powerful prime minister and foreign minister, Shaykh Hamad bin Jasim Al Thani—are nearly as powerful as the ruler. This in part explains why Qatar hosts both US forces and Al Jazeera, the controversial satellite station often critical of US policy. The second difference, a consequence of the first, is the relative instability the ruling family has experienced in the years since independence. The current emir, Shaykh Hamad, came to power by overthrowing his father, Shaykh Khalifah bin Hamad Al Thani, in a bloodless coup in 1995, then survived a countercoup attempt in 1996. His father, in turn, came to power in 1972 by overthrowing his cousin, Shaykh Ahmad Al Thani. Shaykh Hamad has since reconciled with his father, although not apparently with the entire family. Upon taking power, Shaykh Khalifah named his son Jasim crown prince but changed his mind in 2003, passing the title on to his fourth son, Tamim.

The pace of political liberalization in Qatar has been slow. The provisional constitution of 1970, which governed political life in Qatar until it was replaced in 2003, provided for a Council of Ministers and an Advisory Council, stipulating that the former was to be appointed by the ruler and that the majority of the latter was to be elected by the general population. However, after taking power in a coup in 1972, the new emir simply appointed an Advisory Council with little authority.

Liberalization reappeared after the Gulf War. In January 1992, fifty leading Qataris petitioned the emir to establish an assembly with legislative powers and to institute economic and educational reforms. His response was only to broaden modestly the Advisory Council's membership.

After Shaykh Hamad took power in 1995, he began tentative steps toward political liberalization. In 1999, 2003, 2007, and 2011, Qatar held relatively free and open elections for a twenty-nine-member advisory Central Municipal Council, albeit one with few powers. Suffrage was extended to women, despite modest opposition in the form of a petition signed by twenty-two Islamic scholars. Female candidates ran in the elections, and one woman won a seat in the 2003 and 2007 elections.

In 1999 the emir established a constitutional committee, which submitted a draft constitution in 2002. In April 2003, Qatar's new constitution was adopted by popular referendum, replacing the provisional constitution drawn up with Qatar's independence in 1970. The new constitution came into force in 2005. It called for the creation of a partially elected legislative body and offered protections for civil, political, and social rights. The emir announced in 2006 that in 2007 he would hold, for the first time ever, the Advisory Council elections stipulated in the constitution (to comprise forty-five members, two-thirds of whom were to be elected by popular vote). Election dates have been set, then postponed, three times, most recently in 2010 when elections were tentatively rescheduled for 2013. The Advisory Council would have authority to propose legislation, review budgets, interpellate ministers, and issue no-confidence votes against ministers. Political parties remain banned.

The government also introduced some press freedoms. After taking power, Hamad revoked censorship of the news media and dissolved the Ministry of Information. In 1995 he established Al Jazeera, a satellite news station, revolutionary at the time because it introduced frank and provocative news reports, commentaries, and debates. It was welcomed enthusiastically by a viewing public accustomed to coverage of state visits and broadcasts of official speeches. Al Jazeera offended many Arab (and non-Arab) governments, but it also inspired a host of other satellite stations in the Gulf. Al Jazeera, however, has been careful not to criticize the Qatari government or the Al Thani family. During the Arab Spring, some criticized Al Jazeera for coverage sympathetic to the government's positions. While formal censorship was lifted in 1995 and the Ministry of Information abolished, considerable self-censorship by reporters and editors in practice limits the amount of free expression. Many journalists criticized a new press law, drafted in 2002, because, among other things, it allowed journalists to be imprisoned for their writing.

The right to peaceful public assembly is restricted. Public demonstrations and political parties are banned. Permission is required for public gatherings and demonstrations, and the government grants these reluctantly. Nongovernmental organizations require government permission to operate, and most groups have had license requests refused. In 2004 the government did issue a new labor law, giving Qataris the right to form trade unions and engage in collective bargaining (including the right to strike). It also offered businesses a clearer legal framework for employment. There is a Chamber of Commerce and Industry.

Qatar is divided administratively into ten municipalities (*baladiyat*). However, since the majority of the population lives in the capital, local government is of little practical importance.

Since the early days of oil, when political opposition was frequently sharp and ideological, opposition forces have become much less vocal. There may simply be less simmering discontent in Qatar than elsewhere, but for whatever reason, liberals and even Islamists have not been an important political force. Aside from a 2005 suicide car bomb attack by an Egyptian on a theater popular with Western expatriates, neither terrorism nor militant Islam has made an appearance (although there have been reports that Qatar's interior minister hosted some Islamist terrorists in the 1990s). Perhaps preemptively, Qatar does host a number of conservative Islamic clerics, most notably Yusuf al-Qaradawi, known widely for his weekly show on Al Jazeera. The Arab Spring had little impact on Qatar domestically. In March 2011 Qatar detained Sultan al-Khalaifi, a human rights activist and blogger. But overall Qatar remained calm. Nonetheless the government did offer a preemptive raise in salaries for state employees. Qatar did, however, play an early and extremely active part in supporting Libya's rebel forces and NATO's military campaign in Libya. Al Jazeera also provided extensive coverage of the Arab Spring as it emerged and spread throughout the region

Social cleavages do exist in Qatar. The old merchant class has historically exerted less influence on government affairs than its larger and older counterparts in Kuwait, Dubai, and even Bahrain. As revenues have accumulated and as many members of the ruling family have become more interested and involved in business themselves, the traditional separation of Al Thani–dominated government and merchant class–dominated business has begun to disappear. The Al Thani and the business community, through a symbiotic process, have increased their collaboration in many areas relating to Qatar's economic growth.

Tribal divisions remain important. Qatar has about eighteen tribes linked through marriage. In 2005 the government stripped members of the al-Murrah tribe in southern Qatar of their nationality because of their alleged connection to the 1996 coup attempt; this act was reversed in 2006.

The most important division is that between Qataris and foreign workers. The 2004 labor law did not address domestic workers (e.g., drivers and maids) at all and barred all expatriate workers from union activities.

Economic liberalization and diversification have proceeded steadily over the last decade. Shaykh Hamad took power in 1995 with an agenda of economic reform, eager to deal with the lack of transparency and accountability that had led to corruption so massive in the 1980s that it was undermining the country's economic growth. Shaykh Hamad clamped down on corrupt business practices and introduced standards for transparency and accountability in both the public and the private sectors.

These measures were accompanied by development programs to streamline and expand the economy. A key target was the oil sector. The emir invited international oil companies to help locate and develop new oil fields, investing in advanced oil-recovery systems to extend existing fields and expanding production of the country's huge natural gas reserves. Qatar's oil exports more than doubled in a decade. Much of the additional income was invested in natural gas projects. As a result, Qatar, which ran deficits in the 1990s, began experiencing some of the highest economic growth rates in the region, earning more from gas than from oil. Qatar has also invested in energy projects abroad, most notably in a $1.5 billion oil refinery in Zimbabwe.

The drop in oil prices in 2008, coupled with the deepening global recession, reduced Qatar's budget surpluses, prompting the head of its sovereign wealth fund, one of the world's largest, to announce a six-month hiatus, a pause for reflection, in March 2009. Nonetheless, Qatar remained in a far better financial situation than many of its neighbors.

Qatar has moved, albeit more cautiously than its neighbors, into other areas, such as tourism. In 2004 the government announced several education reforms, including the inauguration of a new Education City that presently hosts branches of several US academic institutions, among them Cornell's Medical School and Carnegie-Mellon and Texas A&M universities.

Qatar's state security forces were merged into one force in June 2003. They remain under the direct control of the emir. Qatar's military is the second smallest in the region (after Bahrain). Qatar also has a paramilitary royal guard in the Ministry of Defense and a regular police force.

Like many Islamic countries, Qatar's legal system is an amalgam of Islamic law and Western civil legal procedures. Islamic law is applied mainly as family law, based on the conservative Hanbali school of Islamic jurisprudence. In 1999 Shaykh Hamad established the High Judicial Council, which advises on judicial appointments and legislation concerning the judicial system. In October 2004, long-promised court reform unified Qatar's dual court system (of sharia and civil courts). In 2007 an Administrative Court and a Constitutional Court were established.

Qatar's human rights record is mixed. Those most subject to abuse are foreign workers, especially domestic workers. The abuse faced by these workers was documented extensively in a Human Rights Watch report in June 2012.

UNITED ARAB EMIRATES

Political Environment

The UAE is a loose federation of seven emirates—Abu Dhabi, Dubai, Ajman, Fujayrah, Sharjah, Ras al-Khaymah, and Umm al-Qaywayn—located along the Strait of Hormuz. The emirates vary a good deal in size and wealth. Abu Dhabi is the largest, covering nearly 90 percent of the UAE's territory. It is also the wealthiest, possessing most of the UAE's gas and oil reserves. Dubai, although running out of oil, has become an important business hub for the region and is the second wealthiest emirate.

The most distinctive characteristic of the various shaykhdoms is tribal affiliation. Six principal tribal groups inhabit the country: the Bani Yas, a confederation of nearly a dozen different tribes, two branches of which (the Al Bu Falah and the Al Bu Falasah, respectively) provide the ruling families of Abu Dhabi and Dubai; the Manasir, who range from the western reaches of the UAE to Saudi Arabia and Qatar; the Qawasim, two branches of which rule Sharjah and Ras al-Khaymah; the Al Ali (also Al Mu'alla) of Umm al-Qaywayn; the Sharqiyin in Fujayrah; and the Al Nu'aim in Ajman. All the tribes are Sunni. Despite this tribal identification, only a small percentage of the national population is still nomadic.

Other cleavages are politically less salient. Dubai, with its long history as a trading center, has long had a powerful merchant class with a network linked to the Indian subcontinent and Iran. Before the emergence of oil as the dominant factor in the region's economy, Dubai's merchants were major free traders, smuggling gold and other luxury items from picturesque dhows that concealed powerful engines capable of outrunning the coast guard vessels of a half dozen countries.

UNITED ARAB EMIRATES

Capital city	Abu Dhabi
Chief of state, 2012	President Khalifah bin Zayid Al Nuhayyan
Head of government, 2012	Prime Minister and Vice President Muhammad bin Rashid Al Maktum
Political parties, 2012	None
Ethnic groups	Emirati (19%), other Arab and Iranian (23%), South Asian (50%), other expatriates, includes Westerners and East Asians (8%)
Religious groups	Sunni Muslim (80%), Shi'a Muslim (16%), other (4%)
Export partners, 2011	Japan (16.1%), India (14%), Iran (10.9%), South Korea (5.5%), Thailand (5.4%), Singapore (4.4%)
Import partners, 2011	India (19.8%), China (13.9%), United States (8.2%), Germany (4.6%)

Political Economy

Oil drives the economy of the UAE. Nearly 10 percent of the world's known oil reserves are located in the UAE, and given the country's relatively small population, it has one of the highest per capita incomes in the world. Abu Dhabi accounts for more than 85 percent of the UAE's oil production and more than 90 percent of its reserves. Before oil, Abu Dhabi Town was little more than a mud-brick village. Today it is the largest city in the UAE and by far the most advanced in terms of administrative and social welfare services. Abu Dhabi has also worked to diversify its economy, mainly with light industry, such as food processing, and some heavy industry, such as cement production. Despite its wealth, Abu Dhabi was late in developing modern financial institutions. In 1991 it experienced a major financial scandal when regulatory authorities in seven countries abruptly terminated the operations of the Bank of Commerce and Credit International (BCCI), in which the ruling family of Abu Dhabi held a controlling interest. It was learned that bank authorities had committed major fraud prior to the Al Nuhayyan family's purchase of the bank's shares. The affair was settled in 1998 when Abu Dhabi authorities paid $1.8 billion to compensate the bank's creditors.

The BCCI scandal prompted the strengthening of the UAE Central Bank and stricter regulation of the country's financial sector. In 2005, Abu Dhabi followed Dubai's lead in seeking to attract foreign investment by enacting legislation allowing 100 percent foreign ownership of investments in its Industrial City. One of the most important innovations by the UAE federal government was the establishment of the UAE Offsets Group, which mandates that foreign firms winning defense contracts must invest a percentage of the value of their contracts in joint ventures with local partners. In this way, a number of significant projects, ranging from a shipbuilding company to a health-care center, have been undertaken. The UAE, with Abu Dhabi in the lead, has also developed a vast network of global investments. Nonetheless the UAE faces economic problems similar to those confronting the other GCC states: unemployment, emiratization, education, and housing shortages.

Of all the GCC entities, Dubai has perhaps the most ambitious and unusual strategy of economic development. Before the discovery of oil in Abu Dhabi in 1958, only Dubai and Sharjah had developed an extensive entrepôt trade. Dubai began to eclipse Sharjah both politically and commercially when Sharjah's harbor began to silt up in the 1940s. The conditions for perpetuating the former's economic edge over the latter were practically ensured when Dubai succeeded in dredging its own inlet (or "creek," as it is called locally), allowing larger ships to make Dubai a port of call. Dubai's merchants reinvented themselves as modern business executives in a global economy. Dubai remains an entrepôt for goods and services, based on its free market economy. The other emirates have business communities that are tied more closely to the state. Building on its history as a trading entrepôt, Dubai created a niche for itself as a regional banking and tourism center. In 1979 Shaykh Rashid began building the world's largest man-made harbor at Jabal Ali. In the 1980s Dubai, building on family business ties to Iran, became an important source of connections for that country during the Iran-Iraq War, connections that remain strong despite a dispute between the UAE and Iran over three Gulf islands. As US-led sanctions against Iran have deepened, this connection has grown stronger.

Despite Abu Dhabi's preeminence as the UAE's major oil producer, Dubai has received more attention abroad with its grandiose projects and open market economy. Dubai has an indoor ski slope and the world's largest mall. In early 2010, the Dubai Khalifa, the world's largest building, was opened. Dubai's location as a halfway point between Asia and Europe and its wide-open, free market economy have enabled it to become a major upscale winter tourist center. To encourage tourism, Dubai hosts international golf and tennis tournaments and is building a Dubai Sports City. Dubailand, a theme park twice the size of Disney World, is planned. Dubai has also embarked on a $1.6 billion shopping and entertainment project called Dubai Festival City.

The major factor behind Dubai's renaissance, however, was its free market economy and use of Gulf oil revenues to develop itself as a major global banking and investment center. But this could be a two-edged sword. A key to success was to establish modern financial standards of transparency and accountability to replace traditional, unregulated free market commercial standards. This has been an evolutionary process. In 2002, the government hired a retired Bank of England regulator to help draw up a financial regulatory system. And in 2004, the Dubai government established the Dubai International Financial Center (DIFC) to attract private investment institutions. Licensed firms operating in the DIFC and other enclave free trade centers benefit from no taxes on profits; no restrictions on foreign ownership, foreign exchange, or repatriation of capital; and access to operational-support and business-continuity facilities. In addition, Dubai aims to become a regional sales, distribution, and trading center for goods sold over the Internet. Dubai also suffered the most from the 2008 recession, which hurt the financial and investment sectors, caused some dramatic declines in property values, and forced the suspension of many domestic construction projects. In 2009 Abu Dhabi began taking steps to rescue financially strapped Dubai.

Sharjah produces modest quantities of gas and condensate and, like Dubai, has undertaken extensive development projects, most recently focusing on centers of higher education. The contrast between these three affluent shaykhdoms and the other four remains substantial, though the gap has decreased somewhat as the federal government, largely financed by Abu Dhabi, has funded numerous development projects in the poorer states. The abundance of new income, the lack, to date, of a strong centralized planning authority with the power to veto or modify individual shaykhdoms' development ventures, and, most importantly, the continuation of intense competition among the various rulers for prestige have resulted in the duplication of many facilities, such as international airports.

Oil has transformed the class structure of the UAE, as it has those of the other Gulf states. The most important demographic impact of oil has been the influx of foreign workers. The indigenous inhabitants of the UAE account for less than one-fifth of the total population, with that percentage lower still in the wealthier emirates. After the Gulf War, the largely Arab foreign population was replaced predominately with labor from the Indian subcontinent. Of all the GCC states, the distance between expatriates and nationals is perhaps greatest here. The presence of so many nonnationals has created a strong sense of Emirati identity.

Political Structure and Dynamics

The internal politics of the emirates' ruling families have historically been replete with intrigue and jockeying among contenders for the limited positions of official power. Before the establishment of the UAE, many local rulers fell victim to assassination at the hands of brothers, cousins, or sons. Abu Dhabi, the richest of the emirates, has been ruled by the Al Nuhayyan family for over three centuries. In 1966 a palace coup in Abu Dhabi brought a new ruler, Shaykh Zayid, to power. He had the broad support of many who thought that his brother and predecessor, Shaykh Shakhbut, was not up to the task of ruling Abu

Dhabi. In 1972 the UAE's minister of education, Shaykh Sultan bin Muhammad al-Qasimi, assumed the position of ruler in Sharjah following an abortive palace coup in which his predecessor was murdered. In 1987, Shaykh Abd al-Aziz bin Muhammad al-Qasimi tried to seize power from his brother, the ruler of Sharjah, an event that threatened the union's integrity, both because it raised the question of the legitimacy of all the rulers in the UAE and because Abu Dhabi initially backed the usurper and Dubai backed the incumbent. The UAE's Federal Supreme Council (FSC) temporarily defused the crisis by arranging a compromise sharing of power, with Shaykh Sultan remaining ruler.

Recent successions have been smoother, however. In 2004, Shaykh Zayid, who had ruled Abu Dhabi, was succeeded on his death by Shaykh Khalifah, the crown prince and oldest of his nineteen sons. Even so, Khalifah's brother Shaykh Muhammad administers much of the day-to-day business of Abu Dhabi and the UAE. In 1990 the ruler of Dubai, Shaykh Rashid bin Sa'id Al Maktum, was succeeded peacefully on his death by his son Maktum, who appointed his brother Muhammad, the de facto ruler, crown prince. When Maktum died in 2006, his brother Shaykh Muhammad took over. The current rulers are Khalifah bin Zayid Al Nuhayyan (Abu Dhabi), Muhammad bin Rashid Al Maktum (Dubai), Sultan bin Muhammad al-Qassimi (Sharjah), Sa'ud bin al-Qassimi (Ras al-Khaymah), Humaid bin Rashid Al Nu'aimi (Ajman), Hamad bin Muhammad al-Sharqi (Fujayrah), and Rashid bin Ahmad Al Mu'alla (Umm al-Qaywayn). In October 2010 Shaikh Saqr bin Muhammad al-Qasimi, ruler of Ras al-Khaymah, died, and a brief succession struggle ensued when his eldest son, Crown Prince Shaikh Khalid, returned from exile attempting to wrest leadership from his half brother, Shaikh Sa'ud, whose bid was recognized by the government of the UAE.

The UAE is ruled as a federation of these families. The UAE's constitution, drafted in 1972 and made permanent in 1996, provides for federal legislative, executive, and judicial bodies. The head of state, the president, is chosen by the seven members of the FSC for a five-year term. The first president and architect of the federation, Shaykh Zayid, served as president from independence until his death in 2004. His son and successor, Shaykh Khalifah, was chosen shortly afterward to be president of the UAE. The ruler of Dubai is the vice president. The FSC meets four times a year. It is charged with formulating and supervising all federal policies, ratifying UAE laws, approving the country's annual budget, ratifying international treaties, and approving several appointments. In procedural matters, a simple majority vote is sufficient for passage of any resolution. However, on substantive issues, Abu Dhabi and Dubai have veto power. Thus, on any substantive vote, five member states, including the two leading shaykhdoms, must approve a resolution in order for the motion to have the force of law. The constitutional allocation of a preponderance of political power to Abu Dhabi and Dubai has been a major point of contention among the other shaykhdoms.

The Federal National Council (FNC) is an appointed consultative assembly with advisory powers. In accordance with the relative size of their constituent populations, eight seats each are apportioned to Abu Dhabi and Dubai, six each to Ras al-Khaymah and

Sharjah, and four each to the remaining three members. The FNC's duties are limited mainly to discussing and approving the budget, drafting some legislation, and serving as a forum for discussion and debate of policies and programs under consideration by the government. This last duty is of no small significance because of the absence of political parties, trade unions, and other kinds of voluntary associations familiar to Westerners. The constitution would permit the FNC's evolution into an elected body exercising real legislative functions.

Although the powers of the presidency are subordinate to those of the FSC, Shaykh Zayid was relatively successful in keeping together what has been the Arab world's foremost example of regional political integration. His success was due in part to Abu Dhabi's preeminence as the most pro-federation state in the union but also to his own strong personal dedication to the UAE's development. Abu Dhabi has thus far been a willing hegemon: many of the federation's operations are almost completely funded by Abu Dhabi.

Nonetheless, even without Shaykh Zayid's influence, the kinds of economic and security concerns that initially helped bring the seven shaykhdoms into a federation endure. The habits of working together are well established, and the advantages of doing so are demonstrable. It seems likely that the UAE will continue to muddle through as a loose federation for the indefinite future.

The government of the UAE responded to the Arab Spring with both carrots and sticks. The carrots, though modest, came early. In February 2011 the government announced it would expand the electorate to its advisory body from 7,000 to almost 80,000. In March the government announced it would invest $1.6 billion in the poorer emirates. In November the government announced pay raises for state employees. The sticks soon followed. In March 160 Emiratis signed a modest petition calling for free and democratic elections and reform of the FNC. In the following months the government's response to dissent grew increasingly harsh. It dissolved the boards of the lawyers' and teachers' associations after they issued a joint statement calling for pro-democratic reforms. It arrested five pro-democracy activists, some of whom had signed the March petition, sentencing them in November to two to three years in prison (later pardoning one). The government also signed a contract with Blackwater to create a special operations force. In December 2011 it revoked the citizenship of six Islamist activists. In May 2012 it detained fifteen more.

Each emirate exercises a degree of independence. Each has its own independent police force. The intelligence services, while formally under one umbrella, operate largely independently. The UAE military is not completely unified. In 1976 several Emirati military forces were formally united and placed under the single command of the Union Defense Force. However, the two principal shaykhdoms, Abu Dhabi and Dubai, did not fully integrate their defense forces into the union force; indeed, the latter has created its own central military region command. Moreover, Fujayrah, Ras al-Khaymah, Sharjah, and Umm al-Qaywayn maintain their own national guard forces. The UAE's military forces number about 65,000. As in other GCC states, many of the nationals working in the police and military are from more recently settled Bedouin families.

The UAE's federal judiciary was established in 1971, but federal judicial structures emerged only slowly. The federal judiciary still does not apply to Dubai and Ras al-Khaymah. In 1973 a Supreme Federal Court was established, and in the following years some judicial matters were transferred from the emirates to the federal level. In 1983 a comprehensive law governing the federal judiciary was issued, although individual emirates retained varying degrees of judicial autonomy. Ras al-Khaymah and Dubai chose not to cede any jurisdiction to the federal courts. The other emirates ceded most, but not all, jurisdiction. All the emirates retained their own sharia courts with jurisdiction over personal-status matters. In 1983 a Federal Supreme Judicial Council was created to play an advisory role to the Ministry of Justice, which retains oversight of the court administration. The federal system is three-tiered, with primary courts, appeals courts, and a supreme court. The Supreme Court serves as the highest court of appeal and also adjudicates disputes among individual shaykhdoms and between individual shaykhdoms and the federal government. It also determines the constitutionality of federal or Emirati laws when challenged.

Like the federal bureaucracy, the judiciary depends heavily on foreign residents' expertise. Efforts to staff the courts with trained native UAE jurists have been only partially successful. Judges are appointed by the president and serve indefinite terms. Emirati judges may not be dismissed without serious cause. Nonnational judges serve on renewable contracts.

The country's legal system places special emphasis on Islamic law but is drawn from several sources, including Western ones. In February 1994, Shaykh Zayid ordered that a number of serious crimes, including murder, theft, adultery, and drug offenses, be tried in sharia courts rather than civil courts. Ras al-Khaymah experienced a flurry of controversy in the 1990s when an Egyptian judge briefly attempted to enforce certain corporal punishments found in Islamic law.

The UAE's record on human rights is mixed. Although foreign workers flock to the Emirates because of the higher wages, many are subjected to human rights abuses, including unsafe working conditions, nonpayment of wages, long hours, and poor living conditions. Many of the workers are in virtual debt bondage to recruiting agencies. As in the other Gulf countries, female domestic workers are at particular risk of abuse. Foreign workers have staged public protests, typically over nonpayment of wages. In 2006 the government announced that it would amend the labor law with the goal of improving the conditions of foreign labor after public protests in Dubai and a Human Rights Watch report critical of the problem brought unwanted international attention. The abuse of young boys working as camel jockeys was formally banned in 2005. In 2009 an incident involving the videotaped torture, apparently by Shaykh Issa bin Zayid Al Nuhayyan, brother of Abu Dhabi's crown prince, of an Afghan business partner brought the human rights issue to public attention. The government is not a signatory to most human rights treaties and has not responded to repeated efforts by human rights groups to organize inside the country.

The UAE has thus far largely resisted regional trends toward political liberalization. Politics within the shaykhdoms traditionally have been tribe based and autocratic, even if tempered by consultation, consensus, and adherence to the principles and norms enshrined in Islamic law. Considerable debate over the development of a more responsive participatory system of government has been vigorously and extensively covered in the press. In 2003 Dubai formed district municipal councils to encourage a degree of public participation. In 2005 Shaykh Khalifah announced that half the seats in the FNC would be elected at some point in the future. Instead, in 2006 the government allowed an appointed group of fewer than 7,000 Emiratis to vote for half the members of the consultative FNC.

Most associational life is banned in the UAE. All private associations must be licensed by the government, which rejects most applications. Political parties and trade unions are illegal. In recent years, however, a handful of professional and student associations have been allowed to emerge. In 2005, the Abu Dhabi Chamber of Commerce and Industry, in an experiment with limited democracy, elected fifteen of its twenty-one seats. The media is relatively free of formal censorship, but considerable self-censorship occurs. The government has blackballed journalists whose views it does not like and has used the Anti-Terrorism Act of 2004 to restrict freedom of expression. A proposed media law in 2009 received criticism from Human Rights Watch and other groups over its press and speech restrictions.

OMAN

Political Environment

Located on the southeastern reaches of the Arabian Peninsula, the Sultanate of Oman has an area two or three times greater than Kuwait, Bahrain, Qatar, and the UAE combined: 82,000 square miles. Perhaps a quarter of Oman's population lives in the Greater Capital Area, which includes Muscat, the capital; Matrah, a major port; and Ruhi, the country's commercial hub. The main city of inner Oman is Nizwa, the traditional religious center of interior Oman. Sur, south of Muscat, is an important fishing port, and Salalah is the largest city and principal port of Dhufar, the southernmost province. Dhufar consists of three ranges of low mountains surrounding a small coastal plain and is separated from the rest of Oman by several hundred miles of desert. Oman proper consists of inner Oman and the coastal plain, known as the Batinah. Inner Oman contains a fertile plateau and the oldest towns in the country. Separating this region from the Batinah is the Hajar mountain range, stretching in an arc from northwest to southeast and reaching nearly 10,000 feet in height at the Jabal al-Akhdar (Green Mountain). The majority of Oman's population is found along the Batinah coast, which has the country's greatest agricultural potential.

Most Omanis are Arab Muslims. Perhaps half are Ibadhi Muslims, members of the only remaining branch of Kharijism, which originated in Islam's first schism, predating the Sunni-Shi'a split. Most of the remainder of the population is Sunni, including many

SULTANATE OF OMAN

Capital city	Muscat
Chief of state, 2012	Sultan and Prime Minister Qaboos bin Said al-Said
Head of government, 2012	Sultan and Prime Minister Qaboos bin Said al-Said
Political parties, 2012	None
Ethnic groups	Arab, Baluch, South Asian, African
Religious groups	Ibadihi Muslim (75%), other (25%)
Export partners, 2011	China (30.5%), South Korea (11%), United Arab Emirates (10.6%), Japan (10.5%), India (10.1%), Thailand (5.4%), United States (4.7%)
Import partners, 2011	United Arab Emirates (27.8%), Japan (12%), United States (6.1%), India (5.3%), China (4.3%), Saudi Arabia (4.1%), Germany (4%)

Baluchis, originally from the coastal area of Iran and Pakistan, who live along the Batinah coast. Many merchants of the capital region and the coast are Indians, either Hindus or Khojas (a community of Shi'a Muslims). There are also Persians and other groups of Shi'a Muslims, including some originally from Iraq or Iran. Dhufar and the surrounding desert are home to several groups whose primary language is South Arabian. Shihuh tribes, a group of mixed Persian-Arab ancestry, inhabit the northern, strategically important exclave of the Musandam Peninsula at the Strait of Hormuz.

Like the other GCC states, Oman has in modern times experienced an influx of migrant labor, principally from other Arab states and the Indian subcontinent. Oman's modest level of wealth has, however, enabled it to avoid the situation of Kuwait, Qatar, and the UAE, where foreigners outnumber the indigenous population. Omanis constitute over 90 percent of Oman's estimated population of 3.5 million.

Oman has experienced more rapid development than any of the other GCC states in the last few decades owing to its starting point. Economic development was almost totally neglected in Oman until the accession of Sultan Qabus in 1970. Since that time it has progressed steadily. In the early 1980s construction was completed on copper mining and refining facilities, and in 1984 two cement plants began operations. Since the mid-1980s Omani development policies emphasizing light industry (e.g., food processing) have been promoted at industrial zones in Muscat, Sohar, and Salalah. Agriculture generates less than 3 percent of gross national product but employs as much as half the labor force, although official figures are much lower.

Despite some diversification, modern Oman remains largely dependent on its meager and dwindling oil revenues. Oil accounts for some 40 percent of Oman's GDP. Oil exports began in 1967, and in the 1970s the large oil field of Qarn Alam was discovered at the edge of the Empty Quarter. But by the 1980s, oil flow had declined significantly. Production fell further from about 800,000 barrels a day at the turn of the millennium to 633,000 in 2006. By some estimates, Oman will run out of oil in less than twenty years. Moreover, oil in Oman is difficult to extract, and so Petroleum Development Oman has invested heavily in enhanced oil recovery. Natural gas production, however, has added to Oman's revenues in recent years. As a result, Oman began economic diversification and Omanization well before the other GCC states. Economic development funds for various projects have been carefully spread across the regions, with industrial poles in Salalah, Sohar, and Sur. A $15-billion tourism project has begun in Madinat al-Zarqa, and Vision 2020, Oman's long-term development plan, envisions opening nearly a dozen resorts across the country in coming years, developing a niche in eco- and heritage tourism. As part of a broader process of economic liberalization in 2004, the sultan permitted foreign ownership of land in some designated tourist areas. Although the economy was briefly buoyed by the higher oil prices in 2007, the subsequent recession and lowering of prices had a more notable impact on Oman than its GCC neighbors.

Political Structure and Dynamics

The Al Bu Sa'id family has ruled Oman since the eighteenth century. In the early twentieth century, a movement to restore an Ibadhi imamate had led to substantial autonomy for the interior of the country. Qabus's father, Sultan Sa'id bin Taimur (r. 1932–1970), with the assistance of British forces, largely reunified the country in the 1950s. This reunification was completed under Sultan Qabus, who took power in a nearly bloodless coup in 1970 and changed the name of the country from the Sultanate of Muscat and Oman to the Sultanate of Oman.

The southernmost province of Dhufar, annexed in the late nineteenth century after it had been quasi-autonomous for years, became the site of an insurrection in the early 1960s. By 1968 leadership of the rebellion had been seized by the Marxist-oriented Popular Front for the Liberation of the Occupied Arabian Gulf (which changed its name in 1971 to the Popular Front for the Liberation of Oman and the Arab Gulf and in 1974 to the Popular Front for the Liberation of Oman). Supported by Soviet and Chinese aid channeled through South Yemen, the insurrection occupied large areas of the province by the early 1970s. The rebellion was finally put down in 1975, with British advisers and

Iranian troops playing key roles in assisting Omani light infantry and tribal militia forces. Sultan Qabus assured Dhufari loyalties thereafter by dispensing generous development funds to the province.

As in the other GCC states, the sultan relies on his relatives, cousins, and uncles, who control many (although not always the most important) ministerial and other governmental posts. However, compared with the other GCC states, the sultan has shared far less power with his family, or indeed with anyone. Qabus himself, in addition to being prime minister, holds the portfolios of defense, finance, and foreign affairs. This may make for a difficult transition, should power remain in the ruling family. The childless sultan has named no heir apparent, leaving Oman alone among the GCC states with no clear successor. He has asked that his family choose a leader from two candidates he has selected, to be revealed upon his death. They are suspected to be sons of Qabus's uncle, Sayid Tariq bin Taimur, who has played an important role in government for many years.

Over the past twenty years, Oman's political structure has evolved toward increasing popular participation in government. In 1981, Oman established a consultative assembly to advise the sultan on matters of social, educational, and economic policy (defense and foreign policy were excluded). The members, appointed by the sultan, were drawn from the tribal and merchant communities as well as from government. Initially forty-five members served on the council; the total was raised to fifty-five in 1985. This first experiment in representative government lasted for a decade.

In November 1990 the sultan established a new Consultative Assembly (Majlis al-Shura) to replace the 1981 body. Regional representatives from each of the fifty-nine districts would nominate three candidates, and the deputy prime minister for legal affairs would select one to serve, subject to the sultan's approval. In 1994 the Consultative Assembly's membership was expanded from fifty-nine to eighty, and women could for the first time be nominated (two were selected in 1995). Although lacking legislative powers, the council was empowered to review social and economic legislation, to help draft and implement development plans, and to propose improvement in public sectors. Ministries were required to submit to the council annual reports on their performance and plans and to answer questions from council members. The council could summon ministers to discuss any issue within the purview of their respective ministries. Moreover, the council was required to refer to its appropriate committees questions and suggestions from citizens on public issues and subsequently to inform the correspondents of the actions taken.

In 1996 Sultan Qabus issued a Basic Statute of the State, which defined the system of government and is, in effect, the sultanate's constitution. The document vested substantial authority in the sultan but also set out a legislative and a judicial branch. In principle, it also guarantees citizens a set of basic civil rights.

The legislature, the Council of Oman, consists of an appointed upper house, the Council of State (Majlis al-Dawla), and an eighty-two-member elected lower house (Majlis al-Shura). In 1997, 2000, and 2003, the government held elections to the body, expanding suffrage until by 2003 it extended to virtually all adult nationals. Elections were next held in 2007 and 2011. Among those elected were three activists involved in the Arab Spring protests (see below). The council's mandate remains narrow, primarily restricted to economic and some social matters, but it does enjoy the right to interpellate ministers and provides a forum for public debate. The voting age is twenty-one (lowered from thirty in the 2000 elections). Members of the council are elected to three-year terms and may serve successive terms.

The Arab Spring arrived in Oman in earnest in February 2011 when thousands of typically more quiescent Omanis protested, largely over economic issues such as jobs, wages, inflation, and corruption. Demonstrations began in Sohar, spread to Muscat and beyond, and continued into May. As in the other GCC states, the protesters stopped short of demanding the ruler's ouster. The government's response was mixed. At times it was quite forceful, including even firing on the opposition. The government also introduced modest reforms such as a cabinet reshuffle in March and promises of new government jobs. In October Sultan Qabus issued a royal decree expanding the powers of the Majlis al-Shura, requiring the Council of Ministers to refer draft laws to the council. Economic reforms also followed: raising the minimum wage, introducing unemployment benefits, and raising government pensions. The unrest led to promises of aid from the GCC. Still, dissent continued. In December 2011 twenty-two imprisoned protesters went on a hunger strike. In May 2012 a wave of strikes occurred in the oil sector. The arrest of strikers led to more dissent, now for the first time including direct criticism of Sultan Qabus, and more arrests.

The judiciary is supervised by the Ministry of Legal Affairs, established in 1994. A 1999 Judicial Authority Law began a restructuring of the judicial system. Sharia courts have jurisdiction over personal-status matters; other cases (civil, criminal, and commercial) go to the regular courts. Oman has a three-tiered court system: courts of first instance, six appeals courts, and a supreme court. The sultan is the final court of appeal. State security courts have been used on occasion for political dissidents.

Articles 32 and 33 of the 1996 Basic Statute guarantee free association; however, the 1984 Press and Publications Law allowed the government to censor publications. The Consultative Assembly approved a new Press and Publications Law in 2002. Political parties are banned. Some professional and other associations exist, among them the Chamber of Commerce and Industry.

The government has a mixed human rights record. In 1994 state security forces arrested hundreds of regime opponents, including higher-ranking government officials and members of prominent families, alleging they were Islamists (a claim others dismissed since many of those arrested were Shi'as and Ibadhis). They were charged with sedition but later pardoned.

In early 2005 the government again arrested dozens of dissidents (academics, civil servants, and Islamic scholars). They were convicted of sedition in May 2005 by a state security court. In June 2005 the sultan again pardoned thirty-one of them. More arrests occurred during the Arab Spring protests.

Oman is large enough for meaningful local government. In 1976 the sultan reorganized regional and local governments by establishing thirty-seven (later fifty-nine) districts (*wilayat*), one province (Dhufar, historically a separate sultanate that enjoys more local autonomy than other regions), and a municipality that embraces the capital. The districts are administered by governors appointed by the sultan. They collect taxes, provide local security, settle disputes, and advise the sultan.

Oman has a military of about 45,000. Its domestic forces consist of the Royal Police and a small tribal national guard.

There are four politically important groups in Oman: the ruling family, the tribes, the expatriate advisers, and the merchant class. They occupy a number of key ministerial and other government posts. Traditionally the tribes have also played a significant role in the Omani political process. Under Qabus's father, Sultan Sa'id bin Taimur, manipulation of tribal rivalries was a major element in ruling the country. Qabus, on the other hand, has tried to decrease the power of the tribes through development of local administration, such as local government councils. Although the tribes' influence may be reflected in the election of council candidates, especially in rural areas, their power has declined considerably.

FOREIGN POLICIES OF THE EASTERN ARABIAN STATES

The eastern Arabian states share similar foreign policy interests, regional national security threats, and global economic interests. As a result, there is a degree of coordination among all the states and with Saudi Arabia, by far the largest and most powerful state in the Arabian Peninsula.

At the same time, the differences in the pace and breadth of development in each state far outweigh the similarities. Full political independence and the discovery of oil occurred at different times; there are wide differences in geography, demographics, proved oil reserves, military and security capabilities, and the impact of rapid modernization on traditional social and political values and norms. For example, although Gulf oil policies are carried out based on consensus through OPEC, the GCC as a multilateral institution is little more than a consultative body in the Arabic context of *tashawwar,* which means simply soliciting an opinion with no attempt to reach an overall consensus.

The eastern Arabian states have long understood that their security lies outside their direct control. They are small and militarily weak; yet their wealth draws the often unwanted attention of the outside world. As a result, they have all looked to larger, more powerful allies for national security. Regionally, that has been Saudi Arabia, also a GCC member. Bilateral relations with Saudi Arabia have been hampered by a great deal of resentment among the smaller states, however, due to what is often seen as its patronizing and domineering attitude toward them. And, at any rate, they have felt the need for alliance with a stronger power against potential regional antagonists such as Iraq under Saddam and republican, Shi'a Iran.

Historically, Britain played that role. But with the departure of Britain and advent of the United States as a superpower, the latter has taken over that role. This has created some tension, however, due in large part to domestic antipathy toward the close US relationship with Israel and the US failure to create a just settlement of the Palestinian-Israeli conflict. In short, while the eastern Arabian states rely to a great extent on the United States for their national security, they try to avoid being dependent on it. This is done by diversifying arms purchases and training to include many sources.

At present, the greatest security threat is from Iran, based on a complex set of factors. Iranian governments have always aspired to leadership in the Gulf. A second factor is sectarian. Iran is Shi'a, which some Sunni Arabs see as heretical and which those states with large Shi'a populations, such as Bahrain, fear could undermine their regimes. Furthermore, the US overthrow of the regimes in Iraq and Afghanistan provided an opportunity for Iran to seek influence in Iraq. Finally, there is concern over Iran's nuclear program and the possibility that Israel, with or without US support, might use military force in Iran.

As already noted, the global recession of 2008 hurt all the eastern Arabian states. By and large, however, it has had a positive result in increasing transparency and accountability in the marketplace. The price of oil declined, but the price elasticity of oil is high, and as economic recovery proceeds, revenues will recover. The same should be true for financial markets both at home and abroad. The greatest unknown at the time of this writing is how long it will take.

FUTURE PROSPECTS

The prospects for political stability in the small GCC states are, with the exception of Bahrain, good. All of the states have felt the impact of the global financial crisis and the Arab Spring, but absent a very deep drop in oil prices, the GCC states are better positioned than most to ride out these storms. Each state has institutionalized a system of family rule that is responsive to the concerns of the major actors in society and manages succession, though for Oman the succession crisis may move the country away from family rule and toward something resembling republicanism. Kuwait continues to experience a degree of gridlock, but not serious instability, as monarchical and democratic forces struggle against each other.

BIBLIOGRAPHY

Lawrence Potter, ed., *The Persian Gulf in History* (New York: Palgrave MacMillan, 2009), is an excellent place to begin. A number of useful edited volumes on the Gulf have come out recently, including Anoushiravan Ehteshami and Steven Wright, eds., *Reform in the Middle East Oil Monarchies* (Reading, UK: Ithaca Press, 2007); Joshua Teitelbaum, ed., *Political Liberalization in the Gulf* (New York: Columbia University Press, 2008); and Paul Dresch and James Piscatori, eds., *Monarchies and Nations: Globalisation and*

Identity in the Arab States of the Gulf (London: I. B. Tauris, 2005). Older overviews worth consulting include Khaldoun Hasan al-Naqeeb, *Society and State in the Gulf and Arab Peninsula: A Different Perspective* (London: Routledge, 1990); Rosemarie Said Zahlan, *The Making of the Modern: Kuwait, Bahrain, Qatar, the United Arab Emirates, and Oman* (Ithaca, NY: Garnet, 1999); F. Gregory Gause, *Oil Monarchies: Domestic and Security Challenges in the Arab Gulf States* (New York: Council on Foreign Relations Press, 1994); and Liesl Graz, *The Turbulent Gulf: People, Politics and Power* (New York: I. B. Tauris, 1992).

Two books covering multiple countries are Laurence Louer, *Transnational Shi'a Politics: Religious and Political Networks in the Gulf* (New York: Columbia University Press, 2008), focusing on Kuwait, Bahrain, and Saudi Arabia; and Michael Herb, *All in the Family: Absolutism, Revolution, and Democracy in the Middle Eastern Monarchies* (Albany: State University of New York Press, 1999).

Several books offer more detailed treatment on individual states. These include Fred H. Lawson, *Bahrain: The Modernization of Autocracy* (Boulder, CO: Westview Press, 1989); Jill Crystal, *Kuwait: The Transformation of an Oil State* (Boulder, CO: Westview Press, 1992); Malcolm C. Peck, *The United Arab Emirates: A Venture in Unity* (Boulder, CO: Westview Press, 1986); and Calvin H. Allen Jr., *Oman: The Modernization of the Sultanate* (Boulder, CO: Westview Press, 1987). See also Christopher Davidson, *The United Arab Emirates: A Study in Survival* (Boulder, CO: Lynne Rienner, 2005) and his *Dubai: The Vulnerability of Success* (New York: Columbia University Press, 2008). Two volumes on the UAE provide thoughtful essays: Joseph A. Kechichian, ed., *A Century in Thirty Years: Shaykh Zayed and the United Arab Emirates* (Washington, DC: Middle East Policy Council, 2000), and Edmund Ghareeb and Ibrahim Al Abed, *Perspectives on the United Arab Emirates* (London: Trident Press, 1997). Frauke Heard-Bey, *From Trucial States to Emirates*, rev. ed. (London: Longman, 1996), is a detailed account of the process by which the UAE emerged. Christopher Davidson's *Dubai: The Vulnerability of Success* (New York: Columbia University Press, 2008) and *Abu Dhabi: Oil and Beyond* (New York: Columbia University Press, 2009) are excellent additions.

Joseph A. Kechichian's *Oman and the World: The Emergence of an Independent Foreign Policy* (Santa Monica, CA: RAND, 1995) and his *Political Participation and Stability in the Sultanate of Oman* (Dubai: Gulf Research Center, 2006) add usefully to the literature on that country, as do Francis Owtram, *A Modern History of Oman* (London: I. B. Tauris, 2004), and Marc Valeri, *Oman: Politics and Society in the Qaboos State* (New York: Columbia University Press, 2009). Jill Crystal, *Oil and Politics in the Gulf: Rulers and Merchants in Kuwait and Qatar* (New York: Cambridge University Press, 1995), looks at politics in those two states. An excellent new history is Allen Fromherz's *Qatar: A Modern History* (Washington, DC: Georgetown University Press, 2012). Al Jazeera has generated its own books, among them Marc Lynch, *Voices of the New Arab Public* (New York: Columbia University Press, 2007); Hugh Miles, *Al-Jazeera: The Inside Story of the Arab News Channel That Is Challenging the West* (New York: Grove Press, 2005); and

Mohammed el-Nawawy and Adel Islander, *Al Jazeera: How the Free Arab News Network Scooped the World and Changed the Middle East* (Boulder, CO: Westview Press, 2002).

There are several other good treatments of the internal politics of Kuwait, including Mary Ann Tetreault, *Stories of Democracy: Politics and Society in Contemporary Kuwait* (New York: Columbia University Press, 2000); Pete Moore, *Doing Business in the Gulf: Politics and Economic Crisis in Jordan and Kuwait* (Cambridge: Cambridge University Press, 2004); Anh Nga Longva, *Walls Built on Sand: Migration, Exclusion and Society in Kuwait* (Boulder, CO: Westview Press, 1999); and Deborah Wheeler, *The Internet in the Middle East: Global Expectations and Local Imaginations in Kuwait* (Albany: State University of New York Press, 2005).

Two very good analyses of the Gulf Cooperation Council are Erik R. Peterson, *The Gulf Cooperation Council: Search for Unity in a Dynamic Region* (Boulder, CO: Westview Press, 1988), and John Sandwick, ed., *The Gulf Cooperation Council: Moderation and Stability in an Interdependent World* (Boulder, CO: Westview Press, 1987). Also recommended is Joseph W. Twinam, *The Gulf, Cooperation and the Council: An American Perspective* (Washington, DC: Middle East Policy Council, 1992).

John E. Peterson, *Defending Arabia* (New York: St. Martin's Press, 1986), although dated, provides an excellent background and introduction to security issues in the Gulf. Anthony H. Cordesman's *The Military Balance in the Gulf* (Washington, DC: Center for Strategic and International Affairs, 2001) presents a detailed analysis of the military balance and force trends in the region. Security issues are dealt with in David E. Long and Christian Koch, eds., *Gulf Security in the Twenty-First Century* (Abu Dhabi: The Emirates Center for Strategic Studies and Research, 1997).

In addition to more general journals, the Centre for Gulf Studies at Exeter (social sciences.exeter.ac.uk/iais/research/centres/gulf) publishes the *Journal of Arabian Studies* as well as other resources. Jadaliyya offers a regular Arabian Peninsula Media Roundup (http://www.jadaliyya.com/pages/index/9853/arabian-peninsula-media-roundup) and an Arabian Peninsula page (http://arabianpeninsula.jadaliyya.com). In the region, the Emirates Center for Strategic Studies and Research offers publications at its website (www .ecssr.ac.ae), as do the Gulf Research Center (www.grc.ae) and the Doha Institute (http://english.dohainstitute.org). The best general portal to the Gulf remains Gary Sick's Gulf2000 (http://gulf2000.columbia.edu).

7

REPUBLIC OF YEMEN

Robert D. Burrowes

The Republic of Yemen (ROY) is the product of the unification of North Yemen and South Yemen in May 1990. It covers an area of 207,286 square miles (530,000 square kilometers), less than three-fourths the size of France, and its population is approaching 25 million. The ROY occupies the southernmost corner of the Arabian Peninsula. The location of the two Yemens on the world's busiest sea lane, at the entrance to the Red Sea, where Asia meets Africa, gave them strategic significance from the age of imperialism through the Cold War. More relevant today are the facts that Yemen shares a long border with oil-rich Saudi Arabia, serves as a bridge between Arabia and the Horn of Africa, and is well placed to spread or contain global revolutionary Islam.

HISTORICAL BACKGROUND

Arabia Felix

Yemen has been dotted with human settlements for several thousand years, perhaps since humans first came out of Africa. Geography largely determined Yemen's history after the rise of great civilizations in Egypt, Mesopotamia, and the Mediterranean basin. Roughly from 1000 BCE to 500 CE, this corner of Arabia provided the caravan route to these civilizations for highly prized goods from South Arabia, East Africa, and India, among them spices, myrrh, and frankincense. These were the centuries of the several pre-Islamic trading kingdoms astride the "frankincense trail" along the edge of the desert from the Arabian Sea northwest to the Nabatean city of Petra and beyond. These kingdoms included Saba, ruled from Marib by Bilqis, allegedly the Queen of Sheba (Saba). The last of the kingdoms was Himyar, the only one ruled from the Yemeni highlands rather than the desert's edge. The Sabean and Himyarite kingdoms embraced much of historic Yemen. Over these early centuries, the ideas of Yemen as a place and the Yemenis as a people probably emerged.

Occupying what Roman cartographers called Arabia Felix, these states depended for their prominence and prosperity upon their ability to protect and tax the passage of prized goods. When the Romans occupied Egypt in the first century BCE, they soon learned

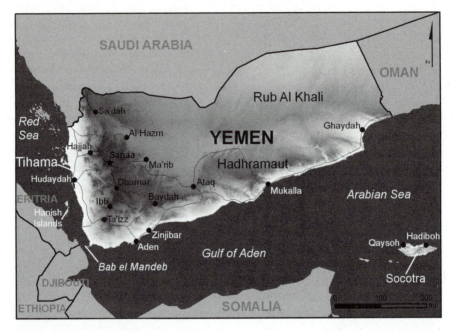

Republic of Yemen

both the secret of the monsoon winds and the true source of the luxuries they desired. They then made the Red Sea their primary avenue of commerce, sending the interior of Yemen into a decline from which it never recovered. Indicative of the decline, weakened indigenous regimes were unable to prevent Yemen's occupation by Christian Abyssinia and the Sassanids of Persia in the centuries before the rise of Islam.

The Islamic era, beginning in the seventh century CE, contains many events critical to the making of Yemen and the Yemenis. The force with which Islam exploded out of nearby Mecca made almost inevitable the early Islamization of Yemen. Yemeni converts provided many of the first soldiers of Islam, those who marched north and then west across North Africa. In the late ninth century CE, the founding of an indigenous dynasty in Yemen, the Zaydi (Shi'a) imamate, ended Abbasid rule from distant Baghdad, freeing Yemen to develop in relative isolation its own variant of Arab-Islamic civilization.

The occupation of Yemen by the Ottoman Turks in the sixteenth century and the Turks' expulsion after a long struggle led by the imamate over the next century served to deepen a sense of Yemeni identity. Despite the rapid growth of the coffee trade on the coast at al-Mukha (Mocha), the interior highlands of Yemen remained largely cut off from and unknown to the rest of the world from the mid-seventeenth to the mid-nineteenth centuries. During this period western Europe was transformed and came to exercise control over much of the rest of the world.

The Two Yemens: 1839–1999

The process by which one Yemen and Yemeni people, albeit still vaguely defined, became two Yemens began with both Great Britain's seizure of Aden in 1839 and the second Ottoman occupation of North Yemen in 1849. By the time the Turks and the British had delineated the border between their domains in 1904, the bifurcation of Yemen and development of two polities and political cultures were well under way. Politics in the north, led by the imamate, turned increasingly on opposition to Ottoman rule. In the south, politics revolved around Britain's position in Aden and efforts to extend its sway beyond Aden's environs.

Defeat in World War I forced Ottoman withdrawal from North Yemen. During the first six decades of the twentieth century, two willful and able imams, Yahya Hamid al-Din and his son Ahmad, acted to forge a monarchical state in North Yemen, much as the kings of England and France had centuries earlier. They strengthened the state, enabling them to expand their domain and considerably secure the borders and interior. Their claim to and defense of Yemen fostered a nascent Yemeni nationalism.

The two imams isolated North Yemen's traditional Islamic culture and society. The result was a "backward" Yemen, quite frozen in time, and a tiny but increasing number of Yemenis who, exposed to the outside world, wanted progress and blamed the imamate for its absence. This produced the chain of events that resulted in revolution in 1962, the imamate's abolition, and the declaration of the Yemen Arab Republic (YAR).

The history of the YAR can be divided into three periods: first, the wrenching first five years under President Abdullah al-Sallal (1962–1967), which were marked by military rule, a long civil war in which an Egyptian military presence backed the republicans and Saudi Arabia backed the royalists, and—above all—the sudden, irreversible opening of Yemen to the modern world; second, a ten-year period (1967–1977) distinguished by the republican-royalist reconciliation ending the civil war, adoption of the 1970 constitution and the holding of elections under President Abd al-Rahman al-Iryani, and the brief attempt by President Ibrahim al-Hamdi to build the state and turn it to the task of modernization; and third, the twelve-year tenure of President Ali Abdallah Salih, a soldier and tribesman, and the change from political and economic weakness to political stability, the discovery of oil, and the prospect of oil-driven change and prosperity.

President Salih consolidated his rule by defeating a leftist rebellion and by creating his ruling party, the General People's Congress (GPC). Important though Salih's era was, the 1967–1977 period provided needed breathing space for a Yemen so buffeted by change during the five years after 1962 that it was unable to retreat into the past and ill-equipped to go forward.

South Yemen's history after the British occupation of Aden in 1839 was different. Of critical importance were Britain's focus on Aden and its neglect for decades of the dozen statelets in the hinterland. As a consequence, no single polity embraced what became the People's Democratic Republic of Yemen (PDRY) at independence in 1967. Instead, it

REPUBLIC OF YEMEN

Capital city	Sanaa
Chief of state, 2012	President Abd Rabu Mansur Hadi
Head of government, 2012	Prime Minister Muhammad Salim Ba Sindwah
Major political parties (seats in most recent election, 2003)	General People's Congress (238), Islamic Reform Grouping (47), Yemeni Socialist Party (6), Nasserite Unionist Party (3), National Arab Socialist Ba'th Party (2), Independents (5)
Ethnic groups	Predominantly Arab, but also Afro-Arabs, South Asians, Europeans
Religious groups	Predominantly Shafi'i (Sunni) and Zaydi (Shi'a) Muslim, small numbers of Jews, Christians, Hindus
Export partners, 2011	China (27.3%), Thailand (12.4%), India (10.9%), South Korea (9.8%), Japan (5.6%), United States (5.4%), South Africa (4.5%), United Arab Emirates (4.3%)
Import partners, 2011	United Arab Emirates (18.5%), China (11.6%), Saudi Arabia (8.7%), Kuwait (6.5%), India (6.4%), France (4.6%), United States (4.1%)

consisted of Aden Colony—a partly modern city-state and world-class port—and a vast, remote, and politically fragmented hinterland.

At independence, the infrastructure barely holding the country together consisted of unpaved roads, airstrips, and the telegraph. Most of what little market economy existed centered on Aden and its environs, and this in turn was plugged less into the hinterland than into international commerce. This modern sector was dealt devastating blows in 1967. The blocking of the Suez Canal during the Arab-Israeli War nearly halted port activity, and Britain's withdrawal ended both aid and the economic activity tied to its presence.

The history of independent South Yemen has four periods: first, the period of takeover and consolidation (1967–1969), a phase in which the National Liberation Front (NLF) established control over the country at the same time that power within the NLF passed from the nationalists to the socialist wing; second, the period of uneasy coleadership of Salim Ruba'i Ali and Abd al-Fatah Isma'il (1969–1978), distinguished by the efforts of these two rivals to transform the Yemeni Socialist Party (YSP) into a vanguard party, to organize the country around "scientific socialism," and to align the PDRY with the socialist camp and liberation movements; third, the era of Ali Nasir Muhammad (1980–1985), a period marked by consolidation of power in a single leader and growing moderation in both domestic and external politics; and fourth, after the violent end of the Ali Nasir era, a period of collective leadership (1986–1990) in which a weak, decapitated YSP had to cope with worsening economic conditions and declining aid from the Soviet Bloc.

The era of the PDRY saw considerable conflict and violence, including executions and assassinations. Nevertheless, the regime had some notable successes: it established order in the country, made progress in bridging the vast gap between Aden and the hinterland, and made good use of limited resources to advance literacy, health care, and women's rights.

Yemeni Unification and the ROY

Although long desired by many, unification in May 1990 took most Yemenis and non-Yemenis by surprise. The Salih regime took the initiative in the late 1980s, but both sides got caught up in the process in 1989 and 1990; new political parties, organizations, newspapers, and magazines sprang up and occupied the new, open public space. Under transition terms, Ali Abdullah Salih became president and Ali Salim al-Baydh, YSP's secretary-general, became vice president. San'a was declared the capital. The two cabinets merged, with positions shared equally between the GPC and YSP, and the parliaments were merged and renamed the Council of Deputies.

The transition period ended with the 1993 parliamentary elections. The GPC won about twice as many seats as either of its main opponents, the YSP and the Yemeni Reform Grouping (Islah), a party formed at unification by anti-YSP tribal shaykhs and conservative Islamists. The GPC, YSP, and Islah formed a "grand coalition" cabinet, and other top positions were allocated roughly on a 2:1:1 basis. Shaykh Abdullah ibn Hussayn al-Ahmar, head of Islah and an ally of President Salih, became the council's speaker.

The honeymoon between the GPC and YSP had actually ended with acrimony in 1992. Their closing of ranks for the 1993 elections was quickly replaced by bitter conflict. The hostility rapidly escalated, punctuated by violence and second thoughts about unification.

Rapidly worsening economic conditions in the early 1990s had helped fuel the political conflict. Less than three months after unification, Yemenis focusing on that process were blindsided by Iraq's occupation of Kuwait. Yemen refused to join the effort to expel Iraq by force, and in reprisal the United States, Saudi Arabia, and other Gulf Arab states slashed foreign aid. Far more damaging, the Saudis expelled about 800,000 Yemeni workers, thereby cutting off the remittances upon which Yemen depended and creating for the first time massive unemployment.

Many efforts to stop the conflict were made and failed. What followed was the brief War of Secession in mid-1994. The ROY survived, as largely northern forces loyal to President Salih prevailed over southern forces led by most of the YSP leaders. Militant Islamists and forces loyal to Ali Nasir supplemented the northern side.

War of Secession Through 2010

The War of Secession over, the Salih regime faced the need both to deal with an economy in free fall and to reintegrate the defeated south into the ROY. The regime acted quickly on the latter, granting amnesty to all but the secession's top sixteen leaders and urging those who had fled abroad to return to Yemen. Most did.

Yemen's economy was halved by the costs of unification, the War of Secession, and, above all, the loss of remittances. Massive unemployment and rising poverty indicated that the economy had ceased to be viable and sustainable. In mid-1995, the regime adopted major financial and economic reforms, which initially seemed to be effective.

On the political side, President Salih was reelected by parliament in late 1994. Abdu Rabbu Mansour Hadi, a southern general who had opposed secession, became vice president. A new coalition government was also approved, which included the GPC and Islah—but not the YSP. In 1997, a still-reeling YSP boycotted parliamentary elections. Winning a huge majority, Salih's GPC then chose to rule alone, with the result that Islah became the major opposition party. Shaykh al-Ahmar remained speaker, demonstrating his and Islah's ambiguous relationship to President Salih. Two years later, in 1999, the GPC used its dominance in parliament to prevent a revived YSP from running its leader in the ROY's first direct popular presidential elections. Virtually unopposed and backed by Islah, Salih was elected to a new term.

Peaceful elections notwithstanding, politics had become increasingly acrimonious and divisive by the late 1990s, and behind this lay the effects of the grim state of the economy on most Yemenis. Unemployment persistently held at about 40 percent, as did the percentages of those malnourished and living below the poverty line. The middle class shrank and was pauperized. Most Yemenis were just trying to make ends meet and openly expressed their anger.

These conditions probably contributed to increased violence involving al-Qaida and other Salafi groups in the late 1990s. The kidnapping of twelve tourists in 1998 ended in the deaths of four, and the suicide bombing of the USS *Cole* in Aden in October 2000 killed seventeen US sailors. These events became more salient in 2001 after the suicide bombings of the World Trade Center and the Pentagon—9/11—and the US declaration of a war on terror.

Despite the upsurge in Islamist violence and worsening economic conditions, the GPC reaffirmed its dominance in the 2003 parliamentary elections. The party increased its majority, taking more than two-thirds of the seats. Islah remained in second place, but with fewer seats than before. The YSP, returning after boycotting in 1997, made a very modest comeback. Al-Ahmar remained speaker.

Against this backdrop, several opposition parties moved haltingly toward creating a unified opposition to the Salih regime. In late 2002, they created the Joint Meeting Parties (JMP), consisting of five members: the YSP, Islah, the Nasirist party, the Union of Popular Forces, and al-Haqq (Truth). The parties that counted were Islah and the YSP. Their initial task was to resist the tendencies of the YSP to go it alone and of Islah to form temporary alliances with the GPC, and with the later two parties' compliance, the JMP's five members increasingly began to speak and act together.

By 2005, attention turned to the 2006 presidential and local council elections. Both the GPC and the JMP drew up reform programs. The JMP's program was very critical of the regime's economic performance. In early 2006, President Salih, yielding to "popular demand," reversed his decision not to run. For its part, the JMP chose a credible candidate who waged a vigorous campaign. Despite this, President Salih again won decisively, and the GPC also swept the local council elections. The JMP remained intact after the elections, pledged to hold the regime accountable, and began planning for the parliamentary elections in 2009 and the next presidential contest in 2013.

By this time, however, electoral politics were being eclipsed by more confrontational and violent actions. The Houthi Rebellion erupted in June 2004 in Sa'da in the far north. Led by Husayn al-Houthi, a Zaydi sayyid (descendent of the Prophet), the Houthis' chants of "Death to the Israelis, death to the Americans" masked a deeper dissatisfaction with their social and political lot during the Salih era. Before a truce in September, many lives were lost and homes destroyed. Partly as a result of the regime's harsh response, the rebellion erupted several times over the next four years, each time growing more violent. Despite a truce in 2008, conflict turned into all-out war in 2009 and continued thereafter. President Salih named his response Operation Scorched Earth.

Beginning in mid-2007, a rash of protests and demonstrations, some of them violent, occurred across South Yemen. Initially these events involved military officers angered by being forced into retirement on meager pensions after the War of Secession. This activity soon broadened to include civil servants, lawyers, teachers, professors, and unemployed youth protesting against what they saw as the north's systematic exploitation of the south since 1994. The actions of the newly proclaimed Southern Mobilization Movement (SMM, Hiraak) and the regime's harsh reactions continued throughout 2008 and grew more violent in 2009.

The Houthi Rebellion and the protests in the south challenged the legitimacy of the Salih regime and unification. Some protesting southerners, moving beyond charges of unfairness, began asserting that unification was occupation and called for secession. Even more fundamentally, some of the Houthis questioned the very idea of republicanism, explicitly calling for restoration of the Zaydi imamate.

As if this were not enough, bombings by al-Qaida and its allies occurred in the diplomatic quarter of San'a in 2008. This violence spread to Wadi Hadhramaut later in the year, targeting tourists and security forces. The suicide bombing at the US embassy in September, taking nineteen lives, was only the worst event. In early 2009, a new al-Qaida in the Arabian Peninsula (AQAP) announced itself, merging al-Qaida's Yemeni and Saudi branches. It later declared jihad against the regime and expressed support for the SMM and the Houthis. The Salih regime's response to the terrorist acts was swift and harsh, reaching a peak in late 2009.

The GPC and JMP had negotiated for months on electoral and other political reforms in advance of the 2009 parliamentary elections. In February 2009, with the violence continuing on all fronts and the threat of a JMP election boycott looming, the GPC and JMP agreed to a two-year postponement of elections. The violence continued through 2010, despite President Salih's warning that conflict with the southern secessionists, AQAP, and the Houthis could result in many—not just two—Yemens.

Yemen's Arab Spring

In early 2011, political dynamics changed dramatically in response to events in Tunisia. Beginning in late January, popular protests by mostly young people new to politics erupted throughout Yemen. Moribund civil society organizations revived, and new ones were created. The organized opposition got on board. The growing movement quickly climbed to another level in March, when the regime responded with extreme violence to peaceful protests in San'a. Ali Muhsin al-Ahmar, long President Salih's chief supporter and likely successor, turned his crack military brigade against the regime. The unrelated al-Ahmar tribal family, led by Shaykhs Sadiq and Hamid, soon did the same with its well-armed tribal forces.

Deeply concerned, the Gulf Cooperation Council (GCC) in April 2011 proposed a transition plan under which President Salih would resign in exchange for immunity for himself, his family, and his colleagues; this plan was soon endorsed by the United Nations, the United States, and other key parties. Under the package, presidential power was to be transferred to Vice President Hadi, who was to appoint a national unity government drawn equally from the GPC and the JMP. This was to be followed within three months by the uncontested "consensus" election of Hadi to the presidency, at which time Salih would formally cease to be president. The next two years were to involve an organized "national dialogue," the drafting of a constitution based on that dialogue, a referendum on the constitution, electoral reform, and finally presidential and parliamentary elections in early 2014. At the outset, a military commission was to be created and charged with the task of unifying the military and security forces and subjecting them to state control.

Over the next several months, President Salih agreed to sign the transition package three times—and reneged each time. During these months, heavy fighting occurred in and around San'a and Taiz, raising fears that Yemen was on the verge of slipping into civil war. In addition to forces loyal to Salih, the fighting involved those of Ali Muhsin, the al-Ahmars, and other tribal leaders.

In June 2011, President Salih was severely injured in an assassination attempt. Under great domestic and international pressure, he finally signed the package on November 23. Vice President Hadi immediately assumed power and, in early December, appointed the national unity government. In January, Salih left for the United States, as parliament had granted him immunity and approved Hadi as sole candidate for the presidency. On February 21, despite calls by the SMM and Houthis for a boycott, Yemenis turned out in large numbers to vote for Hadi.

With Hadi's election, however, regime change was only partial. Not out of the picture, ex-president Salih returned on February 25, claiming leadership of the GPC. His son, Ahmad, remained commander of the powerful Republican Guards, his half brother remained head of the air force, and three of his nephews continued in top security and military positions. As importantly, many family members and others close to Salih remained in control of major economic entities dominated by the military.

President Hadi, judged something of a cipher since becoming vice president in 1994, proved to have some backbone—and, perhaps more importantly, the support of many Yemenis, some quite influential. Over the first half of 2012, he set up the military commission and the outreach committee charged with getting all groups on board for the national dialogue conference. More tellingly, he ousted or reined in some of ex-president Salih's allies in the military and security services, including his half-brother and two of his nephews. In August, he stripped Salih's son of control over part of the Republican Guards. Allegedly corrupt and close to the ex-president, the head of the national airline was also ousted.

Although most of the parties and other actors initially endorsed the transition plan, they were increasingly at odds over its details and implementation. In particular, efforts to get all actors on board for the dialogue without preconditions bogged down. Many of the protesting youth, criticizing the transition as designed to preserve existing elites, remained dubious or alienated. The Houthis and the SMM imposed, removed, and then reimposed conditions for their participation. There was the question of whether dialogue was possible with a GPC led by ex-president Salih and of what role Ali Muhsin could or should play. The JMP seemed on the verge of coming apart, with Islah and Hamid al-Ahmar, in particular, on the verge of going their own ways. In general, once Salih was ousted from the presidency, the fragile consensus diminished, largely replaced by narrowing self-interest and increased conflict within and between parties and coalitions.

Beginning in early 2011, the redeployment of forces to the north to defend the Salih regime—or, as some said, to prove Salih's indispensability in the war on terror—had left a security vacuum in much of the south. Ansar al-Shariah, a mix of al-Qaida elements and local Salafis, quickly occupied and began to administer most of Abyan and much of Shabwa provinces. The regime's control also was challenged in parts of Aden and Wadi Hadhramaut. In April 2012, President Hadi launched a military campaign and, with assistance from civilian militias, recovered most of this territory over the next two months. Control of this territory remained tenuous, and the campaign triggered suicide attacks by AQAP elsewhere in the country.

Preoccupied with transition politics and the conflict with the Islamists, the Hadi government neglected the growing humanitarian crisis as well as long-term economic and social issues. Postponement of the Friends of Yemen donors' conference until September 2012 was indicative of the latter. In the meantime, those in command of the economy, who had served most Yemenis so poorly during the last two decades of the Salih regime, remained in place.

The year 2012 also saw a further breakdown in public safety and order. Kidnappings, theft, and random violence increased. Extreme shortages of electricity and water persisted. Many lacked the money to buy food, even when it was available.

Political Environment

Geography

Yemen is marked by a high, steep, jagged mountain range that forms the western and southern edges of a high plateau that descends gradually east and north into the desert interior and to the Saudi border. The mountains rise abruptly about twenty-five miles inland from a flat coastal desert plain, the Tihama. They parallel the Red Sea, running north to south along the length of North Yemen, abruptly turn ninety degrees near the old border between the two Yemens, and then head east parallel to the Gulf of Aden for part of the length of South Yemen. The northern highlands, averaging several thousand feet and including the highest point on the Arabian Peninsula, have a largely semiarid but otherwise temperate climate. By contrast, the southern uplands are lower and quite verdant. The Tihama and the southern coast are hot and humid much of the year.

Groundwater and surface runoff are in very short supply in most of Yemen. However, the annual monsoon winds blow inland after picking up moisture from the sea; the mountains then force the warm air to rise, cool, and drop its moisture. This considerable, albeit erratic, seasonal rainfall in the mountains and highlands in the spring and summer accounts both for intensive cultivation of crops, much of it in streambeds and on steep, terraced hillsides, and for the relatively dense population in these areas. The highlands in North Yemen are loftier and more extensive than those in South Yemen, explaining the former's greater rainfall, more intensive and extensive agriculture, and considerably larger population. By contrast, the eastern two-thirds of South Yemen are all but uninhabitable, except for coastal fishing villages and ports and, deep in the interior, the well-populated Wadi Hadhramaut. Half again larger in area than North Yemen, South Yemen has about one-fourth as many people—roughly 5 million. In the north nearly all of the population is sedentary, and this is only slightly less so in the south. What nomads there are mostly live on the edge of the desert near Saudi Arabia.

Regions and Population Centers

Yemen has six major regions. The northern highlands include much of the upper half of North Yemen and are bound on the west by the mountains. The southern uplands consist of the lower half of North Yemen and include Taiz and Ibb provinces. The coastal Tihama runs the length of North Yemen, between the Red Sea and the mountains. The arid east, on the edge of the desert, consists of the remote provinces of Marib, al-Jawf, and Shabwa. Far to the south are Aden and the area running from the Arabian Sea up to the mountains between the two Yemens. To the east is large, arid Hadhramaut province and Wadi Hadhramaut. Finally, farther to the east are the culturally distinct Mahra region, bordering Oman, and the otherworldly island of Socotra.

The country has four major cities: San'a, Aden, al-Hudayda, and Taiz. Aden and al-Hudayda are the major ports, Aden's being natural and world-class. There are several large towns: Sa'da, far to the north; Dhamar, Yarim, and Ibb, in the middle region; Mukalla, on the southern coast; and in Wadi Hadhramaut, the trio of Shibam, Seiyun, and Tarim. The population of South Yemen is highly concentrated in a few places—in Mukalla and the towns of Wadi Hadhramaut, in the highlands northeast of Aden, and, above all, in Aden and its environs. By contrast, the much larger population of North Yemen is more widely scattered over many towns, villages, and hamlets. Still, Taiz and al-Hudayda have experienced much growth, and San'a's exploding population approaches 2 million.

Economy

Yemen has long been, and remains, an extremely poor country, the poorest in the Arab world. For centuries its economy was largely self-sufficient, based mainly on subsistence agriculture. Although North Yemen moved quickly from self-sufficiency to dependence on the outside world after 1962, as part of South Yemen had done earlier, farming and animal husbandry remain chief sources of livelihood for a majority of the population—even though they contribute only a small percentage of total gross domestic product (GDP). Fishing, trade, and traditional artisanship are also important. Modern industry remains rare, marginal, and small in scale. Finally, the viability of the Yemeni economy after the 1960s increasingly depended on remittances and the employment of Yemenis abroad. In sharp decline after 1990, remittances still contribute to the economy. In 2009, Yemen's estimated annual per capita income was about $1,250—less than $3.50 per day.

Until the mid-1980s, Yemen had no exploited natural resources of consequence other than its fisheries, and these were barely tapped. Modest amounts of oil were discovered in the north, in Marib, and first exported in 1987. At the time of unification in 1990, larger amounts of oil were discovered in Masila, an area northeast of Mukalla in the Hadhramaut. Oil production peaked at 465,000 barrels per day in 2003 and then began to decline. Predictions have reserves depleted by 2020. The development of Yemen's modest gas reserves in Marib got under way in 2005, and liquefied natural gas exports began in late 2009.

Culture and Society

Nearly all Yemenis are Muslim Arabs. Christian communities disappeared early in the Islamic era. Most of the sizable Jewish community migrated to Israel shortly after that country's creation in 1948; only a few hundred Jews remain, mostly in and north of San'a. The once large and powerful Isma'ili Shi'a population was reduced through persecution over the centuries to an insignificant, though reviving, minority in the mountains between San'a and al-Hudayda.

The establishment of the Zaydi imamate stamped the northern highlands and their towns and tribes with the Zaydi strand of Shi'a Islam. By contrast, the two-century rule of the Rasulids, beginning in the twelfth century, stamped South Yemen and the southern uplands and coast of North Yemen with the Shafi'i form of Sunni Islam. There remains an old and still politically and socially salient cleavage between the Zaydis and Shafi'is. The Zaydis, although only a minority, dominated politics and cultural life in North Yemen for centuries through the Zaydi tribes and the imamate. With unification and the addition of South Yemen's almost totally Shafi'i population, the numerical balance shifted dramatically away from the Zaydis, who now make up little more than 20 percent of the combined population. Nevertheless, the Zaydis remained overrepresented in the government and armed forces. While sectarianism has not played a prominent role in Yemeni politics for generations, the Houthi Rebellion and the Salafi response to it suggest it remains a possibility.

For millennia, tribal ties have been the most important basis of social organization and identity in the northern highlands, in the mountainous region between the two Yemens, and in remote parts of the Hadhramaut. Two large tribal confederations predominate in the northern highlands, the Hashid and the Bakil. Less important is the Madhhij confederation, east of the other two.

While many people in other parts of Yemen claim some tribal affiliation, these ties are less important as bases of identity and solidarity than the extended family, locality, class, caste, and occupation. Atop the traditional nontribal social system was the sayyid caste—those Zaydis and Shafi'is who claimed descent from the Prophet. The imams had to be Zaydi sayyids. Beneath this caste was the *qadi* class, usually learned Zaydis and Shafi'is who served as judges, administrators, teachers, and religious figures. In the middle was the relatively large and varied class of peasants, merchants, shopkeepers, and artisans. At the bottom were two groups: the *muzayyin* class that provided the butchers, barbers, and those who performed other "demeaning" tasks, and, at the bottom, the *akhdam* caste of servants, street sweepers, and popular musicians.

Despite great differences in status, North Yemen's economy of scarcity fostered a social system that was not marked by great inequality. The imams did live better than most other Yemenis, but not that much better. After the 1962 revolution, inequality increased both within the modern sector and between that sector and traditional Yemen, much as had happened in British-ruled South Yemen earlier in the century. In the PDRY after 1970, the regime's Marxist ideology and economic scarcity served to temper the inequality that usually accompanies early stages of development. Moreover, the tendency of long-entrenched one-party states to widen class divides was countered by relatively wide access to education, health care, and housing and by efforts to integrate the rest of the country into more-modern Aden.

Rugged terrain, widely separated population centers, and primitive means of transportation and communication have made for diversity among the considerably homogeneous Yemeni people. Although Arabic is spoken by nearly all, there are several dialectical differences, most notably between the dialect of North Yemen's highlands and that of the southern part of North Yemen and Aden. Beyond language, other sociocultural and regional differences abound. The subtlest and most important is the difference between northerners from the highlands and southerners from the southern half of North Yemen and Aden. The former are stereotyped as having strong tribal ties, claiming a warrior tradition, and, at least in the past, being more parochial. The latter are stereotyped as being of nontribal peasant origins, peaceful or docile, engaged in commerce, and more traveled and cosmopolitan. Going east, many people in Wadi Hadhramaut reflect the cultural influence of Southeast Asia, with which they have long social and commercial ties. The people of Mahra and Socotra share a non-Arab language and culture. Finally, the people of the coastal desert and ports reflect the long racial and cultural influences of nearby Africa—Somalia and Ethiopia—and Aden still carries hints of India and the British Raj.

POLITICAL STRUCTURE

The ROY's constitution, ratified by the people in 1991, closely resembles the YAR's 1970 constitution. However, in the absence of a tradition of constitutional government in Yemen, the constitution neither closely reflects political reality nor tightly constrains the use of power—it is not yet a "living constitution." Free speech, the right to organize, and the other rights it enshrines are largely aspirational, and the system of courts and appointed judges does not constitute an independent judiciary.

The constitution originally called for a plural executive, a feature that was changed in 1994 to a singular presidency and a Council of Deputies, the 301 members of which are chosen by voters in single-member constituencies. The terms of office for legislators and the president were four and five years, respectively, and were changed to six and seven years in 2001. In addition to its legislative duties, the Council of Deputies selected the president, a provision that was changed in 1994 to direct popular election. A second chamber, the Shura Council, appointed by the president and with mostly advisory powers, was created in 1997. The constitution provided for provincial and local council elections and for the appointment of provincial governors by the executive. Local elections were finally held in 2001 and again in 2006. The selection of governors was changed to elective, and their first election was held in 2008.

Opponents of the Salih regime had persistently demanded fundamental constitutional changes, and these demands became central in the post-Salih transition. Key proposals would increase legislative power at the expense of executive power and institute some form of federalism and local autonomy. Some would replace the presidential system with parliamentary government, base elections on proportional representation, and give the Shura Council legislative power equal to that of the Council of Deputies.

In a break with the YAR's theoretical no-party system and the PDRY's one-party system, the 1990 constitution explicitly allowed for a multiparty system. The GPC came to dominate politics in the YAR and the ROY. Islah, with its organization, cadre, and grassroots support, remained a potential challenge to the GPC. The YSP, with some of the ideology and organization of its glory days, retained a base of support in the south and in pockets of the north. For their part, the Ba'th and Nasirist parties had little popular support, lived in the pan-Arab past, and were of no real consequence. Tiny conservative Islamic parties, such as al-Haqq and the Union of Popular Forces, were just that—tiny. With the exception of the Ba'th, these parties formed the JMP in 2002. All parties, including the GPC, were challenged and put to the test by the events of 2011 and 2012, and the post-Salih era is marked by party fragmentation and reconfiguration.

Unification witnessed the explosive growth and freedom of newspapers and magazines, while radio and television remained government monopolies. Organized interest groups—civil society or nongovernmental organizations (NGOs)—sprang up by the hundreds and openly voiced their concerns. Although the print media and NGOs remained outspokenly critical, the Salih regime learned over the years how to subvert them through an array of carrots and sticks. Yemen's Arab Spring has reinvigorated them.

The three parliamentary elections have been, to a degree, free and fair. Arguably, the 1993 elections were the most significant because the new Council of Deputies at that time was a focus of attention—even excitement—and accordingly of some influence in the new ROY. By contrast, the 1997 and 2003 elections were for a legislature that, formal powers notwithstanding, was rarely assertive and served largely as a rubber stamp. Perceiving it as irrelevant, the public paid little attention to the legislature, diminishing its role in public discourse and as a shaper of public opinion. This tendency was reinforced by the events of 2011 and 2012.

The military played an important role in the PDRY and a dominant one in the YAR and the ROY. Although falling short of the *makhabarat* (secret police) states elsewhere in the Arab world, both Yemens had security services that were strong and deeply involved in politics. Despite pledges to dismantle them at unification, the security forces have had a strong and growing role since 1994. In particular, the Political Security Organization became a force of real consequence. Nevertheless, compared to some other Arab states, there was relatively little physical repression in the ROY.

POLITICAL DYNAMICS

Yemen's political dynamics since unification have largely revolved around three issue clusters: the shift from remittances to rents and kleptocracy, economic crisis and failed economic reform, and Yemeni political Islam and global revolutionary Islam.

From Remittances to Rents and Kleptocracy

Many North Yemenis remember the decade through the mid-1980s as the halcyon years, the best of times. Remittance money flooded into the country from those working abroad, mostly in Saudi Arabia. The remittances were distributed widely, with some going directly or indirectly to nearly all families in all parts of the country. In the late 1980s, oil revenues began to flow in, as did considerable foreign aid. By contrast, the PDRY's situation was very different. Its people experienced a smaller flow of remittances, a drastic cut in aid from a faltering Soviet patron, and the failure of expected oil revenues to materialize.

The creation of the ROY in 1990 held out to most Yemenis hope for a stronger and more prosperous Yemen. Months later, Iraq's occupation of Kuwait dashed these hopes. Most foreign aid to Yemen was terminated; more importantly, Saudi Arabia expelled its many Yemeni workers. The expulsion virtually destroyed Yemen's remittance economy and left it with massively increased unemployment—which had profound political implications.

The Salih regime that took shape in the YAR in the 1980s is best described as an oligarchy. Most of the relatively small number of people who got the little there was to get—be it political power or economic well-being—came from North Yemen's northern highlands. They had strong tribal or military (or security) connections, or both. To the military-tribal complex that accumulated power in the YAR was added in the early 1980s a northern commercial-business element, the result of an informal affirmative action program that favored northerners over their long-dominant colleagues from the southern uplands, especially Taiz. The ties between the military-tribal and business leaders found institutional expression in the Military Economic Corporation that dated back to the mid-1970s.

From 1990 until 1994, unification interrupted this trend toward the concentration of power in the hands of these northern oligarchs. However, it resumed and increased after the War of Secession, as that event eliminated or weakened politicians from the former PDRY. Moreover, as a result of increasing oil revenues and aid, the state quickly became the principal source of wealth and private gain for the well-placed and fortunate few. Transformation of the republican state into such a source—something the relatively impoverished imamate had not been—had begun modestly when aid began to flow into the YAR in the mid-1970s. But this trend had been countered by remittances that were spread widely and, most importantly, did not pass through the state.

By the end of the 1990s, the end of the remittance system and the rise in oil revenue and development aid had combined to rapidly transform the ROY into a variant of oligarchy, a kleptocracy—government of, by, and for the thieves. Occupants of key government offices through which these funds flowed were able to use their positions in the state—these "profit centers"—to extract a price for providing services or permissions. Those close to occupants of key offices were also enriched, the reaping of riches being a matter of connection as well as location.

Graft, bribery, and other forms of corruption came to pervade all levels of a steeply sided pyramid of patronage. At the broad base of this pyramid are the hundreds of thousands of government employees who are paid extremely low salaries and have to take petty bribes—have to "eat money"—to make ends meet. High up the pyramid, perhaps the most visible measures of this corruption are the growing number of high-end SUVs and virtual castles on the outskirts of San'a, most of which are owned by government officials on modest salaries.

This nouveau aristocracy of shaykhs, officers, and businessmen has a strong sense of entitlement. Its second generation is now slipping into key positions and questions even less its entitlement. This small part of the total population is on the take—and without apology. Some sense that this cannot last much longer and that they must get as much as they can while the getting is still good. Although some public servants choose not to participate in this system, and others are simply not in offices through which much money flows, they do not define the new order.

The ROY also exhibits arrested statehood, a legacy of North Yemen's history. The imamate, although dominant, did not approximate Max Weber's classic definition of a state; it did not have a monopoly on the legitimate use of violence in its territory. In this regard, the description of the Hashid and Bakil tribal confederations as "the wings of the imamate" is suggestive. These tribes and their leaders conceived of themselves, and were conceived of by others, as outside the imamate and not subjects of the state.

The YAR's modernists were prevented by events after the 1962 revolution from creating the state to which they aspired. Conclusion of the civil war in 1970 dictated that the republic that prevailed would be a conservative one; it would preserve much of the traditional order, in particular, a prominent role for the tribal leaders and tribal system. Subsequently, President al-Hamdi's failed attempt at modern state building allowed arrested statehood to persist into the Salih era.

Reflecting this history, Yemen's state today is in vital ways more like the imamate than a modern state. It is severely limited in terms of what it has the power to do and where it can do it. This arrested statehood is both the cause and effect of the tribal-military-business regime that remained in place as of this writing. The weak state nicely suited a regime inclined to minimize efforts at state building, especially those that require reining in rampant corruption and incompetence.

Economic Crisis and Reform—and Crisis

By late 1994, Yemen's economy was in free fall and well on its way to becoming nonviable and unsustainable, despite the steady rise of oil revenues. The situation was extremely grim. GDP for 1995 was reduced to less than half that of 1990. The value of the Yemeni riyal had plunged, raising the cost of goods, especially needed imports. Because of the massive unemployment and loss of remittances, gross inequality and abject poverty were increasing at alarming rates.

In mid-1995, the Salih regime agreed with the International Monetary Fund (IMF) and World Bank to a program of economic stabilization, structural reforms, and IMF/World Bank aid. The premise was that significant IMF/World Bank aid and the major reforms upon which that aid was conditioned would begin to turn the Yemeni economy around. This and the stamp of approval of these bodies would begin to attract other aid donors and, most importantly, private investors, both Yemeni and non-Yemeni. The promise was that the belt-tightening initially required of the Yemeni people (e.g., elimination of subsidies for essentials) would produce an economic setting that would attract investment, stimulate business, and create jobs. Initially, the public accepted this trade-off.

At first, Yemen's collaboration with the IMF/World Bank on reform closely followed the best-case scenario. In the first year, the Salih regime put in place stabilization measures and the initial set of structural reforms designed, among other things, to rein in inflation. In late 1996, the regime took a cautious first step to lift subsidies for essential goods, repeating this process in 1997 and 1998. In return, the IMF/World Bank loaned Yemen roughly $1 billion to support reform projects over these years. In addition, they helped organize two donors' conferences that yielded pledges of another $2 billion. IMF commitments also paved the way for a big reduction of Yemen's foreign debt.

The IMF/World Bank reform program faltered in late 1997, in part because of political protests and sharply declining oil revenues. Perhaps more importantly, some of the new reforms reached beyond the majority and directly threatened the interests of the privileged and highly placed. Among them were measures designed to fight corruption, increase transparency, make the courts more effective, and reform the banking and financial sectors. Many of the well-off simply lost whatever appetite they had had for reform.

Nevertheless, a new IMF/World Bank agreement calling for further reforms was negotiated in 2000. It required the complete lifting of most subsidies and the loss of many jobs through a downsizing of the civil service and the privatizing of bloated public corporations. Within a year, however, the program was virtually abandoned. Most of the measures agreed to were implemented partially and half-heartedly, if at all. Reforms of the judiciary and the civil service lagged, and the rampant corruption in the public and private sectors was barely addressed.

As a consequence, Yemen failed to attract foreign and Yemeni investors in the late 1990s and after. Wealthy Yemenis who had jumped in early, especially those with origins in Wadi Hadhramaut, quickly retreated after bad personal experiences or hearing the woeful tales of others. Many foreign investors decided that the risks relative to potential gains were too great, based partly on well-publicized cases of corruption, nepotism, and political favoritism.

As with the IMF/World Bank program, major development projects failed to move forward rapidly or fell short of expectations. The Aden free zone and container port project, touted in the early 1990s as Yemen's most important, promised to create many jobs and much wealth. In operation in 2000, after numerous delays, the project produced modest results due to regional security problems and serious mismanagement and corruption. Similarly, the development of Yemen's natural gas reserves was delayed until 2005 partly by fighting between two groups of Yemeni politicians, each with its own multinational gas developer as client.

Despite higher oil revenues in 2005, due to soaring prices, the overall performance of the economy did not improve. The growth rates for GDP and job creation were at best barely keeping up with the high population growth rate of about 3.5 percent. The levels of the unemployed, the malnourished, and those living below the poverty line persistently held at about 40 percent. The pauperization of the shrinking middle class continued, and the modern institutions in which they worked and had placed their hopes were hollowed out. The gap between the few rich and the many poor widened visibly. The education system declined, and medical services were in shorter supply and of poorer quality. On the personal level, most Yemenis lost hope, ground down by the effort to make ends meet. More and more people were openly expressing anger and seemed ready to act on it.

Arguably, Yemen's economy and society had ceased to be viable and sustainable by 2010. As importantly, despite public pronouncements, the Salih system seemed to lack the will and capacity to adopt and implement reforms needed to accomplish what needed to be done. Behind this lack were Yemen's oligarchs—its kleptocrats—and the pyramid of patronage they had come to depend upon. The limited capacities of the state made it unlikely that they could effect needed change, even if they wanted to. They seemed unable to act in terms of their own self-interest in survival, much less in the interest of the Yemeni people.

Political Islam in Yemen

Modern political Islam came to North Yemen when the Muslim Brotherhood started a branch there in 1947. The Brotherhood survived the 1962 revolution and persisted into the republican era; indeed, in the 1970s, it was regarded as a major threat due to its organization and grassroots support. Its top leader in the 1970s was Abd al-Majid al-Zindani, the spiritual leader of Islah since 1990.

The growth of political Islam in Yemen and the role of al-Zindani in that process were largely the result of Saudi Arabia's systematic use of Islam for foreign policy purposes. First, the Saudis tried to influence the YAR in the 1970s and 1980s by promoting their brand of Salafi fundamentalism, Wahhabism, through schools and "scientific institutes." Second, the Saudis in the 1980s recruited a large number of Yemenis for jihad against the Soviet forces in Afghanistan, a struggle that served as the incubator for the next generation's global revolutionary Islamists. Al-Zindani, working with the Saudis, was involved in promoting Salafism in Yemen and then in the jihadist project in Afghanistan.

When Soviet forces withdrew from Afghanistan in 1989, many radicalized, battle-hardened Yemeni "Afghani Arabs" came home. In 1990, many got caught up in the politics of unification and the first Gulf War, the latter causing them to perceive the Americans and Saudis as Islam's main enemies. Some created the Yemeni Islamic Jihad (YIJ).

As political conflict between the GPC and the YSP escalated after 1991, President Salih often ignored the killing of southern leaders by returning militants with old scores to settle. Ali Muhsin folded many of the Afghani Arabs into units of the northern army, and many of them participated in the War of Secession in 1994, placing the Salih regime in debt to them. Thereafter, when the regime balked at their demands, armed conflict occasionally occurred between them and the security forces.

In the mid-1990s, preoccupied with the YSP, President Salih viewed militant political Islam largely as a troublesome domestic matter. The YIJ bombing of a hotel in Aden at the end of 1992 targeted American military personnel staying there. Yemeni forces responded with the arrest of Tarik al-Fadhli, an Afghani Arab leader of YIJ and heir to one of the sultanates abolished in 1962. Al-Fadhli "escaped" and soon pledged loyalty to President Salih.

Some of al-Fadhli's colleagues who refused to follow him created the Aden-Abyan Islamic Army (AAIA), a group with which the Salih regime waged a low-intensity fight through the rest of the 1990s. In late 1998, the death in Abyan of four tourists kidnapped by the AAIA suggested that the Islamists posed a broader threat to the Salih regime. The sequence of events had started days earlier with the arrest of several armed young Muslims from Britain. The AAIA's kidnapping of the tourists had been requested by the father of one of those jailed, a militant ulema in London. This strained British-Yemeni relations. Alarmed, the government quickly tried and executed the kidnappers' leader.

The Salih regime became increasingly concerned with al-Qaida after militants bombed the USS *Cole* in Aden in fall 2000. In late 2001, Yemeni troops failed in an attempt to eliminate Qaid Sinan al-Harithi, an al-Qaida leader and the alleged mastermind of the *Cole* bombing. Major events rocked the regime in 2002: the suicide bombing of the French oil tanker *Limburg* off Yemen's southern coast; the killing of al-Harithi with a rocket from a US drone in a strike coordinated with the regime; the assassination by a militant of YSP's thinker-activist, Jarullah Omar; and the murder two days later of three American medical missionaries by another militant, a colleague of Jarullah's assassin. In mid-2003, the AAIA ambushing of a military convoy led to a battle in which several militants were killed. Among them were individuals involved in the *Cole* and *Limburg* bombings who had recently escaped from prison.

On another front, President Salih moved in 2002 to bring the Salafis' "scientific institutes" under government control and to close down unofficial religious schools. The state also removed militant ulema from mosques, replacing them with moderates. Both efforts triggered outcries over interference and censorship.

Having pledged full support for the US war on terror, President Salih had to balance meeting US demands with a domestic political landscape marked by Yemeni nationalism, strong Islamic sensibilities, and growing anti-American feelings. As importantly, military officers and politicians inside the regime were themselves Islamists or politically tied to them (e.g., Ali Muhsin). From the *Cole* bombing and 9/11 on, President Salih carefully picked his way with difficulty among these often contradictory forces.

In late 2002, criticized by both secular nationalists and Islamists, President Salih authorized creation of a religious dialogue council responsible for reeducating persons charged with terrorist activities. Between then and 2005, a few hundred went through rehabilitation, were released, and often received jobs in the military. This program did lessen some of the domestic pressure on President Salih.

The coming of the Houthi Rebellion illustrates the complexities Islamic politics posed for President Salih. Husayn al-Houthi, who had helped found al-Haqq and was elected to the Council of Deputies in 1993, also founded a network of Zaydi schools and a youth movement, the Believing Youth. President Salih had supported al-Houthi's efforts, concerned as he had become about the assertiveness of the Salafis with whom he had earlier allied himself in his struggle with the YSP. But when the Houthis began challenging the regime, the president directed the governor of Sa'da to crack down on the movement—and he did. In response, al-Houthi launched his rebellion. Thereafter, the large, indiscriminant military response, led by Ali Muhsin, served to deepen and perpetuate the rebellion.

During the struggle to oust President Salih in 2011, the activities of the Houthis and AQAP were overshadowed by the activities of mostly non-Islamist actors. In the south, however, Ansar al-Shariah proclaimed a caliphate over territory it had occupied. In the summer of 2012, President Hadi launched a two-month military campaign that recovered most of this territory. This triggered lethal AQAP suicide attacks against military and security forces in San'a and elsewhere in the country.

Foreign Policy

The regional relations of both Yemens focused largely on their rich, worried, and overbearing neighbor, Saudi Arabia. Imamate Yemen lost a short war with the newborn Saudi Kingdom in 1934, forcing it to cede control of "the northern provinces," Asir, Najran, and Jizan. After the Yemeni Civil War, in which the Saudis supported the royalists, their strategy became one of controlling the republicanism on their border by making the YAR dependent on them for aid. Nevertheless, the YAR got a good bit of aid over the years and retained a good bit of independence. As the PDRY moved toward Marxism and supported rebellion in Oman, the Saudis worked to undermine their radical neighbor. Above all, they did what they could to discourage Yemeni unification, especially if a united Yemen were dominated by the Marxist south.

Generally, the two Yemens and inter-Yemeni relations were viewed in Cold War terms by the two superpowers and treated accordingly. During the civil war, the Soviet Union supported the YAR. By 1970, however, the victorious YAR was successfully seeking good relations with—and aid from—the West while maintaining close ties to the Soviets. As the PDRY moved left, it became dependent economically and politically on the Soviet Bloc. Both relied heavily on the United Nations and other multinational bodies for aid.

Creation of the ROY in 1990 and increasing conflict between the GPC and the YSP over its future added a new dimension to Yemen's external relations. In 1992, Saudi Arabia approached the YSP and offered support if it sought to secede. During the War of Secession in 1994, the Salih regime tried to stall a UN cease-fire until its forces had won, fearing that a troop pullback would mean de facto separation. Saudi Arabia, which by then was aiding the secessionists materially, urged the United States to support a quick cease-fire. President Salih's representative worked successfully to hold the United States off until Aden had fallen.

Thereafter, the ROY placed priority on undoing the damage caused by its failure to join the effort to expel Iraq from Kuwait in 1990. This mainly involved efforts to restore good relations with Saudi Arabia, Kuwait, and the United States. Good relations meant foreign aid and, in terms of Yemen's neighbors, the possibility of jobs, remittances, and a neighborhood safer for foreign investment and tourism. These efforts were superseded in 1995 by armed conflict with newly independent Eritrea over a cluster of Red Sea islands. Although angered by Eritrea's seizure of the islands and capture of Yemeni forces, Yemen dealt in a statesmanlike way with a situation that, if allowed to spin out of control, could have scared off investors and tourists. The dispute was submitted for international arbitration and resolved amicably in 1998, with most of the islands going to Yemen.

Among the Arab Gulf states, Kuwait was the most reluctant to forgive. Persistence by Yemen finally resulted in the reestablishment of diplomatic relations in 2000. Over the second half of the 1990s, relations with Qatar, the United Arab Emirates, and Oman also improved. The Salih regime campaigned hard to join the GCC, but its requests were denied. It was, however, allowed to join some agencies, and full membership was held out as a future possibility.

Ambivalent about reconciliation after 1994, Saudi Arabia financed vocal Yemeni dissidents in London and elsewhere. In addition, subsidies paid to the tribes helped enable them to carry out the many kidnappings that made foreigners wary. Clearly, however, the biggest obstacle to restoring good relations between the two neighbors remained their long, undemarcated border, for decades a source of violent incidents. Rather suddenly, but after years of negotiations, this thorn in the side of Saudi-Yemeni relations was removed in June 2000 in an agreement covering the entire border. Yemen gave up all claims to the provinces seized by Saudi Arabia in 1934, and the Saudis made some concessions along the long desert border east to Oman.

Thereafter, some Saudi aid began to flow, and some Yemeni workers were allowed to return to the kingdom. With terrorist bombings in Riyadh in 2003, the Saudis increased pressure on Yemen regarding security along their porous shared border. Over the next few years, the neighbors strengthened their extradition treaty, exchanged dozens of prisoners, and agreed to undertake joint operations to block border infiltration and smuggling. Nevertheless, the Saudis did become annoyed as it became apparent that Yemeni frontier forces were sometimes party to border violations. In early 2006, the escape of twenty-three terrorists from the security prison in San'a, apparently with inside help, alarmed and angered the Saudis, as did similar, less dramatic events over the next two years.

Late in the decade, however, faced with the Houthi Rebellion, the creation of the AQAP, and the possibility that the growing chaos in Somalia could be replicated in Yemen, the Saudis found themselves in the unfamiliar position of providing major support to the Salih regime and the ROY. It is rumored that the Saudi kingdom provided as much as $2 billion in 2009 to cover the budget shortfall caused by declining oil revenues. Beginning in November 2009, moreover, the Saudis took cross-border military action by the Houthis as reason for unleashing sustained air strikes and some ground actions against them. Coordinated with the Yemeni military's Operation Scorched Earth, the Saudi intervention amounted to part of an effort to defeat the Houthis once and for all.

Long concerned about turmoil in Somalia, the mass exodus of refugees to Yemen, and the US tendency to view events in the Horn of Africa solely in terms of its war on terror, President Salih convened a summit in 2002 with the presidents of Sudan and Ethiopia. This led to the formation of the San'a Forum for Cooperation, which thereafter met annually and later included the presidents of Djibouti and Somalia. Over the rest of the decade, the forum addressed, with little effect, the worsening situation in Somalia, the intervention by Ethiopia and the United States in that country, Eritrea's conflicts with Ethiopia and Djibouti, and the dramatic increase in Somali piracy and the international community's naval response.

The US drastically reduced relations with the ROY after it failed to support action against Iraq in 1990. Relations began to thaw in mid-1994, during the War of Secession, when Washington sided with a unified Yemen. In 1995, the United States strongly backed the IMF/World Bank aid-for-reform package with Yemen and, in something of a first, publicly chastised Saudi Arabia for attempting to pressure oil companies to refrain from activity near the two countries' disputed border. Military ties increased modestly in 1997 with, for example, the refueling of US warships in Aden. Still, the rebuilding of strong relations, desired by Yemen, was low on the US list.

Two events caused the United States to reorder priorities: the bombing of the USS *Cole* in 2000 and, far more crucial, the suicide bombings of 9/11. The latter made US-Yemeni relations more salient and made global revolutionary Islam and terror the main focus of those relations. Days after 9/11, President Salih flew to Washington and pledged full support for the war on terror. US military aid increased significantly. For its part, the Salih regime stepped up its effort against militants in Yemen.

Thereafter, the dynamics of US-Yemeni relations revolved around Washington's insistence on Yemen's full support in the war on terror and its attempt to do as much as politically possible to meet this demand. The Salih regime clearly wanted to avoid repeating the punishment meted out in 1990. Still, the new relationship was uneasy. President Salih tried to do what Washington wanted, but in a manner politically palatable to the Yemeni public. When caught between the two, he usually chose to risk angering Washington rather than his domestic audience. For example, when Washington sought to connect the dots in the *Cole* investigation back to Osama bin Laden, President Salih balked out of fear that the dots might come uncomfortably close to colleagues in high places.

The United States has been insensitive to the Salih regime's political situation. When al-Harithi was killed in 2002 by a missile deep in Yemeni airspace, Washington's public self-congratulations embarrassed and angered the regime. The response was similar when a popular ulema from San'a was entrapped by the FBI in Germany in 2003, extradited to the United States, and then convicted of financing terrorism. In 2004, over Yemeni objections, Washington placed Islah's Shaikh al-Zindani on its list of supporters of terrorism and later asked Yemen to extradite him. Finally, the detaining of many Yemenis at Guantánamo since 2001 was hard for the regime to explain to its people. As non-Yemeni detainees were released, leaving a big plurality of Yemenis, the issue became a source of growing acrimony. Washington's preference that Yemeni returnees from Guantánamo go to Saudi Arabia for rehabilitation clearly indicated that the United States did not believe Yemen up to the task.

The US invasion of Iraq in 2003 was a political nightmare for President Salih. He tried, with difficulty, to distinguish between Washington's action in Iraq and the effort against terror, opposing the former and supporting the latter. He was not helped by President George W. Bush's efforts to equate the two. Nevertheless, beginning in 2003, there was a stream of very senior visitors from the US government, usually bringing praise and promises of additional aid. In 2004, the United States lifted a ban on supplying new military equipment to Yemen and raised the possibility of again refueling warships at Aden.

In early 2006, however, questions about Yemen's willingness and ability to do its part in the effort against terrorism were raised anew by the escape of convicted al-Qaida figures involved in the *Cole* and *Limburg* bombings. Thereafter, US confidence was shaken further when it was learned that, after release from prison, three graduates of the "national dialogue" process had turned up as jihadists in Iraq, and other convicted terrorists were freed or placed under loose house arrest.

By 2000, the United States had strained to make President Salih something of a symbol of democratization and economic reform in the Middle East. By 2004, however, a growing number of donors had begun to criticize Yemen over economic reform and governance—and acted on the criticism. The IMF and World Bank expressed displeasure with Yemen's failure to completely lift subsidies and implement civil service reforms. They warned that aid remained contingent on Yemen's keeping its part of the aid-for-reform bargain.

The donor community, now joined by the United States, kept up the pressure. In October 2005, the US ambassador flatly asserted that Yemen's progress toward democracy had stalled. A month later, President Salih was surprised in Washington when told that Yemen was no longer eligible for a Millennium Challenge grant because of failures regarding corruption, governance, and individual freedom. Shortly thereafter, the World Bank announced a one-third reduction of its aid for the same reasons. In early 2006, the ambassadors of Yemen's top donors—the United States, the United Kingdom, Germany, and the Netherlands—met with President Salih and told him that their countries wanted to see measures taken quickly to address these problems.

Attacks on Western targets in San'a in 2008, especially on the US embassy, and evidence that the new generation of AQAP leaders was willing to wage jihad in Yemen restored lagging cooperation between Washington and Yemen. High-level visits increased, and projected military assistance in 2009 was about double that of 2007. In 2009, the United States sent CIA antiterrorism specialists and Special Forces commandos to train Yemeni forces, restored economic aid, and authorized a three-year, $120-million "stabilization program" to create jobs and improve health-care and other social services.

In December 2009, based on intelligence that AQAP was about to launch attacks on Western targets in San'a, Yemen carried out a series of arrests and a major air attack on bases in Abyan and Arhab, aided by US "firepower, intelligence, and other support." Days later, another air strike in Shabwa targeted an alleged meeting of top AQAP leaders, producing many casualties. The new collaboration seemed warranted by the failed attempt to blow up a jet over Detroit on Christmas Day 2009 by a Nigerian who had been groomed for the mission in Yemen in 2004. However, increased collaboration came at the risk of perceptions of Yemeni subservience to an increasingly unpopular United States, and civilian casualties threatened to lessen support for both the United States and the Salih regime and to win support for and recruits to AQAP, the Houthis, and the SMM.

In September 2011, Anwar al-Awlaki, a high-profile al-Qaida ideologue and alleged mentor of a number of would-be terrorists, was killed in a US drone strike in Shabwa. He was a US-born American citizen, as was another operative killed in the attack. However, given that Yemenis were preoccupied with the struggle to overthrow President Salih, these events did not seriously affect US-Yemeni relations.

In 2012, President Hadi cooperated with the United States on the issue of terrorism more fully and less ambiguously than had President Salih. With US assistance, President Hadi's forces recovered territory lost to Ansar al-Shariah in 2011. However, while Washington pledged to support regime change and development in post-Salih Yemen, the war on terror seemed to trump these matters when push came to shove. For example, after President Salih stepped down, the United States initially argued that for security reasons his son and nephews should retain their military and security positions.

PROSPECTS

The tasks facing President Hadi and the transitional government are daunting. To realize the goals of Yemen's Arab Spring, they must quickly complete the regime change that began in late 2011. Ending the Salih regime means removing the rest of his family members and close associates in the military and security services and possibly forcing some of them into exile. It probably means that Ali Muhsin and his close associates must also be neutralized politically as well. More generally, the military and security services must be brought under the control of the state, meaning the ministers of defense and interior and, indirectly, the president. Moreover, the capacity of the state must be increased if it is to do what needs to be done to better meet the wants and needs of most Yemenis.

These tasks must be accomplished in ways that do not unite the still strong remnants of the Salih regime in armed struggle—a fight to the death. Even if the remnants of the Salih regime are dealt with successfully, Yemen will still be subject to strong centrifugal forces—especially the Houthi Rebellion and the southern secessionist movement—which must be addressed now. Yemen was close to state failure and civil war by 2010 and remains extremely fragile. Lebanon, Somalia, and Afghanistan attest to how quickly fragile polities can unravel.

These difficult political changes must be made at the same time that the current humanitarian crisis is addressed. The extremely high levels of poverty, hunger, and displacement have continued down to the present and are intolerable and unbearable.

President Hadi's government must also begin to address the need for long-term economic development, and to this end it must begin dismantling the kleptocracy that the Salih regime became and the systemic corruption and staggering economic inequality it spawned. Given the degree of its penetration by the state during the Salih era, the economy will still be dominated by remnants of the Salih regime even with the removal of those in state positions. These are the same kleptocrats who fifteen years ago blocked the demanding IMF/World Bank reforms that are still needed to make Yemen attractive for investors and to begin making the economy and society viable and sustainable again.

Even with greatly improved governance and high levels of external funding and technical assistance, it will take great effort for Yemen to become much more than minimally viable and sustainable. Its known oil reserves are nearly depleted, and its known gas reserves are modest. Other possible natural resources, long talked about, have yet to materialize.

More importantly, and making this a race against time, Yemen's water resources are rapidly being depleted. In the absence of managed water use, its once-ample aquifers are being drawn down far more rapidly than they can be replenished. At the same time, its population growth rate remains one of the highest in the world. Simply put, Yemen risks running out of the water required to sustain its projected population. The Hadi transitional government must at least begin to address these challenges.

BIBLIOGRAPHY

For North Yemen's political history, see Robert W. Stookey, *Yemen: The Politics of the Yemen Arab Republic* (Boulder, CO: Westview Press, 1978); Manfred W. Wenner, *Modern Yemen, 1918–1966* (Baltimore: Johns Hopkins University Press, 1967); and Robert D. Burrowes, *The Yemen Arab Republic: The Politics of Development, 1962–1986* (Boulder, CO: Westview Press, 1987).

For South Yemen's political history, see Robert W. Stookey, *South Yemen: A Marxist Republic in Arabia* (Boulder, CO: Westview Press, 1982), and Helen Lackner, *PDR Yemen* (London: Ithaca Press, 1985). For both Yemens, see Fred Halliday, *Arabia Without Sultans* (London: Penguin, 1974), and Robin Bidwell, *The Two Yemens* (Boulder, CO: Westview Press, 1983).

For politics before and since unification, see Sheila Carapico, *Civil Society in Yemen* (Cambridge: Cambridge University Press, 1998); Paul Dresch, *A History of Modern Yemen* (Cambridge: Cambridge University Press, 2000); Sarah Phillips, *Yemen's Democracy Experiment in Regional Perspective: Patronage and Pluralism* (New York: Palgrave Macmillan, 2008); and Lisa Wedeen, *Peripheral Visions: Publics, Power, and Performance in Yemen* (Chicago: University of Chicago Press, 2008).

For external relations, see Fred Halliday, *Revolution and Foreign Policy: The Case of South Yemen, 1967–1987* (Cambridge: Cambridge University Press, 1989), and F. Gregory Gause III, *Saudi-Yemeni Relations: Domestic Structures and Foreign Influence* (New York: Columbia University Press, 1990).

For tribes and tribalism, see Paul Dresch, *Tribes, Government and History in Yemen* (Oxford: Oxford University Press, 1989), and Steven C. Caton, *Peaks of Yemen I Summon: Poetry as Performance in a North Yemeni Tribe* (Berkeley: University of California Press, 1990). For law, religion, culture, and society, see Brinkley Messick, *The Calligraphic State: Textual Domination and History in a Muslim Society* (Berkeley: University of California Press, 1993); Bernard Haykel, *Revival and Reform in Islam: The Legacy of Muhammad al-Shawkani* (Cambridge: Cambridge University Press, 2003); and Shelagh Weir, *A Tribal Order: Politics and Law in the Mountains of Yemen* (Austin: University of Texas Press, 2007). For qat, see John G. Kennedy, *The Flower of Paradise: The Institutionalized Use of the Drug Qat in North Yemen* (Dordrecht, Holland: D. Reidel Publishing, 1987).

For an encyclopedia/bibliography, see Robert D. Burrowes, *Historical Dictionary of Yemen,* 2nd ed. (Lanham, MD: Scarecrow Press, 2010). And for good reads, see Steven C. Caton, *Yemen Chronicle: An Anthropology of War and Mediation* (New York: Hill and Wang, 2005), and Tim MacIntosh Smith, *Yemen: Travels in Dictionary Land* (London: John Murray, 1997).

For websites, see *Yemen Times* (www.yementimes.com), *Yemen Observer* (www.yobserver.com), Chatham House—Yemen Forum (http://www.chathamhouse.org/research/middle-east/current-projects/yemen-forum), and Brookings—Yemen (http://www.brookings.edu/research/topics/yemen).

8

REPUBLIC OF LEBANON

William Harris

HISTORICAL BACKGROUND

Lebanon's commercial self-image, sense of history, and even genetic markers trace back to the Phoenician traders who gave the world the first alphabet and set out across the Mediterranean from the coast of Mount Lebanon more than 3,000 years ago. Tyre, Sidon, and Jbail (Byblos) were early Phoenician centers, while Tripoli was a later Phoenician foundation, Baalbek a Hellenistic provincial town, and Beirut a Roman veterans' colony. The Ituraean hill clans of Mount Lebanon proved recalcitrant for many decades after Roman occupation around 60 BCE. The population of both the coastal towns and the hills gradually converted from paganism to Christianity, particularly from the third century CE onward, and there is evidence of Arab tribal infiltration of Mount Lebanon in late Roman times.

Modern Lebanon's character as a conglomeration of sectarian communities began with the Islamic conquest of the Roman Levant between 636 and 640 CE. Mount Lebanon and its surrounds witnessed an influx of Muslim Arabs in the seventh and eighth centuries and conversion of part of the local population to Islam. Sidon, Beirut, and Tripoli became citadels of Sunni Islam on the seafront against Byzantium, while dissident Shi'a communities arose in the central and southern hills. The latter reflected the limited ability of the Umayyad (660–750) and Abbasid (750–1258) regimes to exert authority in the Lebanese hills.

Simultaneously, Mount Lebanon continued to host a substantial Christian population. In the late seventh century, a new Christian sect penetrated the area from northern Syria. These Maronites originated around the monastery of Maro in the Orontes valley and, by the ninth century, were the predominant Christian group in Mount Lebanon. Orthodox Christians were reduced to minorities in the Sunni ports and a few rural pockets.

Like the Christians, the Muslims of Mount Lebanon diversified as Abbasid authority contracted after the mid-ninth century. Twelver Shi'as dominated the coastal hills south of

223

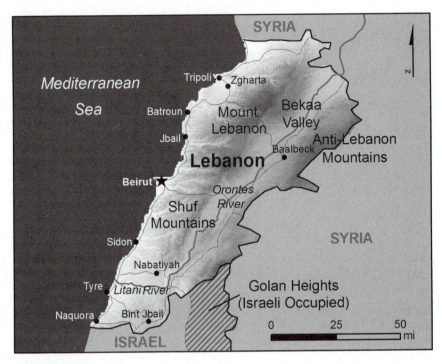

Republic of Lebanon

Sidon and much of the Bekaa valley. In contrast, the more mystical Isma'ili version of Shi'ism, with belief in a line of seven imams, gained sympathizers in the southern Bekaa and the hills near Beirut. When the Isma'ili Fatimid caliph al-Hakim died in Egypt in 1021, a call went out to his followers to give him allegiance as a manifestation of the divine on earth. The Tanukh chiefs of central Mount Lebanon took up the call, thus establishing the Druze sect.

The Seljuk Turks overthrew Twelver Shi'a influence in Iraq and pushed back Isma'ili Fatimid rule in Syria, heralding renewed Sunni Islamic domination of the Levant, later confirmed by the Mamluks of Egypt and the Ottoman Turks. The Crusader presence in Mount Lebanon for almost two centuries (1099–1291) gave the mountain communities—Maronites, Druze, and Shi'as—a critical opportunity to consolidate and play between the Frankish coast and the Muslim interior. By the time of Sultan Baybars and the Mamluk ascendancy, the Maronites, Druze, and Shi'as were entrenched.

After capturing Tripoli (1109), Beirut (1110), and Tyre (1124), the Frankish Crusaders dominated Mount Lebanon through the Kingdom of Jerusalem, from Beirut southward and to the County of Tripoli in the north. The Druze lords were divided in their alliances, with those in the Shuf having good relations with the Franks in Sidon and those inland from Beirut leaning toward the emirate of Damascus. The majority of the Maronites sided with the Franks, and their patriarchate entered a de facto union with the Roman Catholic Church. Some Christians in the north even aided Muslim incursions. Despite Salah al-Din's defeat of the Kingdom of Jerusalem in 1187, the Crusader revival of the early thirteenth century upheld this pattern of affairs until the Mamluk offensives of 1265 to 1291.

All the mountain communities were subject to Mamluk suspicion and punishments in the late thirteenth century, but the new Sunni Muslim masters of the Levant soon relented regarding the Druze and Maronites. They concentrated their hostility on the Shi'as of the Kisrawan hills, which weakened the Shi'a presence there and facilitated later Maronite immigration.

The Ottoman conquest of the Levant in 1516 did not suit some Druze, particularly the Ma'n lords, and they rebelled throughout the sixteenth century. The Ottomans sought to manage the Druze, Turkmen, and Shi'a chiefs of Mount Lebanon, Tripoli, and the Bekaa valley by a mixture of coercion and sharing out of administrative appointments. In 1593, they made the Druze leader Fakhr al-Din Ma'n, who pretended to be a Sunni Muslim, governor of the subprovince of Beirut-Sidon. In the early seventeenth century, Fakhr al-Din carved out a personal principality including all of modern Lebanon, at different stages deposing the Ottoman governors of Tripoli and Damascus. After 1607, he hosted refugee relatives of the rebellious Kurdish lord of Aleppo, Ali Janbalad. One of these married into the Druze community to found the Jumblat family, later Druze leaders. Fakhr al-Din also reopened Mount Lebanon to Europe and aligned himself with Tuscany. Most significantly, Fakhr al-Din associated with leading Maronites, particularly the Al Khazens, and encouraged Maronite peasants to move south toward the Druze areas. At the same time, the Vatican restored its relations with the Maronite Church with the 1598 establishment of a college in Rome to train Maronite priests. Fakhr al-Din's ambitions were too much for the Ottomans, who overthrew and executed him in 1635. Nonetheless, Istanbul tolerated the continuation in central Mount Lebanon of the Ma'n family's de facto principality, which became more entrenched after the Shihab relatives of the Ma'ns took it over in 1697.

In the eighteenth and early nineteenth centuries, the balance among the communities of Mount Lebanon and its surroundings changed. The Druze declined vis-à-vis the Maronites, who prospered from silk production and trade with Europe. The Shihabs, as the preeminent Ottoman tax farmers, identified with their Maronite allies. The leading branch of the family converted from Sunni Islam to Maronite Catholicism. Further, in the late eighteenth century, the Ottoman governor of Acre, Ahmad al-Jazzar, devastated Shi'a southern Lebanon. Shi'as were suspect because of their relations with Iran following the Safavid conversion of Iranians to Twelver Shi'ism—with Lebanese Shi'a assistance—in the sixteenth century.

After 1820, Bashir II Shihab repressed the Druze chiefs, most prominently Bashir Jumblat, and backed Muhammad Ali of Egypt against Istanbul. The Maronite Church, which flourished under the Shihabs, encouraged Maronite peasants against Maronite and

REPUBLIC OF LEBANON

Capital city	Beirut
Chief of state, 2012	President Michel Sulayman
Head of government, 2012	Prime Minister Najib Miqati
Coalitions and parties (share of vote in most recent election, 2009)	*March 8 Coalition* (54.7%): Development and Resistance Bloc, Free Patriotic Movement, Loyalty to the Resistance Bloc (includes Hezbollah), Nasserite Popular Movement, Popular Bloc, Syrian Ba'th Party, Syrian Social Nationalist Party; *March 14 Coalition* (45.3%): Democratic Left, Democratic Renewal Movement, Future Movement Bloc, Kataeb Party, Lebanese Forces, Tripoli Independent Bloc; *Independents*: Democratic Gathering Bloc, Metn Bloc
Ethnic groups	Arab (95%), Armenian (4%), other (1%)
Religious groups	Muslim (59.7%), Christian (39%), other (1.3%)
Export partners, 2009	United Arab Emirates (11.6%), South Africa (9.3%), Iraq (7.4%), Saudi Arabia (6.8%), Turkey (6.2%), Syria (6%), Egypt (5.4%), Switzerland (4.9%)
Import partners, 2009	United States (10.3%), Italy (9.5%), France (8.9%), China (8.3%), Germany (5.2%), Turkey (4.1%)

Druze landlords. Bashir II's Egyptian allies occupied Syria in 1832, and the Shihabi principality collapsed when the British sponsored an Ottoman restoration in 1840. Druze fear of the Maronite advance through the Kisrawan into the Druze districts interacted with Maronite peasant ferment to plunge Mount Lebanon into twenty years of turbulence, exacerbated by Ottoman weakness and manipulation. Sunnis and Shi'as also resented the Christian commercial gains from European penetration. In 1860, the animosities exploded into a Maronite/Druze war in the mountains east and south of Beirut. Despite Maronite numerical superiority, Druze skill and cohesion carried the day. Druze massacred thousands of Christian males, including many non-Maronites. The legacy of the trauma persists to the present.

Ironically, the massacres brought European military intervention and a political settlement to Christian advantage. Most of Mount Lebanon became an autonomous province (*mutasarrifiyya*) with a non-Lebanese Christian governor appointed by the sultan with the consent of the five great European powers. The arrangement involved a prominent role for an elected administrative council, with fixed representation for each major sect and a Christian, but not a Maronite, majority. The autonomous province had a Christian majority of over 80 percent, with Maronites alone comprising over half of the population. It did not incorporate the port cities or the Bekaa, which remained parts of regular Ottoman provinces. It was not ideal from the Maronite perspective, but it provided a stable environment until 1914 and a platform for more ambitious scenarios.

Contacts between Lebanon and the West intensified between 1860 and 1914. Foreign missionaries spearheaded an educational and intellectual florescence. Presbyterians from the United States founded the American University of Beirut in 1866, and French Jesuits established Saint Joseph University in 1875. Economically, Beirut profited from European trade with the Syrian interior, but Mount Lebanon stagnated and could not support the growing Maronite population. Increasing numbers of Christians moved into Beirut, where Sunni Muslims became a minority by the 1850s. After 1880, thousands of Maronites and other Christians left for the United States, Latin America, and Australia. About one-third returned after 1900, bringing new cultural horizons.

World War I terminated four centuries of Ottoman rule in the Levant, and wartime famine emphasized to the Maronites the inadequacy of the Ottoman autonomous province. An Anglo-French agreement allocated Mount Lebanon and its surroundings to the French, who in 1920 created the political entity of Greater Lebanon—the modern Lebanese territorial state—under a mandate from the League of Nations. At the insistence of France's Maronite friends, this area encompassed not just the former autonomous province but also Beirut, Tripoli, Sidon, southern Lebanon, the Bekaa valley, and the Akkar region in the north. France hoped that a larger Lebanon would be more economically and strategically viable. The expansion brought substantial numbers of Sunnis and Shi'as into the new state, reducing the Christian preponderance to a razor-thin majority of 51 percent, according to modern Lebanon's first and last census in 1932. It also stimulated lasting hostility from the new Syrian state founded by the French in the interior.

In Beirut, France sponsored a more complex version of the sectarian power sharing inaugurated in the Ottoman autonomous province. By the 1930s, Sunnis and Shi'as had become reconciled to Greater Lebanon, while many Maronites had grown less patient with French domination. The French mandatory authorities promulgated a constitution in 1926, allowing the Lebanese to elect a parliament and choose a president, but they suspended the constitution in 1932 and 1939. Friction with the French led many Lebanese to embrace alternative political philosophies, especially socialism and Arab and Syrian nationalism. The French High Commission in Beirut established the

economic and bureaucratic infrastructure of modern Lebanon, though the French con-
centrated investment in port facilities, electricity, and roads in Beirut and central Mount
Lebanon, neglecting the Sunni and Shi'a peripheries. World War II brought the end of
French rule. The British army seized Lebanon in 1941 after the German occupation of
France and, in 1943, forced the Free French to grant independence to the Lebanese.

POLITICAL ENVIRONMENT

Physical Geography

Lebanon comprises four major geographical regions: a coastal plain, Mount Lebanon, the
Bekaa valley, and the Anti-Lebanon Mountains. The coastal plain varies in width from
about eight miles (twelve kilometers) in the north to almost nothing in places. Most of the
major towns of the country are on this plain, including the three largest: Beirut, Tripoli,
and Sidon. Mount Lebanon, from the Akkar in the north to the Barouk range and the hills
of Jabal 'Aamil in the south, rises abruptly from the plain. The highest peaks of the
coastal massif are inland from Tripoli and Beirut, within fifteen miles (about twenty kilometers) of the coast. These stand between 8,000 and 10,000 feet (2,500 and 3,000 meters)
and carry heavy snow in winter and spring.

The fertile Bekaa valley lies between Mount Lebanon and the Anti-Lebanon range. It
is a trench, with much of the floor about 3,000 feet above sea level, bounded by fault lines
that express Lebanon's vulnerability to earthquakes. It is widest north of Baalbek, where
it gives rise to the Orontes River, which flows north into Syria. In most of the valley, however, the Litani River is the main water source. The Litani flows southward, making a
right-angle turn west toward the Mediterranean about twelve miles (less than twenty kilometers) north of the Israeli border. To the east, the Anti-Lebanon Mountains are partly in
Lebanon and partly in Syria; the boundary between the two countries departs from ridge-
lines in places and is not well demarcated. These mountains are a little lower than Mount
Lebanon and receive much less rainfall. At 9,232 feet (2,900 meters), Mount Hermon on
the Syrian-Lebanese-Israeli border is the highest peak.

Mount Lebanon receives the most reliable rainfall in the Levant. Lebanon is the only
country in the region self-sufficient in water resources, though high population density
and poor regulation of use have led to severe pollution problems.

People

In the Middle East, Lebanon represents a unique coalescence of Christian and Muslim
communities and of Western and Islamic influences. Its mountains have been a refuge for
minority religious groups, and its large Christian population and central coastal position
in the Levant have made it a gateway for European cultural and economic penetration
since the seventeenth century. Almost all Lebanese identify strongly with their country in

its modern territorial configuration, but their interpretation of what it means to be Lebanese varies with communal affiliation. Maronites often emphasize ties with the West as making Lebanon different from the Islamic neighborhood, Sunnis see Lebanon as a distinctive component of a wider Arab and mainly Sunni environment, and Shi'as view Lebanon as a vehicle for their own community, with Iranian as well as Arab ties. About 95 percent of Lebanese have Arabic as their mother tongue, though some speak another language at home. The differences among the confessional groups, however, remain great. In Lebanon, religion is more than a belief system; it is a major element in self- and family identity, apart from influencing interpretations of national identity.

Christians and Muslims comprised roughly equivalent portions of the population through the late Ottoman period until the mid-twentieth century. Maronite dynamism maintained the Christian share, despite the outflow to the wider world after about 1860. Between the 1920s and the 1990s, however, higher Muslim fertility and continued Christian emigration caused a substantial shift. Surveys and estimates indicate that by the 1990s Christians made up less than 40 percent of resident Lebanese. At the same time, strong differentiation between Sunni and Shi'a Muslims meant that Lebanon remained a country without a majority community. Shi'as, trailing Maronites and Sunni Muslims in the 1932 census, had become the largest single community by the 1990s. As for the early twenty-first century, a decline in Shi'a fertility and increases in Muslim emigration imply that population proportions may again be stabilizing. This would leave Shi'as at about one-third of the total, Sunnis above one-quarter, and Maronites below one-quarter within a Christian fraction of 35 to 38 percent. The Druze represent about 5 percent. Translated into numbers, Lebanon's present population of at least 4 million, excluding Palestinians, encompasses roughly 1.3 million Shi'as, 1.1 million Sunnis, and 800,000 Maronites, or in comprehensive terms, 2.4 million Muslims, 1.4 million Christians, and 200,000 Druze. All estimates are speculative, and the communities dispute the details.

The Palestinian refugee population is another problematic factor. This dates back to the major Palestinian influx of 1948 and 1949, accompanying the creation of Israel. There are perhaps 350,000 Palestinians in Lebanon, half of them living in squalid refugee camps alongside the main coastal cities. Palestinians, overwhelmingly Sunni Muslim, amount to almost 10 percent of Lebanon's population. Shi'as and Christians, in particular, bitterly oppose citizenship grants and permanent Palestinian settlement because of the implications for communal balances. The impact of grants of Lebanese citizenship to tens of thousands of Syrians and Palestinians in 1992, forced through under Syrian hegemony, is not entirely clear, but it was detrimental to Maronites and Shi'as.

Seven of Lebanon's seventeen officially recognized sectarian communities have what might be termed "political weight." The main poles are of course the three "great" communities, each above 20 percent of the population: Maronite Christians and Sunni and Shi'a Muslims. Then there are four other communities with politically guaranteed ministerial positions in Lebanese governments: the Druze, the Orthodox Christians, the Greek Catholics, and the Armenians.

Among Christians, Maronites represent both the demographic majority and the source of political leadership. Lebanon would not exist without the will of this vigorous mountain Christian community to be separated politically from its Islamic neighborhood. To a greater degree than the smaller Christian sects, Maronites are extensively represented among poorer and lower-middle-class Lebanese. They have a powerful political, professional, and commercial elite, and they remain the bulk of the population in most of eastern Beirut and the northern half of Mount Lebanon.

Orthodox Christians constitute the second-largest Christian community (around 300,000). Traditionally they are a more urban population than the Maronites, with a dispersed distribution throughout the Levant. Not having a compact territory like the Maronites, they are more used to being a minority and have had more interaction with Sunni Muslims. Orthodox Christians are more comfortable with Arab identity than many Maronites; some leading late-nineteenth-century Arab nationalists were Orthodox. Also in 1932, an Orthodox Christian, Antoun Sa'adeh, founded the Syrian Social Nationalist Party, which promoted a greater Syria including Syria, Lebanon, Jordan, and Israel. Since the 1960s, however, the powerful Islamic emphasis in Arab nationalism has led most Lebanese Orthodox to gravitate toward the Maronites while still presenting themselves as more open to Muslims and other Arabs. Away from Beirut and Tripoli, Orthodox Christians inhabit the Koura district, parts of the Matn above Beirut, and Marjayoun near the border with Israel.

Greek Catholics in Lebanon (perhaps 150,000) date from the eighteenth century, when a number of Orthodox Christians in Ottoman Syria went into communion with Rome. They have tended to follow the Maronite political lead, though without enthusiasm. They mainly live in eastern Beirut and the Bekaa valley town of Zahle, with a scattering of villages elsewhere, in less defensible locations than the Maronite heartland. Armenians number about 100,000, living overwhelmingly in eastern Beirut. As non-Arabs, they are ethnically distinct from other Christians and Lebanese, and they maintain their separate cultural identity. They came to Lebanon during and after World War I, as refugees from Anatolia, and Maronites welcomed them as buttressing the Christian sector. Armenians have kept a distance from Lebanese political factions, supported the forces in power, and looked for freedom to manage their own community. Many left Lebanon in the 1975–1990 war years, when they came under mounting pressure to take sides.

Until the 1980s, the Maronite political advantage in post-Ottoman Lebanon and Muslim resentment of it obscured the divide between Sunnis and Shi'as. Sunni politicians played a double game: they went into partnership with Maronite leaders to command Lebanon in the 1943 National Pact, and they championed Muslim demands for political adjustment, seeking to contain radical elements. This worked as long as they could direct their own community and Shi'as remained rural, quiescent, and obedient to their semifeudal chiefs. The game foundered in the late twentieth century when leftist and Palestinian groups attracted Sunni loyalty and as Shi'as moved to Beirut, overtook Sunnis in numbers, and coalesced under new sectarian political movements. Sunnis differ from both

Maronites and Shi'as in their long-standing urban concentration in Beirut, Tripoli, and Sidon, with only limited rural extension in the Bekaa and northern Lebanon, and in their closer ties with the Arab world. Sunnis have desired that Lebanon play a larger role in Arab affairs, a stance not favored by Maronites, and that Sunni Arab states influence Lebanon's domestic affairs, sometimes against Shi'a as well as Christian interests.

Through the first four decades of Lebanese independence after 1943, the Shi'as were politically underrepresented and economically disadvantaged, compared with Christians, Sunnis, and Druze. For most, migration in the 1960s and 1970s from southern Lebanon and the Bekaa to the southern neighborhoods of Beirut—from the periphery of the country to the periphery of the capital—simply meant exchanging rural poverty for urban poverty. Young Shi'as eventually reacted to the coldness of other Lebanese and to manipulation by the Palestinians cohabiting their home areas by turning to their own militant sectarian organizations. In the 1980s, they also acquired foreign patrons to match the Western connections of Maronites and the Arab ties of Sunnis: the new Shi'a Islamic revolutionary regime in Iran and the Alawite/Ba'thist rulers of Syria. The 1989 Ta'if Agreement gave Shi'as parity with Sunnis in parliament and increased the powers of the Shi'a speaker of the Chamber of Deputies. Syrian hegemony over Lebanon in the 1990s provided an umbrella under which Shi'as increased their political, bureaucratic, and hence economic shares, while Iran pumped money into the religious wing of the community. The price was subordination to Syrian and Iranian agendas and the complicity of a new class of bourgeois Shi'a politicians with their Sunni and Maronite equivalents in the corrupt and repressive "second Lebanese republic."

Still politically frustrated, Shi'as buttressed their national influence after 1990 by force of arms. In contrast to other Lebanese militias of the 1975–1990 period, which were disarmed and disbanded in 1991, the Islamic Resistance, the armed wing of Hizballah (Party of God), enhanced its weaponry. Hizballah's justification was resistance to Israeli occupation of Lebanese land, and the movement took credit for Israel's unilateral withdrawal and the collapse of Israel's ally, the South Lebanese Army, in May 2000. This consolidated Hizballah's standing as Lebanon's largest, most disciplined political movement after 1990, with social service provisions for Shi'as and unrivaled foreign backing. In the 2000, 2005, and 2009 parliamentary elections, Hizballah and the more secular Amal movement commanded the Shi'a population of southern Lebanon, the northern Bekaa valley, and the southern suburbs of Beirut. The elections, however, emphasized that Hizballah was a sectarian party, stuck in a minority. Its maintenance of its arms after 2000, at the expense of state sovereignty, became controversial for the non-Shi'a majority of Lebanese.

Suspended between the Muslims and Christians, the Druze community is in a peculiar position. The Druze faith derives from Islam but is not really Muslim, and the old Druze mountain partnership with the Maronites came to grief in 1860. Estrangement from Maronites and discontent with the limited prospects for Druze ascent in post-1920 Lebanon led Druze leaders, above all Kamal Jumblat, to champion political revisionism. Here the

Druze joined Sunni Muslims, leftists, and Palestinians and forged ties with Soviet Russia. Since Lebanon's independence, the Druze have seemed most comfortable in alignment with Sunnis and the smaller Christian communities, which they perceive as nonthreatening. They feel challenged by the two larger mountain communities, the Maronites and Shi'as. Nonetheless, the historical intimacy of Druze and Maronite clans retains resonance, whereas the Shi'a rise has mainly stimulated fear. Limited Druze numbers are to a degree offset by the strategic location of the community, in the Shuf hills above Beirut, straddling the main road from Beirut to Damascus, and on the slopes of Mount Hermon, between southern Lebanon and the Bekaa valley. The Druze community is the most tightly knit in the country, is generally well educated but not wealthy, and has a martial reputation.

Even before their coreligionists, Lebanese relate to their extended families and villages. Because one does not normally marry outside one's religion, family and religious identification are mutually reinforcing. The family was long the vehicle of political advancement, plugging into wider clan and patronage networks. Family associations have also provided support functions elsewhere performed by the state. In August 2012, the Shi'a Mekdad clan conducted reprisal kidnappings and flaunted the family's "armed wing" when a Syrian opposition faction seized a family member in Damascus. Nonetheless, the war years after 1975 saw a weakening of the family in political affairs, with raw money power, sectarian parties, and obeisance to Syria and the security apparatus becoming better promotion routes by the 1990s.

Economic Conditions

Lebanon's entrepreneurial talent, which some date to the Phoenicians, is mainly a product of European commercial influence in late Ottoman times and the maintenance of the country's merchant economy while other Arabs indulged in semisocialist experiments. Merchants, shopkeepers, artisans, and service workers flourished under Lebanon's unfettered free market system until the warfare of 1975 to 1990.

After independence and before 1975, the Lebanese enhanced their regional economic role, benefiting from economic and political developments elsewhere. The independence of Israel cut economic ties between the Arab world and most of the former British Mandate for Palestine, leaving a large gap that the Lebanese filled. For example, the terminal for the Iraq petroleum pipeline was transferred from Haifa to Tripoli. More generally, overland transport and communications that might have traversed the southern Levant were funneled into Beirut. International corporations and banks established regional headquarters in the Lebanese capital, and the economy boomed.

The Lebanese took advantage of the growing wealth of the Arab oil states. Beirut supplied entertainment and investment as well as a transit point for goods and services. Arabs from the Gulf countries flocked to Beirut and the nearby mountain villages each summer. The Lebanese provided their guests with recreation, banking arrangements, and European shopping in an Arab environment. Many Arabs bought homes in the mountains or invested in Beirut. Lebanon's schools and universities educated the children of Arab leaders.

In the decade before the collapse into chaos in 1975, Lebanon experienced rapid industrial growth. The oil refineries at Zahrani and Tripoli had previously been the leading industry. In the 1960s, a manufacturing belt began to grow in the poorer suburbs of Beirut, mostly small enterprises producing light consumer goods, textiles, or processed foods. The agricultural sector gradually declined as Lebanese tended more toward urban living. Nonetheless, many people continued to earn incomes from their small landholdings or tenant farms. Lebanon's topography offers a variety of environments, and apples, citrus fruits, olives, olive oil, and grapes remain significant export items. Otherwise, the most interesting aspect of the pre-1975 Lebanese economy was its perennial trade deficit, with imports regularly five times the value of exports. Remittances from Lebanese emigrants, including workers in the oil-producing states, and hard currency from Lebanon's service sector offset the deficit.

Fifteen years of warfare from 1975 to 1990 punctured Lebanon's economic ascent and status as a regional hub. Successive rounds of hostilities devastated commerce and industry, and crucial middleman functions relocated to Cyprus, the Persian Gulf, and Jordan, though they remained partially in Lebanese hands. Communications and water and electricity provision deteriorated. The difficulty of maintaining infrastructure did not end with the war years. Israeli air raids up to 2000 damaged electricity facilities, and the Israeli-Hizballah confrontation weakened business confidence.

Rafik Hariri became head of the Council of Ministers in late 1992. Hariri, an extraordinarily successful Lebanese Sunni businessman, had amassed a fortune in Saudi Arabia. Lebanese and international observers hoped that Hariri would entice foreign, Arab, and Lebanese diaspora investment to the country to restore its former standing. The Syrian regime hoped that Hariri would make its command of Beirut suitably lucrative.

Hariri's government undertook a vigorous program of reconstruction. The cost of Hariri's projects far exceeded Lebanon's capacity to pay, and Syrian hegemony, corruption, and political uncertainty contributed to a tepid response from potential investors. As a result, the Lebanese government borrowed large sums of money at inflated interest rates, principally from the domestic banking sector. When Hariri came to office, the national debt was about $900 million; in 1998, it reached $18 billion and ballooned to $43 billion by 2008, when it stood at 180 percent of gross domestic product (GDP). Debt servicing ate up more than half the national budget after the mid-1990s. Despite liberal government deficit spending, economic growth was only modest, unemployment was substantial, income gaps stretched, and the once-robust middle class saw its economic status erode. Hariri's reconstruction projects were impressive but focused on parts of Beirut, leaving much of Lebanon untouched. Most disturbing was the number of educated and skilled Lebanese workers who emigrated during and after the war years.

By 1998, Hariri's star was behind a cloud, and the Syrian leadership shifted its favor to the new Maronite president, Emile Lahoud. Hariri resigned, and through the next two years, he and his team endured a cynical campaign of denigration. Nonetheless, the new government had no solutions to Lebanon's predicament. Hariri could at least pull strings in the wider world, and in the fall of 2000, he and his allies won the parliamentary elections, imposing his return as prime minister.

Thereafter, Hariri found himself unable to satisfy international reform requirements. The state apparatus remained venal and ramshackle. Hariri's achievement in the first five years of the new century was simply to keep Lebanon afloat—his personal standing enabled the government to restructure debt and keep borrowing. Vigorous support for Lebanon from the UN Security Council mitigated the shock of Hariri's assassination in February 2005. The economy faltered in 2005–2006 with the political standoff between pro- and anti-Syrian regime camps and about $4 billion in damage from the July–August 2006 Israel-Hizballah hostilities. On the other hand, the Syrian military departure and international favor for Hariri's adviser Fuad Siniora as the new prime minister gave hope, and in 2006 remittances alone more than outweighed war damage. Lebanon sailed through the 2008–2009 global recession unscathed. Its banks had avoided risky financial instruments; regional backers of Shi'a and Sunni factions, principally Iran and Saudi Arabia, directed money into the country; and Gulf Arab tourism boomed.

In 2011, GDP growth slumped to 1.5 percent from 7 percent the previous year because of the turmoil in Syria. Like politics, the economy marked time, awaiting a Syrian outcome. The slowdown in tourism, construction, and financial services, accompanied by complete distraction of the new Hizballah-dominated government toward the Syrian crisis, highlighted continued severe deprivation among a large part of society and persistent infrastructural decrepitude, notably in electricity provision.

POLITICAL STRUCTURE

The system of government bequeathed to Lebanon by the French in 1943 was modeled after that of France but took into account Lebanese sectarian peculiarities. The principal pillars of the system are the 1926 constitution and the 1943 informal National Pact, as modified by the 1989 Ta'if Agreement. Judicial institutions apply French-style civil law. Ordinary courts have criminal and civil wings, with benches of judges at three levels—first instance, appeal, and cassation. There are also administrative courts, military tribunals, a judicial council, and a constitutional court. Legal personnel are competent, but political pressure has subverted the legal authorities.

Beyond the state, each sectarian community has its own religious institutions, with personal-status issues (e.g., marriage, divorce, and inheritance) subject to religious codes—not civil law. Such institutions—for example, the Maronite Church and patriarchate, the office of the Sunni chief mufti, and the Higher Shi'a Islamic Council—control extensive property and their own courts. Spiritual leaders can have significant political influence.

Lebanon's National Pact of 1943, which originated as an understanding between the Maronite Bishara al-Khoury and the Sunni Muslim Riyadh al-Solh, has been the framework of the country's confessional politics. Most prominently, it was an oral agreement about allocation of top posts. Since 1943, the president, chosen by parliamentary vote for a single six-year term, has been a Maronite. The president nominates a Sunni Muslim as prime minister on the basis of consultation with the parliamentary deputies, and the prime minister forms a cabinet, since 1989 half Christian and half Muslim/Druze. The speaker of the Chamber of Deputies is a Shi'a, and his deputy is an Orthodox Christian. Ministerial portfolios are allocated according to confessional shares, as are many other positions in the executive, legislative, and judicial branches. The army commander is customarily a Maronite, and there is a religious balance among security service chiefs.

Lebanon's legislature, the Chamber of Deputies, elaborates the sectarian political system. Parliamentary seats are distributed on both a confessional and a geographical basis. Deputies come from geographical districts. Each district has a specified number of seats allocated by religion, and all citizens registered in a district vote for candidates for all the seats. For example, the Shuf constituency used for the 2000 and 2005 elections returned three Maronites, one Greek Catholic, two Druze, and two Sunnis. This was in rough proportion to the demographic distribution of registered voters, a large number of whom no longer lived in the district. Similarly, many Beirut Shi'as vote in southern Lebanon, not Beirut, because they remain registered in their original villages.

Religious sects concentrate sufficiently to justify constituency-based sectarian seat allocation. Tripoli and Sidon are overwhelmingly Sunni; Zgharta, Kisrawan, and Jbail are similarly Maronite; Tyre, Nabatiyah, and Baalbek have Shi'a majorities; and the Koura is predominantly Orthodox. Even in areas of mixed population, villages tend to belong primarily to a single religious group. In Beirut, Christians, Sunnis, and Shi'as live in separate neighborhoods. The representative system established under the departing French adapted democracy to Lebanese demography.

Apart from confessional political shares, the 1943 National Pact also addressed the conflicting external orientations of the Lebanese. A majority of Christians, particularly Maronites, looked toward Western nations as protectors. Their Lebanese nationalism contrasted with Arab nationalism. Muslims often viewed Lebanese nationalism as a denial of Lebanon's Arab face. To Christians, Muslim pan-Arabism sacrificed Lebanese, particularly Lebanese Christian, interests to Islamic and Arab goals.

The National Pact attempted a compromise between Lebanese and Arab nationalists. The Maronite side agreed not to try to alienate Lebanon from the Arab world or to draw Lebanon too close to the West. The Sunni Muslim side recognized Lebanon's uniqueness and agreed not to pressure the government to become overly involved in the affairs of Arab states. The 1989 Ta'if Agreement upset this aspect of the National Pact, clearly placing Lebanon in the Arab context. Here the Lebanese nationalists suffered a setback, but the new turning of Christians, Sunnis, and Druze toward Western powers in 2005 to throw off Ba'thist Syria indicated that the issue remained alive.

In general terms, the Ta'if Agreement recalibrated the political system. Sixty-two of seventy-three surviving members of the 1972 Lebanese parliament, the last elected before the war years, met in Ta'if, Saudi Arabia, from September 30 to October 22, 1989, to adjust the constitution to reconcile Muslim grievances with Christian fears. They modified the balance of power while perpetuating most of the 1926 constitution and the National Pact. First, the agreement reduced the executive power of the presidency in favor of the Council of Ministers headed by the Sunni prime minister. Second, it gave greater influence to the Chamber of Deputies and its Shi'a speaker. For example, the president could no longer veto legislation; he could simply require it to be presented a second time. Third, the agreement changed parliament's composition. It altered the ratio of Christian to non-Christian deputies from 6:5 to parity and established equality between Sunnis and Shi'as. The number of deputies was increased from 99 to 128 in 1992. The sixty-four Christian seats became allocated as follows: thirty-four to Maronites, fourteen to Orthodox, eight to Greek Catholics, six to Armenians, one to a Protestant, and one to other Christians. The sixty-four non-Christian seats were to include twenty-seven Sunnis, twenty-seven Shi'as, eight Druze, and two Alawites.

Up to 2005, the Lebanese and Syrian regimes warped implementation of Ta'if. In 1995 and 2004, Syria forced extended terms for Presidents Ilyas Hrawi and Emile Lahoud in defiance of the constitution. On the parliamentary level, the Lebanese authorities set aside the Ta'if provision for using large electorates, instead mixing large and small constituencies to ensure seats for Syria's friends. Elections between 1992 and 2005 subjected many Christian deputies to non-Christian voter majorities. They also undermined traditional leaders in favor of Syria-aligned political parties, for example, Hizballah and Amal.

Despite abuses, Lebanon's constitution has guaranteed basic rights, including equality before the law, personal liberties, political rights, and freedom of the press, association, speech, and assembly. Beirut remains a regional publishing center, noted for the vigor of its print media. From 1990 to 2005, Syria-dominated Lebanon went through a dark period of constricted public freedoms. Senior politicians and the security agencies interfered in elections within the union movement and professional organizations. On the other hand, business and banking associations resisted coordination, preserving effective electoral practices. The basic culture of political pluralism provided the platform for a powerful rebound of civil society.

As regards gender in politics, emancipation of women is still not reflected in political participation. Women received the vote in 1953, and the army opened the gate to female officers in 1992. Yet the number of women in parliament is miserably low: 4 out of 128 deputies after the 2009 elections, down from 7 in 2005. In 2009, two female parliamentarians, Nayla Tueni (Orthodox) and Bahiya Hariri (Sunni), owed their prominence to being, respectively, the daughter and sister of murdered male politicians. Strida Ja'ja' (Maronite) is the wife of politician Samir Ja'ja'. Three belonged to the pro-Western March 14 bloc, and one, Gilberte Zouein (Maronite), to Michel Aoun's group. One bright spot is female participation in the legal profession; in late 2009 Amal Haddad became president of the Beirut Bar Association, and Joyce Thabet became the Lebanese deputy prosecutor for the special international tribunal for the Hariri murder case.

As for the military institution, Lebanon moved from a small Maronite-dominated army, largely neutral in political affairs until the 1960s, to a larger force incorporating militia personnel in the 1990s, with a more representative officer corps. Under Syrian hegemony after 1990, the army command of General Emile Lahoud, military intelligence, and the public security directorate were all politicized in favor of Syria. The restructured army brigades, however, kept popular legitimacy and respect as a nonpolitical armed force. After the 2005 and 2009 polls, they could be relied on to uphold elected governments.

POLITICAL DYNAMICS

Lebanon's history since independence from France in 1943 has gone through four phases. From 1943 until 1975, "confessional democracy" prevailed, with little change in the social order and political control in the hands of traditional communal leaders. There were, however, strains with demographic shifts in favor of Muslims in general and Shi'as in particular, combined with intrusion of Middle Eastern regional politics. Between 1975 and 1990, disorder reigned, with hostilities involving local parties and foreign powers. The country disaggregated into sectarian cantons and zones of Syrian, Israeli, and Palestinian occupation, with state institutions barely surviving. Between 1991 and 2004, the Lebanese state resurfaced, and calm returned, except on the border with Israel, at the price of Syrian steerage. In 2005, Lebanon entered a new phase of shaky autonomy.

1943–1974

The confessional democracy that flourished through the 1950s and 1960s had virtues. It reflected the reality of sectarian allegiances but softened their impact. Relatively small electoral districts gave weight to local and personal ties, often across sectarian lines, which buffered against political radicalism and foreign entanglement. A traditional politician had to provide services for constituents and, to have national reach, join a coalition with counterparts from other communities. Competing electoral lists were multisectarian, with Maronites against Maronites and Sunnis against Sunnis rather than Christians against Muslims. Votes in parliament rarely broke along religious lines.

Apart from the rigidity of sectarian quotas, the most prominent defect of confessional democracy was the discouragement of national parties. Any nationwide bloc of deputies tended to be a factional coalition under a senior politician (for example, the National Bloc of Bishara al-Khoury), not an organized ideological party with a coherent program. Ideological parties, like the Communists, Syrian Social Nationalists, and Ba'thists, had little success unless boosted by family loyalties. Only two parties broke the mold to a limited extent, because they combined ideology with traditional leadership. The Progressive Socialist Party of Kamal Jumblat brought together leftists and a traditional Druze following. The Phalange integrated Lebanese nationalism, a social welfare dimension, and the partisans of the Jumayyil family. Both reached into other sects, but there was no doubting their respective Druze and Maronite foundations.

In consequence, parliaments were highly fragmented. A bloc of fifteen members was considered large, and presidents and prime ministers could never rely on the party backing accepted in the West as a normal underpinning of government. Regimes depended on unstable coalitions, and Presidents Camille Chamoun and Fuad Shihab both fell back on intelligence service manipulation of politics. Nonetheless, most Lebanese were satisfied most of the time that their basic concerns—security and a share of government largesse—were accommodated.

A brief breakdown occurred in 1958, when both Christians and Muslims felt that the National Pact was being violated. President Chamoun feared the pull of Egyptian president Gamal Abdel Nasser's populist Arab nationalism on Lebanese Sunni Muslims. He wished to move closer to the West to protect Lebanon's independence. Muslims viewed this as a challenge to Lebanon's Arab identity. Chamoun also sought to extend his presidency, which aroused rejection from Christian rivals as well as Muslims. The creation of the United Arab Republic between Egypt and Syria in February 1958 raised the temperature. Largely but not exclusively intercommunal fighting ensued between pro- and anti-Chamoun forces. US military intervention in July 1958 gave frightened Lebanese leaders a chance to pull back from the brink. Chamoun stepped down at the end of his normal term, and Maronite army commander Fuad Shihab became president. Shihab had a mild reformist agenda and was on good terms with Nasser.

Shihab and his chosen successor, Charles Helou, calmed the political arena amid economic prosperity through the 1960s. Shihab enlarged the state, promoted investment in peripheral areas, and brought more Muslims into the bureaucracy. However, the 1960s saw destabilizing developments in both Lebanon and the wider Levant. Shihab's reforms stimulated Shi'a aspirations at a time when mass migration brought poorer Christians and Shi'as from the countryside to the booming metropolis. Beirut acquired new suburbs, with Shi'as open to radical leftist influence and Maronites less under the thumb of traditional bosses. The 1960s saw the Shi'a arrival in modern politics, at first under the moderate leadership of Musa Sadr. Beirut's boom sharpened Lebanon's income disparities, producing hostility to the Sunni and Christian bourgeoisie even when many Shi'as found their incomes improving.

The June 1967 Arab-Israeli War introduced critical additional factors. To begin with, the defeat of the Arab states ended the quiescence of Lebanon's Palestinian Arabs, who had come to the country as refugees in 1948 and 1949. For almost two decades the Palestinians had left confrontation with Israel to regular Arab armies and hardly stirred in and around their refugee camps until initiating some paramilitary activity in the early 1960s. The Lebanese army and intelligence agencies watched them, and the Lebanese elite discriminated against their middle class. Israel's 1967 triumph provoked the Palestinians into guerilla action along the Israeli border with Lebanon and into militarization in Palestinian strongholds along the Lebanese coast.

In southern Lebanon, the accelerating tempo of Israeli-Palestinian hostilities impelled more Shi'as to move to Beirut and nourished Shi'a discontent with Lebanese realities. In the late 1960s and early 1970s, many younger members of the community joined Palestinian-Lebanese leftist armed groups. More broadly, Lebanese Sunni and Druze activists, most prominently Kamal Jumblat, saw alignment with Palestinian military capability not just as an affirmation of Arabism but also as a weapon to compel the Maronites to accept new political arrangements reflecting Muslim numbers. Traditional Sunni leaders, including prime ministers, did not dare defy the Palestinian-Lebanese leftist alignment. This alignment paralyzed the Lebanese state, meant the Lebanese army could not uphold state sovereignty, and railroaded the Lebanese regime into the 1969 Cairo Accord, giving Palestinian fighters operational freedom in parts of Lebanon.

Christians responded belligerently to what many interpreted as an existential threat. The failure of the Lebanese army to contain the Palestinians led the Phalange and the Chamounists to build up private arsenals. Christian paramilitaries ignored traditional Christian leadership and recruited among Beirut's newer Maronite residents, as well as in Mount Lebanon. Events in 1970 and 1971 intensified the crisis. The Jordanian crackdown on Yasir Arafat's Palestine Liberation Organization (PLO) in the Jordanian civil war left Lebanon as the only Arab country in which Palestinians could organize freely. The PLO leadership and thousands of fighters shifted from Jordan to Lebanon, further upsetting the Lebanese balance and exciting the Lebanese Left against "Maronite hegemony." At the same time, the takeover of Syria by Hafiz al-Asad and stabilization of the Syrian Ba'thist state inaugurated prolonged Syrian interference in Lebanese politics, at first in favor of the Palestinians and the Lebanese Left. In this delicate environment, Lebanon acquired an unpromising new president, Sulayman Franjiyah. President Franjiyah's policies after 1970 were a bewildering mixture of a hard line against the Palestinians; surrender to his old friend Hafiz al-Asad, advantaging the Palestinians; and the dismantling of Shihab's security apparatus, the eyes and ears of the Lebanese state. This signaled to all sides that they had best look to their own resources and prepare for a showdown.

1975–1990

In early 1975, sporadic incidents between armed Christians and Palestinian militants exploded into fighting in and around Beirut that involved the PLO and the Lebanese leftists. Through 1976, Christian militias carved out a de facto canton in northern Mount Lebanon, and the Palestinians took command of western Beirut and much of southern Lebanon. Despite Christian fears of Syrian Ba'thist designs on Lebanon, President Franjiyah invited Syrian military intervention to forestall PLO advances and Israeli action. Syrian forces, with US and Israeli acquiescence, thereupon deployed through most of Lebanon to contain Syria's Palestinian "allies," except for a zone in southern Lebanon covered by an Israeli "red line."

By 1978, the Christian militias, tired of their brief partnership with Damascus, had compelled the Syrians to retreat from much of the Christian area and turned to Israel. Meanwhile, the Lebanese army fragmented, largely along religious lines, and northern Maronites loyal to the pro-Syrian Franjiyah family split from other Christians. In March 1978, Israel launched a large incursion into southern Lebanon against the Palestinians and established a border strip inside Lebanon under its influence. The latter defied UN Security Council Resolution 425, which demanded Israeli withdrawal.

Between 1978 and 1982, the Palestinians under Arafat's PLO strengthened their position in western Beirut and the south, using their Lebanese allies and their prestige in the Arab world to loosen Syria's grip. The Christian militias in eastern Beirut and its hinterland coalesced into a supermilitia, the Lebanese Forces (LF), under the charismatic Bashir Jumayyil, while the Syrians consolidated their presence in the Bekaa valley and northern Lebanon, Syria's strategic buffers. Within the Shi'a community, the disappearance of Musa Sadr on a visit to Libya, discontent with Palestinian behavior, and the 1979 Iranian revolution stimulated truculence.

The country seemed to be disintegrating, though a battered Lebanese government persisted, shored up by the international community. Only the coffers of the Palestinian "state within the state" averted economic collapse. Lebanon was fundamentally destabilized, with its communities and leaders polarized by domestic quarrels and conflicting external alliances. Its affairs were a free-for-all among the Palestinians, Israel, Syria, and the wider Arab world, and its location on the Arab-Israeli front line raised the stakes. In 1981, a hard-line Israeli government, Maronite wooing of Israel to service Bashir Jumayyil's presidential ambitions, Palestinian bombardment across the Israel-Lebanon border, and Syrian installation of surface-to-air missiles in the Bekaa valley predisposed Israel to an adventure.

Israel's invasion of Lebanon up to Beirut in June 1982, in advance of Lebanon's scheduled 1982 presidential election, certainly changed the Lebanese scene, but mostly against Israel's interests. Israel achieved the expulsion of Arafat and his PLO fighters from Beirut and degradation of Palestinian significance in Lebanon. However, although Israel also dealt a military blow to Syria, eliminating the surface-to-air missile batteries and crippling the Syrian air force, subsequent events proceeded in Syria's favor. For Damascus, Bashir Jumayyil's September 1982 election as president with Sunni and Shi'a support, reflecting Muslim disenchantment with the Palestinians and Bashir's distancing of himself from the Israelis, was intolerable. Bashir would divorce Lebanon from Syria, and his cunning only made him a greater menace. Bashir was assassinated before he could take office, precluding any chance of a Lebanese order favorable to Israel. Members of Bashir's LF went on a rampage in the Sabra and Shatila Palestinian refugee camps, massacring hundreds of Palestinians and others in an area under Israeli control. Israel was blamed and had to retreat from western Beirut under international opprobrium.

The Lebanese parliament elected Bashir's older brother Amin to the presidency, and Amin turned to the Americans. The United States mobilized a multinational force, including American marines, to buttress Lebanese state authority in western Beirut, but the United States and Amin Jumayyil ran into trouble through 1983. Amin refused to make political concessions to the non-Christians, in particular spurning Nabih Birri's Shi'a Amal movement (founded by Musa Sadr in 1974). This assisted the Syrians in reasserting their influence among Muslims and Druze. Damascus was thus able to block implementation of a May 17, 1983, Lebanese-Israeli agreement, laboriously brokered by the United States, for a conditional Israeli withdrawal.

In September 1983, the Israelis pulled out of the Shuf hills above Beirut, without coordination with the resuscitated Lebanese government and army. Druze forces under Walid Jumblat moved against Christian militiamen who had infiltrated the area, in the process expelling 150,000 Christians. Jumblat also joined the Syrians against the US presence. Lebanese Muslims and Druze viewed the United States as supporting Amin Jumayyil's resistance to reform, while Syria and its Soviet backers determined to remove the "NATO base" in Beirut. The Ronald Reagan administration, unwilling to commit more troops, fell back on naval bombardment, and on October 23, 1983, Shi'a suicide truck bombers killed 241 US marines and 60 French soldiers in their Beirut compounds. In February 1984, Shi'a militias overran western Beirut, the Lebanese army again split, and Amin Jumayyil's regime was reduced to the Christian heartland. The US-led multinational force pulled out, and Lebanon returned to decomposition, with the Israelis, Palestinians, and Christians in disarray vis-à-vis the surges of the Syrians, Shi'as, and Druze. Lebanon's Sunnis were in a pathetic situation: the leading component of the Islamic bloc before 1975, they exchanged subjection to the PLO for subjection to Shi'a and Druze militia bosses in the early 1980s.

After September 1983, the Israelis dug in south of the Awali River and across the southern Bekaa valley. This convinced the Shi'as, who had welcomed Israel's defeat of the PLO, that Israel had in mind permanent occupation of southern Lebanon and confiscation of the Litani River waters. Israeli obstinacy interacted disastrously with Shi'a assertiveness. Through late 1983 and 1984, resistance and repression inflated sectarian religious zeal already well fueled by Iran's new Shi'a Islamic revolutionary regime. Various radical tendencies combined to form Hizballah, which in February 1985 announced its arrival with a manifesto against Israel and in favor of an Iranian-style Islamic state. By June 1985, when the Israelis retreated from most of southern Lebanon to a new border buffer zone south of the Litani River, Israel had acquired a new enemy more tenacious than the PLO.

Elsewhere in Lebanon, the remainder of Amin Jumayyil's presidential term, up to late 1988, was characterized by paralysis. The Syrian recovery stalled in the face of Christian stiffening, intrusion by Iran and Iraq, and local conflicts among Lebanese Muslims and Palestinians. Syria's Hafiz al-Asad, who privately viewed the Israeli expulsion of Arafat from Lebanon as positive and completed the job by removing the PLO from Tripoli in November 1983, still feared Palestinian autonomy. Through the mid-1980s, he supported the Shi'a Amal movement in its sieges of Palestinian camps in Beirut and Sidon. Residual

Palestinian forces, no longer a deciding factor in Lebanon, received a dribble of aid from the Christian LF, the Druze, and Hizballah, who all wished for more freedom vis-à-vis Damascus. The ascent of the Shi'a community shuddered to a halt as Amal and Hizballah competed viciously for supremacy. Anarchy engulfed western Beirut, and militants linked to Hizballah and Iran kidnapped Westerners.

After 1985, the major issue in Lebanon was Syria's aspiration for hegemony and blockage of that aspiration by the Christian leadership in eastern Beirut. The Maronite "canton" housed the Lebanese presidency, the high command and heavy weaponry of the army, and the LF, Lebanon's largest militia. Its existence also buttressed its smaller Druze counterpart in the Shuf hills. In the late 1980s, Saddam Hussein of Iraq, looking for revenge against Syria for its alliance with Iran in the Iran-Iraq War, shipped arms to both the LF and the army command. The weaknesses of the canton included its multiheaded leadership and its unpopularity, even among its 800,000 inhabitants, after the ruinous hostilities of 1982 to 1985 brought destitution and the collapse of the Lebanese currency. President Amin Jumayyil and the Maronite patriarchate prevented the mutual jealousies of the militia and army from getting out of hand, but the end of Amin's term in 1988 brought a crisis.

Christian leaders refused a presidential candidate backed by Syria and the United States, which had come to view Ba'thist Syria as a stabilizing force. At the last moment, President Jumayyil reluctantly appointed army commander Michel Aoun as prime minister with executive power until presidential elections could be held. Damascus and Sunni prime minister Salim al-Huss rejected this move, leaving Lebanon with two governments. Aoun had romantic nationalist sentiments and conceived an overthrow of militias, cantons, and foreign occupations in favor of restored state legitimacy, spearheaded by his army brigades. This was highly popular, and Aoun boasted a following among Shi'as and Sunnis as well as Maronites. It also guaranteed collisions with the Syrians, the Druze, and, inside eastern Beirut, the LF militia.

In March 1989, General Aoun launched a "war of liberation" against Syrian forces. This comprised destructive artillery exchanges in which the Syrians had the advantage. Aoun hoped to precipitate international intervention. He gained some Arab sympathy and embarrassed Hafiz al-Asad but also alienated the United States, which saw him as a threat to stability in the region. International intervention, therefore, was not to Aoun's benefit. The United States and the Arab states promoted the Ta'if gathering of Lebanese parliamentarians in October 1989, which agreed on constitutional adjustments, a presidential election, and Syrian assistance to extend the authority of the new regime. The Lebanese deputies elected Rene Mu'awad president on November 5. Mu'awad, however, was not to Syria's taste. He was assassinated three weeks later, whereupon parliament reconvened in the Bekaa and voted for Syria's candidate, Ilyas Hrawi.

Only General Aoun now stood in the way of Syrian command of Lebanon. The LF militia longed to be rid of the general and colluded with Damascus. In February 1990, Aoun went to war with the LF in eastern Beirut and Mount Lebanon, a fight that split and weakened the Maronites. In a supreme irony, Asad's bitter foe Saddam Hussein enabled Syria to administer the coup de grâce. After Saddam invaded Kuwait in August 1990, the United States felt it needed Syria in the coalition against Iraq. In exchange for support, Asad obtained an American green light to suppress Aoun, and the Syrian army overran the Ba'abda presidential palace on October 13, 1990. Aoun proceeded to the French embassy and exile in France, and Lebanon fell under Syrian Ba'thist hegemony.

1991–2004

The Syrian regime did not waste time tightening its hold on Lebanon. In 1991, all Lebanese militias apart from Hizballah disbanded, and the Lebanese army began reorganizing under Syrian supervision and its amenable new Maronite commander, Emile Lahoud. The Treaty of Brotherhood, Cooperation, and Coordination, signed on May 22, 1991, provided for deep Syrian intrusion into Lebanese policy making. It established a semifederal Higher Council between the two countries, with committees for prime ministerial coordination, foreign affairs, security, and economic policy. A Defense and Security Pact followed, banning any activity "in all military, security, political, and information fields that might endanger or cause threats to the other country." All American hostages held in Lebanon were released, and Palestinian militants in Sidon and Tyre were limited to the refugee camps, with subjection to Syrian supremacy. Peace settled over the country, apart from Hizballah's contest with Israel.

Lebanon's government and post-Ta'if parliament were packed with Syria's allies and clients. Parliamentary elections in 1992 and 1996 produced results predetermined by gerrymandering and systematic abuses. The LF found itself marginalized, and when its leader, Samir Ja'ja', declined to join the regime, he was charged with various crimes and imprisoned in the basement of the Ministry of Defense. From 1992 on, the Syrians operated through an executive troika of President Ilyas Hrawi, Prime Minister Rafik Hariri, and Speaker of Parliament Nabih Birri, who squabbled with one another while Hariri worked on economic reconstruction, vital for the stability of Syrian hegemony. Hafiz al-Asad, backed by the Lebanese regime, ignored the Ta'if stipulation for a 1992 redeployment of Syrian forces away from Beirut.

In the late 1990s, Asad patronized domination of Lebanon by a Syrian-style security machine under Emile Lahoud, elevated from the army command to the presidency in 1998. Lahoud, together with the chief of Syrian military intelligence in Lebanon, ran the security machine on behalf of Damascus, closely constraining Hariri, who returned as prime minister in 2000 after spending the first two years of Lahoud's term in opposition. Syria's Alawite overlords found it difficult to circumvent Hariri, especially after his parliamentary electoral gains in 2000, but suspected his associations with the West, Saudi Arabia, and "old guard" personalities inside the Syrian regime. The distrust intensified when Bashar al-Asad took over as Syrian president after the death of his father. Unlike his father, who floated above the Lebanese arena, Bashar descended into the fray. While preserving correct relations with Hariri, he favored Lahoud and developed a personal rapport with Hizballah secretary-general Hassan Nasrallah.

The presidential change in Syria coincided with Israel's May 2000 abandonment of its "security zone" in southern Lebanon under Hizballah pressure. The legacy for Syrian hegemony was ambiguous. On the one hand, through the 1990s Israeli bombardments helped to radicalize the Shi'a community to a point where it was hard to imagine Shi'a give-and-take with anyone, including the rest of Lebanon. Syria could therefore still rely on the Shi'as in any problems with Hariri and others. To ensure a common front, in 1996 Syria forced Hizballah and Amal together into a single parliamentary bloc. Despite the friction between the two organizations, general Shi'a resentment encouraged cooperation. Shi'as felt that the Ta'if adjustment of parliamentary seating was only an initial step toward the 40 or more deputies they were worth in the 128-member chamber.

Syria and Hizballah also stirred a fresh border grievance against Israel to justify Hizballah's keeping its weapons and persisting with "resistance." They claimed that a corner of the Israeli-occupied Golan Heights adjacent to Lebanon, the Shebaa Farms, was really Lebanese, and so Israeli withdrawal was incomplete. The United Nations, which certified Israel's May 2000 withdrawal as fulfilling Security Council Resolution 425 of 1978, was unimpressed, defining the Shebaa Farms as Syrian territory. The United Nations required that Syria confirm Lebanese sovereignty in writing, which the Syrians avoided doing. Nonetheless, the Lebanese government endorsed the claim, thereby also endorsing Hizballah as a private army with command of the border zone facing Israel. Continued trouble with Israel in turn assisted continued Syrian command of Lebanon.

Against all this, the Israeli withdrawal encouraged Lebanese questioning of Syrian hegemony. The Syrian-Lebanese security machine that ran the country and circumscribed Prime Minister Hariri after 2000 was not just a repressive apparatus unprecedented in Lebanon's modern history but also a racketeering combine that siphoned enormous sums, perhaps hundreds of millions of dollars, out of the Lebanese economy. Druze and Sunni voices joined Christian discontent, and Druze leader Walid Jumblat welcomed Maronite patriarch Nasrallah Sfeir, a persistent critic of Damascus, to the Shuf in August 2001. Bashar al-Asad managed to keep the lid on the situation, assisted by continued US indulgence of Syria's role in Lebanon, until the George W. Bush administration turned against him after March 2003 because of his encouragement of attacks on US forces in Iraq. This preceded the final months of President Lahoud's six-year term in 2004, when Hariri and Jumblat, backed by the United States and France, expressed their hostility to an unconstitutional extension.

2004–2011

Syria's president was not to be deterred. He wanted Lahoud, disliked Hariri, and felt the United States was too bogged down in Iraq to take a stand. His security chiefs opposed any change that might disturb their racketeering in Lebanon. Deploying heavy intimidation toward the Lebanese, in late August 2004 he compelled Hariri to assemble the Lebanese parliament to give Lahoud three extra years, sparking an extended crisis. The United States and France mobilized the UN Security Council to pass Resolution 1559 ordering the Syrian army out of Lebanon and demanding dissolution of remaining militias, meaning Hizballah. Hariri, alienated from Lahoud and Bashar al-Asad, worked to consolidate a Lebanese majority against Syria in scheduled May 2005 parliamentary elections. On February 14, 2005, Hariri and twenty-two others were killed in a massive explosion in central Beirut. Subsequent competitive demonstrations exposed a dangerous rift in Lebanese society. On March 8, Hizballah brought out half a million to emphasize Shi'a existence and favor Syria. On March 14, 1 million Sunnis, Christians, and Druze gathered to remember Hariri and condemn Syria, widely blamed for the assassination. In April 2005, Bashar bowed to the international community, and Syrian uniformed forces departed Lebanon, ending a presence of three decades.

Syria's formal withdrawal in the aftermath of the Hariri assassination terminated Syrian hegemony in an unexpected manner. Syria, however, retained its allies and exerted influence through intelligence personnel and infiltration of weaponry across the border, particularly among Hizballah, radical Palestinian organizations, and Lebanese Sunni Islamists. The Iranian leadership declared that it was in "one trench" with Bashar al-Asad. In April 2005, UN Security Council Resolution 1595 established the international organization's first-ever murder inquiry to identify Hariri's assassins. Subsequent investigation pointed to the Syrian-Lebanese security machine and the inner recesses of the Syrian regime.

While the murder investigation ground on, accompanied by further killings of anti-Syrian personalities, Lebanese politics took new twists. General Michel Aoun returned from exile in May 2005 and broke with Hariri's son Saad and Walid Jumblat over their unwillingness to endorse him for the presidency. The May–June parliamentary elections gave the Hariri-Jumblat camp a majority in parliament (72 seats out of 128), but Aoun took the Maronite heartland (21 seats). Together with the Amal-Hizballah bloc and its non-Shi'a clients (35 seats), Aoun blocked the "new majority" drive to remove President Lahoud. In February 2006, Aoun reached an understanding with Hizballah that reflected Maronite and Shi'a suspicions of the Sunni Hariri bloc and its Saudi backers. New prime minister Fuad Siniora, from the new majority, faced a daunting task in dealing with Aoun and Hizballah, the latter entrenched inside his government. Syria's ruling clique maneuvered vengefully in the background, looking to smash the resurgent Lebanese autonomy backed by the United States and France.

On July 12, 2006, Hizballah raided across the Israel-Lebanon border, kidnapping two Israeli soldiers and killing three in an unprecedented action. Hizballah claimed that this was to compel release of Lebanese and Palestinian prisoners. However, it bore the signs of a bid by the Hizballah-Syria-Iran coalition to turn the tables on opponents inside and outside Lebanon—to rescue Ba'thist Syria, pivot of the coalition, from the Hariri murder inquiry and to enable an effective coup d'état by Hizballah against the new majority commanding the Lebanese government. It stretches credulity to suppose that Hizballah did not coordinate with its senior partners in an operation guaranteed to bring a large-scale Israeli response. In the six years after Israel's withdrawal to the international boundary in 2000, Syria and Iran provided Hizballah with up to 15,000 rockets of various calibers, and the party's armed wing turned southern Lebanon into a fortress where the Lebanese state and army had no sway. In 2006, Hizballah was ready to give Israel a military surprise.

Over five weeks, Israel used aerial bombardment and, later, hesitant ground penetration to degrade Hizballah, causing devastation and around 1,000 deaths in the Shi'a areas of Lebanon. Hizballah sent a steady shower of missiles into Israel until the cease-fire and could claim success simply by maintaining itself against a massively larger regular army.

The balance after the August 14 UN-sponsored cease-fire was ambiguous. Hizballah had to accept Lebanese army deployment to the border, stiffened by a more robust UN force. The Lebanese army thus appeared in areas from which it had been absent for decades. UN Security Council Resolution 1701 fingered Hizballah for initiating hostilities and indicated the need to monitor the Syria-Lebanon border. On the other hand, Hizballah could simply conceal weaponry, and Iran supplied cash for Hizballah-led civilian reconstruction, challenging the Lebanese state. Lebanon's Shi'as clustered around Hizballah, but resentment of Hizballah's seizure of decision making for war and peace dominated elsewhere.

Henceforth, Lebanon split between two political camps, named for the demonstrations of March 2005: the anti-Syrian March 14 new majority, led by Saad Hariri and Walid Jumblat, and the March 8 bloc of Hizballah, Amal, and the Aounists, aligned with Syria and Iran. Each bloc was cross sectarian but with a basic divide of Sunni and Druze (March 14) versus Shi'as (March 8), with Christians fragmented. In November 2006, pro-Syrian ministers resigned from the government to stop endorsement of the UN protocol for a mixed international-Lebanese tribunal to prosecute those responsible for the Hariri murder and associated killings. The government, however, retained its two-thirds quorum, passed the protocol, and persevered as a March 14 rump. The March 8 camp declared it illegitimate and began a street campaign against it.

Prime Minister Siniora's rump cabinet endured from November 2006 until May 2008. It survived more murders of March 14 parliamentarians; an uprising of Sunni Islamists, probably inspired by Syrian military intelligence, in the Nahr al-Bared Palestinian refugee camp near Tripoli; and a six-month vacuum in the Lebanese presidency after Emile Lahoud finally left office in November 2007. The UN Security Council bypassed the paralyzed Lebanese parliament and unilaterally established the special tribunal for Lebanon in June 2007. Because the March 8 camp blocked all March 14 civilian candidates for the presidency, the latter bloc gave its reluctant support to army commander Michel Suleiman. Hizballah, which had positive relations with Suleiman, did not oppose him. The March 8 camp, however, demanded veto power in a new national unity government in exchange for allowing parliament to hold a presidential electoral session. The impasse only ended with violence in May 2008. Hizballah, Amal, and the Syrian Social

Nationalists overran mainly Sunni western Beirut after the government tried to shut down Hizballah's illicit communications system, and the Arab League brokered a political compromise in Doha. Suleiman became president, and March 8 received its blocking capability in a new coalition cabinet under Fuad Siniora.

A hiatus ensued in the run-up to the June 2009 parliamentary elections. Nothing further emerged from the Hariri murder inquiry, although the special tribunal came into physical existence in March 2009. Indictments faded into a hazy future, which demoralized March 14 and spurred March 8 into a belligerent electoral posture. Hizballah's use of "resistance" weaponry against other Lebanese in May 2008 hung over everyone, and the Aounists hoped small Christian constituencies from the resuscitated 1960 electoral law would facilitate gains. March 14, however, held fast in the elections; Sunnis mobilized, and enough Christians opposed Aoun to stop him advancing. Results replicated the outgoing parliament: seventy-one seats for March 14 and fifty-seven for March 8, with Hizballah retaining its command of the Shi'a.

Saad Hariri received the commission to form a government, but Walid Jumblat decided to break with March 14 and make up with Syria's allies. Jumblat drew his conclusions from "engagement" of the Syrian regime by new US president Barack Obama, lost hope in the special tribunal, and looked to fortify his position by balancing between March 14 and March 8. His defection gutted the election result. Saad could only stabilize a coalition cabinet by going to Damascus to meet Bashar al-Asad. It was an abject obeisance and availed him little. Through 2010 the coalition proved predictably useless for anything beyond administrative routine. Meanwhile the special tribunal at last looked like it would produce indictments in the Hariri case, with Hizballah members suspected of implementing the murder. Hizballah and Syria demanded that Saad Hariri disown the tribunal, which he refused to do. Consequently, in January 2011 March 8 pulled out of the coalition. In June 2011, nominated by Hizballah, Aoun, and Jumblat, Tripoli Sunni politician and businessman Najib Miqati acquired a parliamentary majority for a government subordinate to Hizballah.

Lebanon and the Syrian Uprising

Lebanon was never a candidate for an upheaval such as those that toppled the autocrats of Tunisia and Egypt in early 2011. Lebanon already featured the pluralism that the crowds in Tunis and Cairo sought to attain. Its sectarian compartments and lack of a majority population—together unique in the Middle East—also guaranteed that no national crowd could be mobilized, just competing crowds with competing agendas. Nonetheless, the country swiftly and completely became hostage to the uprising in neighboring Syria after March 2011, because the Syrian regime and opposition plugged into Lebanon's March 8 and March 14 camps, respectively.

Whichever way the struggle between Bashar al-Asad and a large part of Syria's population developed, it would determine power in Lebanon. Hizballah, with four of its members indicted by the special tribunal in June 2011, was suddenly on the defensive, a dramatic turn from tipping over Saad Hariri only a few months before. If Bashar fell, the central cog in the Hizballah-Syria-Iran alignment would be gone, and Hizballah would be isolated. Party chief Nasrallah backed repression in Syria. Conversely, Bashar's fall and a Sunni takeover in Damascus would greatly boost the Sunni and Christian March 14 leaders; his survival would condemn them to constriction. Druze leader Walid Jumblat returned to his former proclivities. He denounced regime atrocities in Syria and backed regime change there, though he stopped short of derailing the Miqati government. Prime Minister Miqati and President Suleiman, caught in opposing headlights, declared official Lebanon's abstention from the whole affair. Many feared that disintegration of Syria might also tear Lebanon apart.

The Sunni-Shi'a cauldron bubbled, but leaders of both communities worked to keep a lid on it. Tension boiled over between Sunnis and Alawites, the community of the Asads, in Sunni-majority Tripoli, where sporadic clashes caused about sixty deaths between June 2011 and August 2012. The presence of Syrian refugees, increasing in number from about 8,000 in June 2011 to around 90,000 in August 2012, together with Free Syrian Army elements linked with local Sunnis, also raised the temperature. Rudderless while awaiting an outcome in Syria, the Lebanese government floundered into little turf conflicts. Aounist Christians clashed with their Shi'a allies over jobs in the electricity sector, and their followers burned tires and blocked roads. Nonetheless, the country had avoided a breakdown by early 2013, and commerce continued to function.

Events quickened in summer 2012, while the Syrian regime tried to smash the armed opposition in Damascus and Aleppo. President Suleiman, perhaps sensing that Bashar was in trouble and looking to his own legacy, became more assertive, protesting Syrian regime shelling into Lebanese territory and dismissing Syrian claims about Lebanese supplying weapons to the Syrian opposition. In early August Lebanese security services caught former minister Michel Samaha, a Maronite adviser to Bashar al-Asad, redhanded in a plot with Syrian intelligence to murder Christian and Sunni personalities and to plant bombs to ignite sectarian strife in northern Lebanon. The damning evidence was a real blow to the pro-Bashar March 8 camp, with Hizballah already embarrassed by its powerlessness regarding Shi'as abducted in northern Syria. Hizballah indicated its frustration by standing back from kidnappings of Syrians in Shi'a areas in mid-August 2012, but undermining a government that it had created made no sense. Also, if Bashar eventually went down with Hizballah and Iran was tarred by association with him, how many Shi'as would want to follow the party into communal siege?

FOREIGN POLICY

Lebanon matters. The country is located in the core of the Arab world, and Mount Lebanon is the dominant topographic feature of both the coast of the Levant and the land bridge between Eurasia and Africa. The external associations of each of Lebanon's three "great" communities—the Maronites with France and the West, the Sunnis with major Arab states, and the Shi'as with Iran—compound the strategic significance of the mountain. Modern geopolitical fragmentation in the Levant gives the strategic significance special salience. Lebanon offers access to the Arab-Israeli front line and overshadows the Syrian capital. Beyond the Levant, the Lebanese people, with their formidable technical and commercial dexterity and their far-flung diaspora, represent a regional and global human resource. No other Arab country has a reach that remotely compares with the worldwide presence, wealth, and influence of perhaps 10 million overseas Lebanese. Even in its region, Lebanon's smallness is deceptive—the fortunes of democratic politics, a free media, and economic liberalism in Beirut reverberate throughout the Middle East.

The variety of Lebanon's external connections and the salience of Lebanon for external powers have meant that the country's stability has been constantly at risk. Lebanese governments have often preferred to avoid strong foreign alignments, within or beyond the Arab world. Deviation from this approach has invariably brought trouble, either because of strong opposition within one or more of the country's major communities or because of the hostility of significant external powers exercised through their Lebanese sympathizers. In the 1950s, President Chamoun's relations with the West were suspect to many Muslims, and Egypt's influence on Muslims was in turn suspect to most Christians. After 1967, regime compromises with the Palestinians led Christians to arm themselves, and Maronite relations with Israel and Iraq later contributed to Syria's determination to manipulate its local allies to achieve hegemony. After 1985, Hizballah's ties to revolutionary Iran stimulated a variety of counterpressures on Lebanon from the United States, Israel, and Syria. Lebanese regime leaders of the 1990s had no choice but to follow Damascus in foreign policy, but subservience rankled for much of the public. After 2000, the mounting Christian, Sunni, and Druze alienation from Ba'thist Syria was bound to bring a day of reckoning. The reckoning came in 2005, but Syria and Iran were able to operate through the Shi'as to encourage a schism over the convergence of the majority in the new Lebanese government with the United States and France.

As regards Arab-Israeli affairs, Lebanese governments paid lip service to anti-Israeli stances through the 1950s and 1960s but had little taste for activism. Israeli transgressions of Lebanese territory from the 1970s on, however, hardened Lebanese attitudes. Even many Christians viewed Israel as partly responsible for Lebanon's Palestinian problem, for the 1983–1984 Christian disasters in the Shuf hills, and for Shi'a radicalism. In the 1990s, most Lebanese wanted calm on their southern border and resented being coerced by Damascus into serving as Syria's surrogate front line, but they felt little impetus toward an Israeli-Lebanese peace treaty. Syrian pressure to ensure that Lebanon did not seek to emulate the PLO and Jordan in making a separate deal with the Israelis was really unnecessary. In 2006, Walid Jumblat spoke for the non-Shi'a majority when he favored Lebanese army deployment along the border and Hizballah disarmament, with application of the 1949 Lebanese-Israeli armistice agreement, not a formal peace, as long as conditions did not permit a general Arab-Israeli settlement.

Lebanon's principal foreign policy issue in the early twenty-first century stemmed from its principal domestic issue—the Lebanese state's lack of a monopoly of force on much of Lebanese territory. Lebanon could pass as a proper territorial state from independence in 1943 until the early 1970s. Thereafter, for one-third of a century, the procession of sectarian cantons, foreign occupations, and Syrian hegemony meant that Lebanon was simply a territorial shell within which the Lebanese regime was a subordinate actor. The Lebanese state reasserted itself in 2005, but its authority remained partial, dependent on backing from the international community. Syria's grudging military evacuation enabled Lebanon to restore state command of the north and the Bekaa valley, but Syrian aid to various parties and "security islands" continued. Apart from Hizballah's grip on southern Lebanon, these included the Ain al-Helwe Palestinian refugee camp in Sidon, which hosted Palestinian and Lebanese Sunni extremists, and Palestinian outposts on the Syrian border. Ba'thist Syria could also liaise with the Shi'a Amal movement, Hizballah's unenthusiastic "partner," as well as the Maronite Franjiyahs of Zgharta and disaffected Sunni and Druze personalities. In December 2008, the discontented General Aoun, who led the largest Christian parliamentary bloc and gave cross-sectarian cover to Hizballah's private army, made a reconciliation visit to Syria, his old enemy.

Bashar al-Asad's regime girded itself with its Lebanese allies to confront the UN Security Council, mobilized by the United States, France, and Britain to buttress Lebanon's territorial integrity. Security Council Resolution 1559 of September 2004, which required Lebanese state monopoly of force, led to Resolution 1680 of May 2006 "strongly encouraging" Syria to establish diplomatic relations with Lebanon. The novel feature was the Lebanese official demand for embassies, putting aside reluctance to challenge Damascus. The Syrian leadership maintained that diplomatic relations were superfluous between "sister states," but by 2008 Syria had no choice but to concede the embassies.

In 2005, Prime Minister Fuad Siniora, heading a government with an anti-Syrian regime majority deriving from Lebanon's first free parliamentary elections since 1972, returned Lebanon to an international credibility unknown since the 1960s. Within the constraints of its Western-Arab and Muslim-Christian dualities, Lebanon had played an active role in international affairs from the 1940s to the 1960s. It was a founding member of both the United Nations and the Arab League and had been a respected partner of the conservative, Western-oriented group of Arab states, including the Arabian Peninsula monarchies, Jordan, and Morocco.

The Hariri murder affair and the 2006 Israeli-Hizballah fighting led to a level of international intervention in the country unique in the world—the UN murder inquiry and the special tribunal, the enlarged UN Interim Force in Lebanon, the UN Border Assessment Team, and special UN envoys to report on implementation of Security Council Resolutions 1559 and 1701, all in addition to the older UN Truce Supervision Organization for the 1949 armistice and the UN Relief and Works Organization for the Palestinian refugees.

Prime Minister Siniora did his best to cement relations with the US administration, which increased aid to the Lebanese army. He faced Shi'a suspicion of US support for Israel. Lebanon's new majority also had to cope after May 2007 with French president Nicolas Sarkozy's flirtation with Damascus, as well as with uncertain support from Saudi Arabia and Egypt, while Iran and Syria underwrote the opposition. Siniora scored impressive international financial promises at the Paris III donors' conference for Lebanon in January 2007, but with delivery conditional on reforms.

New turns of the wheel in Lebanon's external environment could suddenly tip the domestic balance. US overtures to Bashar al-Asad in 2009–2010 destroyed the Lebanese domestic position of Siniora, Saad Hariri, and the pro-Western camp. The Syrian uprising of 2011–2012 threw everything into uncertainty and held out the prospect of a stunning reversal.

Looking ahead, Lebanon sits on multiple fault lines—Sunni/Shi'a, Arab/Iranian, Arab/Israeli, Christian/Muslim, and Western/Islamic. The domestic and international juggling operations required to secure decent pluralist politics for the long term are Sisyphean tasks, and the chances of success or failure to a large degree depend on events beyond Lebanon.

BIBLIOGRAPHY

For Lebanon's history before 1920, the best starting point remains Kamal Salibi, who offers surveys grounded in Arabic sources. These include *The Modern History of Lebanon* (New York: Praeger Publishers, 1965) and *A House of Many Mansions: The History of Lebanon Reconsidered* (London: I. B. Tauris, 1988). Abdul-Rahim Abu Husayn gives insights into the sixteenth and seventeenth centuries in *The View from Istanbul: Ottoman Lebanon and the Druze Emirate* (London: I. B. Tauris, 2004). Ilya Harik's *Politics and Change in a Traditional Society: Lebanon 1711–1845* (Princeton, NJ: Princeton University Press, 1968); Richard van Leeuwen's *Notables and Clergy in Mount Lebanon: The Khazin Sheikhs and the Maronite Church* (Leiden: E. J. Brill, 1994); and Stefan Winter's *The Shi'ites of Lebanon Under Ottoman Rule, 1516–1788* (Cambridge: Cambridge University Press, 2010) provide coverage of communal developments into the eighteenth century.

Modern Lebanon's emergence from the 1840s on is well covered. Cesar Farah's *The Politics of Interventionism in Ottoman Lebanon, 1830–1861* (London: I. B. Tauris, 2000) and Leila Fawaz's *An Occasion for War: Civil Conflict in Lebanon and Damascus, 1860* (London: I. B. Tauris, 1994) dissect the sectarian turbulence of the mid-nineteenth century. Fawaz also supplies urban social context in *Merchants and Migrants in Nineteenth-Century Beirut* (Cambridge, MA: Harvard University Press, 1983). Engin Akarli's *The Long Peace: Ottoman Lebanon, 1861–1920* (Los Angeles: University of California Press, 1993) analyzes the autonomous province of Mount Lebanon.

Lebanon's transition from French mandatory rule after 1920 to independence after 1943 has received careful attention. Kais Firro and Raghid al-Solh investigate the ideological underpinnings of modern Lebanon in *Inventing Lebanon: Nationalism and the State Under the Mandate* (London: I. B. Tauris, 2003) and *Lebanon and Arabism: National Identity and State Formation* (London: I. B. Tauris, 2004), respectively. These supplement Meir Zamir's two-volume study of Lebanon, *The Formation of Modern Lebanon* (London: Croom Helm, 1985) and *Lebanon's Quest: The Road to Statehood, 1926–39* (London: I. B. Tauris, 1997).

Treatment of Lebanon's progression through the 1950s and 1960s toward breakdown in the mid-1970s is fragmented. An overview benefiting from the academic perspectives of the post–Cold War era is lacking. Samir Khalaf dissects Lebanese integration of representative politics with sectarian influences and patronage networks in *Lebanon's Predicament* (New York: Columbia University Press, 1987), and Wade Goria reviews political personalities in *Sovereignty and Leadership in Lebanon, 1943–76* (London: Ithaca Press, 1986). Studies of the Bishara al-Khoury and Camille Chamoun presidencies (1943–1958) include Eyal Zisser's *Lebanon: The Challenge of Independence* (London: I. B. Tauris, 2000) and Caroline Attié's *Struggle in the Levant: Lebanon in the 1950s* (London: I. B. Tauris, 2004). Nasser Kalawoun discusses Lebanon's interaction with Gamal Abdel Nasser's Egypt in *The Struggle for Lebanon: A Modern History of Lebanese-Egyptian Relations* (London: I. B. Tauris, 2000). The best analysis of Lebanon's difficulties after the 1967 Arab-Israeli War is Farid el-Khazen's *The Breakdown of the State in Lebanon, 1967–1976* (Cambridge, MA: Harvard University Press, 2000).

For the economic and social circumstances of late-twentieth-century Lebanon, consult Caroline Gate's *The Merchant Republic of Lebanon: Rise of an Open Economy* (London: I. B. Tauris, 1998) and Michael Johnson's *All Honourable Men: The Social Origins of War in Lebanon* (London: I. B. Tauris, 2001). Kamal Dib examines the social-economic interface in his *Warlords and Merchants: The Lebanese Business and Political Establishment* (London: Ithaca Press, 2004), while Latif Abul Husn's *The Lebanese Conflict: Looking Inward* (Boulder, CO: Lynne Rienner, 1998) interprets communal affairs and interactions.

The modern emergence of the Shi'as is covered in Fouad Ajami's *The Vanished Imam: Musa al-Sadr and the Shi'a of Lebanon* (Ithaca, NY: Cornell University Press, 1985); Majid Halawi's *A Lebanon Defied: Musa al-Sadr and the Shi'a Community* (Boulder, CO: Westview Press, 1992); and Augustus Richard Norton's *Amal and the Shi'a: Struggle for the Soul of Lebanon* (Austin: University of Texas Press, 1987). Roshanack Shaery-Eisenlohr, *Shi'ite Lebanon: Transnational Religion and the Making of National Identities* (New York: Columbia University Press, 2008), interprets Shi'a outlooks. On the Druze, Robert Brenton Bett's *The Druze* (New Haven, CT: Yale University Press, 1988) and Fuad Khuri's *Being a Druze* (London: Druze Heritage Foundation, 2004) deserve note. In contrast, the Maronite and Sunni communities have not received adequate attention in the English-language literature since Michael Johnson's *Class and Client in Beirut: The Sunni Muslim Community and the Lebanese State, 1840–1985* (London: Ithaca Press, 1986).

Much has been written about the war period from 1975 to 1990. See Samir Kassir's *La guere du Liban: De la dissension nationale au conflit régional, 1975–1982* (Paris: Karthala, 1994) and Itamar Rabinovich's *The War for Lebanon, 1970–1983* (Ithaca, NY: Cornell University Press, 1984). Theodor Hanf's *Co-existence in Wartime Lebanon: Death of a State and Birth of a Nation* (London: I. B. Tauris, 1993) provides an encyclopedic overview. William Harris's *New Face of Lebanon* (Princeton, NJ: Markus Wiener, 2006) and Elie Salem's *Violence and Diplomacy in Lebanon: The Troubled Years, 1982–1988* (London: I. B. Tauris, 1995) concentrate on the 1980s.

Inevitably, analysis of post-1990 trends remains tentative. In Barry Rubin, ed., *Lebanon: Liberation, Conflict, and Crisis* (New York: Palgrave Macmillan, 2009), the chapter authors contribute a multifaceted survey. Nicholas Blanford gives the Hariri story in *Killing Mr. Lebanon: The Assassination of Rafik Hariri and Its Impact on the Middle East* (London: I. B. Tauris, 2006). Oren Barak assesses the military in *The Lebanese Army: A National Institution in a Divided Society* (Albany: State University of New York Press, 2009). Nizar Hamzeh's *In the Path of Hizballah* (Syracuse, NY: Syracuse University Press, 2004) and Nicholas Blanford's *Warriors of God: Inside Hezbollah's Thirty-Year Struggle Against Israel* (New York: Random House, 2011) provide data on Lebanon's "state within the state." Michael Young's *The Ghosts of Martyr's Square: An Eyewitness Account of Lebanon's Life Struggle* (New York: Simon & Schuster, 2010) reviews the half decade after the 2005 Hariri murder.

Several English-language websites may be mentioned. LebWeb (www.lebweb.com) is the best Internet guide. It includes links to Lebanese government sites and political factions, as well as Lebanon's Arabic newspapers, for example, *An Nahar* (centrist) and *Assafir* (leftist/Arabist). Lebanonwire (www.lebanonwire.com) offers a worthwhile subscriber service. For current affairs in English, consult Now Lebanon (www.nowlebanon.com), Beirut's *Daily Star* newspaper (www.dailystar.com.lb), and Naharnet (www.naharnet.com). For economic updates, it is hard to beat the monthly Lebanon country report of the Economist Intelligence Unit (www.eiu.com).

9

SYRIAN ARAB REPUBLIC

Raymond Hinnebusch and David W. Lesch

HISTORICAL BACKGROUND

Syria could genuinely be called a crossroads of history because of the numerous civilizations and religions that have established themselves in this ancient territory. Damascus, the capital of the Syrian Arab Republic, is one of the oldest continually inhabited cities in the world. But the modern identification of Syria as an Arab and Muslim territory began with the seventh-century Muslim conquest. Under the Umayyad caliphate founded in Damascus in 661, Syria was the center of a vast Arab empire. Subsequently it became a province of successive Muslim empires ruled from Baghdad or Cairo and finally, under the Ottomans, from Istanbul.

Syria became extremely important to the Ottoman sultan as one of the Arab territories that remained under real Ottoman control until World War I. As Ottoman power began to decline in the eighteenth and nineteenth centuries, a new class emerged in Syria of urban notables who functioned as local authorities and intermediaries with Ottoman officials. These notables became important political players in Syria for the remainder of the nineteenth century and well into the twentieth. The Arab Muslim majority in Syria, already resentful of the privileges the minority Christians in the area received from sympathetic European powers, avidly supported the pan-Islamism espoused by Ottoman Sultan Abd al-Hamid II. In return, the Sublime Porte assisted in the development of Syria's agricultural and commercial sectors. This mutual give-and-take reinforced the long-standing links between the empire and Syrian cities such as Damascus and Aleppo.

As the Ottoman Empire became subject to more pressure from the Europeans, Ottoman-led "defensive modernization"—and responses to it—were felt in Syria. Syria became a focus of a proto-Arab nationalist response to European encroachment and modernization, engendered by the so-called Arab awakening, an Arabic literary movement centered in the Levant in the second half of the 1800s, and strengthened in reaction to "Turkification" policies after the Young Turk revolution of 1908, which generated in Syria a desire for more representative government and Arab autonomy within the empire.

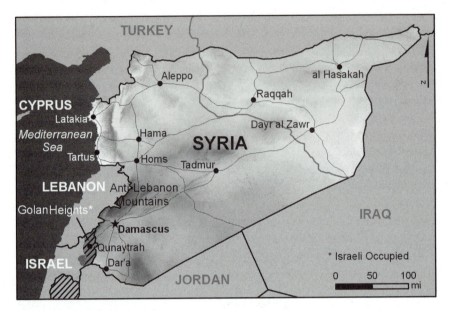

Syrian Arab Republic

When World War I erupted in 1914, Istanbul feared that Arab nationalism could be used as an ideological wedge to break Syria free from the Ottoman Empire, and it dealt harshly with the Arab nationalists. Indeed, an Arab revolt, which some Syrians supported, while more remained loyal to Istanbul, was led from the Hijaz by Sharif Hussein and his son Faisal. The British had negotiated with Hussein to launch the revolt in return for vague promises (embodied in the Hussein-McMahon correspondence) of Arab independence in a state including much of what is now Syria, but they had made contrary promises to their French allies in the Sykes-Picot Agreement. Damascus was taken by British and Arab forces in October 1918, and Faisal was installed as head of a short-lived Syrian kingdom. However, the British abandoned Faisal, leaving Syria to fend for itself against French troops, which occupied the country in July 1920 after overcoming armed resistance.

The immediate outcome of the British-French occupation of *bilad ash-sham*, or greater Syria, was the creation of four ministates, with present-day Lebanon, Jordan, Iskanderun (Alexandretta)/Hatay, and Palestine/Israel separated from the remaining Syrian rump. Syrians perceived these areas to have been artificially separated from Syria as a result of European manipulation.

The resulting state was indeed an arbitrary construction. The Mediterranean Sea is Syria's only natural border, while the others were for the most part drawn by the European powers. The country's longest borders are those with Turkey to the north (822 kilometers) and Iraq to the east (605 kilometers). The eastern four-fifths of Syria constitute a large, mostly semiarid and desert plain—in essence the northern extension of the Arabian

Desert. As such, nearly 80 percent of all Syrians live in the western 20 percent of the country, with the bulk residing in a north-south line of cities (Aleppo, Hama, Homs, Damascus) that generally separates the more fertile western areas of the country from the semiarid and desert plain. The borders that became modern Syria cut off many parts of the country from their traditional mercantile and cultural links in neighboring areas. However, a number of cross-border affinities and ties persisted and are most apparent in the common Syrian mantra regarding Lebanon: "two lands, one people." These cross-cultural identities have had political implications over the years that have at times complicated Syria's relations with its neighbors.

In addition to dismembering the country, the French further adopted a divide-and-rule policy to prevent any coherent opposition from congealing against them. The remainder of French-mandated Syria was therefore divided into five zones: Latakia was carved out for the Alawites, Alexandretta for the Turks, and Jabal Druze for the Druze; the Sunni Muslims were divided between Aleppo and Damascus.

SYRIAN ARAB REPUBLIC

Capital city	Damascus
Chief of state, 2012	President Bashar al-Asad
Head of government, 2012	Prime Minister Wael al-Halqi
Legal political parties, 2012	National Progressive Front (includes Arab Socialist Renaissance [Ba'th] Party), Socialist Unionist Democratic Party, Syrian Arab Socialist Union, Syrian Communist Party, Syrian Social Nationalist Party, Unionist Socialist Party
Ethnic groups	Arab (90.3%), Kurds, Armenians, and other (9.7%)
Religious groups	Sunni Muslim (74%), other Muslim, mainly Alawite and Druze (16%), Christian (10%)
Export partners, 2011	Iraq (38.8%), Italy (7.9%), Germany (7.1%), Saudi Arabia (6.5%), Kuwait (4.2%)
Import partners, 2011	Saudi Arabia (14.5%), China (10.1%), United Arab Emirates (7.1%), Turkey (6.7%), Iran (5.3%), Italy (5%), Russia (4.5%), Iraq (4.3%)

French rule was generally regarded by Syrians as oppressive. French was introduced in the schools at the expense of Arabic, and the unstable French franc became legal tender. Embittered Syrian nationalists played upon these obvious symbols of the French presence and won widespread support in their opposition to French rule. Traditional ethnic and religious leaders also opposed French rule, leading to a series of minor rebellions. The most serious rebellion began in the summer of 1925, when rebel Druze tribesmen drove the French out of the towns and villages in Jabal Druze. French military superiority, however, most notably on display with the bombardment of Damascus, had squashed the revolt by the end of the year.

Although Franco-Syrian relations remained tense, differences subsequently played out for the most part in the political arena. In 1936 a Franco-Syrian treaty conceded an elected parliament and some self-government under a French governor. However, cession of the province of Iskanderun to Turkey in 1939 to keep the latter neutral in World War II incensed the Syrians. The weakening of the Western imperial powers in World War II provided the Syrians with the opportunity to gain full independence. When the Free French ousted the pro-German Vichy governor in the summer of 1941, they promised full independence in order to win Syrian support. Although an elected nationalist government came to power in 1943 under President Shukri al-Quwatli, full independence was not achieved until 1946, when the last French soldiers reluctantly withdrew under British pressure after having again bombarded Damascus.

Despite the antagonistic relationship between the French and most indigenous Syrians, the mandate period significantly influenced the educational system (particularly the private schools), the judicial system, and many important sectors of the economy. Even French language, fashion, cuisine, and architecture are still easily recognizable in Syria. A French practice having enduring political consequences was the recruitment of Alawites into the local military force in numbers far exceeding their percentage of the population. For the traditionally persecuted Alawite sect, joining the military, looked upon with derision by most other Syrians for its tacit cooperation with the French, was one of the few available avenues for upward social mobility. After independence, as the military became politicized and a vehicle for acquiring power, the Alawites were in an advantageous position to advance within the political system. Another enduring outcome of the mandate was the deepening of economic dependence upon Europe, as the French tried to make the country a market for its industries and a site for its investors while orienting Syrian agricultural exports to Europe.

After independence, political power was assumed by a group of politicians from great urban landed or merchant families who had held local power under the Ottomans and gained some nationalist legitimacy from their long struggle against French suzerainty. However, this older generation of Syrian leaders came to be seen by the younger generation as corrupt and failing to deliver on their promise of real independence. The new generation rejected not only the old elites but also their Western liberal ideologies.

The seminal event precipitating the delegitimation of the first-generation elite was the first Arab-Israeli war, from 1947 to 1949. The Syrian government at the time, led by Shukri al-Quwatli, was utterly discredited by its corrupt and inept mishandling of a war that resulted in a humiliating defeat for the Arab combatants, most of whom, including Syria, were more concerned about the strategic designs of rival Arab states than about co-ordinating military strategy against Israel. The discontent among the populace and in the military following the war created an opening for the entrance of the army into Syrian politics, beginning with the seizure of power in March 1949 by a military junta led by General Husni al-Zaim.

Syria's political instability was even more evident in the two successive coups of 1949, ending with Colonel Adib al-Shishakli taking power in December. Al-Shishakli ruled first from behind the scenes, then later as president, until he was ousted in another military coup in 1954. Internal instability also reflected the penetration of the country—via propaganda, money, and guns—by rival Arab and global powers during the Cold War, making Syria a battleground between pro-Western Iraq, which sought to bring the Arabs into the anti-Soviet Baghdad Pact, and Arab nationalist Egypt, which advocated Cold War neutrality.

The 1947 parliamentary elections demonstrated the growing cleavages in the Syrian polity as well as the increasing public disenchantment with mandate-era politicians. They also marked the appearance of what would become the most important political force in Syria, the Ba'th Party, an ardently nationalistic group with a pan-Arab, socialist doctrine. The Ba'th Party arose from the ideological meeting of the minds of three Syrians—Michel Aflaq, a Christian Arab; Salah al-Din Bitar, a Sunni Arab; and Zaki al-Arzuzi, an Alawite—who agreed on the need for Arab unity, independence from imperialism, and "Arab socialism." The Ba'th Party might have remained an ideological party of the periphery were it not for its association with the parliamentary deputy from Hama, Akram al-Hawrani. He ultimately provided the muscle for the Ba'th with his close ties with various elements of the Syrian military, which would soon become the final political arbiter in the country. The relationship was symbiotic, for al-Hawrani's Arab Socialist Party needed the ideological foundation the Ba'th provided. The formal merger occurred in late 1952, making the Ba'th Party a serious contender for power. It was able to force upon whatever government was in power the increasingly popular demands of anti-Zionism and neutral-ist Arab nationalism. The other important actor on the radical Left was the Communist Party, which benefited from Soviet support for Syria against Western pressures to align with the Baghdad Pact. The Communists also opposed so-called capitalist reactionaries and imperialists. Although the Ba'thists were suspicious of the Communists because their ideology was alien and their actions were dictated by an outside power, the two groups often cooperated against the conservative oligarchy and its Western backers.

The Ba'th Party steadily increased its share of seats in parliament and disproportion-ately influenced Syria's foreign policy orientation, which veered toward the Soviet Union and pan-Arab nationalism. This culminated in Syria's ill-fated union with Egypt in February 1958, in the creation of the United Arab Republic (UAR). The UAR failed because the two countries simply did not fit, economically or politically. Gamal Abdel Nasser and his Egyptian cohorts came to dominate the "province" of Syria in a manner distasteful to a number of Syrian parties, not least of which was the Ba'th, which had originally pushed for the merger yet soon became marginalized by pro-Nasserist elements. Finally, in September 1961, following yet another coup by parties representing the traditional elite in Damascus, Syria seceded from the UAR. However, the restored parliamentary regime was not really representative of the direction of Syrian politics, leaving a vacuum that would be filled by the Ba'th Party. The nationalist Left was now fragmented between those who demanded unconditional reunion with Egypt (Nasserites) and the Ba'th, now wary of Nasser.

The Ba'th Party formally came to power in Syria in March 1963 via a military coup by Ba'thist officers, who from that time dominated the party and regime. Originating in a conspiracy by a handful of military officers, the Ba'th regime started as an "army-party symbiosis," built on a narrow base and facing opposition across the whole spectrum of political society, from Nasserites to Islamists to liberals. Internally, the regime was wracked by power struggles over ideology and personal ambition between the first-generation leaders, Aflaq and Bitar and their military partisans, and a younger generation of radical leftists championed by General Salah Jadid. Since sectarianism played a prominent role in the construction of rival coalitions in this and subsequent power struggles, officers from the minority Alawi sect emerged as a dominant clique, owing to their disproportionate recruitment into the army and party and also to class and regional divisions among the Sunnis.

In 1966 an intra-Ba'th coup brought Jadid's radical wing of the party to power. The regime started breaking out of its isolation thorough a "revolution from above" that broke the economic hold of the oligarchy, won the support of peasants with land reform, and created through nationalizations a public sector employing major segments of the middle and working classes. Embracing the Soviet Union and espousing a more assertive anti-Israel policy, the Jadid regime sought nationalist legitimacy by championing Palestinian fedayeen operating against Israel and seeking to push Nasser into a more assertive policy toward Israel. This reckless policy culminated in the 1967 Arab-Israeli War, in which Israel captured the Sinai Peninsula and Gaza Strip from Egypt, the West Bank (including Arab East Jerusalem) from Jordan, and the Golan Heights from Syria. Jadid later oversaw Syria's intervention in the September 1970 Jordanian civil war, also known as Black September. This led to his removal by moderate elements in the Ba'th leadership led by Hafiz al-Asad, an Alawite military officer who at the time was minister of defense and commander of the air force. Asad was formally elected president by public referendum in March 1971.

Hafiz al-Asad's coup ushered in the consolidation of the Ba'th regime. Under the radical Ba'thists who preceded him (1963–1970), the regime had already broken the control of the dominant classes over the economy and mobilized workers and peasants via its so-cial reforms, notably land reform. Asad now constructed a "presidential monarchy" that concentrated power in his own hands. He used his control of the army to free himself of dependence on the Ba'th Party's ideologues and placed a core of largely Alawite personal followers in the security apparatus to give him autonomy from the army. Secure in control of the party and army, he co-opted the private bourgeoisie through limited economic lib-eralization; elements of the Damascene Sunni bourgeoisie entered into tacit business al-liances with Alawite military elites. Penetrating society, the party organization and its auxiliaries incorporated a popular following from both Sunni and non-Sunni villages. Thus, Asad built a cross-sectarian coalition whose effectiveness proved itself in defeating the major Islamic fundamentalist uprising of 1978 to 1982. To build his regime, Asad also depended on external resources—that is, Soviet arms, with which he built up the army, and Arab oil money, with which he expanded the bureaucracy and co-opted the bour-geoisie. Asad tried to legitimize his regime as a bulwark of the Arab cause against Israel, and his relative success in the 1973 Arab-Israeli War provided a legitimacy bonus that al-lowed him to entrench his leadership.

Major subsequent watersheds in Hafiz al-Asad's presidency included the 1970s eco-nomic expansion, spurred by economic liberalization and an influx of Arab oil money; Syria's post-1974 involvement in Arab-Israel diplomacy, brokered by the United States; and the 1976 Syrian intervention in Lebanon. The 1980s were a period of major stress on the regime, with a serious insurgency led by the Muslim Brotherhood (al-Ikhwan al-Muslimun) from 1978 to 1982; an intensified threat from Israel's 1982 invasion of Lebanon, after which Syria became bogged down in a struggle with Israel and its Ma-ronite allies over control of Lebanon; a 1984 bid for power by Hafiz's brother Rifat, when the former fell ill; economic decline, as Arab aid fell after 1986; and Western iso-lation of Syria for its alleged support of terrorism. These stresses were accompanied by decreasing tolerance for dissent, a decline in ideological life in the Ba'th Party, and the growing power of the *mukhabarat* intelligence services and various praetorian guard units that defended the presidency. In the 1990s, Syria lost its Soviet superpower patron but veered, in compensation, toward the United States, joining the anti-Iraq coalition in the 1990–1991 Gulf War and the subsequent Madrid peace process with Israel under US auspices. The resulting windfall of Gulf Arab aid and brief emergence from interna-tional isolation, combined with new early-1990s economic-liberalization measures, sparked a brief economic boom that had petered out by the death of Hafiz al-Asad in June 2000.

The succession of Bashar al-Asad to the presidency in 2000 marked the transforma-tion of Syria into a *jumrukiyya*, or family republic. Bashar's project was to "modernize authoritarianism"—to adapt it to the age of globalization by initiating a move toward a market economy, accompanied by limited relaxation of political controls over society and a foreign policy reorientation to the West. This project, however, became hostage to Syria's new conflicts with the West over Iraq and Lebanon. It also had major social costs, generating crony capitalism, a reneging on the populist social contract, and growing societal inequalities that prepared the way for the uprising that began in March 2011.

POLITICAL ENVIRONMENT

Demography and Society

The population of Syria numbers a little over 22 million, 35 percent of which is below the age of fourteen. The capital and largest city in Syria, Damascus, has a population of approximately 2.52 million, Aleppo has 2.98 million, Homs has 1.27 million, and Hama has 854,000. Approximately 90.3 percent of the population is Arab, including some 400,000 Palestinian refugees. As such, Arabic is the official and most widely spoken language. Kurds make up 5 to 9 percent of the population, depending upon the source. Many Kurds still speak Kurdish, and most live in the northeastern portion of the country, although sizable numbers reside in the major cities. Armenians, clustered primarily in and around Aleppo, and a smattering of other ethnicities, such as Turkmen, Circassians, and Jews, make up the remaining small percentage of the population.

Sunni Muslims account for 74 percent of the population, with Alawites at 12 percent, Christians (of various sects, although the largest is Greek Orthodox) at 10 percent, Druze at 3 percent (mostly located in southwestern Syria in the Jabal Druze region), and Jews and some small Muslim sects (e.g., Ismailis, Twelver Shi'a) at 1 percent. The Alawites, originating in the Latakia mountains, are an obscure offshoot of Shi'a Islam; they venerate Ali ibn Abi Talib, the cousin of Muhammad, and integrate some Christian and Zoroastrian rituals and holidays into their faith. Considered heretical by Sunni Muslims and even most Shi'a Muslims, followers of Alawite Islam were a persecuted minority in the area for centuries before becoming part of the new ruling elite under the Ba'th.

Political Economy

Until the second half of the nineteenth century, Syria had a largely self-sufficient agrarian and trade-based economy. Its agrarian economy was, however, also somewhat precarious: of Syria's 71,504 square miles (185,170 square kilometers), arable land amounts to only about one-quarter of the total. Rainfall is seasonal, most of it coming in the winter months and falling in the northern and westernmost parts of the country, while the semiarid steppe and desert regions receive less than two hundred centimeters (eight inches) of rain per year. Although 80 percent of Syria's agriculture is rain-fed, the government in recent years has invested heavily in developing irrigation systems to maintain crop production during drought years. Cotton is Syria's largest cash crop, accounting for approximately 50 percent of agricultural gross domestic product (GDP). The agricultural sector also produces large quantities of wheat, barley, sugar beets, and olives.

During the late Ottoman and French periods, Syria developed a largely agricultural export economy dependent on imports of manufactured goods. After World War II, a burst of growth in mechanized agriculture and light industry took place, but it appeared to have exhausted itself by the late 1950s. A strong feeling therefore developed among Syrians that state intervention was necessary to overcome economic dependency, push ahead industrialization, and effect a more equitable distribution of national wealth, which was monopolized by the landed oligarchy. In consequence, the 1963–1966 period under the Ba'th was characterized by large-scale nationalizations of banks and big industries and a land reform that limited the size of the great estates and redistributed the surplus to landless peasants.

The path of state capitalism in Syria, however, resulted in a bloated and inefficient public sector that for over four decades provided the support base for the ruling regime. Regime survival drove economic policy, and the public sector was used as a source of patronage to feed a pervasive clientelist network, primarily in the military, bureaucracy, and other elements of society tied to the state apparatus. Hafiz al-Asad also used arbitrariness as a method of control; the 1986 foreign-currency law, ostensibly intended to crack down on black market foreign-currency exchanges, is a case in point. When the economy faced endemic crisis beginning in the 1980s, Asad embarked on a program of "selective liberalization." It had to be "selective" because if either Asad (father or son) were to liberalize too much or too quickly, the public-sector patronage system keeping the regime in power could be undermined. Nevertheless, state employees were adversely affected by economic liberalization, with a decrease in real wages due to currency devaluation, a reduction of subsidies, and under Bashar al-Asad some covert privatization that threatened job security.

In addition to the continuing burden of an overly dominant public sector, a number of other problems inhibited economic growth in the remaining private sector: the absence of a tradition of large-scale domestic capital investment, leading to a proliferation of small-scale enterprise with often outdated technology and investment in nonproductive areas; the lack until recently of a private banking system and stock market to organize capital; an inadequate regulatory regime; insufficient transparency; a corrupt and politicized judiciary; and the ubiquitous necessity of *wasta* (intermediaries). Protected by high tariffs, most domestic industries did not have to become competitive enough to export.

Syria's selective liberalization in the 1990s had some success, buoyed by grants and investment from Arab Gulf states, particularly Saudi Arabia and Kuwait. Domestically, Investment Law No. 10 of May 1991 offered investors duty-free privileges for the import of capital goods and other materials. However, this measure was not followed up with other necessary reforms, and the business environment in Syria became typically captive to the deteriorating situation in the Arab-Israeli arena.

The economic challenges facing the country when Bashar al-Asad came to power were manifold. Syria had not managed to advance beyond the group of lower-middle-income countries, with purchasing power parity income per capita of only $5,100 in 2011. Syria needed to rapidly expand its labor market to absorb a projected annual labor force increase of 4 percent, due primarily to high population growth. Syria's GDP was highly dependent on the agrarian and oil sectors. It produces approximately 300,000 barrels of oil per day, but since 2000 this has declined, and Syria is forecast, barring significant discovery of new oil reserves, to become a net oil importer soon.

Syrians agree on the need for deep, systemic economic reform, though there is no consensus about the pace of change and what changes should be implemented. At the Ba'th Party regional congress in June 2005, President Bashar al-Asad proposed the adoption of a "social market economy" in which a market economy would be combined with social safety nets to help those who might fall through the cracks during and after the transition process. In this transition, Syrian officials wanted to emulate the Chinese model, in which a strong central government regulates the economy, the public sector is reformed to be competitive in global markets, and a parallel private sector expands the market economy. Bashar prioritized educational reform because the deficit in skills hampers Syria's ability to integrate itself into the globalized economy. Private banks and a stock market were approved, and tariffs with Turkey and the Arab countries were slashed. Much more structural reform was needed, but this was retarded by bureaucratic inertia, external conflicts, and the isolation from the West that Syria faced after opposing the 2003 US invasion of Iraq. The culture of caution that exists in Syria ensured that change would occur only at an incremental pace. The risk, which was eventually realized, was that economic deterioration would engender political instability.

POLITICAL STRUCTURE

Hafiz al-Asad consolidated an authoritarian regime that concentrated personal power in a "presidential monarchy." The presidency became the main source of public policy and enjoyed powers of command, appointment, and patronage over the ruling party, army, intelligence agencies, and government bureaucracy. The president is elected to a seven-year renewable term after nomination by the Ba'th Party's Regional Command (al-Qiyadah al-Qutriyah) and the parliament. Hafiz al-Asad was confirmed by unopposed referenda five times, and his son Bashar has been confirmed twice, in 2000 and 2007. Second only to the presidency in policy making is the Regional Command, the top collegial leadership body, roughly divided between senior military commanders, senior cabinet ministers, and top party officials. It endorses policy initiatives and commands the party apparatus, which has systematically penetrated all other institutions of state and civil society. Intraelite politics plays out largely in the relationship between the presidency, the party, and the heads of the multiple security agencies.

A major test of the regime's institutions was the succession upon the death of President Hafiz al-Asad in 2000. However, the party and army elite closed ranks and, to prevent a power struggle, confirmed Bashar al-Asad as the new president. Initially Bashar had to share power with the "old guard"—his father's lieutenants, powerful security barons, and party bosses—who expected him to govern as first among equals. Not having risen from within the regime, Bashar initially lacked a power base. But the presidency gave him unmatched powers of appointment, which he used to replace the older generation with younger officials beholden to himself. His presidency became the source of a spate of economic reform proposals, often delayed by the Regional Command but eventually approved by parliament. Finally, at the 2005 Ba'th Party congress, Bashar engineered the replacement of his rivals in the party hierarchy. This narrowed the inner circle of the regime by excluding such Sunni party bosses as former vice president Abdul Halim Khaddam and some intelligence barons and their private-sector partners. In 2007, Bashar was inaugurated for a second seven-year term, his personal power consolidated.

Second only to the president in coercive power are the heads of the multiple intelligence or security services (*mukhabarat*), whose function is surveillance of possible threats from external enemies, the domestic opposition, the army, and each other. While they are instruments through which the president controls the other power centers, they have significant powers of their own in that they vet all candidates for office and promotion. They also have extralegal power, allowing them to become powerful political brokers whose support ambitious politicians and prominent businessmen seek. They control or co-opt large parts of society via networks of informers and the dispensing of semilicit privileges.

The regime rests on three overlapping pillars of power: the party apparatus, the army, and the government bureaucracy, headed by the Council of Ministers. Although subordinated to the presidency, the Ba'th Party apparatus remains a key pillar of the regime. It has over 11,000 cells (*halaqat*) located in villages, factories, neighborhoods, and public institutions and grouped into 154 subbranches at the district (*mantiqah*) or town level, which are combined into eighteen branches (*furu`*) in the provinces (*muhafazat*), big cities, and major institutions such as universities. A parallel structure exists inside the army and security services. At the national level, a party congress of some 1,200 delegates resolves intraelite conflicts and approves major new policies. A ninety-member Central Committee includes the senior regime elite of party functionaries, ministers, generals, security chiefs, governors, heads of syndicates, and university presidents. The Central Committee elects a fifteen-member Regional Command, whose members either preside over internal party organization and finance or oversee bureaus supervising the military and security agencies, peasants and agriculture, economic affairs, education, unions, and youth. In 2000, party membership numbered nearly 2 million, including teachers, students, state employees, peasants, and workers—an overwhelmingly middle- and lower-class constituency. The party also controls syndical organizations such as worker, peasant, and professional unions and chambers of commerce and industry. These institutions give the regime roots in society and bridge sectarian and urban-rural gaps. Their debilitation in the 2000s, when the president perceived the party as an obstacle to his economic reforms, helps account for the antiregime mobilization of 2011.

The military is another main pillar of the regime. When Ba'th officers brought the party to power in 1963, they inevitably became an equal or senior partner in the new military-party state. But Hafiz al-Asad effectively subordinated the military to his authority. He established firm control over appointments and dismissals of senior officers and created presidential guard units and special forces charged with regime defense and recruited on the basis of political loyalty and (Alawite) sectarian affiliation. Alawite Ba'th officers hold a disproportionate number of top operational commands, especially of potentially coup-making armored units. The larger army, charged with external defense, is more depoliticized and professionally disciplined. The professional officer corps is represented in the president's inner circle by the minister of defense and chief of staff. The continued loyalty of the military explains the ability of the regime to survive in the face of the mass uprising that began in 2011.

The function of the government bureaucracy, headed by the prime minister and the cabinet (Council of Ministers), is to implement the policy of the president and the party, which together appoint cabinet ministers. However, the bureaucracy is so inefficient and colonized by vested interests that it has become more an obstacle than an instrument of the president's economic reforms.

There is no effective separation of powers. The parliament (People's Assembly) merely responds to government initiatives and normally approves government legislation. Deputies mainly act as brokers between officials and their constituents—notably those seeking favors. Although formally elected by popular vote, the regime has manipulated the composition of parliament: two-thirds of the seats are reserved for candidates of the National Progressive Front, an alliance of the Ba'th Party and several small leftist and nationalist parties. In order to co-opt elements outside its power base, the regime has allowed independent candidates, mostly from the urban bourgeoisie, to contest the remaining seats. The judiciary is politicized through party control of appointments. The legal process suffers from corruption and interminable delays in litigation and fails to guarantee the rule of law, civil liberties, and property rights. Hence, redress of grievances typically rests on access to informal clientelistic connections. Judicial reform and independence are widely recognized as essential to Bashar al-Asad's reform project. One of the regime's prime weapons against internal dissent is Decree 51 of 1963, which declared a state of emergency. Lifting of the emergency law and abolition of the associated extraconstitutional Supreme State Security Courts are two of the prime objectives of Syrian humans rights and democracy activists, but the regime has always claimed they are justified by Syria's "living in a dangerous neighborhood."

POLITICAL DYNAMICS

Politics in Ba'thist Syria has taken varying forms. In the 1963–1970 period, it turned on ideological conflicts between Left and Right within the party, settled at party congresses or by intraparty military coups. Once Hafiz al-Asad consolidated the regime, politics as usual took the form of conflicts over the evolution of economic policy among politicians, technocrats, and business representatives and a search for collective group redress through the party and corporatist institutions or for individual privileges through personal connections, notably in the security forces and party apparatus. Contestation over the larger direction of the country occurred during periods of crisis, such as the failed 1978–1982 Islamic revolution and after the 2000 presidential succession, when the new president was struggling to establish his authority, and the degree of liberalization was being contested between the president and the party. In both periods, nonregime actors— Islamists and liberals—sought to reshape Syrian politics with limited success. The uprising of 2011 ushered in a violent contest to shape Syria's future.

The Ba'th Regime and Political Islam

Political Islam provided the strongest and most durable opposition to the Ba'th regime. While the regime was initially rooted in the rural areas, the Islamic opposition was concentrated in traditional urban quarters, led by politicized ulema (religious scholars) and the Muslim Brotherhood, whose members were typically recruited from urban merchant families. In the 1960s, they denounced the secularism of the regime and protested the state takeover of foreign trade and restrictions on imports, which deprived merchants of business. From 1977 to 1982, the Muslim Brotherhood instigated a violent insurrection against the regime; corruption, sectarian favoritism, Hafiz al-Asad's 1976 confrontation with the Palestinians in Lebanon, and Sunni resentment of minority domination generated fertile conditions for it. The Brotherhood attacked the Alawites as unbelievers and, reflecting the worldview of the *suq* (bazaar), called for an Islamic economy based on free enterprise. The revolt was concentrated in the northern cities and towns, especially Hama, a historic center of Islamic piety and of the great Sunni landholding families curbed by Ba'thist land reforms. By contrast, the Damascene bourgeoisie, enriched by the disproportionate share of public money expended in the capital, remained quiet during the uprising. The insurrection failed, owing to its fragmented and largely unknown leadership and the urban bias of its social base. The regime, backed by its rural base, remained cohesive, and the security apparatus, led by Alawite troops with a stake in regime survival, mounted a repressive campaign marked by the 1982 sack of Hama, in which an estimated 15,000 to 30,000 people were killed.

With the Brotherhood's supporters jailed and its leaders exiled, a less politicized, less oppositional Islamization of society was tolerated by the regime. Hafiz al-Asad sought to tame political Islam through an alliance with moderate Islam, represented by the Grand Mufti Kaftaro and Muhammad Sa'id al-Buti, who preached a moderate Islam and opposed Islamist violence against the regime. Bashar al-Asad continued this strategy as a counter to both radical Islamists and the secular opposition, resulting in the spread of Islamic schools and charities, conservative attire, and mosque attendance. This largely nonpolitical Islam, concentrating on personal piety, rejecting violence, and mobilizing around nonpolitical issues such as opposition to liberal reform of Syrian family law, seemed unthreatening to the regime. While the majority of the ulema, recruited from the *suq* merchant class and seeing the acquisition of wealth as a sign of God's favor, had rejected Ba'thist socialism, they were appeased by Bashar's increasingly neoliberal tangent, and some benefited from the Gulf money attracted by the Islamic financial institutions allowed by the regime. The offloading of welfare responsibilities onto the private charities the ulema controlled helped co-opt and empower them. Bashar also built alliances with the interlocked business and religious elite of formerly oppositionist Aleppo, which benefited from his economic opening to Turkey.

At the same time, the regime sought to control Islam. It appointed the senior ulema, such as muftis and imams of the big mosques, and benefited from the divisions between the Damascus and Aleppo ulema, the Sufi orders and their Salafi critics, and conservative imams and modernists, further dividing them by repressing some and favoring others. The regime sought to regulate Islamic institutions and assume some control over the distribution of *zakat* (charitable donations) and attempted to reintroduce limits on public displays of piety. The government's coming to terms with political Islam initially enhanced stability. But for what is sometimes called a "regime of minorities," the consequent erosion of secularism carried real dangers, which manifested themselves in the Islamic color of much of the 2011 uprising.

Presidential Succession, Stalled Democratization, and "Authoritarian Upgrading"

Bashar al-Asad's July 2000 succession was widely welcomed. Politically inexperienced, he was not thought to threaten the incumbent elite. As an Asad, he assured the Alawites that he would not betray his father's heritage. Yet among the public, especially the younger generation, he was popular, seen as uncorrupted and as a modernizer, who, in his inaugural speech, invited constructive criticism of the regime. According to Volker Perthes, however, Bashar's intention was to "modernize authoritarianism." His project required limited political liberalization and more rule of law, but not democratization. He initially hoped to liberalize politics, at least to the extent this would help legitimize his position and advance economic reform. However, when Bashar encouraged civil society to express constructive criticism as a way to strengthen his reformist agenda in the 2000–2001 Damascus Spring, hard-line opposition figures framed political change in zero-sum terms by attacking the legacy of Hafiz and spotlighting the corruption of regime barons. Regime hard-liners were strengthened, and Bashar shut down the experiment.

In principle, Bashar could have struck an alliance with the loyal opposition to further the kind of limited political liberalization that helped other Arab rulers control the opposition, and he could have strengthened his hand against the old guard by allowing the formation of a bourgeois neoliberal party. Such moves arguably would have increased his regime's co-optative capabilities, but democratization was never in the cards. No democratic coalition emerged pushing for it. Democracy activists among the intelligentsia suffered from fragmentation, resource scarcity, and relative isolation from mass society. The chaos and sectarian conflict in Iraq and the fear—ignited by Kurdish riots in 2004 and the rise of Islamist militancy—that democratization would spread the "Iraqi disease" to Syria led the public to put a high premium on stability. This generated for the regime what might be called "legitimacy because of a worse alternative." The continuing struggle over Palestine and the Golan also allowed the regime to justify a national security state and provided nationalist legitimacy that seemed to substitute for democratization. The business class, dependent as it was on the state for opportunities (contracts, licenses) and for disciplining the working class and rolling back populism, had no interest in a democratization that could empower the masses to block economic liberalization. Even regime reformers believed their economic reforms would be blocked if the masses were empowered by the vote; indeed, the first stages of Bashar's economic-reform program meant a rollback in the populist social contract and a stage of crony capitalism that was incompatible with the regime winning a free election and could only be sustained by authoritarian power. Not least, the minority Alawite elite feared that sectarian voting (as in Iraq) would allow the Sunni majority to drive it from power. Indeed, their mortal enemy, the Muslim Brotherhood, had the best potential to mobilize mass support.

As a substitute for democratization, Asad embarked on a process of "authoritarian upgrading," the fostering of alternative constituencies—to substitute for the alliance with workers and peasants that the regime was abandoning—which could be balanced against each other. The regime co-opted reforming technocrats. The new rich and the urban middle class were encouraged to develop their own civil society organizations, such as junior chambers of commerce, or to join several government-sponsored nongovernmental organizations. Critics of the regime were treated more leniently and even encouraged to voice constructive criticism, albeit within boundaries highlighted by episodic instances of selective repression. This was meant to provide a safety valve for discontent, but it also increased consciousness of abuses without opening institutionalized channels of real redress. Similarly, the introduction of the Internet and mobile telephones was seen by Asad, who had been president of the Syrian Computer Society, as an essential tool of economic modernization, which the regime also used to mobilize supporters and legitimize itself. But these moves also gave political activists the ability to build networks, overcome atomization, and publicize abuses. They paved the way for the 2011 uprising.

The Syrian Uprising of March 2011

The seeds of the uprising that began in March 2011 can be seen in the policies by which Bashar al-Asad sought to fix the vulnerabilities of the regime he inherited from his father, notably through economic reform. The root of the regime's problems was that its survival required both nationalist legitimacy and continuing investment. However, the regime's nationalist foreign policy (opposing Israel and the invasion of Iraq), while winning domestic support, brought economic isolation from the West—a main source of capital and technology. This drove the regime's efforts to find alternative sources of revenue via tax cuts and currency and trade liberalization, designed to attract Syrian expatriate capital and surplus liquidity from the Arab Gulf. The drive to evade isolation and increase access to resources sidelined the ideal of a social market economy. The actual policy of Bashar's reforming technocrats was little different from neoliberalism, with its prioritizing of capital accumulation and growth to the neglect of equality and distribution.

The removal of subsidies on agricultural inputs, the decline of farm price supports, and the neglect of the system of agricultural planning and cooperatives, combined with the terrible drought of 2007 to 2009, led to agricultural decline. Poor neighborhoods around the cities burgeoned with an influx of drought victims and Iraqi refugees. In addition, urban real estate speculation unleashed by the influx of Gulf capital, together with an end to rent controls conceded to the landlord class, drove the cost of housing beyond the means of the middle strata. The conspicuous consumption of the new urban rich was at odds with Syrian traditions and alienated those in the surrounding, deprived suburbs. The president was warned that the people perceived the state to be abandoning the poor for the sake of the rich. Free trade agreements ending tariff protection devastated small manufacturers in the suburbs. Parallel to this, authoritarian upgrading fostered alternative constituencies, mostly in the big cities. The regime co-opted big segments of the business class and ulema, traditional centers of opposition to the Ba'th.

In addition, to advance his postpopulist reforms, Asad had concentrated power in the presidency in an extended struggle with the old guard. In uprooting the old guard, he reduced obstacles to his reforms but also weakened powerful interests with clientelistic networks that incorporated key segments of society into the regime. This shrank the scope of elites incorporated into the regime, making the president overly dependent on the presidential family, Alawi security barons, and technocrats lacking bases of support. Also, seeing the party apparatus and the worker and peasant unions as obstacles to economic reform, Asad debilitated them; since they were the regime's organized connection to its rural and Sunni constituency, its social base shrank, becoming more minoritarian and more upper-class. As the party's penetration of neighborhoods and villages declined, citizens who would once have gone to local party or union officials for redress or access increasingly approached tribal, sectarian, or religious notables. In short, seeking to consolidate power within the regime he inherited, Asad unwittingly weakened its capacity to sustain his power over society. Overconcentrating patronage in the hands of the presidential family and thereby narrowing loyalties from party to family core is a dangerous move for authoritarian regimes.

The security forces' overreaction to protests, starting in Dera, in an atmosphere created by the overthrow of authoritarian presidents in Tunisia and Egypt provided the spark for the uprising. While demonstrators at first called for political reform, after a heavy-handed regime response in which over 1,000 demonstrators were killed, they began to call for the president's resignation and an end to the regime. Had Asad reacted with democratic concessions instead of repression, he might have won a free election as a reformer.

Given the minority core of the regime, however, making sufficient democratic concessions to appease the opposition must have appeared too risky, especially since debilitation of the regime's former cross-sectarian base was making it a sectarian-family regime with limited vote-getting capacity.

The uprising continued because there were enough grievances to fuel it among a plurality of the population, while a minority supported the regime as a better alternative than civil war. The uprising was geographically concentrated outside the capital, beginning in the rural peripheries and then spreading to small towns, suburbs, and medium-sized cities. It took on a distinctly Sunni Islamic character. Centers of grievance were mixed areas where Alawis and Sunnis lived together, such as Latakia, Banias, and Homs. The regime's supporters included crony capitalists, urban government employees, and minorities, especially Alawis and to a lesser degree Christians, who, not suffering from the restrictions typical in other Muslim countries, were rallied through exploitation of their fear of Salafi Islam. The main cities, Damascus and Aleppo, where the investment boom, surge in tourism, and new consumption were concentrated, remained largely quiescent months into the uprising—although their suburbs were often hotbeds of revolt. The regime was able to mobilize significant counterdemonstrations in these cities, whose middle classes originally saw Bashar as a reformer and, while disillusioned by his repression of the protestors, preferred a peaceful democratization and feared instability and the loss of their secular, modern lifestyle if traditional rural or Salafi insurgents seized power.

The opposition's initial strategy was to mobilize demonstrations on such a broad scale that the army would become exhausted or divided, to exaggerate or provoke violence so as to discredit the regime and prompt foreign intervention, and to damage the economy enough to turn the bourgeoisie against the regime. The regime's repressive response had the effect not of deterring but of spreading the protests, with massive demonstrations filling the streets of medium-sized cities. In August 2011, as many as 1 million demonstrators flooded the streets. However, in a newly intensified crackdown, tanks were used to pacify medium-sized cities such as Hama, Homs, and Deir ez-Zor, and the security forces concentrated on arresting and assassinating activist leaders. By September, these measures seemed to have sharply reduced the numbers involved in street protests to perhaps between 25,000 and 30,000. Also, the regime's determination not to lose control of peripheral areas—which could, as in Libya, become centers of an alternative government backed by outside powers—led to some of the harshest repression in areas such as Tel Kalakh and Jisr ash-Shaghour.

What the opposition had hoped to provoke—a major split in the regime or army—had not happened over a year into the insurgency. However, the uprising had become more violent by early 2012, as the crackdown provoked armed resistance led by deserters from the army. The regime lost control over some areas, leaving a vacuum filled by a combination of civil society and criminality. Rustum, Harasta, Idlib, and Jabal Zawiya emerged as strongholds of opposition. Although opposition fighters were not able to hold such areas against army assaults, neither could the regime keep them pacified when its forces withdrew.

Various external initiatives to halt the violence failed. An Arab League observer force arrived in Syria in December 2011, but extensive violence continued, and the mission ended in failure. In April 2012, the UN Security Council agreed on a peace plan and authorized the dispatch of UN observers to Syria, which, together with a cease-fire, was supposed to lead to political dialogue and a power transition. However, this initiative also failed to stop the violence, with neither side prepared to compromise or negotiate.

In 2012 rebels proved better able to challenge the regime, which responded with greater violence. Levels of insurgent violence increased as the rebels, bolstered by arms and training, improved their combat capability and coordination and increasingly challenged the regime, killing around a hundred security personnel daily. Armed ambushes of the security forces and attacks on their bases by military defectors increased. The regime's siege of Homs, where the armed opposition was entrenched, involved bombarding neighborhoods at a high cost in civilian casualties. In June and July, massacres in several Sunni villages on the fringes of the Alawite heartland were thought by some to be an attempt at sectarian cleansing aimed at making this area a fallback bastion for the regime should it lose control of the country. A weakening of the regime's core was signaled by high-level defections, notably by a Republican Guard commander from the Ba'thist Tlas family, which had long worked with the Asads. The bombing of a government building, killing four senior security officials, in the heart of upper-class Damascus signaled the failure of the regime's defenses and suggested opposition penetration at the heart of the security apparatus. In July and August 2012, major insurgent infiltrations of Damascus and Aleppo further undermined any pretense of normality, which was crucial for the regime to maintain support from the uncommitted. The regime responded with helicopter gunships and even jet fighters, indicating its inability to contain the insurgency. The sense of insecurity among the urban middle- and upper-middle classes greatly intensified, and many who could exit did so. The death toll from the intervention stood at 19,000 by July. Some 200,000 refugees had fled to neighboring countries, and 1.2 million Syrians were forced to flee their neighborhoods to escape the fighting. By summer 2012, Syria had descended into full-scale civil war, with no end in sight.

Foreign Policy

Syrians consider their country the birthplace of Arab nationalism, and its tenets have considerably influenced Syria's foreign policy. This has manifested itself in Syria's role as the self-proclaimed leader of the anti-Israeli front in the Arab world, the most consistent proponent of the Palestinian cause, and the beacon of anti-imperialist pan-Arab neutrality in the region. Syria's sponsorship of Palestinian guerillas against Israel and inter-Arab rivalry for Arab nationalist leadership were factors in the outbreak of the 1967 Arab-Israeli

War, in which Syria lost the Golan Heights to Israel. Ever since, recovery of this territory has been the primary driving force behind Syrian foreign policy.

The Golan Heights is geostrategically important for two reasons. First, control of the territory would give Syria the strategic advantage of looking down upon northern Israel—unless the Heights were demilitarized, as seems likely in any settlement. Second, as long as the Golan remains in Israeli hands, the Israeli military will be positioned only a short distance from Damascus on the flat, open Golan plateau. Mount Hermon, at the Golan's northwest corner, peers over much of southern Lebanon, northern Israel, southern Syria, and the Golan Heights itself. The Golan is also a major water source, as tributaries spring fed on the slopes of Mount Hermon feed through it into the Sea of Galilee and the Jordan River, on which Israel depends.

Hafiz al-Asad and the Struggle with Israel: From War to Failed Peace

A realist, Asad was convinced Israel would never withdraw from the occupied territories unless military action upset the post-1967 status quo. The main thrust of his policy after coming to power in 1970 was therefore preparation for a conventional war to retake the Golan. Toward this end, the rebuilding of the shattered Syrian army was his first priority. He therefore maintained Syria's close alliance with the Soviet Union to secure arms, and he put aside the radicals' ideological cold war to forge new alliances with the Arab oil states to secure the financing needed for a military buildup. Finally, he struck a strategic alliance with Anwar Sadat's Egypt, the most militarily powerful of the Arab states, which shared Syria's interest in recovery of the occupied territories.

Egypt and Syria went to war with Israel in 1973 to break the stalemate over the occupied territories. Although Syria failed to recover the Golan militarily, Syria and Egypt gained enhanced political leverage from their challenge to the pro-Israeli status quo and from the Arab oil embargo. Asad sought to exploit this new leverage to focus international pressure on Israel to withdraw from the occupied territories. He accepted Henry Kissinger's mediation of the Golan Heights disengagement negotiations while also conducting a war of attrition on the front with Israel as part of a "fighting while talking" bargaining strategy. He saw Syria's resulting 1974 disengagement agreement with Israel as a first step in total Israeli withdrawal from the Golan. However, Sadat's subsequent separate deals with Israel undermined Syrian diplomatic leverage and shattered the Syro-Egyptian alliance needed to pressure Israel into a comprehensive settlement.

Syria's 1976 intervention in the Lebanese civil war against the Palestine Liberation Organization (PLO) was widely interpreted as serving Syrian reasons of state and even a "Greater Syria" project. Indeed, Asad aimed to head off various threats in Lebanon to Syria's position in the struggle with Israel. He used the civil war to insert Syria as Lebanon's arbiter, balancing between the various sides and tilting one way or the other depending on the strategic situation. He blocked a defeat of the Maronite Christians to deter their alignment with Israel. He prevented the emergence of a radical, Palestinian-dominated Lebanon that could give Israel an excuse to intervene militarily, possibly seizing southern Lebanon and positioning itself to threaten Syria's soft western flank. Syria's intervention allowed Asad to station his army in the Bekaa valley against this danger. Later, however, as the Maronites allied with Israel, Syria tilted toward Palestinian forces confronting Israel in southern Lebanon.

The Lebanon intervention was also part of Asad's attempt to construct a Syrian sphere of influence to substitute for the Egyptian alliance in the military and diplomatic struggle with Israel. Syria had always viewed Lebanon as a lost part of Greater Syria that should serve its Arab strategy. Moreover, whoever controlled Lebanon was in a strong position to control the PLO and hence the Palestinian card: Syria's bargaining leverage in the Arab-Israeli conflict would be greatly enhanced if it enjoyed the capacity to veto any settlement of the Palestinian problem that left Syria out or to overcome rejectionist Palestinian resistance to an acceptable settlement. The intervention did demonstrate Syrian moderation to the United States and Israel, better positioning Asad for such a settlement. But in continuing to insist on Palestinian rights and a comprehensive settlement, Asad passed up a chance to follow Sadat down the road of separate peace. Syria's role and alliances in Lebanon enabled it to put pressure on Israel through Hizballah. In time, Syria's presence in Lebanon also served as a source of patronage to reward key regime supporters.

Once Sadat's separate peace with Israel had exhausted the 1970s peace process and taken Egypt out of the Arab-Israeli power balance, Syria felt increasingly vulnerable. Asad used the Arab aid Syria received as the main remaining frontline state to finance a military buildup aiming at parity with Israel: the threat of an Israel emboldened by the neutralization of its southern front had to be contained, while the resumption of peace negotiations depended on restoration of the Arab-Israeli power balance. In the meantime, Damascus obstructed all attempts at partial or separate Israeli agreements with other states that tried to circumvent Syria: if Syria could not achieve an Arab-Israeli peace to its liking, it could at least prevent others that damaged its interests or Arab rights—hence Syria's role in the collapse of both the 1983 Lebanese-Israeli accord and the 1985 bid by Yasir Arafat and King Hussein of Jordan for negotiations with Israel under the Reagan Plan.

At the same time, the 1979 Islamic revolution was transforming Iran from an ally of Israel and the United States into a fiercely anti-Zionist state and potential Syrian ally in the Arab-Israeli power balance. Asad condemned the Iraqi invasion of Iran, predicting that it would divide and divert Arabs from the Israeli menace. His stand with Iran was vindicated after the 1982 Israeli invasion of Lebanon, when the effectiveness of the Iran-sponsored Islamic resistance to Israel helped foil a mortal threat to Syria. Nevertheless, sensitive to Arab opinion, Asad actively discouraged Iranian threats to Iraqi territory.

Asad's adhesion to the Western-led war coalition in the 1990–1991 Gulf War was driven by multiple considerations of realpolitik. Saddam Hussein had made himself a considerable nuisance to Asad, notably supporting challenges to Syria's position in

Lebanon; and success in Kuwait would enhance Saddam's capacity to seek revenge for Syria's stand with Iran in the Iran-Iraq War. Adhesion to the Gulf coalition gained US and Israeli tolerance of Asad's 1990 military intervention to establish a Pax Syrianna in Lebanon. Standing with Saudi Arabia revitalized the subsidy channel from the Gulf oil states that had dried up with the decline of oil prices and, enabling Syria to break out of Arab isolation due to its alignment with Iran, put Syria back at the heart of a renewed Cairo-Damascus-Riyadh axis.

Ultimately, however, Syria's decision to join the anti-Iraq coalition was most definitively shaped by the emerging breakdown of the bipolar world. By the 1990s, the withdrawal of the Soviet Union as a reliable protector and arms supplier deprived Syria of the ability to pose a credible threat of war against Israel and left it vulnerable to Western animosity for its obstruction of the peace process in the 1980s and particularly for its alleged resort to terrorism, which Israel could exploit to justify an attack on Syria. Asad understood that Syria's struggle with Israel would henceforth have to take a chiefly diplomatic form, and that required détente with the United States, which alone had leverage over Israel. Asad needed to get the United States to accept Syria as the key to peace and stability in the Middle East, and the Gulf War presented an opportunity to trade membership in the coalition—whose credibility arguably required Syria's nationalist credentials—in return for US promises to broker an acceptable Arab-Israeli settlement.

After the war Asad joined the Madrid peace process—a strategic decision to do what was necessary to obtain an acceptable settlement with Israel. This was made much easier after the Oslo Accords relieved Damascus of the responsibility to make its recovery of the Golan Heights contingent on the satisfaction of Palestinian rights. In the peace negotiations, Asad aimed to minimize the "normalization of relations" and security concessions Israel expected in return for the Golan. But once Israel signaled its willingness to return the Golan, Syria put forth a formula under which the more land Israel conceded, the more peace it could have, and made several concessions, such as stating its willingness to open diplomatic relations after a settlement and its acceptance of demilitarized zones on the border that would favor Israel. In fact, the two sides came very close to a settlement. But a final deal was obstructed by Israel's demands to keep its surveillance station on Mount Hermon and its insistence on keeping 5 percent of the Golan's territory adjoining Lake Tiberias.

Foreign Policy Under Bashar al-Asad

Bashar al-Asad came to power in the same year as the collapse of Syria's peace negotiations with Israel. His legitimacy was contingent on his faithfulness to his father's mission of recovering the Golan, but he inherited a deteriorating strategic situation: a new Turkish-Israeli alliance and growing opposition to Syrian forces remaining in Lebanon following Israel's withdrawal from southern Lebanon in 2000. Without its former Soviet arms supplier, Syria could not sustain the conventional military balance with Israel, and a growing technological and airpower gap opened between the two countries. In response, Bashar tried to construct compensating alliances: he sought a strategic opening to Europe, negotiating Syrian membership in the Euro-Mediterranean Partnership. At the regional level, Syria initially remained in loose alliance with Saudi Arabia and Egypt, improved relations with Turkey, and in 2001 started an opening to Saddam Hussein's Iraq.

Toward Israel, Asad affirmed that Syria was willing to resume peace negotiations if Israel acknowledged Yitzhak Rabin's commitment to a full withdrawal to the June 4, 1967, borders on the Golan. But once the rise of Ariel Sharon to power in Israel had pushed a settlement off the agenda, Asad revived Syrian militancy, insisting that a Syrian-Israeli settlement had to be linked to the establishment of a Palestinian state, allowing Palestinian Hamas and Islamic Jihad to maintain offices in Syria, and supporting Hizballah operations against Israeli forces in Shebaa Farms, a disputed enclave in southern Lebanon. Given the strategic imbalance with Israel, Syria now relied on "nonconventional" deterrence strategies—Hizballah's asymmetric warfare capability and Syrian missiles with chemical warheads—but Israel still made several limited retaliatory strikes on Syrian positions. Syria made massive arms deliveries to Hizballah during its summer 2006 conflict with Israel, thereby helping deprive Israel of a military victory in Lebanon. But Bashar also pursued Turkish-brokered peace talks with Israel, which were aborted by Israel's 2009 attack on Gaza.

Syrian-US relations dramatically declined under the George W. Bush administration. After 9/11, Bush announced that all states not with the United States in the war on terror were foes. Syria objected to the US designation of what it regarded as national liberation movements—Palestinian militants and Hizballah—as terrorist. It regarded these groups as "cards" in its struggle with Israel and evaded US demands that it cease its support for them. Syrian-US relations worsened further when Syria helped Iraq evade US attempts to isolate Baghdad by reopening the closed oil pipeline between the two states, gaining the Syrian treasury a badly needed billion-dollar annual windfall and enabling Saddam to evade UN sanctions.

The immediate catalyst of a crisis in US-Syrian relations was Syrian opposition to the 2003 US invasion of Iraq. At the United Nations and in the Arab League, Syrian diplomats attempted to delegitimize the invasion. Asad allowed Arab resistance fighters to move across Syria's border into Iraq and gave refuge to Iraqi Ba'th officials. His defiance of Washington over the war reflected Syria's Arab nationalist identity and was costly for the regime. Washington attacked Syrian economic interests in Iraq and moved against its position in Lebanon. However, while Hafiz al-Asad had been rewarded for siding with the United States in the 1991 war with a US commitment to pursue the peace process, no such offer was on the table in 2003. And while Iraq had been the aggressor against another Arab state in 1990, an Arab state was the victim of imperialist aggression in 2003, as Syrians saw it. Indeed, Syrian public opinion was so inflamed against the 2003 US invasion that regime legitimacy dictated opposition. This was a more important consideration for Bashar al-Asad, whose rule was still unconsolidated, than it had been for his father in 1990.

After triumphing over Saddam Hussein, the United States presented Damascus with a list of nonnegotiable demands that threatened Syria's vital interests: to end support for Palestinian militants, dismantle Hizballah, withdraw from Lebanon, and cooperate with the occupation of Iraq—in short, to give up its cards in the struggle over the Golan, its sphere of influence in the Levant, and its Arab nationalist stature in the Arab world. Syria did end its overt support for the resistance in Iraq but otherwise sought to trade coopera- tion over Iraq for US respect for Syrian interests, notably in the conflict with Israel. US difficulties in Iraq gave Syria a certain space for maneuver between defying and submit- ting to US demands. However, the cost of defiance was US economic sanctions that ob- structed aspects of the regime's economic liberalization by discouraging Western banks and companies from doing business in Syria.

In 2005, Syria's role in Lebanon became an issue of conflict with the West. The United States and France engineered UN Security Council Resolution 1559 calling for Syria to withdraw its military forces from that country. Syria reluctantly acquiesced. After the as- sassination of former Lebanese prime minister Rafik Hariri, the United States and France set up an international tribunal to investigate Syria's role in the killing, which Damascus saw as an effort to foment regime change in Syria. After Syria withdrew from Lebanon, that country became a battleground in a wider struggle pitting the United States, France, and Saudi Arabia against Hizballah, backed by Syria and Iran. In May 2008, Hizballah demonstrated its power by taking over western Beirut, leading to the formation of a na- tional unity government in which Hizballah held veto power over any moves by Lebanon against Syria.

A major consequence of Syria's stands in the Iraq and Lebanon conflicts was a shift in regional alignments, with Syria becoming estranged from its traditional Arab partners, Egypt and Saudi Arabia. Bashar was highly critical of these countries' acquiescence in the US invasion of Iraq, and they, in turn, blamed Syria and Iran for the 2006 Israel-Hizballah war and the Hariri assassination. By 2006, a battle for the Middle East was being waged between two axes—a "moderate" one led by the United States and backed by the Euro- pean Union, Saudi Arabia, Egypt, and Jordan, with Israel an unofficial partner, and a "re- sistance front" led by Iran and Syria, aligned with Hizballah and Hamas and enjoying wide support in Arab public opinion. Iraq, Lebanon, and Palestine were the main battle- grounds for the rival alliances. As Syria faced isolation in the West as a pariah state, its links with Iran and other members of this "radical" axis strengthened.

At the same time, Syria moved into close alignment with formerly hostile Turkey. In the 1990s the two states had come to the brink of war, as Syria supported the Kurdistan Workers' Party (PKK) against Turkey to pressure Ankara into giving it a greater share of Euphrates River water controlled by new Turkish dams upstream. Turkey and Israel also had cooperated closely in opposition to Syria and Iran. Military threats by Turkey in 1996 caused Syria to abandon its support for the PKK, and Turkish-Syrian relations then im- proved. The empowerment of Iraqi Kurds with the US-Iraq wars of 1991 and 2003 gradu- ally drove Turkey and Syria closer over the shared threat of Kurdish separatism. Turkey refused US demands to isolate Syria and even brokered Syria-Israel peace negotiations in defiance of the United States. By the end of 2008, Bashar had outlasted his main nemesis, George W. Bush, and was enjoying a cautious improvement in relations with Europe and the United States under the new administration of Barack Obama.

The 2011 uprising, however, reshuffled the cards and unleashed a struggle for Syria. Syria is a pivotal Arab state. When united under Hafiz al-Asad, it became a regional player able to punch well above its weight. When divided, as in the 1950s and again with the 2011 uprising, it becomes an arena for struggle among external forces, all trying to use Syria to shift the regional balance of power in their favor.

At stake in the 2011 uprising are Syria's relations with the West, specifically the balance between the pro-Western Sunni axis, led by Saudi Arabia, and the Iran-led "resistance front." While the uprising is essentially indigenous, external forces have tried from the beginning to use it to their advantage. Qatar has used Al Jazeera to amplify antiregime protests. The Saudis have funneled money and arms to Syrian tribes and, with the United States, smuggled into the country sophisticated mobile phones able to bypass government-controlled networks. In November 2011, Qatar and Saudi Arabia took the initiative in prompting the Arab League to take unprecedented moves to isolate Syria, which, together with European sanctions, were aimed at drying up the regime's access to economic resources and breaking its coalition with the business class. An anti-Asad coalition, led by the United States, France, Saudi Arabia, and Turkey, began financing, training, and arming insurgents and infiltrating them into the country. As Syria became a failed state, it became a magnet for jihadis and al-Qaida militants, some funded or armed from the Gulf. Its links to its Shi'a partners—Hizballah to the west and Iraq and Iran to the east—were the Asad regime's only chance of slipping out of this tightening stranglehold. Meanwhile, Russia and China, antagonized by the West's use of a UN humanitarian resolution to promote regime change at their expense in Libya, protected Syria from a similar scenario. Whichever way the current version of the struggle for Syria goes, it will, as formerly, be decisive in the parallel struggle for the Middle East.

BIBLIOGRAPHY

A good general book on Syrian history is John Devlin's *Syria: Modern State in an Ancient Land* (Boulder, CO: Westview Press, 1983). Also see Moshe Maoz, Joseph Ginat, and Onn Winckler's edited volume, *Modern Syria: From Ottoman Rule to Pivotal Role in the Middle East* (Brighton, UK: Sussex Academic Press, 1999). On the World War I and French mandate periods, see Philip S. Khoury's classic *Syria and the French Mandate: The Politics of Arab Nationalism, 1920–1945* (Princeton, NJ: Princeton University Press, 1987). For an insightful examination of domestic political developments and movements during the transition from Ottoman to French rule, see James L. Gelvin's *Divided Loyalties: Nationalism and Mass Politics in Syria at the Close of Empire* (Berkeley: University of California Press, 1999).

On Syria's political development in the twentieth century, see the following works: Hanna Batatu, *Syria's Peasantry, the Descendants of Its Lesser Rural Notables, and Their Politics* (Princeton, NJ: Princeton University Press, 1999), and Raymond A. Hinnebusch, *Authoritarian Power and State Formation in Ba'thist Syria: Army, Party, and Peasant* (Boulder, CO: Westview Press, 1990). Also see Raymond Hinnebusch, *Syria: Revolution from Above* (London: Routledge, 2001); Itamar Rabinovitch, *Syria Under the Ba'th, 1963–1966: The Army-Party Symbiosis* (Tel Aviv: The Shiloah Center for Middle Eastern and African Studies, 1972); and Nikolaos Van Dam, *The Struggle for Power in Syria: Politics and Society Under Asad and the Ba'th Party* (London: I. B. Tauris, 1996).

On Syria's foreign policy in the post–World War II period, see Patrick Seale, *The Struggle for Syria: A Study of Post-War Arab Politics 1945–1958* (New Haven, CT: Yale University Press, 1986); David W. Lesch, *Syria and the United States: Eisenhower's Cold War in the Middle East* (Boulder, CO: Westview Press, 1992); Moshe Maoz, *Syria and Israel: From War to Peacemaking* (Oxford: Oxford University Press, 1995); Itamar Rabinovitch, *The War for Lebanon: 1970–1985* (Ithaca, NY: Cornell University Press, 1985); Naomi Weinberger, *Syrian Intervention in Lebanon* (Oxford: Oxford University Press, 1987); Muhammad Muslih, *Golan: The Road to Occupation* (Washington, DC: Institute for Palestine Studies, 2000); and Anoushiravan Ehteshami and Raymond Hinnebusch, *Syria and Iran: Middle Powers in a Penetrated Regional System* (London: Routledge, 1997). Good accounts of the Syrian-Israeli peace process are Helena Cobban, *The Israeli-Syrian Peace Talks: 1991–96 and Beyond* (Washington, DC: US Institute of Peace Press, 1999), and Itamar Rabinovitch, *The Brink of Peace* (Princeton, NJ: Princeton University Press, 1998).

Two good, if sympathetic, biographies and examinations of Syria under Hafiz al-Asad are Patrick Seale, *Asad of Syria: The Struggle for the Middle East* (London: I. B. Tauris, 1988), and Moshe Maoz, *Asad, the Sphinx of Damascus: A Political Biography* (London: Grove/Atlantic, 1990). A less sympathetic portrayal is Eyal Zisser, *Asad's Legacy: Syria in Transition* (New York: New York University Press, 2001). On Syria under Bashar al-Asad, see David W. Lesch, *The New Lion of Damascus: Bashar al-Asad and Modern Syria* (New Haven, CT: Yale University Press, 2005); Flynt Leverett, *Inheriting Syria: Bashar's Trial by Fire* (Washington, DC: Brookings Institution Press, 2005); Volker Perthes, *Syria Under Bashar al-Asad: Modernisation and the Limits of Change* (London: Oxford University Press, 2004); and Alan George, *Syria: Neither Bread nor Freedom* (London: Zed Books, 2003).

Syria's economic situation is covered in an excellent work by Volker Perthes, *The Political Economy of Syria Under Asad* (London: I. B. Tauris, 1995). Also see Eberhard Kienle, ed., *Contemporary Syria: Liberalization Between Cold War and Cold Peace* (London: British Academic Press, 1994). On Syria's culture and society, see Richard T. Antoun and Donald Quataert, eds., *Syria: Society, Culture, and Polity* (Albany: State University of New York Press, 1991); Lisa Wedeen, *Ambiguities of Domination: Politics, Rhetoric, and Symbols in Contemporary Syria* (Chicago: University of Chicago Press,

1999); Umar F. Abdallah, *The Islamic Struggle in Syria* (Berkeley, CA: Mizan Press, 1983); and Sami Moubayed, *Steel and Silk: Men and Women Who Shaped Syria, 1900–2000* (Seattle, WA: Cune Press, 2006).

Useful websites dealing with Syria include the following: Syria Comment (http://syriacomment.com), Syria Report (www.syria-report.com), Syrian Studies Association—Syrian Links (www.ou.edu/ssa/links.htm), Syria Online (www.syriaonline.com), Syria Daily (http://syriadaily.com), and Syrian Center for Political and Strategic Studies (www.scpss.org).

10

HASHIMITE KINGDOM OF JORDAN

Curtis R. Ryan

Despite its central role in the history of the Arab-Israeli conflict and peace process and its geopolitical importance to major powers from the Cold War era to the present, Jordan remains in many ways a young state with ancient roots. Since its perhaps inauspicious beginnings, Jordan has developed into a modern state that has long defied predictions of its imminent demise. What began as the British Mandate for Transjordan in 1921 evolved into the Emirate of Transjordan at the time of independence from Britain in 1946 and finally into its current form as the Hashimite Kingdom of Jordan in 1949. The Hashimite monarchy has throughout its existence pointedly emphasized its Arab heritage as well as its Islamic lineage, especially the direct Hashimite family line descending from the Prophet Muhammad.

HISTORICAL BACKGROUND

Like many other postcolonial states in the Middle East, the Hashimite Kingdom of Jordan has largely artificial boundaries, drawn by European imperial powers. In the aftermath of World War I, Britain and France divided the territories of the former Ottoman Empire between themselves. As part of the Sykes-Picot wartime agreement between Britain and France, the territory that is modern Jordan came under British tutelage. In 1921, having secured the League of Nations' official mandate for the territories of Palestine, Transjordan, and Iraq, the British government created the Emirate of Transjordan through agreement with its new ruler, Emir Abdullah (later King Abdullah I) of the Hashimite family. Thus, the Hashimites only emerged as rulers in Jordan in the third decade of the twentieth century, having earlier ruled Mecca and the Hijaz territory of western Arabia.

The Hashimites had fought with the British in the Great Arab Revolt against the Turkish Ottoman Empire during World War I. But shortly after the war ended, the Hashimites were defeated and expelled from Arabia by their rivals, the Saudis, who ultimately carved out the modern Kingdom of Saudi Arabia, to which they attached the family name. In the postwar mandate period, the British government decided to install two brothers of the House of Hashim, Abdullah and Faisal, respectively, in their mandates of Jordan and Iraq.

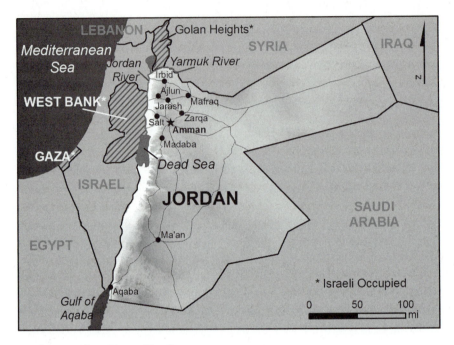

Hashimite Kingdom of Jordan

This move was in large part intended as a reward for Hashimite support in the Arab revolt against the Ottoman Empire during World War I. The British thus established new borders and new dynasties for both Transjordan and Iraq. The latter dynasty was overthrown and eliminated in a bloody coup in Baghdad in 1958, but well into the twenty-first century, the Hashimite monarchy continued both to reign and rule in Jordan.

The Kingdom of Jordan is therefore one of the many successor states of the Ottoman Empire. But the territory east of the Jordan River has a history dating back several millennia of being the crossroads between the Mediterranean, the Orient, and Arabia. The ancient biblical kingdoms of Gilead, Moab, and Edom were largely located in what is now Jordan. Because of its relatively remote (albeit strategically important) location, the area was usually the last conquered and the first abandoned as the great ancient empires ebbed and flowed. At various times, Egyptian, Hittite, Assyrian, Persian, Greek, Roman, and Byzantine armies each occupied the region.

Of all the peoples of antiquity, the Nabataen Arabs were most likely the direct ancestors of modern Jordanians. Shortly after 800 BCE, the Aramaic-speaking inhabitants of Petra created their kingdom along the key north-south trading routes, maintaining their independence until they were conquered by the Romans under Pompey in 64 BCE.

In sociological terms, the Islamic conquest of the area had the greatest impact. The Battle of Yarmuk in 636 CE expelled the Byzantine Christians and laid the groundwork for the establishment of Islam as the religious and cultural foundation for the majority of the people. At various times the area was ruled from Damascus, Baghdad, Cairo, Jerusalem, and Istanbul. Under Ottoman rule, southern Jordan was governed as part of the Hijaz, while the north was included in the Damascus governorate.

The Emergence of Modern Jordan

The modern Jordanian state emerged following the collapse of the Ottoman Empire during World War I. Arab tribesmen under the leadership of Emir Faisal, son of Sharif Hussein of the Hashimite family of the Hijaz (now Saudi Arabia), and advised by the famous Lawrence of Arabia, marched northward against Ottoman forces. The Hashimite-led forces fought as part of the Great Arab Revolt against the Ottoman Empire. But after the war, the Hashimites lost control of Arabia to the rival Al Saud family. Britain then established two brothers of the Al Hashim, Faisal and Abdullah, respectively as rulers of the British Mandates for Iraq and Transjordan.

The establishment of a governmental system for the new Emirate of Transjordan took much time and effort on the part of the British. Being politically cut off from Syria, with whose government its people had been traditionally associated, Jordan lacked a national identity and had practically no economic base. The few Arab administrators in Jordan had fled from the French in Damascus and were generally more concerned with reasserting Arab control in Syria than with making Jordan an independent, self-sufficient state. Less than 3 percent of the land was under cultivation. With virtually no other economic assets in the country, the new government was heavily dependent on British economic support.

With the assistance of a small group of British officials, Jordan under Emir Abdullah made slow progress toward true independence. At first, the administration was simple. Abdullah ruled with the advice of a small executive council. British officials handled defense, foreign affairs, and finance. A major step toward real independence came with a new treaty in 1928 that gave greater authority to the emir and his officials. However, London retained the right to oversee finance and foreign policy, and British officers still controlled the Jordanian army, known then as the Arab Legion. The Organic Law of 1928 made the first move toward a representative government by providing for a legislative council to replace the old executive council. In 1946, Jordan and Britain reached a new agreement whereby a constitution replaced the Organic Law of 1928, and Abdullah was recognized as king of Jordan. Two years later, London agreed to continue paying a subsidy in return for British access to two military bases.

The rising crisis in Palestine became the dominant concern of the fledgling state. Abdullah's policy toward Palestine differed from that of other Arab states. In fact, he met secretly with Zionist leaders, including Golda Meir, in an attempt to work out some modus vivendi with the Jews in Palestine. Nevertheless, when Israel declared independence, Jordan's army occupied areas of Palestine adjacent to Jordan that had been allocated to the Arabs in the UN Partition Plan of 1947. Abdullah's forces were the most successful of the

HASHIMITE KINGDOM OF JORDAN

Capital city	Amman
Chief of state, 2012	King Abdullah II
Head of government, 2012	Prime Minister Fayez al-Tarawneh
Political parties, 2012	Arab Ba'ath Socialist Party, Ba'ath Arab Progressive Party, Call Party, Democratic People's Party, Democratic Popular Unity Party, Islamic Action Front, Islamic Center Party, Jordanian Communist Party, Jordanian National Party, Jordanian United Front, Life Party, Message Party, National Constitution Party, National Current Party, National Movement for Direct Democracy
Ethnic groups	Arab (98%), Circassian (1%), Armenian (1%)
Religious groups	Sunni Muslim (92%), Christian (6%), other (2%)
Export partners, 2011	Iraq (15.3%), United States (14.7%), India (12.5%), Saudi Arabia (9.6%), Lebanon (4.4%)
Import partners, 2011	Saudi Arabia (22.4%), China (10.6%), United States (6.2%), Italy (5.1%), Germany (4.2%), Egypt (4.1%)

Arab armies. When the fighting halted, the Arab Legion held perhaps 20 percent of Palestine, including East Jerusalem.

On April 24, 1950, Abdullah unilaterally annexed the portion of Palestine called the West Bank. Most Arabs joined the Palestinians in believing that Abdullah had betrayed them by annexing part of Palestine. Jordan became a pariah among the Arab states, with only the fellow Hashimite regime in Iraq offering support. At the same time, Abdullah alone among the Arab rulers extended full citizenship rights to the Palestinians. Nevertheless, many Palestinians detested him for what they perceived to be his self-serving action and betrayal of their desire to obtain Palestinian national rights. As King Abdullah was leaving the al-Aqsa Mosque in Jerusalem on July 20, 1951, he was assassinated by a Palestinian nationalist.

Jordan Under King Hussein

After his death, Abdullah was succeeded by his eldest son, Talal, under whom a new constitution was promulgated in January 1952. Talal, however, had a long history of mental illness and under his doctor's advice abdicated in favor of his son Hussein, who was still a minor. A regency council of three was formed to govern for several months until the young Hussein reached majority and assumed the throne in May 1953.

King Hussein ruled Jordan from 1953 until his death in 1999 and therefore became one of the longest-serving monarchs of the twentieth century. The king had served for so long, in fact, that his imprint remains indelibly marked on the evolution of Jordan as a modern state. For most of the modern history of the Hashimite Kingdom of Jordan, most Jordanians knew only one king as architect of the kingdom's domestic development and foreign policy. King Hussein consolidated the Hashimite regime in Jordan and defended it against internal and external challenges, neither of which were in short supply.

Hussein thwarted attempts by nationalist army officers to overturn the monarchy in the 1950s. In the 1960s, Jordan was drawn into the June 1967 Arab-Israeli War. That military disaster carried even more profound social, economic, and political implications, as Jordan lost control of the entire West Bank—including East Jerusalem and its holy places—to Israeli forces. The 1967 debacle also led hundreds of thousands of Palestinian refugees to flee across the Jordan River, joining the thousands already there since the 1948 Palestine War. The changing demographics and regional tensions soon exploded within the kingdom itself in the form of the 1970–1971 Jordanian civil war. The internal struggle pitted the guerrilla forces of the Palestine Liberation Organization (PLO) against King Hussein's regular army. The royalists won the war, but at a very high cost, particularly in Palestinian lives. Although PLO forces were thereafter expelled from the kingdom, the scars of that bitter conflict remained for many decades.

Jordan managed largely to avoid the 1973 Arab-Israeli War, with the regime arguing that another wartime loss would spell the end of Jordan entirely. Token forces were sent to support the Syrian front, but for the most part Jordan remained outside the fighting. The kingdom also remained outside the postwar peace process between Egypt and Israel. In the 1980s, regional tensions and war threatened once again, only this time to the east of Jordan. The 1980–1988 Iran-Iraq War created a new set of challenging circumstances for Jordan. As the war dragged on, Jordan increased its support for Iraq. This policy coincided with the policies of the Gulf states and the US administration. Jordan provided Iraq with a safe port, strategic depth, and a good trading partner. But if Iraq was Jordan's strongest regional ally in the 1980s, it seemed to be more of a liability with the onset of the 1990s.

Jordan's most serious international challenge in almost two decades resulted from the August 2, 1990, Iraqi invasion and occupation of Kuwait. The overwhelming majority of Jordanians supported Iraq against the allied coalition. Facing such strong domestic sentiments, the Hashimite regime attempted to bridge the divide between its traditional Western allies and Iraq. King Hussein shuttled between various capitals in a failed effort to avert war. But Jordan's fence-straddling policy alienated virtually all of its local and global allies, at great cost to the kingdom. The United States, Western allies, Gulf Arabs, Egyptians, and Syrians sharply criticized Jordan's actions. Foreign assistance all but evaporated. The Gulf states expelled 300,000 Jordanians, and an allied armada searched ships entering and leaving the port of Aqaba. Despite the international criticism, King Hussein's popularity soared at home.

In the immediate aftermath of the war, the Hashimite regime played on Jordan's vital role in any Arab-Israeli peace settlement by enthusiastically accepting terms for multilateral negotiations to begin in 1991 in Madrid. Jordanians and Palestinians initially formed a joint delegation to the peace talks before eventually shifting to distinct negotiating teams in Palestinian-Israeli and Jordanian-Israeli peace talks. After Israel and the PLO reached a breakthrough in the Oslo Peace Accords in 1993, the Jordanians pushed for a full and formal peace treaty with Israel. Jordan and Israel made their peace official in 1994, and Jordan was able to utilize the peace process to reestablish its warm ties with the United States and Europe. By the late 1990s, Jordan had also restored diplomatic relations with and financial aid from each of the Arab Gulf monarchies, including Kuwait and Saudi Arabia.

In February 1999, King Hussein of Jordan passed away after a long battle with cancer. He was succeeded by his son, King Abdullah II. This royal succession marked the latest in a series of dramatic transitions in Jordanian politics over the last decade of the twentieth century. These included a process of limited democratization (from 1989), several rounds of economic adjustment and restructuring as the kingdom came to terms with globalization (also from 1989), and the signing of a peace treaty with the State of Israel (in 1994). As the kingdom entered the twenty-first century under King Abdullah II, these three transitions remained the central and most controversial issues in Jordanian politics.

Political Environment

The Land

The Hashimite Kingdom of Jordan sits on part of the north Arabian plateau, which Jordan shares with Syria to the north, Iraq to the east, and Saudi Arabia to the south. No natural frontiers exist between Jordan and its Arab neighbors. The western border of Jordan is the Great Rift Valley, through which the Jordan River flows. From an average of 600 to 900 meters (2,000 to 3,000 feet) on the plateau, the landscape plummets to well below sea level in the valley. The Great Rift Valley also includes the Dead Sea and the Gulf of Aqaba to the south. Jordan's only coastline is a twelve-mile stretch on the Gulf, including the port of Aqaba. Beyond the Great Rift Valley lie Israel and the West Bank highlands.

More than four-fifths of Jordan is desert or semidesert, receiving less than four inches of rain annually. Jordan's population is concentrated in the western part of the kingdom where rainfall, averaging about twelve to sixteen inches annually, permits some farming. All of Jordan's major cities—Amman, Irbid, and Zarqa—are concentrated in this area. Some attempt has been made to expand the area of settlement and cultivation. Of particular note are reforestation projects north of Amman and the East Ghor irrigation canal project in the Jordan River valley. As part of the terms of its 1994 peace treaty, Jordan began importing water from Israel.

The People

Most Jordanians are of Arab heritage and may be roughly divided into two principal groups: Palestinian Jordanians and East Bank Jordanians (sometimes called Transjordanians). Palestinian Jordanians trace their roots to west of the Jordan River, in historic Palestine, and arrived in Jordan in several waves of refugees during and after the 1948 and 1967 Arab-Israeli wars. East Jordanians trace their lineage to east of the Jordan River, and many have roots in the key tribes and clans that originally allied with the Hashimites to create the modern Jordanian state.

Since 1948, Jordan alone among the Arab states has given full citizenship to Palestinians. No official distinction is made between Palestinian and East Bank Jordanians, and all Jordanians share the same legal rights. Grievances remain, however, particularly among Palestinians, who often feel that theirs is a secondary status in Jordanian society. Others, both Palestinian and Jordanian, feel that these distinctions are no longer important. Generally speaking, East Bank Jordanians dominate much of the government, public-sector industry, and military, while Palestinians are heavily represented in private-sector businesses and in the various professions. For many in the regime, however, the East Bank Jordanians remain the rock upon which the Hashimite monarchy was built.

Most Jordanians are Sunni Muslims, although a small Christian minority also exists. Among the Palestinians, the percentage of Christians is higher. Many East Bank Jordanians are members of one of several hundred Arab tribes. Even though Bedouins are a small minority of the overall population, Bedouin values and traditions continue to have an important influence on society. The few who continue to live a nomadic life, as well as those who have settled in towns, maintain these values. In Jordan, more than any other state in the Fertile Crescent, tribal elements provide a disproportionate number of recruits for the military and are guaranteed representation in parliament.

Two minority groups—Christians and Circassians—have also provided backing for the Hashimites. Jordan's Christian population is mainly urban and has lived in the area for centuries. Predominantly Greek Orthodox and Greek Catholic, most are descendants of very early converts to Christianity, whereas others allegedly descend from the Crusaders.

The Circassians settled in Jordan in the last decades of the nineteenth century. They were part of the approximately 1 million Muslims who fled the Caucasus region when the Russians captured it from the Ottomans, and they were given land by the Ottoman sultan in what is now Israel, Jordan, and Syria. The Circassians are Sunni Muslims; they have traditionally been loyal to the monarchy and have held very senior positions in the government. They are particularly numerous in the armed forces and police force. Jordanian Circassians are divided into two major groups: the Adigah and the Chechen. Both groups of Circassians, like Bedouins and Christians, are guaranteed representation in parliament.

Economic Conditions

Despite its harsh climate, Jordan historically was an agricultural country. The loss of the West Bank in the 1967 war, however, dealt a harsh blow to Jordan's economy. Before 1967, the West Bank accounted for 60 to 80 percent of the country's agricultural land, 75 percent of the gross national product, 40 percent of the government's revenue, and nearly 33 percent of its foreign-currency income. With the loss of the West Bank, the hope for self-sufficiency all but vanished.

Nevertheless, the East Bank did have significant economic assets, including industry and mining. The national power plants and important phosphate mines were in the East Bank. In addition, most of the larger manufacturing facilities were located between Amman and Zarqa. These included textiles, leather, batteries, food processing, brewing and bottling, and cigarette manufacturing.

Although possessing no oil of its own, Jordan indirectly benefited from the rapid rise in the price of oil during the 1970s. Subsidies from Arab oil-producing states and remittances from Jordanians working in those states helped provide necessary capital. High rates of growth transformed the Jordanian economy to the point that the service sector became larger than industry and agriculture combined.

With the economic slowdown in the oil industry during the 1980s, the economic growth rate declined to less than 5 percent. Remittances from workers abroad, however, remained fairly constant, as Jordanian workers were not as heavily involved in construction and other sectors of the Arab Gulf economies, which were drastically reduced. Subsidies from the Arab states to the Jordanian government were cut in half, contributing to the difficulties. With steadily declining foreign aid, the kingdom faced a series of shortfalls in the government budget in the late 1980s. By 1988, Jordan's debt was twice its gross domestic product.

By March 1989, the government felt it had no recourse but to turn to the International Monetary Fund for financial help. That help was forthcoming, but only in return for a severe economic-adjustment program, which included cutbacks in state subsidies of staple foods and other products, leading to skyrocketing prices and ultimately to political unrest as well. Riots erupted throughout the country to protest the economic measures and government corruption. The regime, caught off guard by the intensity of the unrest, moved to stave it off by sacking the government, restoring some subsidies, and announcing the resumption of elections and more meaningful parliamentary life in the kingdom. Thus, a positive outcome emerged from decidedly negative circumstances, as the kingdom embarked on its program of limited democratization. That program was not even a year old, however, when another external shock jolted the Jordanian economy. On August 2, 1990, Iraqi forces invaded Kuwait, triggering a major regional and global crisis.

By the time the 1991 Gulf War was over, the crisis had created still more challenges for the Jordanian economy. Subsidies from the oil-producing states were eliminated. Iraq, Jordan's largest trading partner and source of petroleum, lay in ruins and was under boycott by the international community. And 300,000 Jordanian citizens were forced to leave the Gulf states, causing the loss of hundreds of millions of dollars in remittances and placing a major strain on social services within the kingdom.

Paradoxically, however, the return of wealthier Palestinian and East Jordanians with capital created a brief but significant economic stimulus. Many had significant savings that increased foreign-currency deposits from $1.4 billion in February 1991 to $3.2 billion in July 1992. Furthermore, the need to provide housing and other services for the former Gulf residents significantly stimulated construction and other industries. Although the Jordanian economy exceeded expectations following the Gulf crisis, serious problems remained. Political estrangement from the Gulf states continued for almost a decade, with significant economic repercussions. Iraq remained under the UN embargo, depriving Jordan of a primary market. Large numbers of returnees were unable to find work.

By the time of the royal succession in 1999, however, Jordan had managed to restore diplomatic ties with all six Arab Gulf monarchies and had revived part of the earlier economic partnership between Jordan and the Gulf states. Under King Abdullah II, Jordan strengthened its economic and military ties to both the United States and the European Union by securing a free trade agreement with the United States and joining the European Free Trade Agreement. In 2000, Jordan joined the World Trade Organization. King Abdullah's regime clearly sees Jordan's economic and political future as closely tied to these powerful Western states and organizations. Ultimately, hopes for an improved economy will rest on these economic relationships, on peace in the region, and on maintaining and expanding the opportunities for Jordan's well-educated population to find employment throughout the region.

King Abdullah II has made clear that economic development is his main priority. His regime has created free trade and investment zones in the area around the port of Aqaba while encouraging extensive foreign investment and tourism in the kingdom. Abdullah has also been particularly zealous in emphasizing information technology as a key part of Jordan's economic and social development. Unlike many of its neighbors, Jordan has also supported nongovernmental organization (NGO)–oriented sustainable-development projects, including protecting nature preserves while also developing these areas for ecotourism. Yet, for all the many development projects, Jordan remains a small and relatively poor country; hence, it remains largely dependent on outside sources of financial aid and concessionary sources of oil. Still, Jordan's influence and approach to world politics has never been limited by its size and relative lack of resources. This is perhaps best illustrated by the fact that the World Economic Forum, an annual global gathering of some of the world's most influential business and political leaders, is now routinely held in Jordan in the kingdom's Dead Sea resort area.

POLITICAL STRUCTURE AND DYNAMICS

Jordan is a constitutional monarchy. Promulgated in 1952 during the brief reign of King Talal, the constitution gives increased authority to parliament. Nevertheless, the monarch retains ultimate authority over the legislative, executive, and judicial branches.

Executive power is primarily vested in the king. He appoints the prime minister and members of the cabinet and has the power to dismiss members of the cabinet. When parliament is suspended, the king assumes its responsibilities. The king's considerable powers include the right to sign and promulgate laws, veto legislation, issue royal decrees (with the consent of the prime minister and four cabinet members), approve amendments to the constitution, command the armed forces, and declare war. In addition, he appoints and dismisses judges. The question of royal succession is also addressed in the constitution. The throne is guaranteed through the eldest male in direct line from King Abdullah I.

Jordan is divided into five provinces or governorates: Amman, Balqa, Irbid, Karak, and Ma'an. Each province is administered by a governor appointed by the king. At the national level, Jordan has a bicameral parliament. The senators in the upper house, the Assembly of Notables (Majlis al-'Ayyan), are appointed by the king, while the deputies in the lower house, the Assembly of Deputies (Majlis al-Nuwab), are directly elected. The prime minister originates legislation and submits proposals to the lower house. The approval of the upper chamber is necessary only when the lower house accepts a proposal. Should only one of the houses of parliament pass a bill, the two meet together to resolve their differences. Jordan maintains full adult suffrage. Women have had the right to vote and run for office since 1973.

There are three sources of Jordanian law: sharia (Islamic law), European codes, and tradition. The Jordanian constitution and the Court Establishment Act of 1951 mandate a judiciary to reflect these sources of law. Three categories of courts are outlined in the constitution: regular civil courts, religious courts, and special courts. The civil courts system, which is heavily based on Western law, has jurisdiction in all cases not specifically granted to the others. The religious court system has responsibility for personal status and communal endowment. Sharia courts have responsibility for Muslims, whereas the various Christian sects have their own councils. The special courts have responsibility for tribal questions and land issues. The king retains the right to appoint and dismiss judges and pardon offenders.

Parliament, Elections, and Political Change

The 1967 war radically transformed the Jordanian political landscape. Half the elected representatives in parliament had come from the now Israeli-occupied West Bank. The decision of the Arab states at Rabat in 1974 giving the PLO sole responsibility for the destiny of the West Bank further clouded the issue of West Bank representation in parliament, which King Hussein subsequently dissolved. In 1978, he replaced that body with a sixty-member National Consultative Council. Members of the council were appointed by the king for two-year terms. Powers were limited to reviewing bills, and views were not binding. The council was reappointed in 1980 and 1982.

By January 1984, King Hussein had determined that circumstances had changed. It was again in Jordan's perceived interest to increase its influence on the West Bank, open the political system to increasingly well-educated and prosperous citizens, and renew the search for peace with Israel. In order to accomplish these objectives, the king recalled parliament, including representatives from the West Bank. As it was not possible to hold elections on the West Bank, the parliament amended the constitution, allowing elections to be held on the East Bank with West Bank deputies to be chosen by parliament. After the outbreak of the 1987 Palestinian intifada (uprising) against Israeli occupation, the Jordanian regime made a move that it had been debating for decades, renouncing its claims to the West Bank.

Within Jordan, however, the need to open the political system was made very clear by widespread political unrest in April 1989. Eighty deputies were elected from the five governorates of East Bank Jordan. Parties were not allowed to participate. Although all candidates were officially independent, many were known to be affiliated with various parties or groups.

The results of the election in November 1989 alarmed many regime loyalists, as opposition candidates fared very well. Thirty-four of the eighty seats in the chamber went to candidates identified with the Muslim Brotherhood and to independent Islamists. Together they formed the single largest bloc in parliament. Leftist and Arab nationalist candidates won another thirteen seats.

The Jordanian establishment had to adjust its policies in order to adapt to changes in popular opinion. As a means of establishing a national consensus, the king appointed a sixty-member commission that included leaders from all factions, from leftists to Islamic fundamentalists. The commission wrote a national charter, which was a political compact having in many ways as much authority as the constitution. The charter addressed all aspects of state and society and stressed the importance of political pluralism, equality for women, education, a social safety net, and updated labor laws. In agreeing to the national charter, the political opposition in Jordan had endorsed increasing pluralism and political liberalization. In doing so, it also accepted the legitimacy of the ruling Hashimite monarchy. The king endorsed the charter in June 1991 and ended the remaining elements of martial law the following month. In the spirit of the national charter, parliament drafted a law legalizing political parties as a preliminary step toward national elections.

The elections of 1993 resulted in a more moderate parliament. Traditional elements were strengthened and Islamic groups and leftists were weakened, although Islamists and their allies continued to be the single largest bloc. The loss of seats for the opposition, however, was due in large part to the new and controversial electoral law that limited voters to one vote each. The previous electoral law had allowed each voter to vote as many times as there were representatives for their district. Thus, voters in Irbid in 1989 had been able to vote for up to nine representatives from their city for the national parliament. The Muslim Brotherhood utilized this system to run blocs of candidates up to the exact number of seats in a district. That way, they were able to exploit the plurality-based system to gain representation well above their percentage of the overall national vote. But the 1993 electoral law had virtually the reverse effect. The one-person, one-vote restriction was coupled with adjusted new districts that tended to enhance representation in traditionally pro-Hashimite areas—such as rural rather than urban districts. This question of districts and representation remained a bone of contention between the regime and the opposition long afterward.

Prior to the next round of elections in 1997, the regime imposed more restrictive media rules, cutting back on much of the openness that had been achieved since 1989. In 1997, an eleven-party opposition bloc boycotted the parliamentary elections to protest the electoral law, media restrictions, continuing economic-adjustment policies, and normalization of relations with Israel. The electoral boycott led, naturally, to a relatively pliant pro-regime parliament. In effect, the issues that prompted the 1997 electoral boycott remained the central points of debate in Jordanian politics more than a decade later.

Liberalization and Deliberalization

Despite several rounds of parliamentary elections since 1989, Jordan's political party system remains weak, with parties largely associated with particular personalities or charismatic figures.

In 1989, the first modern round of parliamentary elections took place in the context of a decades-old ban on political parties. But as political liberalization continued, Jordan promulgated the national charter, repealed martial law, and legalized political parties once again. When the next parliamentary elections were held in November 1993, twenty legal parties participated. The 1993 elections, however, demonstrated the weaknesses of the parties: less than one-third of the elected members were party members; the majority comprised independents who supported the king. Even those who were members of political parties often ran without party affiliation. Family membership and local influence remain far more important than party identification. The sole exception to the rule regarding weak parties is the Islamic Action Front (IAF), which emerged in the early 1990s as the party of Jordan's Muslim Brotherhood. The Brotherhood has operated as a largely loyal opposition within Jordan for more than half a century and thus remains Jordan's best-organized opposition group. In 1997, party representation within parliament declined still further when the eleven-party opposition bloc boycotted the elections.

Following the 1997 electoral boycott, the IAF and indeed most of Jordan's opposition groups—including most secular leftist parties—found themselves with no representation in parliament. This institutional vacuum was filled as the locus of opposition within Jordanian politics shifted increasingly from parties to professional associations (PAs). These organizations—representing engineers, lawyers, pharmacists, and other professionals—held democratic elections for their own leadership posts. More often than not, the PA elections were won by Islamist candidates. Jordanian debates about liberalization and deliberalization therefore came to include not only parties, parliament, and the media but also the professional associations and other aspects of Jordanian civil society.

In 2003, Jordan held national parliamentary elections in an effort to reengage its stalled political-liberalization process. Given this context, the 2003 elections were deemed especially important by both government and opposition. They were the first since 1997, the first since the dissolution of parliament in 2001, and the first under King Abdullah II. In 2003, the political opposition returned to full electoral participation. The regime had postponed the elections for more than two years, initially over a complicated new voter-card system but probably also because of the Palestinian intifada that began in 2000 and the US invasions of Afghanistan and Iraq in 2001 and early 2003.

In June 2003, the elections were finally held under still another electoral law. The new law, announced in July 2001, lowered the voting age for men and women from nineteen to eighteen and increased the number of parliamentary seats from 80 to 104, with new, but still uneven, electoral districts. In February 2003, King Abdullah added to the changes with a new decree adding six more parliamentary seats in a quota to ensure minimal representation for women. In the previous three elections—1989, 1993, and 1997—only one woman had been elected to parliament. Interestingly, the IAF had originally opposed the women's quota but then included for the first time a woman, Hayat al-Musayni, among its slate of thirty candidates. No Jordanian woman won a seat outright in 2003, but Musayni turned out to be the top vote-getter among female candidates overall. Thus, in an ironic twist, the first woman seated in the new 2003–2007 parliament was a conservative Islamist activist. The IAF succeeded in getting seventeen of its party members elected, including Musayni. Aside from the IAF, five independent Islamists were also elected. Most parliamentary seats, however, went to traditional tribal leaders or former government officials. In short, at least 62 seats out of 110 went to loyalist pro-regime figures.

In 2006, Hamas won a sweeping victory against Fatah in Palestinian legislative elections in the West Bank and Gaza. This seemed to inject a "Hamas factor" into the dynamics of government and opposition in Jordan. For many Jordanian Islamists, the Hamas victory was, on the one hand, inspiring; on the other, it also demonstrated their comparative limitations. Hamas's electoral win produced a new Hamas-led government and cabinet. Within Jordan, in contrast, years of Islamist electoral strategies had indeed produced some success, but at no time did the Muslim Brotherhood or IAF have the opportunity to form a government in Jordan. Still, the Hamas victory seemed to embolden more-hawkish elements in the Jordanian Islamist movement, even as it hardened the positions of the state and especially its intelligence services, or *mukhabarat*, against any Hamas-like shift in the politics of Islamism in Jordan. After the Hamas victory, Jordan's IAF reasserted its demand that governments be drawn from parliament rather than appointed by the king. The party also continued to emphasize its more standard policy stances, including demands to implement sharia law and abandon the peace treaty with Israel.

In the next round of parliamentary elections, in November 2007, the Islamists suffered a resounding and controversial defeat. Islamist strength in parliament dropped from seventeen seats to a mere six, and Islamist candidates even lost in such traditional strongholds as Zarqa. The IAF charged the government with vote-rigging and refused to participate in the next election (in 2010), arguing that the electoral system and voting process were designed to prevent Islamist successes.

Despite differences in ideological or even religious orientation, opposition parties of all types in Jordan actually agree on several things. Most have been sharply critical of the peace treaty with Israel and the regime's policies of economic privatization (since this has reduced the social safety net for many Jordanians). Opposition parties also insist that future prime ministers and cabinets should be drawn from parliament in a truer model of a parliamentary system, rather than royally appointed pending only the formality of parliamentary approval. Still, whether rooted in Islamic, pan-Arab nationalist, or secular leftist ideas, political opposition in Jordan has tended to struggle with the regime over policy and the direction of the state, including demands for greater democratization; it has not tended to challenge the nature of the state itself as a Hashimite monarchy.

There was some cause for optimism in the wake of the 2007 elections in terms of efforts at gender equality. Women made up more than 25 percent of the candidates for parliamentary office, with four times as many running as had contested the 2003 elections. Still, success has remained hard to come by, aside from the six members of parliament determined by the women's quota. But in 2007, Falak Jamaani became the first woman to win a Jordanian parliamentary seat outright—without any form of quota. Jamaani, a career army dentist who retired with the rank of major general, had earned a parliamentary seat in 2003 through the quota system. When she ran for reelection in 2007 in her home district of Madaba, she earned an outright victory. Jamaani's victory was hailed by women's-empowerment activists throughout the kingdom as the first major crack in a glass ceiling over women's representation.

Overall, since the initiation of the political-liberalization process in 1989, the Jordanian political system has taken major steps toward pluralism but then reversed or stalled many of them, leaving full democracy an ideal but not a reality. Political parties, NGOs, and independent media are all part of Jordanian society and political life. Yet tensions remain between the security concerns of the regime and the ambitious reformist agenda of many Jordanian individuals and organizations pressing for democratization.

Jordanian media include a plethora of independent newspapers, magazines, and even tabloids. But laws covering the press and publications include ambiguous regulations preventing journalists from harming state security. Since it remains unclear what might be read as "harming" the state, journalists often practice self-censorship in an effort to avoid running afoul of the intelligence services. Similarly, Jordanian civil society has grown so much that one Jordanian NGO, the al-Urdun al-Jadid Research Center, cataloged no less than 1,800 different civil society organizations operating in the kingdom. These include societies and associations for a variety of purposes, such as educational, cultural, professional, environmental, and, of course, political activism. But here, too, the glass appears to be both half full and half empty. There is clearly no shortage of civil society organizations in Jordan. But the whole purpose of civil society is to be independent of the state, while these organizations are registered with and monitored by government ministries.

In general, Jordan under King Abdullah II has pursued a program of liberalization, but the regime has favored economic over political liberalization. And the latter tends to be slowed by any perceived threats to the security of the Hashimite regime itself. Thus, regional tensions have at times served to undermine the domestic reform process, but they can also underscore, or even reinvigorate, existing divisions within Jordanian society. The Palestinian intifada, for example, revived questions within the kingdom about the nature of Jordanian identity itself. Who exactly is a Jordanian? If a Palestinian state were to be established, would Palestinians in Jordan be loyal to that state or to Jordan? This question, though not of great concern to many Jordanians, is asked by powerful conservative East Bank Jordanians and hence matters within domestic politics. Even economic liberalization carries ethnic implications. As the state slowly privatizes various industries, the historically Palestinian-dominant private sector continues to get larger, while East Bank Jordanian dominance of the public sector is under threat.

For its part, the monarchy insists on its stated policy of "Jordan first," arguing that any emphasis on a Jordanian-Palestinian rift is outdated, divisive, and even unpatriotic. King Abdullah and his wife, Queen Rania (who is of Palestinian origin), both argue that intraethnic divisions are part of Jordan's past, not its future. Still, Jordan is wedged between Israel and Palestine to the west and Iraq and Saudi Arabia to the east, so regional crises and violence do still cross the border, threatening to enflame local divisions. The Hashimite monarchy, however, sees economic development as the key to further unifying the kingdom, as King Abdullah's "Jordan first" program implies.

Yet, as noted above, Jordan remains vulnerable to regional tensions and crises. On November 9, 2005, al-Qaida suicide bombers from Iraq struck three luxury hotels in central Amman, killing sixty people—mostly Jordanians—and injuring more than one hundred. Jordanians referred to this horrific event as "our 9/11." Since Jordan, like most countries, writes dates in the order of day, month, and year, this 9/11 reference is also literal, since the attacks took place (presumably on purpose) on the ninth day of the eleventh month. And in 2011 and 2012, when the entire region was rocked by the revolutions and protests of the Arab Spring, Jordan too was affected by protests for change.

Jordan and the Arab Spring

Like their counterparts in many other countries across the Arab world, Jordanian demonstrators have marched almost every Friday since the start of the Arab Spring. Jordanian protestors began their demonstrations even before the January 25, 2011, revolution in Egypt, but unlike the protestors there, who called for the ouster of longtime dictator Husni Mubarak, Jordanian demonstrators were calling for reform rather than regime change.

Specifically, Jordanian activists mobilized to demand the resignation of the prime minister, Samir al-Rifa'i, and his cabinet. Many Jordanians viewed Rifa'i as a neoliberal technocrat and identified him with some of the regime's most unpopular policies, including economic privatization and liberalization efforts that undercut the traditional social safety net. Other protesters decried perceived corruption in state-led business transactions. In February 2011, King Abdullah acquiesced to protesters' demands and dismissed the Rifa'i government.

A succession of short-lived governments under a series of new prime ministers followed. The Rifa'i government had started a second term in office, which barely lasted two months. Its replacement, the government of Prime Minister Marouf Bakhit, lasted only from February to October 2011. Protestors had been calling for deeper levels of democratic reform, but Bakhit seemed to represent an earlier version of Jordan: he was a member of the conservative East Jordanian elite with a strong tribal background and a long career in the military and intelligence services. He did not, in short, appear to represent the reform that so many Jordanians were hoping for.

In October 2011, however, the king dismissed Bakhit and appointed a new prime minister from a very different mold. Awn Khasawneh was not actually a politician but a highly regarded judge on the International Court of Justice. A strong proponent of democratic reform and the rule of law and committed to wiping out corruption, Khasawneh was charged with revising the kingdom's electoral laws, overseeing a series of amendments to the constitution, and establishing, for the first time, an independent commission to oversee and clean up the registration and voting process. He took his role very seriously but riled many antireform hard-liners in the regime and soon found himself at odds with the king himself. Khasawneh argued that the palace was interfering with daily governance and making his job nearly impossible. The king, for his part, argued that Khasawneh was dragging his feet on completing the reform process. Matters came to a head quickly. A mere six months after taking office, Khasawneh made the unprecedented move of resigning while abroad on a state visit to Turkey in May 2012.

Khasawneh was replaced with a veteran politician and former prime minister, Fayez Tarawneh. Tarawneh had previously served during the transition in the monarchy from King Hussein to King Abdullah. He was a longtime member of the Jordanian Senate and had held a host of key positions in the Jordanian government and foreign service. As prime minister, Tarawneh was expected to play a kind of caretaker role, shepherding the reform process along and laying the groundwork for December 2012 elections.

In the lead-up to the elections, the independent electoral commission registered well over 1 million voters. Yet debates continued to rage in Jordan regarding the electoral law and even the relevance of parliament itself. The new law maintained the earlier gerrymandered districts, which essentially overrepresented rural, mainly East Jordanian areas while underrepresenting urban districts with large Palestinian populations. Yet the new law also added parliamentary seats for national lists that would include political parties. While the regime saw this as a major reform concession, Islamists and many leftist political parties argued that the proportion was too small. Instead, they favored a system in which at least 50 percent of parliamentary seats were based on parties and proportional representation. The Islamist movement felt so strongly about this that it called for a boycott of the 2012 elections.

Even as the electoral and parliamentary debates continued, another controversy emerged as the government passed a new series of laws restricting online media and imposing guidelines similar to those governing print media. After September 2012, online news sites would have to register with the government, editors would have to become members of the Jordan Press Association, and publications would be held responsible for content, including comments left by readers. Reform and free speech activists had tried hard, but ultimately unsuccessfully, to block the laws, arguing that they were too elastic and that restrictions on "news sites" could be extended to blogs and social media sites, as these too posted political news. The government insisted that the new rules would not be used to curb blogs or social media, but many users remained unconvinced and genuinely worried that the new restrictions might curb free speech in the kingdom.

Jordanian activists organized an Internet blackout of hundreds of sites for a day in an effort to demonstrate the potential effects of the legislation. Others pointed out that part of Jordan's business and investment strategy was based on its open Internet policies, in contrast to so many other states in the region, and that the new restrictions might unintentionally undermine the kingdom's own economic and political reform goals. The very fact that Internet restrictions had become such a hot political topic underscored how "connected" Jordanians had become. Jordan is well ahead of most of the region, having established itself as a regional center for information and communications technology. As a result, Jordanians—especially Jordanian youth—are connected online via the Internet, cell phones, and social media such as Facebook, Twitter, blogs, and the like.

Youth activists now communicate not only directly but also virtually and have established an impressive pro-reform and pro-democracy Internet presence, particularly via social media. That, together with the fact that most Jordanians are under the age of twenty-five, has to be remembered in any discussion of reform or the kingdom's political future.

Foreign Policy

As Jordanians continued to debate various aspects of the reform question, regional tensions associated with the Arab Spring threatened to spill across the kingdom's borders. Syria's revolution turned into a civil war between regime and rebel forces, with extensive violence. Not surprisingly, large numbers of Syrians fled. Jordan allowed more than 150,000 Syrian refugees into the kingdom but attempted to keep the refugee populations in towns and refugee camps near the border rather than allowing them to disperse throughout the country as waves of Palestinian refugees had over the decades and thousands of Iraqi refugees had after 2003. Conditions were very difficult for the refugees, but the Jordanian government, working with the United Nations High Commissioner for Refugees and other agencies, felt it was doing all that it could reasonably do, especially in the context of its own economic downturn. And Jordanian security agencies and border forces worried that the violence in Syria might destabilize Jordan as well. As usual, the internal stability of the kingdom would hinge not just on its domestic politics but also on its international relations and foreign policy.

From the foundation of the Hashimite state onward, Jordan maintained close strategic ties to Britain and later the United States. After World War II and the onset of the Cold War, Jordan established stronger and stronger links to the United States, as the Western powers came to view Jordan as a conservative bulwark against communism and radical pan-Arabism and a potentially moderating element in the Arab-Israeli conflict. From the beginning, then, Jordan has held close ties to powerful Western states and has in fact depended heavily on foreign aid from these countries to remain afloat.

Jordan's very centrality in Middle East politics and geography also has carried with it real strategic vulnerability. Given its location, Jordan from the outset was deeply involved in the various dimensions of the Palestinian-Israeli and broader Arab-Israeli conflicts. By the time of Jordanian independence in 1946, tensions were peaking in neighboring Palestine between Jews and Arabs over the issue of Jewish and Palestinian aspirations to full statehood. When the United Nations voted to partition Palestine between the two peoples in 1947 and Israel declared its independence the following year, Jordan's Arab Legion was one of the Arab armies that fought Israel, joining fighting that had already begun between Jews and Arabs in Palestine. In that hard-fought campaign— a defeat for the Arab forces—Jordan's Arab Legion held on to East Jerusalem and the West Bank. Jordan later lost both territories in the disastrous 1967 Arab-Israeli War.

While tensions continued in the following years, Jordanian foreign policy avoided direct confrontation with Israel and pursued a resolutely cautious and conservative course. The chief architect of this approach to foreign policy was, of course, the late King Hussein. Under Hussein, and afterward under King Abdullah II, Jordanian foreign policy has been driven by regime security above all things.

In the Jordanian context, regime security consists of not only military but also economic components. As a small and relatively poor state, Jordan relies on external sources of aid and oil and external labor markets. Tourism and foreign investment are cornerstones of King Abdullah's approach to national development, both requiring domestic and regional stability. As a result, King Abdullah has maintained his father's emphasis on cautious foreign policy while also actively pursuing a regional role as a peacemaker. Despite its small size, Jordan sends soldiers on UN peacekeeping operations throughout the world.

In regional politics, meanwhile, King Abdullah has maintained the kingdom's peace treaty with Israel while pressing for a peace settlement between Israel and the Palestinian National Authority. Abdullah has argued to US officials in particular that the Palestinian issue remains the single most destabilizing issue in Middle East politics. The Jordanian government therefore consistently offers its good offices in relations between the United States, Israel, and the Palestinian National Authority. But with periodic Palestinian uprisings against Israel, the instability following the 2003 US invasion of Iraq, and the 2011–2012 revolution in Syria, Jordan's geography has left it wedged between three zones of conflict.

Despite the intensity of regional insecurity, Jordan for the most part has remained stable and secure within its borders, while the regime continues to emphasize economic development, trade, investment, and an active tourism industry as the ultimate keys to Jordan's present and future. These priorities, in turn, have led the monarchy to pursue warm relations with economically influential states, from the Arab Gulf monarchies to the European countries and the United States.

Under King Abdullah, as under King Hussein before him, Jordan has presented itself as a source of regional moderation and stability, and the kingdom has continued to play a foreign policy role far beyond what its small size and limited resources would otherwise suggest. Yet it also remains vulnerable to crises erupting across its borders and even to internal tensions as government and opposition struggle over the question of domestic reform. Despite the importance and even dire security implications of conflict in neighboring states, the kingdom's stability hinges even more on its ability to pursue genuine reform and change. Earlier forms of largely cosmetic change are no longer adequate to accommodate the wave of change represented by the Arab Spring. King Abdullah argues that the Arab Spring is an opportunity rather than a challenge and that Jordan is carving its own unique niche in the midst of regional change. This represents neither revolution nor civil war but rather a model of a monarchy reforming itself for a more stable and democratic future. Whether Jordan succeeds in following a reform path rather than one of revolutionary unrest depends entirely on how convinced Jordan's people are regarding the depth and reality of change.

BIBLIOGRAPHY

For good general histories of Jordan, see Philip Robins, *A History of Jordan* (Cambridge: Cambridge University Press, 2004), and Kamal Salibi, *The Modern History of Jordan* (London: I. B. Tauris, 1998). Robert Satloff's *From Abdullah to Hussein: Jordan in Transition* (New York: Oxford University Press, 1993) examines the emergence of the Hussein regime in the early 1950s. For a detailed analysis of the emergence of Jordan as a country, see Mary C. Wilson's *King Abdullah, Britain and the Making of Jordan* (Cambridge: Cambridge University Press, 1987). On Jordanian development and national identity and debates over these issues within Jordanian politics, see Marc Lynch, *State Interests and Public Spheres: The International Politics of Jordan's Identity* (New York: Columbia University Press, 1999), and Joseph Massad, *Colonial Effects: The Making of National Identity in Jordan* (New York: Columbia University Press, 2001).

Several articles have examined various aspects of the democratization process in the kingdom, including Rex Brynen, "Economic Crisis and Post-Rentier Democratization in the Arab World: The Case of Jordan," *Canadian Journal of Political Science* 25, no. 1 (1992): 69–97, and Glenn E. Robinson, "Defensive Democratization in Jordan," *International Journal of Middle East Studies* 30, no. 3 (1998): 373–387. For an analysis of the 1989, 1993, and 1997 elections, see Curtis R. Ryan, "Elections and Parliamentary Democratization in Jordan," *Democratization* 5, no. 4 (1998): 176–196.

On contemporary Jordanian politics, particularly the democratization process, economic reform, peace with Israel, and the succession from Hussein to Abdullah, see Curtis R. Ryan, *Jordan in Transition: From Hussein to Abdullah* (Boulder, CO: Lynne Rienner, 2002). On economic change, see Peter Moore, *Doing Business in the Middle East: Politics and Economic Crises in Jordan and Kuwait* (Cambridge: Cambridge University Press, 2004).

An interesting and challenging discussion of Palestinian-Jordanian relations within the kingdom can be found in Mustafa Hamarneh, Rosemary Hollis, and Khalil Shikaki, *Jordanian-Palestinian Relations: Where To?* (London: Royal Institute of International Affairs, 1997).

On the Islamist movement within Jordan, see Jillian M. Schwedler, *Faith in Moderation: Islamist Parties in Jordan and Yemen* (Cambridge: Cambridge University Press, 2006); Janine A. Clark, *Islam, Charity, and Activism: Middle Class Networks and Social Welfare in Egypt, Jordan, and Yemen* (Bloomington: Indiana University Press, 2004); and Quintan Wiktorowicz, *The Management of Islamic Activism: Salafis, the Muslim Brotherhood, and State Power in Jordan* (Albany: State University of New York Press, 2000).

On Jordan's international relations and foreign policy, see Laurie A. Brand, *Jordan's Inter-Arab Relations: The Political Economy of Alliance Making* (New York: Columbia University Press, 1994); Marc Lynch, *State Interests and Public Spheres* (New York: Columbia University Press, 1999); and Curtis R. Ryan, *Inter-Arab Alliances: Regime Security and Jordanian Foreign Policy* (Gainesville: University Press of Florida, 2009).

Useful websites on Jordan include those of the Jordanian embassy to the United States (www.jordanembassyus.org); the main English-language daily newspaper in the kingdom, the *Jordan Times* (www.jordantimes.com); the Center for Strategic Studies at the University of Jordan (www.css-jordan.org); the al-Urdun al-Jadid Research Center (www.ujrc-jordan.org); the American Center for Oriental Research (www.bu.edu/acor); the Jordan Tourism Board (www.visitjordan.com); a site dedicated to the memory and accomplishments of the late King Hussein (www.kinghussein.gov.jo); and the official websites of King Abdullah (www.kingabdullah.jo) and Queen Rania (www.queenrania.jo).

11

State of Israel

David H. Goldberg

Israel is a product of Zionism, the Jewish national movement. Since biblical days, Jews of the Diaspora (Jewish communities outside Israel) have hoped to return to Zion, the Promised Land. While some Jews always resided in the Holy Land, the overwhelming majority lived in the Diaspora. Over the centuries Zionism developed spiritual, religious, cultural, social, and historical concepts linking Jews to the land of the historical Jewish state in Israel. The political variant of Zionism that saw the establishment of a Jewish state as a logical consequence of its actions developed in the nineteenth century, partly as a result of political currents then prevalent in Europe, especially nationalism and anti-Semitism—often referred to as the Jewish question.

Historical Background

In 1897, Theodor Herzl, a Viennese journalist who had proposed establishing a self-governing community for the Jewish people in his book *Der Judenstaat* (*The Jewish State*), organized a conference at Basel, Switzerland, to assemble prominent leaders from the major Jewish communities and organizations throughout the world. This assembly shaped a Zionist political movement and established the World Zionist Organization. The Basel Program, which became the cornerstone of Zionist ideology, enunciated the basic aim of Zionism: "to create for the Jewish people a home in Palestine secured by public law" as a response to the Jewish question.

World War I enabled the Zionist movement to make important gains. As a consequence of the war, the Ottoman Empire, which had ruled Palestine since the sixteenth century, was forced to relinquish the territory. With the aid of Chaim Weizmann, a prominent Zionist leader and chemist who contributed to the British war effort, the Zionist organization secured from the British government the Balfour Declaration (1917), stating, inter alia, "His Majesty's Government view with favour the establishment in Palestine of a national home for the Jewish people." By the end of the war, British control had replaced Ottoman rule in Palestine. The League of Nations allocated the Palestine mandate to Great Britain, which controlled the area between 1920 and May 1948.

State of Israel

During the mandate period, the British mandatory government entrusted the elected representative body of the organized Jewish community in Palestine (the Yishuv) with the responsibility for Jewish communal affairs—but not foreign policy or defense—and granted it considerable autonomy. The National Council established institutions for self-government and procedures for implementing political decisions. It also controlled the clandestine recruitment and military training of Jewish youth in the defense force (Hagana), which after independence formed the core of Israel's defense forces.

Prototypical political institutions, founded and developed by the Jewish community, laid the foundation for many of Israel's public bodies and political processes. Several of the semigovernmental organizations that were created—most notably the General Federation of Labor (Histadrut), founded in 1920, and the Jewish Agency (legitimized in Article

4 of the League of Nations Palestine mandate)—continued to play important roles after Israel's independence and contributed to the growth of a highly developed system of Zionist political parties and the consequent prevalence of coalition executive bodies in the Zionist movement and the local organs of Palestine Jewry.

Throughout the mandate period, the Jewish and Arab communities of Palestine were in conflict over the future of the territory. Arab opposition to Jewish immigration and land purchase was manifested in such actions as the Arab revolts in the 1920s and 1930s. British policy vacillated, but restrictions on Jewish immigration became a central element of the British response to intercommunal violence. Unable to find a solution to satisfy these conflicting views, the British eventually turned the problem of the mandate over to the United Nations, which placed the Palestine issue before its General Assembly in the spring of 1947.

The UN Special Committee on Palestine studied the problem and recommended that the mandate be terminated and that the independence of Palestine be achieved without delay; however, the committee was divided over the future of the territory. The majority proposal recommended partition into a Jewish and an Arab state linked in an economic union, with Jerusalem and its environs established as an international enclave—a separate body (*corpus separatum*). The minority recommended that Palestine become a single federal state, with Jerusalem as the capital and with Jews and Arabs enjoying autonomy in their respective areas. On November 29, 1947, the UN General Assembly, over strong Arab opposition, adopted the majority recommendation by thirty-three votes to thirteen, with ten abstentions. The Zionists reluctantly accepted the decision as the best practical outcome. The Palestinian Arabs and other Arabs rejected the vote.

Thereafter the situation in Palestine deteriorated rapidly. Violent disorders, reminiscent of those of the 1920s and 1930s, broke out in all parts of the territory, and as the end of the mandate approached, these degenerated into a virtual civil war. General Sir Alan Gordon Cunningham, the last British high commissioner, departed. Israel declared its independence as a Jewish and democratic state on May 14, 1948. Armies of the Arab states entered Palestine and engaged in open warfare with the defense forces of the new State of Israel. The United Nations secured a truce, and the military situation was stabilized in the spring of 1949 by a series of armistice agreements between Israel and the neighboring Arab states. But no general peace settlement was achieved.

The provisional government of Israel, which was formed at the time of independence and recognized by the major powers, was new in name only. It had begun to function following the adoption of the partition resolution in 1947, and it drew on the experience gained by the Yishuv. After proclaiming Israel's independence, the provisional government repealed the British mandatory restrictions on Jewish immigration to Palestine and the sale of land to Jews and converted the Hagana into the Israel Defense Forces (IDF).

State of Israel

Capital city	Jerusalem
Chief of state, 2012	President Shimon Peres
Head of government, 2012	Prime Minister Benjamin Netanyahu
Major political parties (share of most recent vote, 2009)	Kadima (22.5%), Likud (21.6%), Yisrael Beiteinu (11.7%), Labor Party (9.9%), Shas (8.5%), United Torah Judaism (4.4%), United Arab List (3.4%), Hadash (3.3%), National Union (3.3%), New Movement–Meretz (3%), Jewish Home (2.9%), Balad (2.6%)
Ethnic groups	Jewish (76.4%, of which 67.1% are Israeli-born), non-Jewish, mostly Arab (23.6%)
Religious groups	Jewish (75.6%), Muslim (16.9%), Christian (2%), Druze (1.7%), other (3.8%)
Export partners, 2011	United States (28.8%), Hong Kong (7.9%), Belgium (5.6%), United Kingdom (5%), India (4.5%), China (4%)
Import partners, 2011	United States (11.8%), China (7.4%), Germany (6.2%), Belgium (6.1%), Switzerland (5.4%), Italy (4.2%)

Political Environment

Israel's special role as the world's only Jewish state has had a manifold effect on its political system. Israel is interested in the well-being of Jews everywhere and concerned that all Jews who wish to immigrate be free to do so. Israel's Declaration of Independence proclaims that "the State of Israel will be open to the immigration of Jews from all countries of their dispersion." The Law of Return of July 5, 1950, provides that "every Jew has the right to come to this country as an 'oleh' [Jew immigrating to Israel]," and it has been reinforced by the programs and actions of successive Israeli governments. The "ingathering of the exiles" has received overwhelming support in the Knesset (Israel's parliament) and from the majority Jewish population, and it has been implemented almost without regard to the economic costs and social dislocations caused by the rapid and massive influx of people. Immigration serves Israel's needs by providing the manpower necessary for Israel's security and development and for maintaining Israel's unique Jewish character.

The early immigrants laid the foundations for an essentially European culture in Palestine, and subsequent immigration accelerated the trend of Westernization. The Occidental (overwhelmingly Ashkenazi, referring to Jews of central and eastern European extraction) immigrants developed the Yishuv structure of land settlement, trade unions, political parties, and education in preparation for a Western-oriented Jewish national state. Future immigrants had to adapt themselves to a society that had formed these institutions, and this presented a problem for those who were part of the immigration from non-Western countries, including the massive influx of Jewish communities from Muslim states in the Middle East and North Africa.

Economic, social, and cultural assimilation of the waves of immigrants in a short time would have been a formidable undertaking for a small country even under the most favorable conditions. In Israel, this has been accomplished despite the obstacles posed by limited resources, defense needs, and the diverse composition and character of the new immigrants. Mandatory military service, which emphasizes education, the experience of common living and working, and learning the Hebrew language, facilitates acculturation and encourages evolution in the direction of a unified, multicultural Jewish Israeli society.

Some 24 percent of Israeli citizens in 2012 were Israeli Arabs—that is, Arabs who have lived in Israel since its independence and their offspring. Israeli Arabs confront problems qualitatively different from those facing Jewish immigrants. After the 1949 armistice agreements, most of the areas held by Israel and inhabited by Arabs were placed under military administration. Israel's Arabs were granted citizenship but forbidden to travel into or out of security areas without permission from the military, as a means of preventing infiltration, sabotage, and espionage. As it became evident that Israel's Arab citizens were not a disloyal fifth column, popular pressure for relaxation and then for total abolition of military restrictions grew. The restrictions were gradually modified, and on December 1, 1966, the military government was abolished.

The major long-term challenge for the Arab minority is its social integration. Although Israeli Arabs vote, sit in the Knesset, serve in government offices, have their own schools and courts, and prosper materially, they face difficulties in adjusting to Israel's modern Jewish- and Western-oriented society. The Arabs tend to live in separate villages and separate sections of the major cities. They speak Arabic, attend separate schools, and, with few exceptions, do not serve in the army. Israel's Arab and Jewish communities have few points of contact, and those that exist are not intimate. The societies are segregated and generally hold stereotyped images of each other, often reinforced by the schools, media, and social distance, as well as by the tensions and problems created by the larger Arab-Israeli conflict in its numerous dimensions.

Over time the Arab community has become restive and increasingly politically aware. In the spring of 1976, Israel's Arabs participated in their first general protest and staged the most violent demonstrations to that date in Israel's history. The riots grew out of a general strike that was organized to protest land expropriations. The demonstrations escalated and eventually became broader and more general in their focus.

Israeli Arabs demonstrated greater political activism after the beginning of the Palestinian intifada (uprising) in the West Bank and Gaza Strip in December 1987. They began to identify more strongly with the Arabs in the occupied territories and showed signs of growing nationalism and greater militancy. In October 2000, Israeli Arabs rioted and demonstrated in support of the Palestinians and expressed long-standing grievances. Twelve Israeli Arabs (and one resident of the Gaza Strip) were killed in clashes with Israeli police. A commission of inquiry concluded that specific circumstances, combined with a long-standing grievance in Israel's Arab community concerning unfair treatment and discrimination by the Jewish majority, had triggered the riots. There was a continuing gap between government commitments on the one hand and their implementation on the other.

Despite the existence of a number of Arab political parties, Israeli Arabs have failed to form a significant independent Arab political party to represent the Arab minority in its quest for Arab rights and to express Arab opinions and views. In the absence of such an Arab political party, the Arab Democratic Party, the United Arab List, and the mixed Jewish-Arab Israeli Communist Party, in their various incarnations, have played important roles in the articulation of the Arab perspective. Arab members of the Knesset (MKs) continue to stir controversy by participating in the international campaign to delegitimize the State of Israel and Zionism.

In February 2006, Israel's High Court of Justice held that Israel's Arab citizens are endowed with equal rights and must not be discriminated against in resource allocation and that racism and discrimination must be avoided. The court noted that although Israel is defined as a Jewish and democratic state, any favorable bias in education budgets for Jewish communities must be rejected outright. The democratic nature of the state requires that citizens residing in it have equal rights.

Religion and the State

Israel is a Jewish state, but that does not ensure agreement on the appropriate relationship between religion and the state or between religious and secular authorities, or even on the methods and techniques to be employed by religious authorities for determining "who is a Jew." Since independence, Israel has had to come to terms with the concept of its Jewishness and the question, Who is a Jew? And thus it has had to address what it means to be a Jewish state. Secular and religious authorities and ordinary citizens have faced the question in connection with issues of immigration, marriage, divorce, inheritance, and conversion, as well as in matters related to registration to secure identity cards and the official collection of data and information. The question relates to the application of laws, such as the Law of Return, the Nationality Law, and others passed by the Knesset, and to their interpretation by secular and religious authorities. It remains essential not only to determine "who is a Jew" but to decide who should make such a determination and what criteria should be used.

Although Israel's government is secular, there is no formal wall of separation between religion and the state, as is common in Western democracies. The Ministry of Religious Affairs concerns itself with meeting Jewish religious requirements, such as the supply of ritually killed (kosher) meat, rabbinical courts, and religious schools (yeshivot), as well as with meeting the religious needs of the non-Jewish communities that enjoy religious autonomy. These functions are not controversial. But there is sharp and recurrent controversy concerning the extent to which religious observance or restriction is directly or indirectly imposed on the entire Jewish population. Moreover, the religiously ultraobservant (Haredi) community, constituting about 10 percent of the Jewish population, through its own political parties and its membership in government coalitions has been able to secure government agreement to establish separate school systems, exempt most of its young men and women from army service, and curtail almost all business and public activity on the Sabbath. The less-observant and secular Jews of Israel argue that they do not have religious freedom because of governmental acquiescence to demands of the observant Jewish groups and the limitations placed on the public role of non-Orthodox streams of Judaism in Israel.

Israel utilizes a modified millet system derived from the Ottoman period for distributing authority among religious communities. The various religious communities (Jewish, Muslim, Christian, Druze) exercise jurisdiction in litigation involving personal-status and family law and apply religious codes and principles in their own judicial institutions. Matters that are secular concerns in other states often fall within the purview of religious authorities in Israel. Even though there is no established state religion, all religious institutions have a special status and authority granted by the state and are supported by state funds.

The political reality that has required coalition governments in Israel from the outset has also necessitated inclusion of political parties of the Haredi community in virtually all cabinets as coalition partners. They have sought to control the Ministry of Religious Affairs and usually also the Ministries of the Interior and Education. This has given the religious parties substantial political power and thus an ability to enforce many of their demands and perspectives concerning the role of religion in the Jewish state. The role of religion in Israel's everyday life clearly remains a major social and political issue.

Economic Conditions

Israel's economy has undergone substantial change since independence, and the economic well-being of the people has improved significantly. Israel remains something of an economic miracle, having transformed itself from a semisocialist backwater into a high-tech superpower. A country virtually bereft of natural resources and faced with substantial burdens imposed by massive immigration and Arab/Islamic hostility has achieved a relatively prosperous economic standard. By the beginning of the twenty-first century, Israel had achieved a large economy by regional standards, and its people generally had become prosperous. The standard of living in Israel and the productivity of its labor force are comparable to those in Western European countries. The Israeli people live in one of the healthiest countries in the world, and Israel provides extensive social services for its population. Per capita, there are more technology start-ups in Israel, attracting more foreign venture capital investment, than in any other country in the world.

Israel's small size and its lack of mineral and water resources profoundly affect its economy. Its dearth of energy resources has made it almost completely dependent on foreign supplies of oil, coal, and natural gas. Since the 1980s, Israel's oil imports have contributed significantly to its large balance-of-payments deficit. Two natural gas fields discovered off Israel's coast in 2009–2010, with estimated reserves of 25 trillion cubic meters of gas, could be a game changer for Israel's economy by heightening the country's energy-security outlook.

Extensive irrigation and intensive farming methods have dramatically increased agricultural production for both domestic consumption and export. Israel is a world leader in developing advanced agricultural technology. Israel's agricultural exports include citrus, cotton, vegetables, and dairy products. Industrial export commodities include machinery and equipment, software, cut diamonds, chemicals, and textiles and apparel.

Israel's development can be traced to an investment program financed from outside sources, including US government loans and grants, the sale of Israel bonds, investments, and German reparations and restitution payments. At the same time, charitable contributions from the world Jewish community helped reduce the government's burdens in the social welfare sector, thereby permitting the use of scarce funds for economic projects. Israel's substantial human resources include Nobel Prize winners nurtured by world-class universities.

During its domination of politics from before independence to 1977, the Labor Party pursued socialist economic policies in a mixed economy adapted to the special circumstances of Israel. The government played a central and decisive role in the economy, aided by the Jewish Agency, the United Israel Appeal, the Jewish National Fund, and the Histadrut labor federation. When the nonsocialist Likud came to power in 1977, the system was altered to reduce the government's role in the economy and apply free market principles.

Hyperinflation in the mid-1980s was arrested by an aggressive economic-stabilization program adopted in July 1985. But the economy was soon buffeted by the effects of the Palestinian intifada that started in December 1987, the mass immigration of Soviet Jews that began in 1989, and the crisis resulting from the Iraqi invasion of Kuwait in 1990.

In the early 1990s, Israel's high-tech sector took off, there was a large influx of well-educated immigrants, and prospects for regional peace seemed to improve. These factors combined to fuel the economy's strong performance, which slowed only in the second half of the 1990s. A recovery of economic activity started in the second half of 1999, with a rapid expansion of gross domestic product (GDP) driven by industrial exports in high-technology sectors. Israel had also adopted important structural reforms, including privatization of core industries and reduced controls on foreign companies operating in Israel. Israel made progress in the direction of a more open, competitive, market-oriented economy, although public spending remained a significant proportion of GDP, and top marginal income tax rates remained high.

The outbreak of the al-Aqsa Intifada in September 2000 plunged Israel's economy into a recession. GDP shrank for two years, unemployment reached 11 percent, and tourism all but disappeared. A growing government budget deficit forced an austerity program that, among other factors, cut social welfare benefits. As before, however, conditions began to improve as the violence was contained and security improved.

By 2004, Israel's economy had returned to its robust pre–September 2000 expansion, as investors and businessmen focused on the long-term resilience of the Israeli economy, despite the absence of peace and continuing (though lessened) terrorist attacks. The integration of Israel's economy into the twenty-first-century global economy continued, with imports at 40 percent of GDP and exports at more than 35 percent. Israel's economic growth for 2005 was the highest in the Western world.

Israel's economy was largely unaffected by the 2006 war in Lebanon, despite incessant Hizballah shelling that resulted in massive social disruption, affecting more than 1 million citizens, as well as the short-term collapse of tourism. Similarly, Operation Cast Lead against Hamas in Gaza in December 2008 and January 2009 did not have a discernible impact on Israel's economic performance or outlook. From an economic standpoint, the key was that foreign investment continued as if there had been no hostilities.

Israel's economy emerged largely unscathed from the global financial crisis that began in 2008–2009, with solid fundamentals following years of prudent fiscal policy and a stable banking sector. In the summer of 2011, popular protests arose around vast disparities in wealth, housing prices, the cost of living, and the cost of basic commodities. Israel's government adopted tax reforms to address some of the protestors' grievances, but Prime Minister Benjamin ("Bibi") Netanyahu remained committed to an economic program of austerity, deficit reduction, and deep cuts to all sectors of the state budget, including social welfare.

POLITICAL STRUCTURE

Constitutional Consensus

Israel's system of government is based on an unwritten constitution. The first legislative act of the Constituent Assembly in February 1949 was to enact the Transition Law (small constitution), which became the basis of constitutional life in the state.

The First Knesset (parliament) devoted much time to a profound discussion of the constitutional issue, and on June 13, 1950, it adopted a compromise that has indefinitely postponed the real debate. It decided, in principle, that a written constitution would ultimately be adopted; for the time being, however, there would not be a formal, comprehensive document. Instead, a number of fundamental, or basic, laws would be passed dealing with specific subjects, which might, in time, form chapters in a consolidated constitution. Israel has adopted Basic Laws dealing with various subjects. The Basic Laws (and their amendments) articulate the formal requirements of the system in specific areas of activity, thereby providing a written framework for governmental action.

Several areas of popular national consensus, together with the Basic Laws, define the parameters of Israel's political system. Those disavowing allegiance to these Jewish-Zionist ideals tend to be marginalized. Israel's self-definition as a Jewish state is perhaps the most significant area of consensus, although views diverge on some of its tenets and their interpretation. Accord centers on the "ingathering of the exiles" and ensuring that Israel is a social welfare state in which all share in the benefits of society and have access to essential social, health, and similar services. Foreign and security policy draws from a wide consensus because of its overriding importance in light of continuing Arab/Islamic hostility and the resultant conflict, although there is discord concerning methods and techniques employed. The IDF enjoys an enviable reputation and serves as a national unifying institution—despite vilification by Far Left and Far Right activists because of specific actions and events.

Political Institutions

Israel has a parliamentary political system, in which the government (cabinet) and the parliament (Knesset) are the dominant institutions and the president serves essentially as a ceremonial or symbolic figure.

These core institutions perform the basic political functions of the state within the framework provided by Israel's constitutional consensus. The president is elected by the Knesset for a seven-year term and may not be reelected. He or she is generally a figure of considerable stature with popularity and support among the population. Until 2000, all presidents completed their terms or died in office. In 2000, President Ezer Weizman resigned over criticism about financial improprieties. Weizman was succeeded by former Likud MK Moshe Katzav, who resigned in disgrace in June 2007 amid accusations of sexual harassment. During the six months prior to his resignation, Katzav had been replaced on an interim basis by Knesset speaker Dalia Itzik. In July 2007, the Knesset chose veteran Israeli parliamentarian and statesman Shimon Peres as Israel's ninth president.

The president is head of state, and his powers and functions are essentially representative, though not inconsequential. The president participates in the formation of the government and receives its resignation. The president's powers and functions relating to the formation of the government require consultation with the parties in the Knesset and selection of a member of that body to form a government. Although traditionally the leader of the largest party in the Knesset has been chosen, the president can use his or her discretion to select the person he or she deems most capable of creating a viable coalition government. For instance, after the 2009 elections, Peres tapped Benjamin Netanyahu, leader of the Likud Party, holder of twenty-eight Knesset seats, despite the fact that Tzipi Livni's Kadima Party held twenty-nine seats.

In 1996 the election process changed, and the prime minister and Knesset were chosen by popular vote. This eliminated the president's function of providing the mandate to the prime minister. The change was short-lived; in March 2001 the Knesset eliminated direct election of the prime minister and restored the previous system.

The prime minister is the most powerful figure in Israel's political system. The president entrusts a member of the Knesset with the task of establishing a government, generally with him- or herself as prime minister and a number of ministers who are usually, but not necessarily, MKs.

The government is formally instituted upon obtaining a vote of confidence from the Knesset. It is collectively responsible to the Knesset, reports to it, and remains in office as long as it enjoys the confidence of that body. Only one successful Knesset vote of no confidence has caused the ouster of a government, in March 1990. A government's tenure may also be terminated by the ending of the Knesset's tenure, by the resignation of the government on its own initiative, or by the resignation of the prime minister.

The Knesset is the supreme authority in the state. It is a unicameral body of 120 members elected by national, general, secret, direct, equal, and proportional suffrage for a term not to exceed four years. Voters cast their ballots for parties rather than individual candidates, and each party presents voters with a list, in order of preference, of up to 120 candidates—its choices for Knesset seats. After ballots are cast, seats in the Knesset are determined. From 1949 to 1988, only those party lists that received at least 1 percent of the total number of valid votes cast were represented in the Knesset. The threshold for the 2009 election stood at 2.5 percent. Any list failing to obtain this minimum does not share in the distribution of mandates, and its votes are not taken into account in determination of the composition of the Knesset.

The main functions of the Knesset are similar to those of most modern parliaments. They include expressing a vote of confidence or no confidence in the government, legislating, participating in the formation of national policy, and supervising the activities of the governmental administration. The Knesset, divided into numerous legislative committees, must also approve the budget and taxation, elect the president of the state, recommend the appointment of the state comptroller, and participate in the appointment of judges.

Judicial authority is vested in religious as well as civil courts. The Supreme Court of Israel is unique in that all citizens have the right to direct appeal. The Supreme Court does not formally have the power of judicial review of Knesset legislation, but it has the authority to invalidate administrative actions and declare statutes to be contrary to the law.

The Court's growing activism in this regard has provoked criticism from all points on Israel's wide ideological spectrum. Each major religious community (Jewish, Muslim, Christian) has its own religious court system that deals with an array of matters of personal status.

POLITICAL DYNAMICS

Political life is intense in Israel, political participation is extensive, and political parties play a central role in the political life of the country. Israel's political system is characterized by a wide range of ideological and social viewpoints that are given expression not only in political parties but also in social media and a host of social, religious, cultural, and other organizations. Numerous minority and splinter factions freely criticize the government. This diversity has been most apparent in the existence of multiple parties contesting Knesset elections (and in the factions within most of the major parties) and in the coalition governments that have been characteristic of Israel since its independence. Because Israelis vote not for individuals but for parties in parliamentary elections, the party determines where individuals will be placed on the electoral list and thus who will represent it in the Knesset and in government. Individuals or groups of individuals, no matter how prominent, generally have not fared well when divested of the support of the established parties. In the several instances in which there has been notable success (such as that of the Democratic Movement for Change in 1977 and the Center Party in 1999), the success has tended to be ephemeral. Electoral campaigns are controlled by the established parties, which make the decisions, wage the campaigns, and spend the money. In the final analysis the voter focuses on the party, the party member looks to it for fulfillment of his or her needs, and the politician needs its leaders and machinery to ensure a political future.

Israel's political parties and the blocs they have formed have gone through a substantial number of mergers, splits, disagreements, and reconciliations as a result of the intensity of ideological differences, policy disagreements, and personality clashes. Numerous parties have contested the 120 seats in the Knesset, and many have been successful in winning representation. The complex party structure reflects various dimensions of cleavage, but socioeconomic, religious-secular, and foreign policy/national security issues tend to be the most significant.

The multiplicity of parties, the diversity of views they represent, and the proportional-representation electoral system have prevented any one party from winning a majority of Knesset seats in any of the eighteen elections between 1949 and 2009, necessitating the formation of coalition governments. Prior to the national unity government formed in 1984, only twice had the coalitions been truly broad-based, and those were established in times of national stress: the provisional government formed at independence and the national unity government formed during the crisis preceding the 1967 war and maintained until the summer of 1970. The 1984 national unity government was unique in that it was based on a principle of power sharing between Labor and Likud, the two major political blocs. This experiment was repeated after the 1988 election and lasted until spring 1990. The rigorous discipline of Israel's parties has curbed irresponsible action by individual Knesset members. Continuity of policy has also been enhanced by the reappointment of many ministers in reshuffled cabinets and the permanence of bureaucratic officeholders.

Notwithstanding the varying views and interests, Israel's coalitions have proved remarkably stable. In the 1990s, systemic changes in Israeli society (referred to as "tribalization" by some analysts) resulted in the end of coalition stability in Israeli politics, as the Knesset devolved into numerous relatively small parties, necessitating extensive negotiations in the formation and maintenance of coalition governments.

The requirements of coalition government have placed limitations on the prime minister's ability to control the cabinet and its actions fully. The prime minister does not appoint ministers in the traditional sense; he or she reaches accord with the other parties, and together they select the individuals who will hold the various ministerial portfolios and share in the cabinet's collective responsibility for governing Israel. Similarly, the prime minister does not necessarily have the power to dismiss ministers (although Ariel ["Arik"] Sharon did succeed in dismissing right-wing ministers Avigdor Lieberman and Binyamin Elon in 2004 in a dispute over Sharon's Gaza disengagement plan). The prime minister does, however, possess substantial powers that enable him or her to influence the process by which ministers are selected and removed.

Coalition formation is one of the more interesting and arduous tasks of the prime minister. Each party and each political leader has a complex set of interests and concerns and seeks to maximize gain from participation in, and support of, the prime minister's government. Each party leader wants ministerial slots, concessions on policy matters, and funding for institutions, as well as patronage and positions for party loyalists. The bargaining resulting from the coalition system has permitted the religious parties—National Religious Party/Mafdal, Agudat Israel, Poalei Agudat Israel, United Torah Judaism, and Shas—to gain considerable policy concessions and to play strong roles in government decision making because they were essential to securing a majority in the Knesset.

Despite party proliferation and general political intensity and diversity, Israel's political life has been dominated by a relatively small and cohesive Jewish elite that has been mostly homogeneous in background. Most of its early leaders were European in origin, arrived in Israel during the Second Aliyah (1904–1914), and were personally acquainted, if not intimate. The political elite was predominantly civilian in character and background, although, increasingly, high-ranking military officers have become senior political figures and opinion leaders after completing their military careers. Religious elements have exerted strong influence in the cabinet and Knesset as political parties because of their role in government formation. The elite structure has come to include Moroccan Jews and other Sephardim, as well as native-born Israelis (*sabras*), a reflection of the country's shifting demographics. The rabbinate is not considered part of the political elite, and the religious establishment generally does not intervene directly in politics.

The IDF is virtually unique in the Middle East in that it does not, as an entity, play a role in politics, despite its size, budget, and importance. The military in Israel is subordinate to its civilian masters, both constitutionally and in practice. Individual officers and senior commanders (such as Moshe Dayan, Yitzhak Rabin, Yigael Yadin, Ehud Barak, Yigal Allon, Ariel Sharon, and Shaul Mofaz) have secured important political positions, but they have done so as individuals, only after retiring from active military service and joining political parties, and without the backing of the military as an institution. Their military reputations and popular prestige enhanced their chances for, but did not ensure, significant political careers.

Changing Political Dimensions

The Labor Party, in various incarnations, dominated the political life of the Yishuv and of Israel from the 1920s to the 1970s. The turmoil in Israel's political life at the time of the Yom Kippur War (1973) set in motion forces that created the political "earthquake" (*mahapach*) that led to Likud's replacement of Labor in the 1977 Knesset elections.

Many of the social and political forces set in motion by the Yom Kippur War and its aftermath seemed to coalesce when Israel's electorate went to the polls in May 1977. The largest number of votes went to the Likud, led by Menachem Begin. The Likud emerged as the leading political force, formed the government, and took control of Israel's governmental bureaucracy. The parties constituting the Likud bloc (especially Begin's Herut) had been serving as the opposition since independence, with the exception of their joining the "wall-to-wall" government of national unity from 1967 to 1970. Now Likud established the coalition responsible for establishing and implementing programs and policies, and Begin worked toward implementation of Vladimir Zeev Jabotinsky's revisionist vision, developed decades earlier, of a Jewish state in all of the Land of Israel.

The 1981 Knesset election was not conclusive: the electorate virtually divided its votes between the two blocs but awarded neither bloc a majority of votes or seats in parliament. President Yitzhak Navon granted the mandate to form the new government to Begin, and the latter succeeded in forming a Likud-led coalition. The election highlighted the political dimension of the ethnic issue in Israeli politics: Likud secured the majority (probably some 70 percent) of the Oriental Jewish vote. (Oriental Jews are non-Ashkenazi Jews, primarily of Afro-Asian origin. In Hebrew they are called collectively *Edot Hamizrach*, meaning "Eastern" or "Oriental communities." Generally the term refers to Jews whose origins are in Muslim lands.) Begin's popularity with the Oriental community was a direct result of its previous failure to secure appropriate representation in the Knesset, his courting of the community even as opposition leader, and his responsiveness to its concerns during his first administration. This support of Begin and Likud—an apparent identification by Orientals of a political home—came in lieu of an effective independent Oriental political organization. Likud was widely seen as the party that would assist the Oriental community in emerging from its second-class status.

Begin was a personally popular politician with strong charismatic appeal, and he was an able and skilled political leader. When Begin resigned in the fall of 1983, his foreign minister, Yitzhak Shamir, a relative newcomer to politics, replaced him. The short-lived Shamir government was virtually the same as its predecessor in its membership and pursued a policy of continuity.

In the 1984 election, fifteen of the twenty-six political parties that participated secured seats in the Knesset. The Labor Alignment secured forty-four seats, and Likud secured forty-one. This division in the Israeli body politic contributed to, and complicated the formation of, a government of national unity that was approved by the Knesset in September 1984. The new government inaugurated an experiment in Israeli politics at the basis of which was an agreement by the two dominant parties to share power, with the unusual proviso of a "rotation" of their leaders, Shimon Peres and Yitzhak Shamir, in the positions of prime minister and foreign minister. The national unity government, with the power-sharing and rotation concepts, lasted its full term largely because there was strong public support for its continuation and no politician wanted to be seen as flouting the popular will by bringing it down.

The results of the 1988 election were similar to the inconclusive outcome of the 1984 balloting. Likud emerged with only a slight edge over Labor, winning forty Knesset seats to Labor's thirty-nine. The Oriental Jewish community continued to vote for Likud in greater numbers than for Labor, although there were indications that its support for Likud was weakening and that some were turning more to the Sephardic ultra-Orthodox Shas and other religious parties.

The establishment of a new and different national unity government in December 1988 was a complicated process, but after weeks of maneuvering, Likud's Yitzhak Shamir was able to establish a government in which he would remain prime minister throughout its tenure. Labor's Shimon Peres was appointed finance minister, a position that would give him little international visibility and little opportunity to generate popular support within Israel. Yitzhak Rabin retained the post of defense minister throughout the government's term; this became especially important after the outbreak of the intifada in December 1987.

In early 1990, Labor quit the Shamir government. This led to the only successful vote of no confidence in the Knesset's history. Labor's Shimon Peres was granted a mandate from the president to form a successor coalition but failed. Shamir ultimately established a narrow coalition (in June 1990) supported by parties and individuals from the political Right and the religious bloc.

The Iraqi Scud missile attacks during the 1991 Persian Gulf War soon tested the new government—and Shamir's leadership. The government showed remarkable restraint and did not respond militarily to the attacks, largely in response to US President George H. W. Bush's urging.

After the Gulf War, in October 1991, Israel entered into peace negotiations in Madrid to resolve the conflict with its Arab neighbors. In January 1992, after three rounds of bilateral talks, the right-wing Tehiya and Moledet parties, which together held five Knesset seats, resigned from the government over Shamir's willingness to discuss an interim agreement on Palestinian self-rule in the West Bank and Gaza Strip. The defection of the two parties deprived the coalition of a parliamentary majority, and agreement was reached to schedule Knesset elections for June 1992.

The election was contested by twenty-five political parties, representing virtually all points of the political spectrum. Commentators called the outcome of the election another political earthquake, in the sense of revolutionary change, as in 1977. This time Labor, led by Yitzhak Rabin (who had unseated Shimon Peres in a leadership primary), was the victor, winning forty-four Knesset seats, ending a decade and a half of Likud rule. Likud lost eight seats, falling to thirty-two. The religious parties fell from eighteen to sixteen seats; more importantly, they lost their traditional role as kingmakers.

The crucial element in the outcome of the election was the creation of a blocking majority of sixty-one Knesset seats, which meant that Shamir would not be able to reconstruct a Likud-led nationalist-religious right-wing coalition. Rabin moved quickly to forge a coalition that included the left-wing Zionist Meretz (with twelve seats) and Shas.

Labor's return to control of the Knesset and government generated an initial euphoria among many in Israel, and external observers were hopeful that the peace process might be reinvigorated. This soon proved to be the case, as seen in the signing of the Oslo Accords in September 1993. Some movement also took place in Israel's negotiations with Syria. But Rabin was assassinated in November 1995 by Yigal Amir, a right-wing religious student who considered him a traitor for relinquishing territory promised by God to the Jewish people and occupied by Israel in the 1967 war.

The 1996 elections were held under a changed electoral process that allowed Israelis to cast two ballots, one for a party list for the Knesset and one for direct election of the prime minister. Shimon Peres, who succeeded the assassinated Yitzhak Rabin as prime minister and Labor Party leader, campaigned on the theme of continuity and expansion of the peace process. Peres was narrowly defeated by the Likud's Benjamin Netanyahu, who focused on the need for security as the first imperative, with peace achievable at the same time. Netanyahu formed a Likud-led coalition government that included secular-nationalist and religious parties. Netanyahu's tenure in office was marked by a fractioned Knesset and coalition government. He suffered from discord on both domestic and foreign policy issues, especially the peace process. Although negotiations with the Palestinians moved slowly, eventually there were the Hebron Agreement (January 1997) and the Wye River Memorandum (October 1998), which were approved separately by narrow margins in the Knesset. However, Netanyahu could not keep his restive coalition together, and agreement was reached to hold new elections for both the Knesset and the prime ministership in the spring of 1999.

Ehud Barak—former IDF chief of staff and newly chosen leader of the One Israel bloc, comprising Labor and two small parties—was elected prime minister in May 1999, defeating Netanyahu in the direct election. However, One Israel was able to obtain only twenty-six seats in the Knesset election, and this led to the formation of a broad and disparate coalition. Barak faced a very divided Knesset. Israel's two traditionally dominant political parties, Labor/One Israel and Likud, together held fewer than half the seats in the Knesset; thirteen parties, representing virtually all points on the political spectrum, initially shared the remainder. Barak succeeded in cobbling together a coalition of these diverse political units. Its longevity was questioned from the outset, but it seemed to hold together as Barak began efforts to achieve his goals of peace and security.

After June 2000, the coalition unraveled. Barak's government was reduced from 75 of the Knesset's 120 seats in July 1999 to only 30 seats as of August 2000. Barak soon called for a new, special direct election of the prime minister. This time he faced Ariel Sharon, who had replaced Netanyahu as Likud leader.

Election 2001 occurred against the background of weeks of intense Palestinian violence that followed Palestine Liberation Organization (PLO) leader Yasir Arafat's rejection of Barak's diplomatic offer at Camp David II (July 2000). Sharon won overwhelmingly, primarily because he suggested a different way to ensure security for the average Israeli.

Sharon understood Israeli concerns about security. Israelis sought, and Sharon promoted, "security and peace." Sharon made clear in his campaign that the Oslo process was dead and that the security of Israelis was the central requirement and objective of his administration. The two elements overlapped in his demand that an end to Palestinian violence must precede a return to negotiations, which would not be restricted by the Oslo process. For a large number of Israelis, Ehud Barak had failed to deliver significant movement on the peace process, despite substantial concessions to the Palestinian position, and many saw erosion in their personal security as the al-Aqsa Intifada adversely affected the situation of the average Israeli.

Sharon's government, approved by the Knesset on March 7, 2001, was broad based, including Likud, Labor, and Shas, as well as a number of smaller secular-nationalist and religious parties. For the first time, the government included an Israeli Arab minister. The government reflected a broad Israeli national consensus that the time was not ripe to achieve a peace treaty with the Palestinians. Supporters and opponents of the Oslo process joined in a cabinet whose clear first objective was to stop the violence and restore security to the average Israeli.

The coalition government collapsed on October 30, 2002, when Labor Party ministers resigned in a dispute over the reallocation of social funding to settlement activity in the West Bank and Gaza Strip. Sharon sought alternative Knesset support for the government from religious and right-wing nationalist parties.

Sharon retained the leadership of the caretaker government and added new members to it. Former Likud prime minister Benjamin Netanyahu became foreign minister, and Shaul Mofaz became defense minister. Mofaz, an Iranian-born Jew, was a former IDF chief of staff who had advocated sending Yasir Arafat into exile. His inclusion was widely seen as shifting the government more to the right on terrorism and security issues.

The 2003 elections resulted in another major victory for Sharon, with Likud taking thirty-eight Knesset seats compared with only nineteen seats for Labor, now under the leadership of Amram Mitzna, a former IDF general and the popular mayor of Haifa. Sharon emerged with a stronger mandate to deal with the Palestinians and the security issue, while Labor suffered its worst election defeat and shrank to its smallest size ever. Clearly, Likud was again the dominant power in Israeli political life.

Sharon presented the coalition government to the Knesset on February 27, 2003, his seventy-fifth birthday. The coalition initially comprised only the barest of majorities: 61 of 120 seats in the Knesset, although an agreement was reached to include another party that brought an additional seven seats, thereby according Sharon a comfortable majority. Sharon noted that his government's mission would be to deal with the worsening economic situation and resolve the conflict between Israel and the Palestinians.

In a lengthy interview published in *Ha'aretz* in April 2003, Sharon spoke of "painful concessions" to help achieve peace and suggested giving up some Jewish settlements in the occupied territories—"steps that are painful for every Jew and painful for me personally. . . . If we reach a situation of true peace, real peace, peace for generations, we will have to make painful concessions." He continued, "We are talking about the cradle of the Jewish people. Our whole history is bound up with these places. Bethlehem, Shiloh, Beit El. And I know that we will have to part with some of these places. As a Jew, this agonizes me." He emphasized that he would not make concessions that would jeopardize Israel's security.

On December 18, 2003, Sharon announced that Israel would take unilateral steps to ensure the country's security in the absence of a Palestinian partner for peace. He warned that Israel would end negotiations and take unilateral disengagement measures if the Palestinian Authority (PA) did not take action to halt terrorism and there was no progress toward a negotiated peace within the next few months.

On April 14, 2004, President George W. Bush essentially recognized Israel's right to retain some West Bank settlements. Bush referred to "new realities on the ground," suggesting that it was unrealistic to expect the outcome of final-status negotiations to be a full and complete return to the 1949 armistice lines and that the so-called right of return of Palestinian refugees to Israel was effectively ruled out. Bush called Sharon's plan to disengage unilaterally from Gaza "historic" and "courageous."

The last months of 2004 and the first months of 2005 focused on the Gaza disengagement plan, which called for dismantling all twenty-one Israeli settlements in the Gaza Strip and four small, isolated ones in the northern West Bank, beginning in July 2005. It pitted all elements of Israeli society against one another and developed along all of the political and religious fault lines, overshadowing other aspects of national life. Ultimately, Sharon prevailed.

Overshadowing everything was the death of Yasir Arafat on November 11, 2004. On January 9, 2005, the Palestinians went to the polls to elect a successor as head of the Palestinian Authority. Mahmoud Abbas (Abu Mazen), who had already replaced Arafat as chairman of the PLO, won the election handily and seemed to bring a new approach to the conflict with Israel that suggested prospects for new openings and opportunities. Even as he reaffirmed his support for the intifada as a vehicle of Palestinian resistance against Israel, Abbas implied that violence and the Palestinian resort to arms were counterproductive. This suggested prospects for an improvement in relations with Israel.

Arafat's death and the opportunity presented by Sharon's disengagement proposal led Labor, again under Shimon Peres, to rejoin the coalition government on January 10, 2005. Labor was convinced that Sharon's Gaza disengagement plan was a crucial step toward a settlement with the Palestinians and could fail without Labor's support. The Knesset voted approval of a new coalition led by Sharon by a vote of fifty-eight to fifty-six with six abstentions. On February 20, 2005, the cabinet approved Sharon's plan to unilaterally withdraw Israeli settlers and soldiers from the Gaza Strip.

Over the summer of 2005, Israel's occupation of the Gaza Strip ended fully. The settlers were evacuated, the settlements demolished, the troops withdrawn, and the military positions abandoned and destroyed. Palestinian control of Gaza replaced Israeli (since 1967) and Egyptian (1949 to 1967) control.

In a speech to the UN General Assembly on September 15, 2005, Sharon spelled out a critical principle to guide future Israeli policy concerning the territories and the nature of Israeli-Palestinian relations: "The right of the Jewish people to the Land of Israel does not mean disregarding the rights of others in the land. The Palestinians will always be our neighbors. We respect them and have no aspirations to rule over them. They are also entitled to freedom and to a national, sovereign existence in a state of their own."

Ariel Sharon, one of Likud's principal founders, increasingly frustrated by rebellion and opposition within the party, resigned on November 12, 2005, and created a new "centrist" political party, Kadima (Forward), which he would lead in the 2006 Knesset elections. Sharon took with him a number of Likud ministers and MKs and was joined by some leading Labor Party members and other prominent Israelis. Sharon said he left Likud because he did not want to waste time with political wrangling or miss the opportunities presented by Israel's withdrawal from Gaza. This political earthquake set in motion changes within the Israeli political system, with a new center emerging under Sharon's leadership.

Amir Peretz, a Moroccan immigrant and head of the Histadrut Labor Federation, defeated Shimon Peres for leadership of the Labor Party in November 2005. Peretz appealed to Israel's working class and Sephardic Jews of Middle Eastern descent and origin. Peres subsequently left Labor to join Sharon's new Kadima Party.

The Knesset was disbanded officially on December 8, 2005, preparing the way for the next Knesset election, to be held on March 29, 2006. Thirty-one parties presented lists of candidates.

On the night of January 4, 2006, Sharon suffered a major stroke and fell into a coma. Unexpectedly, his career was over, and Israel was in search of new political leadership, as was the peace process.

Sharon's incapacitation, followed by the Palestinian elections of January 25, 2006, posed a major challenge for the Israeli body politic. The election results were as much a repudiation of the PLO mainstream Fatah movement (for corruption and ineffectiveness) as they were a vote for the Islamic fundamentalist Hamas and its stated political objectives. Nevertheless, for Israel it raised a basic question: how to deal with a Palestinian government whose dominant party (and prime minister) was Hamas, an organization whose charter calls for the end of Israel.

In early April 2006, with no change expected in Sharon's condition, the Kadima-led coalition deemed him officially and permanently incapacitated and unable to discharge his duties of office. They chose Ehud Olmert to serve as interim prime minister.

The 2006 election marked the beginning of a new and significant period in Israel's political life. The voter turnout was only 63.2 percent—low by Israeli standards. Twelve parties gained sufficient votes to pass the 2 percent threshold required to win seats in the Seventeenth Knesset.

The election results were an earthquake that dramatically altered Israel's political landscape. The new Kadima Party, without its founder Ariel Sharon, won twenty-nine seats, and its new leader, Ehud Olmert, was tasked with forming the new government. Labor was the second-largest party, winning nineteen seats. Likud, which had dominated Israeli politics and was basically the party in power for more than a quarter century, with some brief interludes, shrank in size and influence. The Left-Right and religious-nonreligious balance in the Knesset seemed to focus on a centrist approach.

On May 4, 2006, the Knesset approved Israel's thirty-first government, headed by Ehud Olmert. The cabinet was large and included a curious mix of individuals. Olmert served for the first time as prime minister. Tzipi Livni became only the second woman (after Golda Meir) to serve as foreign minister. Labor Party leader Amir Peretz became minister of defense, despite a lack of significant military experience.

Olmert noted that he preferred negotiations with the Palestinians for a solution, but only with a Palestinian Authority that upheld all previous agreements with Israel and fought terror. If it continued to be led by terrorist factions, it would not be a partner in negotiations; nor would there be practical day-to-day relations. Failing a change—"We will not wait forever"—Israel would act without an agreement to establish defensible borders and ensure a solid Jewish majority. In the government policy guidelines, Olmert noted that major settlement blocs in the West Bank would be part of the sovereign State of Israel forever. The disengagements from the Gaza Strip and northern settlements in the West Bank were a prelude to Olmert's "convergence" proposal, which would move tens of thousands from settlements scattered throughout the West Bank to several settlement blocs near the Green Line.

Olmert's tenure in office was beset by crises from the outset. The kidnapping of one Israeli soldier (Gilad Shalit) by Hamas in June 2006 and two more (Ehud Goldwasser and Eldad Regev) by Hizballah in July, as well as Israel's poorly conceived objectives in the Second Lebanon War (July–September 2006), underscored for many Israelis the political and military inexperience of the prime minister and especially of Defense Minister Peretz. The Winograd Committee of Inquiry, established to investigate deficiencies in Israel's prosecution of the Second Lebanon War, was strongly critical of the wartime decision making of Olmert and Peretz. However, while finding failings in their management of the war, the committee determined that, concerning the crucial cabinet decisions affecting the IDF's prosecution of the war, Olmert and Peretz had acted on the merits and "on the basis of the facts before them."

Asserting that the mountain of allegations of corruption and financial impropriety rapidly piling up against him had been the product of a "political witch hunt," Olmert on July 31, 2008, announced that he would resign as prime minister following the Kadima Party's primary on September 17, 2008. Unable to form a new coalition, the new Kadima leader, Tzipi Livni, recommended to Israel's president that new Knesset elections be held. Agreement was reached to hold the elections on February 10, 2009. Under Israeli law, Olmert and the incumbent government remained in office, pending the formation of a viable successor government. In this caretaker capacity, the Olmert-led government prosecuted Operation Cast Lead, the twenty-three-day IDF counterterrorism operation against Hamas in the Gaza Strip from December 27, 2008, to January 18, 2009.

Much change occurred in Israel's political landscape in the run-up to the 2009 elections. Following Ariel Sharon's dramatic departure, on December 19, 2005, Benjamin Netanyahu was chosen again to lead the Likud Party. Similarly, Ehud Barak was elected again to lead the Labor Party on June 12, 2007, succeeding Amir Peretz. Barak also took over Peretz's position as defense minister in the governing coalition.

The 2009 election campaign focused exclusively on security and peace issues. Kadima leader Tzipi Livni endorsed the basic principles adopted at the November 2007 Annapolis Conference, including expedited bilateral negotiations leading to a viable two-state solution coupled with a "zero-tolerance" approach to Hamas rocket attacks from the Gaza Strip. By contrast, Netanyahu and Likud were skeptical of the Annapolis efforts, calling instead for a return to the "performance-based roadmap" initially formulated by US President Bush in 2002.

Livni's Kadima Party won twenty-eight seats in the elections, one more than Netanyahu's Likud. The right-wing Russian Yisrael Beiteinu Party rose to third place in the Knesset with fifteen seats, pushing a controversial agenda that called on Israeli Arabs to take a voluntary "loyalty oath" to the Jewish state, while Labor took thirteen seats. Shas won eleven seats.

Having considered the overall configuration of the new Knesset, and after consulting the parties, President Shimon Peres invited Benjamin Netanyahu to form Israel's thirty-second government. The new government, approved by the Knesset in March 2009, was a broad-based coalition giving Prime Minister Netanyahu a solid majority of 69 seats in the 120-seat Knesset. A separate agreement brought MKs from the Ashkenazi Haredi United Torah Judaism party (three seats) into the coalition as deputy ministers and chairs of influential Knesset committees.

Domestically, Netanyahu shepherded an economy backed by solid fundamentals, following years of prudent fiscal policy and a stable banking sector. The economy was bolstered by an energetic high-tech sector, strong foreign investment, and the prospect of game-changing offshore gas-field discoveries.

Two issues challenged Netanyahu's government on the domestic front. In the summer of 2011, popular protests led by students and involving elements of Israel's traditionally quiescent middle class arose over vast disparities in wealth between rich and poor sectors of Israeli society, the concentration of wealth, housing prices, the cost of living, and the price of basic commodities. The government appointed a committee headed by economist Manuel Trajtenberg to address the protestors' grievances. By Trajtenberg's own admission, the tax reforms adopted by the government would not satisfy the protesters' demands for a fundamental restructuring of Israel's socioeconomic order. On July 14, 2012, Moshe Silman, a fixture at earlier protests in Haifa, set fire to himself to protest the "governmental injustice" that he charged had caused his impoverishment and desperation. Silman died six days later, and a second self-immolation victim died shortly thereafter. Prime Minister Netanyahu expressed regret for such "personal tragedies" but remained committed to an economic program of austerity, deficit reduction, and deep cuts to the state budget, steps seemingly at stark variance with the protestors' grievances.

Also dominating Netanyahu's domestic agenda was the challenge of addressing the inequality inherent in the systematic exemption of Haredi men and women from military service in Israel, which had been given legal expression through the Tal Law of 2002. On February 12, 2012, Israel's High Court of Justice ruled against the constitutionality of the Tal Law. Netanyahu pledged that his government would formulate new legislation that would guarantee "a more equal sharing of the burden on all parts of Israeli society."

On May 2, 2012, Netanyahu called for early Knesset elections to preempt pressure about the exemptions from the religious parties in his coalition. Days later, Netanyahu shocked the Israeli body politic by striking a deal with Shaul Mofaz to have the Kadima Party enter the government, giving the coalition 94 of 120 seats in the Knesset.

Concluding robust legislation for integrating Haredim into the IDF was a key element of the Likud-Kadima coalition agreement. Netanyahu appointed a committee chaired by Kadima MK Yochanan Plesner, but Netanyahu abruptly dissolved the committee on July 2, 2012. Plesner nevertheless released the committee's recommendations, which included (1) imposing the principle of universal service on all Israeli citizens, (2) imposing individual liability on anyone trying to evade service, (3) mandating the draft of Haredi men, and (4) applying the principle of universal service to the Arab sector via civilian national service opportunities.

Kadima leader Shaul Mofaz viewed committee recommendations as a "historic opportunity" to bring equality to military service in Israel and demanded their immediate adoption. Netanyahu favored their incremental adoption, a process more amenable to the Likud's Haredi coalition partners. Kadima quit the coalition on July 17, citing severe disappointment with Netanyahu's handling of the military exemptions.

There was much movement in Israel's political landscape in 2011–2012. In mid-January, the Labor Party split in a dispute about whether to quit Netanyahu's coalition over the pace of negotiations with the Palestinians. Party leader Ehud Barak and four other MKs quit Labor to form the new Haatzmaut (Independence) faction and stayed in the coalition, with Barak remaining defense minister. MK and former journalist Shelley Yachimovich succeeded Barak as Labor Party leader, defeating Amir Peretz in a September 2011 primary. Despite widespread relief at the safe return of IDF soldier Gilad Shalit on October 18, 2011, after more than five years of Hamas captivity, there was widespread debate about the Netanyahu government's decision to exchange Shalit for 1,027 Palestinian prisoners, including many "with Jewish blood on their hands." In January 2012, veteran journalist and media personality Yair Lapid announced his intention to create a new centrist political party. Early surveys suggested that Lapid's Yesh Atid (There Is a Future) could steal votes from Center-Left and Center-Right secular parties in the election for the Nineteenth Knesset, scheduled for no later than spring 2013. MK and former IDF chief of staff Shaul Mofaz ousted Tzipi Livni as leader of the Kadima Party in a primary on March 27, 2012. As discussed above, Mofaz then briefly took Kadima into Netanyahu's coalition government.

FOREIGN POLICY

The primary objectives of Israel's foreign and security policies remain the quest for peace through negotiations (with the Arab states and the Palestinians) and the assurance of security in a region of hostility through an effective defense capability. The goals of peace and security derive from the continuing conflict with the Arab states, the Palestinians, and Iran and Iran-sponsored Islamist terrorists, which remains the preeminent problem confronting Israel. It affects all of Israel's policies and activities, both domestic and foreign. Israel recognizes that peace and cooperation with the Palestinians and the neighboring Arab states are vital for the long-term survival and development of the Jewish state, and this remains the cornerstone of its foreign policy.

During its first thirty-four years of existence, between 1948 and 1982, Israel fought six wars with Arab states and the PLO. Between 1987 and 2006, two intifadas brought violence and terrorism to Israel. In 2006, Hizballah initiated a thirty-four-day war that engulfed Israel and Lebanon. From December 2008 to January 2009, Israel fought a twenty-three-day war with Hamas in an effort to stop the smuggling of weapons into the Gaza Strip and to end rocket attacks on Israeli towns and cities. Wars, countless skirmishes and terrorist attacks, and incessant, vituperative rhetoric, combined with the Holocaust and Arab hostility during the mandate period, have all left their mark on Israel's national consciousness. Israel spends, on a continuing basis, a major portion of its budget and GDP on defense and defense-related items and has, by regional standards, a sizable standing army and reserve force widely considered to be of great quality and capability. It is believed to have nuclear weapons. Israel's military power is substantial but not unlimited and is constrained by its own demography and economy, as well as by international factors.

Israel's quest for peace with its Arab neighbors dates from its establishment. Although Israel accepted the UN Partition Plan (UN General Assembly Resolution 181[II]), the Arabs opposed the partition of Palestine, and the Arab League declared war in response to Israel's declaration of independence upon termination of the British mandate. The armistice agreements of 1949, following the first Arab-Israeli war, were intended to facilitate a transition to "permanent peace in Palestine." Negotiations did not begin, and Israelis soon became preoccupied with the need for security. The Suez War of 1956 reinforced that concern and was waged in response to Egyptian president Gamal Abdel Nasser's calls for Israel's destruction.

The Six-Day War of 1967 generated dramatic change in Israelis' perceptions of their security situation. The realities of Arab hostility, the nature of the Arab threat, and the difficulties of achieving a settlement became more obvious. Belligerent threats from the Arab world, especially Egypt, engendered realistic Israeli concerns of politicide—the destruction of the state. Israel's preemptive military strike proved successful in preventing the imminent threat of an Arab military invasion; Israel staved off defeat and achieved a militarily secure position. The dynamic of the conflict changed as a result of the Israeli victory: Israel occupied the Sinai Peninsula of Egypt, the Gaza Strip, the West Bank, East Jerusalem, and the Golan Heights of Syria. Israel adopted the position that it would not withdraw from those territories until negotiations with the Arab states had led to peace agreements that recognized Israel's right to exist and accepted Israel's permanent status and borders. The Arab view was articulated in the Palestine National Covenant of 1964, which called the creation of Israel "null and void," and in the "three no's" resolution of the Arab League summit meeting in Khartoum in September 1967: "no peace with Israel, no recognition of Israel, no negotiations with it."

Throughout the period between the Six-Day War and the October 1973 Yom Kippur War, the focal point was the effort to achieve a settlement of the Arab-Israeli conflict and secure a just and lasting peace. In those attempts, based on UN Security Council Resolution 242 of November 22, 1967, the regional states, the superpowers, and the main instrumentalities of the international system were engaged. Israel focused its attention on peace and security objectives and developed positions concerning the occupied territories, the Palestinians, and related questions. Although some of the diplomatic efforts were promising, peace was not achieved. In 1969 and 1970, Israel and Egypt engaged in a lengthy and costly war of attrition along the Suez Canal, in which Soviet pilots flew operational missions over the Canal Zone in support of Egypt.

The Yom Kippur War created a new environment for the quest for peace and the development of Israeli foreign policy. Israel's position deteriorated with the outbreak of the fighting, as various states condemned the country and some severed diplomatic relations.

In the wake of the Yom Kippur War, modifications of Israel's foreign policy were relatively minor. The primary goals remained the achievement of an Arab-Israeli settlement and the assurance of security in the interim. This constancy resulted, in part, from Israel's collective conception of its fundamental international position—and the limited policy options that flowed therefrom—which was not substantially altered. Israel's view of itself as geographically isolated and lacking dependable allies, its geographical vulnerability, and its need to acquire and produce arms for self-defense were reaffirmed by the Yom Kippur War.

After the 1977 elections, the Likud-led coalition headed by Menachem Begin maintained Israel's focus on the goal of establishing peace, which would include the formal end of war, full reconciliation and normalization, and an open border over which people and goods could cross without hindrance. On the matter of the territories taken in 1967, the new government could rely on a consensus among Israelis opposing a return to the armistice lines of 1949, thus ruling out total withdrawal, although there was debate among Israelis about the final lines to be established and the extent of compromise. The focus of the territorial debate was the West Bank, known by many Israelis as the biblical Judea and Samaria. There was a substantial difference between the Likud view, which opposed relinquishing any territory, and the compromise views articulated by Labor and others to Likud's left. The Labor-led coalition governments between 1967 and 1977 had generally tried to limit Jewish settlements to those that could serve a security function and had sought to avoid confrontation between the settlements and the local Arab populations. Menachem Begin's Likud government elected in 1977 altered that policy. It supported settlement in the area as a natural and inalienable Jewish right. The broadest and most articulate consensus continued to revolve around the question of a Palestinian state and the PLO. Israel's refusal to negotiate with the PLO and its opposition to the establishment of an independent Palestinian state on the West Bank and in the Gaza Strip were reaffirmed.

Israel's national consensus focused on the need for peace, and the main obstacle appeared to be the continuing Arab unwillingness to accept Israel or negotiate with it. This was modified as a result of the November 1977 initiative of Egyptian president Anwar Sadat to visit Israel and inaugurate direct bilateral negotiations. The negotiations culminated in the Camp David summit meeting of September 1978 at which Egypt, Israel, and the United States agreed to two frameworks for continued negotiations. The primary objective of post–Camp David negotiations was to convert the two frameworks into peace treaties. Despite efforts to secure the involvement of other Arab states, none agreed to participate. The parties concentrated their efforts on the Egypt-Israel Peace Treaty, which was signed at the White House on March 26, 1979.

The Egypt-Israel Peace Treaty was a significant accomplishment that represented a first step toward a comprehensive Arab-Israeli settlement and regional stability. Peace was established, but it was often a "cold" peace in which long-standing mistrust had not been replaced by the warmth of friendly relations.

Begin also fulfilled his government's pledge regarding the Golan Heights. In December 1981, the Knesset adopted the Golan Heights Law, which extended Israel's "law, jurisdiction, and administration" to the area. Begin cited Syrian president Hafiz al-Asad's refusal to negotiate a peace treaty with Israel as the main reason for the decision.

The Egypt-Israel peace process was soon overshadowed by the sixth Arab-Israeli war: the 1982 War in Lebanon. The continued presence in Lebanon of surface-to-air missiles transferred there by Syria remained an Israeli security concern. So were PLO terrorist attacks in northern Israel from bases in southern Lebanon and terrorist attacks against Israeli and Jewish targets worldwide, despite a US-arranged cease-fire in the summer of 1981. On June 6, 1982, Israel launched a major military action against the PLO in Lebanon. The military objectives were to assure security for northern Israel, destroy the PLO infrastructure that had established a state within a state ("Fatahland") in southern Lebanon, eliminate a center of international terrorism, and eradicate the PLO from Lebanon so that its territory would not serve as a base of operations from which Israel could be threatened. The operation's political objectives were not as precise. The goal was to weaken the PLO so that it would no longer be as significant politically, but there was also the hope that a new political order might lead Lebanon to consider becoming the second Arab state to make peace with Israel.

In many respects the results of the war in Lebanon were ambiguous. The achievements were primarily in the military realm: the PLO was defeated, and its military and terrorist infrastructure in Lebanon was destroyed. Israel's northern border was more secure, although Israeli troops who remained in Lebanon became targets for terrorists, and numerous casualties resulted. The political achievements were less tangible. Despite some losses in credibility, the PLO remained the primary representative of the Palestinians, and Yasir Arafat, now operating from Tunis, soon rebounded to his preeminent position. Although an agreement between Israel and Lebanon calling for Israeli withdrawal and for the normalization of relations between the two countries was concluded in May 1983, it was soon unilaterally abrogated by Lebanon under Syrian pressure.

Little occurred in the foreign and security policy domains until the outbreak of the first intifada in 1987. Palestinians in the Gaza Strip began a wave of violent protests and riots on December 8, 1987, that quickly spread to the West Bank and Arab areas of Israel. The initial effect of the intifada on Israel was to reinforce the sharp cleavages dividing the public between those who believed the Palestinian problem had to be resolved through territorial compromise and those who believed Israel could have both peace and the territories.

Dialogue was opened in December 1988 between the United States and the PLO in the wake of Arafat's acceptance—to US satisfaction—of UN Security Council Resolutions 242 and 338, calling for recognition of Israel and renunciation of terrorism. This development added to the growing internal and external pressures on the Yitzhak Shamir–led coalition government to work on a constructive policy to deal with the intifada and to advance the peace process.

On May 14, 1989, the government adopted a proposal (suggested publicly months earlier by Defense Minister Yitzhak Rabin) to have West Bank and Gazan Palestinians elect their own representatives to peace talks. Over the months, the United States worked to narrow the differences between Israel and the Palestinians over the election initiative and to start direct negotiations. The diplomatic maneuvering had the effect of exacerbating political differences in the national unity government. In March 1990, the government fell in a Labor-sponsored vote of no confidence over Likud's unwillingness to respond affirmatively to US proposals. Yitzhak Shamir formed a new Likud-led, narrow, right-wing religious coalition in June 1990.

When Iraq invaded Kuwait in August 1990, much of the world's attention was diverted from the Arab-Israeli conflict—despite Iraq's firing of thirty-nine Scud missiles at Israeli cities. After the Persian Gulf War ended, US President George H. W. Bush announced that "the time had come to put an end to the Arab-Israeli conflict."

The October 1991 Madrid Conference did not achieve a substantive breakthrough, although it broke the procedural and psychological barriers to direct bilateral negotiations between Israel and its neighbors by having Israeli and Egyptian, Jordanian-Palestinian, Lebanese, and Syrian delegations meet at an opening public session and deliver speeches and responses.

The Madrid meetings were followed by a series of bilateral talks between 1991 and 1994. Progress was measured chiefly by the continuation of the process rather than the achievement of substantive accords on the issues in dispute. In the bilateral discussions, the Israeli-Palestinian and Israeli-Syrian negotiations proved to be both the most central and the most difficult. In the case of Syria, the central issues were peace, security, and the future of the Golan Heights. In the Israeli-Palestinian discussions, the disagreement centered on the Palestinian desire for an independent state in the West Bank and Gaza Strip and Israeli opposition to that goal.

Labor's victory in the 1992 Knesset elections was widely heralded as a significant and positive factor that would alter the regional dynamic and the prospects for peace. Secret negotiations between Israel and the PLO began in Oslo in the spring of 1993 and led to an exchange of mutual recognition in September 1993, soon followed by the formal signing, on September 13, 1993, of a Declaration of Principles—a first step and a crucial and historic breakthrough. Additional implementing agreements were signed in Paris and Cairo in spring 1994. In October 1994, Israel and Jordan signed a formal peace treaty, ushering in an era of peace and normalization of relations between the two states.

The 1996 shift from Labor to Likud brought with it a change in the substance and style of Israel's peace-process strategy and tactics. Under Rabin and Foreign Minister Shimon Peres, Israel had made gains in its quest for peace and the normalization of relations with the Palestinians and neighboring Arab countries. Nevertheless, the outcome of the 1996 elections, held against a background of terrorist bombings, indicated that the majority of Israelis perceived Labor's peace strategy as riskier than Likud's and, consequently, had voted in favor of what they envisioned to be a more controlled and balanced approach. The Likud's Benjamin Netanyahu promised Israeli voters that he would achieve a "secure peace" and that, while he accepted the reality of the Oslo framework for Israeli-Palestinian negotiations (and in that context negotiated the Hebron and Wye River agreements), he would never accept a Palestinian state.

Labor's resumption of power in July 1999 generated optimism that there could be renewed progress in the peace process. Ehud Barak transferred some control over territories in the West Bank to the Palestinian Authority. He also hinted that he might return virtually all of the Golan Heights to Syria in exchange for peace. But negotiations held in Shepherdstown, West Virginia, in early 2000, with US President Bill Clinton participating, and in Geneva, Switzerland, in March 2000, involving Clinton and Syrian president Hafiz al-Asad, failed to produce an agreement. At the time of Asad's death in June 2000, the process had reached a stalemate, despite rumors of substantial agreement in principle between Asad and Barak.

In May 2000 Barak fulfilled his pledge to unilaterally withdraw Israeli forces from Lebanon back to an internationally accepted international border, a fact confirmed by the UN Security Council. Nevertheless, Lebanon and Syria continued to stress that Israel's withdrawal was incomplete.

A summit took place at Camp David in the summer of 2000, at which Clinton, Barak, and Arafat focused on a comprehensive peace agreement by which Israel would relinquish territory occupied in the 1967 war and the Palestinians would agree to live alongside Israel in peace. Despite intensive efforts and some areas of accord, no agreement was reached. Arafat rejected Barak's (and Clinton's) compromise proposals. The failure of the Camp David II summit and the ensuing Palestinian violence brought the Oslo process to a halt. The Clinton administration was followed by that of George W. Bush; Ariel Sharon replaced Ehud Barak as Israel's prime minister. The peace process that had marked the decade of the 1990s was replaced by violence—the al-Aqsa Intifada broke out in September 2000 and continued in the ensuing years. The problem was further exacerbated in the wake of the al-Qaida terrorist attacks in New York and Washington on September 11, 2001, when Palestinian terrorists escalated their attacks against Israeli civilians. The assassination of an Israeli cabinet minister in October 2001 and large-scale attacks inside Israel targeting Israeli civilians elicited a strong Israeli military response. Israel's goal was to root out the terrorists and force Arafat and the Palestinian Authority to arrest them.

Sharon made it clear in the 2001 election campaign that the Oslo process was dead and that the security of Israel (and Israelis) was his government's paramount concern and central objective. He asserted that the violence must stop before negotiations could take place. Given continuous violence and the lack of confidence between Israel and the PLO, the peace process remained moribund.

Despite the unilateral Israeli withdrawals from Lebanon in 2000 and the Gaza Strip in 2005 to the recognized international frontiers, no progress was made on the diplomatic process. And despite a UN Security Council resolution calling for its disarmament and dismantling, Hizballah remained armed.

Israel's occupation of Gaza ended completely in the summer of 2005. Yet prudence dictated that Israel maintain control of its ground and air borders with Gaza to guard against attack by irredentist Palestinian elements. Israel instituted a naval blockade on Gaza after the January 2006 Palestinian elections brought to power Hamas, a group dedicated to Israel's destruction, and after Hamas failed to meet the conditions for achieving normalized relations set out by the Middle East Quartet—the United States, European Union, Russia, and United Nations. Israel's control of Gaza's borders and the IDF's occasional incursions into Gaza in pursuit of terrorists or missile-launching sites had been used by Hamas and other Gaza-based groups to justify escalating missile attacks into Israel. A similar rationalization had been used by the Fatah-led Palestinian Authority in the West Bank as part of its international campaign at the United Nations to delegitimize the State of Israel and Zionism.

The lack of movement in Arab-Israeli diplomacy and continued tensions along Israel's borders with Lebanon and the Gaza Strip were replaced in the summer of 2006 by conflict. On June 26, Palestinian terrorists tunneled under the international border between Israel and Gaza, attacked an Israeli patrol, killed two soldiers, and kidnapped a third (Gilad Shalit). Israel responded by attacking a series of terrorist and infrastructure targets in the Gaza Strip, but the kidnapped Israeli soldier remained in captivity. Hizballah, on July 12, initiated a cross-border raid from Lebanon into Israel, killing several Israeli soldiers and kidnapping two others (Eldad Regev and Ehud Goldwasser). The Hizballah raid was followed by thirty-four days of fighting that ended on August 14, 2006. Subsequently, Hassan Nasrallah, the leader of Hizballah, acknowledged that he had not thought that the capture of the two Israelis would lead to a war of that magnitude at that time.

As with previous wars in 1973 and 1982 that ended without clear and overwhelming Israeli success, there developed after the 2006 Lebanon War a series of perceptions in Israel concerning wartime "failures." There were protests and demonstrations, as well as calls for inquiries to evaluate the management of the conflict and the IDF and Israel's political leadership. This was due partly to the substantial attacks on Israeli territory, with more than 3,000 missiles fired by Hizballah into northern Israeli cities and towns, but also because of the number of Israeli soldiers wounded and killed and the substantial attacks on, and damage suffered by, the civilian population, as well as the inconclusive results of the war. When the fighting ended, the two kidnapped Israeli soldiers remained in their captors' hands, and Israel's image as an overwhelmingly successful military power seemed diminished.

Israel's deterrence capacity was to some extent restored in Operation Cast Lead, the IDF operation against Hamas in Gaza in December 2008 and January 2009. There was almost unanimous public support in Israel for the operation as necessary to end the unrelenting Hamas rocket fire on Israeli population centers and the smuggling of weapons into Gaza. The Gaza operation's prosecution also suggested that Israel's political leadership and the IDF command had internalized the findings of the Winograd Committee inquiry into the major failings that occurred in the 2006 Lebanon War. Nevertheless, Gilad Shalit, the IDF soldier kidnapped by Hamas in 2006, remained in captivity, and the evidence uncovered in Gaza of the increased cooperation between Hamas and Iranian operatives did not portend movement toward greater stability or peace for Israel in the Middle East.

Iran and the strategic implications of the revolutionary changes throughout the Arab world dominated Israel's foreign and security policies during Netanyahu's second term. In a major foreign policy speech on June 14, 2009, Netanyahu described "the nexus between radical Islam and nuclear weapons" centered in Iran as "the greatest danger confronting Israel, the Middle East, the entire world and human race."

In agreeing in September 2010 to resume long-stalled direct talks with the Palestinians, Netanyahu said that the ultimate goal of a two-state solution could not take effect as long as Hamas and Hizballah worked to derail it. He also emphasized the need for the Palestinian side to recognize Israel as a Jewish state.

The Israeli popular consensus was that the Palestinian Authority had chosen to avoid direct dialogue with the Netanyahu government in which substantive concessions might be required of the Palestinian side. The PA's preference was to take Palestinian demands directly to the United Nations, on the assumption that in an environment so skewed toward a pro-Arab perspective, pressure for concessions would be imposed exclusively upon one side: Israel. Israelis continued to debate about the West Bank settlements. But the intensity of this debate was mitigated by Palestinian Authority state-building activities, supported by the Netanyahu government, and renewed security cooperation between Israeli and PA services.

The Netanyahu government faced overwhelming international condemnation over the deaths of nine Turkish human rights activists in the May 31, 2010, boarding of the *Mavi Marmara*. A flotilla of activists had publicly declared their determination to delegitimize Israel by breaking the IDF naval blockade of Hamas-controlled Gaza. The UN investigation charged that excessive force had been used by the IDF in boarding and stopping the *Mavi Marmara*, even as it expressed serious questions about "the conduct, true nature and objectives of the flotilla organizers." An inquiry headed by Israel's state comptroller, Micha Lindenstrauss, discerned "significant and substantive deficiencies" in Prime Minister Netanyahu's decision-making process concerning the *Mavi Marmara* incident. Defense Minister Ehud Barak was also criticized for not anticipating the potential for violent confrontation with the flotilla activists or reviewing the IDF's preparedness for such an eventuality. The flotilla incident caused the disruption of Israel's important strategic relationship with Turkey, which demanded a formal apology from Israel for the deaths of the Turkish activists.

Regarding Egypt, Israel's long-term focus was on the impact of the Muslim Brotherhood's 2011 electoral victory and President Mohamed Morsi's approach to the 1979 Egypt-Israel Peace Treaty. The more immediate concern was the terrorist and missile threat resulting from the Islamist radicalization of Egypt's Sinai region, which was attributed mainly to Hizballah and other Iran-sponsored operatives. Steps taken by Morsi's government (with Israel's cooperation) in the summer of 2012 to crush terrorist activity in

Sinai were reassuring from an Israeli perspective and augured well for the future stability of Israel's crucial bilateral relationship with Egypt.

Israel's concern with the civil war in Syria tended to focus on two issues: the potential remilitarization of Israel's northern border with Syria, including the strategic Golan Heights, which had been peaceful since the Yom Kippur War, and the possible transfer of Syria's vast stockpile of weapons of mass destruction to Hizballah.

Iran's nuclear weapons program preoccupied the Netanyahu government, with statements by senior ministers reinforcing the sense among many Israelis that Iran's nuclearization was the greatest existential threat to the Jewish state since the Six-Day War. The debate within Israel, involving politicians, security experts, and current and former members of the security and intelligence community, revolved around three questions:

1. How long could Israel afford to wait to see if diplomacy and sanctions would deter Iran's leadership from its intended goal of achieving the capability to build nuclear weapons?
2. Could the IDF inflict a sufficiently devastating blow against Iran's nuclear weapons capability to warrant the damage to Israeli civilian, industrial, and military targets anticipated from an Iranian counterattack?
3. Should Israel ever go to war alone, without the support of at least one great power?

The Netanyahu government and the US administration of President Barack Obama shared the ultimate strategic objective of denying nuclear weapons to Tehran. But there were disagreements about specific issues, including the efficacy of sanctions and protracted diplomacy and the timing and nature of military action should diplomacy fail to deter Iran's behavior. Washington provided unprecedented military support to Israel in spring 2012 and repeated pledges that "we're doing everything we can to protect Israel's security," as President Obama put it, in an attempt to reassure the Israeli public and its political leadership. By late 2012, however, much of the international concern had shifted from Iran's progress toward acquiring nuclear weapons capability, despite diplomacy and sanctions, to speculation about an "imminent decision" by the Netanyahu government to launch a preemptive, unilateral strike against Iran's nuclear weapons facilities.

The Search for Friends and Allies

Israel's broader approach to foreign policy began to take shape once it became clear that peace would not follow the 1949 armistice agreements with the Arab states that marked the end of its War of Independence. The continuing Arab threat and Israel's geographical isolation suggested a need for positive relationships with other states. Israel directed its attention beyond the circle of neighboring Arab states to the international community in an effort to establish friendly relations with the states of Europe and the developing world, especially Africa and Latin America, as well as the superpowers, and to gain their support in the international arena. These relationships were seen as having a positive effect on Israel's position in the Arab-Israeli conflict: bilateral political and economic advantages would help to ensure Israel's deterrent strength vis-à-vis the Arabs through national armed power and through increased international support for its position.

At the outset, Israel held a positive view of the United Nations, fostered by that organization's role in the creation of the state. With the increasingly large anti-Israel majority in the General Assembly and the resulting virtually automatic support for Arab and Palestinian perspectives, Israel's views changed markedly, and the United Nations came to be regarded as an unhelpful and often negative factor in the quest for peace and security. The Madrid peace conference and the consequent bilateral and multilateral negotiations involved a large number of other powers. The collapse of the Soviet Union and the disintegration of the Soviet Bloc led to the restoration of Israel's relations with many states that previously had been hostile. All of this contributed to an improved international position for Israel in the 1990s. But with the failure of the Oslo process and the Palestinians' and the Arab states' resort to the United Nations for resolutions to delegitimize the State of Israel and Zionism, this view again was altered. At the onset of the twenty-first century, Israel's perception of the United Nations was marked by ambivalence concerning the role it might play in Israel's foreign policy.

The developed and economically advanced industrialized states of Europe, as well as Australia, Canada, Japan, and Korea, are, and have been, of great importance to Israel because of their political influence and economic significance.

Europe has posed an interesting challenge and presented a significant opportunity for Israeli policy makers. Israel has sought to maintain positive relations with Europe based on their common Judeo-Christian heritage, democratic traditions, and memories of the Holocaust. With Israel seeking links to significant powers for military (aid and arms acquisition) and economic (trade and economic aid) assistance, Europe has seemed a logical choice. A tacit alliance with France was supplemented by links with Great Britain and Germany. Over time Israel has been successful in establishing economic links with the European Economic Community, the European Union, and the Organization for Economic Cooperation and Development, albeit with limitations, and also with various European states on a bilateral level. France proved a valuable supplier of military aid until the Six-Day War in 1967, while Germany, through its moral and material reparations for World War II crimes, was an indispensable factor in Israel's economic development beginning in the 1950s. Israel has also successfully established positive trade, cultural, and political ties with new members of the expanded European Union. Israel's positive relations with Europe have been accomplished despite a discernible increase in anti-Israel tendencies among elements of the Continent's social and cultural intelligentsia.

The emergence of the new states of Africa and Asia in the 1950s and 1960s led Israel to pursue a policy in keeping with Afro-Asian aspirations for economic development and modernization. In an effort to befriend these states and secure their support, Israel's multi-faceted program focused on technical assistance, exchange and training programs, loans, joint economic enterprises, and trade. The program grew dramatically and remains an important element of Israeli foreign policy. It had successes in economic and social terms and proved politically beneficial in various international venues. Support from the developing world helped to prevent the United Nations from adopting anti-Israel measures after the 1967 war, and in the early 1970s a committee of African presidents worked to achieve Arab-Israeli negotiations, albeit without success. The nadir of the policy was reached at the time of the Yom Kippur War in 1973, when virtually all of the African states with which Israel had established ties broke those relations in support of the Arab effort to isolate and delegitimize the State of Israel and Zionism. For some Israelis this reflected a policy failure, although some African states have reestablished close links, and some have sustained informal but significant ties despite their official policy positions.

China and India, with the world's two largest populations and two of the globe's most dynamic economies, have been increasingly important to Israel. Israel was among the first countries in the world to recognize the People's Republic of China in January 1950, but official relations were established only in 1992, with the start of the Oslo process. Since then substantial links have been created in the areas of trade, aviation, culture, and scientific cooperation. Numerous reciprocal visits have taken place, and there has also been progress in the area of arms sales.

India recognized Israel on September 18, 1950, but established full diplomatic relations only in January 1992. Israel had opened a consulate in Bombay in the early 1950s, but its functions and jurisdiction were extremely limited and restricted. Since the 1990s, India and Israel have developed increasingly strong bonds that are reflected both in commercial and military trade and the sharing of intelligence against global Islamist terrorism. India has also become an increasingly popular tourist destination for young Israelis.

Despite substantial effort in these sectors, the centrality of the Arab-Israeli conflict has enlarged and enhanced the role of the superpowers, particularly the United States, in Israeli eyes. From World War II to the 1990s, the superpowers (the United States and the Soviet Union) were the major players in the international system. Israel, like all other states, had to operate within the confines of the Cold War. Both superpowers were also significant because they comprised large segments of the world's Jewish population. Zionism and the "ingathering of the exiles" requires Israel to be concerned with the well-being of Jewish communities elsewhere and their potential to emigrate from imperiled locations to the haven of the Jewish state. Thus, in focusing on relations with the superpowers, Israel was also concerned for what were then the world's two largest Diaspora Jewish communities.

Anti-Semitism was, and arguably remains, an endemic feature of Russian (and Soviet) society and history. Not only were Soviet Jews unable to assist with the birth and consolidation of the Jewish state, but Israel during the Cold War was unable to protect them and could not secure large-scale emigration of those at risk. This began to change only in the last years of the Mikhail Gorbachev era, and immigration to Israel became a continuous flow with the end of the Soviet Union and the Cold War.

The Soviet Union voted for the UN Partition Plan of 1947, accorded de jure recognition to Israel shortly after its independence, supported its applications for UN membership, and gave it moral, political, and material support in the early years after independence. However, relations between the Soviet Union and Israel deteriorated rapidly from 1949 to 1953, and Israel's foreign policy no longer reflected a belief in Soviet friendship and support. Soviet support for and expanded relations with the Arab states by the mid-1950s tended to confirm this perspective. Soviet military and economic assistance to the Arab world, the Soviet Bloc's rupture of relations with Israel in 1967, and the continuation of that break led Israel farther into the Western camp, although it continued to seek the restoration of ties with the Soviet Union and its allies and to promote the well-being and emigration of Soviet Jews.

After the Six-Day War, the Soviet Union attempted to become a more significant participant in the Arab-Israeli peace process but made limited progress until the advent of the Gorbachev era, when more liberal approaches to foreign policy permitted the relationship between Jerusalem and Moscow to improve. Consular contacts and exchanges took place, Soviet Jewish emigration increased substantially, and several East European states restored diplomatic relations with Israel. On October 18, 1991, the Soviet Union and Israel reestablished full diplomatic relations.

Beginning in the early 1990s, some 1 million citizens of the former Soviet Union emigrated to Israel, and there was significant growth in bilateral relations with Russia and several of the former Soviet republics in the cultural and commercial domains. Nevertheless, Israel remains skeptical about Russia's ambitions in the Middle East, as reflected in Moscow's support for Bashar al-Asad's regime in Syria's civil war and its refusal to participate in robust sanctions to encourage Iran to end its pursuit of nuclear weapons.

Once a power providing limited direct support for Israel, the United States has become the world's only superpower linked to Israel in a free trade area and a crucial provider of political, diplomatic, moral, and strategic (security) support, as well as economic aid.

The complex and multifaceted "special relationship" with the United States that had its origins prior to the independence of Israel has centered on continuing US support for the survival, security, and well-being of Israel. During the first decades after Israel's independence, the US-Israeli relationship was grounded primarily in humanitarian concerns, in religious and historical links, and in a moral-emotional-political arena rather than a strategic-military one. The United States declared an arms embargo on December 5, 1947; there was practically no US military aid or sale of military equipment and no formal, or even informal, military agreement or strategic cooperation between the two states. Extensive dealings in the strategic realm became significant only in the 1970s and 1980s. The concept of Israel as a strategic asset was more an outcome of the developing relationship than a foundation for its establishment. US policy on arms provisioning evolved from embargo to serving as principal supplier, and arms (including the maintenance of Israel's qualitative military advantage over its adversaries) became an important tool of US policy to reassure Israel and achieve policy modification.

The two states developed a diplomatic-political relationship that focused on the need to resolve the Arab-Israeli dispute, but although they agreed on the general concept, they often differed on the precise means for achieving the desired result. The relationship became especially close after the Six-Day War, when a congruence of policy prevailed on many of their salient concerns. Nevertheless, the two states often held differing perspectives on regional developments and on the dangers and opportunities they presented. No major ruptures took place, although significant tensions emerged at various junctures.

Israel's special relationship with the United States—which is based on substantial positive perception and sentiment evident in public opinion and official statements and manifest in political-diplomatic support and in military and economic assistance—has never been enshrined in a formal, legally binding document joining the two states in a formal alliance. Israel has no mutual security treaty with the United States, nor is it a member of any alliance requiring the United States to take up arms automatically on its behalf, despite Israel's status as a major non-NATO ally. The US commitment to Israel has taken the form of presidential statements that have reaffirmed the US interest in supporting the political independence and territorial integrity of Israel.

The United States is today an indispensable, if not fully dependable, ally. It provides Israel, in one form or another, with economic (governmental and private), technical, military, political, diplomatic, and moral support. The United States was seen as the ultimate resource against Soviet intervention during the Cold War and remains a central participant in the campaign against Islamic terrorism. It is the source of Israel's sophisticated military hardware, and it is central to the Arab-Israeli peace process.

The United States and Israel have established a special relationship replete with broad areas of agreement and numerous examples of discord. There was, is, and will be a divergence that derives from a difference of perspective based on the environment in which each makes its policies. The United States remains the world's only superpower; Israel is a small regional power. Nevertheless, the two states maintain a remarkable degree of congruence on broad policy goals. Israel continues to focus on the centrality and significance of the ties.

At Israel's birth, the United States seemed to be a dispassionate, almost uninterested midwife—its role was essential and unconventional but also unpredictable and hotly debated in US policy circles. Decades later, some of the policy debate continues, and there are periods of tension in the relationship, but there is little doubt about the overall nature of US support for its small, still-embattled ally.

In separate remarks to the United Nations General Assembly on June 20, 2011, and September 21, 2011, President Barack Obama summed up the relationship in the following terms:

One inviolable principle [will be that] the United States and Israel will always be stalwart allies and friends—that the bond isn't breakable and that Israel's security will always be at the top tier of considerations in terms of how America manages its foreign policy—because it's the right thing to do, because Israel is our closest ally and friend, it is a robust democracy, it shares our values and it shares our principles . . .

America's commitment to Israel's security is unshakeable, and our friendship with Israel is deep and enduring. And so we believe that any lasting peace must acknowledge the very real security concerns that Israel faces every single day. Let us be honest with ourselves: Israel is surrounded by neighbors that have waged repeated wars against it. . . . Those are facts. They cannot be denied. The Jewish people have forged a successful state in their historic homeland. Israel deserves recognition. It deserves normal relations with its neighbors. And friends of the Palestinians do them no favors by ignoring this truth.

Bibliography

Bernard Reich and David H. Goldberg, *Historical Dictionary of Israel,* 2nd ed. (Lanham, MD: Scarecrow Press, 2008) is a convenient reference work. On the Arab-Israeli conflict, see Bernard Reich, ed., *An Historical Encyclopedia of the Arab-Israeli Conflict* (Westport, CT: Greenwood Press, 1996), and Bernard Reich, ed., *Arab-Israeli Conflict and Conciliation: A Documentary History* (Westport, CT: Praeger, 1995).

On the history of Israel, consult Bernard Reich, *A Brief History of Israel,* 2nd ed. (New York: Facts on File, Inc., 2008); Martin Gilbert, *Israel: A History,* rev. ed. (Santa Barbara, CA: McNally and Loftin, 2008); Howard M. Sachar, *A History of Israel: From the Rise of Zionism to Our Time* (New York: Knopf, 1976), and *A History of Israel,* Vol. 2: *From the Aftermath of the Yom Kippur War* (Oxford: Oxford University Press, 1987); Colin Schindler, *A History of Modern Israel* (Cambridge: Cambridge University Press, 2008); and Yehuda Avner, *The Prime Ministers: An Intimate Narrative of Israeli Leadership* (Jerusalem: Toby Press, 2008). The mandate period is discussed in Christopher Sykes, *Crossroads to Israel* (Cleveland, OH: World Publishing, 1965); Geoffrey Lewis, *Balfour and Weizmann: The Zionist, the Zealot and the Emergence of Israel* (New York: Continuum, 2009); Howard Greenfeld, *A Promise Fulfilled: Theodor Herzl, Chaim Weizmann, David Ben-Gurion, and the Creation of the State of Israel* (New York: HarperCollins, 2005); and Jonathan Schneer, *The Balfour Declaration* (London: Bloomsbury, 2010). Shlomo Avineri's *The Making of Modern Zionism: The Intellectual Origins of the Jewish State* (New York: Basic Books, 1981); Arthur Hertzberg's *The Zionist Idea* (Philadelphia: Jewish Publication Society, 1959); and Walter Laqueur's *A History of Zionism* (New York: Holt, Rinehart and Winston, 1972) provide a comprehensive history and examination of the Zionist movement, its origins, and its diverse ideological trends. A useful reference is Charles I. Waxman and Rafael Medoff, *Historical Dictionary of Zionism* (Lanham, MD: Scarecrow Press, 2000).

Studies of Israel's parliament include Asher Zidon, *Knesset: The Parliament of Israel* (New York: Herzl Press, 1967); Eliahu S. Likhovski, *Israel's Parliament: The Law of the Knesset* (Oxford: Oxford University Press, 1971); Gregory S. Mahler, *The Knesset: Parliament in the Israeli Political System* (Rutherford, NJ: Fairleigh Dickinson University Press, 1981); and Samuel Sager, *The Parliamentary System of Israel* (Syracuse, NY: Syracuse University Press, 1985).

Various aspects of Israeli politics and policy have been the subject of specialized studies. These include Myron J. Aronoff, *Israeli Visions and Divisions: Cultural Change and Political Conflict* (New Brunswick, NJ: Transaction Books, 1989); Marcia Drezon-Tepler, *Interest Groups and Political Change in Israel* (Albany: State University of New York Press, 1990); Dan Horowitz and Moshe Lissak, *Trouble in Utopia: The Overburdened Polity of Israel* (Albany: State University of New York Press, 1989); Gregory S. Mahler, *Politics and Government in Israel: The Maturation of a Modern State,* 2nd ed. (Lanham, MD: Rowman & Littlefield, 2010); and Abraham Diskin, *The Last Days in Israel: Understanding the New Israeli Democracy* (New York: Routledge, 2003). Political parties are the particular focus of Peter Y. Medding, *Mapai in Israel: Political Organization and Government in a New Society* (Cambridge: Cambridge University Press, 1972), and *The Founding of Israeli Democracy, 1948–1988* (London: Oxford University Press, 1989); Jonathan Mendilow, *Ideology, Party Change, and Electoral Campaigns in Israel, 1965–2001* (Albany: State University of New York Press, 2003); and Yonathan Shapiro, *The Road to Power: Herut Party in Israel* (Albany: State University of New York Press, 1991).

Studies of the salient domestic, political, economic, and social issues include S. N. Eisenstadt, *The Transformation of Israeli Society* (Boulder, CO: Westview Press, 1985); Adam Garfinkle, *Politics and Society in Modern Israel: Myths and Realities,* 2nd ed. (Armonk, NY: M. E. Sharpe, 2000); Orit Rozin, *The Rise of the Individual in 1950s Israel* (Lebanon, NH: Brandeis University Press/University Press of New England, 2011); Daniel Avnon and Yotam Benziman, eds., *Plurality and Citizenship in Israel* (London: Gibson Square, 2008); and Daniel Gavron, *The Kibbutz: Awakening from Utopia* (Lanham, MD: Rowman & Littlefield, 2000). Studies of Israel's economy include Dan Senor and Saul Singer, *Start-Up Nation: The Story of Israel's Economic Miracle* (New York: Council on Foreign Relations/Grand Central Publishing, 2009); Yair Aharoni, *The Israeli Economy: Dreams and Realities* (London: Routledge, 1991); and Yoram Ben-Porath, ed., *The Israeli Economy: Maturing Through Crises* (Cambridge, MA: Harvard University Press, 1986). The relationship of religion and the state is discussed in Charles S. Liebman and Eliezer Don-Yehiya, *Civil Religion in Israel: Traditional Judaism and Political Culture in the Jewish State* (Berkeley: University of California Press, 1983). For analyses of the history and role of Arabs in Israel, see Jacob M. Landau in *The Arabs in Israel: A Political Study* (London: Oxford University Press, 1969), and Hillel Cohen, *Good Arabs: The Israeli Security Agencies and the Israeli Arabs, 1948–1967* (Berkeley: University of

California Press, 2010). See also Sabri Jiryis, *The Arabs in Israel* (New York: Monthly Review Press, 1976); As'ad Ghanem, *The Palestinian-Arab Minority in Israel, 1948–2000* (Albany: State University of New York Press, 2001); and Laurence Louer, *To Be an Arab in Israel* (New York: Columbia University Press, 2007).

For an overview of Israel's foreign policy, see Aaron S. Klieman, *Statecraft in the Dark: Israel's Practice of Quiet Diplomacy* (Boulder, CO: Westview Press, 1988); Ilan Peleg, *Begin's Foreign Policy, 1977–1983* (Westport, CT: Greenwood Press, 1987); and Bernard Reich and Gershon R. Kieval, eds., *Israeli National Security Policy: Political Actors and Perspectives* (Westport, CT: Greenwood Press, 1988). The eighteen-volume *Israel's Foreign Relations, Selected Documents, 1947–2001* (Jerusalem: Ministry of Foreign Affairs, 1976–2002) provides the major documents of Israel's foreign policy from its inception through 1999; this documentary analysis is extended through Itamar Rabinovich and Jehuda Reinharz's, *Israel in the Middle East,* 2nd ed. (Lebanon, NH: Brandeis University Press/University Press of New England, 2007). Gershon R. Kieval, *Party Politics in Israel and the Occupied Territories* (Westport, CT: Greenwood Press, 1983), provides a detailed analysis of Israel's policy. Bernard Reich, in *Quest for Peace: United States–Israel Relations and the Arab-Israeli Conflict* (New Brunswick, NJ: Transaction Books, 1977), deals with Israel's relations with the United States in the context of the efforts to resolve the Arab-Israeli conflict. Bernard Reich, *The United States and Israel: Influence in the Special Relationship* (New York: Praeger, 1984), examines Israel's crucial links with the United States. Bernard Reich, in *Securing the Covenant: United States–Israel Relations After the Cold War* (Westport, CT: Greenwood Press, 1995), examines the special relationship of these allies. Other studies in this regard include Abraham Ben-Zvi, *Decade of Transition: Eisenhower, Kennedy, and the Origins of the American-Israeli Alliance* (New York: Columbia University Press, 1998); Aaron David Miller, *The Much Too Promised Land: America's Elusive Search for Arab-Israeli Peace* (New York: Random House, 2008); Dennis Ross (with David Makovsky), *Myths, Illusions, and Peace: Finding a New Direction for America in the Middle East* (New York: Viking, 2009); and Michael Oren, *Power, Faith and Fantasy: America in the Middle East, 1776 to the Present* (New York: W. W. Norton & Co., 2008).

Specific aspects of Israeli foreign policy are considered in Jacob Abadi, *Israel's Quest for Recognition and Acceptance in Asia: Garrison State Diplomacy* (London: Frank Cass, 2004); Andrea S. Arbel, *Riding the Wave: The Jewish Agency's Role in the Mass Aliyah of Soviet and Ethiopian Jewry to Israel, 1987–1995* (Jerusalem: Gefen Publishing House, 2001); Gadi Ben-Ezer, *The Ethiopian Jewish Exodus: Narratives of the Migration Journey to Israel, 1977–1985* (London: Routledge, 2002); Colin Schindler, *Israel and the European Left: Between Solidarity and Delegitimization* (New York: Continuum, 2012); Robin Shepherd, *A State Beyond the Pale: Europe's Problem with Israel* (London: Weidenfeld and Nicolson, 2009); Ofra Bengio, *The Turkish-Israeli Relationship: Changing Ties of Middle Eastern Outsiders* (New York: Palgrave Macmillan, 2004); and Uri Bialer, *Cross on the Star of David: The Christian World in Israel's*

Foreign Policy, 1948–1967 (Bloomington: Indiana University Press, 2005). Caroline Glick, *Shackled Warrior: Israel and the Global Jihad* (Jerusalem: Gefen, 2008), and Jonathan Spyer, *The Transforming Fire: The Rise of the Israel-Islamist Conflict* (New York: Continuum, 2010), focus on recent challenges to Israel's foreign and security policy. Some recent works on the Arab-Israeli conflict are Itamar Rabinovich, *The Lingering Conflict* (Washington, DC: Brookings Institution Press, 2011); Dennis Ross, *The Missing Peace: The Inside Story of the Fight for Middle East Peace* (New York: Farrar, Straus, and Giroux, 2004); Efraim Karsh, *Palestine Betrayed* (New Haven, CT: Yale University Press, 2010); and Benny Morris, *1948: A History of the First Arab-Israeli War* (New Haven, CT: Yale University Press, 2008).

Yigal Allon, *The Making of Israel's Army* (New York: Bantam Books, 1971); Amos Perlmutter, *Military and Politics in Israel: Nation-Building and Role Expansion* (London: Frank Cass, 1969); and Yoram Peri, *Generals in the Cabinet Room: How the Military Shapes Israeli Policy* (Washington, DC: United States Institute of Peace, 2006) consider the role of the military. For a general overview of the Israel Defense Forces and their background and development, see Ze'ev Schiff, *A History of the Israeli Army: 1874 to the Present* (New York: Macmillan, 1985).

The government of Israel is a prolific publisher of high-quality materials, such as *Israel Government Year Book* and *Statistical Abstract of Israel*, that would serve the interested reader well. The websites of the government of Israel are a substantial resource, providing access to virtually all official information that a student or researcher could desire. The Israel government portal is www.gov.il. The prime minister's office is found at www.pmo.gov.il. The Knesset site is www.knesset.gov.il. The Israel Ministry of Foreign Affairs website is www.mfa.gov.il. The Ministry of Defense website is www.mod.gov.il. Statistical data for Israel is available through the Central Bureau of Statistics at www.cbs.gov.il.

A number of Israeli newspapers have English online editions. These include *Ha'aretz* (www.haaretz.com), *Yediot Ahronot* (www.ynetnews.com), *Arutz Sheva* (www.israel nationalnews.com), and *Israel Hayom* (www.israelhayom.com). The English-language *Jerusalem Post* publishes its online edition at www.jpost.com. Another English-language newspaper is accessible at the *Times of Israel* (www.timesofisrael.com).

12

THE PALESTINIANS

Glenn E. Robinson

A predominantly Arab-Muslim people ever since the Muslim conquest in the seventh century CE, Palestinians are descendants of the peoples who have conquered the territory over the centuries—including the Jewish tribes that populated the area 2,000 years ago. Palestinians today seek to create a viable and independent state. Due to the lack of an independent state and the presence of only limited autonomy in the West Bank and Gaza Strip, much of the Palestinian story must be told through the lens of historical development, in contrast to the stories of states told in the other chapters of this book.

HISTORICAL BACKGROUND

Much of the Palestinians' history prior to the Roman conquest 2,000 years ago is more speculative than grounded in fact. The population for many centuries prior to the Roman period was largely tribal and often nomadic, although settled agricultural communities were increasingly common. The Old Testament presents many fascinating stories about the Israelite period, but there are few independent sources to confirm the accuracy of these accounts. Alexander the Great conquered the region in 332 BCE when his forces defeated Persia, but he largely ignored the area later called Palestine. The Roman Empire seized control of the region in 63 BCE, and it was Roman rulers who coined the name "Palestine," drawing on Greek and possibly Semitic sources.

As the Roman Empire collapsed in the fourth century CE, control passed to the Byzantine, or Eastern Roman, Empire, which ruled from a distance until the Muslim conquest in 634 CE by tribes from the Arabian Peninsula. The caliph 'Umar's conquest of Jerusalem and Palestine marked the beginning of nearly 1,300 years of continuous Muslim rule, interrupted only by the European Crusades (primarily twelfth century CE). Saladin famously recaptured Jerusalem from the Crusaders in 1187.

The Ottoman Empire

The Muslim Ottoman Empire, based in Istanbul, ruled Palestine indirectly for four centuries, from 1516 to 1920. Regional governors and other local elites had wide discretion to wield power in ways they saw fit, allowing local business leaders, military commanders, and religious figures to become prominent; these were known collectively as the "notable" (*a'yan*) social class. The authority of local notables increased dramatically during the nineteenth century as a result of a number of reforms enacted by the Ottoman Empire in its bid to fend off growing European power. Ottoman policies helped shape Palestine's social structure, which consisted primarily of a handful of notable families holding sway over a largely illiterate peasant society.

In the latter part of the nineteenth century, Jewish immigration, primarily to escape persecution in Europe, increased. By World War I (1914), the Jewish community in Palestine comprised 11 percent of the total population (about 75,000 out of 690,000). That was a visible change from 1880, when Jews made up 6 percent of inhabitants (35,000 out of 485,000). The four historical Jewish communities in Palestine (in the cities of Hebron, Jerusalem, Safad, and Tiberias) were populated primarily by religious, nonpolitical Jews, while most of the new Jewish migrants from Europe after 1880 espoused Zionism. From that point on, two emerging national groups—Jews and Palestinians—claimed the same land as their own, making conflict inevitable.

The British Mandate

With the defeat of the Ottoman Empire in World War I, Great Britain took control of Palestine. Arab leaders thought Palestine would be included in the area promised independence by Sir Henry McMahon, the British high commissioner for Egypt, in letters he wrote during 1915 and 1916 to Sharif Hussein of Mecca. Hussein and McMahon had agreed that the British would support Arab independence from the Turks if the Arabs launched a revolt against the Ottoman Empire, a revolt made famous in the West by the tales of Lawrence of Arabia. In the Balfour Declaration, issued on November 2, 1917, and later incorporated into the British Mandate for Palestine, Britain supported "the establishment in Palestine of a national home for the Jewish people." That proclamation transformed the balance of power between the Arab majority and the Jewish minority, providing the Zionist movement its long-sought legal status.

Much of the British mandate period was marked by instability and conflict. While Zionist forces were trying to establish a foothold in Palestine with British support, Palestinian nationalist forces were just beginning to form, often in opposition to both British imperial rule and Zionist expansionism. A revolt begun in 1935 under the leadership of the Muslim preacher Izz al-Din al-Qassam, a heroic figure for Hamas and other Islamists today, lasted until 1939 and captured the dual nature of Palestinian political discontent. Both British military might and Britain's change in direction in Palestine following the issuance

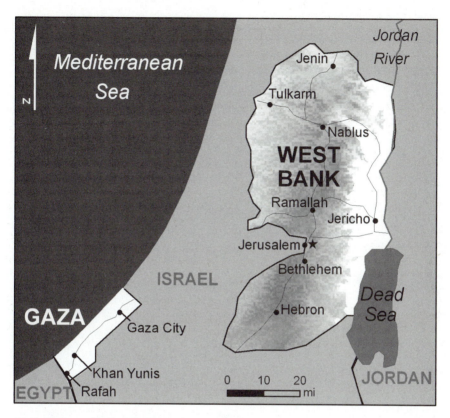

Gaza Strip and West Bank

of its famous 1939 White Paper—essentially abrogating the Balfour Declaration—brought an end to the Palestinian revolt. For Palestinians, it was too little, too late, as Zionist forces by this point had created the institutions of a nascent state.

In 1947, the British announced they were ending the mandate and turning the Palestine issue over to the United Nations. In November 1947, the UN General Assembly approved a partition plan that divided the Palestine mandate into a Jewish state, an Arab state, and an international area in Jerusalem. The Jewish state comprised about 55 percent of the territory, even though Jewish landholdings comprised less than 7 percent of the total land surface. The Jewish state would have nearly as many Arab as Jewish residents. The Arab state would control only about 40 percent of Palestine; deprived of the best agricultural land and seaports, it would retain Galilee, the central mountains (now primarily the West Bank), and the Gaza coast. The United Nations would administer Jerusalem as an international zone.

The Palestinians rejected a partition plan they viewed as unjust but were too weak to defeat the Hagana—the Zionists' main armed militia—and a few months later the armed forces of the self-declared State of Israel. Even prior to the declaration of statehood by Israel, Palestinians were already on the run, with 300,000 (out of an eventual 700,000) now refugees. With the final British withdrawal on May 14, 1948, and the immediate declaration of Israeli statehood, surrounding Arab states invaded Palestine. The Arab armies were no match for the better-trained and better-equipped Israeli forces; when armistice agreements were signed in 1949, only 23 percent of Palestine remained in Arab hands, and an additional 400,000 Palestinians had become refugees. The Egyptian army held the Gaza Strip, and Transjordanian forces held the West Bank, including East Jerusalem.

The first Arab-Israeli war was complicated, with different rationales for each actor, especially among the Arab parties. Zionist leaders and King Abdullah of Jordan (with British agreement) had forged a secret, informal arrangement to divide the lands designated for the Palestinian state, which was implemented in the fighting. The suspected collusion led to the 1951 assassination of King Abdullah by a Palestinian nationalist. Egypt's military intervention seemed designed at least as much to thwart Abdullah's ambitions in Palestine as to defeat Israel. At the time, Egypt and Jordan were the main rivals for power in the Arab world.

Fragmentation and Exile: 1948–1967

Some 85 percent of the mandate's Arab population fled during the 1947–1949 conflict. While the "fog of war" created many reasons for Palestinians to flee their homes, their becoming actual and permanent refugees had a specific beginning. Displaced Palestinians became permanent refugees on June 16, 1948, when Israel's new government decided not to allow any Palestinian refugees to return to their homes in lands under Israel's control or in lands that would come under Israel's control during the remainder of the war. The departure of Palestinians in 1948 from their homes and villages shattered Palestinian society. Most Palestinian refugees went to makeshift camps established by the United Nations. Over time, these camps evolved into squalid, cinder block encampments housing the world's largest refugee population. Of the 1.2 million Palestinian Arabs, over 700,000 became refugees, dispersed to Egypt, Jordan, Lebanon, and Syria. About 500,000 remained in place, of which 150,000 stayed in Israel (primarily in the Galilee region), with the remainder in the West Bank (annexed by Jordan) and the Gaza Strip (administered by Egypt). The situation Palestinians faced in the countries to which they fled varied considerably.

Palestinian society was changed profoundly by this trauma, which Palestinians call *al-nakba* (the disaster). The society was previously highly stratified and largely rural, with a powerful notable social class, a large peasantry, and a small middle class. Palestinian peasants were forced into wage labor, the elite lost the land that underpinned their power, and merchants lost their livelihoods. In time, dispersal transformed Palestinians into a mobile but highly insecure people among whom educational attainment and political activism ranked high as criteria for social standing. The physical dispersion made it difficult to reestablish a coherent political center. Living under different authoritarian regimes and subject to restrictions on political expression, the Palestinians suffered from constant pressure toward fragmentation. Palestinians' political aims evolved significantly. At first they were determined to regain all of Palestine, but beginning in the 1970s, an increasing number conceded that territorial partition—the establishment of a Palestinian state along-side Israel—was the most they could achieve. The concept of partition remains controversial, but for many it seemed the only way to ensure their national survival.

Controls imposed on dispersed Palestinians by the host countries took different forms. In Israel, Palestinians gained citizenship but lived under martial law until 1966. The movement of Palestinian residents was closely regulated, access to education and employment was restricted, and political activities were curtailed. In the Gaza Strip, the Egyptian military government maintained tight control over the restive Palestinians, of whom 80 percent lived in refugee camps. Palestinians living in Syria had the same access to jobs and schools as Syrian citizens, but their ability to travel abroad was curtailed. The Lebanese authorities were especially restrictive, denying Palestinians citizenship and the right either to study in public schools or to obtain permanent employment. Friction developed between the Palestinians, who were largely Sunni Muslim by religion, and those Lebanese politicians who sought to retain the special status of the Maronite Christian minority.

Life was least disrupted in the West Bank, where most people remained in their original homes. Palestinians staffed the administrative and educational systems in Jordan and developed many of the country's commercial enterprises. Palestinians also enjoyed citizenship rights in Jordan, which set Jordan apart from its Arab neighbors. But the regime never trusted them with senior posts in sensitive ministries and the armed forces, and their loyalty to the monarchy remained tenuous. Development priorities in Jordan focused on the East Bank, leading to a mass migration of Palestinians from the West Bank to Amman in the 1950s and 1960s.

The growth of a separate Palestinian nationalism gained traction in the 1960s with the emergence of Palestinian guerilla factions. Al-Fatah, founded in Kuwait in 1959 by the young engineer Yasir Arafat and several colleagues, launched its first raid into Israel on New Year's Eve in 1965. The fedayeen had a twofold strategy: they asserted that self-reliance was the route to liberation and sought to catalyze popular mobilization that would shame the Arab rulers into fighting Israel. When war finally came in 1967 and ended disastrously for the Arab states, the Palestinian guerrilla movement was thrust into the leadership position on the issue of Palestine, eclipsing the leading role that had been played by Amman, Cairo, and Damascus.

The Palestine Liberation Organization and the Palestinian Diaspora: 1967–1993

The 1967 war cut the Palestinian community in two: half of all Palestinians now lived inside the boundaries of old mandatory Palestine under Israeli rule, and half continued to live in the diaspora outside mandatory Palestine, mostly in various Arab countries. The Palestine Liberation Organization (PLO) was initially created in 1964 by the Arab League—in particular, by Egypt's Gamal Abdel Nasser to show that he was "doing something" about reclaiming Palestinian rights. In its early years it was an ineffective organization led by Palestinians tied to Arab regimes, especially Egypt. PLO leaders like Ahmad al-Shuqayri gave fiery speeches but did little to change the situation on the ground.

Shuqayri and other well-to-do Palestinians wrote the PLO Charter, amended in 1968, which called for the elimination of Israel, the creation of a secular Palestinian state in its place, and the return to Europe of Jews who had migrated under the banner of Zionism. It was a maximalist document that reflected Palestinian thinking of the time. In the ensuing decades, PLO thinking would evolve substantially.

The humiliating defeat in 1967 provided the opportunity for the Palestinian guerrilla groups to take control of the PLO and transform it into an autonomous and important umbrella organization that came to represent Palestinian interests in the region and internationally. The guerrilla organizations asserted their newfound muscle at the Fifth Palestine National Council meeting of 1969, where they ousted the old leadership and installed Arafat, head of the largest guerrilla faction, as the PLO's new leader.

As an umbrella organization, the PLO contained many diverse and competing groups. The largest and most important was Fatah, led by Arafat, which espoused a nationalist ideology typical of national liberation movements everywhere. There was little social content to Fatah's ideology, simply a call to regain lost lands. The two other most important constituent groups of the PLO espoused ideologies that were more hard-line Arab nationalist and Marxist in orientation: the Popular Front for the Liberation of Palestine (PFLP), founded by George Habash, a Greek Orthodox physician, and the Democratic Front for the Liberation of Palestine (DFLP), led by Nayif Hawatmeh, a Jordanian from the city of Salt. While Fatah focused on freeing Palestine, the more radical groups believed that only a more general revolution by the Arabs against their own conservative regimes could lead to the liberation of Palestine. The PFLP's spree of civilian-aircraft hijackings in 1970 was intended to launch the revolution.

The PLO began to flex its muscle by creating "states within states." The first ministate was created in Jordan, and King Hussein tolerated it until radical factions within the PLO openly called for the overthrow of his regime and set about implementing revolution. The hijacking of civilian passenger planes to a desert airfield in Jordan, where they were blown up after the passengers and crew had been released, proved to be the breaking point. The Jordanian army defeated the PLO in a bloody showdown in 1970 (later known as Black September), seized control of the refugee camps, and forced the guerrillas to flee to Syria and Lebanon in July 1971.

While the PLO was establishing a base of operations in Lebanon in the early 1970s, high-profile acts of political violence continued. In retaliation for Black September, Palestinian commandos assassinated Jordan's prime minister when he visited Cairo in November 1971. In one of the most infamous terrorist acts in modern history, Palestinians kidnapped and murdered eleven Israeli athletes at the 1972 Munich Olympics. Operations across the Lebanon-Israel border likewise intensified. Palestinian attacks were matched by Israeli bombardments and special operations in villages and refugee camps in Lebanon. Tit-for-tat violence and assassinations continued between Israel and the PLO in Lebanon until 1982, when Israel launched an invasion of Lebanon in an operation designed to eliminate the PLO as a political force.

The PLO's weakness compelled it to reevaluate its strategy. Even during the heady days of revolution between the 1967 war and Black September in Jordan in 1970, the PLO was powerless to reverse Israel's occupation of the West Bank and Gaza Strip, much less to regain all of Palestine. Attempts to organize an armed rebellion in the West Bank failed. Black September demonstrated the futility of confronting Arab regimes that had no interest in furthering the Palestinian cause if it meant the loss of their own power. Recognizing that the balance of power did not favor Palestinian interests, some Palestinians began calling for the establishment of a Palestinian state only in the lands occupied by Israel during the 1967 war: the West Bank, East Jerusalem, and the Gaza Strip.

The October 1973 Arab-Israeli War further consolidated the transformation of PLO policy toward accepting a two-state solution. The 1973 war was a victory for both Arab and Israeli states. The performance of Egyptian and Syrian militaries was strong enough to dim the memory of their humiliations in 1967. Israel's ultimate triumph on the battlefield in 1973, even after it absorbed a devastating initial blow, showed again that the PLO had no chance of defeating Israel militarily. Over the objections of the PFLP and other hard-liners, the 1974 Palestine National Council of the PLO took a major step toward embracing a two-state solution when it pledged to create a "national authority" over any liberated lands of Palestine. Several months later, the Arab League recognized the PLO as the "sole legitimate representative of the Palestinian people," a move that led to the PLO's achieving observer status at the United Nations and Yasir Arafat's speech to the General Assembly in November 1974.

The 1979 peace treaty between Israel and Egypt dramatically altered the geostrategic landscape for the PLO. The PLO rejected Israel's offer, made through Egypt, of autonomy under overarching Israeli control for Palestinians living in the West Bank and Gaza Strip. The rapid expansion of Israel's colonization efforts in the West Bank under Menachem Begin and the Likud Party, in power since 1977, showed Palestinians clearly that Israel was not interested in withdrawing to the 1967 borders and allowing a Palestinian state to develop. Moreover, the peace treaty effectively removed the Arab world's most powerful state from the Arab-Israeli stage, giving Israel a much freer hand in dealing with other Arabs. Egypt under Anwar Sadat was most interested in gaining the return of the Sinai Peninsula and currying favor with the United States, both cornerstones of its new economic-development strategy.

Having neutralized Egypt politically, Israel turned its eyes toward eliminating the PLO. Leaders of Israel's Likud Party believed that crushing the PLO and its state within the state in Lebanon would deprive Palestinians in the West Bank of political leadership, making permanent Israeli control of the West Bank more feasible. Following the October 1981 assassination of Anwar Sadat and the April 1982 Israeli withdrawal from the last part of the Sinai Peninsula, Israel made destroying the PLO its first priority.

No longer feeling vulnerable to Arab counterattack, Israel invaded Lebanon in June 1982. Israeli forces easily defeated the Lebanese, Palestinian, and Syrian forces they encountered on their drive to Beirut. Trapped, the PLO negotiated with the United States an exit of their forces to Tunisia and elsewhere in the Arab world. The American promise to protect Palestinian civilians left behind in Beirut proved hollow, as Lebanese forces, with logistical assistance from the Israel Defense Forces, slaughtered hundreds of refugees in the Sabra and Shatila camps shortly afterward.

Israel's gambit to destroy the PLO by invading Lebanon initially seemed to pay dividends. The PLO was decimated, its remaining forces scattered throughout the Arab world. Its new headquarters was in far-off Tunis, its factions were fighting each other more than Israel, and its prospects for pushing the international community to compel an Israeli withdrawal from the occupied territories seemed dim. Two events proved critical in rescuing the PLO from possible oblivion. First, Palestinians living inside the occupied territories launched their own uprising (intifada) against Israel in 1987. The intifada showed that Palestinians inside the West Bank and Gaza would actively resist Israel's occupation and confiscation of Palestinian lands, even in the face of a badly weakened PLO in the diaspora. The political mobilization of Palestinians that gave rise to the intifada was in part a response by West Bank and Gazan Palestinians to Israel's attempt to destroy the PLO.

Ironically, Israel itself helped rescue the PLO from obscurity when it engaged in secret peace negotiations with the organization in Oslo, Norway, in 1993, at the time when the PLO was extremely weak. During the 1990–1991 Iraq War, the PLO made a serious strategic miscalculation by backing Iraq against a US-led coalition determined to end Iraq's occupation of Kuwait. Kuwait and Saudi Arabia had long been the PLO's chief financial backers through a tax collected on Palestinians living in those countries. Yasir Arafat's public embrace of Saddam Hussein during the war caused Kuwait and Saudi Arabia to end their financial support of the PLO, which went bankrupt, closed a number of offices, and cut financial disbursements to Palestinian families and organizations. The PLO also lost the political support of much of the Arab world for its stance during this first Gulf War.

Because of its extreme weakness, the PLO offered Israel terms in Oslo that Israel had long demanded and the PLO had long rejected. These PLO concessions included a long interim period, no guarantee of ultimate statehood, continued Israeli control of all of Jerusalem during the interim period, and no explicit cessation of Israeli colonization of the occupied territories. Indeed, the number of Israeli settlers in the West Bank and Gaza doubled in the decade following the September 1993 signing of the Oslo Accords and had tripled by 2013. This interim period, viewed as a permanent trap by Palestinian opponents of the Oslo Accords, marked its twentieth year in 2013, with the situation further away then from a final resolution than it had been in 1993.

The Israeli Occupation: 1967–1993

After the 1967 war, developments in the occupied West Bank and Gaza Strip were markedly different from those affecting Palestinians elsewhere. The Palestinians in the occupied territories went through a period of relative political quiescence, even experiencing economic growth, while those in the diaspora were engaging in radical politics, civil war, and displacement. Then, as the PLO gradually moved toward accommodation with its Arab hosts and mainstream nationalism, the "inside" Palestinians increasingly radicalized and mobilized. In particular, three structural changes helped to transform Palestinian society: the opening of Israeli labor markets to Palestinians, the extensive confiscation of Palestinian lands by the Israeli government, and the establishment and expansion of the Palestinian university system.

After the 1967 war, Israel opened its domestic labor market to Palestinians from the occupied territories. Palestinians were recruited to do the unskilled or semiskilled jobs that Israelis refused to do themselves—primarily in the agricultural and construction sectors. This pool of cheap labor was a boon to Israeli businesses, which grew rapidly in the late 1960s and early 1970s. These jobs appealed to Palestinians both because they paid relatively well in comparison to jobs in the occupied territories and because there was an endemic shortage of local jobs. The Palestinians employed in Israel tended to come from the lower classes, primarily the peasantry and refugee camp dwellers. They came in large numbers: shortly after Israel opened its labor market, one-third of the Palestinian labor force in the West Bank and Gaza Strip was employed in Israel. By the 1980s, over 120,000 Palestinians—fully 40 percent of the Palestinian labor force—worked in Israel daily. As much as 70 percent of the Gazan labor force worked in Israel or in Israeli settlements. The result was the virtual disappearance of the Palestinian peasantry and the destruction of many patron-client networks, especially in the West Bank, seriously undermining one of the pillars of social power for the Palestinian elite. This pool of recruits proved crucial in the general political-mobilization campaign of the 1980s and the subsequent intifada.

A second change was the massive Israeli confiscation of land. In the immediate wake of the 1967 war, Israel tripled the size of the municipal boundaries of Jerusalem and then annexed it. Large sections contained within the new boundaries of Jerusalem were unilaterally declared state lands and taken by Israel, often for Jewish settlements. Other lands in East Jerusalem were confiscated on "security grounds," while still other parcels were awarded to Israelis who had claims dating to the pre-1948 period. Those Palestinian claims on land parcels in West Jerusalem, also dating to the pre-1948 period, were not similarly recognized. Those lands not confiscated were in essence frozen, so that the natural expansion of Palestinian neighborhoods was virtually impossible.

Confiscation of land in the West Bank and Gaza Strip was even more extensive. The most common means was to declare parcels of land as state land or as needed for security reasons; recognized private property was also confiscated outright. Often Jewish settlements would be built on the land seized. While large tracts of land in the West Bank and, to a much lesser degree, Gaza were confiscated in the first decade of military occupation, the confiscations were accelerated and were often deliberately provocative after the Likud Party came to power in Israel in 1977. On the eve of the Palestinian uprising in 1987, over half the West Bank and one-third of the Gaza Strip had been confiscated or otherwise made off-limits to Palestinians. In addition to antagonizing the Palestinians, such confiscations directly attacked a second pillar of notable power—control over land—further undermining this elite's legitimacy by showing it to be powerless to stop or slow Israel's land seizures.

The third change was the creation and expansion of a Palestinian university system. Prior to 1972, higher education was a privilege reserved for the Palestinian elite, as only those families could afford to send their children abroad for university. In 1972, the first full-fledged Palestinian university, Birzeit, was established. In subsequent years, more universities were established in Bethlehem, Hebron, Gaza, Jerusalem, and Nablus. In the decade preceding the intifada, the Palestinian university student population grew from a few thousand to between 15,000 and 20,000 annually. The effect was significant, as tens of thousands of Palestinians went through the university and its concomitant political socialization. The composition of the student population at these new universities was striking: 70 percent of the students came from refugee camps, villages, and small towns. From this student population, a new Palestinian elite emerged in the 1970s and 1980s—one that was larger, more diffuse, from lower social strata, more activist, and less urban than the notable Palestinian elite it largely replaced. As a result, Palestinian politics became more confrontational with Israel.

The major strategy of this rising Palestinian elite in the 1980s was to build grassroots organizations designed to mobilize the Palestinian population against the occupation. In turn, these institutions would act as protostate structures, designed to vest authority in Palestinian hands and away from the military government. During this period Palestinians built or expanded most labor unions, student blocs, and women's, agricultural-relief, medical-relief, and voluntary-works committees.

Two international events helped spur the mobilization campaign. First, the Egypt-Israel Peace Treaty shifted the regional balance of power dramatically in Israel's favor. The Palestinians recognized that any positive solution to their dilemma would be a long way off. Thus, the primary objective was to make the West Bank and Gaza difficult for the Israelis to rule and absorb. Second, Israel's 1982 invasion of Lebanon had the unintended consequence of invigorating the emerging elite in the West Bank and Gaza and making it clear that they could no longer rely on the "outside" PLO for salvation—it would have to be accomplished by those Palestinians still living in the occupied territories. While this new elite was widely affiliated with the major factions of the PLO—Fatah, Popular Front for the Liberation of Palestine, Democratic Front for the Liberation of Palestine, and the Palestinian Communist Party—it was significant that the political initiative clearly lay with those on the "inside."

The First Intifada: 1987–1993

In December 1987 a mass uprising against Israeli occupation began. It was a spontaneous event; no person or faction planned it. It was not an armed uprising, nor was it particularly violent. It took the form of thrown rocks, bricks, and occasional Molotov cocktails. Demonstrations, marches, and rallies were employed, especially in the first six months. However, the intifada was primarily about mass organized disengagement from Israel. In political terms, Palestinians denied Israeli authority on any number of issues and created alternative authoritative bodies to govern Palestinian society. The principal locus of authority for over two years was the Unified National Leadership of the Uprising (UNLU), an ever-changing body of local PLO activists who published periodic leaflets directing the intifada. The UNLU's first confrontation with the military government came over strike hours demanded of commercial establishments. The UNLU would instruct merchants to close their businesses at certain hours, while the military government commanded that they stay open during those hours and close for others. The confrontation went on for weeks, until finally Israel relented, and the UNLU was free to set strike hours and days. Its authority in these matters was recognized and widely obeyed, especially in the first two years of the intifada.

Political disengagement was not limited to the UNLU. Alternative structures of authority sprang up everywhere in the form of popular and neighborhood committees. These committees would provide social services to meet needs generated by the intifada, including distributing food during curfews, organizing "popular education" when the schools were closed, planting "victory gardens" to diminish dependence on Israeli agricultural products, organizing guard duty to watch for military or settler attacks, ensuring compliance with strike days, and the like. Some committees undertook more violent activities, particularly the interrogation and execution of alleged collaborators.

Economic disengagement was seen in the boycott of Israeli-made goods and the refusal to pay taxes to Israel in a number of communities, especially the town of Bayt Sahur. Institutional disengagement was illustrated by the mass resignation, at the UNLU's urging, of Palestinian policemen employed by the military government. Perhaps most important was psychological disengagement: the uprising was a vehicle of individual and communal empowerment, whereby, at least for a time, Palestinians believed they could actually roll back the occupation.

After an initial period of confusion, Israel responded to the intifada harshly, using, in the words of then defense minister Yitzhak Rabin, "force, might, beatings" to crush it. Well over 1,000 Palestinians were killed by Israeli forces, with many thousands more injured, and tens of thousands were imprisoned—many without charge or trial. Most important was the strategy of collective punishment, whereby many were punished—through house demolitions, curfews, destruction of crops, and similar means—for the actions of a few. Bringing disproportionate force to bear was a reasonably successful strategy in containing the intifada.

The intifada was also responsible for significant changes in Palestinian society. First, the traditional respect for elders was largely lost. Neither the youth throwing stones nor the more important "mid-generation" building popular institutions had much time for what they regarded as the compromises and concessions of their elders. This was seen clearly in the liberalization of family structures, where clan patriarchs lost their influence in decision making.

Second, the intifada had an antinotable aspect. While Israel was the primary target of the intifada, the old Palestinian elite was the secondary target. The families that had held local power for generations were largely marginalized, continuing a process begun even before the uprising.

Third, the intifada produced the rise to prominence of a powerful Islamist alternative to the secular PLO. The largest Islamist group, the Muslim Brotherhood, had been politically discredited in the years before the uprising because of its cooperation with Israeli authorities. The intifada radicalized the Islamist movement, giving birth in its early days to the Islamic Resistance Movement, or Hamas. Hamas (and the Islamic Jihad group) brought to Palestinian resistance a level of operational violence against Israeli targets that the PLO in the West Bank and Gaza had never employed, gaining converts and splitting Palestinian society. Hamas would continue to grow in strength.

The "outside" PLO in Tunis was as surprised as Israel when the intifada broke out and was not particularly important to the unfolding of events. Rather, Tunis sought to capture and control the intifada, something it never managed to do completely. The PLO funneled resources and advice to the occupied territories in support of the intifada and provided it with greater attention on the world stage. The PLO had not lost its legitimacy, but Tunis was geographically and situationally too far removed from the course of events in the West Bank and Gaza to matter much.

Clearly, though, the PLO was not enamored of the alternative bodies of authority and viewed them and any autonomous political activity as potential threats to its position. As a rule, through lack of support the PLO undermined political actions in the intifada over which it had little control, while it strongly endorsed those activities it could manage. Thus, while the PLO supported the intifada in principle, it often acted to demobilize Palestinian society in the West Bank and Gaza.

The Oslo Accords and Their Failure: 1993–2006

In the aftermath of the 1990–1991 Gulf War, the United States launched a major effort to deal with the Arab-Israeli conflict. In October 1991, the Madrid Conference convened with American, Arab, European, Israeli, Palestinian, and Russian participation. It led to a series of bilateral negotiations in Washington, which made little progress. The return to power of Yitzhak Rabin and the Labor Party in the 1992 Israeli elections, combined with a keen PLO interest in moving toward a peace agreement (and thus extracting itself from the political grave it had dug by backing Iraq in the 1990–1991 Gulf War), provided the basis for diplomatic progress. Secret negotiations begun in Oslo in January 1993 between PLO officials and two Israeli academics linked to the dovish Labor politician Yossi Beilin ultimately led to a breakthrough agreement between Israel and the PLO that was signed on the White House lawn in September 1993.

In addition to producing letters of mutual recognition, the 1993 Oslo Accords—formally known as the Declaration of Principles—established the principles upon which the interim period was to be based and identified the key issues that the parties would need to resolve in a timely manner in order to enter into a final-status agreement. Indeed, the interim period was supposed to have ended in May 1999. The 1993 accord was followed by the Gaza-Jericho Agreement of 1994 that established the Palestinian Authority (PA) in the Gaza Strip and the West Bank city of Jericho. An interim agreement was signed in September 1995. A subsequent agreement that expanded the territory under PA control was signed at Wye River in Maryland in 1998.

The Oslo peace process essentially ended in the summer of 2000. US President Bill Clinton convened a summit meeting at Camp David in July to negotiate a final-status agreement between Israel and the PLO. Accounts of what exactly happened there vary. The dominant Israeli interpretation was that Arafat had rejected a generous proposal and returned to Ramallah to prepare for a new round of fighting. The dominant Palestinian understanding was that Israel was not serious about making peace. Israel offered to return all of Gaza and a large portion of the West Bank to Palestinian control but refused to engage the refugee issue and insisted on control over most of East Jerusalem. Palestinians noted that Israel's proposal for the West Bank left Palestinians with three unconnected cantons (often referred to pejoratively as Bantustans), each surrounded by Israeli territory. Each side came away from Camp David convinced that the other was not interested in a real peace agreement.

The failure at Camp David left both sides simmering in an atmosphere of distrust. Ariel Sharon, then fighting for leadership of the Likud Party (and a staunch opponent of the Camp David negotiations), made a provocative visit on September 28, 2000, to the site of what Muslims regard as the third holiest mosque in Islam, the Haram al-Sharif, which Jews refer to as the Temple Mount, the site of the Temple in Jerusalem. Scuffles and rock throwing degenerated the next day into large demonstrations and clashes with Israeli police, with deadly consequences. The second intifada had begun.

A last effort at peacemaking pursued by Clinton in December and January failed. Ariel Sharon won a resounding victory to replace Ehud Barak as prime minister and was largely successful in ending the uprising, primarily by reoccupation of the West Bank in March and April 2003. A major criticism of the Oslo Accords is that they never specified, even in broad terms, what peace at the end of the road was supposed to look like. Palestinian opponents of the Oslo Accords—such as Hamas and the PFLP—openly criticized Yasir Arafat for falling into a trap, for agreeing to what would become a never-ending interim period with no Palestinian state ever resulting. The breakdown of the Oslo peace process gave credence to this charge in the eyes of many Palestinians.

From the Palestinian perspective, the fundamental problem with the Oslo negotiations was that the parties were negotiating from two different base points. Israel's negotiating posture, in essence, was that the conflict had begun in 1967; thus, the disposition of the West Bank and Gaza Strip was the item to be negotiated. From this vantage point, returning 100 percent of those lands won in the 1967 war would seem one-sided, and seriously discussing refugees from 1948 would not be in order. The PLO's negotiating posture dated the conflict to 1948. As a result, Palestinians believed they had already ceded 77 percent of historic Palestine, so asking for the remaining 23 percent (all of the West Bank and Gaza) constituted a fair and modest proposal. Moreover, finally settling the refugee issue was essential.

Yasir Arafat, under siege in his Ramallah-based, and mostly destroyed, *muqatama* headquarters, fell ill in October 2004 and died in France a month later. Mahmoud Abbas (Abu Mazen) was elected as the new Palestinian president.

The breakdown of the Oslo peace process led to two major Israeli moves. First, Israel began construction of a large barrier along its border with the West Bank. While its architect, Ariel Sharon, maintained the wall was a security barrier, not a political line, Sharon's successor, Ehud Olmert, quickly pledged that the barrier would represent Israel's border with the western half of the West Bank.

Israel's second step was to withdraw from the Gaza Strip in the summer of 2005. The idea of ridding itself of control of Gaza had long been popular among almost all segments of Israel's population. The withdrawal went relatively smoothly, although, since it was done unilaterally, PA president Mahmoud Abbas could not claim political credit for it. Instead, the Palestinian Islamist group Hamas capitalized on the withdrawal as evidence that its policy of armed resistance was paying off.

Fragmentation and War: 2006–2009

Palestinian frustration with the lack of any real progress in ending the occupation and with PA corruption and inefficiencies led directly to the success of Hamas in the 2006 parliamentary elections. Hamas won 44 percent of the national vote (to 41 percent for Fatah) but was able to parlay that plurality, because of an unusual electoral law, into a commanding majority in the Palestinian Legislative Council. Hamas's victory led to a halt in negotiations to end Israel's occupation. Israel froze relations with the PA as it concerned Hamas, though Fatah's Mahmoud Abbas remained president of the PA. The United States and Europe also sought to isolate the new Hamas government.

Fatah did not take lightly the end of years of one-party rule and all the benefits and privileges that went along with its dominion over Palestinian society. Fatah conspired to take back what it viewed as its rightful role, instigating significant social turmoil as a result. Combined with the general breakdown of Palestinian institutions of law and order during the second intifada, lawlessness and factional violence were widespread during

2006 and early 2007. By June 2007, the Hamas government feared that Fatah was planning a coup to take back power. Hamas launched a preemptive putsch in its heartland, the Gaza Strip, routing Fatah in four days of heavy fighting and taking full control over the Gaza Strip. Fatah responded by dismissing the Hamas government and appointing a new government. Palestine was now effectively divided between a Hamas-controlled Gaza Strip and a Fatah-controlled West Bank.

Hamas's seizure of the Gaza Strip immediately led to an Israeli siege, with substantial international support. This wrecked an already fragile economy. General scarcity made those with some resources, such as Hamas, even more important to the population. Hamas's putsch in Gaza also sparked cross-border violence between Israel and Gaza. A July 2008 cease-fire agreement between Israel and Hamas brought four months of relative quiet but no end to the economic strangulation of Gaza, as had been agreed in the cease-fire.

The cease-fire ended on November 4, 2008, the night of the US presidential election. Israel raided Gaza in order to destroy suspected tunnels under the border with Egypt, killing a number of Hamas militants in the process. A cycle of escalating violence ensued, which included Hamas rocket fire into Israel. Matters came to a head on December 27, 2008, when Israel began an aerial bombardment of Gaza, followed on January 3, 2009, by a ground offensive, code-named Operation Cast Lead. While far more Palestinians were killed—about 1,400 to 13 Israelis—the nature of warfare has so changed in the modern era that Israel's unquestioned military supremacy cannot be effectively utilized against what are essentially civilian militia ensconced in a general population.

Even after the war ended, the Israeli siege of Gaza remained in place throughout 2009. Palestinian fragmentation and weakness were apparent, as was Israel's inability to determine outcomes in Gaza effectively. The election of a hard-line government led by Benjamin Netanyahu in 2009 further dimmed the prospects for an end to the occupation anytime soon. Indeed, Netanyahu was effectively able to change the international discussion from Israel's occupation and settlement activity to Iran's potential nuclear ambitions, easing pressure on Israel and leading to record numbers of new Jewish settlers in the West Bank.

POLITICAL ENVIRONMENT

The West Bank (including East Jerusalem) and the Gaza Strip constitute 23 percent of historic Palestine and are separated by Israel. Gaza is a small, densely populated area along the Mediterranean Sea largely inhabited by refugees from the 1948 war and their families. Poverty rates are very high and have been exacerbated by frequent closures of the border with Israel, preventing Palestinians from working as day laborers in Israel. Unemployment is extensive and endemic. Saltwater intrusion into Gaza's aquifer has polluted freshwater supplies, a problem that increasingly threatens public health. Gaza's only river, which flows from the Hebron hills in the West Bank out to the Mediterranean through Wadi Gaza, is seasonal only and badly polluted. Beginning in 2000 with the outbreak of the second intifada, malnutrition in Gaza's children increased sharply. In terms of human misery, the Gaza Strip is one of the most desperate places on earth.

By contrast, the West Bank is larger and less densely populated, with somewhat better health and employment prospects for its residents. The west-facing hills receive significant winter rains that promote agriculture and replenish the western aquifer, a key source of freshwater for both Israel and the Palestinians. A hilly north-south spine separates the relatively lush and populated areas in the western half of the West Bank from the much more arid and sparsely populated eastern half. These hills drop off into the hot and humid Jordan valley. While the valley is below sea level, it is served by the Jordan River and thus generates some agricultural production.

Even in this small territory with about 4 million Palestinians, a number of important social and demographic divisions characterize modern Palestinian society. At the top are the remnants of Palestine's old notable social class, consisting of some of the prominent families. Their wealth and property holdings today are a fraction of what they were a century ago. Palestine's merchant class runs the gamut from small store owners to wealthier businessmen. Under the PA, individuals with important political ties to power often have been rewarded with lucrative state contracts or monopolies that have generated significant wealth in a short time. The higher merchant community feels significant resentment over such corruption and "leapfrogging" over more established businessmen.

The nonlanded, professional middle class rose to political prominence in the 1980s. Usually from modest origins, members of this socioeconomic group used university education as their stepping-stone to relative success. While Israeli confiscation policies did the most to undermine the notable elite in Palestine, the professional middle class likewise had no love lost for what it collectively viewed as a regressive force in Palestinian society. In many cases, members of declining notable families dropped out and joined the professional middle class.

These old and new elite classes in Palestine sit atop large blue-collar and agricultural working classes. Until recent decades, the peasantry had always constituted the largest class in Palestine. Today, peasants and poor farmers remain, but their numbers are dwindling. Most Palestinian peasants became wage laborers following the 1967 war. Throughout the 1970s and 1980s, Israeli construction, service, and agricultural sectors became dependent on Palestinian wage laborers, who themselves preferred to leave their small farms in order to get better wages in Israel. Before Israel's closure policy began in 1993, 40 percent of the Palestinian labor force worked in Israel, almost all as wage laborers. As Israel gradually closed its labor market to Palestinians, these workers rarely returned to agriculture. Many became unemployed.

Another important social cleavage is between refugees and nonrefugees. Generally, refugees have lower social status than nonrefugees. A similar cleavage exists between the West Bank and Gazan populations. Given its poverty and abundance of refugees, the Gaza Strip tends to be seen as a lesser place by those in the West Bank. When the Palestinian Authority was first established in Gaza and then spread in 1995 to most West Bank cities, some West Bankers spoke openly of the *ihtilal ghazawi* (the Gazan occupation). While that regional resentment was a mostly transitory phenomenon, there is no question that the physical separation of the two geographic parts of Palestine, as well as Israel's reluctance to allow Palestinians to travel between them, will keep these two islands moving on different social trajectories. The current political split between Gazan Hamas and the PLO-led West Bank reflects some of these social differences as well.

A demographic cleavage of diminishing importance is that between Muslim and Christian Palestinians. Historically, Christians made up about 10 percent of the total Palestinian population. However, given their privileged relations with European colonizers, Arab Christians have had much higher rates of emigration than their Muslim brethren. For example, while a small minority throughout the Arab world, Arab Christians make up about half of all Arabs who have immigrated to the United States. By 2010, Christians made up less than 2 percent of the Palestinian population in Palestine.

Of significant political importance is the cleavage between "insiders" and "outsiders." The signing of the Oslo Accords in 1993 opened the door for some 100,000 Palestinians associated with Yasir Arafat's Fatah movement to move to the West Bank and Gaza. While most were rank-and-file members of police and security forces and their families, they also included the political elite that came to dominate Palestinian politics after Oslo. They were sometimes called "Tunisians" by Palestinians, since so many came from the old PLO headquarters in Tunisia. The efforts of this outside elite to consolidate power "inside" were central to defining Palestinian politics after Oslo. The Oslo elite tangled in complex ways with the homegrown political activists, or new elite, that had developed in the 1970s and 1980s. Some refer to this struggle as being between the "old guard" and the "young guard."

Palestinian social demography is a complex web of relations and divisions. A myriad of other types of social cleavages are not discussed here, including, for example, relations between urban and rural Palestinians and between tribalized and nontribalized Palestinians. But the dominant factor by far in the Palestinian political and economic environment is Israel. More than any other power or factor, Israel controls the facts on the ground in the West Bank and Gaza. Israel decides if the borders are opened or closed, whether goods and services can move between towns or be exported or imported, whether Palestinians can come or go or even travel internally, whether settlements get built and more land gets confiscated. In short, since 1967, there is simply no important sector of Palestinian life that has not been directly impacted by Israel. The post-1993 Oslo period only altered that reality slightly by granting limited autonomy to the Palestinians. Israel and the decisions it makes about Palestinians will remain the dominant feature of Palestine's political environment for decades to come.

POLITICAL STRUCTURE AND DYNAMICS
UNDER THE PALESTINIAN AUTHORITY: 1993–2013

On paper, the Palestinian Authority was constructed as a democratic polity. Its dominant institution was to be its parliament, known as the Palestinian Legislative Council. The executive branch of the PA under the *ra'is* (president) was designed to be of secondary importance. An independent judiciary, harkening back to the days of British rule, was to play an important role in asserting the rule of law in Palestine.

Palestine had one of the most active civil societies in the Middle East. In the absence of an actual state and in the face of a hostile occupation, Palestinians mobilized around institutions of civil society, including women's and medical committees, human rights organizations, labor groups, and many others. Political factions seemed poised to transition into political parties, including the major factions of the PLO (Fatah, the PFLP, the DFLP, and the People's Party) and even Hamas.

However, the PA evolved into a soft authoritarian regime marked by the centralization and personalization of power. Three dynamics in particular contributed to PA authoritarianism: elite conflict, Palestine's political economy, and the imbalance of power between Palestine and Israel. PA authoritarianism and corruption under Fatah rule provided an opening for Hamas to gain popular support.

Elite Conflict

The Oslo Elites. Post-Oslo Palestine contained two distinct political elites. The Oslo elite (sometimes referred to as the old guard or the Tunisians) consisted primarily of top PLO officials and their networks of supporters who returned to the West Bank and Gaza Strip from Tunisia with the establishment of the PA in 1994. The Oslo elite was represented most dramatically by Yasir Arafat but also included numerous cabinet ministers, high ministry officials, most of the top leaders of the security and police forces, and a number of leading businessmen. Some of the most recognizable names of the Oslo elite are Mahmoud Abbas (Abu Mazen), Ahmad Qurei' (Abu Ala), and Nabil Sha'th.

The New Elite. The second political elite consisted primarily of native-born Palestinians in the West Bank and Gaza who were educated in Palestinian universities and Israeli prisons. These cadres were better educated and more numerous but less wealthy than their Oslo counterparts. This group of political activists has variously been called the new elite, the intifada elite, and the young guard. The new elite and its heirs led both the first intifada (1987–1993) and the second uprising (2000–2004). Activist Marwan Barghouti, imprisoned by Israel for his work with the al-Aqsa Martyrs Brigade, is perhaps the most prominent of the new elite, which also includes the leaders of Hamas.

Both sets of political leaders have strong national and familial ties with each other; however, they are sociologically and philosophically quite distinct, and their visions of the proper political rules of the game differ significantly. These are not differences in policies so much as in how politics gets organized and practiced. In a simple sense, the Oslo elite represents more traditional politics, and the new elite is more modern in its political sensibilities. These differences stem in part from diverse life experiences, but they also have a tactical political component.

When Arafat and the Oslo elite returned from Tunisia, their primary political task was to consolidate their power, and to do that they needed to undermine the new elite. Only the new elite had the proven mobilization skills to thwart the Oslo project from within Palestinian society if it so chose.

The PA—an institution primarily of the Oslo elite, or old guard—had some success in co-opting some members of the new elite and intimidating others. The institutional home of the new elite consisted primarily of the organizations of Palestinian civil society. Indeed, the formation of civil society in modern Palestine was largely a result of the efforts of the new elite in the post-1979 period. The domination of civil society organizations by the new elite is the underlying reason for the persistent PA attacks on its own civil society since 1994.

In order to weaken the new elite, the PA engaged in a politics of antithesis, or the implementation of rules of politics at odds with the strengths of the new elite. Because the new elite based its politics in institutions, the PA emphasized personalism. The cult of personality that was developed around Arafat was the most obvious, but not the only, form of this personalism. In general, one's official office said much less about actual power than one's personal ties to powerful people. Because the new elite practiced diffused, grassroots authority (a practical necessity under occupation), the PA centralized power, deliberately disempowering the grassroots. Because the new elite was more democratic in its political sensibilities, the PA adopted more authoritarian rules of politics.

The al-Aqsa Intifada, the internal Palestinian reform movement, and, most especially, Arafat's death in November 2004 called into question how long the Oslo elite would be the dominant power in Palestine. The Oslo elite bet its political future in Palestine on the success of the Oslo peace process. The failure of that process in Palestinian eyes discredited this elite, opening the door for its rivals to reassume power within Palestinian society. Hamas's electoral victory in the 2006 parliamentary elections was further evidence of the weakening of the Oslo elite in the post-Arafat period.

The tension between these two elite groups is best seen as an evolving dynamic. From the establishment of the PA until the second intifada and concomitant reform movement, the cleavage between these two elites was sharp and formed the decisive component of internal Palestinian politics. The Oslo elite, however, was predominant. The reform movement born of the al-Aqsa Intifada heralded a second stage in the evolution of this elite conflict. The reemergence of the new elite in this period was demonstrated in part by the new prominence of reformers in Palestinian government and the new political alliances that sprang out of the changed circumstances. The sharp and decisive distinction between the Oslo and new elites blurred as the latter reemerged on the political scene, most dramatically with the Hamas victory in 2006. Given the demographic weight of the new elite and the population it represents, the third stage in this evolving dynamic will likely see the consolidation of power by the new elite and the absorption of the remnants of the Oslo elite.

As the new elite consolidates power, cleavages within it will likely emerge. The most obvious cleavage is the ideological one between Islamists and nationalists, Hamas and Fatah. The cadres leading these movements are sociologically identical in terms of their class origins and educational backgrounds, but they are ideologically divided. However, conflict between these two elements was not inevitable. Fatah and Hamas cadres went to school together, spent time in Israeli prisons together, and cooperated tactically for many years. This is not to say that relations have always been warm; they clearly have not. But it is useful to remember that Fatah itself emerged from the Muslim Brotherhood organization in Gaza in the 1950s, long before Hamas and Fatah worked together during the al-Aqsa Intifada. They have regularly shared cultural and ideological frames and symbols, with Hamas openly promoting Palestinian nationalism and Fatah embracing Islamic symbols. The emergence of Fatah's al-Aqsa Martyrs Brigade (Kita'ib Shuhada' al-Aqsa) is a case in point—its very name combines words that have nationalist and Islamic connotations.

Political Economy

A second contributing factor to PA authoritarianism and corruption was the basic political economy established after Oslo—one quite similar to that of the oil-rich states of the Persian Gulf.

The Palestinian Authority can be considered a distributive state because a large majority of its budgetary revenues come from direct payments to the PA from international sources. The most important payment has been the transfer by Israel to the PA of various taxes collected by Israel on Palestinian goods, services, and labor. But these transfers proved unstable, as Israel would periodically cut them off, such as during the second intifada or when Hamas won the 2006 elections. Prior to the uprising, Israeli payments to the PA amounted to about $600 million of the PA's $850 million in typical annual budget revenues, or about 70 percent. In terms of their political impact, such direct payments created the same dynamic as oil rents: they helped create and sustain a top-heavy, centralized, authoritarian political structure. In addition, foreign donors contributed a total of about $3 billion in the period from 1994 to 2000. In some cases, these expenditures took the form of direct subsidies to the PA's budget, although more commonly they supported specific projects, which in turn freed up monies for the PA to spend elsewhere. In sum, of the approximately $8 billion spent by the PA directly or on its behalf by foreign donors prior to the al-Aqsa Intifada, about $6.5 billion, or over 80 percent, came in the form of external transfers to the PA.

The taxes that Israel collects for the PA do belong to the legitimate Palestinian government. But the fact that they are collected by another state and simply transferred as a lump sum to the PA treasury has important consequences. That about three-quarters of all government revenues come to the PA as simple transfers has the same type of political impact as in oil-based distributive states. Creating a democracy out of a consolidated distributive political economy is extremely difficult.

Imbalance of Power

A third factor contributing to authoritarianism in the PA was the vast imbalance of power between Israel and the Palestinians. The negotiating process accurately reflected the imbalance of power to Israel's advantage, including Oslo's focus on interim measures only, the absence of powerful policy levers for keeping Israeli withdrawal from Palestinian territory on schedule (Palestinians fully controlled only about 18 percent of the West Bank at the apex of the withdrawal), the doubling of the number of Jewish settlers in the West Bank during the peace negotiations of the 1990s, and Israeli veto power on key issues, such as Jerusalem and refugees, which ultimately scuttled negotiations.

As the weaker party, the PA was a "term taker"—it could accept or reject Israeli offers but had little leverage to compel different terms. Within the Palestinian body politic, this often meant having little choice but to accept—de facto if not de jure—terms and conditions deeply unpopular within Palestinian society. Massive settlement expansion and endemic Israeli closures of Palestinian areas while negotiations were ongoing were the most important exemplars of PA impotence vis-à-vis Israel in the eyes of most Palestinians.

The imbalance of power posed a dilemma for the PA: in order to continue the peace process, it was forced to accept highly unpopular terms and realities. In turn, the PA had to crack down on the growing public dissent that resulted. Even if Arafat and the PA had been inclined to embrace democracy, the fact that elections would have empowered rejectionist elements from the Islamist Hamas within the democratic mainstream of Haidar Abdel-Shafi deterred the Oslo elite from conducting them. For this reason no municipal elections were held from the establishment of the PA in 1994 until 2005, and no parliamentary elections were held between 1996 and 2006.

Hamas Rule in Gaza

Fatah's clumsy authoritarian rule and corruption ultimately affected its political situation in the 2006 elections. While Hamas had boycotted the 1996 parliamentary elections, it ran a full slate of candidates in the January 2006 elections. Hamas ran a disciplined election, never having more candidates than available seats. Fatah-oriented candidates, however, ran in far greater numbers, thereby splitting their votes. As a result, Hamas was able to parlay a small 44 to 41 percent popular vote margin into a substantial parliamentary majority: 74 seats out of 132. Hamas's Ismail Haniya became the new PA prime minister.

Hamas's victory was not only a reaction to Fatah's ineffective rule but also a result of Hamas's policy of continuing armed resistance to Israel's occupation. Fatah had chosen to follow a predominantly political process to end the occupation and create a Palestinian state, and that was seen to have failed. Hamas promised the path of armed resistance, which many Palestinians felt was the only viable means to end the occupation.

Hamas's electoral victory sent shock waves through much of the world. Israel, the United States, and Europe all tried to isolate Hamas, refusing to work with a group they all considered a terrorist organization. While some voices in Fatah encouraged dialogue with Hamas, the bulk of Fatah's leaders supported isolating Hamas as well. Fatah was following the path of other once-dominant parties that have suddenly lost the benefits, privileges, and patronage associated with one-party rule. Fatah decided to try to win back power by any means necessary.

Israel ceased transferring taxes and duties owed to the PA, now that Hamas controlled the purse strings, and subsequently imprisoned without charge dozens of Hamas parliamentarians, cabinet ministers, and high officials. Resentment between Hamas and Fatah led to street clashes in the Palestinian territory, especially in Gaza, throughout 2006 and early 2007.

Matters came to a head in June 2007 following the publication of leaked documents that suggested an impending coup attempt by Fatah, backed by the United States. Hamas struck first, routing Fatah forces in Gaza and consolidating its rule. PA president Mahmoud Abbas then dismissed the Hamas government under questionable legal rules and installed a new government under Prime Minister Salam Fayyad. Fayyad's government had effective control over only parts of the West Bank and no control in Gaza. The West Bank and Gaza were now formally split, with Fatah ruling the former and Hamas the latter.

Hamas rule in Gaza had mixed results. On the positive side, Hamas was given credit for bringing the era of near anarchy to a close and establishing law and order. As part of this effort, Hamas took on clan militias in Gaza that were operating outside the law, often protecting lucrative black market enterprises, including large-scale tunnel operations linking Gaza to Egypt.

On the negative side, Hamas was largely intolerant of challenges to its rule and ideology, continuing its proxy war with Fatah. The international isolation of Gaza under Hamas rule, including Israel's tight siege, brought even more misery to Gaza, although the Palestinian population largely blamed others, not Hamas, for this condition. The conflict between Hamas and Israel contributed to the bloody conflict beginning in December 2008 and continues in the blockade and isolation of Gaza by Israel. Various attempts to end Israel's blockade of Gaza, most notably by Turkish and international activists aboard the *Mavi Marmara* in 2010, have not succeeded.

FOREIGN POLICY

While not a sovereign state, the Palestinian Authority had an active foreign policy during the Oslo period of limited autonomy. Formally, the PA was merely the interim government, and Palestinian foreign policy was conducted by the PLO. In actual fact, the two organizations merged to the point of being indistinguishable.

The PA had different target audiences for its foreign policy. The United States was a key partner, as only the United States had the leverage over Israel essential to achieve Palestinian goals. The European Union was also an important foreign policy partner because it contributed the most aid to the PA and because European powers, especially Britain, could (it was thought) influence Washington on key issues. The Arab states constituted a third target audience because they could help deliver regional support and legitimacy to the Oslo process and Palestinian goals. Finally, there was Israel, the foreign power that held control over all Palestinian lands and must be convinced to relinquish that control. While some Palestinian leaders recognized that it was critical to try to win over domestic Israeli opinion, the PA never was adept at it. Any gains and inroads the Palestinians made were lost entirely with the second intifada.

The PA had three primary foreign policy goals. First, it needed financial resources. The PA had as a core function a patronage role of distributing jobs and resources to key supporters and constituencies. It became the largest single employer (by far) in the occupied territories, employing about 160,000 Palestinians and thus supporting about 20 percent of all Palestinian families in the West Bank and Gaza. Organizational survival was essential, and foreign aid was critical to this. The PA was generally successful in meeting this objective; indeed, it typically received the second-most foreign aid per capita of any polity in the world, following only Israel.

A second foreign policy objective was to ensure that the interim period generated the maximum amount of Palestinian sovereignty over the occupied territories. The PA needed a successful interim period in order to sell the Oslo peace process to a skeptical national constituency and set the stage for final-status negotiations. On this foreign policy objective, the PA was less successful. At its peak, the PA had full control over less than 20 percent of the West Bank; Israel maintained full control over 60 percent of the West Bank, with the remainder being jointly administered. The PA had no control over East Jerusalem at any point. As for Gaza, the PA controlled about two-thirds of the Gaza Strip until 2005, when Israel unilaterally withdrew from all of Gaza. Even after the withdrawal, however, Israel still fully controlled the land and sea borders of Gaza and the airspace above it. The only exception was Gaza's land border with Egypt.

The number of Jewish settlers in the West Bank doubled during the Oslo peace process and tripled after it failed, further pointing out the PA's failure to secure Palestinian lands. Its failure to gain credible control over the occupied territories during the interim period undermined its legitimacy in the eyes of most Palestinians. The consequences of this failure included the al-Aqsa Intifada and the coming to power of the rejectionist Hamas.

A third foreign policy objective for the PA was to put together enough international support to achieve a good final-status agreement. Winning over the United States when it came to key Palestinian positions was considered central to the overall strategy of securing a legitimate Palestinian state. However, the US administration under Bill Clinton rejected the right of return for Palestinian refugees, insisted on significant Israeli sovereignty in East Jerusalem, never pushed Israel to cease its colonization of the West Bank, and advocated Israeli annexation of parts of the West Bank. The US administration of George W. Bush further distanced itself from Palestinian interests by allowing Israeli prime minister Ariel Sharon to implement a series of unilateral measures in the occupied territories that were designed, it was widely believed, to prevent the emergence of a viable Palestinian state. US President Barack Obama's administration used its bully pulpit to push for a two-state solution and pressure the Israeli government of Benjamin Netanyahu to restrict the flood of settlers moving to the West Bank with active Israeli government encouragement, but to no avail. Obama's failure to change the basic dynamic of the conflict led his administration to drop the issue. None of the other international support the PA generated could counterbalance the strong US support of Israel.

The Arab Spring has further complicated PA foreign policy. While the far-reaching reforms demanded in a number of Arab countries were not matched inside the West Bank and Gaza, the Arab Spring has nevertheless been a setback for the Palestinians. Arab attention has been turned dramatically toward domestic issues of democracy and development, while the regional issue of Palestinian rights has been largely forgotten for the present. Egyptians, Tunisians, Libyans, and Yemenis are busy constructing entirely new political systems, while Arabs in Jordan, Morocco, Bahrain, and elsewhere continue to press for change. Syria has entered a long and bloody civil war. While broader Arab concern for the Palestinian issue will not disappear until some resolution is at hand, the Arab Spring has put Palestine on the back burner for the time being.

FUTURE PROSPECTS

The future is bleak for the Palestinians, in large measure because they do not control their own fate. Palestinians in the West Bank and Gaza are essentially powerless in a world of states, and their future will be decided far more by others than by themselves. The fragmentation of Palestine between Hamas rule in Gaza and Fatah rule in the West Bank complicates Palestinian prospects. Palestinians cannot speak with a unified voice in such a situation, which only weakens their ability to affect outcomes and promote their right to self-determination effectively. It may well be that the historical period when a Palestinian state could be constructed has passed. After two decades of promoting a two-state solution, many Palestinians despair that it is any longer possible to achieve. Thus, while Palestinian leaders cling to the fading hope that a two-state solution is possible, a growing number of Palestinians now openly speak of a new phase in their conflict with Israel: that of a postnationalist single state with equal rights for both Jews and Arabs. If such a dream ever comes to pass, it is likely decades in the future. In the meantime, unending conflict, continuing dispossession, and statelessness will likely be the immediate fate of Palestinians.

BIBLIOGRAPHY

The Palestine problem has been studied exhaustively from different political and analytical perspectives. The best broad historical narratives that give excellent overviews of Palestinian history and the conflict with Israel include Charles D. Smith, *Palestine and the Arab-Israeli Conflict,* 7th ed. (New York: Palgrave MacMillan Press, 2010); Baruch Kimmerling and Joel S. Migdal, *The Palestinian People: A History* (Cambridge, MA: Harvard University Press, 2003); James Gelvin, *The Israel-Palestine Conflict: One Hundred Years of War* (New York: Cambridge University Press, 2005); Benny Morris, *Righteous Victims: A History of the Zionist-Arab Conflict, 1881–1999* (New York: Alfred A. Knopf, 1999); Ilan Pappe, *A History of Modern Palestine: One Land, Two Peoples* (New York: Cambridge University Press, 2004); Mark Tessler, *A History of the Israeli-Palestinian Conflict* (Bloomington: Indiana University Press, 1994); and Avi Shlaim, *The Iron Wall: Israel and the Arab World* (New York: Norton, 2000).

Among the few studies of pre-twentieth-century Palestine, Beshara Doumani's *Rediscovering Palestine: Merchants and Peasants in Jabal Nablus, 1700–1900* (Berkeley: University of California Press, 1995) is outstanding for its insight into the political economy of an important town. Also excellent is Alexander Scholch, *Palestine in Transformation, 1856–1882: Studies in Social, Economic and Political Development* (Washington, DC: Institute for Palestine Studies, 1993). Rashid Khalidi examines the evolution of Palestinian nationalism before and after World War I in *Palestinian Identity: The Construction of Modern National Consciousness* (New York: Columbia University Press, 1997), as does Muhammad Muslih in *The Origins of Palestinian Nationalism* (New York: Columbia University Press, 1988).

For overviews of the British mandate period, the reader can study Tom Segev, *One Palestine, Complete: Jews and Arabs Under the British Mandate* (New York: Henry Holt, 2000); J. C. Hurewitz, *Struggle for Palestine* (New York: Norton, 1950); Ann Lesch, *Arab Politics in Palestine, 1917–1939* (Ithaca, NY: Cornell University Press, 1979); Yehoshua Porath, *The Emergence of the Palestinian-Arab National Movement, 1918–1929* (London: Frank Cass, 1974), and *The Palestinian Arab National Movement, 1929–1939* (London: Frank Cass, 1977). Walid Khalidi, ed., *Before Their Diaspora: A Photographic History of the Palestinians, 1876–1948* (Washington, DC: Institute for Palestine Studies, 1984), offers visual evidence of family life, culture, and customs in Palestine.

Gershon Shafir emphasizes the centrality of land to the conflict in *Land, Labor and the Origins of the Israeli-Palestinian Conflict, 1882–1914* (New York: Cambridge

University Press, 1989). Walid Khalidi, ed., *All That Remains: The Palestinian Villages Occupied and Depopulated by Israel in 1948* (Washington, DC: Institute for Palestine Studies, 1992), lists more than four hundred villages destroyed during and after the 1948–1949 war.

Our knowledge and understanding of the events surrounding the 1948 war have been revolutionized by the work primarily of Israeli scholars who gained access to critical documents once Israel and Britain's thirty-year classification rule expired. Among many excellent books that shed light on 1948 are Benny Morris, *The Birth of the Palestinian Refugee Problem Revisited* (New York: Cambridge University Press, 2004), and *1948 and After* (New York: Oxford Clarendon, 1990); Avi Shlaim, *Collusion Across the Jordan: King Abdullah, the Zionist Movement, and the Partition of Palestine* (New York: Columbia University Press, 1988); Ilan Pappe, *The Making of the Arab-Israeli Conflict, 1947–1951* (New York: I. B. Tauris, 1992); Zeev Sternhell, *The Founding Myths of Israel* (Princeton, NJ: Princeton University Press, 1998); and Eugene L. Rogan and Avi Shlaim, *The War for Palestine: Rewriting the History of 1948* (New York: Cambridge University Press, 2001). For an excellent depiction of the city of Jerusalem during the 1948 war, see Salim Tamari, ed., *Jerusalem, 1948: The Arab Neighbourhoods and Their Fate in the War* (Jerusalem: The Institute of Jerusalem Studies and Badil Resource Center, 1999).

The Jordanian dimension of the Palestine problem is analyzed in Shaul Mishal, *West Bank/East Bank: The Palestinians in Jordan, 1949–1957* (New Haven, CT: Yale University Press, 1978), as well as in the book by Avi Shlaim noted above, *Collusion Across the Jordan*. Highly recommended is Adnan Abu Odeh, *Jordanians, Palestinians and the Hashemite Kingdom in the Middle East Peace Process* (Washington, DC: US Institute of Peace, 1999).

The status of Palestinian citizens of Israel has been examined by Sammy Smooha in his two-volume *Arabs and Jews in Israel* (Boulder, CO: Westview Press, 1989, 1992) and by Ian Lustick in *Arabs in the Jewish State* (Austin: University of Texas Press, 1980). Highly recommended is David Grossman, *Sleeping on a Wire: Conversations with Palestinians in Israel* (New York: Farrar, Straus and Giroux, 1993, reissued in 2003 by Picador).

Books on the conditions and political struggles in the occupied territories prior to the first intifada include George Emile Bisharat, *Palestinian Lawyers and Israeli Rule: Law and Disorder in the West Bank* (Austin: University of Texas Press, 1989); Rita Giacaman, *Life and Health in Three Palestinian Villages* (London: Ithaca Press, 1988); and Joost R. Hiltermann's *Behind the Intifada* (Princeton, NJ: Princeton University Press, 1991). Israeli author David Grossman wrote an insightful account of Palestinian life under occupation in the 1980s in *The Yellow Wind* (New York: Farrar, Straus and Giroux, 1988, reissued in 2002 by Picador). A very personal account of growing up under occupation is by the Palestinian lawyer Raja Shehadeh, *Strangers in the House: Coming of Age in Occupied Palestine* (New York: Penguin, 2003).

Moshe Ma'oz, *Palestinian Leadership on the West Bank: The Changing Role of the Mayors Under Jordan and Israel* (London: Frank Cass, 1984), and Emile Sahliyyeh, *In*

Search of Leadership: West Bank Politics Since 1967 (Washington, DC: Brookings Institution Press, 1988), offer insights into local politics. Sara Roy, *The Gaza Strip: The Political Economy of De-development* (Washington, DC: The Institute for Palestine Studies, 1995), provides a comprehensive analysis of Israeli policies that stifled Gaza's economy. Details on legal, socioeconomic, and political conditions are contained in Naseer H. Aruri, ed., *Occupation: Israel over Palestine,* 2nd ed. (Belmont, MA: Arab American University Graduates, 1989). The complexities of life under Israeli occupation are depicted by novelist Sahar Khalifeh in *Wild Thorns* (New York: Olive Branch Press, 1989). Raja Shehadeh writes a penetrating critique of how law was used as a tool of occupation, not justice, in *Occupier's Law* (Washington, DC: Institute for Palestine Studies, 1988).

The intifada of 1987 to 1993 spawned many books, including my own *Building a Palestinian State: The Incomplete Revolution* (Bloomington: Indiana University Press, 1997). While my book covers both the uprising and its political aftermath, other books just focus on the intifada itself, including Zachary Lockman and Joel Beinin, eds., *Intifada* (Boston: South End Press, 1989); Jamal R. Nassar and Roger Heacock, eds., *Intifada* (New York: Praeger, 1990); Zeev Schiff and Ehud Ya'ari, *Intifada* (New York: Simon and Schuster, 1990); and F. Robert Hunter, *The Palestinian Uprising* (Berkeley: University of California Press, 1993). Helen Winternitz illustrates the impact of the uprising on a West Bank village in *A Season of Stones: Living in a Palestinian Village* (New York: Atlantic Monthly Press, 1991).

Yezid Sayigh has written the most detailed history of the PLO, titled *Armed Struggle and the Search for State* (Oxford: Clarendon Press, 1997). Shorter accounts of the Palestinian movement before 1982 can be found in Helena Cobban, *The Palestinian Liberation Organization* (New York: Cambridge University Press, 1984); Alain Gresh, *The PLO: The Struggle Within* (London: Zed, 1985); and William Quandt et al., *The Politics of Palestinian Nationalism* (Berkeley: University of California Press, 1973). Salah Khalaf (Abu Iyad), in *My Home, My Land* (New York: Times Books, 1981), describes his key role in the establishment and growth of the PLO. Rashid Khalidi details the PLO's withdrawal from Beirut in *Under Siege: PLO Decisionmaking During the 1982 War* (New York: Columbia University Press, 1986).

Laurie Brand considers the circumstances facing Palestinians in exile in *Palestinians in the Arab World: Institution Building and the Search for State* (New York: Columbia University Press, 1988). Rosemary Sayigh, *Palestinians: From Peasants to Revolutionaries* (London: Zed, 1979), focuses on the political awakening of Palestinian refugees in Lebanon. Salma K. Jayyusi's comprehensive *Anthology of Modern Palestinian Literature* (New York: Columbia University Press, 1992) captures the spirit of Palestinians living in exile and under Israeli rule.

The rise to prominence of Hamas has generated several recent works detailing the Islamist movement in Palestine, including Ziad Abu-Amr, *Islamic Fundamentalism in the West Bank and Gaza* (Bloomington: Indiana University Press, 1994); Khaled Hroub, *Hamas: Political Thought and Practice* (Washington DC: Institute for Palestine Studies,

2000); Shaul Mishal and Avraham Sela, *The Palestinian Hamas: Vision, Violence and Co-existence* (New York: Columbia University Press, 2000); and Glenn E. Robinson, "Hamas as Social Movement," in *Islamic Activism*, ed. Quintan Wiktorowicz, 112–139 (Bloomington: Indiana University Press, 2003).

Prior to the signing of the Oslo Accords in 1993, a number of authors outlined their visions of a two-state solution to the conflict, including Mark A. Heller, *A Palestinian State* (Cambridge, MA: Harvard University Press, 1983); Mark A. Heller and Sari Nusseibeh, *No Trumpets, No Drums: A Two-State Settlement of the Israeli-Palestinian Conflict* (New York: Hill and Wang, 1991); Jerome M. Segal, *Creating a Palestinian State: A Strategy of Peace* (Chicago: Lawrence Hill, 1989); and Ann Lesch, *Transition to Palestinian Self-Government: Practical Steps Toward Israeli-Palestinian Peace* (Cambridge, MA: American Academy of Arts and Sciences, 1992). In 2005, the RAND Corporation prepared a two-volume set on the requirements for creating a successful Palestinian state: Steven N. Simon et al., *Building a Successful Palestinian State* (Santa Monica, CA: RAND, 2005), and Doug Suisman et al., *The Arc: A Formal Structure for a Palestinian State* (Santa Monica, CA: RAND, 2005).

Studies of internal Palestinian politics and problems during the Oslo process include Joel Beinin and Rebecca L. Stein, eds., *The Struggle for Sovereignty: Palestine and Israel, 1993–2005* (Palo Alto, CA: Stanford University Press, 2006), and Amira Hess, *Drinking the Sea at Gaza* (New York: Owl Books, 2000). Edward W. Said pens a scathing critique of the underlying principles and implementation of the Oslo Accords in *The End of the Peace Process: Oslo and After* (New York: Pantheon, 2000).

Scholars are still contemplating the long-term impact of the al-Aqsa Intifada (2000–2004), but early accounts of the impact on Palestinians include Raja Shehadeh, *When the Birds Stopped Singing: Life in Ramallah Under Siege* (South Royalton, VT: Steerforth, 2003), and Baruch Kimmerling, *Politicide* (New York: Verso, 2006).

Key websites in English on Palestine include Foundation for Middle East Peace (www.fmep.org), United Nations Relief and Works Agency (www.unrwa.org), PLO Negotiations Affairs Department (www.nad-plo.org), Badil Resource Center (www.badil.org), Palestinian Authority (www.palestine-net.com), Palestinian Central Bureau of Statistics (www.pcbs.gov.ps), Palestinian Initiative for the Promotion of Global Dialogue and Democracy (www.miftah.org), Birzeit University (www.birzeit.edu), Palestinian Non-Governmental Organizations Network (www.pngo.net), Jerusalem Media and Communications Center (www.jmcc.org), and Palestinian Center for Policy and Survey Research (www.pcpsr.org).

Online daily newspapers in English that cover Palestinian issues include Beirut's *Daily Star* (www.dailystar.com.lb); Amman's *Jordan Times* (www.jordantimes.com); and Tel Aviv's *Ha'aretz* (www.haaretz.com).

13

ARAB REPUBLIC OF EGYPT

Joshua Stacher

The Arab world's most populated country rose up against its dictator on January 25, 2011. Inspired by protests in Tunisia, Egyptians launched a revolution to reject their political elites and the crony-capitalist economic system that regulated their lives. Beginning in late January, protesters occupied many public squares around the country's towns and cities. The government responded with force, but this failed to contain the mobilization. In fact, increased dissent resulted. Longtime president Hosni Mubarak (r. 1981–2011) made several belated attempts to satisfy the demands of the demonstrators. As this drama unfolded, Mubarak's regime watched the ruling party implode, the state's security forces melt away, and the military ascend to executive leadership. In a matter of eighteen days, popular mobilization had not only constrained the options of longtime elites but brought down Mubarak.

After Egypt's president was deposed, uprisings began in Libya, Bahrain, Syria, Yemen, and other countries to lesser degrees. There is no doubt that significant political change has happened in Egypt. Indeed, in June 2012, Egyptians freely and fairly elected a member of the Muslim Brotherhood, Mohamed Morsi, to become the first civilian president in Egypt's history. Yet change has not rid the country of frustrating continuities. The architects of the Egyptian uprising unleashed a historic social process that continues to unfold. While change has come to Egypt and representative institutions are now more transparent, political power continues to reconfigure itself in familiar authoritarian ways.

For nearly sixty years before the uprising, a centralized executive wielded control over Egypt's governing institutions of state. While the president consulted with other leading elites, the state bureaucracy existed to implement his policies rather than to participate independently. Following Mubarak's downfall, power has become decentralized and a number of groups compete for influence. This prompts several questions: Has a revolution taken place? Why can't all Egyptians compete for state power? Will this produce democracy or some other, more autocratic arrangement? For now, Egypt's removal of an autocratic leader has not led to a wider regime change or democracy. Whether this will occur in the future remains to be seen. We can, however, answer why more expansive and inclusive change has not resulted. Egypt's past is guiding and structuring its current possibilities.

HISTORICAL BACKGROUND

Although Egypt's history stretches back millennia, the country's contemporary political arrangements and institutions have little to do with this long past. Rather, Egypt's current politics is a product of its more recent trajectory.

Modern Egypt emerged out of the Ottoman Empire. Beginning in 1805, the Ottomans' appointed minder was an Albanian named Muhammad Ali Pasha, who ran Egypt as an independent state. Ali devoted his efforts to modernizing the country and ruled until 1848. Enamored with Europe, he sought to create his own army and bureaucracy and worked to establish an industrial infrastructure. Egypt was a rural country with comparative advantages in cotton and other agricultural production. As a consequence, the economy developed in a dependent manner in relation to the center of the international economy: western Europe.

Muhammad Ali's family reigned until 1952. His descendants shared his goal of developing Egypt but did not have the revenue to cover the costs of modernizing society or developing the economy. Successive leaders relied on credit lines from Europe as they pursued grandiose development projects, such as the Suez Canal. These projects eventually bankrupted the country. To offset the lack of development, and under a reforming guise, Egypt's king in 1866 established an impotent parliament.

By 1882, the parasitic imperial powers had called in Egypt's debts and competed to incorporate the strategically located country into their empires. The British became Egypt's colonizer but did not unseat the ruling family. Rather, they used the monarchy as a buffer between themselves and a public eager for self-determination.

Trapped between the population and the colonizer, the king relented and incrementally empowered the parliament. Similarly, courts began to assert themselves and legally challenge the British. Yet, from the time Britain took over in 1882 until the end of World War I, an uneasy relationship became knitted into the polity.

World War I brought down the Ottoman Empire, but Britain continued to support Egypt's monarchy. However, the regional explosion of nationalism required Britain and Egyptian elites to recalibrate. Muslim and Coptic Christian nationalists joined forces to demand greater independence. Together they founded the Wafd Party, which became a powerful political force backed by landowners. Parliament began to exert more influence, as elections became the chief means for the population to resist the empire, reward and constrain the Wafd, and chide the weak king. Finally, after successive waves of negotiation, the British granted Egypt formal independence in 1922. Yet it was a mixed declaration because the British continued to dominate the country's foreign policy and control the Suez Canal. A new constitution was promulgated in 1923, and parliamentary elections were held regularly thereafter.

The political system that emerged during the so-called liberal era (1923–1939) resembled a three-legged stool. The monarch occasionally conspired with parliament against the British, but he more frequently needed British support to stay in power. As the world

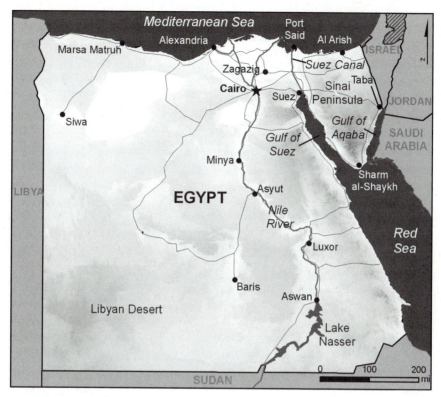

Arab Republic of Egypt

economy sank into depression during the 1930s, Egyptian politics became militarized. Mass movements such as the Muslim Brotherhood and the Wafd Party developed paramilitary wings to counterbalance the armed militias and rising fascism of the political parties. The rate of political assassinations rose. Yet no relief was possible in an unstable system that blended imperialism, weak executive rule, open parliamentary elections, and an underdeveloped economy controlled by a small number of elites. By 1952, less than 1 percent of the population owned over 50 percent of the land, and 44 percent of the people in rural areas were landless. As the era of decolonization began, the colonial experiment in Egypt left a fractured economy and arbitrary, fragmented political institutions.

As Egypt's domestic conditions deteriorated, world powers recognized the newly established State of Israel in 1948. Many in Egypt—as was the norm across the Arab world—were concerned that the Israeli state had come at the expense of the Palestinian people, who were largely forced to migrate to Jordan, Syria, and Lebanon. Demonstrating how out of touch the elites were, King Farouk sent an underequipped army to face off with the numerically superior Israeli forces. Egypt's army was routed, as were the other

ARAB REPUBLIC OF EGYPT

Capital city	Cairo
Chief of state, 2012	President Mohamed Morsi
Head of government, 2012	Prime Minister Hisham Qandil
Political parties (share of most recent vote, 2012)	Democratic Alliance for Egypt (37.5%), Alliance for Egypt (27.8%), New Wafd Party (9.2%), Egyptian Bloc (8.9%), Al Wasat Party (3.7%), The Revolution Continues Alliance (2.8%), Reform and Development Party (2.2%), National Party of Egypt (1.6%), Freedom Party (1.9%), Egyptian Citizen Party (.9%), other (3.7%)
Ethnic groups	Egyptian (99.6%), other (0.4%)
Religious groups	Muslim (90%), Coptic Christian (9%), other Christian (1%)
Export partners, 2011	Italy (8.8%), Germany (5.5%), United States (5.5%), India (5.2%), Saudi Arabia (5.1%), Spain (4.7%), France (4.5%)
Import partners, 2011	China (11.5%), United States (9.8%), Italy (5.6%), Germany (4.9%), Turkey (4.4%), Brazil (4.1%)

Arab armies. The Egyptian population was disappointed, but those sent to fight in the 1948 war were even angrier with the feckless leadership, lack of economic development, and continued foreign meddling in the country's affairs.

The Free Officers Regime

In July 1952, military officers known as the Free Officers launched a coup d'état against the king. They abolished the 150-year-old monarchy and Egypt became a republic. Initially, the military's intervention had ambivalent support from the population.

With King Farouk exiled, the young officers now commanded the state and inherited the legacy of its colonial problems. While Gamal Abdel Nasser would emerge as the leader, one of the group's elders, Mohammed Nagiub, served as the republic's first president in 1953–1954.

During Nagiub's presidency, Nasser was the prime minister. The previous experience under the monarchy created a desire for greater autonomy and genuine independence. The officers did not want Western powers to be able to manipulate Egypt politically, and they wanted to break the shackles of Egypt's dependency so as to encourage national economic development. Yet the new rulers were also politically pragmatic. While they shared the same aim, their opinions and tactics for getting there differed. Important disagreements about Egypt's future ensued. The disputes were not ideological. Rather, they were about who should govern the country: the military or civilians.

The Free Officers quickly fragmented into two groups centered on Nagiub and Nasser. The former favored party and parliamentary politics and a return to civilian governance. Nasser feared that turning the country back over to civilians would lead to the reemergence of divisive political gridlock. He felt that democracy was too cumbersome and the military was best positioned to modernize the country. After a struggle between the rival camps, Nagiub finally resigned and spent the rest of his life under house arrest or away from public life. Nasser became president in 1956.

Despite emerging victorious, Nasser remained pragmatic when eying Egypt's development. To streamline the modernization process, he created a repressive authoritarian state. Dissent was prohibited. Nasser's elaborate and redundant security offices penetrated society in ways that encouraged obedience for the sake of a better Egypt. Nasser cracked down on the Muslim Brotherhood and a budding labor movement. He outlawed political parties and established a single-party machine to regulate politics. He disbanded parliament and reined in civil society organizations. He also slowly but incrementally used the state to take over the economy's commanding heights.

The president became unchallengeable. His ruling party, the Arab Socialist Union (ASU), became the chief vehicle of civilian political life. It was impossible to advance politically or professionally without being an ASU member. All politics became subservient to his office.

The only institution that Nasser left somewhat unfettered was the one from which he recruited his most trusted allies—the military. For most of Nasser's presidency, his friend and colleague Abdel Hakim Amer headed the military. It was the only semiautonomous institution partly because the military's intelligence apparatus competed with the state's civilian security apparatuses.

Nasser also built masterfully on decades of Arab nationalist sentiment, thought, and education. By investing in pan-Arabism, he wooed the expanding middle classes and the poor. In July 1956, Nasser directly confronted the vestiges of the past by nationalizing the Suez Canal, wresting it from the British—a move that is still the single most important event in Egypt's contemporary history. He doubled down on industrialization and pursued projects such as the Aswan High Dam. He used fiery rhetoric against Israel to appeal to his regional base and consolidate power domestically.

Nasser's approach changed starkly after the 1967 war with Israel. Following Egypt's humiliating defeat, he reined in the military and began the process of dismantling his pan-Arab foreign policy since both had been exposed as empty shells. Irrespective of these policy reversals, however, Nasser remains Egypt's most popular president, as well as the one who established the country's centralized presidential system.

After Nasser suffered a fatal heart attack in 1970, his vice president, fellow Free Officer Anwar Sadat, came to power. If Nasser created a strong presidential office, Sadat institutionalized it further. Yet, understanding Sadat's Egypt as a simple extension of Nasser's is erroneous. Sadat inherited Nasser's presidency but not his operational powers. To consolidate his presidency, Sadat reconstituted the political establishment. This led to a professionalization of the military and security apparatus. It also created a political field that, while portending a semblance of pluralism, was far more personalized than Nasser's political structures.

Nasserist politicians and their security networks easily cornered the new president politically. Realizing that he might become a tool in the hands of the party and the military, Sadat launched a so-called corrective revolution to reorient the regime's direction. He arrested powerful politicians and rotated the military's high brass sometimes more than once a year. Grand initiatives became common. Sadat promulgated a new constitution in 1971 and expelled Soviet advisers from Egypt in 1972. He launched a war against Israel in 1973, which, despite being a military defeat, became a diplomatic victory. He liberalized the economy in 1974, opened the Suez Canal in 1975, introduced party pluralism in 1976, and went to Jerusalem in 1977. The capstone was his signing of the Camp David peace accords with Israel in 1979. In the process, Sadat fastidiously worked to align Egypt with the United States, despite being shunned by fellow Arab leaders. He was a bold leader. Yet politics became a revolving door in which survival depended on loyalty to Sadat and acceptance of his initiatives.

There were also many changes to Egypt's legal framework that had political ramifications. Sadat repeatedly vowed to be a rule-of-law president. In addition to promulgating a new constitution, he made parliamentary elections more meaningful. He dismembered Nasser's ASU in 1976 and created a new ruling party in 1978, the National Democratic Party (NDP). In addition, he allowed other parties to be established, namely, the Ahrar (Liberal) and Tugammu (Progressive) parties. Despite unleashing a pluralist experiment, he tightly controlled the leadership of those parties, making them beholden to him. Sadat loosened control over the repressed Muslim Brotherhood so it would dilute the Nasserist trend in the country, and he allowed the judiciary, which had a history of autonomy, to reestablish itself. In the process of implementing these changes, the president personalized politics by depoliticizing political parties and the parliament and professionalizing the military and security apparatus.

Sadat's constant twists and turns made Egypt's political establishment dizzy and created a new wave of dissent. Politicians who challenged Sadat's economic liberalization and political realignments were fired. But this did not stop resistance from below. The population responded by criticizing and contesting Sadat's ability to govern unilaterally. While Egyptians seemed willing to discuss a peace agreement with Israel, the fact that Sadat rammed the Camp David Accords down their throats angered many. Others were concerned about encroaching US patronage and the growing inequality unleashed by economic liberalization. For his part, Sadat seemed unable to understand why his policies created so much opposition. Yet, because he responded to dissent by constructing an expansive security apparatus, repression—not debate—became the norm. Weeks after a roundup of people from all trends, Islamist army officers assassinated the president during a military parade in October 1981. While Sadat is frequently hailed as the president of peace, many Egyptians remain ambivalent about him.

Vice President Hosni Mubarak, a shy and loyal servant of Sadat, became the republic's fourth president after Sadat's assassination. After the tumult of the Sadat years, Egypt settled in for a long period of stagnation under Mubarak. No one could have predicted that this air force officer from a rural background would go on to become Egypt's longest-serving leader since Muhammad Ali (r. 1805–1849). For nearly thirty years, Mubarak fought to maintain the strong presidential system he had inherited. His risk-averse style made politics predictable, despite changes in the landscape. More parties emerged, elections became more contested, a violent insurgency erupted during the 1990s, and the country existed on the brink of serious economic crisis. Yet, Mubarak, the ruling party, the state apparatus, and Egypt's primary external patron—the United States—became unshakable features of politics in Egypt.

During the 1980s, Mubarak oversaw a liberalization of the political scene. Parliamentary elections were contested more openly. Legal parties, such as the Wafd, Labor, Liberals, and Progressives, as well as the outlawed Muslim Brotherhood, gained legislative representation. Yet Mubarak never governed with a parliament that did not have an NDP supermajority of at least 74 percent. The military was also marginalized. Although most provincial governors were former military officers, the ministries were overwhelmingly civilianized. The military was included in huge swaths of the economy to ensure its continued loyalty to the regime.

Mubarak maintained Egypt's close relationship with the United States. He oversaw the continuation of US military and economic aid—an outcome of the Camp David Accords—and played a mediating role between Israel and the Palestinians. Omar Suleiman, Mubarak's chief intelligence officer, watched his portfolio grow after the September 11, 2001, terrorist attacks by working closely with the United States on counterterrorism policy.

Mubarak was a manager, not an innovator. He directed the country through many potentially destabilizing moments. Yet suggesting that the Egyptian state was at peace with its population would be a mistake.

As limited political liberalization occurred during the 1980s, groups outside the formally recognized opposition began to mobilize. Often under the cover of human rights groups, activists began to document the repression of Mubarak's police and dreaded State Security Agency. Mubarak deliberalized the political arena during the 1990s, as the state fought against the Islamist al-Gamma al-Islamiyya insurgency, leading one interior minister to deflect criticism indelicately by saying that Egypt held "less than 10,000 political prisoners."

As Mubarak entered his third decade as president, mobilization against his regime spiked exponentially. The second Palestinian intifada, which began in late 2000, provided an issue around which activists could mobilize. After the attacks of September 11, 2001, Mubarak supported US President George W. Bush's global war on terror and subsequent invasion of Iraq, sparking public disagreement among Egypt's population. Protests about these issues quickly turned into protests against the Egyptian president.

As this mobilization against Mubarak increased, the regime appeared to be preparing for a hereditary succession. After Syria's Bashar al-Asad succeeded his father in 2000, many commentators speculated that Mubarak's younger son, Gamal, had presidential ambitions. While Hosni Mubarak seemed ambivalent, he did not obstruct the project. Rumors also spread that Mubarak's wife was plotting her son's takeover. Gamal Mubarak's meteoric rise was complemented by a restructuring of the NDP around his secretariat. His succession seemed a fait accompli.

Because of the security forces' invasive tactics, it was difficult to judge the size of the opposition in this period. Small pockets of resistance were everywhere. In 2004, a group of activists coalesced into the Egyptian Movement for Change, or Kifaya (Enough). Kifaya sponsored protests with "No to Mubarak" and "No to Hereditary Succession" themes almost weekly during 2005. While Kifaya did not last as a movement, it did provide a model of resistance adopted by other groups, such as April 6 and We Are All Khalid Said. The latter two groups were integral players in the protests that led to Mubarak's resignation in February 2011. The opposition was not solely political, however.

Gamal Mubarak's rise coincided with a shift in the state's economic policies. Although Egypt had pursued an International Monetary Fund (IMF)–sponsored structural-adjustment program since 1991, Gamal aligned himself with a group of technocrats who took over the cabinet in 2004. Prime Minister Ahmed Nazif oversaw the single greatest expansion of neoliberal policies in Egypt's history. The wealth gap between rich and poor grew substantially, despite 7 percent gross domestic product growth rates. Yet, more importantly, this led to the single largest wave of industrial strikes in over sixty years. Over 2 million workers participated in more than 2,100 strikes between 2006 and 2009 alone. The labor sector's mobilization did not connect to the smaller but parallel networks of political dissent. But this activism had an effect—just not on state policy.

Egyptian elites fortified their ranks against this opposition through coercion rather than debate. The interior ministry's budget increased steadily to contain the growing mobilization of the 2000s. While the waves of mobilization never threatened the state's cohesion or Mubarak's presidency, it produced an environment of political learning among the varied opposition movements. These experiences led directly to the popular uprising of January 25, 2011.

The 2011 Uprising

By January 25, 2011, Egypt was boiling politically. Nearly a decade of crushing neoliberal economic reforms and increasing instances of police brutality led to the emergence of a number of contentious protest movements (such as the April 6 Movement and We Are All Khalid Said Facebook groups). Protesters called for a mobilization against Mubarak on the national police holiday—just days after Tunisians had overthrown their dictator. The initial groups of protesters were technologically savvy activist youths, organized in horizontally structured groups in Cairo and Alexandria. Another group of leaderless protesters emerged in provincial towns and cities in the Nile delta and along the Suez Canal. After these groups had pulled off their protests and withstood the repressive police response, other groups joined in the uprising against Mubarak, including the Muslim Brothers, the Salafis, the labor movement, and previously apolitical citizens. Faced with such broad opposition, the military intervened against Mubarak on February 11.

Mubarak's seemingly durable regime collapsed in just eighteen days. In the initial days of unrest, the crowds braved countless canisters of tear gas, buckshot pellets, and water cannons before overwhelming the riot police (al-Amn al-Markazi). Mobilization spread across the country as police stations—where egregious acts of torture and brutality had often occurred—were ransacked. The NDP's national headquarters and several provincial party offices were set ablaze. After the uprising's fourth day, the military moved tanks and armored personnel carriers into the capital's streets.

As the protests continued, many worried that the army might fire on the crowds to save Mubarak. Instead, the generals turned their tanks away from the crowds and toward the palace. Finally, after three speeches by Mubarak failed to empty the occupied squares, the military issued its first communiqué, in which it recognized the "legitimate demands" of the protesters. A group of around twenty senior generals formed the Supreme Council of Armed Forces (SCAF). Mubarak and his family left for exile in Sharm al-Shaykh.

Despite the euphoria after Mubarak's overthrow, Egypt did not experience full regime change. This is because the SCAF hived off parts of the regime in order to save its rump. Mubarak had actually started the process when the protests began by firing the neoliberal economic reformers in his cabinet (and ending his son's presidential aspirations). He also had the hated interior minister, Habib al-Adly, arrested. Between that arrest and pressure from the protesters, the interior ministry no longer possessed political agency. The demise of the neoliberal reformers, the neutralization of the interior ministry, and the weakening of Mubarak and his inner circle meant that the military now was the only institution capable of safeguarding the state. Thus, the SCAF slid into the position of the strong centralized executive. It was able to do so because the military's power increased as the revolutionaries neutralized its institutional revivals. While the SCAF could not govern as Mubarak had, it initially relied on its favorable national reputation.

After Mubarak resigned, the SCAF relied on the state's institutions, which had been disrupted but not broken during the uprising. As time lessened the effects of the protests, continuities in the hierarchies of the state bureaucracy returned. This provided the SCAF with powerful weapons of incumbency, such as the media and the judiciary. The SCAF also sought partnerships with influential domestic political organizations, such as the Muslim Brotherhood, to help restore order, calm worries, and demobilize the population.

The SCAF arranged the transition in ways that would protect its privileged status from future civilian oversight. It commissioned a series of constitutional amendments, made unilateral constitutional declarations, scheduled parliamentary and presidential elections, and proposed writing a new constitution. The generals promised to return to their barracks as soon as a president was elected.

What unfolded over the next sixteen months was a chaotic and often violent transition. It was not unusual for sectarian strife to erupt or for the military to deploy force against protesters—even as Mubarak received a life sentence for failing to stop violence against protesters. In the process, the voices of revolutionary change became marginalized in formal politics. Antilabor discourses, the threat of an economic crisis, and the occasional manufactured security crisis also helped strengthen the rule of the generals.

The military, supported by the state apparatus, and the Muslim Brotherhood proved to be the only organizations capable of exerting influence during the SCAF-led transition. While the NDP had collapsed, many of its leaders' patronage networks remained intact. This did not translate into many parliamentary seats, but the so-called remnants (*feloul*) of the party were capable of running an uncharismatic candidate, General Ahmad Shafiq, who almost won the presidency. Alternatively, the Muslim Brotherhood proved an electoral juggernaut, winning 47 percent of the seats in the parliament elected in November 2011 and January 2012. The more conservative Islamist groups, known as Salafis, won a further 24 percent. Revolutionary candidates only managed to secure 9 out of 508 seats in the first parliament elected after Mubarak. Then, after a June 2012 Supreme Constitutional Court (SCC) decision dissolved that parliament, the Brotherhood watched its candidate, Mohamed Morsi, win the presidency with 52 percent of the vote.

Reducing the narrative of Egypt's post-Mubarak events to a competition between the military and the Muslim Brotherhood, however, does not tell the whole story. While the revolutionary protesters did not achieve their aim of full regime change, and while the prospect of democracy still seems distant, there is no overstating the change that has occurred. After nearly sixty years of rule by military officers, the strong centralized presidency has been dismantled. Whether it will return remains to be seen. Elections, rather than moments when the state rigs a spectacle to make the population feel powerless, are now an irreversible part of political life. Groups, parties, and civil society organizations—ranging from the Trotskyist Left to the Islamist Right—now contest one another, as the remnants of the older autocratic order try to reconstitute themselves. Labor unionists struggle to increase their rights while attempting to eject the Mubarak cronies who have long controlled their factories. New media ventures appear each day with sophisticated investment structures to ensure that wealthy capitalists cannot dominate their editorial lines. Art and cultural productions have been unleashed, making the Ministry of Culture irrelevant.

Despite all the change, however, the military remains an entrenched actor in the economy. Much of the country's economic activity remains off the books and is not transparent. Decades of underdevelopment, illiteracy, a large wealth gap, a broken national health-care system, and crumbling infrastructure challenge the ever-increasing population of 83 million on a daily basis. While the head of state has been changed and the regime has been severely disrupted, it remains to be seen whether political development and inclusivity can become hallmarks of the new Egypt, given the legacies of the past.

Yet a longer historical process has been unleashed that may eventually reconcile tensions between political Islam and representative governance, civil-military relations, and inclusive approaches to national development. While it is impossible to predict how these issues will be resolved, a return to a Mubarak-like state is beyond the realm of possibility. Indeed, the only certain characteristic of Egyptian politics in the coming years will be the ongoing struggle between factions of the state and military, the Muslim Brotherhood, and the revolutionaries.

The contemporary politics of Egypt resembles that of other developing countries that also emerged out of colonial contexts. Egypt had a cohesive national identity, stable borders, and a state apparatus with considerable expertise, particularly in the judiciary and security services. Yet the political system is fragmented. This is in part what the Free Officers tried to rectify through their military intervention. In the process, however, they stitched into the country a peculiar set of privileges and dynamics that continues to encourage military intervention. The post-1952 military regime also established a strong centralized executive, which today's Egypt is debating and struggling against. Egypt's recent past will condition the possibilities for its future.

POLITICAL ENVIRONMENT

Geography

Egypt is located in the northeast corner of the African continent, at the crossroads of North Africa (*Maghreb*), the eastern Mediterranean (*Mashreq*), and the Arab Gulf (*Khaleej*). Egypt's neighbors are Libya, Israel, Palestine, Jordan, Saudi Arabia, and Sudan. The Mediterranean Sea is to its north and the Red Sea to its east. The world's longest river, the Nile, finishes its nearly 6,000-mile journey by emptying into the Mediterranean. The Nile creates some of the most nutrient-rich soil in the world, so even though 95 percent of the country's 83 million people live on only 6 percent of the land, Egypt's agricultural production feeds its people. The country is divided into three distinct parts: the Nile delta, Upper Egypt, and the Sinai Peninsula. The delta is the fan structure that one sees on the map above Cairo. Upper Egypt is the thin line along the Nile below Cairo. (Upper Egypt is in the south because the Nile's water flows from south to north.) The Sinai Peninsula is the appendage separated from the rest of Egypt by the Suez Canal, adjoining Gaza, Israel, and Jordan. Although Cairo and Alexandria are both megacities, the majority of Egyptians live in rural areas.

Religion and Ethnicity

Egypt has one of the most homogenous populations in the Middle East. Most people identify themselves as distinctly Egyptian, a product of the long state-building and modernization processes that have been under way since the reign of Muhammad Ali began in 1805. All Egyptians speak Arabic, though there are small dialectical differences between Cairo and the rest of the country. Upper Egyptians also speak a distinct dialect.

Around 89 percent of the population is Sunni Muslim, and 10 percent is Coptic Christian, or Egyptian Orthodox. There are very small pockets of Protestant Christians and Shi'a Muslims, and less than one hundred Jews now remain in the country. There are also Baha'is in Egypt, but they are unrecognized and unable to attain state documents such as birth and death certificates and national ID cards. While there is discrimination against all minority groupings, it is not systematically practiced by the state, except in the case of Baha'is. Rather, the weakness of the legal system contributes to the ongoing instances of discrimination and violence.

Political Culture

Egyptians have been disciplined by the authoritarian state structure that has conditioned their political participation since 1952. Between 1952 and 1970, the system primarily produced a culture of Arab nationalism that was also anti-Communist. The principal targets of Nasser's repression were leftist movements and Islamists.

Islamism, particularly as defined by the Arab world's largest Islamist group, the Muslim Brotherhood, was revived during Sadat's presidency. Ostensibly encouraged by Sadat to counterbalance residual Nasserist elements, Islamists penetrated many quasi-state institutions and many sectors of civil society. While Egyptians overwhelmingly have a nationalist orientation, an Islamist trend is electorally influential. This trend, however, is not religiously inspired. Rather, the Islamists, particularly the Brotherhood, appeal to Egyptians with a discourse that provides continuity with the old Arab nationalist discourse. Namely, Islamists call for Egypt's national development and autonomy from external powers such as the United States. Despite these rhetorical overtones, many observers and analysts focus exclusively on the religious discourse most Islamists use.

Political culture continues to change in the wake of the uprisings of 2011. More Egyptians are calling for freedom of expression, the right to organize, greater transparency, and more representative government. Despite these calls for change and equality, the post-Mubarak regime appears to be drifting away from these essentially democratizing demands. Thus, the state seems likely to continue to maintain autocratic practices alongside changes in its representative institutions in the near term. Either way, the state will be the most influential actor in producing the political culture of Egypt, while modes of resistance continue to contest the state's hegemonic interpretations.

Economic Conditions

Nasser and the Free Officers inherited an underdeveloped colonial economy in 1952. Outside powers had penetrated Egypt's economy and structured it to serve Europe's markets. The country's new leaders thought that producing economic development was merely a matter of establishing a new order and viewed themselves as the engines of growth. The experiment's fatal flaw was that Nasser and his colleagues linked the state's control of the political arena to economic decision making. Once political considerations began to affect sound economic planning, Egypt's development became the casualty.

Fresh out of the colonial era, many newly independent states watched the United States and Soviet Union compete for clients. Nasser wished to distance Egypt from any potential foreign patrons. He strove to stay neutral in the Cold War and forge a new autonomous path. He was obsessed with attracting outside aid for industrialization projects but did not want to become dependent on donor countries. Given the reluctance of the Americans to help fund the central symbol of Egypt's industrialization push, the Aswan High Dam, Nasser rejected the United States and aligned with the Soviets.

When the Free Officers came to power, their social support was limited. Given this narrow foundation, Nasser used a massive state-led economic-growth program to achieve the dual goals of industrializing Egypt and consolidating the Free Officers' regime. He did this through state intervention and economic populism, which had some popularity at this time.

The Egyptian state began to nationalize privately owned assets, which it then redistributed across society as populist benefits. From a structural point of view, the new military incumbents attacked the existing bases of capital in the country and handed over the gains to previously disenfranchised segments. The state undertook land reform, seizing land from large agriculturalists and giving small lots to the large class of farmers. It also seized factories to eliminate uncontrollable political rivals. These assets gave the state considerable revenue, which it used to provide social benefits. Nasser made populist promises to provide free universal health care, free university education, and guaranteed state employment for graduates.

The population became healthier, schools and universities were packed, and public-sector employment ballooned. Despite the regime's repressive tendencies, many Egyptians experienced unprecedented upward social mobility. Nasser had eliminated political competitors and attracted the population's support. Nevertheless, in the process, he fused political and economic considerations into one indistinguishable entity while erecting a strong centralized executive.

Nasser's foreign policy, especially his nationalization of the Suez Canal in 1956, resonated deeply with the population's desire for Arab self-determination. Nasser established a model that leaders in other developing countries mimicked. Some even call his approach to building a broad populist coalition "authoritarianism of the Left," in contrast to the rightist variant that emerged in Latin America at this time.

Yet popular support was not enough to generate sustainable economic growth. One of the benefits of populist state-led development is that it gives the state access to capital, which it can then distribute. But attacking the owners of capital suppressed domestic investment and especially foreign investment. Thus, in addition to paying for populist entitlements, the state also must become the engine of investment and ingenuity. Such financial commitments become increasingly difficult to maintain. After a few years of growth, the state-led growth model stagnated. But rather than liberalize the economy, Nasser doubled down on the populist experiment.

By the end of the 1960s, the internal tensions and contradictions of Nasser's state-led model had produced a large national debt, a chronic imbalance of loan payments, and a capital-accumulation crisis. The model proved to be a failure, despite improvements in the lives of many. And if this were not enough, Egypt's ongoing conflict with Israel and Nasser's bid to lead the Arab world meant the government also was making substantial military expenditures. After Egypt sank into a military quagmire in Yemen and experienced a humiliating defeat by Israel in 1967, Nasser began to reconfigure the economy. But he died in 1970 before real progress was made. At Nasser's death, Egypt had approximately $6 billion of external debt. Nasser had failed to resolve Egypt's underdevelopment or improve its international economic position.

Sadat drastically altered Egypt's economic policies and ushered in a postpopulist era. Yet, despite the change, Sadat's macroeconomic policies were no more effective than Nasser's. Rather than focus on domestic considerations or painful economic reforms, Sadat used Egypt's economy as an international geostrategic tool to elevate his presidency on the international stage.

Sadat followed Nasser's style of prioritizing politics over the economy and keeping both under tight control. He used the economy and international patronage. He felt that Egypt's salvation was dependent on moving into the American sphere of influence, which, in part, required opening up the economy to US investors. Thus, in 1974, when Sadat launched his *Infitah* economic-liberalization program, he looked for American partnerships to ease the transition. Sadat's liberalization initially was not tepid. He rolled back many populist privileges. He also created a group of crony capitalists who were dependent on his patronage. Thus, loyalty, not an enterprising free market spirit, became a requirement for business success.

The United States hesitated to embrace Sadat fully. US officials were uncertain he really wanted to realign Egypt. Yet, with each reform, Sadat pushed Egypt into American arms. Sadat often pursued liberalization with reckless abandon. In 1977 he unilaterally announced the end of state subsidies on staples such as bread, producing an insurrection from Alexandria to Aswan that lasted three days and nearly ended his presidency. In fact, the military had to reestablish control before Sadat reinstated the subsidies. The population's volatile response to these actions continues to guide economic decision making regarding price controls on gas, bread, and utilities to this day.

Sadat's economic liberalization, coupled with continuing populist commitments, produced a sharp increase in the national debt. In Sadat's eleven years in office, Egypt's debt grew fivefold, to $30 billion. The onslaught of foreign commodities easily eclipsed the market for low-quality, locally produced domestic goods. Money was fleeing the country for foreign goods. Crony capitalists grew wealthy while the poorer segments of society grew more impoverished. The professional middle classes also felt the squeeze of a quasi-liberal economy. The cost of living increased, the currency lost some of its value, and the service sector outgrew the industrial sector. Egypt for the first time became a net importer of grain. Although Sadat initiated a postpopulist era, his extreme economic changes and the continuation of a state-led economic model left the economy stagnant.

Hosni Mubarak inherited Sadat's large external debt, commitment to peace with Israel, and close relationship with the United States. Mubarak muddled through his first decade as president. He was too cautious to roll back the populist social contract for fear of inciting another popular revolt. Egypt remained in a holding pattern despite attempts by the IMF to pursue a structural-adjustment package beginning in 1986. Yet Mubarak refused to budge. Egypt's debt had increased to $48 billion by 1990.

After Iraqi president Saddam Hussein invaded Kuwait in 1990, Egypt was presented with an opportunity to halt its stagnant trajectory. When US officials assembled a multinational coalition to remove Iraqi forces from Kuwait in January 1991, they believed Arab military participation would be crucial and lobbied Egypt strongly to join the coalition. This gave Mubarak negotiating leverage.

Mubarak agreed to contribute troops to the coalition after US and international financial institutions forgave over half of Egypt's foreign debt. Mubarak then approved an IMF structural-adjustment plan in 1991. The plan called for a reordering of Egypt's macroeconomic policies. Land-reform and tenant laws were reversed, union activity and labor rights were restricted, and public-sector ventures were privatized. Egypt's textile industry lost nearly half its jobs as a result. Nevertheless, Mubarak's economic reforms involved more continuity than change. The president's overriding concern was the popular unrest that economic reform might create. Thus, before long, inflation rose, and economic growth slowed.

It seems that in 2004 Gamal Mubarak persuaded his father to turn over the nation's economic portfolio to him. An investment banker by trade, Gamal introduced a new technocratic elite to change the Egyptian economy. The younger Mubarak and his colleagues were true believers in neoliberal trickle-down economics. In June 2004, a cabinet led by

Canadian-trained prime minister Ahmed Nazif launched Egypt's most aggressive economic experiment yet.

Nazif pursed deep neoliberal reforms. Privatization increased, state assets were sold, and subsidies were rationalized, though not eliminated. Other ministers, such as Mahmoud Mohy Eddin, Rachid Mohamed Rachid, and Yosif Boutros-Ghali, guided implementation of these reforms. From the distant view of statistics, they were a success. Egypt regularly produced a 7 percent annual growth rate and was routinely named one of the World Bank's top reformers from 2005 to 2010. The world's most influential financial institutions also touted Egypt as a success.

But the view from inside Egypt was quite different. The wealth gap dramatically expanded. While reform produced impressive economic growth rates, all of the growth was concentrated in the wealthiest part of society. There was no trickle down, despite promises to the contrary. The growing poverty was not lost on anyone. Even a US ambassador noted in a cable to Washington that 35 to 40 percent of the population lived in intractable poverty. Demonstrations and labor activism grew. People resisted the state's withdrawal precisely because it left no alternative for survival.

When the uprising against Mubarak began in January 2011, it was not surprising that so many protesters cited economic inequality as their primary motive for wanting to remove him. The uprising, rather than ending Egypt's crony capitalist nightmare, merely halted it. Nearly all economic activity stopped. The economy contracted by 4.2 percent during the first quarter of 2011, and Egypt experienced its highest level of unemployment in over a decade. The SCAF used the transition to protect its monopolistic economic ventures while relying on the country's decline to stabilize the currency. In the transition's sixteen months, Egypt used up over $21 billion of reserves, as the SCAF put all economic policy initiatives on hold.

Since the election of the Muslim Brotherhood's candidate, Mohamed Morsi, as president in June 2012, many have wondered whether and how he will reverse Egypt's economic decline. Morsi has been industrious in seeking loan forgiveness and securing foreign-investment pledges from economic powerhouses such as China. He appears likely to sign a new IMF agreement for $4.8 billion in loans. But he has also increased public servants' salaries and sought to accommodate some of the labor movement's demands. Thus, it remains unclear what kind of economic policies Egypt's first civilian president will pursue. Given the Muslim Brotherhood's neoliberal proclivities, Morsi will likely push for greater economic liberalization.

This approach would be consistent with the trajectory that Sadat began and Mubarak incrementally continued. Morsi remains captive to the economic system Nasser created, which invites destabilizing political push-back if populist privileges are cut. Although Egypt has the third-largest economy in the Middle East, it also has the largest population. The country has failed to develop a competitive export sector. While the edifices of economic development have changed, the fundamental challenge of job creation remains.

POLITICAL STRUCTURE

After the 1952 military takeover, Egypt's new elites reshaped the state's political structures. Although constitutions and laws dictated how state institutions should operate, the reality often was quite different in practice. Nevertheless, these institutions did operate in distinctive, predictable ways.

Nasser and his successors developed a powerful presidency. Whoever was president between 1956 and 2011 managed and oversaw the bureaucracy, legislature, military, and security services. The only occasional exception in this dynamic was the judiciary. The regular maintenance of this structure kept the flow of power directed toward and from the executive office. It is unlikely that the presidency in Egypt after Mubarak's departure will remain as dominant.

Nasser, Sadat, and Mubarak were careful to maintain and expand presidential authority vis-à-vis the other institutions of state. Maintaining such a hierarchy ensured that the president had autonomy to act while others were constrained. The Egyptian political system was not without institutional competition or debate. However, state institutions were only allowed to contest each other in limited ways. Generally, the new organizations created after 1952 were unable to act without the president's blessing, while institutions created before that time struggled but kept a limited semblance of independence.

The legislature consists of upper and lower houses: the Consultative Assembly (Majlis al-Shura) and the People's Assembly (Majlis al-Sh`ab). Before 2011, two-thirds of the seats in the upper house were elected, and the president appointed one-third. The legislature always had circumscribed authority. Although it was involved in ratifying constitutional amendments and signing treaties into law, the Consultative Assembly submitted to the lower house's authority. Furthermore, the upper house was almost completely dominated by the ruling NDP under Sadat and Mubarak. (It did not exist under Nasser.) Since the 2011 uprising, the Muslim Brotherhood has controlled approximately 45 percent of the seats in the Consultative Assembly. While this normally would not mean much, Morsi's administration has relied on the Consultative Assembly since June 2012, when the SCAF used a Supreme Constitutional Court ruling to disband the People's Assembly.

The lower house traditionally has been the vehicle of legislative authority. Nasser, citing the divisive character of democratic politics, banned parliament. Sadat resurrected the institution in 1971 as he tried to brand himself a rule-of-law president. Despite elections occasionally being open under Sadat and Mubarak, the NDP always enjoyed a supermajority in parliament. This ensured that the president's agenda would always be passed and the speaker of parliament could ignore formal opposition or dismiss it through a vote. This is crucial, since the People's Assembly is empowered to pass legislation, approve the state's budget, question ministers, and approve or renew emergency (martial) law.

Egypt's current People's Assembly has 508 members, 10 of whom are appointed by the president. During the first free elections, held between November 2011 and January 2012, the Muslim Brotherhood took 47 percent of the seats. Salafists won another

24 percent. The remaining seats were spread among ex-NDP members and Wafd, Wasat, and Egypt Bloc candidates. The revolutionaries of 2011 won only nine seats as they began learning how to go from informal street politics to organized campaigning. The SCC ruled that the law governing the election was unconstitutional. The SCAF then implemented the ruling and dissolved parliament in June 2012. Egypt currently is without a parliament, but there are plans to elect a new assembly two months after a new constitution is approved in a popular referendum.

Egypt's judiciary has been the state institution in which most of the fiercest contestation has taken place since 1952. Courts were established in the colonial era and became places where people challenged the colonial authorities. In the process, legal training was developed, and judges became professionalized. By 1952, Egypt's judiciary was more advanced than those in other decolonizing states. Nasser largely left the judiciary to its own devices. In 1969, not long before his death, Nasser purged the judiciary of political opposition. Thus, when Sadat committed himself to the rule of law, he brought the experienced judges back to the bench.

The judiciary's independence became a sticking point for Mubarak. He never disregarded a SCC ruling, but he was selective in his implementation of rulings from the state administrative and cassation courts. Mubarak also relied on the state of emergency (martial law) to try opponents and override legal protections with specially designated courts. He even occasionally used military trials for civilians.

Some judges refused to accept submission to Mubarak. Twice during the Mubarak era they pushed for laws to expand judicial independence. The regime responded with laws that incrementally reduced judicial autonomy, leaving the judiciary somewhat compromised. Many judges are well trained and continue to assert themselves. But others were appointed on the basis of their loyalty to the Mubarak regime or have been co-opted, undermining the overall integrity of the institution. Nevertheless, Egypt's judiciary remains a model in the region.

Given the military's intervention in 1952, it is unsurprising that the armed forces remain the regime's spine. During Nasser's presidency, over a third of all cabinet ministers were from the military. This number decreased to 20 percent under Sadat and 8 percent under Mubarak. Yet military officers were not pushed out of the establishment altogether. They remained the key appointees in crucial provinces, ensuring that the regime's order was maintained.

The military's capacity to participate in politics dwindled between 1952 and 2011. In exchange for the professionalization of its ranks, the military began to control monopolistic market shares in some sectors of the economy. While the military's companies were initially dominant in the public sector, their role has changed over time. They can now be found in the private sector and in public-private joint ventures and at times act as local representatives for foreign investors. The military's companies make everything from staples such as olive oil and bread to heavy industrial items such as tanks. The military also remains in charge of the petrochemical sector and is Egypt's largest landowner.

When political order breaks down, the military emerges as the state's last line of defense. The 2011 uprising provided the military with the opportunity to intervene and eliminate its political and economic competitors. Hence, the military used the uprising to save a part of the regime but also to discredit Gamal Mubarak's economic reform team and the politically ascendant interior ministry. The uprising also allowed the SCAF to largely dictate the terms and sequence of the transition. While many claim that the military has left politics to resume its traditional role since President Morsi's election, this remains to be seen. Morsi seems to consult with the SCAF's generals rather than to govern over them as a powerful executive.

Political Dynamics

Egypt's central political dynamics are products of how its presidents and ruling regimes have designed and manipulated the political arena. The general pattern remains constant across different areas: when the state loosens political restrictions, cooperation improves, and development occurs among the citizens and polity. Yet, when state elites enforce illiberal policies or tighten the reins on organizational and political activities, state repression and opposition fragmentation result. Autocratic design has never eradicated political contestation or opposition challenges. It has, however, split the opposition into two camps: elites and contentious groups. This feature not only helped the uprising gain traction but also became the dominant characteristic of politics after the SCAF-led transition began.

Elections are one area in which this determinant of elite action is on display. Egypt has held regular elections since the days of Sadat. Under Mubarak, elections proliferated. Parliamentary elections occurred in 1984, 1987, 1990, 1995, 2000, 2005, and 2010. Mubarak was also subject to popular referenda in 1981, 1987, 1993, and 1999, before competing in a multicandidate direct election in 2005. When Mubarak was consolidating power, he allowed more open elections. The NDP won 87 percent of seats in the 1984 parliamentary election and 79 percent in the 1987 election. As Mubarak became more powerful, the NDP's parliamentary majority increased to 90 percent in 1990 and 95 percent in 1995. When the SCC in 2000 ruled that judicial supervision of elections was constitutionally mandated, the NDP's majority slipped to 88 percent. In 2005, the Muslim Brotherhood shocked the establishment by winning 20 percent of the seats in parliament, though this was due mainly to the NDP's miscalculations. The final parliamentary election under Mubarak, in 2010, was the most flagrantly rigged and returned a 94 percent NDP majority.

Protesters cited their discontent with the rigged elections during the 2011 uprising. Since Mubarak's overthrow, the population has become "electionized." Between February 2011 and Morsi's election in June 2012, Egyptians had the opportunity to vote on five separate occasions. Gone are the days of a formal ruling party; as a consequence, elections are more representative, despite the organizational advantages of the Muslim Brotherhood and state-affiliated politicians. Turnout proved to be high, signifying a higher degree of citizen buy-in. For example, the 2011 parliamentary elections witnessed a nearly 55 percent turnout rate.

The high-turnout trend was repeated during the presidential elections of June 2012. After none of the original twelve candidates won a majority during the first round, over 52 percent of the population turned out in what was a close second-round vote between the two first-round leaders: Ahmed Shafiq, from the state's networks, and Mohamed Morsi of the Muslim Brotherhood. Morsi won just over 51 percent of the valid ballots cast. Elections in Egypt have changed: now they will be the chief method for legitimating who is in power rather than a display of state power. The problem is that Egypt's increasingly fair elections are not the same as democratization.

Irrespective of how we define civil society, Egypt has enjoyed a long tradition of voluntary civic organizations stretching deep into the Ottoman period. In Egypt, this tradition has comprised mainly religious endowments—Islamic, Coptic, and Jewish. Because of the modernization projects of Muhammad Ali, conditions on the ground had changed greatly by the dawn of the twentieth century. Not only was self-determination laced into society's expectations, but European modes of political organization were also introduced through colonialism. Consequently, a number of civil society organizations were founded. After Britain ceded nominal independence to Egypt, the 1923 constitution encouraged civil society development. Essentially there was no legal registration process for civil society associations. Hundreds of professional associations, syndicates, and women's groups were established.

While the years between 1923 and 1952 proved to be a boon for civil society, this dynamic reversed sharply with the advent of the military regime. Like the formal political sphere, in which Nasser prohibited many formal institutions, civil society also became a target. The regime designed Law 32 of 1964 to constrict nongovernmental organizations (NGOs), which were no longer de facto legal entities. Associational life stalled after Law 32, as the state prohibited the formation of NGOs, limited their organizational ability, and blocked their outreach. Whereas civil society had never before been considered a threat to political elites, Nasser's framing made them appear as such. After Sadat created a formal opposition structure through his party pluralism, citizens who rejected the formal opposition as credible sources of resistance retreated to civil society to participate in politics. Mubarak's presidency bore further witness to this development.

During the 1980s, the Muslim Brotherhood reinvigorated many defunct professional associations and syndicates. Abu Ella Madi, a leading Brotherhood figure during this push, admitted to treating the syndicates like political parties. By the mid-1990s, the Mubarak regime was forced to issue laws and in some cases to sequester syndicates because their political autonomy was increasing. Those not participating in the professional syndicates gravitated to human rights groups to register their discontent. Many challenged the state through human rights organizations and groups that focused on land acquisition and labor conditions. The Mubarak regime responded by updating Law 32 to stifle uncontrolled oppositional politics. Law 84 of 2002 made NGO registration more difficult and gave the state authority over an NGO's ability to receive funding from foreign donors.

Since Mubarak's overthrow, civil society and space for NGOs have expanded, despite some threatening trends. It remains unclear if the Morsi government will attempt to reconsolidate control over civil society or let it be. Associational life in Egypt has always witnessed flows and ebbs, with the authorities granting or blocking civil society activity. While more draconian measures would require the population to recalibrate, none have previously been able to stop people from mobilizing.

Another political dynamic that has been explosive at times is the growing sectarian dimension of Egyptian politics. Egypt is an extremely homogenous population. National identity is well developed, and Egyptians have a strong attachment to the state and country. Roughly 10 percent of the population is Coptic Christian; the Coptic Church has its own hierarchies and is utterly committed to state officials. Worryingly, however, sectarian clashes have increased in recent years. To be fair, the overwhelming number of Egyptians do not think, behave, or operate along religious lines. They tend to treat one another as Egyptians and stand together during instances of political upheaval. For example, during the eighteen days of protest against Mubarak in 2011, Christians and Muslim took turns forming chains to protect each other when they prayed or held mass.

Nevertheless, the final years of the Mubarak era and the year during which the SCAF governed were particularly alarming. Usually, some disagreement or rumor about a cross-religious relationship has provoked strong feelings against members of the other religion. In many communities, particularly in Upper Egypt, this has led to deadly clashes, the destruction of churches, and damage to property. Rather than systematically promote or eliminate discrimination, the state haphazardly encourages it by not using the legal system to punish criminal behavior. Instead, the state has promoted reconciliation councils, where security officials negotiate and broker settlements between those involved. It is a process that neither produces satisfactory justice nor deters other instances of strife. While many feared Morsi's presidency because he was a member of the Muslim Brotherhood, he has neither played on nor mended the sectarian cleavage. Rather, Morsi seems more concerned about being outflanked by more-conservative Salafi Islamists. As long as this dynamic remains unresolved, sectarian conflict is likely to continue.

The lasting legacy of the post-1952 Free Officers regime is that, despite its various shapes and forms, the system produced a centralized presidency with a dependent ruling establishment and institutions. This type of state, because of its monopoly on power, produced an opposition. The regime accepted opposition as long as it agreed to maintain order. Incremental reform helped keep the power brokers in office, including established opposition leaders. Under this dynamic, even banned and repressed groups such as the Muslim Brotherhood were allowed to operate. Those who chose not to work their way through the restricted world of the legal opposition parties, the Brotherhood, and the state had to find new ways to participate. This opposition coalesced in a small group of protest movements during the 2000s. Initially a response to the Palestinian intifada and the Iraq War, groups of activists gathered to criticize Mubarak and the possibility of a hereditary succession. More groups then emerged, exploring social justice and police brutality. Coupled with the labor movement, opposition segments that remained outside the governing structure and formal elite opposition pervaded Egypt by 2011.

While this contentious opposition emerged as the uprising's revolutionary core, these groups have not been sufficiently represented in the post-Mubarak order. Legitimate questions remain about whether the revolutionary forces have had an equal opportunity to help write the new constitution, gain entry into parliament, or even protest peacefully. While the revolutionaries shocked the Egyptian state, and there continue to be daily strikes and sit-ins against the hierarchies that survived Mubarak's fall, it remains unclear whether these voices of change will be incorporated or relegated to a parallel environment of revolution, where they will coexist separately with a reconstituted, exclusive elite arena. While the dynamic elements of Egyptian politics will continue to interact fluidly, it is possible that this last element will remain the most important in the continuing battle for the country's future.

FOREIGN POLICY

Egypt is by far the largest Arab country and sits near the center of the Middle East, so regional and international powers want a friendly relationship with it. Moreover, the Suez Canal provides the shortest distance for shipping goods and commodities between Asia and Europe. The canal was important during the colonial era, and it is no less strategic today. US national security concerns and commitments to Arab states in the Persian Gulf region, as well as the wars in Iraq and Afghanistan, mean the canal also serves as a crucial transportation link for the US military.

Wooing Egyptian presidents has not always been easy. During the Cold War, Egypt under Nasser tried to remain nonaligned. Nasser's strategy was to play one superpower against the other. Essentially, whichever power attached the fewest strings to its diplomatic support and aid could rely on Egypt's friendship. The Soviets proved to be far more amenable to Nasser's insistence on nonconditionality. Thus the Soviet Union provided extensive assistance in constructing the Aswan High Dam, as well as arms and military experts, in exchange for military cooperation. Yet, in many respects, the Egyptian-Soviet relationship remained shallow.

Egypt needed extensive foreign military assistance in this era because of its ongoing state of war with Israel. In 1948, Egypt was part of the Arab attack on the new Israeli state. In 1956, Britain, France, and Israel launched a joint invasion of Egypt, which Nasser weathered until the United States and Soviet Union intervened to stop the aggression. Then in 1967, Israel struck a massive blow that destroyed nearly all of Egypt's air force. A steady war of attrition between Egypt and Israel continued along the Suez Canal after the 1967 war, producing more casualties on both sides. In 1973, Sadat launched one more war against Israel, after his repeated attempts to gain the return of Egyptian land occupied by Israel were rebuffed.

Hostility with Israel was not the only defining feature of Egypt's foreign policy in this era. Nasser used pan-Arabism to project Egyptian power in the region. His speeches, which often invoked Arab independence and unity, resonated deeply in a region whose inhabitants believed they lived in a colonial playground. This type of rhetoric drew acolytes and rivals for Nasser from around the region. The leaders of the other Arab republics, such as Iraq, Syria, Tunisia, Algeria, and Libya, emulated Nasser's project. In fact, Syrian elites in 1958 appealed to Nasser to merge Syria and Egypt, though the resulting United Arab Republic proved to be a short-lived experiment, collapsing in 1961. Yet, during the 1950s and 1960s, pan-Arabism proved to be a mobilizing force that helped many military-based regimes consolidate their authority and punch above their weight. Even though pan-Arabism descended into its own cold war, with some Arab states sabotaging the interests of others, Nasser today remains a popular symbol of Arab strength and autonomy.

When Sadat became president in 1970, a pan-Arab foreign policy was no longer possible. Still reeling from the humiliating 1967 defeat by Israel, Nasser himself began the process of dismantling Arabism as the pillar of Egypt's foreign policy. Sadat then shifted to an "Egypt First" posture. Thinking about "Mother Egypt" now would figure prominently in any foreign policy decisions. The other Arab states were responsible for themselves. To his credit, Sadat followed through. He tried approaching both the United States and Israel about regaining Egypt's occupied land but was unsuccessful. A permanent situation seemed to be settling in. Sadat then ordered a war against Israel to change the status quo. He reportedly told his aides that if the Egyptian army could take back part of the Sinai, he would negotiate return of the rest. For good measure, he invited Hafiz al-Asad of Syria to join in the war. On October 6, 1973, both armies attacked. Egyptian forces advanced but stopped when they no longer had air support. The Syrians were left to fight Israel on their own. While no evidence suggests that Nasser would not have done the same, Sadat's actions revealed Egypt's formal divorce with the pan-Arab era.

The 1973 war was just Sadat's opening salvo. He used the legitimacy he earned in the war to negotiate with the United States and Israel. Initially shocked, US Secretary of State Henry Kissinger was unprepared to move as fast as Sadat wished. To prove his sincerity, Sadat traveled to Israel in 1977, where he offered peace in exchange for land. As Sadat pressed, Egypt drifted firmly into the US sphere of influence. The relationship was consummated when Egypt and Israel signed the Camp David peace accords in 1979. Egypt regained the Sinai Peninsula, as well as $2 billion per year in US aid. This aid was broken into two segments: $1.3 billion for the Egyptian military and $800 million for social and economic development. US aid continues to flow to Egypt to this day, amounting to over $60 billion since 1979.

Egypt's realignment to become an American client during the 1970s fundamentally changed the balance of power in the Middle East. As a consequence, the United States had three core allies: Saudi Arabia with its oil, Israel with its powerful military, and Egypt with its large population. And if pan-Arabism's demise was not already apparent, the peace treaty with Israel became its death knell. Indeed, Egypt was expelled from the Arab

League. Yet, despite Sadat's bold moves, Egypt's foreign policy and dependence on the United States became points of political contestation.

The United States may have bought Egypt's president, but it did not own Egyptians. This continued to be a dynamic under Mubarak and remains so under President Morsi. Status as a weak, dependent US client has created substantial tension between the Egyptian state and its citizens. In many respects, as US-Egyptian military and diplomatic cooperation has increased, a vast security apparatus has been needed to contain the population's objections. Not only was Sadat forced to rely on coercion, but Mubarak expanded it in order to do the regional bidding of the United States. Hence, major foreign policy issues, such as participating in Operation Desert Storm in 1991 or siding with the United States against Saddam Hussein in 2003, proved incredibly contentious for Mubarak. This was highlighted further when Mubarak blamed Hizballah and Hamas for the hostilities in 2006 and 2008–2009 between those groups and Israel. Egypt's close relationship with the United States also led Mubarak to support the US extraordinary rendition program after the September 11, 2001, attacks, under which many suspected militants were tortured.

The foreign policy that Sadat initiated and Mubarak expanded left Washington with a predictable, cost-efficient way to maintain its interests in the region for nearly thirty-five years. But Sadat and Mubarak regularly had to disregard Egyptian public opinion and Egyptians' hopes for empowerment and representative governance in order to maintain their side of the relationship.

Since the 2012 election of Mohamed Morsi, it remains unclear how Egypt will pivot in its relations with the United States. The status quo has been untenable for far too long; yet Egypt has no alternative unless it charts a more nonaligned posture. Given how deeply the United States has penetrated the Egyptian state through key institutions such as the military, it will be difficult for Morsi to completely break this link. Yet, since the president is now popularly elected, Egypt's foreign policy establishment finally has a card to play. Since Mubarak's overthrow, it is no longer possible to preserve the tension between an unaccountable president's submission to the United States and Egyptian public opinion.

While we can expect the Egyptian president will continue to be a US ally and support the relationship's core principles, it is unlikely that Egypt will remain submissive to the United States, as it was in the past. The sooner the United States treats Egypt as an equal partner, the sooner a balanced and functional relationship will be achieved.

BIBLIOGRAPHY

Standard histories of Egypt in the contemporary era include Jacques Berque, *Egypt: Imperialism and Revolution* (New York: Praeger, 1972); Afaf Lutfi Sayyid-Marsot, *A History of Egypt: From the Arab Conquest to the Present,* 2nd ed. (Cambridge: Cambridge University Press, 2007); Joel Beinin and Zachary Lockman, *Workers on the Nile: Nation-

alism, Communism, Islam and the Egyptian Working Class, 1882–1954 (Princeton, NJ: Princeton University Press, 1988); Khaled Fahmy, *All the Pasha's Men: Mehmed Ali, His Army, and the Making of Modern Egypt* (New York: Cambridge University Press, 1998); Timothy Mitchell, *Colonising Egypt* (Berkeley: University of California Press, 1991); Robert Vitalis, *When Capitalists Collide: Business Conflict and the End of Empire in Egypt* (Berkeley: University of California Press, 1995); Ahmed Abdallah, *The Student Movement and National Politics in Egypt, 1923–1973* (Cairo: American University in Cairo Press, 2009); and Timothy Mitchell, *Rule of Experts: Egypt, Techno-Politics, Modernity* (Berkeley: University of California Press, 2002).

On state formation and the post-1952 regime, see Raymond Baker, *Egypt's Uncertain Revolution Under Nasser and Sadat* (Cambridge, MA: Harvard University Press, 1978); John Waterbury, *The Egypt of Nasser and Sadat: The Political Economy of Two Regimes* (Princeton, NJ: Princeton University Press, 1983); Raymond Hinnebusch, *Egyptian Politics Under Sadat: The Post-populist Development of an Authoritarian-Modernizing State* (Cambridge: Cambridge University Press, 1985); Joel Gordon, *Nasser's Blessed Movement: Egypt's Free Officers and the July Revolution* (New York: Oxford University Press, 1992); Robert Springborg, *Mubarak's Egypt: Fragmentation of the Political Order* (Boulder, CO: Westview Press, 1989); Tamir Moustafa, *The Struggle for Constitutional Power: Law, Politics, and Economic Development in Egypt* (Cambridge: Cambridge University Press, 2009); Bruce Rutherford, *Egypt After Mubarak: Liberalism, Islam, and Democracy* (Princeton, NJ: Princeton University Press, 2008); and Samer Soliman, *The Autumn of Dictatorship: Fiscal Crisis and Political Change in Egypt* (Stanford, CA: Stanford University Press, 2011).

On the Muslim Brotherhood, see Richard Mitchell, *The Society of Muslim Brothers* (New York: Oxford University Press, 1969); Asef Bayat, "Revolution Without Movement, Movement Without Revolution: Comparing Islamic Activism in Iran and Egypt," *Comparative Studies in Society and History* 40, no. 1 (January 1998): 136–169; Carrie Wickham, *Mobilizing Islam* (Princeton, NJ: Princeton University Press, 2002); Mona El-Ghobashy, "The Metamorphosis of the Egyptian Muslim Brothers," *International Journal of Middle East Studies* 37, no. 3 (August 2005): 373–395; and Samer Shehata and Joshua Stacher, "The Brotherhood Goes to Parliament," *Middle East Report*, no. 240 (Fall 2006): 32–39.

On informal politics and cultural politics, see Diane Singerman, *Avenues of Participation: Family, Politics, and Networks in Urban Quarters of Cairo* (Princeton, NJ: Princeton University Press, 1996); Jessica Winegar, *Creative Reckonings: The Politics of Art and Culture in Contemporary Egypt* (Stanford, CA: Stanford University Press, 2006); Elliot Colla, *Conflicted Antiquities: Egyptology, Egyptomania, and Egyptian Modernity* (Durham, NC: Duke University Press, 2008); and Samer Shehata, *Shop Floor Culture and Politics in Egypt* (Albany: State University of New York Press, 2009).

On the US-Egyptian relationship, see Jason Brownlee, *Democracy Prevention: The Politics of the US-Egyptian Alliance* (Cambridge: Cambridge University Press, 2012).

On the Egyptian uprising of 2011, see Alaa al-Aswany, *On the State of Egypt: A Novelist's Provocative Reflections* (Cairo: American University in Cairo Press, 2011); Jeannie Sowers and Chris Toensing, eds., *The Journey to Tahrir: Revolution, Protest, and Social Change in Egypt* (New York: Verso, 2012); Joshua Stacher, *Adaptable Autocrats: Regime Power in Egypt and Syria* (Stanford, CA: Stanford University Press, 2012); and Hazem Kandil, *Soldiers, Spies, and Statesmen: Egypt's Road to Revolt* (New York: Verso, 2012).

14

GREAT SOCIALIST PEOPLE'S LIBYAN ARAB JAMAHIRIYA

Mary-Jane Deeb

Libya is situated in North Africa, bordered by the Mediterranean Sea in the north, the Arab Republic of Egypt and the Sudan in the east, Niger and Chad in the south, and Tunisia and Algeria in the west. It has an area of just under 1.8 million square kilometers (685,000 square miles), more than 90 percent of which is desert. Libya comprises three distinct geographical units: Tripolitania in the west, with an area of about 248,640 square kilometers (96,000 square miles); Cyrenaica in the east, with an area of about 699,300 square kilometers (270,000 square miles); and Fezzan in the south and southwest, with an area of about 826,210 square kilometers (319,000 square miles).

Libya has a small population, estimated at 6.7 million in 2012, of which 90 percent live in less than 10 percent of the total area, primarily along the Mediterranean coast. About 70 percent of the population is urban, mostly concentrated in the two largest cities, Benghazi and Tripoli. The majority of the population is of Arab origin, descending from a number of Arab tribes, including the powerful Beni Hilal and Beni Sulaiman, who came originally from the Arabian Peninsula. But Libya is also partly African (in the Fezzan region) and Berber (in the north and central regions). Berbers descend from the original inhabitants of North Africa. Virtually all Libyans are Sunni Muslims.

HISTORICAL BACKGROUND

In the earliest days, the area that is now Libya was visited by Phoenician sailors, who established trading posts along the coastline. Later the Greeks landed. Subsequently, control of part of the area fell to Alexander the Great and later to the Egyptian kingdom of the Ptolemies. Rome annexed Cyrenaica and Tripolitania, and both became part of the Roman Empire. Eventually Pax Romana prevailed, and Libya enjoyed a long period of prosperity and peace. A period of decline began in the fourth century. In the seventh century Arab invaders arrived from Egypt, and most of the Berber tribes embraced Islam. The Arabs who swept across North Africa in the seventh century ruled for nine hundred years, interrupted

State of Libya

by the Normans, the Spaniards, and the Knights of St. John. They were finally replaced in 1551 by the Ottoman Turks, who ruled until 1911. Italy declared war on the Ottoman Empire in September 1911, and Italian troops soon landed in Tripoli and Benghazi.

The Italian conquest faced opposition from the powerful Sanusiya movement, led by Muhammad Idris al-Mahdi al-Sanusi, the grandson of the movement's founder. The Sanusiya was a Muslim reformist movement that started in western Arabia in 1837 and a few years later moved to Cyrenaica. It was primarily a missionary movement whose functions were to spread the call to Islam throughout North Africa and mediate intertribal conflicts. It became a powerful political movement in the last two decades of the nineteenth century, when it sought to curb Ottoman power in the region, and later when it tried to push the Italians out of Libya.

In 1929, Italy officially adopted the name "Libya" to refer to its colony consisting of Cyrenaica, Tripolitania, and Fezzan. Until then it had been known by the name of its capital, Tripoli, although the word "Libya" had been used in early times by the Greeks to denote a much larger area in Africa. Colonization along the coast included the settlement of Italian peasants and consolidation of Italian control. Resistance against Italian control continued until 1932, by which time Fascist rule had subdued all opposition.

World War II interrupted Italy's plans for further colonization. By the end of 1942, British and French forces had swept the Italians out of the country. The North African campaigns of World War II devastated the country, leaving Benghazi partly destroyed. The head of the Sanusiya, Sayyid Muhammad Idris I, who had gone into exile in Egypt in 1922 but continued to support resistance to the Italian occupation, had sided with the British during the war and been promised, at minimum, freedom from Italy. Between 1943 and 1947, the British established a caretaker military administration in Tripolitania and Cyrenaica, and the French set up one in the Fezzan, until the final status of the territories could be settled.

The settlement of the country's future was contained in the Italian Peace Treaty of 1947. Britain, France, the Soviet Union, and the United States were to decide it, with the stipulation that if no agreement was reached, the question would be taken to the United Nations. Each of the powers proposed a different plan, and it was decided that a four-power commission should ascertain the wishes of the Libyans. In 1947, after visiting Libya, the commission ended in disagreement on many of the specifics; however, the members reached accord on the view that although Libyans wanted independence, they were not yet ready to rule themselves. By the summer of 1948, it was clear that the four powers were unable to agree, and the matter went to the United Nations. On November 21, 1949, the General Assembly adopted a resolution that Libya should become an independent state no later than January 1, 1952.

The assembly resolution allowed approximately two years for Libya to prepare for independence. British and French administration continued during much of the period, as Adrian Pelt, the UN commissioner appointed to assist in the transition to independence, helped prepare the institutions of self-government. Eventually, Libya was established as a federation in which substantial autonomy was given to each of the three component units. Libya became independent on December 24, 1951, as the United Kingdom of Libya, made up of Fezzan, Cyrenaica, and Tripolitania, with Sayyid Muhammad Idris I as its monarch.

Kingdom of Libya

The 1951 constitution established the United Kingdom of Libya as a constitutional monarchy. Sovereignty was vested in the nation but entrusted by the people to King Idris and his male heirs. Islam was declared the religion of the state and Arabic the official language. Executive power was granted to the king, whereas legislative power was shared by the king and parliament. King Idris was to exercise his executive power through an appointed prime minister and cabinet, or Council of Ministers, whereas legislative power was vested in a parliament, which he convened and could adjourn (for up to thirty days) or dissolve. The king sanctioned and promulgated all laws and made the necessary regulations through the relevant ministries for their implementation. He could veto legislation,

State of Libya

Capital city	Tripoli
Chief of state, 2012	President Mohammed al-Megarif
Head of government, 2012	Prime Minister Mustafa Abushagur
Political parties (share of most recent vote, 2012)	National Forces Alliance (48.1%), Justice and Construction Party (10.3%), other parties (26.3%), independents (15.3%)
Ethnic groups	Arab and Berber (97%), other (3%)
Religious groups	Sunni Muslim (97%), other (3%)
Export partners, 2011	Italy (21.5%), Germany (13.5%), France (13.4%), China (10.1%), Spain (4.9%), Tunisia (4.6%), India (4.3%)
Import partners, 2011	Egypt (15.5%), Tunisia (11.9%), Turkey (8.1%), China (7.8%), Italy (7.5%), Syria (4.6%), France (4.4%), Germany (4.3%)

and his veto could be overridden only by a two-thirds vote of both chambers of parliament. The king was supreme commander of the armed forces; he could proclaim a state of emergency and martial law, declare war, and conclude peace, with the approval of parliament. In addition, he appointed senators, judges, and senior public servants. The king was supreme head of state, "inviolable," and "exempt from all responsibility."

The cabinet was appointed and dismissed by royal decree on the prime minister's recommendation. Although the cabinet was selected by the king, under Article 86 its members were collectively responsible to the lower house of parliament, and each was individually responsible for the activities of his own ministry. The cabinet was responsible for the direction of all internal and external affairs of state.

Parliament consisted of two chambers. The Senate had twenty-four members (eight from each province), half of whom were appointed by the king. The others were elected by the legislative councils of the provinces. Each served for eight years and could be reappointed or reelected. The House of Representatives consisted of deputies elected by popular suffrage on the basis of one deputy for every 20,000 inhabitants, although each province was required to have at least five members. The deputies served for a maximum of four years. Parliamentary sessions were called by the king in November. During sessions, a bill could be introduced by the king or by one of the chambers; it had to be adopted by both chambers and ratified by the king before becoming law. However, only the king and the House of Representatives could initiate bills involving the budget.

The federal government exercised legislative and executive powers as described in the constitution, which provided a detailed listing of areas for the exercise of its power. In other areas there were provisions for joint powers between the federal and provincial governments. The provinces were to exercise all powers not assigned to the federal government by the constitution. Each province was to have a governor (*wali*) appointed by the king. An executive council and a legislative council were established in each province.

The federal system was a necessary compromise, allowing for a common political authority while preserving some autonomy for the three provinces of Cyrenaica, Fezzan, and Tripolitania. Local affairs were administered independently in each province, and certain powers were reserved for the federal government. The federal structure was abolished in 1963, when a new constitution established a unitary system. The country's name was changed to the Kingdom of Libya, with Idris I remaining the monarch. The provinces surrendered administrative and financial decision making to the national government, whose authority was exercised through ten administrative districts, or *wilayas*.

The shift from the federal to a unitary system did not alter the government greatly because much of the structure established in 1951 remained intact at the national level. The major changes in the revised constitution related to the federal elements contained in the 1951 constitution. Each of the ten administrative districts was headed by a *wali* appointed by the Council of Ministers and empowered to execute the policies of the government in his district. The council also had the power to transfer or dismiss the *walis*. All matters except those dealing exclusively with local affairs were under the direction of the national government.

Although King Idris determined the policies implemented by his ministers, whom he appointed and dismissed at will, he often did not appear involved in the daily activity of the government. He allowed the prime minister and cabinet to adopt policies they deemed appropriate as long as they had the confidence of parliament and stayed within the broad outlines established by the king.

The political circle Idris led was centered in the palace and had special ties to Cyrenaica. Political expression was limited, and political parties were disbanded soon after independence. The ministers were close to and dependent on the monarchy, despite constitutional provisions stating that they were collectively and individually responsible to the lower house of parliament. In the governmental structure, the only significant potential alternative power center was the House of Representatives. It was the only place in which policies were publicly discussed, evaluated, and frequently criticized, and it provided a forum for the opposition to express its views.

In less than two decades, King Idris managed to unify the Libyan state. By means of political alliances and diplomacy, he protected his weak country from external aggression and intervention. He also was able to obtain assistance from Western powers to help Libya feed its people and build schools and hospitals at a time when it was one of the poorest countries in the world.

The discovery of oil and the rise of Egyptian president Gamal Abdel Nasser as a major charismatic figure in the Arab world transformed the Libyan political scene. King Idris was old (he was eighty in 1969, when he was overthrown) and in poor health. He had lost interest in running the day-to-day affairs of his country. His entourage had become progressively more powerful, and its conspicuous wealth was creating great resentment among Libyans. By the late 1960s, significant opposition to the policies and programs of the state was coming from many quarters of Libyan society.

The Revolution of 1969

On September 1, 1969, a bloodless military coup d'état overthrew the government of King Idris (who was out of the country at the time). There was little resistance, even by elements loyal to the king, such as the police and the tribes of Cyrenaica. Although the king made an attempt to secure British assistance to restore him to power, he was unsuccessful, and the monarchy was abolished. Little was known about the coup makers except that they called themselves the Free Unionist Officers and advocated "social justice, socialism, and unity."

In the first few weeks, a number of moderate civilians and army officers were appointed to the first postcoup cabinet. Although strongly nationalistic, these people were not antagonistic to the West and were prepared to develop good relations with Western powers after they evacuated their military bases. Regionally, they were more pro-Arab and spoke more openly of supporting Arab causes, such as Arab unity and the Palestinians. Although socialism and social justice were discussed, the first Libyan cabinet did not plan to nationalize any sector of the economy, and foreigners who lived in Libya were to be allowed to keep their property. The Revolutionary Command Council (RCC), however, headed by a young army officer named Muammar al-Qaddafi, advocated radical economic, social, and political change.

The confrontation between the Free Unionist Officers and the cabinet took place in December 1969, when the prime minister and a number of his cabinet ministers were accused of attempting to overthrow the regime and arrested. The next day all powers were transferred to the RCC, which was made up of the Free Unionist Officers, and it was proclaimed the supreme authority in the land. The direction the political system was to take was decided then.

At the outset Qaddafi attempted to follow in the footsteps of Nasser of Egypt, going as far as to name a party he created the Arab Socialist Union (ASU), like its Egyptian counterpart. In the mid-1970s, however, Qaddafi moved away from Nasserism and invented his own brand of socialism, which he called "natural socialism." He enunciated its principles in his *Green Book*, published in three volumes between 1976 and 1978. He preached complete egalitarianism and the abolition of wage labor and private ownership of land. Trade was exploitative and nonproductive and therefore had to be taken over by the state. He strongly upheld the principles of Arab nationalism and called for support of the Palestinians and the creation of a powerful bloc of Arab states to fight Israel.

Religious reform was a very important part of Qaddafi's ideology. He emphasized that the Qur'an was the only source of Islamic law, or sharia. He claimed that Muhammad, the Muslim prophet, was just an intermediary between God and man and that since the Qur'an was written in Arabic, anyone could read and understand it and did not need a clergyman or imam to interpret it. He cracked down on Islamic militant groups inside Libya and shared intelligence with Algeria, Egypt, and Tunisia on the movements of those groups and their leaders. In February 1994, however, Qaddafi appeared to change course, probably to undermine the rising tide of Islamic fundamentalism, by calling for the implementation of Islamic law in Libya, primarily for criminal offenses but also for marriage and divorce. In the same vein, he called for the revival of the tradition of Sufi brotherhoods as a source of Islamic teachings.

Muammar al-Qaddafi was born in 1942 near Sirte, on the Mediterranean coast. He was the only surviving son of a poor Arabized Berber family belonging to the Qaddafi tribe. At the age of ten he was sent to elementary school in Sirte, and in 1956 he moved with his family to Sebha, where he attended the Sebha Preparatory School. There he created the first command committee with many of the people who would become his closest allies and members of the RCC after the revolution. During that period he also learned about events in Egypt: the 1956 Suez Canal crisis, the evacuation of British forces, and Nasser's agrarian reforms and nationalizations. But perhaps most influential to him would be Nasser's call for a united Arab world.

Qaddafi and his family moved to Misrata in Tripolitania, where he completed high school in 1963. He then entered the military academy in Benghazi. Three of his classmates from Sebha and Misrata joined him there, where they formed the nucleus of the Free Unionist Movement that planned the overthrow of the monarchy. After graduating from the academy in 1965, Qaddafi was sent to England, where he took a six-month signal course. On his return to Libya, he enrolled in the history department at the University of Benghazi, but he was commissioned in 1966 to the signals corps of the Libyan army and never completed his university education. He remained in regular contact with the large network of fellow officers and friends he had developed over the years and built a secret organization that enabled him to carry out the coup in 1969.

Once firmly in control of the government in Libya, Qaddafi began to build his political power base. The first political organization he built, in 1971, was the Arab Socialist Union, which was supposed to mobilize the population in support of the new regime's policies. Half of its members were to be farmers and workers, and its structure was to have local, regional, and national units headed by the RCC. The ASU, however, failed to mobilize popular enthusiasm for the revolution. Consequently, at its Third Party Congress in 1976, it ceased to exist as a political party.

Earlier, in 1973, Qaddafi had attempted to create a "cultural revolution," this time using the Chinese model, to mobilize popular support for the regime by criticizing the government bureaucracy, the bourgeoisie, the RCC, and the cabinet. He advocated the destruction of the bureaucracy, the suspension of all laws, the arming of the people, and a return to the principles of the Qur'an. He called on the people to take over the responsibilities of government. The outcome of this cultural revolution was a period of chaos during which were launched the first "popular committees" that were to involve people directly in the process of governing Libya. Qaddafi claimed that direct democracy was the only real democracy, and, therefore, only through such organizations could Libya become really democratic.

In the second half of the 1970s, when Qaddafi felt that Libyans were again becoming apathetic, he came up with new ideas for political reorganization. In 1977, he formed the revolutionary committees (*lijan thawriya*) that became watchdogs over the political activities of the popular committees and the secretariats of the popular congresses. These revolutionary committees became extremely powerful and quite unruly at times. They arrested people arbitrarily on charges of subversion, settled personal scores, and acted as spies for the government. The experiment with popular committees was reintroduced in the mid-1990s, when "purification committees" were set up to root out corruption in the private-sector retail trade. These committees, in turn, suffered a similar fate, when "volcano committees" were organized in the late 1990s to purge members accused of corruption.

Until 1977, government activities were managed by a cabinet appointed by the RCC. The cabinet comprised mainly civilian technocrats, but RCC members held such critical cabinet posts as defense and interior. After an attempted coup against Qaddafi by RCC members in 1975, the RCC was reduced from its original twelve members to only five. In 1977, in a carefully orchestrated maneuver, a General People's Congress changed the country's name to the Socialist People's Libyan Arab Jamahiriya, proclaimed the establishment of people's power, and vested all official power in itself, abolishing the RCC as the supreme authority but naming the five remaining RCC officers as members of the congress's secretariat. Those five, with Qaddafi as the undisputed leader, continued to be the real power in Libya for the next two decades. The cabinet became the General People's Congress Committee.

In November 1988, Qaddafi announced the restructuring of the military and the creation of a new voluntary paramilitary organization under a separate command. He felt that the army, which had tried to overthrow him on a number of occasions, had become even more threatening after its defeat in Chad in 1987. Consequently, restructuring the army was meant to purge its more dangerous elements. Paramilitary organizations, such as the People's Militia and the Jamahiri Guards, had been in existence since the late 1970s.

Opposition to the regime, however, continued unabated. There were reports of mutinies in the military throughout the 1980s, and one took place in 1993. The reaction was always swift and deadly. In the case of the 1993 mutiny, air force units bombed selected military targets. Monarchist organizations, such as the Libyan Constitutional Union, called for general elections and the return of the monarchy. The best-known organization opposing the Qaddafi regime was the National Front for the Salvation of Libya (NFSL), headed by a former ambassador to India, Muhammad al-Maqaryaf. This organization succeeded in bringing together Islamists and secular pro-democracy opponents of the regime under one umbrella. Some members of the Muslim Brotherhood left the NFSL in 1982, and some secularists left in March 1994 and formed a new opposition organization calling itself the Movement for Change and Reform. The principal organ of the NFSL was *Inqadh* (Salvation), a publication that appeared seven or eight times a year with articles condemning the regime, exposing human rights violations in Libya, and discussing social, economic, and political conditions in the country. The NFSL also published a bimonthly newsletter and broadcast a radio program, *Voice of Libya*, daily from Cairo. The NFSL attempted to overthrow the regime in 1984 with a military attack against the barracks of Bab al-Aziziya. The attack failed, but the NFSL subsequently built a paramilitary wing of the party: the Libyan National Army.

In the 1990s, Islamists became another major opposition force in Libya. They had their roots in older movements, such as the Muslim Brotherhood (Ikhwan), a movement that developed in Libya with the arrival of Egyptian schoolteachers in the 1950s. The Hizb al-Tahrir (Liberation Party) and Jabhat al-Tahrir al-Islami (Islamic Liberation Front) were offshoots of the Muslim Brotherhood. Other Islamic opposition groups included al-Jama'a al-Islamiyah 'Libya' (Islamic Group–Libya), al-Haraka al-Islamiya 'Libya' (Islamic Movement–Libya), and al-Takfir Wal-Hijra (Apostasy and Migration). The Qaddafi regime responded by cracking down on these groups, imprisoning their leaders, and censoring their publications.

The Libyan authorities also imprisoned and assassinated critics of the government who belonged neither to Islamist nor to terrorist groups, such as Dayf al-Ghazal, a prominent Libyan writer and journalist for the London-based online newspaper *Libya al-Yawm*; Abd al-Razaq al-Mansuri, an Internet writer and former bookseller; and Libya's best-known prisoner of conscience, Fathi al-Jahmi, who was incarcerated in March 2002 and later died of a heart ailment left untreated during his imprisonment.

Libya's Second Revolution, 2011

Libya was the third country after Tunisia and Egypt to experience an uprising during the Arab Spring of 2011. On February 15, 2011, the first protests began in Benghazi, when hundreds of protesters gathered in front of a police station and were shot at; several died. Two days later, on February 17, the official date of the start of the uprising, thousands of demonstrators began protesting peacefully throughout eastern Libya, in Benghazi, Ajdabiyah, Darnah, and Zintan. Security forces responded with live ammunition; about a dozen people were killed.

Rather than ending the protests, the government's actions created more anger and led to the takeover of Benghazi by protesters on February 20. Army units joined the rebels and were able to break into the city's well-stocked military garrison and obtain weapons, which they used to fight Qaddafi's forces.

As the takeover of Benghazi was unfolding, a small group including former justice minister Mustafa 'Abd al-Jalil, human rights lawyer 'Abd al-Hafiz Ghoga, and Mahmud Jabril, a Libyan professor teaching in the United States, formed the National Transitional Council (NTC), claiming that they represented the Libyan people. The NTC succeeded in getting European powers and eventually the United States to recognize it as the legitimate interim government and in obtaining military and other forms of aid for the rebels.

On March 17, ten members of the UN Security Council approved Resolution 1973, imposing a no-fly zone over Libya to prevent Qaddafi's forces from bombing civilians. Russia, China, Germany, India, and Brazil abstained from the vote. The resolution authorized international military action to protect civilians. The UK representative pledged that NATO partners and members of the Arab League would act upon this resolution.

Two days later, NATO military operations against Qaddafi's forces began, with air strikes by French jets against Libyan army tanks. British and American forces fired Tomahawk cruise missiles, and British and French forces bombed Libya. Concomitantly, the British navy blockaded Libya's ports to prevent weapons from entering the country. Qatar and the United Arab Emirates were the only two members of the Arab League to participate, providing NATO forces with logistical support. These actions were welcomed by the largely unarmed and untrained Libyan rebels facing Qaddafi's overwhelming military power.

Despite NATO air power, the fighting in Libya lasted eight months. Libyans fought city by city and town by town, encountering resistance not only from Libyans who supported Qaddafi but also from African mercenaries and prisoners purportedly released from jail to fight the rebels. After conquering Cyrenaica, the rebels began moving westward and were joined by others, including Islamists, who wanted to overthrow Qaddafi. Some of the fiercest and longest battles were for the towns of Misrata in Tripolitania, not far from the capital city of Tripoli; the rebels finally took them in May.

The strategy of the rebels was to surround the main holdouts of Qaddafi and his family and supporters in Tripoli, Bani Walid, and Sirte. Throughout August, the rebels fought in and around Tripoli, which fell by the end of the month. Qaddafi went into hiding; his wife, Safia, his daughter, Aisha, and two of his sons, Muhammad and Hanibal, fled to Algiers.

Finally, the rebels converged on Sirte. After more than two months of fighting, Sirte fell on October 20, and Qaddafi was captured and killed, ending his forty-two-year rule in Libya. A month later, on November 19, his son and heir apparent, Sayf al-Islam, was captured. Despite calls by the International Criminal Court (ICC) to have him tried at The Hague on charges of crimes against humanity, the new Libyan authorities insisted that he be tried in Libya.

A new electoral law drafted in January 2012 determined that the General National Congress (GNC) would be made up of 200 seats, 120 of them constituency seats for independent candidates and 80 party seats based on proportional representation. It thus ensured that members of tribes and ethnic minorities, as well as regional representatives, could be candidates without having to run on party lists. On July 7, 2012, over 2.7 million Libyans, an estimated 80 percent of eligible voters, went to the polls. More than 3,000 candidates ran for office, including six hundred women. The elections were monitored by the United Nations Support Mission in Libya, whose special representative, Ian Martin, declared it a "peaceful and democratic transfer of power [from the NTC], which [was] not only a first for this country but an inspiration for others." The largely secular National Forces Alliance won thirty-nine of the eighty party seats, while the Justice and Construction Party, the party of the Muslim Brotherhood, won only seventeen seats. It is unclear, however, what the views of the 120 independent candidates are or how those views will affect the activities of the GNC.

On August 8, 2012, the newly elected members of the GNC took their oath of office at a ceremony in Tripoli, at which Mustafa 'Abd al-Jalil stepped down as head of state and was succeeded by the body's oldest member, Muhammad 'Ali Salim. The NTC was dissolved, and the GNC then elected Yusif Magariaf, the leader of the National Front Party, which had won only three seats, as its interim president. The GNC will have to decide on the composition of the committee that will draft Libya's constitution.

Economic Dynamics

At independence Libya was one of the poorest countries in the world, with an illiteracy rate of over 90 percent and very limited natural resources. The nature and prospects of the Libyan economy changed drastically with the discovery of important petroleum reserves at the end of the 1950s. Although small amounts of oil had been found as early as 1935, not until 1955 was the first major discovery made, at Edjeleh, on the Algerian border. Although the first major oil finds were in western Libya, most of the other important discoveries were in the northeast, primarily in Sirtica. Production and exports continued to increase rapidly over the next decade, rising from 6 million barrels in 1961 to 1.2 billion in 1970.

After Qaddafi seized power, he decided to exert more control over oil production in Libya. In April 1970, serious negotiations began with the major oil companies over a reduction in production, higher prices, and control of the companies' operations in Libya. With expert legal advice, Libya put certain proposals on the table and threatened the companies with nationalization if they did not agree. Several companies refused to give Libya 51 percent control of their operations and left the country, but the majority agreed to renegotiate the terms of their concessions. The outcome was a decline in production and a tremendous increase in revenue for the Libyan government. Whereas in 1969 Libya was producing 1.12 billion barrels of oil and oil revenues totaled $1.17 billion, by 1973 production had declined to 794 million barrels and revenues had risen to $2.22 billion. In 1974, after the Arab oil embargo, Libya produced 544 million barrels and revenues increased to $6 billion.

Throughout the 1980s, Libyan production hovered around 1.1 million barrels per day (bpd), the quota limit set by the Organization of Petroleum Exporting Countries, but it rose to 1.5 million bpd in the early 1990s, when world oil prices were low. By 2005, production was up again, reaching an estimated 1.7 million bpd. Oil revenues declined from $21 billion in 1980 to $10.2 billion in 1991 and $5.7 billion in 1998, after which world oil prices began rising significantly, with Libya's oil revenues growing commensurably. Libya earned an estimated $24 billion from oil exports in 2005, $35 billion in 2008, and $32.4 billion in 2010. In the early 1990s, Libya's proven reserves of crude oil were estimated at 22.8 billion barrels, but after further exploration, these estimates rose to 47.1 billion barrels in January 2012. Libya's reserves are the largest in Africa and among the ten most important in the world. Most of its oil wells are in the eastern part of the country, in the Sirte Basin, but Libya also has access to major offshore deposits on the continental shelf near Tunisia.

The Western Libyan Gas Project (WLGP), which came online in 2004, made it possible to transfer natural gas to Europe via a 520-kilometer underwater pipeline called the Green Stream. In 2005, 10 billion cubic meters of gas were produced (up from 7 billion the previous year); 8 billion were sold to Europe, and 2 billion were consumed domestically. The WLGP is a fifty-fifty joint venture between Italy's Ente Nazionale Idrocarburi (ENI) and Libya's National Oil Company. As of January 2012, Libya had 52.8 trillion cubic feet of proven natural gas reserves.

Libya's major economic activity before the discovery of petroleum had been agriculture. However, only 1.2 percent of Libya's land is arable, and of that, less than 1 percent is irrigated. The agricultural sector still retains its importance and, together with forestry and fishing, represented 7.6 percent of gross domestic product (GDP) and employed 17 percent of the labor force in 1999. However, the country does not produce enough to feed its own population: Libya imports 75 percent of its food requirements.

Water is scarce, and the supply is very irregular in areas where rainfall is its main source. Water for irrigation has been drawn from aquifers in the Jefara Plain at a rate equivalent to six times the amount of rainfall needed to replenish those aquifers. In 1984, a massive water pipeline project, the Great Manmade River (GMMR), was inaugurated at the Sarir Oasis. When completed it will have cost an estimated $30 billion to $35 billion. It is one of the largest civil engineering projects in the world. The first phase of the project was completed in 1994, and 2 million cubic meters of water per day were supplied to Benghazi via a 1,874-kilometer pipeline from fields at Tazerno and Sarir, in east-central Libya. The second phase, completed in 1996, provided 2.5 million cubic meters of water daily to Tripoli from three fields in the southern oasis of Kufra via a 1,551-kilometer pipeline. By early 2011, the GMMR was supplying 6.5 million cubic meters of freshwater per day to the major population centers of northern Libya on the Mediterranean coast; a significant portion of it was used for agriculture. In July 2011, at the height of the uprising, NATO forces bombed the Brega factory that supplies pipes to repair breaks and leaks in the system.

The non-oil manufacturing sector accounted for 35 percent of GDP in 2011, of which 20 percent was generated by construction and services and 3.2 percent by agriculture. The manufacturing sector included not only the processing of agricultural products but also more complex industries, such as petrochemicals, iron, and steel. The only identified non-hydrocarbon mineral deposit in Libya is the iron ore at Wadi Shatti, which has an estimated 2 to 3 billion tons with 25 to 50 percent iron content. In December 2011, Libya's reserves of foreign exchange and gold were estimated at $100.3 billion.

After the 1969 revolution, the RCC redirected the economy toward rapid economic development, a more equal distribution of income and services, greater government economic control, and independence from foreign influence. An increase in literacy was sought through compulsory and free elementary education. The literacy rate, which in 1973 was estimated at 40 percent for the Libyan population as a whole, with a lower rate for women, rose to 76 percent in the late 1990s. By 2010, the percentage of the population over fifteen that could read had risen to 89.2 percent, including 95.6 percent of males and 82.7 percent of females. This is considerably higher than for any other North African country, including Egypt and Tunisia. Secondary schools, universities, and adult and technical education also became more widely available. In 2010, Libya had more than twenty universities and thirty higher institutes of technology.

Upgrading of health standards and other measures to improve the population's well-being also contributed to the improved resource base. The number of medical doctors rose to 1.29 per 1,000 people in 2008, which compares favorably with industrialized countries such as the United Kingdom with 1.66 and Singapore with 1.40. The infant-mortality rate dropped from 160 per 1,000 live births in 1960 to 72 in 1991 and 17 in 2008. Life expectancy rose from 46.7 years in 1960 to 77.3 years in 2009. However, despite these improvements, Libyans complain about the quality of health care, and there were several reported cases of bubonic plague in 2009.

Under the Qaddafi regime, the government's role in the economy became predominant. Libya not only took majority control of the oil companies operating in its territory but also nationalized the local assets of some companies, such as Shell in 1974. Starting in November 1969, it nationalized all foreign banks, including the Arab Bank, Banco di Roma, and Barclay's Bank. By the end of 1970, the number of commercial banks had been reduced to five, three of them state-owned and two state-controlled. Insurance companies had been completely nationalized by 1971 and were merged into two state-owned companies. Basic infrastructural facilities, including major airlines, power plants, and communications, became state-owned and -operated.

Large- and medium-sized industries with foreign owners—primarily Italians, who owned 75 to 80 percent of all industrial plants in Libya—were taken over by the state. Those included tobacco, tanning and leather, textiles, lumber, construction, and food production, including canned sardines and tomatoes and bottled soft drinks. In 1972, agricultural cooperatives were established and gave financial, technical, and marketing assistance to the farmers who joined. The small-business sector prospered at first, as the government adopted a policy of giving contracts to Libyan firms and lending up to 95 percent of the capital to finance indigenous commercial enterprises. Between 1969 and 1976 the government issued 40,000 licenses to new grocery stores in the district of Tripoli alone. Starting in 1971, workers became part-owners and were given a larger share of the profits made by the firms that employed them. Free housing was provided to some, and loans were given to others to buy suitable housing.

Although the government's aim in implementing these policies was to stimulate Libyan entrepreneurship and develop a strong indigenous middle class that would become a powerful political base for the regime, they had different outcomes. Local businesses that were assured of receiving government contracts or loans began to depend more and more on government subsidies and foreign labor and expertise, and many became mere fronts for non-Libyan interests. A number of the large agricultural projects that were meant to modernize and develop the rural sector foundered because of water shortages, poor planning and management, and the small rural labor force. The settlement policy pursued by the government to induce farmers to remain in rural areas was largely unsuccessful, as the rural population continued to migrate to cities, seeking employment and higher standards of living. In the industrial sector, the policies of the government led to an increase in imports of capital goods and raw materials. Because of shortages of skilled manpower and administrative personnel, labor had to be imported as well. In 1975, 58 percent of the managerial and professional manpower in Libya was foreign, as were 35 percent of the technical personnel, 27 percent of the skilled and semiskilled workforce, and 42 percent of unskilled workers. In 2008, the labor force was estimated at 1.8 million people.

The attempt to develop an entrepreneurial middle class failed as well, when the Libyan businessmen with government contracts reaped huge profits and then invested them abroad. What was taking place was not so much the formation of a new middle class of small businessmen supportive of the regime as the consolidation of the economic power of the traditional urban notability, whose members had the skills, experience, and connections to take advantage of government-sponsored programs to enrich themselves. That process, in turn, frightened the Qaddafi regime, which perceived the notables as a major potential source of opposition.

Consequently, the policies of the state became more radical between 1976 and 1980. Qaddafi's *Green Book*, expounding his political and economic philosophy, first appeared during that period. He called on workers to take over a large number of commercial and industrial enterprises. A law was promulgated in 1978 specifying that every family had the right to own a home of its own and that tenants therefore could take immediate possession of their rented homes. Those two injunctions dealt a severe blow to the urban notables, who lost both their commercial establishments and their real estate investments. By some estimates the private sector had invested 41 percent of its capital in real estate. Furthermore, all foreign trade was to be conducted by the state, whereas until then the private sector had been allowed to import goods and sell them in Libyan markets.

In the 1980s, the confrontation that pitted the United States against Libya because of the latter's support for terrorism resulted in the imposition of economic sanctions banning US imports of Libyan oil and exports of high-technology equipment to Libya. After 1985, the United States stopped importing Libyan crude oil products, such as naphtha, methanol, and low-sulfur fuel oil. In 1986, Libyan assets in the United States, estimated at $1 billion to $2 billion, were frozen. These embargoes, bans, and freezes, coupled with a decline in the price of oil, resulted in a major decline in Libya's export revenues.

The outbreak of the Gulf crisis in 1990 led to windfall profits for several months, owing to an increase in crude output and prices. But Libya began facing economic difficulties after 1992, when the UN Security Council imposed major economic sanctions on Libya for its alleged role in the bombing of Pan Am Flight 103 over Lockerbie, Scotland, in 1988. UN Resolution 731 banned flights to and from Libya and prohibited the supply of aircraft or aircraft parts and the sale or transfer of military equipment to Libya. It also called on all UN member states to significantly reduce diplomatic personnel and staff in Libyan embassies on their territories. The UN sanctions were suspended in 1999, after two bombing suspects were turned in to a Scottish court. Only after Libya officially accepted responsibility for the bombing and agreed to pay $2.7 billion in compensation to the families of the victims did the UN Security Council vote to lift the sanctions in September 2003.

Because of its dwindling resources and international trade problems in the early 1990s, Libya was unable to pay the salaries of government officials and armed forces personnel regularly or to maintain 1980s levels of expenditure on health and education. To reduce the deficit and deal with the economic crisis, Qaddafi called for privatization in September 1992 and passed a law urging Libyans to form joint-stock companies and to set up family firms, partnerships, and individual businesses. In March 1993, for the first time since the nationalizations of the 1970s, Libya allowed the establishment of private banks. In July of that year, the government permitted private-sector companies to engage in wholesale trade. In June 2003, Qaddafi announced that Libya's public sector had failed and would be abolished, and he once again called for privatization. He appointed an American-trained technocrat, Shukri Ghanim, as prime minister to oversee privatization. The following year, Ghanim announced that 160 publicly owned companies had been privatized, out of 360 earmarked for privatization. The rest, he claimed, would be transferred to the private sector gradually over the next four years, and some would be open to foreign investors.

The 2011 uprising has had a major impact on the Libyan economy. The International Monetary Fund (IMF) reported in May 2012 that Libya's GDP had contracted by 60 percent in 2011, due to instability in the country. At one point Libya's oil production dropped from 1.3 million bpd to 300,000 bpd. By May 2012, however, the US Energy Information Administration estimated Libya's oil output at 1.4 million bpd. Furthermore, the price of oil rose to an estimated $91 a barrel in 2012, from $58 in 2010, and it is expected to reach $100 in 2013. Based on the rapid recovery of the Libyan economy due to higher oil prices, the removal of trade restrictions, a significant increase in subsidies and wages, and the creation of public- and private-sector jobs, the IMF is predicting a major rebound of the economy, with a 16.5 percent growth rate in 2013 and 13.2 percent in 2014.

FOREIGN RELATIONS

King Idris followed a pro-Western foreign policy. Treaties signed with Britain in 1953 and the United States in 1954 allowed them to maintain military bases and to station forces in Libya in exchange for ensuring Libyan security. Britain and the United States also provided development grants and budgetary subventions to Libya. An agreement with France in 1955 provided for communications facilities in the southwestern desert. Libya also maintained close ties with Turkey and Greece. It joined the Arab League in 1953 but remained basically neutral in inter-Arab and Arab-Western conflicts, following the theory that it was in Libya's security interest not to get involved. The king's decisions not to close the British military bases in 1956 during the Suez Canal crisis and not to participate in the 1967 Arab-Israeli War created resentment among young Libyans, who felt the country was being kept out of Arab affairs and marginalized in the Arab world. Under internal and external pressure to close foreign bases, the government after 1964 publicly supported the early evacuation of these bases but took few practical steps to implement the closures. The issue was brought up again in 1967, and the process of closing bases began in earnest.

Qaddafi regarded the coup of September 1969 as the starting point of Libyan independence. In order to legitimize its power, the RCC gave priority to removing the foreign bases. It could then claim that the new regime had liberated Libya from foreign imperialism. Agreements were reached between the RCC and the US and British governments to evacuate the Wheelus base and the British bases at Tobruk and al-Adam in spring 1970.

Libya's relations with its neighbors under Qaddafi were characterized by numerous attempts at unity. The Tripoli Charter, in December 1969, was the first of seven such attempts to unite, in this case with Egypt and Sudan. Another attempt took place in September 1971, with Egypt and Syria, with the Federation of Arab Republics. Libya and Tunisia announced the formation of a union in January 1974. The plan called for the formation of a single state, the Arab Islamic Republic. The original offer had come from Tunisia, in an effort to draw Libya away from Egypt. Opposition within Tunisia and from Algeria aborted the merger plans. In 1975, Libya and Algeria signed a mutual-defense pact, the Hassi Mas'ud Treaty, which ensured Libya a major regional ally. When Egypt attacked Libya in July 1977 and destroyed Soviet radar installations on the Libyan-Egyptian border, Algeria intervened on Libya's behalf, and the bombing was stopped. In return, Libya supported Algeria against Morocco on the Western Sahara issue and supplied the Polisario Front with both financial and military resources for the next six years. In 1981, Libya merged with Chad in an attempt to put an end to the war between the two countries. Libya also wanted to ensure its dominance of northern Chad. That merger worsened relations with Algeria, which turned toward Tunisia and then Mauritania and signed the Treaty of Brotherhood and Concord in 1983, which did not include Libya. The Arab-African Federation, set up between Libya and Morocco in August 1984, was a reaction in part to the renewed regional isolation of Libya and in part to King Hassan's concern with retaining control of the Western Sahara. The outcome was a significant decline in Libyan support for the Polisario.

In February 1989, Algeria, Libya, Morocco, Mauritania, and Tunisia announced the creation of the Arab Maghreb Union (UMA), meant to foster economic integration on the model of the European community. The countries of the Maghreb wanted to enlarge their markets and find an alternative outlet for their labor. Although they lacked economic complementarity, they set up joint companies and joint projects to increase efficiency and prevent duplication in the manufacturing sector. Libya removed trade barriers with its neighbors, enhancing trade and allowing Libyans to shop in Tunisia for goods they could not find at home. Libya became a major partner in the Arab Maghrebi Bank for Investment and Trade and had a large number of joint projects with its neighbors, including Egypt, in the agricultural, transport, communications, industrial, and petrochemical sectors.

For four decades, Libya's relations with Egypt have been turbulent. After the early closeness with Nasser during the first year of the Libyan revolution, relations deteriorated progressively under Anwar Sadat, culminating in Egypt's bombing of Libya in 1977, partly in retaliation for Libya's subversive activities in Egypt and partly because Libya allowed the Soviets to survey Egypt's military installations by means of radar based on the Libyan-Egyptian frontier. In the 1980s, however, relations with the regime of Hosni Mubarak improved markedly. Tens of thousands of Egyptians sought employment in Libya, and a large number of joint infrastructural, industrial, and agricultural projects were set up between the two countries. Mubarak and Qaddafi shared intelligence on Islamic fundamentalists on both sides of the border, and Mubarak personally interceded on Libya's behalf for the lifting of UN sanctions.

Under Qaddafi, the Libyan government was uncompromising in its stance toward Israel. Qaddafi condemned Zionism as aggressive nationalism and supported the more radical groups among the Palestinians, such as the Popular Front for the Liberation of Palestine–General Command. Although the Libyan leader provided financial, moral, and political support to the Palestine Liberation Organization, he also had strong disagreements with its longtime chairman, Yasir Arafat. After the Camp David Accords of 1978 and the Egypt-Israel Peace Treaty of 1979, Libya became a leader of the "rejection front"—Arab states that denounced any political settlement with Israel. Qaddafi was against the 1993 peace initiative between the Palestinians and the Israelis, but in May 1993 he sent two hundred Libyans on a pilgrimage to Jerusalem and invited Libyan Jews who lived abroad to come and visit Libya. After the second Palestinian intifada (uprising) that began in the fall of 2000, Libya again became very vocal in its criticism of Israel and US policy in the region. Qaddafi also worked actively for over two decades to counter Israeli influence in sub-Saharan Africa.

Libya's relations with the United States deteriorated over the years. Until the 1973 Arab-Israeli War, Qaddafi had merely been critical of US Middle East policies. After the war, Sadat moved closer to the West and to the United States. The Libyan leader, perceiving this as threatening to Libya's security, moved closer to the Soviet Bloc. His support for terrorist groups in various parts of the world caused the United States to stop selling arms and military hardware to Libya. In December 1979, the US embassy in Tripoli was sacked and burned. The Ronald Reagan administration then chose Qaddafi as the principal target of its antiterrorist policy and adopted further economic and political measures to isolate Libya regionally and internationally. This culminated in the bombing of Tripoli in 1986 in retaliation for a terrorist bombing later traced to the radical Palestinian Abu Nidal organization.

In 1991, the United States and the United Kingdom formally charged Libya with the bombing of Pan Am Flight 103 over Lockerbie, Scotland, while France issued arrest warrants for four Libyans accused of participating in a 1988 bombing of a French Union des Transports Aériennes (UTA) airliner over Niger. The Lockerbie and UTA charges led to UN Resolutions 731 and 748 in 1992 imposing sanctions on Libya, including a ban on all flights to and from Libya and a prohibition on the supply of aircraft, aircraft parts, and military equipment of any kind. The United States and Britain demanded that Libya extradite two Libyans accused of the Lockerbie bombing. Libya refused. In the mid-1990s, the United States passed a law imposing sanctions on non-US firms investing in the oil sectors of Libya and Iran, which became known as the Iran-Libya Sanctions Act (ILSA). The European Union, in turn, strongly objected and passed legislation to block the impact of ILSA, making it illegal for European firms to comply with it.

Eventually, in April 1999, the two men accused of the Lockerbie bombing were sent to The Hague to a specially convened Scottish court, where their trial opened a year later. One of the men was found innocent of all charges, but the second, 'Abd al-Basit al-Migrahi, the head of security for Libyan Arab Airlines, was found guilty and sentenced to life imprisonment on 270 counts of murder. Libya appealed the case, and in August 2009 Migrahi was released on compassionate grounds, as he was suffering from terminal cancer. Back in Libya he was hailed as a hero but finally died in May 2012. The UN sanctions against Libya, suspended when the two suspects were turned over to the Scottish court, were finally lifted in September 2003 after Libya agreed to pay $10 million to each of the families of the victims of the Lockerbie bombing.

In December 2003, Libya announced it would end all programs aimed at developing weapons of mass destruction. In the following month it ratified the Comprehensive Nuclear Test Ban Treaty and allowed a compliance-monitoring team to be posted in its territory. In response to these initiatives, the US administration lifted its travel ban and unilateral trade and investment sanctions on Libya and ceased the application of ILSA. It also unblocked Libya's frozen assets, encouraged people-to-people exchanges in education and health, and welcomed Libya's application to the World Trade Organization. In May 2006, US Secretary of State Condoleeza Rice announced that the United States was restoring full diplomatic relations with Libya. In 2007, President George W. Bush appointed Gene Cretz ambassador to Libya, ending a thirty-five-year vacancy in the position. Also in 2007, Libya was elected to the UN Security Council; it even assumed the presidency of the council for a month in January 2008.

Libya's Arab Spring uprising in 2011 once again changed that country's relations with the West. When it became clear that Qaddafi was not prepared to give up power and that he was using all means at his disposal, including airpower, to destroy the opposition—killing many civilians in the process—the West decided to act. First France and then the United States recognized the NTC as the legitimate interim government of Libya, thereby delegitimizing Qaddafi and his administration internationally; next, they moved the debate to the United Nations. On March 17, the UN Security Council voted to establish a no-fly zone and authorized international military action to protect civilians. NATO then began air attacks against Qaddafi's forces and blockaded Libyan ports. Qatar and the United Arab Emirates provided logistical assistance. These actions were crucial to the overthrow of the Qaddafi regime.

Libyan-Soviet relations became closer after the rapprochement between Egypt and the West that began in 1974. Relations were based primarily on mutual interest rather than ideology, as Qaddafi had been consistently critical of communism. Libya needed a stable supplier of arms and a strong ally to balance US influence in Egypt. The Soviet Union acquired a client that could pay its bills and was strategically located, with the longest coastline on the southern Mediterranean. A sharp drop in oil prices and Libya's inability to pay its debts later soured relations between the two countries. For a time, oil was used to pay some of Libya's debts, estimated at $4.5 billion. Russia respected the sanctions and refused to sell arms to Libya until it handed over the two Lockerbie bombing suspects. After that, Russian-Libyan relations improved significantly, and trade between the two countries resumed. In April 2008, Russian president Vladimir Putin visited Libya, the first such visit by a Russian head of state since 1985. He agreed to suspend Libya's debt in return for its signing a number of military and civilian agreements, including a $3.4 billion contract to build a railway between Sirte and Benghazi on the Mediterranean.

Libya's relations with western Europe improved gradually during the 1990s and more rapidly after the lifting of UN sanctions in 2003. Energy was a major determinant in these relations, as Libya exports oil and gas to western Europe and imports foodstuffs, capital goods, medicine, and other commodities. Royal Dutch/Shell, the energy giant, announced an agreement with the National Oil Corporation of Libya in May 2005 to rejuvenate and upgrade the existing liquefied natural gas plant at Marsa Brega on the Libyan coast and to explore for gas in five areas in the Sirte Basin region. Italy's ENI S.p.A. and Azienda Generale Italiana Petroli (AGIP) oil and gas companies were exploring for and producing oil, as were Austria's OMV 4, France's Total, Spain's Repsol, Greece's Hellenic Petroleum, British Petroleum, and the British Gas Group. As of 2006, Tamoil, an oil-refining, marketing, and distribution company controlled by Netherlands-based Oil Invest and partly owned by Europoil, a group of private Libyan investors, owned 2,967 service stations in Germany, Italy, the Netherlands, Spain, and Switzerland, as well as refineries in Germany, Italy, and Switzerland.

Qaddafi supported Muslims in Africa and Asia politically, financially, and culturally. He aided Muslim insurgents in the Philippines, built mosques and schools in Niger and Mali, and gave financial aid to a large number of states, including Burundi, the Central African Republic, Gabon, Indonesia, Malaysia, Pakistan, Togo, and Uganda. The Organization of African Unity (OAU) passed a resolution in June 1998 declaring that its member states would no longer recognize the UN embargo on flights to and from Libya and the UN sanctions against Libya unless the United States and United Kingdom agreed to try the Libyan bombing suspects in a neutral country. The OAU's action and Nelson Mandela's support for Libya were critical in the final negotiations to hold the Lockerbie trial at The Hague.

In the late 1990s, Qaddafi declared that a "United States of Africa" should be formed to replace the OAU. He convinced the African heads of state of the importance of this idea, and in September 1999 they issued the Sirte Declaration calling for the establishment of the African Union (AU). The declaration was followed by a summit in Lomé, Togo, in 2000 where the Constitutive Act of the African Union was adopted. Two years later, the African Union was launched in Durban, South Africa, by its first president, South African president Thabo Mbeki. The AU has fifty-three member states, including all African states except Morocco (because of its position on the Western Sahara dispute). It is a successor not only of the OAU but also of the African Economic Community. In 2008, Qaddafi was declared "King of Kings of Africa" by more than two hundred African kings and traditional rulers at a meeting in Benghazi, and in February 2009 Qaddafi was elected chairman of the African Union at a closed session in Ethiopia.

After coming to power, Qaddafi sought to associate Libya with revolutionary causes and movements. For more than three decades, Libya headed the list of terrorist states. It was active in various regions of the world, supporting coups and funding and training guerrilla groups and opposition political movements. Qaddafi's administration was implicated in numerous attempts to assassinate rival leaders and opponents of his regime and in support for terrorist groups and movements all over the world. One of Qaddafi's sons, Sayf al-Islam, tried to improve Libya's terrorist state image. He helped negotiate the release in 2000 of European and South African hostages held in the Philippines by the Abu Sayaf rebels. In 2001, he was involved in negotiations to help free Shelters Now aid workers who had been taken hostage by the Taliban government in Afghanistan. In 2003, he negotiated an agreement with France on behalf of Libya to provide compensation to the families of victims of the 1989 UTA plane bombing. Sayf al-Islam stood by his father throughout the Libyan uprising. He was captured in November 2011 by militiamen from the town of Zintan, who are holding him until he can be brought to justice in Libya.

It is too soon to tell where the new government of Libya will steer the country, which has experienced two revolutions in less than half a century. There are clear signs, however, that the new generation wants a more open and representative political system and society, and it may very well achieve its goals in the not-too-distant future.

BIBLIOGRAPHY

Historical works on Libya include John Wright's *Libya* (New York: Praeger, 1969), which focuses especially on the period from 1911 to 1951. Wright's second volume, *Libya: A Modern History* (Baltimore: Johns Hopkins University Press, 1982), covers the period through 1981. E. E. Evans-Pritchard's *The Sanusi of Cyrenaica* (London: Oxford University Press, 1949) provides an important study of Libya's main religious order and its role in the country's development, as does Nicola Ziadeh's *Sanusiyah: A Study of a Revivalist Movement in Islam* (Leiden: E. J. Brill, 1968). Henry Serrano Villard, the first US minister to Libya after independence, gives a general overview in *Libya: The New Arab Kingdom of North Africa* (Ithaca, NY: Cornell University Press, 1956). The UN commissioner in Libya, Adrian Pelt, describes the transformation of Libya from an Italian colony to an independent state in *Libyan Independence and the United Nations: A Case of Planned Decolonization* (New Haven, CT: Yale University Press, 1970). Lisa Anderson covers the social and political history of Libya for a century and a half in *The State and Social Transformation in Tunisia and Libya, 1830–1980* (Princeton, NJ: Princeton University Press, 1986). Majid Khadduri, in *Modern Libya: A Study in Political Development* (Baltimore: Johns Hopkins University Press, 1963), considers the monarchy in detail.

Studies of Libya's political, social, and economic system and foreign policy since 1969 include J. A. Allan, *Libya Since Independence: Economic and Social Development* (London: Croom Helm, 1982); Omar L. Fathaly and Monte Palmer, *Political Development and Social Change in Libya* (Lexington, MA: Lexington Books, 1979); Harold D. Nelson, *Libya: A Country Study,* 3rd ed. (Washington, DC: American University, Foreign Area Studies, 1979); John K. Cooley, *Libyan Sandstorm* (New York: Holt, Rinehart & Winston, 1982); Marius Deeb and Mary-Jane Deeb, *Libya Since the Revolution: Aspects of Social and Political Development* (New York: Praeger, 1982); Mary-Jane Deeb, *Libya's Foreign Policy in North Africa* (Boulder, CO: Westview Press, 1991); Ruth First, *Libya: The Elusive Revolution* (Middlesex, UK: Penguin Books, 1974); Ronald Bruce St. John, *Qaddafi's World Design: Libyan Foreign Policy, 1969–1987* (London: Saqi Books, 1987); Lillian Craig Harris, *Qadhafi's Revolution and the Modern State* (Boulder, CO: Westview/Croom Helm, 1986); E. G. H. Joffe and K. S. McLachlan, *Social and Economic Development of Libya* (Cambridgeshire, UK: MENAS Press, 1982); Jonathan Bearman, *Qadhafi's Libya* (London: Zed Books, 1986); J. A. Allan, *Libya: The Experience of Oil* (Boulder, CO: Westview Press, 1981); Mirella Bianco, *Gadafi: Voice from the Desert* (London: Longman Group, 1975); David Blundy and Andrew Lycett, *Qaddafi and the Libyan Revolution* (Boston: Little, Brown, 1987); Edward Haley, *Qadhafi and the United States Since 1969* (New York: Praeger, 1984); and René Lemarchand, *The*

Green and the Black: Qadhafi's Policies in Africa (Bloomington: Indiana University Press, 1988).

Recent books include Lindsey Hilsum, *Sandstorm: Libya in the Time of Revolution* (New York: Penguin Press, 2012); Bruce St. John, *Libya: From Colony to Revolution* (London: One World, 2012); John Wright, *A History of Libya* (New York: Columbia University Press, 2012); Tim Niblock, *"Pariah States" and Sanctions in the Middle East: Iraq, Libya, Sudan* (Boulder, CO: Lynne Rienner Publishers, 2001); Mansoor El-Kikhia, *Libya's Qaddafi: The Politics of Contradiction* (Gainesville: University Press of Florida, 1997); Dirk Vandewalle, *Libya Since Independence: Oil and State-Building* (Ithaca, NY: Cornell University Press, 1998), and *History of Modern Libya* (New York: Cambridge University Press, 2012); J. Millard Burr and Robert O. Collins, *Africa's Thirty Years War: Libya, Chad, and the Sudan, 1963–1993* (Boulder, CO: Westview Press, 1999); Judith Gurney, *Libya: The Political Economy of Oil* (Oxford: Oxford University Press, 1996); and Ronald Bruce St. John, *Libya and the United States: Two Centuries of Strife* (Philadelphia: University of Pennsylvania Press, 2002).

15

KINGDOM OF MOROCCO

Gregory W. White

HISTORICAL BACKGROUND

Precolonial Morocco

What is today known as Morocco remained largely cut off from the Roman Empire, primarily by the mountains of the Rif and the Atlas range. Indigenous tribes resisted extensive external imperial incursion. Still, the Roman presence was not insignificant, and important occupations were established in Tingis (Tangier) and Volubilis. In turn, the Vandal activities in the fifth century were similarly incomplete, as was the effort of Byzantium to take control of the territory in the sixth century.

The Islamic campaign in the 660s reached as far as the Atlantic, but in 683 the Berber chieftain Kusayla defeated 'Uqba, sending Islamic forces back east to present-day Libya. By 698, however, Arab forces had recaptured the Byzantine footholds on the North African coast. And by the early eighth century, Arab-Islamic power had spread back into Morocco and across the Strait of Gibraltar. Al-Andalus was a medieval Muslim state on the Iberian Peninsula from 711 until 1492.

For centuries, several influential and powerful dynasties dominated northwestern Africa: the Idrissids, who founded Fez in the 780s; the Almoravids, who established Marrakech in the eleventh century; the Almohads, who reigned during the fall of Muslim Spain; the Merenids; the Wattasids; and the Saadians. The scope of these empires was truly astounding. At its height in 1100, for example, the Almoravid state reached from northern present-day Mauritania, east to Algiers, and north into Spain to include Zaragosa.

The completion of the Christian Reconquista of Spain in 1492 changed the political economy of Morocco. The extension of Christian control into North Africa transformed the trans-Sahara slave trade and prompted the emergence of Christian enclaves on the Mediterranean coast: Melilla and Ceuta. In turn, it set the stage for Ottoman efforts to move into the western Mediterranean in the sixteenth century. Both the Saadians and, in its turn, the Alawite dynasty in the seventeenth century ultimately avoided Ottoman

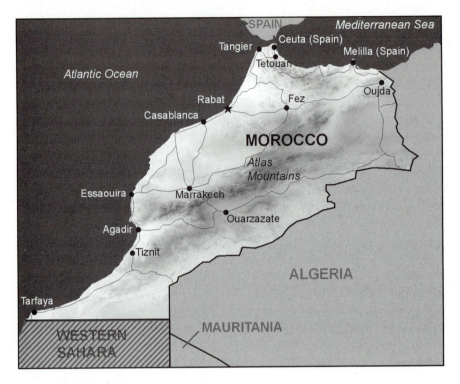

Kingdom of Morocco

penetration. The Alawites established Meknes as their capital and have ruled Morocco until this day.

By the nineteenth century, the country was largely in decline. The French occupation of Algeria in 1830 was met with virtually no response from the ruling Moroccan monarchy. In 1856, a treaty with Great Britain opened the country to free trade and gave Britain control over the Strait of Gibraltar. The Spanish seized control of more coastal islands and rocks in the mid-nineteenth century—to complement their control of Ceuta and Melilla—and fully occupied Tetouan.

From 1873 to 1894, Mulay Hassan fully established the authority of the Alawi Sharifian Empire. After his death, however, the country fell into immediate difficulties, largely owing to mismanagement by Hassan's son, Abd al-Aziz (r. 1894–1908). Under Abd al-Aziz the country incurred a large external debt, undermining its internal sovereignty. By 1904, Spain and France had effectively divided the country; Britain abandoned its claims in exchange for French recognition of British authority in Egypt. By 1908, Moroccans were in revolt against Abd al-Aziz, and his brother, Mulay Hafid, replaced him.

Formal European Colonialism

Mulay Hafid further indebted the country to European creditors. At the same time, dissident tribes in Fez besieged him, and he turned to France for military, political, and economic assistance. On March 30, 1912, Mulay Hafid signed the Treaty of Fez, establishing a French protectorate.

The French colonial presence in Rabat retained the basic structure of the sultan's government. The administration of Marshall Lyautey ruled through a policy of co-optation. Mulay Hafid signed official decrees in his own name, thereby remaining the ostensible authority. Many have noted that the French colonial presence propped up what had become an increasingly dissolute and ineffective monarchy. Had Morocco achieved independence in the 1930s, the Alawite monarchy might have given way to a more republican form of government.

In striking contrast to France's extensive colonial occupation of Algeria, colonialism in Morocco left domestic institutions relatively intact. The traditionally privileged classes were preserved, especially the commercially dominant Arab bourgeoisie in the cities of Fez and in the southern Sousse, as well as Berber tribal notables. And unlike in Tunisia, internal social evolution in Morocco was modest. Upwardly mobile lower-status groups did not infuse sectors of the traditional elite with fresh blood. Few elites received a French education or gained access to professional careers.

Often missing from quick characterizations of Morocco as a former French colony is the fact that Spain colonized the north. Although the Anti-Atlas tribes offered significant opposition, the north exhibited the strongest resistance to European colonialism, with Abd al-Krim al-Khattabi forming a Rifian republic that espoused a mix of nationalism and Salafi (militant Islamist) fervor. His forces delivered a humiliating defeat to a superior Spanish army at the Battle of Anoual in 1921. Nonetheless, the Rif population was ultimately suppressed by 1926, with colonial forces (including a young Francisco Franco) making extensive use of mustard gas. The campaign was brutal. Legend has it that Franco once returned from a raid with the bloody heads of Berber tribesmen as trophies. Today Abd al-Krim's resistance is trumpeted as a source of national honor, a complicated deployment of nationalist symbols given the Berber origin of the uprising.

Emergent Nationalism

Nationalists among the traditional elite eventually capitulated to French demands and reluctantly accepted their status. They retained their national identity, however, and after 1926 their ranks were joined by a small group of populists. Disaffection emerged as well among skilled urban craftspeople who were beginning to suffer because of strong competition from colonial imports. The combination of disgruntled traditional elites, radicalized younger elites, and lower-middle-class elements constituted a powerful nationalist front.

KINGDOM OF MOROCCO

Capital city	Rabat
Chief of state, 2012	King Mohammed VI
Head of government, 2012	Prime Minister Abdelilah Benkirane
Political parties (seats in most recent election, 2011)	Justice and Development Party (107), Istiqlal Party (60), National Rally of Independents (52), Authenticity and Modernity Party (47), Socialist Union of Popular Forces (39), Popular Movement (32), Constitutional Union Party (23), Progress and Socialism Party (18), Democratic Forces Front (9), Democratic and Social Movement (9), Covenant Party (8), Labor Party (4), other (13)
Ethnic groups	Arab-Berber (99%), other (1%)
Religious groups	Muslim (99%), Christian (1%)
Export partners, 2011	Spain (18.6%), France (16.9%), Brazil (6%), United States (4.8%), India (4.5%)
Import partners, 2011	France (15.4%), Spain (14.4%), China (7.7%), United States (7.3%), Saudi Arabia (6.1%), Italy (5.1%), Germany (4.8%)

The national independence movement gained momentum on May 16, 1930, when the colonial authorities issued an infamous *dahir*, known as the Berber Decree, establishing a separate system of customary-law tribunals in Berber-populated parts of the country. It was part of a French effort to isolate the rural areas from the growing nationalism in urban areas. Empowered to deal with civil matters, these tribunals created an artificial division between Arabs and Berbers by removing the latter from the national system of Muslim jurisprudence on civil matters. Berber—or, more appropriately, Tamazight—identity politics remain salient to this day. Henceforward, this chapter will use "Tamazight" given the derogatory etymology of "Berber"—its association with "barbarian"—although it is true that some modern activists sometimes use "Berber" in an ironic, proud, or knowing fashion.

In May 1932, the Kutla al-Amal al-Watani (National Action Bloc) was formed as the first overtly nationalist party in the country. The bloc sought a reform plan that called for autonomy and an end to colonial efforts to craft a distinctive Tamazight identity. Nonetheless, French officials (and Sultan Muhammad Ben Yussuf, or Muhammad V) ignored the plan. The bloc worked peacefully but in vain for reforms within the framework of the protectorate until the French dissolved the party in 1937. In 1943, the Istiqlal (Independence) Party was formed.

After World War II, the Istiqlal enjoyed strong support in the towns and a tacit alliance with the throne. It was challenged, however, by powerful rural chieftains allied with the French, by some traditionalist elements in the cities, and by the heads of some religious brotherhoods. During the late 1940s, the Istiqlal transformed itself into a broad-based independence movement. As the alliance between the Istiqlal and the monarchy became more overt and began to challenge French hegemony, colonial authorities took action. In August 1953, they sent Muhammad V and his family, including his son Hassan, into exile in Madagascar and replaced the king with a more docile relative. Once again, however, the French had miscalculated. Muhammad V became a martyr in the eyes of the population, and the nationalist movement was catalyzed into an all-out fight for independence.

In part because of the turmoil in neighboring Algeria, a quick political settlement was achieved. Muhammad V's return from exile in fall 1955 marked the end of colonial rule. On March 2, 1956, the French regions were joined with the Spanish-controlled areas, and France formally granted independence. In 1957, the country was proclaimed a kingdom.

Early Years of Independence

The monarchy emerged as the major beneficiary of independence. Indeed, Morocco is notable because its struggle for independence revolved around the revival of a monarchy that was rather ineffective prior to colonial rule. The population revered Muhammad V for his *baraka*, or religious blessing. Upon independence, the country enjoyed a sufficient level of institutional stability and a reasonably effective political leadership. The political parties, with the Istiqlal in the lead, provided necessary cadres for the new government. The urban resistance forces were incorporated into the police, and the Army of Liberation, one of the last groups to recognize the monarchy, was absorbed into the Royal Armed Forces. Civil servants were recruited from the former protectorate government and from newly trained Moroccan youth. Over this heterogeneous group, Muhammad V ruled as a symbol of Moroccan unity.

Within five years, however, the working relationship between the king and the political parties had disintegrated. Muhammad V was unwilling to become a constitutional figurehead, and the internally divided Istiqlal leadership was unwilling to accept the secondary role envisioned by the king. Tension between the conservative and radical wings of the Istiqlal reached a breaking point in 1959, when Prime Minister Abdallah Ibrahim joined a group of secular intellectuals and trade unionists to form a new left-wing

424 GREGORY W. WHITE

party, the National Union of Popular Forces (UNFP), closely allied with the large Moroccan Workers Union. The UNFP charged the Istiqlal leadership with not standing up to the king and with indifference to meaningful reforms. The fragmentation of the Istiqlal and the limited appeal of the UNFP outside urban areas, however, greatly facilitated the king's efforts to expand the powers of the monarchy.

Muhammad V dismissed the government of Prime Minister Ibrahim and his predominantly UNFP cabinet in May 1960, naming himself prime minister and making Crown Prince Hassan his deputy. The king suddenly died the following February after minor surgery and was succeeded by his son King Hassan II on March 3, 1961. Hassan, with a law degree from the University of Bordeaux, quickly consolidated power in his own hands and further reduced the political role of the parties. He believed that the role of parties was to organize support for the monarchy, not to represent the electorate in the formulation of public policy. The young king lacked Muhammad V's charisma, however, as well as the advantage of being a nationalist hero.

With a minimum of consultation, but in keeping with his father's public promise, King Hassan II introduced a constitution that was approved in a referendum in December 1962. The promulgation of new constitutions has been a recurring theme of postindependence Moroccan politics. Drawing inspiration from France's Fifth Republic, the first constitution guaranteed political freedoms. Yet its principal provisions solidified the king's power; the king was given the authority to dissolve the legislature and exercise unlimited emergency powers.

In the first national elections in May 1963, Hassan encouraged the creation of parties loyal to the throne, including the Constitutional Institutions Defense Front (FDIC) and a conservative Tamazight party, the Popular Movement (MP). The FDIC was unable to win the majority the king had hoped for. On June 7, 1965, following a series of bloody riots in Casablanca, Hassan invoked Article 35 of the constitution and assumed full power.

This move only exacerbated the unrest that had existed since Muhammad V's death. The gulf between the throne and the opposition parties widened even more in 1965 with the abduction in a Paris café of popular UNFP leader Mehdi Ben Barka. Ben Barka had been sentenced to death in absentia because of his criticism of Hassan's rule. Although his fate was the subject of speculation for years—with Hassan claiming ignorance in interviews—the release of official documents after Hassan's death in 1999 indicate that Ben Barka was tortured to death with French connivance. His body was then flown to Rabat, where it was dissolved in a vat of acid.

Throughout the late 1960s, the police seized newspapers and made many arrests, and sanctioned political activity virtually disappeared. In July 1970, however, the king unexpectedly announced that a second constitution would be submitted for a national referendum in an attempt to shore up his faltering legitimacy. Elections for a new single-chamber *majlis* (parliament) were held immediately after the successful referendum. But the Istiqlal and the UNFP—which had joined together in the Kutla Wataniya (National Front) to oppose ratification of the new constitution—organized a boycott of the elections.

Coup Attempts

The elimination of political opposition failed to prevent—or perhaps prompted—two attempts by military officers to assassinate the king: one in July 1971 at Skhirat and the other in August 1972 in Rabat. Hassan emerged uninjured in both instances, more determined than ever to suppress perceived enemies.

The August 1972 coup attempt provided the country with one of its most notorious political episodes: the death of General Muhammad Oufkir. Oufkir, a former defense minister and longtime ally of Hassan, is now known to have been present at Ben Barka's torture and murder. Nevertheless, Oufkir conspired to overthrow the king, ordering fighter planes to strafe the royal jet as it returned from Europe. Hassan survived the attack, and by evening the general was dead. According to official accounts, Oufkir confessed to the plot and promptly committed suicide. But it appears to have been an "acrobatic suicide," as bullet holes were found in the back of his head. Security forces imprisoned the general's family. They were released in 1991 after nearly twenty years and allowed to leave the country in 1996.

In 1972, Hassan announced a third constitution. Executive power was to be vested in the government and a new chamber of representatives. Two-thirds of the chamber's membership was to be elected by universal suffrage, compared with one-half under the 1970 constitution. The Kutla, caught unprepared, urged a boycott of the constitutional referendum and again accused the government of rigging the balloting. Once the king felt confident that he had reestablished control of the military, he ignored the demands for more political freedom by the muddled opposition parties. Differences between the Istiqlal and the UNFP had reemerged, with internal divisions within the UNFP as well. By the end of 1972, a new, Rabat-based faction under Abderrahim Bouabid had gained sway and renamed itself the National Union of Socialist Forces (USFP).

The Controlled Opening of the Economy in the 1970s and the Western Sahara

At the same time, Hassan slowly began to liberalize trade with Europe. In this way, he combined his ability to outmaneuver opposition parties with economic-liberalization measures that created the impression of change and progress. In 1973, King Hassan undertook additional economic programs designed to increase support for the monarchy, including the distribution of nationalized land (mostly French) among the peasantry. Further, he introduced an ambitious five-year development plan that called for an annual economic growth rate of 7.5 percent. Hassan also launched several foreign policy initiatives designed to defuse domestic unrest, including a strong stand in a fishing dispute with Spain in 1973. Conflict with Spain and, in turn, the European Union (EU) over access to Morocco's abundant Atlantic fisheries persists to this day.

The king also scored a major political victory in 1974 and 1975 by reasserting his country's historic claim to the former Spanish Sahara. This move mobilized popular support from all segments of society and raised Hassan's political fortunes enormously. Both the Istiqlal and the USFP supported reintegration of the Western Sahara as part of their own inherent nationalism, and Hassan's move outflanked the parties.

In particular, Spanish withdrawal from the territory in 1975 set the stage for a major act of political theater, perhaps the central event of Morocco's postindependence history. In November 1975, Hassan organized the *massira*, or "Green March," in which approximately 350,000 civilians assembled on the southern border with the Western Sahara and staged a short symbolic walk into the disputed territory. The event is celebrated annually as a national holiday. Since the northern two-thirds of the Western Sahara contains large deposits of phosphate as well as oil and uranium reserves, the king's actions seemed to portend economic gains. Ostensible political tranquility did not last long, however. An insurgency by the Popular Front for the Liberation of Saguit al-Hamra and Rio de Oro, or the Polisario Front, claiming the right to an independent Sahara, broke out in 1976. The Western Sahara is discussed more extensively below.

Severe droughts ravaged the economy during the 1970s, devastating the agricultural sector and encouraging urban migration. World phosphate prices also began a decline during this period. After placing strong emphasis on phosphate exports to earn foreign exchange, the rentier state grew increasingly indebted (and corrupt) and was forced to reduce public investment in development projects. In the face of such economic difficulties, public discontent reemerged in 1978 and 1979. Unemployment reached as high as 35 to 40 percent of the youth workforce. Labor unrest increased, and militant Islamist groups opposed to the established political order emerged.

The Moribund 1980s

Major riots broke out in Casablanca in June 1981, with attacks on banks, car dealerships, and other symbols of authority and privilege. Security forces were barely able to restore order in some areas, with conservative estimates placing the number of dead protestors at two hundred. The rioting was followed by numerous arrests, including arrests of trade union leaders and even some *majlis* members belonging to the USFP.

In January 1983, there were reports of another military plot against the king. Officers were arrested, and General Ahmed Dlimi, commander of the Saharan forces, was killed in a mysterious car accident. Following Dlimi's death, Hassan fragmented the military command structure. In 1983, Hassan again postponed the elections to the *majlis* as well as elections for provincial and prefectural assemblies, deepening still further public alienation and cynicism. Elections for municipal and rural councils finally took place but were accompanied by serious irregularities, rendering meaningless the victory of Hassan's supporters.

January 1984 brought new riots. They began with strikes by students in Marrakech and spread throughout the country. The security forces killed at least 150 people, and thousands were arrested. Verdicts handed down to Islamists were especially harsh, including thirteen death sentences, the first for political crimes since 1972.

In August 1984, Morocco concluded a union with Libya. The union secured Muammar al-Qaddafi's agreement to withdraw support from the Polisario Front. Moreover, it set in motion a series of economic cooperation efforts, including employment opportunities in oil-rich Libya for Moroccan migrant labor, the purchase of Libyan oil at preferential prices, and several trade agreements. But the Moroccan-Libyan union was not bound to last. After Qaddafi denounced Rabat for its support of Ronald Reagan administration policies—and after Qaddafi's overtures to Algeria—Hassan abrogated the treaty in August 1986.

With the continuing war in the Sahara, the cycle of unrest motivated by economic privation and followed by harsh security measures continued throughout the 1980s. Leftists and Islamists protested the regime from different directions; for its part, the government charged that the Polisario was backing leftist efforts to conduct subversive activities among students and labor. Hassan invariably disregarded specific demands regarding political prisoners but maintained his long-established practice of pardons and amnesties, especially on national or religious holidays.

Although the government has historically been relatively lenient on press freedom, especially in comparison to the Tunisian and Algerian regimes, it has suspended newspaper circulation several times in recent decades. In general, papers have been permitted to criticize the government's economic and social policies so long as they do not mention the king personally or question Moroccan sovereignty over the Western Sahara. In terms of the latitude of civil society organizations, in 1988 the government banned the Moroccan Human Rights Organization (OMDH) because of its plans to hold a constitutive assembly. Other Moroccan human rights organizations are the Moroccan Association of Human Rights, linked to the USFP; Istiqlal's Moroccan League of Human Rights; and the Association for the Defense of Human Rights in Morocco, based in Paris. After international and domestic pressure, however, Hassan finally approved establishment of the OMDH, which held its first assembly in December 1988.

The king also began to secure "contributions" for the construction in Casablanca of the Hassan II Mosque. Completed in the early 1990s, the mosque has a minaret over five hundred feet tall and an internal capacity of 25,000. Many Moroccans take great pride in the mosque's grandeur and beauty, but there were complaints about a cost estimated at US$800 million. Some charge that it would have been much better to devote these resources to development projects rather than to an edifice devoted to a then-living monarch. Additional anxieties have emerged in recent years because of the mosque's majestic location on the Atlantic Ocean; the anticipated rise in sea level associated with climate change will pose challenges for the building's foundation.

The Post–Cold War Era and a Controlled Opening

Lethal food riots in December 1990 associated with International Monetary Fund–sponsored structural-adjustment reforms and the Gulf crisis in 1990 and 1991, the country's situation generally stabilized in the early 1990s because of significant international assistance. Hassan had sent a contingent of soldiers to the Gulf to join the anti-Iraq coalition, prompting much domestic criticism from a population that generally sided with Saddam Hussein. The king adroitly navigated the criticism by allowing protests, with as many as 300,000 people filling the streets of Rabat. The king's stance was rewarded with debt relief and enhanced aid from the EU, Saudi Arabia, the United States, and international financial institutions. Disturbances continued throughout 1991, with riots in April and November led by Justice and Charity (al-Adl Wal-Ihsan), a banned Islamist group.

In 1992, Hassan announced that deferred elections would be held, in part to respond to ongoing criticism from the international community about human rights. In September, a referendum approved a fourth postindependence constitution that allowed the prime minister rather than the king to distribute ministerial portfolios, although the monarch maintained final approval and control over the powerful, sovereign Ministries of Interior, Justice, Foreign Affairs, and Islamic Affairs. After several delays, legislative elections finally took place in June 1993, the first since 1984. Turnout was relatively low, with only about 63 percent of the electorate voting.

The 1993 elections provided a clear example of the system's structural bias, much like the experience in 1977 and 1984. Of the 333 seats in the *majlis*, only two-thirds (222) were elected by popular vote. Local councils, chambers of commerce, and official unions elected the remaining third of the members. This system consistently resulted in a pro-palace legislature because of the conservative tendencies of the local bodies—not to mention fraud and manipulation. In a noteworthy development, however, women were elected to the chamber for the first time: a USFP candidate from Casablanca and an Istiqlal candidate from Fez.

During this period the political system was paralyzed by *attentisme*, or stalemate. Hassan was visibly unwell and traveled to New York to receive medical treatment in 1996. In July 1995, he permitted USFP leader Fkih Basri to return after thirty years of exile. In September 1996, a new referendum for the fifth constitution since independence created a bicameral *majlis* with a directly elected Chamber of Representatives and an upper house known as the Chamber of Councilors. In turn, in November 1997 the first election under the new constitution was held, inaugurating *alternance*, or accountable, competitive government. The opposition had argued for years that if given the opportunity, it would do well in an election, and it did. In March 1998, Hassan appointed the USFP's Abderrahman Youssoufi to the post of prime minister, a move that granted the opposition some power though hardly control of policy.

The Post-Hassan Era

In the end, a full assessment of Hassan's ability to rule under *alternance* was rendered impossible by his death on July 23, 1999, and the accession to the throne of his son, King Muhammad VI. Muhammad quickly distinguished himself by presiding in a less draconian fashion than his father. Moreover, Muhammad began to nurture discussions of human rights. Most notably, he created a climate that allowed exposés of the human rights violations from the *années de plomb* (leaden years) of his father's reign. Muhammad was also dubbed the "king of the poor" because of his trips throughout the country and his willingness to wade into crowds. Some even called him "Al Jawal"—the Moroccan word for the ubiquitous cell phone—because of his high mobility. In 2002, he publicly married a commoner, an engineer from Tetouan. This was in striking contrast to his father, whose wives never appeared in public.

After September 11, 2001, however, the gradual opening began to slow, as the palace increasingly circumscribed the power of the *majlis*. To be sure, elections in September 2002 marked a significant moment in the post-Hassan era, with the Justice and Development Party (PJD) performing very well, becoming the third-largest party after the USFP and the Istiqlal Party. The PJD increased its presence from nine seats in 1997 to forty-two, despite standing in only fifty-six constituencies. Muhammad appointed Driss Jettou as prime minister; this was a striking development, as Jettou was a venerable technocrat with no formal party affiliation. Given the aforementioned exclusion of Justice and Charity, support for Islamists in the country was likely much higher than the elections indicated. Despite a few irregularities and skepticism—particularly on the part of the dismissive Spanish media—the elections were trumpeted internationally as the country's first free elections. The 2002 elections also included a national list of female candidates, guaranteeing that women would hold thirty parliamentary seats.

In turn, the political and social landscape was profoundly rocked by bombings in Casablanca on May 16, 2003, that killed forty-five people. In a royal discourse on May 29, 2003, Muhammad declared the "end of the era of leniency." Following attacks on the Atocha train station in Madrid on March 11, 2004, in which Moroccan nationals were implicated, the political system tightened still further, with antiterrorism legislation being passed later that year.

Concomitant with this tightening were two important developments. First, in January 2004 Muhammad created the Equity and Reconciliation Commission (IER) to formally investigate the human rights violations of the past. It was the first such step in the Middle East and North Africa (MENA). Criticized for its circumscribed purview, underestimation of the number of victims, and unwillingness to name perpetrators, the IER nonetheless publicly investigated rights violations from the Hassan years. It released its report in March 2006, stating that several hundred people had been illegally killed and over 9,000 subjected to human rights abuses during the reign of Hassan. It called for reform of the judicial system and compensation for victims. The event offered, perhaps, some closure for the victims and their families.

A second development was the reform of the family code, known as the *Muddawanna*. In a balancing act with conservative interests, a royal commission announced the changes in 2004 after several years of negotiation and deliberation. The new law reduced men's ability to treat their wives as property. It required a man to inform his wife that he was seeking a divorce and stipulated that he must get permission from a judge before taking a second wife. The legal age for marriage was increased from fifteen to eighteen. The implementation of the juridical reforms has been complicated because the legal system is ill-equipped to deal with and enforce the changes. Not surprisingly, conservative segments were frustrated by the developments. Yet, women's groups criticized the reforms too. Given that four out of five rural women are illiterate and relatively lacking in socioeconomic power, men's right to divorce can lead to severe deprivation and ostracism.

The September 2007 elections marked a turning point for the country in that they demonstrated a significant consolidation of electoral reforms. That said, turnout was below democratic norms; it stood at 37 percent, a sharp decline from 52 percent in the 2002 election and 58 percent in 1997. In addition, the number of spoiled ballots increased to 19 percent from 17 percent in 2002. Reasons for the low turnout and large number of spoiled ballots likely included ongoing voter disaffection, the *majlis*'s marginal position in the political system, and insufficient media coverage. In addition, legislative fraud in the 2006 municipal elections—for which the government arrested perpetrators—enhanced skepticism.

In terms of the actual outcome, the Istiqlal won 11 percent of the vote to garner fifty-two seats, an increase of four from 2002. The PJD also won 11 percent of the vote, increasing its presence by four seats to forty-six. The pro-government Popular Movement won 9 percent and increased its presence by fourteen seats to forty-one. And the National Rally of Independents earned 10 percent of the vote, resulting in thirty-nine seats. The big loser was the USFP, which lost twelve seats from 2002. It earned 9 percent of the vote to hold thirty-eight seats and left the governing coalition. The king appointed Istiqlal leader Abbas El Fassi to be the new prime minister.

In 2009, however, El Fassi appeared to have fallen out of favor, as former deputy interior minister Fouad Ali El Himma organized the Authenticity and Modernity Party (PAM) to contest municipal elections. El Himma is a close associate of the king, and PAM did well in June 2009 elections. In January 2010, there was a cabinet reshuffling, with El Fassi remaining head of government even as the king placed key associates at Interior and Justice.

Also in January 2010, King Muhammad established a new Advisory Commission on Regionalization, designed to implement plans to improve local governance. In a speech, the king emphasized the importance of the Western Sahara territory, which he called the "recovered southern provinces." The king added, "Morocco will not sit by while the enemies of our territorial integrity continue to frustrate the UN process designed to find a realistic, mutually acceptable political solution to this dispute over our provinces, on the basis of our autonomy initiative for the Moroccan Sahara."

The Arab Spring, the Moroccan Exception, and the February 20 Movement

Moroccans joined the entire world in watching the mediatized events of the uprisings in Tunisia, Egypt, and elsewhere. While convention continues to refer to an Arab Spring, there are at least two reasons why the label is awkward. One is the fact that while the monarchy and outsiders have long cast Morocco as Arab, its Tamazight identity is as strong as, if not stronger than, its Arabism. A second reason is that riots and demonstrations took place beyond the so-called Arab world: in Mozambique and Russia in the fall and in China, Greece, Uganda, the United Kingdom, and the United States across 2011. In this regard, Morocco was beset with many of the same concerns of people elsewhere in the MENA region and beyond: rising food and energy prices, broken economies, corrupt affluent classes, and autocratic rulers. One might have predicted that, given the severity of unemployment, poverty, and illiteracy, Morocco would have been far riper for turmoil than, say, Egypt or Tunisia. But the Moroccan state managed to avoid full upheaval.

As a result, much has been made of the so-called Moroccan exception—the notion that somehow Morocco is special because it managed to dodge the revolutionary bullet so evident throughout the region. Exceptionalist narratives focus on the king's charisma and legitimacy as a descendent of the Prophet and Commander of the Faithful, the eschewal of single-party government in the early years of independence, the allowance of a moderately robust press with a few starkly drawn red lines concerning the Western Sahara and the monarchy, the moderate reforms concerning Tamazight identity and the *Muddawanna* in the 2000s, and the king's willingness to explore human rights abuses under his father.

Admittedly, of course, the events were nonetheless framed as "Arab" and regional, and the Arabic language was certainly a crucial vector in the transmission of news. So, as events unfolded in Egypt, Tunisia, Yemen, Bahrain, and Libya, Moroccan society watched intently. Young, Internet-savvy Moroccans also took to protesting, although the target was not so much the regime as affluent elites. At least two Moroccans followed the lead of Tunisia's Mohamed Bouazizi and immolated themselves. By February, unrest had coalesced around the organization of a day of protest, which came to be known as the February 20 Movement. The February 20 protest was followed by smaller, regular protests that continued into 2012. The movement comprises a heterogeneous grouping that covers the spectrum from leftists and Tamazight activists to Islamists from the banned Justice and Charity Party.

In response to the protests, and in a preemptive move, Muhammad gave a royal speech on March 9, 2011, in which he established a royal commission to work on a package of reforms that would strengthen the *majlis* (with the prime minister automatically coming from the party that won the most seats in parliament), as well as deepen respect for human rights, the independence of the judiciary, equality between men and women, and the full recognition of Tamazight. The commission released its findings in June, followed by a hasty referendum on July 1, the sixth in the postindependence era. As with past referenda, the yes vote according to official figures was astoundingly high: 98.5 percent.

While the opposition was very frustrated with the process, elections scheduled for fall 2012 were moved up to November 25, 2011, resulting in a victory for the opposition PJD, which took 107 of the 395 seats in the lower house. The Istiqlal placed second with sixty seats; the National Rally of Independents ended up with fifty-two, the PAM with forty-seven, the USFP with thirty-nine, the Popular Movement with thirty-two, the Constitution Union with twenty-three, and the Progress and Socialism Party (PPS) with eighteen. The February 20 Movement and other Islamists and leftists had called for a boycott, but turnout was 45 percent, a respectable increase from the 2007 figure. Abdelilah Benkirane of the PJD became prime minister and formed a coalition government with the Istiqlal, the Popular Movement, and the PPS.

The new government faces profound social and economic challenges. In addition to the long-standing problems, a new food deficit has become exacerbated, pitting the importance of using the domestic wheat crop against the need to lift import duties. Moreover, the February 20 Movement remains in full force, continuing throughout the summer of 2012 to protest the heavy hand of the monarchy in government.

POLITICAL ENVIRONMENT

Geography

The country's physical geography is remarkably diverse, from the relatively fertile, sun-drenched Mediterranean and Atlantic coasts to the snowcapped Atlas Mountains and deserts in the east and south. The beauty of the country's natural patrimony has impressed Moroccan and foreign travelers for ages. In recent times this has been the source of crucial foreign exchange, as tourists have traveled to Morocco to explore its varied landscape.

Morocco has been plagued by chronic drought in recent decades, undermining efforts to engineer economic growth. In a country where the preponderance of the population works on the land and the government has devoted considerable resources to irrigated agriculture and hydrologically intensive, high-end tourism, the challenges of the water deficit are profound.

The country has enormous phosphate reserves—a key source of foreign exchange during periods of high commodity prices—as well as deep-sea fisheries off the Atlantic coast. The amount of hydrocarbon reserves is a "known unknown." Oil was discovered in Talsinnt in 2000, but it was determined to be not easily accessible or of high quality.

Many breathed a sigh of relief, as the country seemed to have avoided the "resource curse" that afflicts many petroleum producers.

The existence of oil reserves in the Western Sahara—as well as off the Atlantic coast—is another matter. Reserves are abundant. Yet oil-exploration contracts lack sufficient legal standing given the territory's disputed sovereignty; companies operating in the region have been targeted for protest. The US Department of Energy acknowledges that oil claims in the region are controversial, citing the pullout of most foreign firms from the region, with the exception of Kerr-McGee.

Political Culture

A primary feature of Moroccan political culture is distrust. This is visible both in the attitude of the people toward their leaders and in relations among political elites. For decades, Moroccans have viewed the political system as a coercive instrument rather than a basis for cooperative action. The inauguration of *alternance* and the accession of Muhammad VI have changed that dynamic to a certain extent, with greater scrutiny of Hassan's *années de plomb*.

A second, related feature is conspiratorial politics. Political authority is derived only secondarily from formal political offices, and the system thus lacks accepted rules by which decisions are reached. Instead, patterns of patrimonialism dominate political life. A third feature of Moroccan political life is political stalemate, or *attentisme*. Morocco's political culture facilitates the monarch's power, wherein *lèse-majesté*, or criticism of the monarchy, is expressly forbidden.

The powerful Ministry of Interior and Information controls domestic affairs. For years, the ministry was headed by Driss Basri, a confidant of Hassan's. Basri was viewed as the country's most powerful man after Hassan because he controlled such a wide array of governmental powers: police, security, human rights, media and information, electoral mechanisms, and even foreign affairs. In a celebrated move in September 1999, however, Muhammad VI dismissed Basri.

In recent years, the Ministry of Interior has remained very powerful, especially in the clampdown since the 2003 Casablanca attacks. Despite the close continuing ties between Rabat and Washington since September 11, 2001, the US State Department sharply criticized Morocco in its 2006 Human Rights Report, especially regarding press freedom. Freedom House and other international human rights organizations have similarly criticized the country's human rights record and press freedoms.

Judicial and administrative institutions reflect both French and Spanish colonial influences. The country is administratively divided into nineteen provinces and two urban prefectures, Casablanca and Rabat. The provinces are further divided into seventy-two administrative areas and communes. Each administrative area is headed by a governor, who is appointed by and responsible to the king. The Supreme Court is composed of four chambers: civil, criminal, administrative, and social. The king appoints all judges, with the advice of the Supreme Judicial Council. Moroccan courts administer a system that is based on Islamic law but strongly influenced by the French and Spanish legal systems. A separate system of courts administers the Judaic religious laws for Jewish citizens, although today there is only a small remnant of the country's once-prosperous Jewish community.

Economic Conditions

Economic growth remains uneven, albeit respectable for a lower-middle-income country. The average annual growth in gross domestic product (GDP) per capita between 2000 and 2010 was 3.8 percent. The average income per person in 2010 was $2,900, below the MENA average of $3,874 but greater than the $1,619 average for lower-middle-income countries. Half of the population is illiterate, with women's illiteracy as high as 66 percent and in rural areas as high as 80 percent. The country was ranked 130 by the United Nations Development Programme's 2011 Human Development Index.

Foreign debt as a percentage of GDP fell from a high of 112 percent in 1987 to 28 percent in 2010—a positive trend. At the same time, exports of goods and services as a percentage of GDP have increased to 33 percent, rendering the economy vulnerable to exogenous shocks. As a result, the 2008 global financial crisis and the crisis in the Eurozone have had profound reverberations in Morocco. Growth is fragile, as European and North American tourists have eschewed trips abroad and European demand for Moroccan exports has fallen sharply. Rather than the 7 to 10 percent annual growth considered necessary to reduce poverty and unemployment, projections envision an average growth rate of 3.9 percent from 2010 to 2014.

Agriculture remains the largest sector in terms of manpower, employing over half the population. Its economic importance, however, has declined since independence; it comprised only 15 percent of GDP in 2010. This decline has to do in part with land tenure and exports. Wealthy landlords own the best 10 to 15 percent of the land. Although the productivity of this sector exceeds that of subsistence farming, and despite government subsidies, agricultural exports dropped significantly throughout the 1990s. Traditional markets in Europe were limited by the EU's Common Agricultural Policy and its admission of Greece in 1981 and Spain and Portugal in 1986; the EU has become self-sufficient in citrus, olive oil, and wine, which Morocco had long exported. Intellectuals have lamented ruefully that the country enjoyed better trade ties with Europe during colonialism.

Another factor is drought. Morocco experienced some of its worst droughts in the 1970s and 1980s, but it is a perennial concern. Severe drought struck in 2000, again in 2005, and to some extent in 2007. Rains returned in 2008, contributing to the 5.7 percent growth rate that year. But growth rates fell to 4.8 percent in 2009 and 3.7 percent in 2010. Drought mostly affects subsistence farmers, particularly those cultivating more marginal lands in the south and southeast. The Intergovernmental Panel on Climate Change predicts that the Mediterranean basin will be one of the regions of the world most susceptible to climate change in the form of rising temperatures and reduced rainfall.

The principal crops grown by peasant smallholders are wheat, barley, maize, beans, and chickpeas. In addition, there is a large government-owned sugar beet sector to satisfy the domestic market's insatiable appetite for sweets and to reduce sugarcane imports. Livestock productivity and crop yields remain low, and the government imports food from the EU and the United States to meet domestic requirements. The 2004 US-Morocco Free Trade Agreement opened Morocco to US farm exports.

For its part the fishing sector offers some promise, although export markets for the main product, sardines, are highly competitive. Since the 1970s the government has sought to develop the deep-sea fishing fleet that plies the abundant Atlantic waters. In so doing, however, it has come up against the interests of Spain. European boats want to fish in Morocco's territorial waters, and sharp diplomatic disputes have occurred. In 1995 Rabat and the EU signed a fishing accord, but only after protracted dispute. After the accord expired in 2000, negotiations resumed, only to fall apart in 2001. In 2005 Rabat signed a new fishing agreement with the EU, which allowed boats to fish in territorial waters in exchange for €144 million. But this agreement was not renewed in 2011 after the European Parliament rejected a new agreement, arguing that it legitimated Moroccan claims to the Western Sahara. In addition, chronic overfishing in the world's fisheries raises questions about the long-term sustainability of the deep-sea fishing sector.

Manufacturing and industry accounted for 45 percent of GDP in 2010. The main industries are phosphoric acid and fertilizer production and oil refining. Light manufactures such as textiles and leather are growing rapidly. Most industry is concentrated in the Rabat-Casablanca region, along the western seaboard. The mining sector plays an essential role. Morocco holds three-quarters of the world's known phosphate reserves. Its National Phosphate Office has reduced the mining of phosphate rock since 1981 because of low prices on the international market.

Also worth mention is the new economic activity in the north, focused on the Tangier Mediterranean Port, hailed as the largest deep-sea port in Africa. Construction was completed in the summer of 2007, with further phases scheduled in the years to come. It is hoped that the port will dynamize not only Morocco's northern economy but the entire Maghrebi economy.

Finally, tourism remains an extremely important economic sector. The government aggressively markets a romantic destination to high-end travelers; luxurious world-class hotels and top-notch golf courses are found throughout the country. The government continues to promote tourism and has welcomed direct foreign investment in the sector. The results of this effort have been mildly disappointing in recent years. In 2005, 5.8 million tourists visited, of which 2.7 million were Moroccan expatriates returning home during the annual summer visit known as Opération Marhaba. In 2008 the figure increased to 7.8 million, of which 3.6 million were Moroccans. As noted, the global financial crisis prompted a downturn in tourism in 2009, with recovery only spotty in recent years. The country has experienced a housing boom in cities such as Marrakech, with a kind of international gentrification. Foreign investors buy and renovate traditional houses, known as *ryads,* in the old city, rendering housing prices unaffordable for locals, who have to move to suburban and exurban areas.

Fueling grievances against the economic system is the fact that a large proportion of the population is unemployed or underemployed, with estimates of urban unemployment running as high as a third of the population.

POLITICAL STRUCTURE

The Palace and Makhzen

The king is the center of the political, economic, and military system, known as the *Makhzen.* He is the supreme authority—the *emir al-mu'minin,* or "commander of the faithful"—as well as commander in chief of the armed forces. The Dar al-Mulk (Royal Palace) and the four sovereign ministries (Interior, Justice, Foreign Affairs, and Islamic Affairs) are at the core of the *Makhzen.* The king appoints ministers to the sovereign ministries.

The Alawite king's moral authority is based on his role as imam of the Islamic community. Because of his noble religious ancestry and the attendant powers ascribed to him, the Moroccan king satisfies the aspirations of rural Muslims who seek the miraculous qualities inherent in the monarch's *baraka.* Muhammad VI, like his father and grandfather, is thus deeply venerated by the population, who view him as a sharif (descendant of the Prophet) and a dispenser of God's blessing. His legitimacy as a religious leader is said to defuse the potency of political Islamism.

The monarchy's ability to manipulate rival factions—and, when necessary, eliminate them altogether—is an additional source of power. Another source is the fact that the monarch is the nation's most prominent dispenser of patronage. As head of the "economic *Makhzen,*" the royal family is the lead shareholder in the Omnium Nord Africain, a massive holding company with subsidiaries in virtually every economic sector. Using royal patronage, Muhammad balances and dominates the political and economic elite. Many in his inner circle are "engineers," young and often Anglophone technocrats trained in engineering or business abroad before returning home.

Party Structure

The country's party landscape shifts regularly. But there are some constants. On the loyalist right wing are parties known as al-Wifaq (Covenant): the Popular Movement, the Constitutional Union, the National Democratic Party (PND), and the new Authenticity and Modernity Party, founded in 2008. The MP is a Tamazight movement, founded by resistance leaders in 1958 to counter the preponderance of the Istiqlal. The PND is a party of rural notables.

Center-Right parties include the National Independent Rally (RNI), the National Popular Movement (MNP), and the new Democratic and Social Movement (MDS). The RNI was formed in 1977 and soon splintered off from the PND. Like the PND, the RNI consists of rural notables. The MNP was created in 1991, after a 1986 break with the MP, and espouses a more profound Tamazight authenticity. The MDS was created in 1996, after a break with the MNP, and seems very similar to its MNP parent, except for a greater emphasis on participatory democracy. All of the centrist and right-wing parties support the monarchy without question.

On the opposition side, there are the venerable Istiqlal, the USFP, and the Modernist Left Pole headed up by the PPS. Each is affiliated with a trade union, the USFP with the Democratic Workers Confederation (CDT) and the Istiqlal with the General Union of Moroccan Workers.

The Islamist organization Justice and Charity remains outside the Moroccan political process. The movement mixes Sufi mysticism with Salafi theology and combines it all with Muslim Brotherhood–styled social activism. Its now octogenarian leader, Abd al-Salam Yassin, was placed under house arrest throughout the 1980s and 1990s for his mocking condemnations of the monarchy as insufficiently Islamic and beholden to Western interests. In May 2000, however, Muhammad VI released Yassin. His daughter, Nadia Yassin, a former French teacher, has emerged as a forceful and controversial spokesperson in her own right. While outside the political process, Justice and Charity's followers are estimated by observers to be more numerous than those of the moderate PJD—and they are poised to enter politics if allowed.

For its part, the PJD has emerged as the leading force in the *majlis*. In the aftermath of the March 2003 bombing, the PJD took a lower profile in the September local elections. In 2004 the party elected a moderate, Saad Eddine Othmani, as its leader. Othmani was replaced by Abdelilah Benkirane in 2008. In contrast to Justice and Charity, the PJD recognizes Muhammad VI as the legitimate sovereign and—like its counterpart in Turkey with the same name—runs on a platform of social justice and transparency. In addition to the PJD, there are several smaller Islamist groups committed to nonviolent methods: al-Badil al-Hadari (Civilized Alternative), Harakat min Ajli al-Umma (Movement for the Nation), and al-Chebiba el-Islamiya el-Maghrebiya (Moroccan Islamic Youth).

Radical Islamists

Most analysts tend to place radical Islamism under the rubric of Salafiyya al-Jihadia (Jihad for Pure Islam), founded in the early 1990s by Muhammad el-Fizazi. The leader of Salafiyya is the son of a veteran of the Afghan war, Abdelwahab Rafiki, alias Abu Hafs.

Abu Hafs refers to his group as al-Sunna Wal-Jamaa (Teaching of the Prophet and the Community). Estimates of the movement's strength run to around a few thousand members; the number of sympathizers is likely much higher.

One current within the Salafist movement is al-Sirrat al-Moustakim (The Straight Path), which claimed responsibility for the 2003 Casablanca bombing. Another current is al-Takfir Wal-Hijra (Exile and Flight), headed by thirty-year-old Youssef Fikri. The groups target adherents in urban slums and use gang-like enforcement measures to discipline adherents and community members. Inflammatory literature and sermons are also used to disseminate arguments. The government has tried to meet the challenge with some efforts to fight poverty, but much of the response has been coercive. Thousands of suspected Islamist radicals have been jailed since September 11, 2001.

The Moroccan Islamic Combatant Group (MICG) remains salient as well. Tied to al-Qaida in the Islamic Maghreb (AQIM), the MICG networks are mysterious to analysts outside the intelligence community. Many speculate that there may be little formal cooperation; the groups instead have "franchised" al-Qaida's political philosophy and theology. In either case, the government has taken a resolutely hard line against radical Islamism. Morocco is often mentioned as one of the countries participating in the extraordinary US rendition program.

The establishment of Azawad in 2012 in northern Mali portends uncertainty for Morocco, as it provides a base for AQIM's operations. Alarmed predictions of AQIM's reach and influence in the region should be treated skeptically; at the same time, it would be naïve to underestimate the potential for regional instability.

The Military and Security Structure

The military, once viewed as a staunch pillar of the monarchy, has on occasion been a serious threat to the king. Although the king is the head of the Royal Armed Forces and served in that capacity for years as crown prince, the prospect that the military will remain indifferent to the profound social and economic dislocations occurring in Moroccan society can never be certain. Shortly after assuming the throne in 1999, Muhammad launched an inquiry into corruption within the armed forces, but he backed off when it became apparent that the military would not countenance such examination.

The greatly expanded size and combat experience of the army in fighting the Polisario Front add to the potential military threat to the king. Although resolution of the Western Sahara continues to elude the parties to the conflict, the "military *Makhzen*" continues to resist being diminished. Contending with demobilized military units may be a difficult source of pressure on the economy. The exact number of Moroccan troops in the Western Sahara is not known, although it is estimated at more than 100,000. According to the International Institute for Strategic Studies, the defense budget is US$2 billion, or 3.7 percent of GDP.

Despite these developments, the military will most likely remain supportive of the regime, not only because of the monarch but also because of close ties with NATO. Ties with NATO and relations with Western governments are discussed below under "Foreign Policy."

Civil Society Organizations

Important political institutions include the National Union of Moroccan Students (UNEM) and the various labor unions. Since the 1960s, the UNEM has been extensively involved in radical activities directed against the government. In recent years student activism has taken on a decidedly Islamist cast, with supporters of Yassin's Justice and Charity and other Islamist currents frequently active in protests. Students protested government policies in Casablanca in 1998 and in Marrakech in 2000. Unemployed graduate students regularly protest their status, gaining media attention and highlighting the economy's difficulties in generating employment.

The Moroccan trade union movement acquired extensive organizational conviction and solidarity as a result of its struggles against colonialism. The Moroccan Workers Union (UMT) was the sole trade union confederation until 1960, when the Istiqlal organized a rival union, the General Union of Moroccan Workers. In the late 1970s, the CDT, a socialist-oriented union with ties to the USFP, overtook the UMT in prominence and militancy.

Despite the UMT's historic role and the CDT's occasional success in opposing the government, the political and economic climate remains unreceptive to the development of a vigorous labor movement. High levels of unemployment make unions insecure and vulnerable. In the face of the March 2000 implementation of the EU Association Accord, the signing of the 2004 US-Morocco Free Trade Agreement, and Tunisia's success in maintaining a relatively cowed labor movement, the Moroccan government constantly seeks to contain its labor forces in order to make its economy attractive to investors.

The country's nongovernmental organizations proliferated during the early 1990s and have remained salient. Organizations devoted to women's rights, human rights, education, health care, AIDS, and Tamazight rights have all staked claims on the political process and the opening of the country's political system, with the February 20 Movement being the most recent and noteworthy emergence. Their political efficacy remains in question, however, and many organizations quickly become programmatically and financially exhausted. But they add up to a relatively vibrant civil society, especially in comparison with many other countries in the MENA region.

POLITICAL DYNAMICS

The Western Sahara demands special attention in any consideration of Morocco. Despite the rise of Saharawi nationalism in the 1950s and 1960s, Spain did not relinquish control until the Madrid Accord of November 14, 1975. With the accord, Spain ceded the colony to Mauritania and Morocco, setting the stage for the Green March.

Spain withdrew its last remaining troops on February 26, 1976, and the next day the Polisario Front declared the area the Saharan Arab Democratic Republic (SADR). It also initiated a guerrilla war against Morocco and Mauritania. Initially Hassan devoted his energies to crushing the Polisario, sending in troops and authorizing erection of a massive defensive sand wall to inhibit guerrilla operations. By the mid-1980s over 80,000 troops were deployed in the territory. Nevertheless, victory eluded Hassan. Algeria and Libya supported the Polisario, the former providing the group safe haven across the Algerian frontier. Libyan support ceased in 1984 with its "union" with Morocco.

In 1984, the SADR won a diplomatic victory by becoming a member of the Organization of African Unity (OAU). In 1986, the United Nations and the OAU together hosted indirect talks, with Mauritania (which had renounced its claim in 1978) and Algeria invited as observers. Although the SADR was initially successful in diplomatic terms, Morocco continued to dominate militarily. Importantly, although nearly eighty countries now recognize the SADR—most recently South Africa in 2004 and Kenya in 2005—no global power broker does so. The United States does not; nor does any member of the EU, China, or Russia.

This position enabled Hassan to balk at accepting UN Resolution 40/50 advocating direct negotiations between the SADR and Morocco. With France's ongoing, constant support, Morocco was said to have a permanent seat on the UN Security Council. In the 1980s, however, Hassan began to receive additional support from the United States. The United States and Morocco conducted joint military exercises off the coast of the Western Sahara in 1986. In 1987, the United States approved the sale to Rabat of one hundred M-48A5 tanks suitable for desert terrain. Morocco extended new walls to the Mauritanian border in the south of the territory.

By August 1988, both sides had accepted a UN plan for a cease-fire and a referendum in which the Saharawis would choose between independence and union with Morocco. The plan was delayed, primarily because the Polisario Front wanted Morocco to withdraw its troops before the vote, which Rabat refused to do. In April 1991, the Security Council authorized establishment of the UN Mission for the Referendum in Western Sahara (MINURSO) to monitor the cease-fire and balloting. Since 1991, the cease-fire has held.

Since 1991, the United Nations has tried to get both sides to agree to arrangements for a referendum. Beginning in 1997, former US secretary of state James Baker served as negotiator. Rabat, for its part, devoted its efforts to delaying a vote while consolidating its superior position on the ground. The June 2001 Baker Plan was a significant departure from previous frameworks in that it called for several years of autonomy for the territory, to be followed by a referendum in which Moroccans who had settled in the territory since 1975 would vote along with UN-approved residents. The vote would come down to a choice between independence, integration, and a "third way" (i.e., autonomy under Moroccan sovereignty). Initially, Rabat, Washington, and Paris embraced the proposal, but the "third way" received sharp criticism from Algeria and various international observers. In exasperation, Baker resigned from his efforts in 2004. Yet, while the numbers would be weighted in Morocco's favor, Rabat ultimately resumed its recalcitrance because it could not be confident that the vote would go as it wished. It argued that sovereignty was nonnegotiable.

In 2010, the UN special envoy for the Sahara, Christopher Ross, expressed frustration with the ongoing stalemate. By 2008, the United Nations had resumed its sponsorship of periodic peace talks between the parties, but with no progress whatsoever. In January 2012, Morocco joined the UN Security Council for a two-year term, leading to still further skepticism that progress could be obtained.

In sum, the question of Moroccan sovereignty over the "Southern Province" will likely remain front and center for years to come. It is the terrain on which intractable questions of decolonization, nationalism, and regional and international diplomacy are certain to play out.

FOREIGN POLICY

Foreign policy decisions are made by the king and a small group of personal advisers within the military, political, and economic *Makhzen*.

The most immediate concern appears to be Europe. Morocco's interests in the Mediterranean stem from geopolitical and economic realities as well as historical conditioning. The country's formal association with the EU dates back to 1969; in 1976, a trade and cooperation agreement gave industrial products privileged access to Europe, as well as reasonably generous financial aid protocols. In 1987, Morocco applied to join the EU, an effort quickly rejected by the European Commission. The 2000 Association Accord with the EU brought the country into still closer contact, establishing a free trade arrangement designed to liberalize trade over a twelve-year period, except, crucially, regarding agricultural commodities.

Europe's 1995 Barcelona Process was renamed Union for the Mediterranean in 2008. Morocco has held a principal position in the EU's foreign policy; it is the largest recipient of funds under the Mesures d'accompagnement (MEDA) of the Barcelona Process. Under MEDA I (1995–1999), Morocco received €660 million. For MEDA II (2000–2006), Morocco received €812 million.

Not surprisingly, France is a particularly important focus of diplomatic efforts with Europe, given the Moroccan elite's close affinity with the former metropole. Former president Jacques Chirac was a very close friend of Rabat. His successor, Nicolas Sarkozy, visited Morocco in 2007 along with French business executives to sign business contracts and jump-start efforts on the Union for the Mediterranean. The first foreign head of state received by François Hollande at the Élysée Palace after his election in May 2012 was none other than Muhammad VI. Any political differences the socialist Hollande has with Sarkozy are not evident when it comes to Morocco and, by extension, the Western Sahara.

France has traditionally viewed Morocco as a lynchpin in its *politique Africaine*. Many French senior citizens retire in Morocco. Low housing costs, perceptions of a simpler lifestyle, and the sun have all prompted such a trend. Enterprising Moroccans speak of building assisted-living communities for retirees, a potential source of foreign exchange and employment in the health-care sector.

Relations with Spain are another story. Franco and Hassan appear to have had a decent working relationship, with mutual interests in keeping their respective authoritarian structures intact. Despite some tension over competition with Spanish agriculture and fisheries, Moroccan-Spanish relations improved steadily after Franco's death in 1975. Spain is Morocco's second-largest trading partner, after France. Spanish-Moroccan relations were cemented by Hassan's visit to Spain in September 1989 and by the signing of a friendship treaty in 1991 during Spanish king Juan Carlos's visit to Rabat. In addition, Madrid and Rabat have collaborated on such projects as underwater electricity links, financial-sector ties, and the Maghreb-Europe Gas (MEG) pipeline. The MEG runs from Algeria through Morocco, across the Strait of Gibraltar, to Spain and Portugal. Gas from the pipeline is being used to power an independent power project in Tahaddart, near Tangier.

On the political front, however, Spanish public opinion has sharply criticized Morocco on the Western Sahara. And as Spain began to experience dynamic economic growth in the 1990s and "reborder" itself as part of Europe, a condescending attitude toward Morocco deepened. For Spanish political culture, Morocco is a foil that represents the past: absolutist, backward, undeveloped. By the late 1990s, tension had become quite palpable on an array of issues: drugs; access to deep-sea fisheries; security; the status of Ceuta, Melilla, and islands along Morocco's Mediterranean coast; and, above all, immigration. Tensions came to a head in July 2002 when six Moroccan gendarmes set up tents and raised a flag on Leyla, a small, uninhabited island three hundred meters off the coast near Ceuta. In response, Spanish warships deployed special forces and removed the police. Morocco had claimed that its initial action was necessary to fight clandestine migration and drug running to Spain. The Spanish government, however, claimed that the island, known to the Spanish as Perejil, was one of its possessions. After lengthy negotiations involving US Secretary of State Colin Powell, the Spanish forces withdrew, leaving the island once again uninhabited—except by goats and birds.

The election of José Luis Rodriguez Zapatero in March 2004—which removed José María Aznar's Popular Party from office a few days after the Atocha train bombings—restored greater comity between the two countries. In September 2005, efforts by non-Moroccan migrants to scale fences in Ceuta and Melilla returned the enclaves to the international news and exacerbated tensions. Immigration remains an issue that transcends the domestic-international divide. Europe's demand for immigrant labor is facilitated by restrictive policies that depress wages. For Morocco, emigration provides a valuable opportunity to obtain crucial remittances from overseas workers. That said, although the Popular Party returned to power in November 2011 under the leadership of Mariano Rajoy, relations continue to trend upward.

With respect to the MENA region, Morocco has long played a provocative role. In addition to its rocky relationship with Qaddafi during his rule, Morocco has a robust diplomatic presence in the region. Viewed as moderate by Washington, Morocco has had relatively close diplomatic relations with Israel, even in the face of full-throated popular criticism of Israeli occupation of the West Bank and Gaza. Fully one-fifth of the Israeli population is of Moroccan origin, and efforts to dynamize trade and investment between the countries wax and wane. Further east, Morocco has had close diplomatic ties with the region's monarchies, especially Jordan as well as the Sunni monarchies in the Gulf. In May 2011, the Gulf Cooperation Council (GCC) extended invitations to Morocco and Jordan to join the regional grouping—a geographically bizarre move, but a geostrategically savvy one on the part of the region's autocratic monarchies.

The 1990–1991 Gulf crisis, the Israeli-Palestinian conflict, and the 2003 Iraq War highlighted the stark discontinuity that exists between elite and popular attitudes about the government's pro-Western orientation. In 1991 mass demonstrations in support of Iraq were held in major cities. Nonetheless, the United States and Europe rewarded Morocco's contribution of a contingent of 6,000 soldiers to the anti-Iraq coalition with military aid and economic assistance. In September 1991, Hassan traveled to Washington, DC, and signed a $250-million agreement securing twenty military aircraft. Shortly after the Algerian military crackdown in January 1992 nullifying the election victory of Algeria's Islamic Salvation Front, a team of US military experts visited Rabat. Throughout the 1990s and into the first decade of the twenty-first century, Morocco deftly played the "security card," requesting support for its economy and society in order to preclude the emergence of an Islamist threat. Morocco also has bought commercial aircraft from the United States. In 1993, Royal Air Maroc ordered twelve Boeing aircraft worth $525 million, despite heavy pressure from France to buy its Airbus. In 2001 Morocco agreed to purchase four Airbus aircraft, but only after it had purchased twenty-two Boeing planes in 2000.

Since the early 1980s the Royal Armed Forces have maintained close collaboration with NATO, conducting bilateral exercises with France, Spain, and the United States and securing much-needed military assistance. In a celebrated move in the summer of 2004, the George W. Bush administration proffered non-NATO ally status, elevating the country to an august club that includes Australia, Egypt, Israel, Japan, Jordan, and Pakistan. The designation entitles Rabat to priority delivery of defense matériel and access to generous loans. Additionally, the country is a player in Washington's Trans-Sahara Counter Terrorism Initiative.

In regional affairs, the monarchy has also long sought to play a mediating role in Arab politics, hosting a number of important Arab summits. Hassan's July 1986 meeting with Israeli prime minister Shimon Peres in the mountain resort town of Ifrane was the first public meeting between Arab and Israeli leaders since the 1981 assassination of Egyptian president Anwar Sadat. Despite harsh criticism from Algeria, Libya, and Syria, however, Egypt, Jordan, the Palestine Liberation Organization (PLO), and other moderate Arab states backed the move. In January 1989, Syria resumed ties broken off after the

Peres-Hassan meeting. Morocco's relations with Egypt also accelerated after Egypt's readmission into Arab League affairs in 1989. Hassan proudly hosted the 1989 Arab League summit in Casablanca.

In the 1990s, Hassan sought to persuade Arab countries, particularly Saudi Arabia, to develop ties with Israel in the context of the peace process. In a striking illustration, he welcomed the Israeli leadership to Rabat the day after the September 1993 PLO-Israeli accord was signed. Morocco was keen throughout the 1990s to encourage Israeli investment in the Moroccan economy, particularly from the large population of Israeli citizens of Moroccan descent. After the collapse of Palestinian-Israeli peace negotiations in the fall of 2000 and the emergence of the second Palestinian intifada, however, diplomatic and economic relations between Morocco and Israel stagnated. In March 2005, relations improved somewhat, as the king met with Israeli deputy prime minister Peres.

Since 1989, some of Morocco's greatest efforts in the region have been devoted to the establishment of the Arab Maghreb Union (UMA). An agreement setting up the UMA was signed in February 1989 in Marrakech. Morocco's energies in the early years of the UMA were devoted to improving relations with Algeria and to a lesser extent Mauritania in connection with the conflict in the Western Sahara—to little avail. In 1994, borders with Algeria were closed again, and relations have remained deeply strained. Even the meeting between the king and Algerian head of state Abdelaziz Bouteflika at the Arab League in March 2005 did little to diminish skepticism. In October 2005, after the conflagration at the fences at Ceuta and Melilla, Morocco accused Algeria of funneling sub-Saharan migrants to the enclaves. Relations with Tunisia's Zine al-Abidine Ben Ali were cordial, if not warm. Prime Minister Benkirane has established good relations with Tunisia's new prime minister, Hamadi Jebali. Qaddafi was always regarded with suspicion. But in August 2012, Benkirane also welcomed Libya's new prime minister, Abdul Raheem al-Keeb, to Rabat.

BIBLIOGRAPHY

Pre-independence Morocco is analyzed in Robin Bidwell, *Morocco Under Colonial Rule* (London: Frank Cass, 1973); Edmund Burke, *Prelude to Protectorate in Morocco* (Chicago: University of Chicago Press, 1976); and Janet Abu-Lughod, *Rabat: Urban Apartheid in Morocco* (Princeton, NJ: Princeton University Press, 1980). Richard Pennell, *Morocco Since 1830: A History* (New York: New York University Press, 2001); Michel Le Gall, "The Historical Context," in *Polity and Society in Contemporary North Africa*, ed. I. William Zartman and Mark Habeeb, 3–18 (Boulder, CO: Westview Press, 1993); and Benjamin Stora, "Algeria and Morocco: The Passions of the Past, Representations of the Nation That Unite and Divide," in *Nation, Society and Culture in North Africa*, ed. James McDougall, 14–33 (London: Frank Cass, 2003), are valuable. A French-language classic is Abdallah Laroui, *Les origines sociales et culturelles du nationalisme marocain (1830–1912)* (Casablanca: Centre Culturel Arabe, 1993).

For analyses of Morocco's ostensible exceptionalism in the context of the events of 2011, see Bruce Maddy-Weitzman and Daniel Zisenwine, *Contemporary Morocco: State, Politics, and Society Under Mohammed VI* (New York: Routledge, 2012). For analyses of the political system, see James Sater, *Civil Society and Political Change in Morocco* (New York: Routledge, 2007); John Entelis, *Culture and Counterculture in Moroccan Politics* (Boulder, CO: Westview Press, 1996); and Abdellah Hammoudi, *Master and Disciple* (Chicago: University of Chicago Press, 1997). John Waterbury, *The Commander of the Faithful* (New York: Columbia University Press, 1970), is a classic work on the nature of elite politics. Ellen Lust-Okar, *Structuring Conflict in the Arab World* (London: Cambridge University Press, 2005), compares the country to Jordan. A classic French-language work is Remy Levau, *Le fellah marocain: Défenseur du trône* (Paris: Presses de la Fondation Nationale des Sciences Politiques, 1985).

For controversial treatments of the monarchy, see Gilles Perrault, *Notre ami le roi* (Paris: Gallimard, 1992); Malika Oufkir and Michéle Fitoussi, *Stolen Lives: Twenty Years in a Desert Jail* (New York: Hyperion, 2001); and Christine Daure-Serfaty, *Letter from Morocco*, trans. Paul Raymond Côté and Constantina Mitchell (Lansing: Michigan State University Press, 2003). Hassan II's own perspective, as well as information about political life, is presented in his memoirs, *Hassan II: La mémoire d'un roi, entretiens avec Eric Laurent* (Paris: Plon, 1993). Abdeslam Maghraoui, "From Symbolic Legitimacy to Democratic Legitimacy: Monarchic Rule and Political Reform in Morocco," *Journal of Democracy* 12, no. 1 (2001): 73–86, is perceptive.

For considerations of the politics of human rights and democratic reforms set in a comparative context, see Susan Slyomovics, *The Performance of Human Rights in Morocco* (Philadelphia: University of Pennsylvania Press, 2005); Susan Waltz, "The Politics of Human Rights in the Maghreb," in *Islam, Democracy and the State in North Africa*, ed. John Entelis, 75–92 (Bloomington: Indiana University Press, 1997); and Sieglinde Gränzer, "Changing Human Rights Discourse: Transnational Advocacy Networks in Tunisia and Morocco," in *The Power of Human Rights*, ed. Thomas Risse et al., 109–133 (Cambridge: Cambridge University Press, 1999).

For analyses of Islam, see Henry Munson, *Religion and Power in Morocco* (New Haven, CT: Yale University Press, 1993); François Burgat, *The Islamic Movement in North Africa*, trans. William Dowell (Austin: University of Texas Press, 1993); Dale Eickelman, *Knowledge and Power in Morocco* (Princeton, NJ: Princeton University Press, 1985); and Elaine Combs-Schilling, *Sacred Performances in Morocco* (Chicago: University of Chicago Press, 1989). Accounts of Morocco's Jewish community are provided in Emily Gottreich, *The Mellah of Marrakesh: Jewish and Muslim Space in Morocco's Red City* (Bloomington: Indiana University Press, 2007). Rahma Bourquia and Susan Gilson Miller, eds., *In the Shadow of the Sultan* (Cambridge, MA: Harvard University Press, 1999), offers an array of discerning essays.

Studies on the role of women include Fatima Mernissi, *Dreams of Trespass* (New York: Addison-Wesley, 1994); Deborah Kapchen, *Gender on the Market* (Philadelphia:

University of Pennsylvania Press, 1998); Alison Baker, *Voices of Resistance* (Albany: State University of New York Press, 1998); Mounira Charrad, *States and Women's Rights* (Berkeley: University of California Press, 2001); Laurie Brand, *Women, the State, and Political Liberalization* (New York: Columbia University Press, 1998); and Loubna Skalli-Hanna, *Through a Local Prism: Gender, Globalization and Identity in Moroccan Women's Magazines* (New York: Rowman & Littlefield, 2006). Katherine Hoffman, *We Share Walls: Language, Land and Gender in Berber Morocco* (New York: Wiley-Blackwell, 2008), examines crucial dimensions of Tamazight politics too.

Analyses of the country's economic situation are available in Will Swearingen, *Moroccan Mirages* (Princeton, NJ: Princeton University Press, 1986); Serge Leymarie and Jean Tripier, *Maroc: Le prochain dragon?* (Casablanca: Eddif, 1992); and Gregory White, *On the Outside of Europe Looking In: A Comparative Political Economy of Tunisia and Morocco* (Albany: State University of New York Press, 2001). An intriguing book is Muhammad VI's doctoral dissertation, Mohamed Ben El-Hassan Alaoui, *La cooperation entre l'Union Européenne et les pays du Maghreb* (Paris: Éditions Nathan, 1994). Morocco's position in the global economy is treated by Shana Cohen, *Searching for a Different Future: The Rise of a Global Middle Class in Morocco* (Durham, NC: Duke University Press, 2005). Its experience with immigration is engaged by Laurie Brand, *Citizens Abroad: Emigration and the State in the Middle East and North Africa* (New York: Cambridge University Press, 2006), and David McMurray, *In and Out of Morocco: Smuggling and Migration in a Frontier Boomtown* (Minneapolis: University of Minnesota Press, 2000).

The war with the Polisario Front is carefully documented and discussed by John Damis, *Conflict in Northwest Africa* (Stanford, CA: Hoover Institution Press, 1983), and Stephen Zunes and Jacob Mundy, *Western Sahara: War, Nationalism and Conflict Irresolution* (Syracuse, NY: Syracuse University Press, 2010).

Finally, Marvine Howe, *Morocco* (New York: Oxford University Press, 2005), provides an accessible overview of the country. Brian Edwards, *Morocco Bound* (Durham, NC: Duke University Press, 2005), offers a stimulating analysis of America's cultural and political relationship with the Maghreb from World War II until the 1970s.

Useful websites include the government's press agency (www.map.ma/en) and official website (www.maroc.ma/PortailInst/An/home). The National Company for Radio and Television (www.snrt.ma) began a website in the early 2000s devoted to Moroccans living abroad; it streams daily news clips in Spanish, Amazight, French, and Moroccan Arabic. The pro-government *Le matin du Sahara* is available at www.lematin.ma. For news within Morocco from a more critical perspective, *Tel quel* is available online at www.telquel-online.com. *Morocco News Line* (www.morocconewsline.com) has interesting content.

Several parties have their own newspapers. The Istiqlal publishes news in *Al Alam* (www.alalam.ma). The USFP's news is available in French online at www.libe.ma.

L'Economiste is an independent weekly available at www.leconomiste.com. *Al-Sabah* is also independent, at www.assabah.press.ma. Finally, the official TV station 2M is available at www.2m.ma. Radio Méditerranée Internationale is a Tangiers-based radio station that broadcasts online at www.medi1.com; it plays an eclectic mix of music (African, Middle Eastern, European, and American) and broadcasts official news in Arabic and French.

16

PEOPLE'S DEMOCRATIC REPUBLIC OF ALGERIA

Azzedine Layachi

HISTORICAL BACKGROUND

Algeria's political history is both a reflection and a product of its struggle for national identity, a struggle made difficult by the pervasive influence of foreign invaders. Invaded in the early seventh century by the Arabs, Algeria in the twenty-first century reflects both the Arab tradition and the culture of the indigenous Berber (Tamazight) tribes. Its central location on the Mediterranean, making it an outpost for piracy until well into the eighteenth century, has led it to absorb many other cultural traditions. People of French, Greek, Italian, and Spanish descent have constituted a substantial part of the Algerian population throughout its history.

Until the sixteenth century, the Maghreb region of North Africa consisted of a large number of autonomous and independent tribes. The Berbers are its oldest inhabitants. The Phoenicians established themselves there in the 1100s BCE, followed by the Romans in 146 BCE and the Vandals in 439 CE. In 533 Algeria was annexed by the Byzantine Empire, and in the seventh century the Arabs conquered it and made it part of the Arab-Islamic Empire. After being ruled by several Arab-Islamic dynasties, Algeria in 1518 became part of the Ottoman Empire, which united it in a loose configuration of tribes and protected it against the imperial ambitions of the Europeans. In 1830 Algeria was conquered by the French, who controlled it until 1962.

Throughout recent centuries, the Arab-Islamic tradition served as a powerful unifying tool in Algeria's struggle against foreign domination, most notably in the war for independence against France from 1954 to 1962. Nonetheless, the integrationist policy pursued by France heavily instilled Algeria with French values and culture and is partially responsible for the nature of contemporary Algerian politics, which is split between Western-oriented elites and the masses, who identify more with their Arab, Berber, and Islamic cultures. Algerian political culture and tradition continue to reflect the impact of these diverse traditions and their varied effects on the country's history.

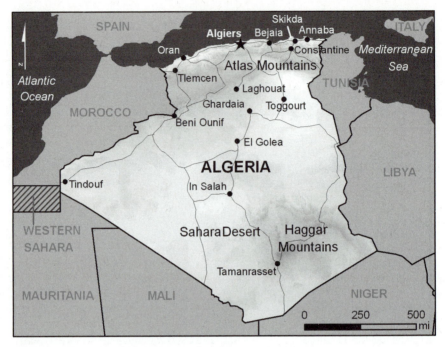

Democratic and Popular Republic of Algeria

France is often credited with the definition and consolidation of Algeria's modern state, but elements of statehood already existed under the Ottoman Empire. It took France more than forty years to conquer and subdue the whole country, and its "civilizing mission" dramatically transformed the entire political and economic structure of the region.

In colonial Algeria the European settlers were mostly peasants, working-class people, army officers, and bureaucrats who profited from the prosperous arable land along the coast. Within fifty years of French occupation, more than 150,000 Europeans had settled in Algeria, and the indigenous population had lost its independence, its freedom, and most of its land through seizure, expropriation, and property laws favoring Europeans. Moreover, by 1900 more than 3 million natives had died from mass repression and disease. France's "total colonialism" policy engendered antagonism among the inhabitants and gave rise to a nationalist movement.

The Nationalist Struggle

From 1830 to about 1870, traditional Algerian nationalists resisted colonial rule. The most prominent leader of that era was Amir Abd al-Qadir, who set about establishing a

Muslim state in all land in the interior not occupied by the French. However, he had been imprisoned and sent into exile in Syria by 1847, and all Algerian territory was soon firmly under French control. In the 1850s the French government declared the territory part of France, and Algerians officially became French subjects, though not citizens. The extension of French authority triggered more nationalist revolts in the 1870s, but these were suppressed and followed by more land confiscations, onerous taxes, and tighter control of the indigenous people. These and other punitive actions were intended to terrorize Algerians into submission and procure land and money for colonization. French atrocities were documented in several eyewitness accounts and in reports such as one issued by a French royal commission in 1883 that stated,

> We tormented, at the slightest suspicion and without due process, people whose guilt still remains more than uncertain. . . . We massacred people who carried passes, cut the throats, on a simple suspicion, of entire populations which proved later to be innocent. . . . [Many innocent people were tried just because] they exposed themselves to our furor. Judges were available to condemn them and civilized people to have them executed. . . . In a word, our barbarism was worse than that of the barbarians we came to civilize, and we complain that we have not succeeded with them![1]

Early Algerian resistance movements, such as Jeunesse Algérienne and Féderation des Elus Musulmans, wanted full assimilation and the integration of Algerians into the French community without surrender of their Muslim identity. (Existing laws required Muslims to renounce Islamic law in favor of the French civil code.) However, when the demand for equality with Europeans in Algeria remained unanswered and reformist efforts became irrelevant, a number of parties called for independence in the 1920s. In early 1954 the Comité Révolutionnaire d'Unité et d'Action (CRUA) was created by dissidents from earlier movements, ex-soldiers in the French army, and miscellaneous groups of dedicated men disillusioned with the French administration and unafraid of violence. In October 1954 CRUA was transformed into a political organization, the Front de Libération Nationale (FLN), and its military arm, the Armée de Libération Nationale (ALN).

On November 1, 1954, the FLN issued a proclamation calling on all Algerians to rise and fight for their freedom. The revolution had begun. A provisional government was formed in 1958, but fighting continued until a cease-fire agreement was signed at Evian, France, on March 19, 1962. The Evian Accords stipulated a national referendum on independence that was to include both European colonists and indigenous Algerians. On July 1 the overwhelming majority voted for independence, and Algeria officially became independent on July 5, 1962.

PEOPLE'S DEMOCRATIC REPUBLIC OF ALGERIA

Capital city	Algiers
Chief of state, 2012	President Abdelaziz Bouteflika
Head of government, 2012	Prime Minister Abdelmalek Sellal
Political parties (seats in most recent election, 2012)	National Liberation Front (221), National Democratic Rally (70), Green Algeria Alliance (47), Socialist Forces Front (21), Workers Party (17), Front for Justice and Development (7), Algerian Popular Movement (6), New Dawn Party (5), Change Front (4), National Party for Solidarity and Development (4), other (41), independents (19)
Ethnic groups	Arab-Berber (99%), European (less than 1%)
Religious groups	Sunni Muslim (99%), Christian and Jewish (1%)
Export partners, 2011	United States (23.3%), Spain (12.2%), Canada (9.5%), France (9.5%), Brazil (5.4%), Netherlands (5.4%), Germany (4.3%), Italy (4.1%)
Import partners, 2011	France (18.5%), China (10.4%), Italy (9.5%), Spain (8%), Germany (4.5%)

Postindependence Algeria

Soon after independence, serious divisions within the nationalist leadership and rank and file threatened the success of the revolution and left a weak organization to lead the country. The absence of a unifying revolutionary ideology, the lack of an uncontested leader, and the factional fighting that had characterized the revolutionary years carried over into the postindependence period. The tactical unity that had marked the FLN's efforts for independence broke down, and a vicious power struggle began. The three major contestants were the Algerian provisional government, the *wilayat* command councils, and the external army (ALN). Factional rivalries remained an intrinsic feature of Algeria's postindependence politics.

On September 26, 1962, the Algerian National Assembly elected Ahmed Ben Bella premier of the new Democratic and Popular Republic of Algeria. His government was formed from the ranks of the military and close personal and political allies. A new constitution made the president military commander in chief, head of state, and head of government. It also preserved the hegemony of the FLN as the single political party.

The most pressing task of the new government was to restore normality to the war-torn country. The mass exodus of Europeans had caused a severe shortage of highly skilled workers, technicians, educators, and property-owning entrepreneurs; many people had lost their jobs after their French employers left.

The concentration of power in the hands of Ben Bella caused factionalism within the leadership to resurface. Ben Bella owed his position to his legacy as "historic chief of the revolution." He had been a key figure in the struggle against French colonialism and spent several years in French prisons. However, in postindependence Algeria, his inability to manage the various rivalries and controversies facing his regime, his ouster of traditional leaders, his repeated attacks on the Union Générale des Travailleurs Algériens (UGTA), and his failure to transform the FLN into an effective mass party eventually led to his ouster. He was overthrown on June 19, 1965, in a bloodless coup by Colonel Houari Boumediene, who had helped put him in office in 1962.

The political transition was smooth and efficient. All political power was transferred to Boumediene and his military-dominated Council of the Revolution, which was the only functioning national political institution. The constitution and the National Assembly were suspended, and Boumediene was named president, head of government, and minister of defense. He relied on the support of the mujahideen (veterans of the war of independence) and a technocratic elite drawn partially from the military. The new regime promised to reestablish the principles of the revolution, end corruption and personal abuses, eliminate internal divisions, and build a socialist economy based on industrialization and comprehensive agrarian reform.

A new national charter, approved by referendum in June 1976, reaffirmed Algeria's socialist orientation, recognized the FLN as the only legal party, and implicitly maintained the authoritarian system. A new constitution, approved by referendum in November 1976, reestablished the national legislature (the Assemblée Populaire Nationale). A month later, Boumediene was elected president with more than 95 percent of the vote on a single-candidate ballot. He was head of state and government, commander in chief, minister of defense, and secretary-general of the FLN. In the parliamentary elections of February 1977, all candidates were FLN members. The diverse membership of the new assembly and its high proportion of industrial and agricultural workers were lauded as the final steps in the creation of a socialist state.

Boumediene died suddenly in late 1978 of a rare kidney ailment. His legacy included a consolidated state, a stable political system, a rapidly industrializing economy, an extensive state-centered socialist program, and an expanding petroleum and gas export industry. He also left a political vacuum. His charismatic leadership and political acumen were very much responsible for Algeria's economic and political development during the 1970s. Rabah Bitat, the National Assembly president, was named interim president until a special FLN congress, following the army's recommendation, selected Colonel Chadli Bendjedid as presidential candidate. He was elected to office in January 1979.

Through a policy of "change within continuity," President Bendjedid consolidated his power and took full control of the state, party, and military apparatus. By the end of 1984 he had completed a process of "de-Boumedienization," firmly secured his position and powers, and consolidated state authority. Reelected in 1985, he faced many challenges, including a declining economy due to the inefficiency of oversized industrial complexes, neglect of the agricultural sector, rapid population growth, increasing unemployment, and a sharp drop in energy prices. In response, Bendjedid initiated economic liberalization, which included a shift in domestic investment away from heavy industry toward agriculture, light industry, and consumer goods. State enterprises were broken up into smaller units, and several small state-owned firms were privatized. Subsidies were reduced, and price controls were lifted. The fiscal deficit was attacked by cutting government spending, and an important anticorruption campaign was launched. Other changes included opening the economy to limited foreign investment, expanding and revitalizing the private sector, shifting away from the Soviet Union toward the West in strategic considerations, and lowering Algeria's once high profile in global and Third World affairs. These policies allowed Bendjedid to eliminate much of the old guard opposition still loyal to Boumediene's policies.

Bendjedid's economic reforms exacerbated an already dismal situation. They increased unemployment, raised prices, and reduced industrial output. The upper class profited from economic liberalization while the burden of reform fell mostly on the masses. A wide generation gap increased between the elites, who based their legitimacy on their war credentials, and the masses, 70 percent of whom were under the age of thirty and had no memory of the independence war. By the late 1980s Algeria was highly polarized.

In the first week of October 1988, the crisis exploded amid the most violent public demonstrations since independence. Weeks of strikes and work stoppages were followed by six days of violent riots in several cities, targeting city halls, police stations, post offices, state-owned cars, and supermarkets—anything seen to represent the regime and the FLN. It was a demonstration against the leadership, corruption, declining living standards, increasing unemployment, food shortages, and persistent inequality and alienation. The riots were quickly suppressed by the military, and a state of siege was declared. Hundreds of rioters were killed.

On October 10, President Bendjedid promised new political reforms, which were approved in a referendum on November 3 and embodied in a constitutional amendment approved in a referendum in February 1989. The reforms included the separation of party and state, restructuring of executive and legislative authority, strengthening of presidential power, elimination of the ideological commitment to socialism, free local and national elections, freedom of association, and a reduced role for the military in politics.

These riots and the resulting reforms constituted the most important changes in postindependence Algeria. This was later termed as the "Algerian Spring," in relation to the

2011 Arab Spring that happened many years later across the Arab world. The political system and ruling elite were severely challenged and shaken by the sudden political mobilization of society. Throughout the 1990s, several armed groups contested the legitimacy of the state and sought to overthrow it. Furthermore, the state, bankrupted by failed economic policies, reluctantly turned to International Monetary Fund (IMF)–sponsored structural-adjustment and neoliberal reforms. During that same period, socioeconomic conditions worsened even further, due to the combined effects of the internal war and structural adjustment. Relative peace and stability had returned by early 2000, but the challenges remain important, and many have not yet been addressed.

POLITICAL ENVIRONMENT

Algeria is located in the center of the Maghreb region. It is only a few hundred miles from the southern coast of France and even closer to Spain and Italy. Its strategic importance stems from several factors, including its vast territory (it is the second-largest country in Africa, after Sudan), linking sub-Saharan Africa to the Mediterranean; its 1,200 kilometers of Mediterranean shoreline; its vast petroleum and gas reserves; and its important mineral resources, including phosphate, coal, iron, lead, uranium, and zinc.

Algeria's 91,935 square miles of land is 85 percent desert. Two ranges of the Atlas Mountains divide it into three regions: the Tell, along the Mediterranean lowlands on the coast; the High Plateau, south of the Tell and north of the Sahara; and the Sahara, which is the largest region. Only 3.2 percent of Algeria's land is arable, located mostly in the northern lowlands.

The Tell region has mild, rainy winters and hot, dry summers, though the coast is quite humid. On the High Plateau, summers are hot and dry, and winters are colder, with some rain. Snow falls regularly on some mountains in the winter. The Sahara is hot by day and cool at night. In the spring, a hot, dry wind from the south, the sirocco, blows across the desert and causes strong sandstorms. Rainfall is rare in the Sahara, and some desert areas may not see rain for up to two decades.

More than three-fourths of Algeria's 37 million citizens live in northern cities and towns. The rest live in the desert. The population is young, with 25.4 percent under fifteen years of age and 70 percent below thirty. Most Algerians are Muslims of Arab-Berber stock. Arabic is the official language, though French is widely spoken and used in business. In 2004, under pressure from Berber militants, the government made the Berber language (Tamazight) a second national language. Berbers live throughout North Africa, with the heaviest concentrations in Morocco and Algeria. Their presence in North Africa goes back 4,000 years. While most Berbers were "Arabized" and converted to Islam following the Arab-Muslim invasions of the seventh and eleventh centuries, many have maintained the Berber language and cultural traditions. In postindependence Algeria, ethnicity became politicized as a result of the state's control over culture and language, its imposition of Arabic as the sole official language, and its repression of minority culture and language.

Distinctive Political and Cultural Factors

Extensive "Arabization" programs and the masses' identification with Islam and the Arab ethnos also conflict with the elites' secular outlook and ideology. Some of this tension dates from the colonial era, when the French used secularization to "divide and conquer." The elite-mass divide remains a constant source of hostility and mistrust that reflects historical experience and cultural and ideological values.

One consequence of this is the political and military leaders' pervasive lack of trust in the masses. That distrust reappeared in response to the emergence of opposition parties in 1989. In addition, personal rivalries and clashes among the leaders themselves have long substituted for legitimate political discourse. Political ambitions are served better by personal loyalties than by purely political objectives and opinions.

Despite the persistence of these elite attitudes, tolerance for limited "legitimate" dissent and discourse has gradually emerged. Since the late 1980s, the leadership has increasingly recognized the validity of popular participation and political discussion. In the 1980s and early 1990s, remarkably open and candid debates occurred over the National Charter (ideological roadmap) and the restoration of local and national representative legislatures, evolving into a radical liberalization program that permitted the emergence of competitive political parties. Although tolerance for opposition may be only superficial, achieving legitimacy has become increasingly important, even if this means including the opposition.

An even more paradoxical feature of Algerian political culture is an innate distrust of those in power. Tolerance for rebellion and sporadic violence, however, sometimes conflicts with more conformist attitudes about appropriate behavior. The revolutionary experience and authoritarian leadership resulted in a strange dichotomy between populism and centralized rule. On the one hand, the colonial and war experiences exerted a profound impact on perceptions of the proper role of government—the need for a strong, centralized state to achieve economic and political development. On the other hand, Algerian political culture remains strongly committed to the populism that fueled the revolution. Algerian populism is a belief in the will of the people, a belief that in part subsumes the purely political. It places justice and morality above all other norms and emphasizes the importance of a direct relationship between the leadership and the people. This relationship, which is not dependent on intermediary political structures, accounts for the phenomenal success of the charismatic leadership of Boumediene.

Although there appears to be more commitment to the rhetoric and symbolism of nationalism and socialism than to their substance, most policies appeal heavily to nationalism to justify interventionist policies and government actions. The entire revolutionary period looms large in the minds of Algerians and reinforces the nationalist cause. The preservation of national unity and of the Algerian nation supersedes all other commitments and affiliations. In fact, the military leadership has used the commitment to national unity since 1992 to screen opposition groups for legalization. The 1989 constitution legalized many political parties on the condition that they never "violate national unity, the integrity of the territory, the independence of the country or the sovereignty of the people" (Article 40).

Algeria is a Muslim country with a primarily secular state. Islam is part of the cultural and political tradition dating back at least to the independence war, when the revolutionary rhetoric of the FLN drew upon the unifying force of religion to strengthen national cohesion and opposition to colonial rule. Islam directly contributed to a uniquely Algerian form of socialism under Boumediene and a conservative political outlook. Conservative policies regarding personal, family, religious, and moral affairs have predominated, despite sweeping secular and modernizing policies in the economic sphere. The populist Islam that arose in the 1980s and 1990s in virtually every segment of Algerian society finds its roots in the nation's conservative and traditional mass political culture.

Economic Conditions

Upon assuming office in 1965, President Boumediene began an extensive industrialization program and established government control over most, if not all, foreign trade, manufacturing, retail, agriculture, utilities, and banking. All major foreign business interests and most domestically owned businesses were nationalized. By the early 1970s, almost 90 percent of the industrial sector and more than 70 percent of the industrial workforce were under state control.

From 1970 to 1973, nearly 45 percent of capital investment was in the capital-intensive industrial sector, about 40 percent went to social and economic infrastructure, and only 15 percent went to agriculture. The "Agrarian Revolution" aimed to create a system of cooperatives. However, with insufficient funding and infrastructure, agriculture declined as a percentage of gross national product.

In the second four-year plan (1974–1977), the agricultural sector and small to mid-sized industries were encouraged, but the emphasis on heavy industry remained unchallenged. However, due to poor design, many large-scale industrialization projects, instead of providing the impetus for national development, eventually became a source of economic drain. Industrialization was driven more by nationalist sentiments than by considerations of economic efficiency. Falling energy prices in the 1980s left Algeria with substantial deficits and an underdeveloped agricultural sector, which led to frequent food shortages, dependence on food imports, and urban migration.

President Bendjedid's economic reforms aimed at breaking down the massive state enterprises into manageable and efficient entities, with the hope that gradually removing restrictions would help the private sector grow. These early reforms were motivated more by pragmatism and administrative concerns than by a genuine commitment to liberalization.

In 1986, economic reformers recognized the need to prepare for a postpetroleum era and include the foreign sector in Algeria's economic revitalization. Foreign investment had up to then been strongly circumscribed or prohibited outright, as it was considered a threat to the country's independence. Restrictions on both foreign and domestic investment were loosened, money and credit laws were restructured, contract laws were revised, the central bank was given full independence, and a system of banks specializing in trade finance and capital investment was established. The state started disengaging from the economy, making significant progress toward a market-driven economy.

Despite these changes, the economic crisis deepened, threatening political stability. High unemployment, urbanization, an unbalanced industrial sector (concentrated mostly on heavy industries), highly polarized and dualistic economic conditions, and rapidly declining export revenue eroded the state's welfare capacities and its ability to maintain security and stability. A massive foreign debt, unpredictable global prices, and a high level of external dependence (on both food imports and petroleum-product exports) left the country dangerously vulnerable.

Reform failure and a sharp drop in hydrocarbon export earnings in the late 1980s worsened the economic situation and hindered the state's ability to finance generous services and subsidies. As the state retreated from more areas, a growing black market made up for the empty shelves of the state distribution networks, corruption and private appropriations of state funds by some officials multiplied, and political and social challenges remained unchecked. Socioeconomic conditions were made even worse by the political instability that followed the cancellation of elections and the overthrow of Bendjedid in January 1992. The resulting conflict disrupted reform attempts, damaged economic infrastructure, hindered internal and external business relations, and stimulated population movements from the areas affected the most by political violence. It was in this context that the government reluctantly opted for a structural-adjustment program to help halt the economic decline, provide temporary debt-servicing relief, and attract foreign investment.

Structural Adjustment

The 1994 structural-adjustment program had stabilized the economy by 2000, and foreign investors began showing interest in nonhydrocarbon areas. Inflation was brought down from 30 percent in 1995 to 2 percent in 2006. The fiscal budget and trade balance produced surpluses, due mostly to increased hydrocarbon revenue. Hard currency reserves increased from $1.5 billion in 1993 to $200 billion in 2012. The country's external debt, which had reached $33 billion in 1996, was almost totally paid off by 2012. After years of poor performance, the gross domestic product (GDP) growth rate improved substantially, rising from –2.2 percent in 1993 to 5 percent in 2008. In 2012, GDP per capita reached $7,000, up from less than $2,000 in the 1990s.

Despite these positive aggregate results, the structural-adjustment reforms carried a heavy social cost. The country's currency was devalued by 40 percent, and the remaining subsidies on primary consumption items were drastically cut. More than 500,000 workers had been laid off by 1998. Unemployment, which had climbed to 35 percent in the 1990s, declined to 10 percent in 2012, though youth unemployment remains high at

20 percent. A 2006 report on poverty issued by Algeria's Security Services indicated that social inequality had increased, with less than 20 percent of the population controlling more than 50 percent of the country's wealth. However, the 2010 Human Development Report placed Algeria among ten countries designated as "top movers"—countries that achieved the greatest improvements in human development when compared to their 1970 levels—and ranked it 96 out of 187 countries.[2]

The "shock therapy" sponsored by the IMF and World Bank did not fulfill its overall promises. Fear of the social cost and opposition by vested interests created strong resistance to the reforms by the largest labor union (the UGTA), civil and professional associations, public-enterprise managers, small private entrepreneurs hurt by high interest rates and currency devaluation, and the few big private import-export businesses, whose informal monopolies reform threatens.

Artificially sustained long past its viability by centralized control and fortuitous energy exports, the economy is now trying to rechannel its energies and focus. In the 2000s the government initiated several public investment programs worth around $500 billion, aimed at economic revival, employment generation, housing, and infrastructure. The privatization of public enterprises picked up speed in the mid-2000s but is still far from its professed goals. A plan to privatize the first bank, Crédit Populaire d'Algérie, was postponed indefinitely in 2007, and a plan to open Sonatrach, the only public hydrocarbons company, to private capital was also canceled, due to domestic opposition.

As for agriculture, it has gradually taken on more importance in economic policy, as state collectives have been privatized, a new agricultural bank has been established, and funds have been allotted for irrigation. Agricultural productivity has increased sharply, with a growth rate of 7.5 percent. In 2011, the agricultural sector's share of GDP was 12 percent, and it employed 14 percent of the workforce. Its major challenge remains recurring drought.

Nonhydrocarbon industrial output remains dismal, and most public enterprises still run deficits. Hydrocarbons, which dominate the economy and are likely to continue to do so, account for 98 percent of Algeria's export earnings and 60 percent of budget revenues. However, as the price of oil recently hovered around $100 a barrel, Algeria's hydrocarbons' revenue increased steadily, reaching around $50 billion a year. Reforms in the areas of taxation, public expenditures, public debt, and the banking system have been moving very slowly. Market-oriented change in these and other areas is needed to achieve Algeria's ambition to join the World Trade Organization and is required by the free trade agreement Algeria signed with the European Union in 2002. Foreign investment reached $1.8 billion in 2008, but only a small fraction was in nonhydrocarbon activities. The World Bank's 2012 Ease of Doing Business Index ranked Algeria 143 out of 148 economies. One of the many reasons foreign investment has declined in all sectors since the mid-2000s is the investment law amendment of 2006, which made Algeria less attractive as a place for capitalist pursuits. Even the energy sector is reeling, to the point of undermining the contracted gas export capacity.

In the wake of social upheaval in the region in 2011, the government, fearing a social explosion, engaged in yet another blitz of public spending. Even before that, in 2010, the government had launched a five-year, $286-billion investment program in infrastructure, low-income housing, and job creation. More money was committed in 2011, after the riots of early January, but all this may not lead to much-needed structural reforms and may fuel inflation, which has increased from 4 percent in 2010 to 7 percent in 2012. Also, this costly program led the IMF to warn Algeria about its growing budget deficit. Short of diversification and liberalization of the economy and better investment laws, much of this effort may end up as populist impulses that fail to create adequate jobs for the educated youth.

POLITICAL STRUCTURE

Algeria's war of national liberation left in place a competitive authoritarian political structure controlled by the main actors in the national liberation movement. This structure then evolved into a triangular system of government in which the military, party, and state apparatus share power and continually compete for it.

The constitution concentrated virtually all powers of the Algerian state into the executive branch, which remained the supreme institution, both formally and effectively. The president's role as head of state, head of government, commander of the armed forces, defense minister, and head of the FLN ensured that he had virtually unlimited power. The republican nature of the state was regularly reaffirmed, as were the Islamic character and socialist commitment of the country. The FLN was recognized as the "only authentic representative of the people's will" and controlled all mass associations from 1968 until 1989.

All this changed after the social upheaval of 1989. After that, Algeria's political structure evolved toward a competitive, pluralistic multiparty polity. However, most political institutions remain fairly powerless. For example, the power of the presidency during Abdelaziz Bouteflika's first term (1999–2004) was still subordinate to that of the military, but after a showdown with the army, which almost cost him a second term, Bouteflika managed to wrest some concessions from the military, notably less outright interference in politics.

The Military

The Algerian military (Armée Nationale Populaire) has remained a constant, if inconsistent, force in Algerian politics, at some times quite visible, at others more discreet. In the early years of independence, the military, endowed with organizational capacity and technical competency, quickly occupied the power vacuum left by traditional and religious forces, whose power bases were almost completely undermined by the revolution.

The Algerian army has always presented itself as the "guardian of the revolution" and guarantor of the country's integrity and stability. Historically it has maintained a discretionary role in politics, interfering when conditions "necessitated" it to ensure stability and security. However, following the brutal suppression of the October 1988 riots, the army found its image severely discredited and quickly retreated from politics. In June 1991, the military saw the civilian leadership crisis as an occasion to reassert its historically predominant role in politics. It had as little faith in the government of Bendjedid as it had taste for the Islamists. In January 1992, it overturned the elections won by the Islamists, the constitutional framework, and the president's authority.

During the 1990s civil war, the army was accused of carrying out massacres and failing to prevent mass killings by the Islamists. New publications and eyewitness accounts accused high officers of crimes against humanity perpetrated by their troops and then attributed to the Islamists.

Officially, the military establishment is committed to a democratic project and a republican form of government. In the 2004 presidential election, it announced for the first time that it would not play a role in choosing the next president. Despite a lack of full support from the military, Bouteflika won with a wide margin against an unorganized and divided opposition. When he sought a third term and a constitutional amendment ending term limits in 2009, the army did not seem to mind. With no real rival candidate and the army's tacit acquiescence, he won a third term with 90 percent of the vote.

There are many signs that the military is eagerly working to professionalize itself and reduce its interference in politics and economics. Its increasing interaction with the US military and NATO may help this transformation. Furthermore, the sudden retirement in August 2004 of General Mohamed Lamari, the military chief of staff, and the appointment of General Larbi Belkheir, the president's chief of staff, as ambassador to Morocco allowed Bouteflika not only to appoint new individuals to top positions but also to start asserting the preeminence of the civilian leadership over the military.

The Islamists

For the Algerian political leadership, the Islamist movement has been a constant source of agitation. Recognizing the powerful message and capabilities of the movement, the regime has alternated between suppressing and befriending the Islamist leadership. The Ministry of Religious Affairs was established to control the mosques and oversee the appointment of imams (prayer leaders). However, urban growth led to a rapid proliferation of mosques and neighborhood associations, which the government could not contain, and created the opportunity for an independent Islamist movement to emerge. The Islamist message was accompanied by extensive voluntary social work and charitable action in areas such as education, garbage pickup, and aid for the poor, the sick, and the elderly. These social services fostered a loyal and extensive mass political base that the Islamists could draw upon once independent political parties were legalized in 1989. Although more than one Islamist organization emerged, the Front of Islamic Salvation (FIS) became the only national challenger to the FLN. The FIS was led by Abassi Madani, a moderate, Western-educated university professor, and Ali Belhadj, a high school teacher from a poor urban neighborhood known for his fiery rhetoric and radical views. The contrast in their styles reflected the pluralistic nature of their party.

Despite its victories in the 1990 municipal and 1991 legislative elections, as well as its impressive skills at political mobilization, critics argued that the FIS had profited from the discontent of unemployed youth in the urban slums and that, apart from its dubious sociological roots, it lacked the organizational and technical capabilities to lead an effective government.

The FIS presented an alternative to the existing regime at a time when there was none. Its electoral success constituted a large protest vote against the existing rulers by those who were less than confident of the party's governing capabilities.

Following the state's crackdown in the early 1990s, the Islamist movement became increasingly radical. Splits in the FIS leadership and membership separated moderate "pragmatists" from hard-liners. This division led to the emergence of a number of radical, armed Islamist groups. After the FIS was banned in 1992, most of its leaders were in jail or in exile, and many others and their followers either defected to more radical Islamist groups or retreated from political activity altogether.

A newly radicalized Islamist opposition emerged to contest by force and terror the authority of the state and claim power in the name of electoral victory. The Armed Islamic Group (GIA), the Armed Islamic Movement, the Islamic Salvation Army (the military wing of the FIS), and the Salafist Group for Preaching and Combat (GSPC) engaged in a daily terror campaign, killing security personnel and civilians, including journalists, professors, poets, doctors, union officials, opposition party leaders, citizens suspected of cooperating with the state, women not abiding by the commandments of the Islamists, and foreigners. They also destroyed infrastructure, including telephone centers, public utility vehicles, and schools. State countermeasures also left scores of people dead, hundreds jailed, and thousands unaccounted for. Within a few years, Algeria had descended in a vicious spiral of violence. By 2001, some 200,000 people had been killed. However, the Islamist rebellion failed to achieve its objective, and its crude violence negatively affected the Islamists' standing in people's minds.

While nonviolent, moderate Islamist parties were allowed to partake in national politics in the mid-1990s, support for them had declined by the 2002 parliamentary elections, due partly to the general irrelevance of opposition parties and to internal conflict within the Society of Peace Movement (MSP), a moderate Islamist party formerly known as Hamas, and Ennahda (Movement for Islamic Renaissance), also a moderate Islamist party. The MSP lost thirty-one of its sixty-nine seats, and Ennahda kept only one of its thirty-four seats. However, a new party—a breakaway from the latter—Harakat al-Islah al-Watani (Movement for National Reform), known as Islah, obtained forty-three seats. Overall, the number of seats controlled by the Islamists declined from 103 to 82. In the November 2005 elections in 143 municipalities, Islamists obtained only seven seats.

Table 16.1   Results of the 1997, 2002, and 2007 Parliamentary Elections

Party	1997 (% of votes)	1997 Seats	2002 (% of votes)	2002 Seats	2007 Seats
Front de Libération Nationale (FLN)	16.1	69	35.27	199	136
Rassemblement National Démocratique (RND)	38.1	156	8.23	47	61
Mouvement de la Réforme Nationale (MRN/Islah)	—	—	9.50	43	3
Harakat Moujtama'a al-Silm (MSP/HMS)	16.7	69	7.05	38	52
Independents	5.0	11	4.92	30	33
Parti des Travailleurs (PT)	2.1	4	3.33	21	26
Ennahda (MRI)	9.9	34	0.65	1	5
Front des Forces Socialistes (FFS)	5.7	20	—	—	—
Rassemblement pour la Culture et la Démocratie (RCD)	4.8	19	—	—	19

Sources: www.mae.dz, http://electionworld.org/election/algeria.htm, and www.aps.dz/fr/legislatives2.asp.

In the May 2007 parliamentary elections, the Islamists lost twenty-two of the eighty-two seats they had won in 2002. The pro-government FLN and National Democratic Rally (RND) parties similarly lost forty-nine seats but remained the dominant parties. Between 2002 and 2007 the process had come full circle, with the FLN back in control of parliament and supportive of the executive branch, headed by Bouteflika. In the May 2012 elections, the Islamists, which had formed an Algeria Green Alliance (comprising MSP, Islah, and Ennahda), lost more seats in parliament, taking only forty-nine (see Table 16.1).

As a protest movement or part of the governing establishment, moderate Islamists will continue to take advantage of the inclusionary opening. However, it seems that the Islamist moment in Algeria has come and gone, leaving these formations in a much weaker position than their counterparts elsewhere in North Africa.

Civic Associations

Following its legalization in 1989, the FIS was but one of many political parties. By the time campaigning opened for the country's first multiparty elections, sixty-two parties existed, some of which were led by noted exiled political leaders and historic war figures, such as Ahmed Ben Bella (Movement for Democracy in Algeria) and Hocine Aït Ahmed (Front of Socialist Forces, or FFS).

Civic associations also proliferated and became a vibrant part of Algerian political life. Many organizations—mainly those of journalists, women, and human rights advocates—played a significant role in Algeria's brief democratic experiment during 1989 to 1991 and actively challenged the regime.

In the spring and summer of 2001, a series of protests against the regime erupted in the Kabylie region east of Algiers, following the killing of a young man imprisoned by the paramilitary gendarmerie. From these events was born what became known as the Citizen Movement, which demanded, among other things, the recognition of Berber as a national and official language. It was a unique movement, started by grassroots, traditional village and tribal leadership structures called the *aarch*, which were revived because of the failure of institutional outlets to provide for expression of popular demands and grievances. The movement bypassed the two Berber-based parties, the FFS and the Rally for Culture and Democracy.

Notwithstanding its cultural demands, the movement was directed against the entire regime, its repressive nature, and its unresponsiveness. The bulk of the Berberist movement had positioned itself in opposition to both Islamism and the regime. While most demands of the Kabylie movement were not met, the Berber language was finally made an official national language. Beyond this movement, the civil society that was incipient in the late 1980s and early 1990s fell victim to resilient authoritarian rule, which, after quelling radical Islamism, muzzled most civil society voices through repression, co-optation, infiltration, and control.

POLITICAL DYNAMICS

Political Liberalization

Following the riots of October 1988, political reforms significantly altered the configuration of the state and opened the way for political liberalization. Constitutional reforms promised a "state of law" and removed all references to the socialist commitment. They deprived the FLN of its single-party status and its official role as the "guardian of the revolution."

Presidential authority, by contrast, was further enhanced. As head of state, head of the Higher Judicial Council, commander in chief of the military, and presiding officer over all legislative meetings, the president was given effective control over all state institutions.

He has the power to appoint and dismiss the prime minister and all other nonelected civilian and military officials; he is the only figure authorized to initiate constitutional amendments and may bypass parliament with national referenda.

The Law Relative to Political Associations of July 1989 extended the right to form political parties to all organizations committed to national unity and integrity and explicitly prohibited parties of a specifically religious, ethnic, or regional character. This last preclusion was laxly enforced. A reform of the law in 2011 added restrictions on obtaining and using funds from abroad, something that would seriously hinder the operation of local offices of global nongovernmental organizations.

The first multiparty elections for local and regional offices, held on June 12, 1990, delivered a decisive blow to the FLN. The FIS secured 853 of the 1,520 local councils (55 percent) and 32 of the 48 provincial assemblies (67 percent). The FLN won only 487 local and 14 provincial constituencies. When new multiparty parliamentary elections were held on December 26, 1991, the FIS won 188 seats out of 430 in the first round, followed by the FFS with 25 seats and the FLN with merely 16 seats. The runoff elections never took place, due to the military intervention that canceled the vote and banned the FIS in early 1992. The two FIS leaders, Abassi Madani and Ali Belhadj, had been arrested earlier and sentenced to twelve years in prison, which they served fully.

President Bendjedid was forced by the army to resign on January 11, 1992. The country was temporarily ruled by a High State Council headed, at first, by Defense Minister General Khaled Nezzar. Thereafter, the country experienced its worst crisis since independence. The state pursued a strategy of crackdown, control, and containment of the Islamists and other opposition groups. Thousands of alleged militants were imprisoned in makeshift camps in the Sahara; scores were killed, and a state of war set in. For many years, the regime was unable to assemble a civilian government that commanded the confidence and respect of all Algerians. Independence war hero Mohamed Boudiaf was invited to return from exile in Morocco and lead the country in January 1992; however, he was assassinated six months after his appointment as president. He was followed by Ali Kafi, whose one-year presidency was largely symbolic. The appointment on January 31, 1994, of retired general Lamine Zeroual as president stimulated some hope for improved economic and security conditions. In the first free presidential election in 1995, Zeroual won a six-year term with 61 percent of the vote. It was hoped that his new electoral legitimacy would help solve the crisis, but violence against civilians increased even more.

A 180-member National Council of Transition (CNT) was established as an advisory body in the absence of a working parliament. The CNT served as an institutional framework for passing legislation and was filled with representatives of parties, trade unions, managers' associations, professional organizations, and other civic associations. As attempts at dialogue with the jailed FIS leaders failed, the state turned to a firmer repression of radical Islamists while opening up to moderate opposition parties, both religious and secular. In January 1995, most opposition parties (including the banned FIS) met in Rome and agreed on a platform for resolving the crisis. The initiative failed when the government rejected the document.

In 1996, additional constitutional amendments reinforced the powers of the president and prime minister and created a second parliamentary chamber, the Council of the Nation, with one-third of its members appointed by the president and the rest elected by indirect suffrage. The amendments also declared Islam the state religion, prohibited the creation of parties on a "religious, linguistic, racial, gender, corporatist or regional" basis, and outlawed the use of partisan propaganda based on these elements.

Elections in June 1997 produced Algeria's first multiparty parliament. The main winners were the RND, the MSP, Ennahda, and the FLN. The RND, FLN, and MSP constituted a pro-government coalition that controlled an absolute majority and twenty-one ministerial posts, seven of which went to the Islamists. This coalition survived until 2012, when the Islamist MSP decided to drop out and join the opposition with the hope of capturing more votes in the wake of the Arab Spring. This strategy failed, and the MSP lost substantially.

President Zeroual, who faced strong resistance from the regime's hard-liners when he attempted a discreet dialogue with the jailed FIS leaders, resigned in early 1999, well before the end of his term. Former foreign minister Abdelaziz Bouteflika quickly became the candidate favored by the military and many others. Two days before the vote on April 15, 1999, the other six candidates withdrew, angered by electoral irregularities. Bouteflika, the only candidate, won by 73 percent of the vote, with support from the military and the FLN, RND, and MSP. For him it was a triumphant return from a twenty-year self-imposed exile.

Violence and terror, which had started to subside during Zeroual's tenure, continued to diminish, and security improved markedly after an amnesty program called the National Concord—approved by referendum in September 1999—invited armed Islamists to give up the fight and avoid prosecution. The first to take advantage of this was the Army of Islamic Salvation, which had been observing a unilateral cease-fire since October 1, 1997. The National Concord was not part of a comprehensive political solution but merely a judicial action that allowed alleged terrorists to be freed with impunity.

A national referendum in September 2005 approved another open-ended amnesty program, the Charter for Peace and National Reconciliation, which came into effect in February 2006. Many more rebels surrendered and others were released from jail, but a small number remained active, causing occasional violence. Like its predecessor, this amnesty was widely criticized not only for preventing the prosecution of rebels who had committed grave crimes against civilians but also for absolving state agents responsible for similar offenses. Furthermore, many of those who surrendered have returned to armed rebellion by joining the GSPC, which officially declared its allegiance to al-Qaida in 2006 and became part of that network, renaming itself al-Qaida in the Islamic Maghreb (AQIM). Since then, AQIM has conducted several violent attacks against security forces and foreign personnel in Algeria, Mauritania, Morocco, Tunisia, and Mali.

President Bouteflika also tried to further the return to normalcy by holding regular elections. In the parliamentary elections of May 30, 2002, and to the surprise of many observers, the FLN was the biggest winner with 199 seats, up from 69 in the previous parliament and 15 in the 1991 elections.

The 2002 elections were marked, however, by people's growing apathy toward the political process in general and political parties in particular, both religious and secular. People lost faith in many of the parties created since 1989 because of their internal dissention and their marginalization within the political process. Some opposition leaders were co-opted through election to parliament or appointment to high office, reducing both their ability to oppose the regime and their popular appeal. It seemed that because economic and political promises went unfulfilled by the new opposition, people placed their hope back in the most established party, the FLN. This apathy was resoundingly expressed in the 2007 and 2012 parliamentary elections; the first had a mere 35 percent voter turnout rate, the lowest in Algeria's history, and the second had a 43 percent turnout. Turnout in the November 2012 local elections was only 44 percent.

The Missing Spring

When the Arab Spring upheaval began in Tunisia in December 2010, the situation in Algeria was already tense, due to dire socioeconomic conditions and lasting political malaise and inertia. On January 3, 2011, riots broke out in Algiers and other major cities, following rumors that the prices for basic food staples were about to rise again, due to new regulations intended to reign in the substantial informal market. The riots were spontaneous and focused primarily on the rising cost of living due to diminished state subsidies and a stagnant, low minimum wage. The rioters were also angry at the state for acute shortages of affordable housing, failing educational and health systems, rampant corruption, and cronyism and nepotism in the bureaucracy and public companies. Their demands included better living conditions, lower food prices, jobs, and respect.

Riots in Algeria have become such a regular occurrence that not a single day passes without more than one taking place over a problem that neither the local authorities nor the state addresses. However, the riots of January 2011 were not limited to a single locality or a local issue; they took place simultaneously in several cities across the country. In contrast with the Tunisian and Egyptian protesters, the rioting Algerian youth were not supported by labor unions, political parties, or civic associations. The riots lasted only four days, ending as soon as the government announced a low price ceiling on basic food, tabled impending market regulations, and promised to address grievances about jobs, housing, marginalization, and the contempt (*hogra*) bureaucrats and state security agents showed for the youth. On February 12, a peaceful protest demanding political change finally started in Algiers. It was led by the newly created National Coordination for Change and Democracy (CNCD), which included small political parties and a few civic associations. It was led by the small Rally for Culture and Democracy party and demanded democracy, an end to the state of emergency, liberalization of the political and media fields, and the release of people arrested during the January 2011 riots. However, this movement was short-lived, as it was not able to assemble due to heavy security restrictions and its failure to attract enough people.

The Arab Spring left Algeria unmoved for several reasons, including the traumatic war of the 1990s, which was still fresh in people's memory; the belief that Algeria's security forces would not hesitate to repress a popular revolt, as they had in 1988 and the 1990s; the absence of a single leader on whom to focus the protest, like Zine al-Abidine Ben Ali in Tunisia and Hosni Mubarak in Egypt; and the inability of the opposition to create a wide and sustained mass movement against the ruling regime.

Although Arab Spring protests were thus limited in Algeria, a growing number of other types of protests and localized riots occurred throughout 2011 and 2012. These actions have affected several towns and villages and many professional sectors. Strikes led by independent unions (i.e., those not affiliated with the UGTA) have occurred in the education, health, and legal sectors, the civil service, and several industries, including the parastatal oil and gas company Sonatrach. The strikers' demands have included pay raises to keep up with inflation, parity with public-sector salaries (which had recently increased by 25 to 50 percent), improved work conditions, and better health insurance and pension programs.

Another sad form of protest also has become prevalent: suicide, especially by self-immolation, apparently in emulation of Mohamed Bouazizi, who set himself on fire in Tunisia in December 2010, initiating the Arab Spring. The growing number of these suicides has generated neither public interest nor the concern of government officials. A final form of protest involves the growing phenomenon of illegal migration to Europe via the sea. This dangerous form of exit—commonly known as *harga*—has caused many deaths, yet remains an attractive alternative for many people with no hope of a decent life in Algeria.

The government's response to this internal malaise and external pressure has included lifting of the nineteen-year-old state of emergency, promise of yet another constitutional reform, changes in the electoral system and media laws, and gender balance in political institutions. In June 2011, a National Commission of Consultation on Political Reforms provided recommendations in these areas that were approved by the government and parliament. By spring, twenty-one new parties were legalized, further diluting the power of both secularist and Islamist parties, and a new quota system was established for women's presence on electoral lists and in parliament. This helped 145 women gain election to parliament in May 2012—31 percent of the 462 deputies, up from a mere 7 percent in the previous parliament.

Political and Economic Prospects

Algeria's aggregate economic indicators have improved markedly in the last decade. The improved environment has started to stimulate domestic investment, though foreign investment has declined.

The government's most pressing task undoubtedly is to resolve the country's pressing socioeconomic problems. A great number of technocrats and members of the political elite want to enact serious—albeit stringent and painful—reforms, but a consensus on the form, depth, and timing of reform has been elusive. Also, fears about the potentially negative consequences of severe economic change for an already discontented population have produced hesitation and inconsistency. More recently, fear of an Arab Spring revolt has further pushed the elite toward conservative economic policies.

The state is caught in the difficult position of having to resolve serious socioeconomic problems while opening the economy to global capital, enacting more austerity measures, and maintaining strict budgetary discipline. Already the implementation of some neoliberal reforms is causing friction between the state and society, as witnessed by the recent strikes and recurring unrest in towns and villages throughout the country. This unrest has become a regular occurrence in an environment marked by failure of the institutions of political representation and justice, as well as a combined fear of the winds of change represented by the Arab Spring and instability in nearby Libya and Mali.

A resolution of the crisis requires sound and timely economic reforms and major changes in political institutions and informal political practices. Conditions that could help thrust Algeria in the right direction include its lucrative hydrocarbon assets, its large industrial base and pool of skilled workers and technocrats, a multiparty system that can help nurture tolerance and compromise, and a thriving independent press that can serve as a forum for public policy debate and push for accountability.

The military's role in politics must be curtailed, and the powers of the presidency must be balanced with those of parliament, which needs to exercise its legislative, oversight, and investigative functions. The judicial system needs to become independent and made to guarantee basic freedoms and protection against abuses of power. Notwithstanding the power of conservative forces—both secular and religious—a united core of reformist elites, backed by constitutional and popular legitimacy, is needed to get Algeria out of its current predicament. Unfortunately, the prospects for this were not hopeful in 2012, when parliamentary elections, instead of ushering in real change, reproduced instead something akin to the old one-party system by allowing the conservative, nationalist, pro-government FLN and RND parties to win an absolute majority of seats. Their victory was presented as a plebiscite on security and stability in the country, in light of the instability prevalent in Libya, the Sahel region (especially Mali), Egypt, Yemen, and Syria.

In short, at the end of 2012, Algeria did not seem to be heading toward substantial reforms. The governing system remains authoritarian, albeit softened by the 1990s war, and concerned about the possible impact of popular upheavals and instability in North Africa and the Sahel. The reform measures announced or enacted in 2011 met with cynicism from an incredulous audience for whom the country's fundamental problems are embedded in the nature of its political and economic systems. If any other serious reform is to take place, it may have to wait until the 2014 presidential election. President Bouteflika's recent illness has left the outcome of this election uncertain, creating both anxiety about and hope for the country's future.

FOREIGN POLICY

Algeria's revolutionary tradition has strongly influenced its foreign policy. Its anticolonial revolution against France was extended to encompass a challenge to imperialist powers worldwide. This lent Algeria a prominent position in the Maghreb, the Arab and Middle East region, and the Third World more broadly. Pursuing an independent, if often abrasive, course in its foreign policy, Algeria acquired an influential role in world politics—a role that far exceeded its resources and capabilities. Gradually, however, internal economic and political problems and changing global circumstances restricted Algeria's foreign policy. Strategic, economic, and political interests in its region began to take precedence over its ideological commitment to Third World causes. Political liberalization further increased the constraints. Algeria's foreign policy came to reflect the actions of a state accountable to its citizens and their perspectives, as evidenced by the dramatic reversal of the government's position on the 1990 Iraqi invasion of Kuwait.

Algeria's relations with its Maghrebi neighbors were strained after independence and remained so throughout the 1970s, especially with Morocco, whose conservative ideological orientation conflicted with Algeria's socialist orientation. In the 1980s, however, political and economic liberalization in Algeria drew the two countries closer, and relations improved dramatically, only to deteriorate again in 1994 after Morocco accused Algeria of supporting an armed Islamist attack in a Marrakech tourist hotel and imposed visa requirements on Algerian visitors. Algeria responded by closing the common border.

A treaty in 1989 established an economic and political Arab Maghreb Union (UMA) between Algeria, Libya, Mauritania, Morocco, and Tunisia. However, regional integration remains elusive and remote as Algeria and Morocco continue to disagree on a host of issues, especially the Western Sahara problem. The instability caused by the popular revolts of 2011 in Tunisia and Libya pushed the implementation of the union project further away.

Despite its membership and founding role in the Organization of African Unity (OAU), Algeria is still much more closely affiliated with its Arab neighbors and southern Europe than with the African countries to the south, except on issues concerning instability and insecurity in the Sahel region, with which Algeria shares more than 1,000 miles of border. It remains involved in the OAU more out of tactical considerations than genuine commitment and has often utilized the organization to further its distinctly self-informed views. Algeria hosted the 1999 OAU summit, assumed the OAU presidency for one year, and committed itself to an active role in conflict resolution in Africa—mediating a peace agreement between Ethiopia and Eritrea—and in negotiations with the industrialized countries over African debt.

After the OAU gave way to the African Union in 2001, President Bouteflika became involved in the New African Partnership for Africa's Development. In July 2009, Algeria hosted the second pan-African cultural festival; the first had been held in 1968. Well before the 2012 conflict that left first Tuareg rebels and then Islamist groups in control of northern Mali, Algeria had served frequently as a mediator between Malian Tuaregs and their government. Algeria favored a negotiated solution to the conflict in Mali, but the UN Security Council in October 2012 called for joint military action by Mali's neighbors—including Algeria—if a peaceful solution to the conflict could not be found soon. Algeria fears such a development because it may cause an influx of refugees and become a source of instability and insecurity within its own borders.

Algeria has been an active member of the League of Arab States since immediately after independence in 1962, but its involvement in Middle Eastern and Arab affairs has been limited mainly to supporting the Palestinian cause. Its historical and ideological commitment to self-determination fostered a strong affinity with the Palestinians. The Iraqi invasion of Kuwait in August 1990 and the subsequent retaliation by Western coalition forces produced substantial popular support for Iraq, leading the regime to quickly backpedal from its initial neutral position. In the context of the Arab Spring, Algerian officials were concerned about the spread of popular upheavals, especially in Libya and Syria. They were also concerned with the NATO intervention in Libya and did not warm up to the new Libyan leadership until well after Muammar al-Qaddafi was gone. Algeria vehemently rejects the idea of a similar intervention in Syria.

Political and economic liberalization at home and a moderate foreign policy have substantially improved Algeria's relations with Europe and the United States in recent decades. In January 1981, Algeria mediated the release of the fifty-two US hostages from Iran. Western powers likewise have shown increasing tolerance for the resolutely authoritarian nature of the Algerian state, which has moved toward the West in its economic orientation and affiliation. The West's growing need for energy and the common fight against Islamist violence have led to increased interaction and diplomatic improvement.

France undoubtedly is Algeria's most significant foreign partner. More than 20 percent of all Algerian exports and imports head to or originate in France. There are close to 2 million Algerians living in France, and many Algerians speak French, creating a tremendous cultural overlap. However, French-Algerian relations have not always been cordial. Algeria's high level of dependence on France and its desire to be free of that dependency have complicated relations between the two countries. France's support for Morocco on the Western Sahara issue and "exploitative" French trade and economic initiatives have repeatedly strained bilateral relations. As with many countries, however, diplomatic relations are largely determined by economic ones, in this case by gas and oil exports. Despite problematic political relations, economic ties have persisted since Algeria's independence. Undoubtedly the most sensitive issue in French-Algerian relations is that of Algerian emigration to France. French policies toward Algerian immigrants have been less than consistent, and popular sentiment in France has generally been biased against people of North African origin. Xenophobic flare-ups between French ethnocentrists and migrant workers are common.

Algerians and their government were unhappy with a 2005 law passed by the French parliament that described the French colonization of Algeria as positive. The Algerian government requested a repeal of the law and a formal French apology for colonization and the brutality that accompanied it. The law, which jeopardized a planned treaty of friendship between the two countries, was later repealed. Algeria agreed in 2008 to support French president Nicolas Sarkozy's proposed Union for the Mediterranean, whose regional cooperation structures and aim remain vague.

Algeria's wide range of contacts qualifies it as one of the few countries in the world to maintain a truly independent position in the international arena. Throughout the most difficult years of the Cold War, Algeria remained actively involved with both the Soviet Union and the United States. Since Bouteflika came to power, Algeria has actively tried to balance its relations with Europe with increasing interaction with the United States. The events of September 11, 2001, provided both the United States and Algeria with a newfound affinity: the fight against Islamist terrorism. Algeria became a key US partner in the war on terror, notably because of its experience in fighting armed Islamists and its intelligence on radical Islamists and their international networks. At the economic level, the traditional American focus on investment in Algerian hydrocarbons has slowly extended to other economic sectors. However, despite this newfound friendship between the governments of the two countries, many Algerians still hold a negative attitude toward the United States because of its unconditional support for Israel and its 2003 invasion of Iraq.

NOTES

1. Cited in Pierre Nora, *Les Français d'Algérie* (Paris: Julliard, 1961), 88.
2. UNDP, "2010 Human Development Report," November 2010, http://hdr.undp.org/en/humandev/lets-talk-hd/2010–11b.

BIBLIOGRAPHY

A good analysis of contemporary Algerian history is found in John Ruedy, *Modern Algeria: The Origins and Development of a Nation* (Bloomington: Indiana University Press, 1992). A more polemical account sympathetic to the Boumediene regime and its socialist policies is found in Mahfoud Bennoune, *The Making of Contemporary Algeria, 1830–1987* (Cambridge: Cambridge University Press, 1988).

On Algeria's war of national liberation, the best account remains Alistair Horne, *A Savage War of Peace: Algeria, 1954–1962* (London: Penguin Books, 1979). Competent interpretations also can be found in David Gordon, *The Passing of French Algeria* (New York: Oxford University Press, 1966), and Alf Andrew Heggoy, *Insurgency and Counterinsurgency in Algeria* (Bloomington: Indiana University Press, 1972). The war's psychocultural consequences are evocatively treated in Frantz Fanon, *The Wretched of the Earth* (New York: Grove Press, 1963), and *A Dying Colonialism* (New York: Grove Press,

1967). An excellent publication with French and Algerian contributors is Mohamed Harbi and Benjamin Stora, eds., *La guerre d'Algérie, 1954–2004: La fin de l'amnésie* (Paris: Robert Lafont, 2004). An excellent reference book is Naylor Phillip Chiviges, *Historical Dictionary of Algeria* (Lanham, MD: Scarecrow Press, 2006).

A good sociological analysis of colonial and postcolonial Algeria is Pierre Bourdieu, *The Algerians* (Boston: Beacon Press, 1962). Questions of culture, women, and society are treated in Ali El Kenz, *Algerian Reflections on Arab Crises* (Austin: University of Texas Press, 1991). The following works deal with the Berber question: Amar Ouerdane, *La question berbère dans le mouvement national algérien: 1926–1980* (Sillery, Quebec: Septentrion, 1990); Ernest Gellner and Charles Micaud, eds., *Arabs and Berbers: From Tribe to Nation in North Africa* (Lexington, MA: Lexington Books, 1972); Azzedine Layachi, "The Berbers in Algeria: Politicization of Ethnicity and Ethnicization of Politics," in *Nationalism and Minority Identities in Islamic Societies,* ed. Maya Shatzmiller, 193–228 (Montreal: McGill University Press, 2005).

Treatments of Algeria's modern political history from elite perspectives are found in William B. Quandt, *Revolution and Political Leadership* (Cambridge, MA: MIT Press, 1969); David and Marina Ottaway, *Algeria: The Politics of a Socialist Revolution* (Berkeley: University of California Press, 1970); John P. Entelis, *Algeria: The Revolution Institutionalized* (Boulder, CO: Westview Press, 1986); and Rachid Tlemçani, *Élections et élites en Algérie: Paroles des candidats* (Algiers: Chihab, 2003).

The role of the military is treated in I. William Zartman, "The Algerian Army in Politics," in *Soldier and State in Africa*, ed. Claude E. Welch (Evanston, IL: Northwestern University Press, 1970); John P. Entelis, "Algeria: Technocratic Rule, Military Power," in *Political Elites in Arab North Africa*, ed. I. William Zartman et al., 92–143 (New York: Longman, 1982); and Hugh Roberts, *Commanding Disorder: Military Power and Informal Politics in Algeria* (London: I. B. Tauris, 2002).

On the internal war of the 1990s, the following are noteworthy: Habib Souaidia, *La sale guerre* (Paris: Découverte, 2001), which presents a strong indictment of the Algerian military in particular and the regime in general; Nesroulah Yous, *Qui a tué à Bentalha* (Paris: Découverte, 2000); Luis Martinez, *The Algerian Civil War, 1990–1998* (London: Hurst & Co., 2002); and Hugh Roberts, *The Battlefield Algeria, 1988–2002: Studies in a Broken Polity* (London: Verso, 2002). Regarding the loss of popularity of the Islamist parties, see Mokrane Ait Ouarabi, "Est-ce la déconfiture des partis islamistes?" *El Watan*, November 17, 2005.

Analyses of Algerian political and economic development, including the role of Islamism, can be found in Azzedine Layachi, "Political Liberalization and the Islamists in Algeria," in *Islam, Democracy and the State in Algeria*, ed. Michael Bonner, Megan Reif, and Mark Tessler, 46–67 (New York: Routledge, 2005); Azzedine Layachi, "Algeria: Crisis, Transition and Social Policy Outcomes," in *Social Policy and Development: The Middle East and North Africa*, ed. Massoud Karshenas and Valentine Moghadam, 78–108 (New York: Palgrave Macmillan, 2006); Azzedine Layachi, "Domestic and International

Constraints of Economic Adjustment in Algeria," in *The New Global Economy: North African Responses*, ed. Dirk Vandewalle, 129–152 (New York: St. Martin's Press, 1996); Azzedine Layachi, "The Private Sector in the Algerian Economy," *Mediterranean Politics* (Summer 2001): 29–50; Azzedine Layachi, "Reinstating the State or Instating Civil Society: The Dilemma of Algeria's Transition," in *Collapsed States: The Disintegration and Restoration of Legitimate Authority*, ed. I. W. Zartman (Boulder, CO: Lynne Rienner, 1995); Azzedine Layachi, "Reform and the Politics of Inclusion in the Maghrib," *Journal of North African Studies* (Autumn 2001): 15–47; Azzedine Layachi, "The Algerian Economy After Structural Adjustment," *Middle East Insight* (November–December 1999): 25–28; Andrea Liverani, *Civil Society in Algeria: The Political Functions of Associational Life* (London: Routledge, 2008); Martin Evans and John Phillips, *Algeria: Anger of the Dispossessed* (New Haven, CT: Yale University Press, 2007); Amar Benamrouche, *Gréves et conflits politiques en Algérie* (Paris: Karthala, 2000); John P. Entelis and Phillip C. Naylor, eds., *State and Society in Algeria* (Boulder, CO: Westview Press, 1992); and François Burgat and William Dowell, *The Islamic Movement in North Africa* (Austin: University of Texas Press, 1993).

The best works on Algerian foreign policy include Nicole Grimaud, *La politique extérieure de l'Algérie* (Paris: Karthala, 1984), and Robert Mortimer's articles in *African Studies*, March 1984; *Orbis*, fall 1977; and *Current History*, 1991, 1993, and 1994. The chapter on foreign policy in Helen C. Metz, *Algeria: A Country Study* (Washington, DC: Library of Congress, 1995), is straightforward and comprehensive.

17

TUNISIA

Christopher Alexander

In early December 2010, Tunisia appeared to be the same island of stability it had been for the previous twenty-three years. Then a young man named Mohamed Bouazizi set himself on fire in front of a government office in a town called Sidi Bouzid. Bouazizi worked on the streets as an illegal fruit and vegetable vendor. He was angry because a police officer had confiscated his wares, and local officials refused to hear his complaint. His desperate act touched off protests that spread quickly to other towns and then to the capital city. Less than two weeks after Bouazizi died, President Zine al-Abidine Ben Ali became the first authoritarian victim of the Arab Spring.

Of all the Arab countries that have experienced dramatic political change since the close of 2010, Tunisia offers the best chance for a successful transition to democracy. But there is no guarantee. Tunisia faces difficult choices and challenges.

HISTORICAL BACKGROUND

Tunisia's location makes it a natural crossroads. Sicily sits forty miles off its northern coast, and its southern tip plunges into the Sahara. The Phoenicians chose a site near modern Tunis to establish the city of Carthage in the eighth century BCE. Tunisia offers some of the finest examples of Roman architecture and artwork from the second and third centuries CE.

Arab invaders brought Islam and the Arabic language to Tunisia in the mid-600s. Over the next several centuries, governments based in Tunis exercised meaningful authority over the northern and coastal areas of the country. Even after the Ottoman Turks pulled Tunisia into their empire in 1574, governors in Tunis, known as *beys*, continued to enjoy substantial independence.

By the early 1800s, the European scramble for colonies, backed by new military technologies, had tipped the regional balance of power in Europe's favor. The Ottoman sultan invested large sums to modernize the economy, administration, and military. Across the empire, Ottoman governors initiated similar reforms in order to defend their own independence against both the Europeans and the Ottoman government. Borrowing to fund

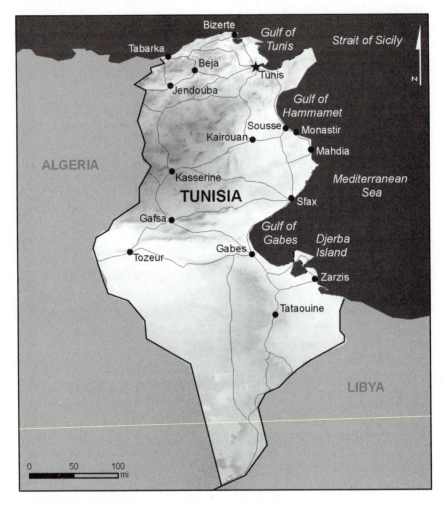

Republic of Tunisia

these reforms generated deeper debt that made the region's governments even more vulnerable to European control. France's influence in Tunisia grew steadily after it occupied Algeria in 1830. In an effort to protect its investments in Tunisia and to shield Algeria from Italian and British ambitions, French forces marched across the Algerian border in 1881 and forced the *bey* to accept treaties that turned Tunisia into a French protectorate.

From Protectorate to Independence

The *bey* maintained his position under the protectorate, but a French resident-general wielded the real power behind the throne. A French adviser stood behind each Tunisian minister, and France maintained control over Tunisia's foreign policy. The French did not destroy local economic and social institutions to the degree that they did in Algeria. In fact, French economic activities laid the foundations for a modern infrastructure in several key sectors. The French also created educational institutions that exposed a generation of young Tunisians to European values. At the same time, though, French owners took the best agricultural land. French manufactured goods pushed out many traditional Tunisian workshops. French administrators dominated the civil service.

A protonationalist movement began to stir in the first decade of the twentieth century. The Young Tunisians did not demand independence. Rather, they criticized France for not honoring its promise to help Tunisia develop in ways that would benefit Tunisians. Following World War I, the Destour Party (from the Arabic *dustur*, or "constitution") took up these same themes. But the party's legalistic demands and its suspicion of a mass movement that might threaten the leaders' privileged positions prevented the Destour from building a broad base of support. In 1934, a young, French-trained lawyer named Habib Bourguiba led a breakaway faction of younger party members. Their new party, the Neo-Destour, created a more aggressive movement that focused on social and economic issues and openly demanded independence.

After World War II, the Neo-Destour developed a strategy that negotiated Tunisia to independence in stages. Party leaders built the Neo-Destour into a national party that mobilized Tunisians across classes, regions, and ideologies. The party, allied with the Tunisian General Labor Union (UGTT), built strong international support for their cause. They used calibrated strikes, mass demonstrations, and small-scale violence to influence French public opinion and maintain pressure on the government. In 1955, France granted Tunisia internal autonomy. In March 1956, Tunisia declared its independence.

Bourguiba's Tunisia

Although Bourguiba rallied a broad coalition in the struggle for independence, the Neo-Destour was deeply divided when that goal had been achieved. Bourguiba and his allies represented a progressive wing of the party that reflected the influence of French socialism and its secular values. But they were not doctrinaire socialists. They wanted to pursue pragmatic policies that would generate growth and distribute it more equitably. To their left, more rigorous socialists wanted the government to adopt a development strategy based on state control of the economy. To the right, a conservative wing of the party was suspicious of Bourguiba's secularism and his European orientation.

In the early 1960s, concern about the conservative opposition and the failure of the private sector to generate growth prompted Bourguiba to tack left. The state adopted centralized planning and assumed a larger role as an owner and planner in the industrial and agricultural sectors. In 1964 the Neo-Destour changed its name to the Destourian Socialist Party (PSD). The regime also became more authoritarian. The government outlawed all parties except the PSD, and the party and the state became virtually indistinguishable.

REPUBLIC OF TUNISIA

Capital city	Tunis
Chief of state, 2011	President Moncef Marzouki
Head of government, 2011	Prime Minister Hamadi Jebali
Political parties (seats in most recent election, 2011)	al-Nahda (89), Congress Party for the Republic (29), Popular Petition (26), Democratic Forum for Labor and Liberties (20), Progressive Democratic Party (16), Democratic Modernist Pole (5), The Initiative (5), Afek Tounes (4), Tunisian Workers' Communist Party (3), other (20)
Ethnic groups	Arab (98%), European (1%), Other (1%)
Religious groups	Muslim (98%), Christian (1%), Jewish and other (1%)
Export partners, 2009	France (29.4%), Italy (19.2%), Germany (10.3%), Libya (6.6%)
Import partners, 2009	France (21%), Italy (17.5%), Germany (8.8%), Spain (4.9%), China (4.7%), Russia (4.5%)

This party-state apparatus tightened its control over lower levels of government, the media, and civil society organizations.

In the late 1960s, cracks began to appear in Bourguiba's political order. The economy had deteriorated over the course of the decade. Protests broke out in response to economic hardship and the government's authoritarianism. In 1969, Bourguiba sacked his planning minister and steered the economy back to the right.

The economic crisis, the government's abrupt turn from left to right, and the deepening authoritarianism created three pockets of dissent. Within the PSD, liberals argued that the party needed to become more open to a wider range of views. Bourguiba briefly tolerated broader discussion within the party. However, when he insisted on installing his allies in the PSD's political bureau, and when he orchestrated his election as president for life in 1974, Bourguiba made it clear that he was not prepared to share power.

On the left, a wide range of socialist and Marxist ideologies gained popularity on university campuses and in the trade union. As it became clearer that Bourguiba would not support a more liberal political system, and as economic inequality increased, leftist activists turned the trade union into a militant opposition force.

On the right, a small collection of Islamic scholars established the Association for the Safeguard of the Quran (ASQ). These early Islamists represented the large number of Tunisians who had never been comfortable with Bourguiba's secularism. They believed that the government's quick turn from left to right reflected an absence of clear guiding principles. They also argued that the government should stop relying on imported ideologies and build a political and economic system consistent with Tunisia's Muslim identity.

Bourguiba tolerated the ASQ as a counter to the Left as long as it focused on cultural and religious issues. But as the Left gained traction by emphasizing economic and political grievances, it became harder for the ASQ to remain on the political sidelines. Islamist leaders began to openly support the opposition's demands for democratic reform, human rights, and economic justice. This marked the beginning of a working relationship between Islamists and secular democrats that deepened over the next three decades.

Bourguiba's Fall

By the early 1980s, Bourguiba and the PSD had lost much of their historic legitimacy. Security forces had fired on striking workers and arrested much of the union leadership in 1978. Two years later, Libyan-backed rebels tried to ignite a rebellion by attacking the town of Gafsa. The party had become a rigid administrative machine led by an aging president and a clutch of self-interested elites jockeying to succeed him. In a bid to restore public confidence, Bourguiba allowed non-PSD candidates to run in legislative elections. The government also legalized the Tunisian Communist Party (PCT), the Movement of Democratic Socialists, and the Popular Unity Party.

These measures did little to restore public support. Electoral rules made it impossible for opposition candidates to win seats in the National Assembly. Additionally, the government refused to legalize a new party called the Islamic Tendency Movement (MTI). The MTI was the product of the ASQ's politicization over the previous decade. It also reflected the Islamists' desire to enter the legal political process. The economy added to popular frustrations. Riots erupted when debt forced the government to raise prices for basic commodities in January 1984.

By 1985, the government's crackdown on the union and the inability of the secular opposition parties to build broad support had created a void. Through their work on university campuses, secondary schools, and underprivileged neighborhoods, the Islamists created a grassroots organization that filled that void. Bourguiba could not manipulate the MTI in the same way he managed the union and the secular opposition parties. Consequently, he launched a fierce campaign to destroy it. In response, the MTI concluded that it had no choice but to use violence to protect itself and to topple the regime. By the fall of

1987, Tunisia teetered on the brink of civil war. On the night of November 7, Bourguiba's prime minister, Zine al-Abidine Ben Ali, invoked Bourguiba's senility to justify a bloodless coup.

Ben Ali's Honeymoon

Ben Ali did not bring many of Bourguiba's assets to the presidency. He was not charismatic. He was not a longtime politician with extensive networks in the ruling party. He was a military man whose rise to power coincided with the escalating conflict between the government and the Islamists.

Nevertheless, Ben Ali had removed Bourguiba without bloodshed and broken the spiral toward civil war. More importantly, he seemed committed to real reform. In his first year he amnestied thousands of political prisoners, invited exiles to come home, met with opposition party leaders, eliminated the presidency for life and the state security court, ratified the United Nations antitorture convention, and relaxed press restrictions. He talked about the importance of political competition and freedom of conscience and expression. He signed a new National Pact between the government and sixteen political parties and organizations. To reflect this new spirit of inclusion and reform, the PSD changed its name to the Democratic Constitutional Rally (RCD).

These initiatives earned praise at home and abroad. However, the April 1989 elections brought the honeymoon to an end. In the months leading up to the vote, Ben Ali refused to modify the electoral code in ways that would give the opposition parties a meaningful opportunity to compete against the RCD. He also set the opposition parties against one another by proposing that they all run with the RCD on single lists and split the seats in parliament on the basis of a predetermined formula. This arrangement guaranteed the opposition some seats, but it also allowed Ben Ali to devise a formula that guaranteed a large RCD majority.

Ben Ali also refused to legalize the MTI. Hoping to participate in the first elections, the MTI reiterated its rejection of violence and its commitment to multiparty politics. It praised Ben Ali for saving the country and softened its position on women's rights. The party also changed its name to the Nahda (Renaissance) Party to comply with a rule that forbade religious references in party names. Despite these reforms, Ben Ali and RCD hard-liners remained uncertain about Nahda's strength and intentions. But they wanted to encourage Nahda to continue on its moderate course. The government offered a compromise. Nahda members could run as independents; the government would revisit Nahda's legalization after the party developed a clearer program.

The election results provided stark evidence of the balance of power in the country. Thanks to the electoral rules, the RCD won all 141 seats in the National Assembly. Independent Islamist candidates won 14 percent of the national vote and more than 30 percent of the urban vote. The secular opposition parties received less than 5 percent. The whole experience demonstrated that Ben Ali was not the democrat he had professed to be and that the Islamists remained the strongest opposition force in the country. Hard-liners in the regime reached an additional conclusion. Flirting with the Islamists was a dangerous game. Ben Ali should stop playing it and destroy them.

Deepening Repression

Ben Ali's repression intensified over the long decade of the 1990s into the early years of the new century. The internal security apparatus grew larger. Surveillance, censorship, dirty tricks, campaigns to incriminate opposition figures, arrests, torture—these became the hallmarks of the government Tunisians had hoped would lead them toward democracy.

To some degree, Ben Ali was playing to his strengths as a former security chief. Algeria's civil war stoked fears that violence would spread to Tunisia. He also felt pressure from party bosses who did not want to give up their privileges for the sake of democratic reform. The government's continued refusal to legalize Nahda led many Islamist leaders to conclude that they had no choice but to use their base to push the government. As the protests increased, so did the arrests. Many Tunisians made the difficult decision to tolerate Ben Ali's authoritarianism if it saved the country from chaos and allowed the economy to perform better than any other in the Maghreb.

While the repression intensified, the government also tried to create the appearance of reform. In 1994 and 1999, Ben Ali allowed non-RCD candidates to run for president. However, the electoral rules and the conduct of the elections made it impossible for anyone else to pose serious competition. Similarly, changes in the electoral code created the impression of reform in the National Assembly. In reality, the rules continued to pit the opposition parties against each other. The government used money, rigged elections, and occasional arrests to co-opt the trade union. The occasional arrest of a journalist or confiscation of an edition prompted the press to self-censor.

By the late 1990s, fear and apathy had depoliticized Tunisian society. The government had jailed, co-opted, or driven into exile anyone who criticized it. Because the environment became too difficult for collective protest, the locus of opposition activity shifted to journalists and human rights activists. They could call attention to the government's abuses without organizing large numbers of people. In May 2002, the government organized a referendum that raised the maximum age for the president and abolished the limit on the number of terms a president may serve. In a vote denounced widely for its corruption, 99.5 percent of the voters approved these changes. The reforms also granted the president immunity from prosecution for all acts carried out in office. Against this backdrop, Tunisia seemed an unlikely place for a revolution.

The Jasmine Revolution

Early discussions of the rebellion against Ben Ali presented it as a spontaneous, leaderless explosion, mobilized primarily through social media. In reality, the revolt was the product of political and economic developments that unfolded over the first decade of the new century.

Economic deterioration was one of the most important factors. In the years leading up to the revolt, Tunisia's economy struggled in the face of successive years of drought and intense competition for global textile markets. While growth rates did not plummet dramatically, they did not climb enough to keep pace with a growing population of educated young people.

By itself, slow growth would not have created a revolution. But it was tied to another critical factor—corruption. In the years leading up to the revolt, Tunisians became increasingly aware of the degree to which Ben Ali's family was robbing the economy. It is one thing for people to live in a system where everyone pays bribes and trades favors that are part of a faceless thing called "the system." It is another thing entirely when people who are struggling with unemployment and inflation hear stories about extravagant wealth amassed by the president's wife or brother-in-law through extortion and sweetheart deals.

Together, economic hardship and growing perceptions of the regime as a thuggish mafia family alienated a range of constituencies. The government offered nothing to a new generation of young people whose expectations were shaped by the world they saw on the Internet. At the elite level, the extortion and other strong-arm tactics began to squeeze members of the ruling party. In addition to feeling the pinch personally, they began to see how corruption was limiting economic growth. Investors and entrepreneurs became hesitant to start new ventures because they knew that the president's family would take its cut.

Tunisians across regions and classes began to lose confidence in Ben Ali's ability to manage the country. The security argument that he used in the 1990s no longer worked. There was no organized Islamist threat in Tunisia, and Algeria's civil tensions had calmed. By the new century, the economy posed the primary challenge. Ben Ali seemed to have no strategy beyond staying in power and lining his family's pockets.

Political developments helped to convert the frustration into action. After 2000, many Nahda activists began to emerge from jail, having served their sentences. They also began to reconstitute grassroots networks. At the same time, journalists and human rights activists were attracting more attention to the regime's human rights abuses. Ben Ali retaliated against these activists, but he also felt pressure from foreign governments and from within his own regime to create some space for opposition activity. Between 2001 and 2005, Ben Ali allowed the secular opposition parties to operate a bit more freely as long as they did not join forces with the Islamists.

This agreement broke down in 2005. Frustrated by Ben Ali's continued abuses and by the constitutional changes that allowed him to stay in power, Nahda, the Progressive Democratic Party (PDP), Ettakatol, and the Tunisian Communist Workers Party (POCT) established the October 18 Coalition for Rights and Freedoms in Tunisia. The October 18 platform articulated principles that guided these parties as they worked together to oppose

Ben Ali. All of the parties expressed their commitment to a democratically elected government. They demanded the release of political prisoners and protected freedoms of conscience and association. Nahda agreed to respect Tunisia's progressive code for women's rights, the nonpoliticization of places of worship, and freedom of conscience. The secular parties agreed to recognize Tunisia's Arab and Muslim identity.

The October 18 parties, along with activists in the labor movement and several illegal parties, steadily increased their protests against Ben Ali. In January 2008, phosphate miners in the south staged a four-month strike that turned into a rebellion against the government. A similar uprising broke out in the southern border town of Ben Guerdane in 2010. By the time Mohamed Bouazizi set himself on fire in December 2010, Tunisia was primed for rebellion. Activists were waiting for some incident that they could exploit to generate protest against the government. These activists did not directly cause the protests that broke out after Bouazizi's dramatic act. But they were in place, ready to sustain the protests and help them spread.

Social media did not cause the revolt but did help it grow. As the protests spread, marchers and bystanders used cell phone cameras to record them as well as clashes with security forces. When they posted the videos on Facebook pages, Al Jazeera picked them up and broadcast them back to a national television audience. This created a shared experience, a common protest narrative that cut across classes and regions. Twitter allowed protesters to share information about the shifting locations of protests.

On the night of January 13, Ben Ali went on national television and tried to restore order. He said he had heard the protesters' message. He promised to reduce prices and not to run for reelection. Crowds in the streets made it clear that he had offered too little too late. When the commander of the army said he would not order his troops to fire on protesters, Ben Ali and his family fled to Saudi Arabia.

Building a New Order

Ben Ali's departure created an unprecedented political void in Tunisia. For the first time since independence, Tunisians did not know who would run the country. The RCD could not step in. The president, not the party, had always run the country. Additionally, Ben Ali's rule had thoroughly discredited the RCD.

Immediately after Ben Ali fled, Prime Minister Mohamed Ghannouchi invoked Article 56 of the constitution to step into the presidency. Article 56 declared that the prime minister would assume power if the president could no longer serve. Very quickly, however, lawyers and civil society leaders argued that this arrangement might allow Ben Ali to return. Article 56 was intended for cases in which the president was temporarily unable to serve. Invoking Article 57, on the other hand, would definitively remove Ben Ali from office. But it required the speaker of the parliament, not the prime minister, to become interim president. Barely twenty-four hours after Ben Ali's departure, Mohamed

Ghannouchi stepped back into the premiership and turned the interim presidency over to Fouad Mbazaa.

Mid-January through late March 2011 was a critical period in Tunisia's transition. The interim government granted amnesty to political prisoners, invited exiles to return, froze the RCD's assets, and began legalizing new political parties. The government also created commissions that began designing political reforms and investigating the crimes of the former regime. Despite these important developments, Tunisia remained very unsettled. Many activists protested that the interim government included too many people from the old regime. Their strikes and marches forced Ghannouchi to overhaul his government, but that government still did not put forth a compelling reform plan.

Ghannouchi's plan relied on the existing constitution. It called for Tunisia's transition to begin with an election for a new president. Once in place, a new government would revise the constitution. Civil society activists believed that this was a dangerous sequence. It would allow an elected president to assume power under an unreformed, patently undemocratic constitution that concentrated unchecked power in the executive's hands. The new president could then use that constitution to subvert the transition.

Instead, democracy activists argued that the transition must begin with constitutional reform. Tunisians should elect members to a Constituent Assembly, which would write a democratic constitution. Once the new constitution was ratified, voters would go back to the polls and elect a new president and a new National Assembly.

In February, these activists organized themselves into a Committee for the Safeguard of the Revolution. The committee set itself up as a watchdog organization that pressured the government to develop a truly democratic reform plan and protect it from remnants of the old regime. By the end of the month, their continued protests had forced Ghannouchi out of office. Beji Caid el-Sebsi became Tunisia's new prime minister.

Caid el-Sebsi moved quickly to resolve the issues that had gridlocked the transition. The interim government legalized Nahda as a political party and accepted the opposition's plan for reforming the constitution before holding presidential elections. The government also established a new Commission for the Realization of the Objectives of the Revolution, Political Reform, and Democratic Transition. The new commission combined the government's reform commission with the Committee for the Safeguard of the Revolution. This fusion gave civil society organizations and opposition parties a direct role in crafting the country's reforms.

The commission worked through the spring to devise rules for the Constituent Assembly elections. This process generated intense suspicion and competition among Islamist and secular parties. Secular activists argued that they had made the revolution. Labor, women's movements, human rights activists, and progressive parties had mobilized the masses and defined the dominant themes of the revolt: dignity, individual freedom, equality for all citizens. Secular activists also accused Nahda of doublespeak. They said that when Nahda leaders talked to foreigners or to the general population, their message emphasized tolerance, freedom of conscience, separation of government and religion, and the protection of women's rights. But when Nahda leaders talked to their base, they criticized secular values and pledged to govern in accordance with Islamic principles.

Nahda countered that the secularists were scared of Nahda's strength. In the months after Ben Ali's fall, Nahda had rebuilt its organization across the country. This growth and Nahda's reputation as the best-known party in the country created a strong expectation that Nahda would do well in the first elections. Nahda argued that most of the members of the reform commission came from the secular Left and were trying to rig the electoral rules in their favor.

This tension between Nahda and secular organizations shaped debates over several issues related to the Constituent Assembly elections. In fact, Nahda withdrew from the reform commission in June 2011. But it never rejected the new process, and the parties agreed on some key points. For example, the new electoral code required all party lists to offer an equal number of male and female candidates. The reform commission also voted to exclude from the elections RCD officials who had held senior positions during Ben Ali's last decade.

Protracted haggling between the parties delayed the elections from July to October 23. This extension created more time for the electoral field to grow. By late summer, the government had legalized nearly one hundred parties. However, most Tunisians and outside observers believed that the election turned on the contest between two parties, Nahda and the Progressive Democratic Party (PDP).

The PDP was a Center-Left party, one of three opposition parties that Ben Ali legalized in 2001. Despite its legal status under the old regime, the PDP enjoyed strong credibility for its role in the October 18 opposition front. PDP leaders believed that most Tunisians did not want to live under an Islamist government. Convinced that a strong anti-Islamist message would allow it to dominate the elections, the PDP ran an uncompromising campaign against Nahda and refused to join a coalition with other parties.

On October 23, 54 percent of eligible voters cast ballots in the election. Just over 40 percent of those voters supported Nahda. This gave the party 89 of the 217 seats in the Constituent Assembly. The next two largest vote getters were the Congress for the Republic (CPR), with twenty-nine seats, and Ettakatol, with twenty seats—two secular parties that had participated in the October 18 coalition and said openly that they would join a coalition government with Nahda. The PDP won only 4 percent of the vote. Tunisian voters had given Nahda a clear, but not overwhelming, victory. More importantly, they had voted for cooperation rather than polarization.

A Slow Start

The coalition partners began their work by deciding how to share power between them. Despite its victory, Nahda did not claim the presidency. Party leaders understood that many Tunisians feared that Nahda would try to dominate the new government. Instead, the three parties agreed that Moncef Marzouki from the CPR would serve as interim president of the republic. Mustapha Ben Jaafar, from Ettakatol, would serve as president of the Constituent Assembly. Hamadi Jebali, representing Nahda, would become prime minister.

The parties negotiated the powers that each of these positions would exercise, but that agreement has not prevented disputes. Late in the spring of 2012, the Libyan government requested that Tunisia extradite Baghdadi al-Mahmoudi, Muammar al-Qaddafi's former prime minister. Marzouki and several members of his cabinet refused extradition on the grounds that Mahmoudi would not receive a fair trial in Libya. In June, however, Jebali extradited Mahmoudi on the grounds that Tunisia could not refuse Libya while pressing Saudi Arabia to extradite Ben Ali. Jebali also reversed Marzouki's decision to dismiss the director of Tunisia's central bank. These disputes and ambiguity about the assembly's powers beyond writing the constitution slowed the government's response to pressing socioeconomic challenges. This, in turn, fueled protests across the country.

The major challenges facing the assembly involved its work on the new constitution. The assembly created six commissions, each charged with a specific set of constitutional issues. The chairs of these commissions formed the drafting committee that would submit the completed constitution to the full assembly. If the draft receives a two-thirds majority vote in the assembly, it will become Tunisia's new constitution. If it fails to receive enough votes, it will be returned to the commissions for revisions. The revised draft will go back to the assembly for another vote. If it fails again to receive a two-thirds majority, the draft will go to the public for a national referendum. A simple majority vote in that referendum will ratify the new constitution.

Assembly leaders hoped to complete the constitution by October 2012 so Tunisians could elect a new legislature in March 2013. However, the commissions made slow progress. Nahda held a majority of the seats on all of the commissions, and many issues generated conflicts between Nahda and the other parties.

As soon as the drafting process began, it bogged down in one fundamental issue: the role of religion in public life. Article 1 of Tunisia's current constitution defines Tunisia as a "free, independent, and sovereign state. Its religion is Islam." This intentionally vague language allowed a wide range of interpretations. Many Islamists wanted to rewrite Article 1 in a way that would establish sharia as an important source of Tunisian law.

Article 1 generated considerable tension from January through March 2012. Islamists and secularists marshaled their forces in the streets and on university campuses in an effort to influence the language of the new constitution. In late March, Nahda leaders officially declared that they would not press for language that makes sharia a source of law. They would support the existing language and the compromise it represents. Although much of Nahda's rank and file supported more-religious language, party leaders wanted to make good on their promise not to alienate secularists by creating an Islamic government.

A full draft of the new constitution became available to the public on August 8, 2012. It reflects compromises by both secular and Islamist camps. For example, the draft preamble describes Tunisia as a country founded on the fundamentals of Islam, but an open and moderate Islam. The draft also extends the freedom of religious practice beyond Islam, Judaism, and Christianity. At the same time, the draft includes prison sentences for "blasphemy," maintains the death penalty, and outlaws normalized relations with Israel. The draft also includes language that some Tunisians say describes women as "complimentary" to men. Others say that the language describes women as "partners." Thousands took to the streets to protest this language shortly after the draft became public.

Opposition politicians hope to use the coming period of review and debate to modify the text before the ratification vote. Many observers believe this process will delay final ratification until April 2013. This, in turn, would delay new elections—a prospect many Tunisians fear will increase the strikes and protests that continue to disrupt the economy and undermine public confidence in the transition process.

POLITICAL ENVIRONMENT

Just under 11 million Tunisians live in an area slightly larger than the state of Georgia. Nearly 70 percent of them live in urban areas along the northern and eastern coasts. These areas enjoy a Mediterranean climate that supports citrus, vegetable, and olive agriculture. The Dorsal, an extension of the Atlas Mountains, cuts across northern Tunisia. North of the mountains lies a region of rolling hills and wheat cultivation. South of the mountains, steppe gives way to the desert that dominates the country's southern region. This diversity does not generate easy wealth. While Algeria and Libya derive considerable income from oil and gas exports, Tunisia's primary exports are clothing, textiles, phosphates, and agricultural goods—products with lower prices and competitive global markets.

Tunisia is also more homogeneous than its Maghreb neighbors. Arabic-speaking Sunni Muslims make up 98 percent of the population. French colonial policies and urbanization long ago eliminated tribes as meaningful political actors or sources of identity for most Tunisians. Consequently, Tunisia does not have to manage the religious, tribal, linguistic, or ethnic cleavages that complicate politics across much of the region.

This does not mean that Tunisian society is free of cleavages. Region and family have been very important factors in politics. For example, because Bourguiba and many of his allies came from the Sahel, that region became synonymous with political power in the postindependence period. Even today, towns and regions have particular reputations. To say that a person is from Sousse, Kairouan, Jerba, or Sfax is to disclose more about that individual than his or her place of origin. While these reputations are based on old stereotypes, they shape perceptions and create poles of solidarity. In a political system dominated by a vast patronage apparatus, one needs to be part of a clientele network. Shared family and regional ties provide a basis for trust and reciprocity in these networks.

One of the most important cleavages separates the more developed coastal areas from the poorer interior. Postindependence development policies concentrated Tunisia's modern economic activity along the coasts. This bias generated strong grievances among Tunisians in the interior, but it is important to note that the resentment was not purely economic. More conservative Tunisians in the interior resented the condescending domination of coastal elites whose values and lifestyles frequently seemed more European than Tunisian. These tensions between the coast and the countryside helped spark the rebellion against Ben Ali in December 2010. They also played a role in Nahda's October 2011 electoral victory.

These demographic, geographic, and economic realities exert a powerful influence on politics. The country's small size and narrow resource base leave Tunisia no choice but to pursue growth through foreign investment, tourism, and exports to global markets. These realities and Bourguiba's progressive philosophy also explain Tunisia's steady commitment to education. Today, Tunisia's adult literacy rate is 80 percent. For people aged fifteen to twenty-four, literacy is 97 percent. From the government's perspective, education has built a modern society with an attractive labor force.

At the same time, Tunisia's educated population creates challenges. Like other countries in the region, Tunisia has developed a pronounced youth bulge. Half the population is younger than twenty-five years old. Unemployment among recent university graduates hovers stubbornly around 40 percent. These young people grew up believing that education is the key to advancement. Television and the Internet have exposed them to lifestyles in Europe and North America. The economy's failure to generate jobs and living standards that meet these expectations is a powerful source of tension. It made young people one of the primary constituencies in the revolt against Ben Ali, and it makes job creation a primary challenge for the current and future governments.

These factors also helped to shape a political culture that emphasizes national unity and generally eschews violence. Beyond the homogeneity and the historical memory that create a shared identity, most Tunisians share a concern that violence scares away tourists and investors and invites meddlesome neighbors. Until Ben Ali, Tunisians had taken pride in the fact that their government did not rule as brutally as many others. Indeed, the revolt against Ben Ali gained strength after security forces fired on demonstrators precisely because this kind of violence was so shocking to Tunisians.

POLITICAL STRUCTURE

The Prerevolution Constitution and Ruling Party

Tunisia's prerevolution constitution described the state as a republic with executive, judicial, and legislative branches. After 2002, the legislature became a bicameral institution, with a larger lower house (the Chamber of Deputies) and a smaller upper house (the Chamber of Councilors). The constitution allowed Tunisians to vote in elections for the president, for members of the Chamber of Deputies, and for local mayors and municipal councils.

These institutions created a democratic facade. Behind it, the president wielded unchecked power over all other institutions. At the head of those institutions stood the ruling party. Despite its various names, the party always functioned as a highly structured organization, rooted in party cells in every neighborhood or village and led by a Political Bureau at the top. Because of the party's internal diversity, and because Bourguiba used it as a patronage machine, Tunisia entered independence with a strong president and a party that did his bidding.

Because the president controlled the party, and the party controlled the National Assembly, the president also controlled the legislature. Even though the constitution contained language that talked about rights and liberties, it also said that citizens must exercise those rights in accordance with the law—a law created by a legislature under the president's control. In this way, Tunisia could have a constitution that appeared to be quite liberal on the surface, but it also could have laws that stripped rights of substantive meaning. Because Tunisia did not have a constitutional court, and because the government appointed judges, the judicial branch could never declare a law unconstitutional or provide recourse to political activists.

The party and the state became indistinguishable, with overlapping structures at the national level in each of the 24 governorates and 264 districts and in every municipality and village. This bureaucratic machine dominated every aspect of Tunisian political life. One of the clearest examples of this domination came in 2002, when over 99 percent of voters approved changes to the constitution that abolished presidential term limits and raised the maximum age of presidential candidates. Ben Ali eliminated the presidency for life shortly after he replaced Bourguiba. Then he used his control of the political process to reinstate it in a different way.

Although elections took place under Bourguiba and Ben Ali, they provided no real opportunity to challenge the ruling party or the president. After the government banned the Communist Party in 1963, the PSD was the only legal party organization in the country until Bourguiba legalized a small number of parties in 1983. From that time through 2011, the government allowed a small handful of parties to operate legally and to contest elections. However, the government's use of discriminatory electoral laws, media control, coercion, and fraud made it impossible for other parties to win more than token representation.

Ben Ali allowed other candidates to run against him for president in 1999, 2004, and 2009. But restrictive candidacy rules and other means of electoral control allowed him to win embarrassingly large margins. Ben Ali faced two challengers in 1999 and three in both 2004 and 2009. He won over 90 percent of the vote in the first two contests and 89 percent in 2009.

Although the ruling party monopolized formal power in Tunisia until 2011, other parties have played critical roles in the country's development. Most of these parties fall into two categories—secular parties, most of which have a Center-Left or social democratic orientation, and Islamist parties—with important differences between them.

Secular Parties

From the late 1960s through the early 1990s, four parties dominated Tunisia's political opposition. The oldest was the Tunisian Communist Party (PCT), founded in 1934. Although the government outlawed the party in 1963, it continued to have a strong influence in the leftist opposition, particularly in the student and labor movements. After the end of the Cold War, the PCT changed its name to the Ettajdid (Renewal) Party and abandoned Marxism for a less doctrinaire Center-Left identity. In 1993, Ettajdid became one of the legal opposition parties under Ben Ali.

The Democratic Socialist Movement was established in 1978 by liberals who had left the PSD. Its respected leadership and its articulate demands for reform made it the most credible secular opposition party in the 1980s and early 1990s. Subsequently, internal divisions over how to respond to Ben Ali's authoritarianism weakened the party. The Popular Unity Party represented a vague mingling of socialist and Arab nationalist ideas. The Progressive Socialist Rally was established in 1983 by a group of young leftist activists; Ben Ali legalized it in 1988. In 2001, the party adopted a more centrist message and changed its name to the Progressive Democratic Party (PDP).

In the 1990s, Ettajdid, the PDP, and three newer parties emerged as the critical players in Tunisian political life: the Tunisian Communist Workers Party (POCT), the Congress for the Republic (CPR), and Ettakatol. The POCT was a Far Left party that formed in 1986. Along with Nahda, the POCT suffered some of the harshest repression under Ben Ali. Ettakatol and the CPR are social democratic parties with roots in Tunisia's human rights movement. Ettakatol was established in 1994 by Mustapha Ben Jaafar, the current president of the Constituent Assembly. The CPR was created in 2001 by a group of human rights activists that included Moncef Marzouki, Tunisia's current interim president.

Between 2001 and 2005, intensified repression and constitutional revisions that allowed Ben Ali to run for additional terms forged a closer alliance between Nahda, the PDP, the POCT, and Ettakatol. That alliance became the October 18 coalition, which played a vital role in laying the foundations for the 2010 rebellion. Consequently, these are the parties that entered postrevolution politics with the strongest credibility. Many of the small new parties knew that they would not win many votes. But if parties were to be the critical players in a democratic system, then becoming a party was the way into the game. A party could join coalitions with others or bargain for positions in larger parties that might subsume them.

Some party consolidation has already begun. On the left, the POCT changed its name to the Tunisian Workers Party and joined with Ettajdid to create a new Democratic and Social Way. In the center, the PDP and several other parties joined the Republican Party. In June 2012, Beji Caid el-Sebsi formed The Call for Tunisia, which involves secular liberals and some former RCD members who were excluded from the October elections. The Call reflects a feeling among many secular Tunisians that they must create a united front against the Islamists. It also reflects concern that the current government lacks the experience to address Tunisia's socioeconomic challenges.

Islamist Parties

The Nahda Party has been the most popular opposition party in Tunisia since the mid-1980s. Ben Ali's repression prevented Nahda from playing a major role in the 2011 revolution. However, the speed with which it rebuilt its organization and its victory in the first elections demonstrate the power of Islamism in contemporary Tunisia.

Since the late 1960s, Tunisia's Islamist mainstream has emphasized its desire to restore Muslim values in a country that has been heavily influenced by Western European culture. Tunisia might have thrown off French rule, but the country's postindependence leaders were steeped in the secular values of the former colonial power. From the Islamists' perspective, these values bred a condescending arrogance in leaders whose policies did not reflect the needs and values of the majority of the population.

Two basic principles have guided the Islamist mainstream's work. First, the movement must adapt its methods to the reality of Tunisian culture and politics. It cannot apply a strategy taken from some other context or from some abstract ideological program. Second, mainstream leaders have emphasized that Islamic values must spread from the bottom up. Capturing the state and compelling beliefs or behaviors would force that government to become as authoritarian as Bourguiba's or Ben Ali's. Over time, education and social work can Islamize society more effectively than government edicts. This position reflects more than the mainstream's religious philosophy. It also reflects an understanding that Nahda must be sensitive to secular Tunisians whose political and economic cooperation is vital to the country's development.

The politics of the 1970s and 1980s pulled the movement deeper into the broader struggle against authoritarian government. That struggle, in turn, helped the movement forge ties to other opposition organizations. Many of those organizations espoused goals and values diametrically opposed to those of the Islamists, but pragmatists in both camps recognized that they all shared a common interest in pushing authoritarian rulers until they either reformed or fell. The Islamist mainstream has always understood that it cannot lead Tunisia on its own. It must have the cooperation of other parties.

Nahda's strategy reflects this pragmatism. Since the early 1980s, the Islamist mainstream has worked steadily to become a political party that works within the legal political process. Nahda leaders also have repeatedly declared their commitments to human rights, pluralism, freedom of expression and religious belief, democratic competition, and women's rights. This moderation puts party leaders in a delicate position. On the one hand, these positions allow Nahda to maintain relationships with secular parties and reassure voters who fear an Islamism that imposes values or laws grounded in sharia. On the other hand, this moderation exposes Nahda's leaders to criticism from more conservative elements in the party's base and from other Islamist parties.

Three parties in particular have emerged on Nahda's right flank. The Islah (Reform) Front is the most moderate of the three. It advocates sharia and an Islamic state, but it rejects violence and is willing to participate in the legal political process. Islah's willingness to accept the rules of democratic competition earned it the right to compete in the next elections. The other two organizations remain illegal in Tunisia. Hizb al-Tahrir is a transnational Salafist organization that rejects the legal political process and supports the restoration of a caliphate that spans national boundaries. Ansar al-Shariah was established in spring 2011. Both organizations call for sharia. They reject democratic institutions and oppose Nahda's moderation. In early 2012, these organizations mobilized protesters to pressure Nahda to adopt sharia as a source of law in Tunisia. After Nahda rejected this idea, Salafists continued to organize protests to undermine Nahda's credibility. Many secular Tunisians fear that pressure from the Salafists will force Nahda to the right when Tunisians go back to the polls in 2013.

Civil Society Organizations

Civil society organizations have played a vital role in Tunisia's political life. Many of these organizations began as creations of the ruling party. During the nationalist struggle and in the early years after independence, the government established unions to mobilize and control students, workers, farmers, and other constituencies. Over time, many of these organizations became collecting points for various kinds of opposition movements. Since the political parties could not challenge the government, activists infiltrated organizations with social bases and turned them into opposition movements. In the late 1960s, the student union became a powerful center of leftist opposition. The workers' union, the UGTT, became the most powerful opposition force in the country in the 1970s and early 1980s.

Other civil society organizations began as independent organizations that the government allowed during its periodic efforts to placate demands for reform. The most important of these organizations focused on human rights. In 1976 activists established the Tunisian Human Rights League (LTDH), the first human rights league in Africa or the Arab world. Relations between the LTDH and the government improved when Ben Ali came to power and initiated some of the reforms that the LTDH had demanded. In 1989, Moncef Marzouki, the man who currently serves as Tunisia's president, became president of the LTDH.

The relationship deteriorated as Ben Ali's repression intensified in the 1990s. In 1992 the government passed a law that required organizations to admit anyone who wanted to join. The government passed this law so that members of the RCD could infiltrate civil society organizations. For the rest of Ben Ali's rule, the LTDH struggled with the challenges created by internal dissension and the government's efforts to freeze the organization's activity. In 1998, Marzouki, Mustapha Ben Jaafar, and other activists created a new organization, the National Council for Liberties in Tunisia. Through the last decade of Ben Ali's rule, the council waged a steady struggle for human rights and for its own existence. Several of the council's leaders became targets of repression.

Women's organizations have made critical contributions to Tunisia's development. Despite the 1956 Personal Status Code, which grants Tunisian women a wide range of rights, many Tunisian women feel that a deep patriarchy continues to shape the country's political, economic, and social life. During Bourguiba's rule, the National Union of Tunisian Women functioned as the primary, albeit government-controlled, women's organization.

After Ben Ali came to power, Tunisian women established two independent organizations. The Association of Tunisian Women for Research on Development became an important center for research on the economic and social status of women. It also established active partnerships with global women's organizations. The Association of Democratic Women became an influential voice for gender equality, democracy, social justice, and secularism. These concerns inevitably generated ties to other opposition organizations. Women's organizations played a vital role in the rebellion against Ben Ali. Since January 2011, they have worked diligently to protect and expand women's rights in a more democratic system.

These organizations and others representing journalists, lawyers, judges, and students have been Tunisia's greatest democratic asset. They have not escaped government efforts to co-opt or splinter them, but they have maintained steadier pressure for democratic reform than any other kind of organization in the country. Their history of activism and cooperation has been critical to Tunisia's democratic transition since Ben Ali fell. Their pressure forced the postrevolution government to make a clean break with the former regime. They also worked together on the reform commission that crafted new institutions that allowed Tunisia to hold a credible democratic election in less than one year.

The Military

Unlike its counterparts in many Arab countries, Tunisia's military has never been an important political player. It did not win Tunisia's independence. It did not seize power in a coup. Bourguiba was keenly aware of the threat to civilian rule that strong militaries posed in many Arab countries. He also believed that building a large military would consume resources that the government should invest in economic growth. Bourguiba kept the army and its budgets small. He did not involve military leaders in the ruling party or the state administration.

The army's status did not change when Ben Ali became president. The country's elite would not have supported a stronger role for the army. Turning the military into a power base also would have consumed resources that Ben Ali needed to invest in economic reform and cultivating other bases of support. The repressive force under Ben Ali was not the army. It was a separate internal security force run by the interior ministry and by the president.

Thus, Tunisia's military has been noteworthy for what it has not done in the political arena. At no time was this truer or more significant than in the closing hours of Ben Ali's rule. As the crowds grew in the streets of Tunis, the military tipped the balance in the protestors' favor by pulling out of key positions and refusing to fire on them. These decisions turned the army and its commander into national heroes. Thus far, the army has not inserted itself publicly into the new political process. However, many Tunisians wonder what the army might do if civilian politicians are unable to construct a stable order or if an elected government begins to violate the country's republican values.

After Bourguiba and Ben Ali, there is broad support for a system that creates meaningful legislative oversight of the executive. Similarly, there is broad agreement on the need for a high court that can pass judgment on the constitutionality of laws and for a more democratic method of amending the constitution. All of this is part of the effort to create a system that prevents the return of an all-powerful president who can bend or ignore the law at his pleasure. Finally, the new constitution likely will decentralize greater authority to the governorates and make the security sector more accountable.

Despite these points of agreement, Tunisia's leading parties differ on other important institutional issues. Nahda supports a parliamentary system in which the government is led by a prime minister and the party or coalition of parties that holds a majority in the national legislature. Nahda argues that this system prevents excessive presidential power. Nahda also knows, however, that this system serves the interests of parties with strong name recognition and national organizations. Many of the secular parties prefer a presidential system or a system that combines elements of both. They argue that parliamentary systems are unstable because the prime minister is subject to changing alliances in the parliament. A country facing difficult socioeconomic challenges needs more effective executive leadership.

POLITICAL DYNAMICS

From one perspective, Tunisian politics has been very nonideological. As noted earlier, the ruling party never developed a clear ideological perspective. Bourguiba and Ben Ali ruled as nonideological pragmatists who cared primarily about protecting their own power and maintaining the freedom to pursue whatever policies they thought best at any given moment.

From another perspective, ideology has been a critical part of Tunisian politics. The fact that the government lacked a coherent ideology made its socioeconomic deficiencies and its authoritarianism all the more objectionable. The government could not claim that its inefficient authoritarianism served some greater project. As a result, political opponents in Tunisia sought not only to change the government but also to give it a substantive ideology.

Three basic ideologies have dominated Tunisian politics. On the left, the Communist Party, the Tunisian Communist Workers Party, and an array of illegal organizations have espoused a range of ideas, from conventional communism to more extreme forms of Maoism. The Center has given rise to a host of socialist and social democratic parties. Thus far, Islamist parties have monopolized the Right.

These parties have dominated the formal political process. With the exception of Nahda, however, they have not generated great enthusiasm across the general population. Because political change was the prerequisite for any other change, most party programs emphasized the same core demands for political reform. Voters saw little difference between the secular parties whose programs focused on political issues that mattered little to people struggling with inflation or unemployment.

As noted earlier, violence has been relatively uncommon in Tunisian politics. This general observation does not minimize the significance of the repression that characterized periods of Bourguiba's rule and certainly Ben Ali's. However, in comparison to many other countries in the region, violence has less commonly been a tool for both the government and its opponents.

Instead, Tunisia's political dynamic has emphasized co-optation, divide-and-conquer tactics, and strategic alliance building. Bourguiba was very adept at banishing troublesome leaders to the political wilderness, then bringing them back into new positions on terms that made them dependent on him. Bourguiba also exploited rivalries between leaders to split organizations and then reunify them on terms that served his interests. Both Bourguiba and Ben Ali used these tactics to divide and co-opt the labor movement and opposition parties. In the 1970s and 1980s, party bosses who wanted to position themselves in the struggle for the succession made alliances with protest movements whose support would enhance their influence.

These dynamics create challenges for Tunisia's transition. Multiple generations have been socialized to believe that this is how one engages in politics. Most of the country's political organizations have struggled with personal rivalries that produce schism, winner-take-all understandings of what it means to exercise power and shape institutions, suspicion that one's allies are making alliances with one's foes, and majoritarian notions of democracy that leave little room for the idea of loyal opposition. These dynamics undermine the growth of parties that can inspire voters, especially young ones, to join the political process. Tunisia's transition depends mightily on new institutions—a new constitution, a new electoral law, and an independent and transparent judicial process. But democracy is a game of rule-governed competition. Parties are the central players in that game. New institutions will matter little if no one is willing to play by the rules.

Foreign Policy

Three basic goals have guided Tunisia's foreign policy: (1) maintaining independence without building a strong military, (2) preventing other actors in the region from allying with the government's domestic opponents, and (3) attracting foreign aid and investment.

Tunisia has pursued these goals with a resolutely pro-Western foreign policy. Even during the independence struggle, Bourguiba intended to make France Tunisia's most important long-term partner. He also recognized that the United States could pressure France to grant Tunisian independence and provide additional development assistance. Bourguiba never tried to play the United States and Soviet Union against each other for the sake of extracting aid from both. He also distrusted pan-Arabism as a threat to Tunisia's sovereignty. As early as the mid-1960s, Tunisia advocated a two-state solution in Palestine.

These positions and Tunisia's small size left the country vulnerable, particularly after Algeria opted for a socialist development strategy and closer ties to Soviet Bloc countries and Qaddafi made Libya a bastion of pan-Arabism. Bourguiba needed to defend Tunisia's independence, but he did not want to pay the economic and political costs required to build a strong military. French and US commitments to Tunisia's security provided deterrence without requiring large military expenditures.

These policies served Tunisia well. France and the United States have provided substantial economic, political, and military assistance since independence. The rise of Islamist movements across the region increased Tunisia's importance to Washington and Paris in the 1990s. In the latter years of Ben Ali's rule, however, his relations with France and the United States became more strained. Algeria's war had calmed, and Ben Ali had eliminated Islamism as a threat inside Tunisia. Yet his repression became more brutal, corruption became more visible, and economic growth slowed. Ben Ali no longer provided a firewall against an imminent Islamist threat, and he was no longer a poster boy for liberal economic growth. In the fall of 2010, WikiLeaks released the contents of US diplomatic cables that provided a frank description of corruption, repression, and mismanagement under Ben Ali. Those cables encouraged the opposition by showing that the United States had lost confidence in Ben Ali.

Tunisia has also cultivated strong ties to Europe beyond France. In 1995, Tunisia became the first Maghrebi state to sign an association agreement with the European Union. The agreement initiated a transition period that culminated in Tunisia becoming the first southern Mediterranean country to join the European Free Trade Area in 2008. Tunisia received greater access to European markets and financial assistance to help firms become more competitive. However, Tunisia also had to lower tariffs on European manufactured goods, a policy that took a heavy toll on Tunisia's manufacturing sector.

Hoping to enhance their bargaining power with Europe and increase inter-Maghreb trade, the five Maghrebi heads of state established the Arab Maghreb Union (UMA) in 1989. Tunisia's small size and narrow resource base give it a particularly strong interest in economic integration. However, inter-Maghreb trade still accounts for a very small portion of the region's total trade. Maghreb governments have preferred to pursue separate trade relations with Europe. Politics has also presented stumbling blocks. Tensions between Algeria and Morocco over the Western Sahara, ideological diversity across the region's governments, fear that integration might facilitate the spread of Islamism, and Qaddafi's difficult relations with the West reduced the UMA to an organization in name alone.

It is too early to know how Tunisia's foreign policy will evolve in the future. Tunisia has been proud to offer inspiration and rhetorical support to other antiauthoritarian rebellions. The interim government allowed anti-Qaddafi rebels to run guns and supplies across Tunisian territory. Tunisians provided safe haven to Libyan rebels and refugees. For the most part, however, the hard work involved in building a new political order has dominated the new government's agenda over the past eighteen months. In any event, Tunisia's foreign policy is not likely to change dramatically. The factors that led Tunisia to pursue good relations with the West and cooperation with its Maghreb neighbors remain powerful today.

BIBLIOGRAPHY

An excellent historical overview is Kenneth J. Perkins, *A History of Modern Tunisia* (Cambridge: Cambridge University Press, 2004). An overview that shaped much of this chapter is Christopher Alexander, *Tunisia: Stability and Reform in the Modern Maghreb* (London: Routledge, 2010).

On politics under Bourguiba, see Lisa Anderson, *State and Social Transformation in Tunisia and Libya, 1830–1980* (Princeton, NJ: Princeton University Press, 1986); Charles A. Micaud, Leon Carl Brown, and Clement Henry Moore, *Tunisia: The Politics of Modernization* (New York: Praeger, 1964); Clement Henry Moore, *Tunisia Since Independence: The Dynamics of One-Party Government* (Berkeley: University of California Press, 1965); Lars Rudebeck, *Party and People: A Study of Political Change in Tunisia* (New York: Praeger, 1969); Derek Hopwood, *Habib Bourguiba of Tunisia: The Tragedy of Longevity* (New York: St. Martin's Press, 1992); Russell Stone and John Simmons, eds., *Change in Tunisia* (Albany: State University of New York Press, 1976); John P. Entelis, "L'héritage contradictoire de Bourguiba: Modernisation et intolérance politique," in *Habib Bourguiba: La trace et l'héritage*, ed. Michel Camau and Vincent Geisser, 223–247 (Paris: Karthala, 2004); Russell A. Stone, "Tunisia: A Single Party System Holds Change in Abeyance," in *Political Elites in Arab North Africa*, ed. I. William Zartman et al., 144–176 (New York: Longman, 1982); I. William Zartman, ed., *Tunisia: The Political Economy of Reform* (Boulder, CO: Lynne Rienner, 1991); and Michel Camau, ed., *Tunisie au present: Une modernité au-dessous de tout soupçon?* (Paris: CNRS, 1987).

On politics and economics in the 1990s, see Iliya Harik, "Privatization and Development in Tunisia," in *Privatization and Liberalization in the Middle East*, ed. Iliya Harik and Denis J. Sullivan, 210–231 (Bloomington: Indiana University Press, 1992); Gregory White, *A Comparative Political Economy of Tunisia and Morocco: On the Outside of Europe Looking In* (Albany: State University of New York Press, 2001); Emma Murphy, *Economic and Political Change in Tunisia: From Bourguiba to Ben Ali* (New York: St. Martin's Press, 1999); Nicole Grimaud, "Tunisia: Between Control and Liberalization," *Mediterranean Politics* 1, no. 1 (1996): 95–106; Stephen J. King, *Liberalization Against Democracy: The Local Politics of Economic Reform in Tunisia* (Bloomington: Indiana University Press, 2003); Melani Cammett, *Globalization, Business Politics and Development: North Africa in Comparative Perspective* (Cambridge: Cambridge University

Press, 2007); Eva Bellin, "Contingent Democrats: Industrialists, Labor, and Democratization in Late-Developing Countries," *World Politics* 52 (January 2000): 175–205; Eva Bellin, *Stalled Democracy: Capital, Labor, and the Paradox of State-Sponsored Development* (Ithaca, NY: Cornell University Press, 2002); and Melani Cammett, "Fat Cats and Self-Made Men: Globalization and the Paradoxes of Collective Action," *Comparative Politics* (July 2005): 379–400.

On the status of women, see Mounira A. Charrad, *States and Women's Rights: The Making of Postcolonial Tunisia, Algeria, and Morocco* (Berkeley: University of California Press, 2001); Emma C. Murphy, "Women in Tunisia: A Survey of Achievements and Challenges," *Journal of North African Studies* 1, no. 2 (Autumn 1996): 138–156; Barbara Larson, "The Status of Women in a Tunisian Village: Limits to Autonomy, Influence, and Power," *Signs: Journal of Women in Culture and Society* 9, no. 3 (1984): 417–433; Laurie Brand, *Women, the State, and Political Liberalization: Middle Eastern and North African Experiences* (New York: Columbia University Press, 1998).

On political Islam in Tunisia, see Emad Eldin Shahin, *Political Ascent: Contemporary Islamic Movements in North Africa* (Boulder, CO: Westview Press, 1988); Susan Waltz, "Islamicist Appeal in Tunisia," *The Middle East Journal* 40, no. 4 (1986): 651–670; Marion Boulby, "The Islamist Challenge: Tunisia Since Independence," *Third World Quarterly* 10 (April 1989): 590–614; Mark Tessler, "Political Change and the Islamic Revival in Tunisia," *Maghreb Review* 5, no. 1 (1980): 8–19; Elbaki Hermassi, "La société tunisienne au miroir islamiste," *Maghreb-Machrek* 103 (April–June 1984): 39–56; John P. Entelis, ed., *Islam, Democracy and the State in North Africa* (Bloomington: Indiana University Press, 1997); Azzam S. Tamimi, *Rachid Ghannouchi: A Democrat Within Islamism* (New York: Oxford University Press, 2001); François Burgat, *The Islamic Movement in North Africa*, trans. William Dowell (Austin: University of Texas Press, 1993); and Mohamed Elhachmi Hamdi, *The Politicisation of Islam: A Case Study of Tunisia* (Boulder, CO: Westview Press, 1998).

On human rights in Tunisia, see Ahmed Manaï, *Supplice tunisien: Le jardin secret du général Ben Ali* (Paris: La Découverte, 1995), and Nicolas Beau and Jean-Pierre Tuquoi, *Notre ami Ben Ali* (Paris: La Découverte, 1999).

On Ben Ali's presidency, see Michel Camau and Vincent Geisser, *Le syndrome autoritaire: Politique en Tunisie de Bourguiba à Ben Ali* (Paris: Presses de Sciences Po, 2003); John P. Entelis, "The Democratic Imperative vs. the Authoritarian Impulse: The Maghrib State Between Transition and Terrorism," *The Middle East Journal* 59, no. 4 (2005): 537–558; Christopher Alexander, "Authoritarianism and Civil Society in Tunisia," *Middle East Report* (October–November 1997): 1–7; Michele Penner Angrist, "Parties, Parliament, and Political Dissent in Tunisia," *Journal of North African Studies* 4, no. 4 (Winter 1999): 89–104; Eva Bellin, "Civil Society in Formation: Tunisia," in *Civil Society in the Middle East,* Vol. 1, ed. Augustus Richard Norton, 120–147 (Leiden: E. J. Brill, 1995); Mark J. Gasiorowski, "The Failure of Reform in Tunisia," *Journal of Democracy* 3, no. 4 (1992): 85–97; Vincent Geisser, "Tunisie: Des élections pour quoi faire? Enjeux et 'sens' du fait électoral de Bourguiba à Ben Ali," *Maghreb Machrek* 168 (April–June 2000): 14–28; Kamel Labidi, "Tunisia: Independent but Not Free," *Le Monde Diplomatique* (March 2006): 1–4; Olfa Lamloum, "Tunisie: Quelle 'transition démocratique'?" in *Dispositifs de démocratisation et dispositifs autoritaires en Afrique du Nord*, ed. Jean-Nöel Ferrié and Jean-Claude Santucci, 121–147 (Paris: CNRS Editions, 2006); Olfa Lamloum and B. Ravenel, *La Tunisie de Ben Ali: La société contre le régime* (Paris: L'Harmattan, and 2002); Moncef Marzouki, *Le mal arabe: Entre dictatures et intégrismes: La démocratie interdite* (Paris: L'Harmattan, 2004).

On the UMA, see Ahmed Aghrout and Keith Sutton, "Regional Economic Union in the Maghreb," *Journal of Modern African Studies* 28, no. 1 (1990): 115–139; Claire Spencer, *The Maghreb in the 1990s: Political and Economic Developments in Algeria, Morocco, and Tunisia* (London: International Institute for Strategic Studies, 1993); and I. William Zartman, "The Ups and Downs of Maghrib Unity," in *Middle East Dilemma: The Politics and Economics of Arab Integration*, ed. Michael Hudson (New York: Columbia University Press, 1999).

On the rebellion against Ben Ali and its aftermath, see Alfred Stepan, "Tunisia's Transition and the Twin Tolerations," *Journal of Democracy* 23, no. 2 (2012): 89–103.

The number of Internet resources on Tunisia has grown dramatically. Useful sites include Tunisia Live (www.tunisia-live.net), an English-language site established shortly after the revolution by a group of independent young journalists; Nawaat (www.nawaat.org), an independent collective blog established in 2004 to provide an outlet for dissident voices under Ben Ali; and Jeune Afrique (www.jeuneafrique.com), a website affiliated with one of France's best magazines for coverage of Africa and the Arab world.

Index